VALUATION

**MEASURING AND
MANAGING THE
VALUE OF
COMPANIES**

WILEY FINANCE

VALUATION

MEASURING AND MANAGING THE VALUE OF COMPANIES

THIRD EDITION

McKinsey & Company, Inc.
Tom Copeland
Tim Koller
Jack Murrin

JOHN WILEY & SONS, INC.
New York • Chichester • Weinheim • Brisbane • Singapore • Toronto

This book is printed on acid-free paper. ∞

Copyright © 1990, 1994, 2000 by McKinsey & Company, Inc. All rights reserved.

Published by John Wiley & Sons, Inc.
Published simultaneously in Canada.

No part of this publication may be reproduced, stored in a retrieval system or transmitted in any form or by any means, electronic, mechanical, photocopying, recording, scanning or otherwise, except as permitted under Section 107 or 108 of the 1976 United States Copyright Act, without either the prior written permission of the Publisher, or authorization through payment of the appropriate per-copy fee to the Copyright Clearance Center, 222 Rosewood Drive, Danvers, MA 01923, (978) 750-8400, fax (978) 750-4744. Requests to the Publisher for permission should be addressed to the Permissions Department, John Wiley & Sons, Inc., 605 Third Avenue, New York, NY 10158-0012, (212) 850-6011, fax (212) 850-6008, E-Mail: PERMREQ@WILEY.COM.

This publication is designed to provide accurate and authoritative information in regard to the subject matter covered. It is sold with the understanding that the publisher is not engaged in rendering professional services. If professional advice or other expert assistance is required, the services of a competent professional person should be sought.

Library of Congress Cataloging-in-Publication Data:

McKinsey & Company, Inc.
    Valuation : measuring and managing the value of companies / Tom Copeland, Tim
Koller, Jack Murrin — 3rd ed.
        p. cm. — (Wiley frontiers in finance)
    Includes index.
    ISBN 0-471-36190-9 (cloth : alk. paper)
    ISBN 0-471-36191-7 (paper ed.)
    ISBN 0-471-39748-2 (cloth with CD)
    ISBN 0-471-39749-0 (CD)
    ISBN 0-471-39750-4 (Web spreadsheet)
    ISBN 0-471-39751-2 (workbook)
        1. Corporations—Valuation—Handbooks, manuals, etc.   I. Copeland, Tom.
II. Koller, Tim.   III. Murrin, Jack.   IV. Title.   IV. Series.

    HG4028.V3 C67 2000
    658.15—dc21

                                                                    00-036651

Printed in the United States of America.

10   9   8   7   6   5   4   3   2   1

About the Authors

The authors are all current or former partners of McKinsey & Co., Inc., and co-leaders of its corporate finance practice. Collectively, they have served more than 400 companies in 40 countries on corporate strategy, mergers and acquisitions, and value-based management.

McKinsey & Company, Inc., is an international top management consulting firm. Founded in 1926, McKinsey advises leading companies around the world on issues of strategy, organization, and operations, and in specialized areas such as finance, information technology and the Internet, research and development, sales, marketing, manufacturing, and distribution.

Tom Copeland, a former partner of McKinsey & Co., was co-leader of the firm's corporate finance practice. Before joining McKinsey, he was a professor of finance at UCLA's Anderson Graduate School of Management. He was also an adjunct professor at New York University and is currently senior lecturer at the Massachusetts Institute of Technology. Tom is co-author of two leading textbooks, *Financial Theory and Corporate Policy* and *Managerial Finance.* He is currently leader of a corporate finance practice. He received his PhD from the University of Pennsylvania and his MBA from Wharton.

Tim Koller is a partner at McKinsey & Co. and has been a co-leader of the firm's corporate finance practices in both the United States and Europe. He was formerly a vice president at Stern Stewart & Co., a financial consulting firm. He received his MBA from the University of Chicago.

Jack Murrin co-founded and co-led McKinsey's corporate finance practice, serving as a partner in the firm's New York and London offices. He has subsequently held senior strategic and financial positions at leading companies, most recently as senior managing director and head of corporate development at Bankers Trust Corp. Jack, a certified public accountant, holds an MBA from Stanford Business School.

Preface

The first edition of this book was published in 1990, yet it continues to attract readers around the world. We believe that the book has succeeded because it is grounded in universal economic principles. While we continue to improve and update the text as our experience grows, the fundamental principles do not change. They are valid across time and geography.

Our message is simple: Companies thrive when they create real economic value for their shareholders. Companies create value by investing capital at rates of return that exceed their cost of capital. This applies equally to U.S., European, and Asian companies. It applies equally to mature manufacturing companies and high-growth Internet companies. Only the implementation details are different.

When companies forget these simple truths, consequences are evident: hostile takeovers in the United States in the 1980s, the collapse of the bubble economy in Japan in the 1990s, the broad Southeast Asian crisis in 1998, and the persistent slow growth and high unemployment in Europe. While the underlying drivers of these events can be traced to a number of factors—most often inappropriate government policies or structural deficiencies—the lack of focus on value creation by managers is a key link in the chain leading to economic malaise or crisis.

We wrote this book for managers (and future managers) who want their companies to create value. It is a how-to book. We hope that it is a book that you will use again and again. If we have done our job well, it will soon be transformed with underlining, margin notations, and highlighting. This is no coffee-table book.

THE NEED TO MANAGE VALUE

In the last two decades, two kinds of thinking and activity—corporate finance and corporate strategy—have come together with a resounding crash.

Corporate finance is no longer the exclusive preserve of financiers. Corporate strategy is no longer a separate realm ruled by CEOs. Participants in the financial markets are increasingly involved in business operations through leveraged buyouts, hostile takeovers, and proxy contests. At the same time, chief executives have led their companies to become increasingly active players in the financial markets through mergers and acquisitions, restructurings, leveraged buyouts, share repurchases, and the like. Financing and investment are now inextricably connected. In the Internet world, for example, having a high share value is essential for making acquisitions and attracting talent.

This new reality presents a challenge to business managers: the need to *manage value* and to focus as never before on the value their corporate and business-level strategies are creating. In the quest for value, they find that they must consider such radical alternatives as selling the "crown jewels" or completely restructuring operations. And they need more systematic and reliable ways to look for opportunities in the turbulence resulting from the confluence of strategy and finance. As a result of restructuring, for instance, companies create new opportunities to acquire assets and businesses that may be worth more to them than to their original owners.

WHY THIS BOOK

This book began life as a handbook for McKinsey consultants. This beginning is reflected in the nature of the book. While the book draws on leading edge academic thinking, its purpose is practical application. It aims to demystify the field of valuation and to clarify the linkages between strategy and finance.

We believe that clear thinking about valuation and skill in using valuation to guide business decisions are prerequisites for success in today's competitive environment. Value needs to be understood clearly by CEOs, business managers, and financial managers alike. Too often, valuation has been left to experts. It has been viewed as a specialized discipline, rather than as an important tool for running the business better.

In this book, we hope to lift the veil on valuation by explaining, step-by-step, how to do it well. We spell out valuation frameworks that we use in our consulting work, and we bring these frameworks to life with detailed case studies that highlight the practical judgments involved in developing and using valuations. Most significantly, we discuss how to use valuation to make decisions about courses of action for a company.

This book can be used by a wide audience, including:

- *Business managers.* Now more than ever, leaders at the corporate and business-unit levels need to know how to assess the value of alternative strategies. They need to know how much value they can create through restructuring and other major transactions. Beyond this, they need to instill a managing-value mindset throughout their organizations.

- *Corporate finance practitioners.* Valuation approaches and the linkage between finance and strategy are important to chief financial officers, merger and acquisition specialists, corporate financial professionals, and corporate development managers and strategists. Value—how to assess it, create it, and communicate it—lies at the core of their roles and responsibilities.

- *Investors, portfolio managers, and securities analysts.* These professionals should find this volume a useful guide to applying cash flow valuation approaches. This is the purest form of fundamental securities analysis, since it links the value of the company directly to the economic returns it can generate from its businesses and assets.

WHEN TO USE IT

First and foremost, this book is written for those who want to improve their ability to create value for the stakeholders in their business. It will be of most use when you need to do the following:

- Estimate the value of alternative corporate and business strategies and the value of specific programs within those strategies. These strategies include such initiatives as new product introductions, capital expenditures, and joint venture agreements.

- Assess major transactions such as mergers, acquisitions, divestitures, recapitalizations, and share repurchases.

- Use value-based management to review and target the performance of business operations. It is essential to know whether and to what extent a business—as currently performing and configured—is creating value. Equally important is the need to understand which operating drivers have the greatest prospects for enhancing value.

- Communicate with key stakeholders, especially stockholders, about the value of the business. Our fundamental premise is that the value of a company derives from its ability to generate cash flows and cash-flow-based returns on investment. Many companies could do a much better job than they now do of communicating with the market and other players about the value of their plans and strategies. But first they need to become value managers themselves, and to understand what value they are creating and why.

INTELLECTUAL FOUNDATIONS

One of us was asked by the editor of *Le Figaro* in Paris, "What is new about your approach?" As far as the methodology is concerned, the answer is practically nothing. Valuation is an age-old methodology in finance with its intellectual origins in the present value method of capital budgeting and in the valuation approach developed by Professors Merton Miller and Franco Modigliani, both Nobel laureates, in their 1961 *Journal of Business* article entitled "Dividend Policy, Growth and the Valuation of Shares." Our intellectual debt is primarily to them, but others have gone far to popularize their approach. In particular, Professor Alfred Rappaport of Northwestern University (co-founder of ALCAR) and Joel Stern (of Stern Stewart & Co.) were among the first to extend the Miller-Modigliani entity valuation formula to real-world applications and to develop and market computer tools for making this an easy task for companies.

STRUCTURE OF THE BOOK

The book is organized into three parts. Part One provides a managerial perspective on valuation and managing shareholder value. Part Two is a step-by-step approach to valuing a company. Part Three deals with more complex valuation issues and special cases.

In Part One, we discuss the link between business strategies and value. In Chapter 1, we make the case that managing shareholder value is a central role and challenge for senior managers. In Chapter 2, we develop a picture of what it means to be a value manager. We do this through a detailed case study based on the actual experiences of a CEO who needed to restructure his company and build a new managing-value philosophy throughout it. Chapter 3 summarizes the basic principles of value creation through a simple case example, focusing on the intuition behind the approach, not the mathematics. Chapter 4 attempts to sort through the confusing jargon about various metrics that you will come across by providing a simple, yet comprehensive framework. Chapter 5 provides the empirical evidence supporting our discounted cash flow view of valuation. Chapter 6 describes the softer aspects of implementing value management. Finally, Chapter 7 provides an overview of value creation in the context of mergers, acquisitions, and alliances.

Part Two—Chapters 8 through 13—is a self-contained handbook for doing valuations of single-business companies. In it we describe a general approach to discounted cash flow valuations and how to implement it. This includes how to analyze historical performance, forecast free cash flows, estimate the appropriate opportunity cost of capital, identify sources of value, and interpret results. As a further aid to the practitioner, we walk through the valuation of a company (Heineken) from the outside, using publicly available information.

Part Three—Chapters 14 through 22—is devoted to valuation in more complex situations. We have included chapters on valuing high growth Internet companies, multibusiness companies, cyclical companies, banks, and insurance companies. Three chapters deal with issues related to valuation outside the United States: valuing foreign subsidiaries, valuing companies outside the United States, and valuing companies in emerging markets. Finally, we explore the application of option pricing theory to assets, liabilities, and investment decisions.

WHAT'S NEW ABOUT THE THIRD EDITION

In the 10 years between the first and third editions, we have gained experience applying valuation in our consulting work and have received considerable feedback from readers. Building on these experiences, we have extensively rewritten and updated core chapters, adding more detail on practical issues that managers and analysts face. We have updated most of the examples and empirical analysis. We have also added six new chapters. Entirely new chapters have been added on valuing Internet companies, valuing cyclical companies, and valuing insurance companies. Valuing companies in emerging markets now warrants its own chapter. Finally, we have created two chapters early in the book, one that provides a nonmathematical, intuitive overview of the principles of value creation, and one that provides an overarching framework for cutting through the confusion of management performance metrics.

VALUATION SPREADSHEET

An Excel spreadsheet valuation model is available on CD-ROM. This valuation model is similar to the model we use in practice. Practitioners will find the model easy to use in a variety of situations: mergers and acquisitions, valuing business units for restructuring or value-based management, or testing the implications of major strategic decisions on the value of your company. We accept no responsibility for any decisions based on your inputs to the model. If you would like to purchase the spreadsheet, ISBN 0-471-39749-0, please call 1-800-225-5945 or visit www.WileyValuation.com to purchase the model via web download.

TOM COPELAND
TIM KOLLER
JACK MURRIN

Acknowledgments

No book is solely the effort of its authors. This book is certainly no exception, especially since it grew out of the collective work of McKinsey's corporate finance practice and the experiences of consultants throughout the world.

First, we would like to thank Ennius Bergsma. Ennius initiated the development of McKinsey's corporate finance practice in the mid-1980s and was instrumental in bringing the three authors together. He encouraged us to turn our original internal McKinsey valuation handbook into a real book for an external audience. He mustered the internal support and sponsorship that we needed to make this happen. Ennius has always been a key discussion partner for us. He also co-wrote Chapter 1, *Why Value Value?*

Fred Gluck deserves our special thanks. Fred played a vital role in creating a knowledge building culture within McKinsey. As the firm's Managing Director, he was like a godfather to many of us and our colleagues. Fred was a vocal supporter of creating a strong corporate financial advisory practice at McKinsey.

For the third edition, we would like to thank several people who worked closely with us on key chapters. David Krieger prepared the analysis and valuation of Heineken that appears throughout the book. Susan Nolen contributed to Chapter 6, *Making Value Happen*, drawing from an internal project she was leading. Mimi James guided us through the complexities of valuing companies in emerging market countries in Chapter 19. Alice Hu brought us into the Internet world, helping us write Chapter 15, *Valuing Dot.coms*. Marco de Heer's thesis on valuing cyclical companies formed the basis for Chapter 16. Vladimir Antikarov and Phil Keenan were steadfast thought partners for the option pricing work in Chapter 20. Gabriel Garcia and Mimi James were instrumental in developing Chapter 22 on valuing insurance companies. Valerie Udale and Annemarie van Neck updated the Excel valuation model, making it easier to navigate and more flexible.

Alice Hu, Irina Grigorenko, Kim Vogel, David Twiddy, Chris Jones, David Wright, and Sandeep Vaswani provided analytical support and number crunching for the third edition. We would also like to thank Petri Allas, André Annema, Olivier Berlage, Richard Dobbs, George Fenn, Marc Goedhart, Kevin Kaiser, and Pieter de Wit for ideas, formulas, and debates.

We would like to reiterate our thanks to all those who contributed to the first two editions. We owe a special debt to Dave Furer for help and late nights developing the original drafts of this book more than 10 years ago. The first two editions and this edition drew on work, ideas, and analyses from Carlos Abad, Buford Alexander, Pat Anslinger, Ali Asghar, Bill Barnett, Dan Bergman, Peter Bisson, the late Joel Bleeke, Steve Coley, Johan Depraetere, Mikel Dodd, Will Draper, Christian von Drathen, David Ernst, Bill Fallon, Russ Fradin, Alo Ghosh, Keiko Honda, Phil Kholos, Shyanjaw Kuo, Kurt Losert, Bill Lewis, Perry Moilinoff, Mike Murray, Juan Ocampo, John Patience, Bill Pursche, Frank Richter, David Rothschild, Silvia Stefini, Konrad Stiglbrunner, Ahmed Taha, Bill Trent, Jon Weiner, Jack Welch, and David Willensky.

For help in preparing the manuscript and coordinating the flow of paper, e-mails and phone calls between four countries and seven time zones, we owe our thanks to our assistants, Marlies Zwaan and Betsy Bellingrath. Geoff Andersen designed the updated and attractive exhibits that accompany the text.

Allan Gold edited the manuscript and kept reminding us that we were writing for the reader, not for ourselves. Allan was also a great sounding board for weary authors. Nancy Nichols also contributed to the editing of the book.

The University edition of this book includes end-of-chapter questions and an instructor's resource guide based on material in this book. Additionally, a professional workbook accompanies this book. We would like to thank Bill Foote for preparing the pedagogy for the University edition and for creating the *Valuation Workbook*. This workbook is an important complement to the text for practitioners and students alike.

We couldn't have devoted the time and energy to this book without the support and encouragement of McKinsey's corporate finance and strategy practice leadership, in particular Christian Caspar and Ron Hulme. We also thank Alan Kantrow for his sage counsel.

Thank you as well to our editors at Wiley, Pamela van Giessen and Claudio Campuzano, and to Nancy Marcus Land and her staff at Publications Development Company for copyediting and production.

Finally, thank you to Maggie Copeland, Melissa Koller, and Wendy Murdock, our most important supporters. This book truly would not have been possible without your encouragement and understanding.

T. C.
T. K.
J. M.

Contents

VALUATION

**MEASURING AND
MANAGING THE
VALUE OF
COMPANIES**

Part One

Company Value and
the Manager's Mission

1

Why Value Value?

This book is about how to value companies and use information about valuation to make wiser business decisions. Underlying it is our basic belief that managers who focus on building shareholder value will create healthier companies than those who do not. We also think that healthier companies will, in turn, lead to stronger economies, higher living standards, and more career and business opportunities for individuals.

There has always been, and continues to be, vigorous debate on the importance of shareholder value relative to other measures such as employment, social responsibility, and the environment. The debate is often cast in terms of shareholder versus stakeholder. At least in ideology and legal frameworks, the United States and the United Kingdom have given the most weight to the idea that shareholders are the owners of the corporation, the board of directors is their representative and elected by them, and the objective function of the corporation is to maximize shareholder value.

In continental Europe, an explicitly broader view of the objectives of business organizations has long been more influential. In many cases, it has been incorporated into the governance structures of the corporation form of organization. Under Dutch law, for example, the board of a Structural N.V.—effectively a large corporation—is mandated to ensure the continuity of the business, not to represent shareholders in the pursuit of value maximization. Similar philosophies lay at the foundation of corporate governance in Germany and Scandinavia.

Our principal aim in this book is *not* to analyze, resolve, or even stoke the debate between shareholder and stakeholder models. However, we believe managers should focus on value creation for two reasons. First, in most developed countries, shareholder influence already dominates the agenda

---

Our thanks to Ennius Bergsma, who co-wrote this chapter.

of top management. Second, shareholder-oriented economies appear to perform better than other economic systems and other stakeholders do not suffer at the hands of shareholders.

ASCENDANCY OF SHAREHOLDER VALUE

Early in 2000, Vodafone AirTouch acquired the German conglomerate Mannesmann, the first major hostile takeover of a German company by a non-German company.[1] This event signaled the broadening acceptance of the shareholder value model in Europe. It might now be argued that managers in most of the developed world must focus on building shareholder value. Four major factors have played a role in the ascendancy of shareholder value:

1. The emergence of an active market for corporate control in the 1980s, following the apparent inability of many management teams to respond effectively to major changes in their industries.
2. The growing importance of equity-based features in the pay packages of most senior executives in the United States and many in Europe as well.
3. The increased penetration of equity holdings as a percentage of household assets, following the strong performance of the U.S. and European equity markets since 1982.
4. The growing recognition that many social security systems, especially in continental Europe and Japan, are heading for insolvency.

The Market for Corporate Control

In 1982, the U.S. economy started to recover from a prolonged period of high inflation and low economic growth. Many industrial sectors required major restructuring. For example, the invention of the radial tire had more than doubled the effective life of tires, leading to huge overcapacity. Rather than eliminating excess capacity and taking cash out of the business, most major tire manufacturers continued investing heavily, setting themselves up for a rude awakening later in the decade.

At the same time, pension funds and insurance companies began to provide increasingly large pools of funds to new kinds of investors, principally leveraged buyout (LBO) groups such as Kohlberg, Kravis, and Roberts (KKR) and Clayton, Dubilier, and Rice. In 1981, of 2,328 mergers and acquisitions in

---

[1] Technically, Mannesmann agreed to a negotiated transaction, but only when it was clear that the shareholders would vote in favor of Vodafone AirTouch.

the United States, 99 were in the form of leveraged buyouts.[2] By 1988, this number had climbed to 381, of a total of 4,049. Probably more important than the hard numbers was the perception of what was happening in the marketplace. The size of the leveraged buyouts had become huge, with the RJR-Nabisco transaction topping the charts at $31.4 billion. This was only four years after the first leveraged buyout exceeding $1 billion, KKR's purchase of the conglomerate Wometco in 1984. While many leveraged buyouts were friendly, the vehicle lent itself to hostile acquisitions as well. Indeed, the most visible hostile transactions in the late 1980s were LBOs, of which RJR-Nabisco was a leading example.

The structure of a leveraged buyout, combined with the emergence of high-yield bonds as a major funding instrument, put much of corporate America within range of hostile takeovers. Not surprisingly, companies that were not dealing effectively with major changes in their industry became targets. In the tire industry, BF Goodrich and UniRoyal were restructured on a friendly basis, but Goodyear and GenCorp (the owners of General Tire) came under attack.

This emergence of the market for corporate control provoked a backlash from established enterprises and their executives. By 1984, the Business Roundtable, an organization that represents the largest corporations in the United States, had already issued a working paper that supported the stakeholder view of corporate governance, largely echoing the prevalent point of view in Europe. By the end of the decade, an increasingly large and vocal opposition to the market for corporate control—as embodied by highly leveraged and hostile transactions—led to its curtailment, but only temporarily.

By the end of the 1990s, the buyout market was again hot, except this time most of the deals were friendly. Managers had learned the lessons of shareholder value and weren't waiting for hostile bidders. At the same time, the LBO had moved to Europe. Many European buyout groups were formed and American firms began to look for deals in Europe as well.

How do LBOs create value? The argument runs along these lines: Many mature, established industries that have been subject to hostile takeovers generate high levels of free cash flow. Some companies in this situation, such as those in the tire, oil and gas, and consumer packaged goods industries, often do not have sufficient attractive investment opportunities. Nevertheless, the natural inclination of an enterprise is to reinvest its cash, rather than give it back to shareholders. Such an approach can result in bad investments that reduce shareholder value. The poor investments take these forms: Money is invested in businesses that the company knows, but are not attractive, or in businesses it does not know and is unlikely to succeed in.

---

[2] G. Baker and G. Smith, *The New Financial Capitalists: Kohlberg Kravis Roberts and the Creation of Corporate Value* (Cambridge, England: Cambridge University Press, 1998).

Outside intervention is an instrument through which this economically suboptimal allocation of cash resources can be stopped. In the case of an LBO, this occurs through substituting equity with debt, forcing much of the free cash flow out of the enterprise and back into the capital markets in the form of interest and principal payments. This need not be done through outside intervention; it can also be accomplished voluntarily through a leveraged recapitalization, where a company takes on debt and uses the proceeds to repurchase a large proportion of its own equity.

What both situations have in common, though, is that they usually lead to significant increases in value accruing to existing shareholders. Indeed, if the corporate objective is shareholder value maximization, spending on unattractive investments is much more likely to be curtailed than if managers are following some other objective, such as employment preservation.

To summarize, the restructuring movement of the 1980s was a reaction to the inability of many corporations to adjust and change direction as their traditional product and market opportunities matured or became otherwise unattractive. The instrument through which much of this restructuring took place was the market for corporate control. The basic premise of the market for corporate control is that managers have the right to manage the corporation as long as its market value cannot be significantly enhanced by an alternate group of managers with an alternate strategy. Accordingly, the key driver for change was the poor performance of a company in terms of shareholder value.

The Increased Role of Stock Options

In the mid-1970s in the United States, there was growing concern about the perceived divergence between managers' and shareholders' interest. In part, this feeling reflected anxiousness over 10 years of falling corporate profitability and stagnant share prices. The concern was also fueled by the increasing attention paid to stakeholder model arguments, which, in the eyes of shareholder value proponents, had become an excuse for inadequate performance. Meanwhile, a number of academics became interested in management's motivation in decisions relating to the allocation of resources, a branch of research known as agency theory. In 1976, Jensen and Meckling published a paper, "Theory of the Firm: Managerial Behavior, Agency Costs, and Ownership Structure."[3] They laid out how over the previous decades corporate management had pursued strategies and projects that were not likely to optimize resources from a shareholder's perspective

---

[3] M. Jensen and W. Meckling, "Theory of the Firm: Managerial Behavior, Agency Costs, and Ownership Structure," *Journal of Financial Economics* (October 1976), pp. 305–360.

and called for redesigning management's incentives to be more closely aligned with the interests of the shareholders. Stock options had been a component of the pay packages of most senior executives in the United States, but the size of option grants coupled with the anemic performance of the stock market as a result of high inflation, effectively made them weak motivators of managerial behavior.

The situation changed in the early 1980s. The emergence of the LBO, and especially the management buyout, created instances where both the performance of the company in shareholder value terms and the pay packages accruing to executives as a result of their equity holdings became very large and noted by the public. At about the same time, in 1982, the U.S. Federal Reserve Board embarked on a program that drastically reduced inflation, which in turn prompted a sustained rise in equity values. As a result of this confluence of factors, the role of stock options in executive pay soared. As illustrated in Exhibit 1.1, by 1998, the estimated present value of stock options represented 45 percent of the median pay package for chief executive officers of public corporations.

Over the same period, boards of directors had come under increased criticism for perceived negligence in representing shareholder interests (which, at least under the legal requirements in the United States, they were supposed to do). A movement developed to require that nonexecutive board members have an equity stake in the companies they represented so that they would be more inclined to pay attention to shareholder returns, if only for self-interest. By the late 1990s, 48 percent of medium and large

Exhibit 1.1   Elements of Median CEO Pay Package in USA[1]

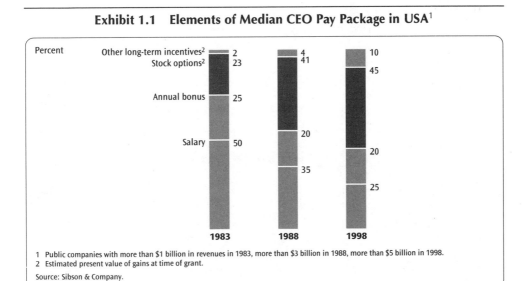

1 Public companies with more than $1 billion in revenues in 1983, more than $3 billion in 1988, more than $5 billion in 1998.
2 Estimated present value of gains at time of grant.

Source: Sibson & Company.

companies had a stock grant or option package for board members, in contrast to virtually none in 1983.

The widening use of stock options has greatly increased the importance of shareholder returns in the measurement of managerial performance. Such developments are not limited to the United States. Stock options and share grants have become important elements of executive pay in England and France. As the competition for executive talent becomes global, it seems likely that the use of stock options will become more and more popular in most open economies.

The Popularization of Equity

The remarkable performance of U.S. and European equity markets since the early 1980s not only contributed to the popularization of stock options in executive pay packages, but also to the increase in stock ownership by households in many countries. This is not to say that many U.S. and non-U.S. households have become active investors in individual equities. What has happened is that growing segments of the population are becoming shareholders through mutual funds and retirement programs. Among the most vocal proponents of shareholder value are the managers of major retirement systems, such as the California Public Employees Retirement System, which has $130 billion in assets under management, a large part of which is in equities.

As shown in Exhibit 1.2, equities are by far the largest asset class in which pension funds are invested in the United States and the United Kingdom, with 58 percent and 76 percent, respectively, in 1996. The difference compared to countries like Germany, with 8 percent, and Italy, with 3 percent, is quite striking. But the situation in these countries is changing rapidly, with an increasing proportion of pension assets moving into equities.

Exhibit 1.2   Pension Fund Asset Allocations

1996 ($ billion)

	USA $	USA %	France $	France %	Germany $	Germany %	Italy $	Italy %	Netherlands $	Netherlands %	UK $	UK %	Japan $	Japan %
Cash	225	5	8	12	9	7	12	17	8	2	43	4	112	10
Bonds	1,130	25	36	54	61	47	21	29	105	30	142	14	538	46
Equities	2,618	58	16	24	10	8	2	3	107	31	784	76	360	31
Other	546	12	7	10	49	38	38	52	130	37	61	6	155	13

Source: Investment Company Institute.

A shareholder culture seems to be developing in many European countries. This has been prompted partly by privatization of large government monopolies in areas such as telecommunications, where governments became active marketers of the shares of these companies. Noteworthy was the German "Deutschland Aktienland" (Germany: Country of shares) campaign in support of the privatization of Deutsche Telekom. The subsequent strong performance of the shares of the privatized companies gave a boost to the popularity of stock investment in these countries.

Exhibit 1.3 illustrates how significant equities have become in terms of market penetration in the United States, covering both direct and indirect share ownership through mutual funds, retirement accounts, and defined contribution plans. While in 1975, 25 million people, representing 12 percent of the population, owned equity shares, by 1995 this number had surged to 69 million and 26 percent, respectively. Under these circumstances, the old notions of labor versus capital are losing currency. No longer is the shareholder someone else: The shareholder is us. As a consequence, the ideological tension that fired the debate on shareholders versus stakeholders is diminishing. With more and more people as shareholders, the support for shareholder value as the objective function for a corporation is gaining momentum.

Pension Insolvency

The fourth contributing factor for the increasing importance of shareholder value is the time bomb ticking away under the public pension systems of most developed countries. In these countries, mandatory public pensions represent the largest part of the income of retirees, with Germany and Sweden leading with respectively 95 percent and 91 percent of retiree income derived from public pensions. Most of these public plans are set up as pay-as-you-go systems where contributions by workers today are used to pay

---

Exhibit 1.3   Ownership of Equity Shares in the United States

	People (millions)	Share of population (percent)
1975	25.3	11.9
1980	30.2	13.5
1985	47.0	20.1
1990	51.4	21.1
1995	69.3	26.3

Source: New York Stock Exchange "Share ownership," various editions.

the retirement of current retirees. This system worked fine as long as there were relatively few retirees in relation to contributing workers. This is changing.

In 1990, for example, there were almost two workers in Germany to support one retiree. By 2035, this number will drop to one retiree per worker. As a consequence, the average contribution rate for a German worker to the mandatory public pension system will rise to 34.1 percent of gross wages in 2035 if no actions are taken, compared with 19.7 percent in 1996. This is the stuff of which revolutions are made.

Although avoiding a pension crisis is possible, there are no easy fixes. Most analysts agree that these countries have no choice but to move to some form of funded pension system, where at least a part of the premiums that workers pay are actually set aside for their retirement. The challenge is how to make it through the transition from pure pay-as-you-go to partially or wholly funded. While there are several variations of funded pensions systems, they all lead to the same conclusion—there is no solution *unless the savings in the funded part of the system generate attractive returns.*

With this in mind, one solution would be to increase premiums by a sufficient amount to build a surplus that can be reinvested, with the combination of premiums and investment returns covering the future shortfall. Here is a simplified example of how this might work in Germany. If the additional premiums were invested in German government bonds, which historically have yielded real returns of about 4 percent, the necessary incremental premium would amount to 3,103 marks, a 13 percent reduction in disposable income. If, on the other hand, these savings were invested in Germany's private sector, where real long-term returns between 1974 and 1993 have averaged 7.4 percent, these premiums would drop to 2,068 marks. If the German private sector were as successful as its U.S. equivalent, which generated real long-term returns in the same period of 9.1 percent, the annual premiums would drop to 1,706 marks, a reduction in disposable income of just 7 percent.

Thus, in combination with measures such as gradually increasing the retirement age, the burden can be reduced to a level where political consensus becomes feasible, if the investment funds generate good returns. Defusing the pension fund bomb dictates that the private sector be held to a standard where generating high returns on invested capital and creating opportunities to invest additional capital at high returns is of paramount importance. It is not coincidental that California's public employee retirement fund is one of the most vocal advocates of creating shareholder value in the United States, and has made it clear that it expects shareholder value to be a priority in other markets.

If the funded plans are to work and intergenerational competition is to be avoided—whether in Germany or other developed nations—then there must be steady pressure on companies to generate shareholder value.

SHAREHOLDER-ORIENTED ECONOMIES PERFORM BETTER

We doubt that the strong economic performance of the United States since the mid-1980s would have taken place without the discipline of shareholder capitalism and an increasingly sharp eye by many participants in its economy on creating shareholder value.

The U.S. corporate focus on shareholder value tends to limit investment in outdated strategies—even encourage divestment—well before any competing governance model would. Schumpeter's "creative destruction" is fostered by a bottom-line focus. Moreover, it is hard to claim (as many have at times, albeit often managers of poorly performing companies) that the capital markets are shortsighted compared with other corporate governors—the high number and value of technology and internet companies going public in recent years attests to this. Foolish maybe, but shortsighted? Certainly not.

But what about actual economic performance? Economists widely agree that the dominant measure of an economy's success is GDP per capita. As Exhibit 1.4 shows, the United States—the world's most capitalist, shareholder friendly economy—has a lead of more than 20 percent over other major countries. Up to 1975 other countries were catching up, but this convergence has since stopped. If anything, the lead of the United States has been widening.

Exhibit 1.4   GDP per Capita

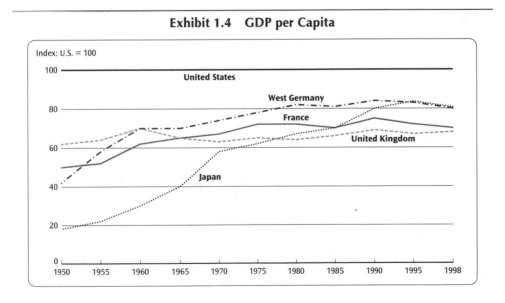

From 1994 to 1997, the McKinsey Global Institute carried out a series of research projects to analyze the differences in GDP per capita between the United States and other countries. The research, which focused on the United States, Germany, and Japan, attributed the U.S. advantage to much higher factor productivity, especially capital productivity (see Exhibit 1.5). How can the United States be outperforming other countries with a savings rate that is often deplored as wholly inadequate? The answer is what happens to those savings. In the United States they are invested in more productive (i.e., economically profitable or value creating) projects than in either Germany or Japan. As shown in Exhibit 1.6, financial returns in the corporate sector in the United States between 1974 and 1993 were dramatically higher than in Germany or Japan.

This is not to say that the shareholder value system is always perceived as fair. Job losses from restructuring disrupt lives. At the same time, one can argue that an economy's ability to create jobs, or its lack thereof, is the better measure of fairness. On that score, the track record of the United States compared with the other countries speaks for itself.

Exhibit 1.5   Sources of Differences in Market Sector GDP per Capita

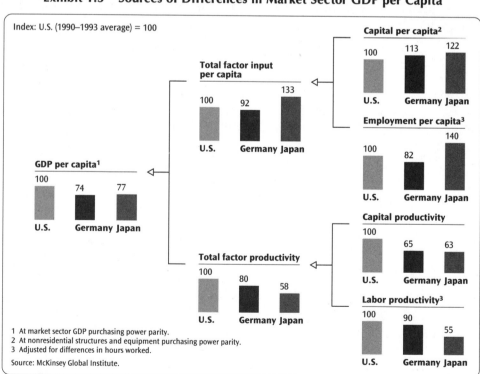

Index: U.S. (1990–1993 average) = 100

1 At market sector GDP purchasing power parity.
2 At nonresidential structures and equipment purchasing power parity.
3 Adjusted for differences in hours worked.

Source: McKinsey Global Institute.

Exhibit 1.6   Annual Financial Returns in Corporate Sector 1974–1993[1]

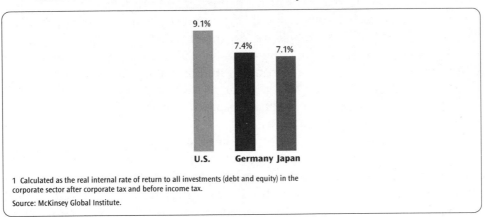

1 Calculated as the real internal rate of return to all investments (debt and equity) in the corporate sector after corporate tax and before income tax.

Source: McKinsey Global Institute.

Two centuries ago, Adam Smith postulated that the most productive and innovative companies would create the highest returns to shareholders and attract better workers, who would be more productive and increase returns further—a virtuous cycle. On the other hand, companies that destroy value would create a vicious cycle and eventually wither away.

Exhibit 1.7   Market Value Added (MVA) and Productivity

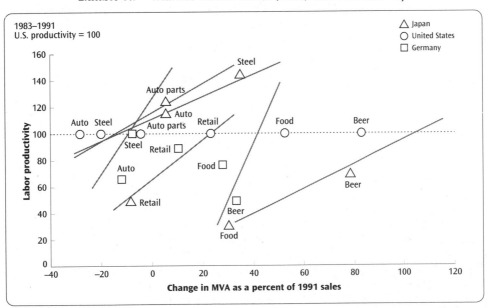

In today's terms, we believe that a company that focuses on building shareholder value is served well by being a good corporate citizen. Why? Simply because such a company will create more value for its shareholders. Consider the employee stakeholders. A company that tries to fatten its profits by providing a shabby work environment, underpaying employees, and skimping on benefits will have trouble attracting and retaining high quality employees. With today's increased labor mobility and more educated work-force, this kind of a company will be less profitable. While it may feel good to treat people well, it's also good business.

The empirical record also strongly supports the conclusion that share-holder wealth creation does not come at the expense of other stakeholders. For the second edition of this book, we analyzed the relationship among labor productivity, increases in shareholder wealth, and employment growth across a range of industries in the United States, Japan, and Germany. Those results are shown in Exhibits 1.7 and 1.8. Our conclusions are that companies with higher labor productivity are more likely to create more value than those with lower productivity, and that these gains do not come at the expense of employees in general. Companies that are able to create more value also create more jobs.

Exhibit 1.8   Market Value Added (MVA) versus Employment Growth

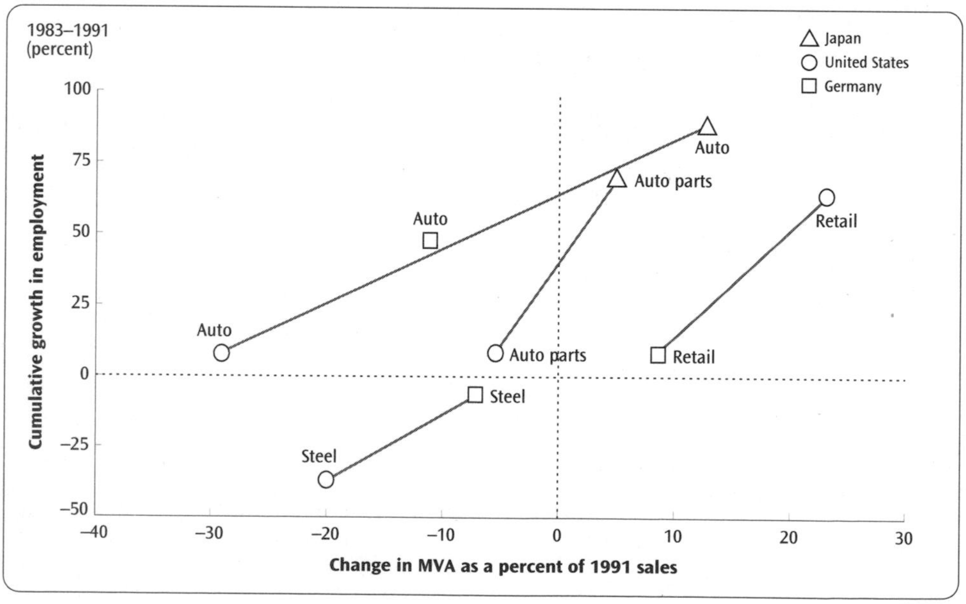

SUMMARY

The ascendancy of shareholders in most developed countries has led more and more managers to focus on value creation as the most important metric of corporate performance. Is this good? The evidence seems to point in the direction that a shareholder value focus not only is good for shareholders (a group that increasingly includes all of us) but also good for the economy and other stakeholders.

2

The Value Manager

In Chapter 1, we argued that value creation is the ultimate measure of performance for a management team. This chapter explains, primarily through a case example, what it means to manage for maximum value creation—in other words, to be a value manager.

BECOMING A VALUE MANAGER

Becoming a value manager is not a mysterious process that is open to only a few. It does require, however, a different perspective from that taken by many managers. It requires a focus on long-run cash flow returns, not quarter-to-quarter changes in earnings per share. It also requires a willingness to adopt a dispassionate, value-oriented view of corporate activities that recognizes businesses for what they are—investments in new productive capacity that either earn a return above their opportunity cost of capital or do not. The value manager's perspective is characterized by an ability to take an outsider's view of the business and by a willingness to act on opportunities to create incremental value. Finally, and most important, it includes the need to develop and institutionalize a managing value philosophy throughout the organization. Focusing on shareholder value is not a one-time task to be done only when outside pressure from shareholders emerges or potential acquirers emerge, but rather an ongoing initiative.

The process of becoming value-oriented has two distinct aspects. The first involves a restructuring that unleashes value trapped within the company. The immediate results from such actions can range from moderate to spectacular; for example, share prices that double or triple in a matter of months. At the same time, the price to be paid for such results can be high. It can involve divestitures and layoffs. Management can avoid the need for cataclysmic change in the future by embracing the second aspect of the managing value process: developing a value-oriented approach to leading and managing their companies after the restructuring. This involves establishing priorities based on value creation; gearing planning, performance measurement, and incentive compensation systems toward shareholder value; and communicating with investors in terms of value creation.

By taking these steps to ensure that managing value becomes a routine part of decision making and operations, management can keep the gap narrow between potential and actual value-creation performance. Consequently, the need for major restructuring that goes with large performance gaps will be less likely to arise. Those who manage value well can guide their companies in a series of smaller steps to the higher levels of performance that even the most comprehensive of restructurings cannot match.

In the balance of this chapter, we illustrate the integrated application of value management principles by presenting a case example distilled from the real-world experiences of client executives with whom we have worked. Our purpose is to show the process of transforming a company in terms of value to shareholders and management philosophy. The case serves as an overview of and framework for the application of the more detailed valuation approaches developed in the main body of this book.

EG CORPORATION CASE

PART 1: SITUATION

In early 1999, Ralph Demsky took the helm of EG Corporation as chairman and CEO. For the previous 10 years, Ralph had been president of Consumerco, EG Corporation's largest division. Consumerco had been the original business of EG before it entered other lines through acquisition. Major institutional shareholders had recently become dissatisfied with EG's performance.

The EG Business

EG Corporation had sales of just over $3.5 billion in 1998. The company was in three main lines of business—consumer products, food service, and furniture—with its Consumerco, Foodco, and Woodco divisions.

Consumerco manufactured consumer products and sold them through a direct salesforce to grocery and drugstores throughout the United States. It had a dominant market share (more than 40 percent) in the majority of its product lines, all of which had a strong branded consumer franchise.

Woodco was a mid-sized competitor in the highly fragmented furniture business. Woodco had been created through acquisitions and consisted of eight separate smaller companies acquired over 10 years. All served the mid- to lower priced end of the market with complementary product lines. The Woodco companies sold their products under their original brand names. As of early 1999, the companies were still operated as autonomous units, but EG had begun to combine the companies into one unit, consolidating separate administration, sales, and production functions to the extent feasible. EG also planned to establish an umbrella brand to tie together the wide range of Woodco product offerings and establish a base for adding new lines.

Thus far, the Woodco businesses had turned in uneven financial results. Management capability in the eight businesses varied widely. Moreover, Woodco's business performance was to differing degrees dependent on keeping up with the latest in furniture styling and fashion. Some of the companies were skilled in this area, but the disastrous consequences of missing the trends had been brought home over the years by their uneven performance. Despite this, Woodco's management was convinced that EG could build a large and successful business. The managers believed consolidation would reduce Woodco's operating costs significantly and strengthen the company's management control over the businesses. They thought the new common sales and marketing thrust would lead to increased volumes and higher margins. The Woodco management's convictions were lent some credence by the existence of several other players in the industry that earned consistently high returns, achieved in part by rationalizing less-efficient companies that they had acquired.

Foodco, EG's third main division, was in the food service business. Foodco operated a small chain of fast-food restaurants, as well as providing food service under contract to major corporations and other institutions around the country. It had been essentially built up from internal growth plus a few small acquisitions over the last five years. The former CEO had viewed Foodco as a major growth vehicle for EG and had backed aggressive expansion plans and the associated capital spending. As of early 1999, EG's Foodco unit was earning a profit but was still in the early stages of its development plan. It was a small player in the restaurant business and had only a few institutional food service accounts. In both businesses, it faced formidable competition, but management believed that its operating approach and EG Corporation's Consumerco name recognition, which was being used as the branding proposition for Foodco, would establish Foodco as a major factor in the industry.

Beyond Consumerco, Foodco, and Woodco, EG Corporation owned a few other smaller businesses: a property development company (Propco), a small consumer finance company (Finco), and several small newspapers (Newsco). No one currently employed by EG could recall why EG had acquired these businesses. They had been added to the portfolio in the 1970s. All were earning a profit, though they were small by comparison with EG's three main divisions. (See Exhibit 2.1.)

EG's Financial Performance

Overall, EG Corporation's financial performance had been mediocre for the last five years. Earnings growth had not kept pace with inflation, and return on equity had been hovering around 10 percent. Part of the problem was that EG had been hit with unfavorable "extraordinary items" that had depressed bottom line results. Beyond this, though, the company had failed to deliver on overall commitments for growth and operating earnings in its businesses for the last few years.

Exhibit 2.1   EG Corporation—Businesses

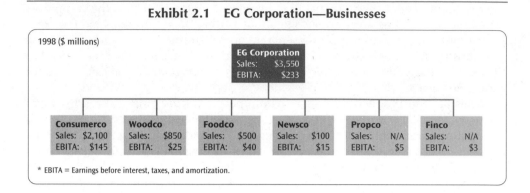

* EBITA = Earnings before interest, taxes, and amortization.

From an investor's standpoint, the company's stock price had lagged the market for the last several years. Analysts bemoaned the company's lackluster performance, especially in view of its strong brand position in Consumerco. They were disenchanted with the slow progress in building profits in other parts of the company. Some security analysts had gone so far as to speculate that EG would make a good breakup play. EG Corporation's board and senior management were frustrated by their inability to convince the market that EG should be more highly valued.

Ralph Demsky's Perspective

Ralph Demsky was familiar with EG's worrisome corporate situation and had been a vocal advocate of a sharper focus on shareholder value for EG for several years. Ralph was convinced that great opportunities existed for EG to boost its value. Upon retirement of the previous chairman and CEO, the board had tapped Ralph to lead EG because of his controversial ideas and his strong operating track record leading Consumerco.

Ralph knew he needed to act fast. His plan was first to uncover and act on any immediate restructuring opportunities within EG. Then for the longer term, he would put in place management systems and approaches to ensure EG did not pass up rich opportunities.

PART 2: RALPH AS RESTRUCTURER

During the first week of his tenure as CEO, Ralph began a project to assess restructuring opportunities within EG. He wanted to take action soon to build value for EG's shareholders and to convince the market that EG could be worth more than its current market value.

To carry out the project, he structured a task force with himself as chairman, the chief financial officer (CFO), and the other heads of the businesses. Analysts from the finance staff supported the valuation work, while each business-unit head was responsible for getting the work on his or her business done. The team met twice a week to review progress, develop conclusions, and—importantly—keep up the tempo of the work. Ralph expected the project to provide actionable recommendations within six to eight weeks.

Ralph had thought long and hard about doing the review with a smaller team, perhaps consisting of him, the chief financial officer, and several financial analysts, to maintain secrecy and speed up the process. However, he had rejected this alternative for several reasons. First, he wanted to draw on the best judgment of his senior managers about the prospects for their businesses. Second, he wanted to involve them from the outset because they would play a key role in carrying out the business improvements that were sure to be identified. Finally, he wanted them to learn the process by doing it, since he planned to undertake a similar thorough review annually.

As an analytical framework, Ralph envisioned investigating the value of EG's existing businesses along six dimensions, which he thought of as forming a restructuring hexagon (see Exhibit 2.2). The hexagon analysis would start with a thorough understanding of EG's current market value. Then the team would assess the "as is" and potential value of EG's businesses with internal improvements, the external sale value of the businesses, growth opportunities, and the opportunities to increase value through financial engineering. All these values would be tied back to EG's value in the stock market to estimate the potential gain to EG's shareholders from a thorough restructuring. The comparison would also help to identify gaps in perceptions between investors and EG management about prospects for the businesses. When their analysis was complete, Ralph and his team would have a thorough, fact-based perspective on the condition of EG's portfolio and their options for building value.

Exhibit 2.2   Restructuring Hexagon

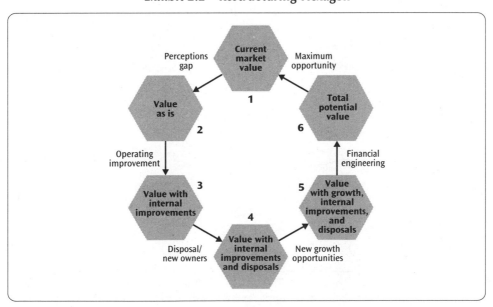

Current Valuation

The first thing Ralph did was to review EG's performance from the standpoint of its stockholders. He already knew that EG had not performed particularly well for its shareholders in recent times and that operating returns had not been as good as everyone had hoped. But Ralph wanted to be more systematic in his review of the market's perspective. His team set about examining EG's performance in the stock market, its underlying financial performance, how it had been generating and investing cash flow, and the market's implicit assumptions about its future performance.

What Ralph found was disturbing—and revealing. EG's return to investors had indeed been below the market overall and below the returns for a roughly assembled set of "comparable" companies (see Exhibit 2.3). When he looked at the current valuation of EG relative to peers, he was disappointed, but not surprised, that his company was also valued lower relative to the book value of invested capital (Exhibit 2.4).

What also stood out from the analysis were a couple of events that had knocked down the value of EG relative to the market. In the period 1992 to 1997, EG had made several acquisitions to establish and build the Woodco furniture businesses. Ralph noticed a decline in EG's share price relative to comparable companies and the market around the date of each acquisition. In fact, when the team calculated the impact of these declines on the total value of EG, they realized that the decline in EG's total value was about equal to the dollar amount of the premiums over market price EG had paid to acquire the companies. Evidently, the stock market did not believe EG would add any value to the acquired businesses. It had

Exhibit 2.3   EG Corporation—Shareholder Returns versus Comparables

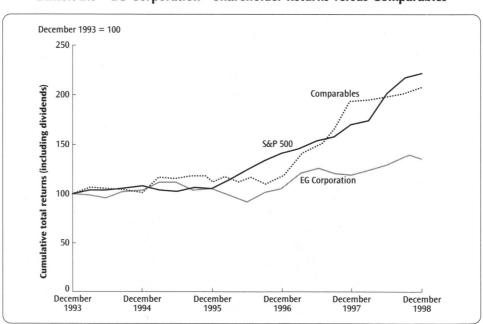

Exhibit 2.4   EG Corporation—Comparative Current Valuation

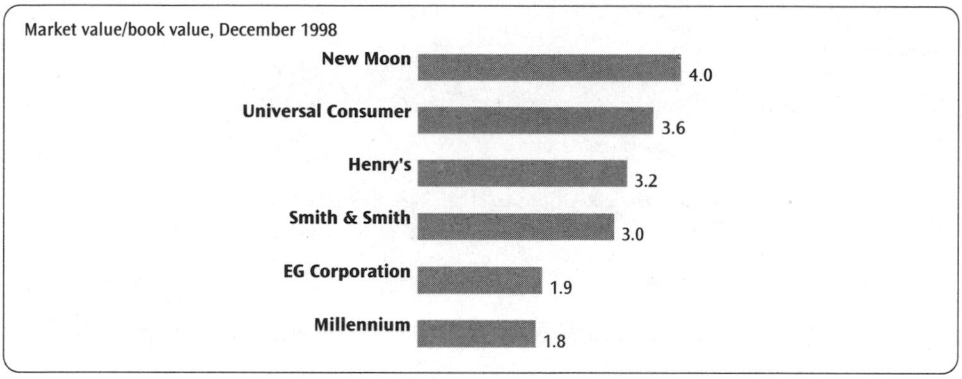

Market value/book value, December 1998

New Moon	4.0
Universal Consumer	3.6
Henry's	3.2
Smith & Smith	3.0
EG Corporation	1.9
Millennium	1.8

viewed the acquisition premiums EG had paid as a damaging transfer of value from EG investors to the selling shareholders in the acquired companies.

Ralph thought that this made sense. Since EG had not in fact done anything to these companies since they were purchased, there was no reason for them to be worth any more than their pre-acquisition value. It didn't seem to matter that the deals had been carefully structured and financed in part with debt to avoid diluting EG's earnings per share. The market had seen through those gimmicks.

Looking next at the financial results of each of EG's businesses, the team noted that Consumerco had generated high, stable returns on invested capital (35+ percent) for the last five years. However, the businesses' earnings were only growing at the pace of inflation. EG's Woodco business had suffered steadily declining returns. The earnings of the Foodco business, on the other hand, were growing, but returns on investment were low because of high capital investment requirements in the restaurants. All of these factors had conspired to depress overall EG returns on capital and hamper growth in profits.

One investment analysis Ralph found especially intriguing was a cash flow map of EG based on information for the last five years (see Exhibit 2.5). What it showed was that EG had been generating substantial discretionary or free cash flow in the Consumerco business, a large portion of which had been sunk into Woodco and Foodco. Relatively little had been re-invested in Consumerco. Moreover, little of the cash had found its way back to EG's shareholders. In fact, on a five-year basis, EG had in effect been borrowing to pay dividends to shareholders. Since Ralph believed that shareholder value derived from the cash flow returns EG could generate, he became increasingly suspicious that EG had taken the cash Consumerco had generated and re-invested it in businesses that might not generate an adequate return for shareholders.

To round out his perspective on EG's valuation by the stock market, Ralph spent a day reading all the reports securities analysts had written recently about the company. He then went to visit several of the leading analysts who followed EG's stock, to gain their perspective on the company's situation. He was surprised at the favorable reception he received. Apparently, the previous CEO had little regard for securities analysts. He had never met with them individually to understand

Exhibit 2.5   EG Corporation—Cumulative Cash Flows

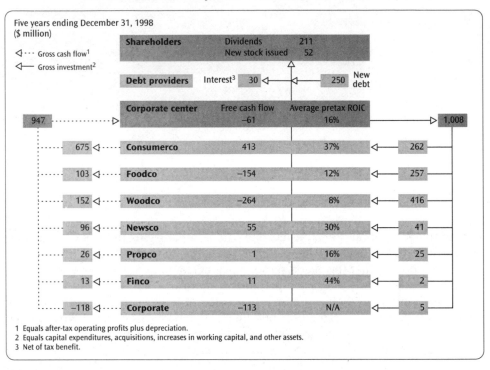

Five years ending December 31, 1998
($ million)

◁ ⋯ Gross cash flow[1]
◁— Gross investment[2]

Shareholders	Dividends	211			
	New stock issued	52			
Debt providers	Interest[3]	30 ◁	◁	250	New debt
Corporate center	Free cash flow	Average pretax ROIC			
947 ⋯▷	−61	16%			▷ 1,008
675 ◁⋯ **Consumerco**	413	37%	◁	262	
103 ◁⋯ **Foodco**	−154	12%	◁	257	
152 ◁⋯ **Woodco**	−264	8%	◁	416	
96 ◁⋯ **Newsco**	55	30%	◁	41	
26 ◁⋯ **Propco**	1	16%	◁	25	
13 ◁⋯ **Finco**	11	44%	◁	2	
−118 ◁⋯ **Corporate**	−113	N/A	◁	5	

1 Equals after-tax operating profits plus depreciation.
2 Equals capital expenditures, acquisitions, increases in working capital, and other assets.
3 Net of tax benefit.

their views. When he did meet with them, it was always to tell them why the stock should be more highly valued, never to listen to what they thought about EG. One of the analysts illustrated why EG lacked credibility with the market by showing Ralph the analysis in Exhibit 2.6. This showed that analysts had to consistently revise downward their earnings forecasts.

What Ralph heard about EG was disturbing, but corresponded with his view of the situation. The analysts thought EG had been complacent for the last five years or more and had pursued new businesses with little regard for the returns to be generated. Moreover, they felt EG would remain an unattractive investment candidate unless Demsky took actions to demonstrate more commitment to creating value for shareholders. However, management would need to see this potential and act on it. They thought some synergies were possible with strategic acquirers for some EG businesses, but the real problem at EG had been a management that was not serious about generating value for shareholders.

EG's "As Is" Value

Ralph's team turned its attention next to assessing the value of each component of the EG portfolio on the basis of projected future cash flows. To do this, the team members developed cash flow models for each business and then set to work assembling key inputs for the projections, many of which were available from each

Exhibit 2.6 EG Corporation—Continuous Earnings Disappointments

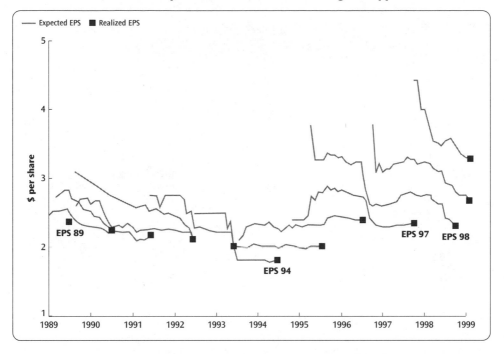

unit's business plan. They needed to know projected sales growth, margins, working capital, and capital spending needs. The finance staff meanwhile developed estimates of the cost of capital for each division.

When they had the inputs assembled, they ran two sets of discounted cash flow valuations as preliminary benchmarks. The first was based on simple extrapolations of the operating results for each business from recent historical performance; in this case, they chose the last three years. They used these projections to estimate the value of each EG business, as well as the cost of corporate headquarters activities and the value of nonoperating investments. Exhibit 2.7 shows the "value buildup" the team used to compare the total value to EG's market value. They noticed several points immediately. First, the total value based on history was substantially below the value of EG in the marketplace. Second, the Foodco food service/restaurant business would be worth far less than the capital EG had invested in it during the last few years, unless performance improved dramatically. Third, the vast majority of EG's value was represented by the cash flow generated by Consumerco. Finally, the corporate headquarters costs, when viewed on a value basis, were a large drag on overall EG value—almost 25 percent.

After reviewing the disturbing results of the historical extrapolations, Ralph asked the team to look at the value of EG assuming the performance estimates in the current business plans were achieved. The results, shown in Exhibit 2.8, were also less than comforting. The total value of EG would be above its market value if the plans came true, but only by about 10 percent. On the face of it this was good news, but Ralph knew that the plans were very aggressive, at least by normal EG

Exhibit 2.7   EG Corporation—Value Based on Historical Extrapolation

	DCF value ($ million)	Invested capital ($ million)	Value created/ (destroyed) ($ million)
Consumerco	1,750	700	1,050
Foodco	300	300	–
Woodco	200	300	(100)
Newsco	175	120	55
Propco	125	140	(15)
Finco	25	55	(30)
Corporate overhead	(425)	0	(425)
Total	2,150	1,615	535
Debt	(300)	(300)	–
Equity value	**1,850**	**1,315**	**535**
Stock market value	2,400		
Value gap	**(550)**		
Percent of stock market value	−23%		

standards. He especially did not like the idea that they would need to do all the hard work implied by the plans just to stand still from their shareholders' perspective. The market took for granted that EG would either improve its performance on its own, or someone would take it over soon and make the needed improvement. Ralph was beginning to think that EG would need to come up with some big ideas to create the impact on the value of his shareholders' investment that he was seeking during his tenure as CEO.

Ralph also was interested to note the change in value of the individual businesses projected by the plans. For example, Consumerco's plan performance would increase its value by about 20 percent, which would have a large impact on EG, given Consumerco's large size. Foodco's value, on the other hand, would actually

Exhibit 2.8   EG Corporation—Value of Business Plans

	Historical extrapolation ($ million)	Business plans ($ million)	Difference (percent)
Consumerco	1,750	2,115	+21
Foodco	300	275	−8
Woodco	200	600	+200
Newsco	175	200	+14
Propco	125	150	+20
Finco	25	35	+40
Corporate overhead	(425)	(425)	0
Total	2,150	2,950	+37
Debt	(300)	(300)	
Equity value	**1,850**	**2,650**	**+43**
Stock market value	2,400	2,400	
Value gap	**(550)**	**250**	
Percent of stock market value	−23%	+10%	

decline despite the fact that its plan involved substantial growth in the number of outlets and overall sales and earnings. To Ralph this could mean only one thing— the returns on investment in the business were too low. Foodco management was more focused on growth than returns. In contrast, the Woodco consolidation looked set to improve the value of the furniture businesses dramatically, while the newspaper, finance, and property businesses would improve somewhat, too.

At this stage, Ralph drew some conclusions. Consumerco would have to do even better, given its large impact on the company. Foodco would need to revamp its strategy to make sure it built value, not simply bulk. Woodco's consolidation was far more important than he had thought and would need to succeed to maintain EG's value. Finally, EG would need to run hard just to maintain shareholder value, and any missteps could spark a collapse in the share price.

EG's Potential Value with Internal Improvements

After looking at EG's value "as is," Ralph's team tried to assess how much each business might be worth under more aggressive plans and strategies. The team first identified key value drivers for each business. The managers estimated the impact on the value of each business of increasing sales growth by 1 percent, raising margins by a point, and reducing capital intensity, while holding other factors in constant proportion. The results, shown in Exhibit 2.9, indicated that the key factors varied by business. Foodco was most sensitive to reductions in capital intensity and increased margins. At current margins and capital intensity, however, Foodco's value would actually decrease if it grew faster. Its growth would be unprofitable with Foodco earning a rate of return on invested capital less than its cost of capital. Woodco was most sensitive to improvements in operating margin, which he hoped would come about as a result of the consolidation of the companies. Consumerco was most sensitive to sales growth. Because of Consumerco's high margin and outstanding capital utilization, each dollar of sales generated large profits and cash flows.

The team next assessed the prospects for each business to improve its performance. One approach it used was simply to compare each EG business with similar companies to gauge relative operating performance. The team also broke down each

---

Exhibit 2.9   EG Corporation—Impact of Changes in Key Operating Measures

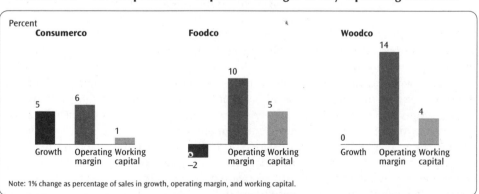

Note: 1% change as percentage of sales in growth, operating margin, and working capital.

of EG's businesses into a business system that allowed it to compare—step by step—relative costs, productivity, and investment for EG versus the competition, based on observations and analyses provided by operating managers in each of the divisions. These analyses, coupled with the financial comparisons, showed that it was reasonable to assume that some of EG's businesses could indeed be made to perform at much higher levels.

Consumerco, despite its already high operating margin, seemed to have room to increase revenue significantly while simultaneously earning ever-higher margins:

- The team discovered that Consumerco had been holding down research and development (R&D) and advertising spending to generate cash for EG's diversification efforts and to buffer the impact of EG's poor performance in other parts of its portfolio. Ralph's team believed that increased spending in the short term would lead to higher sales volumes of existing products, as well as the introduction of additional high-margin products to the marketplace.

- Despite Consumerco's dominant position in its market categories, Consumerco's prices were actually lower than less popular brands. The team's research showed that most category leaders were able to charge higher prices. The team estimated that the value created by price increases would more than offset expected volume losses.

- Consumerco's salesforce was analyzed and the team found that it was less than half as productive as the salesforces at other companies selling through the same channels. Ralph had suspected opportunities here and the analysis confirmed that actions had to be taken to improve salesforce productivity.

- The team determined that cost of goods sold, particularly purchases and inventory management, held additional opportunities. The cost of sales could easily be reduced by one percentage point.

When the team factored in these improvements, they found that Consumerco's value could conservatively be increased by 25 percent, as shown on Exhibit 2.10.

Woodco, the furniture division, also had the potential to improve its performance beyond plan by a large margin, if it could transform itself and perform at the levels of other top companies in its industry. This would likely require a change in Woodco's strategy after the consolidation, to focus less on growth and more on developing higher margins. To do this, Woodco would need to build management information and control systems to keep a tighter rein on its businesses. Woodco would also need to consider sticking more to the basic, mass-market segment of the business where strong operating skills would provide an advantage. This would probably involve abandoning plans to move the business up market. While prices were higher and the potential rewards great in this segment, design skills were of utmost importance. Woodco would be better off focusing on its potentially strong core in the mass-market, basic-furniture segment and maximizing its advantage and returns there. Competitors' performance bore this out. Companies with the highest returns had either a strong operational focus in higher volume segments or played down manufacturing and won with innovative design. Companies who strayed into the middle ground—and there were many of them—turned in only marginal results.

Exhibit 2.10   EG Corporation—Value of Consumerco Internal Improvements

$ millions	
Value per business plan	2,115
Reduce cost of sales by 1 percentage point	115
Reduce cost of sales force	50
Raise prices 3% real (suffer 3% volume decline)	150
Boost sales growth 5% for 3 years with aggressive ad spending	145
Increase R&D yield 25%	65
Value with improvements	2,640

Foodco, EG's restaurant business, looked like it would continue to be a poor performer. The industry was extremely competitive. A few large players were earning respectable returns, but even they were struggling to maintain momentum. Moreover, Foodco appeared to have no advantages to build on. The Consumerco brand, which Foodco was using, was of little or no real value in building the business. Foodco would be unable to develop significant scale economies, at least in the near future. To make matters worse, Foodco had a voracious appetite for capital to build facilities, but was not generating a return on new investment sufficient to cover the opportunity cost of the capital. The team reckoned that the best strategy for Foodco almost certainly would involve cutting back to only its profitable locations and being much more circumspect about growth targets. Even then, it would be necessary to find some way to reduce the cost of capital employed in the Foodco business, either through franchising/management-contract approaches or substantially higher financial leverage. Otherwise, Foodco would likely remain an insignificant contributor to building EG's value.

Similar reviews were carried out for the smaller EG businesses. The team also looked critically at EG's corporate overhead situation and concluded that opportunities existed to reduce costs substantially. EG's corporate staff had grown over the years. The divisions too had added staff to the point where they were functioning largely as freestanding operations. Ralph believed that 50 percent of the corporate costs could be eliminated.

Ralph concluded that the potential internal value of EG's businesses was at least $3.6 billion, which would be 50 percent above its current market value (see Exhibit 2.11). This was before considering any incremental value that might be garnered through the sale of particular EG businesses to owners who might do more with them, as might be the case with the relatively unattractive Foodco business.

Ralph and his team were beginning to feel better about their chances for turning EG into a high-performance company. They were eager to get on to the next step, which was to look at the value of EG as a breakup candidate. They thought

Exhibit 2.11 EG Corporation—Potential Value with Internal Improvements

	Historical extrapolation ($ million)	Business plans ($ million)	Potential value ($ million)	Difference (percent)
Consumerco	1,750	2,115	2,640	+25
Foodco	300	275	300	+9
Woodco	200	600	800	+33
Newsco	175	200	215	+8
Propco	125	150	160	+7
Finco	25	35	35	0
Corporate overhead	(425)	(425)	(225)	NA
Total	2,150	2,950	3,925	+33
Debt	(300)	(300)	(300)	
Equity value	**1,850**	**2,650**	**3,625**	+37
Stock market value	2,400	2,400	2,400	
Value gap	**(550)**	**(250)**	**1,225**	
Percent of stock market value	−23%	+10%	+51%	

that they would also uncover even more ideas for improvement that they could undertake on behalf of their shareholders.

EG's Potential Value with External Improvements

Ralph's team decided to investigate the external value of EG's businesses under four scenarios: sale to a strategic buyer (another company that could realize operating and strategic synergies); a flotation or spin-off; leveraged buyout by management or a third party; and liquidation.

The team started with the easiest values to estimate: what the EG businesses would trade for in the market if spun off as independent companies. To estimate these values, they identified a set of publicly traded companies comparable to each EG business. They used current stock market valuation data (for example, price-to-earnings, market-to-book, market-to-sales ratios) to estimate the value of the EG businesses as freestanding entities. They found that a simple breakup into separate, publicly traded companies would not, at current market prices, provide any gain overall for EG shareholders. Some benefit would result from reduced corporate overhead burden, but the freely traded sum of the parts was less than the current share price of EG.

Likewise, estimates of the value of the businesses as leveraged-buyout candidates did not suggest that EG as a whole would be worth more in parts, especially after taking into account the taxes EG would have to pay on the sale of the units. The Consumerco business with its strong, stable cash flow was a natural buyout candidate, but the other businesses were not.

The final financially oriented valuation Ralph's team considered was a complete or partial liquidation or decapitalization of the businesses. The only EG business of the three larger ones for which this might have made sense was Foodco, because of its real estate holdings. The restaurant property might be sold off piecemeal and the

Foodco restaurant division shut down. To Ralph's team, a number of the units did appear to be worth more for their alternative real estate value than in their current incarnation as restaurants. This did not hold true for Foodco as a whole; the company was worth more as a going concern than in liquidation. The review of Foodco's properties did suggest that management consider closing and selling some of those units, including some that were profitable.

One business the team found might be worth more liquidated than operated was EG's small consumer finance company. Consumer finance had become so competitive that the spread between borrowing costs and the rates earned on new loans did not cover operating costs. The team discovered that the existing loan portfolio might be sold for more than the entire business was worth. In effect, each year's new business was dissipating some of the value inherent in the existing loan portfolio. The team was also sure that it would be relatively easy to sell the portfolio to other financial companies and exit the business entirely.

No links between the finance company and any of the other EG businesses would need to be untangled. EG would also consider the possibility of selling the entire business and searching for ways to make the company stronger, but it seemed likely that it would end up going out of business.

Reflecting on the values generated by a financially driven dismemberment of EG, Ralph saw clearly that the gains from pure financial maneuvering would be limited. The best combination of financial plays for each business did not generate an increment over EG's current market value.

Finally, Ralph reviewed the team's findings on the value of EG's parts to strategic buyers—potential owners who would be able to make the improvements required to increase the value of the businesses. From these analyses, it was evident that Consumerco, EG's largest business, might be worth much more in the hands of another owner than it was now to EG even after Ralph achieved the potential value he had identified earlier. A strategic buyer might see several sources of value in Consumerco. First was the ability to make the improvements to the growth and returns in the business Ralph's team had identified earlier. It was clear to Ralph that these opportunities were evident to any potential acquirer who looked at Consumerco, even using publicly available data. Important too was the potential for cost savings between the consumer businesses of certain potential buyers and Consumerco. For instance, salesforces could be combined and much of Consumerco's direct salesforce eliminated. Potential savings could also be realized in the management of Consumerco itself, since it might be merged into an existing management structure at another consumer products company.

In addition to cost savings, an acquirer might believe it could improve Consumerco's business by injecting more vigorous marketing know-how into the business and improving its new product development activities. Ralph believed that these areas, while difficult to quantify, needed improvement at Consumerco, which was not known for the strength of its marketing team. It had grown accustomed to the high returns its dominant and essentially unchallenged brand recognition provided to its range of products. All these factors together suggested that Consumerco might be worth more than $3.2 billion to a strategic buyer, which was much more than it was currently worth as run by EG (around $2 billion). It was also more than the $2.6 billion potential value of Consumerco to EG that

Ralph's team had estimated previously as the best EG could do with the business. Since Consumerco was a large portion of EG's value, the whole company was at risk of a takeover by a buyer interested in getting its hands on Consumerco.

Potential strategic buyers existed for the other EG businesses too, and Ralph's team did its best to estimate the value of the EG businesses to each company. The team thought Foodco would be attractive to another more established restaurant company that might follow one of two courses of action. On the one hand, it could accelerate Foodco's development and leverage its own management skills to improve the profitability of the Foodco units. Alternatively, it could convert the Foodco sites to its own restaurant concept. Foodco did have quite a few good locations. In fact, it looked as if EG would be better off selling Foodco, since even after paying tax on the proceeds, the business was unlikely to be worth as much under EG's plans.

The Woodco business might be attractive to one of several other companies in the industry that had earned a reputation for buying and improving smaller furniture companies. But it made little sense to sell Woodco when it was in the midst of the consolidation. Any potential buyer would not be willing to take the risk of having the business fall apart in the transition to new ownership. For all practical purposes, the Woodco business would not be salable for 12 to 18 months at anything other than a distressed price. By the end of 18 months, though, EG would be in a good position to evaluate a sale. The business would be streamlined and Ralph would have a better idea about the ability of Woodco's management to improve performance to that of the industry leaders. If Woodco could perform that well on its own, EG would be better off keeping it, and perhaps using it as a base for making additional furniture company acquisitions. If Woodco did not look like it could perform better, it could be sold for a much better price than today.

Exhibit 2.12 shows the conclusions the team drew about estimated values for the EG businesses under the scenarios. The team concluded that, even allowing for difficulty in selling Woodco, EG could be worth substantially more than its current stock price if sold piece by piece to the best potential owners of each business.

New Growth Opportunities

Ralph liked the way the restructuring analysis was coming together. The big missing piece was growth. While he had identified several specific actions to accelerate

---

Exhibit 2.12   EG Corporation—Comparison of External Value Estimates

$ million	Consumerco	Foodco	Woodco	Propco	Finco	Newsco
LBO	2,500	290	NA	NA	NA	180
Spin-off	2,000	280	55	NA	25	140
Liquidation	NA	260	25	130	50	NA
Strategic buyer	3,250	350	155	175	35	190
Highest value	**3,250**	**350**	**155**	**175**	**50**	**190**

the growth of Consumerco in the near term, long-term growth was likely to be modest. Yet he knew that greater long-term growth was imperative to keep managers and investors interested in the company. He also believed that there was tremendous untapped potential in Consumerco's brand name.

Throughout Ralph's years with the company, it always struck him as odd that there was never much discussion about incubating new businesses specifically linked to Consumerco. Radical moves like big acquisitions weren't discussed either. He needed to get long-term growth back on the agenda. A quick analysis showed that if he could find opportunities that generated $500 million to $1 billion in sales, he could increase the market value of Consumerco by $800 million or more. He knew the potential was there, but he wasn't sure yet what the ideas would be. It could be global expansion, it could be new services for retail customers and going directly to the consumer.

With all that was on his plate, Ralph knew that his first priority was EG's restructuring, but he insisted on keeping this long-term potential on the top of everyone's mind. He demanded that all the summary charts of this restructuring analysis prominently display the long-term growth imperative. He was willing to wait six to nine months while the restructuring was under way, but then he had to act on growth.

Potential Value of Financial Engineering

Ralph also urged his CFO to look hard at EG's financial structure and come up with an aggressive plan to take advantage of the tax advantages of debt financing. EG had had a policy of maintaining an AA rating from Standard & Poor's and liked to think of itself as a strong investment-grade company. Ralph knew that many companies had taken on much higher debt levels and performed well. The performance of many had been spectacular, as managers thought harder about how to generate additional cash flow and looked more critically at investment requirements and so-called fixed expenses.

EG had sizable and stable free cash flows that could support much higher debt. The Consumerco business, which generated the bulk of the cash, was recession resistant. Ralph also knew that he did not need much reserve financial capacity given the relative maturity of EG's core business and its limited need for capital. He also believed that EG would be able to get access to funding for a major expansion or acquisition, if it made economic sense. Otherwise, it was probably a poor investment in the first place.

By the CFO's calculations, EG could indeed carry a lot more debt than it did, depending on the interest coverage Ralph wished to maintain. As the financial performance of the EG businesses improved, EG would be able to carry an even higher debt load comfortably. Ralph figured that at a minimum, EG could raise $500 million in new debt in the next six months and use the proceeds to repurchase shares or pay a special dividend. This debt would provide a more tax-efficient capital structure for EG, which would be worth about $200 million in present value to EG's shareholders, assuming a combined federal and state marginal tax rate of about 40 percent.

EG's Restructuring Plan

Ralph's team had analyzed EG's value from multiple perspectives and was in a good position to develop a restructuring plan. As shown in Exhibit 2.13, the team identified, business area by business area, the actions Ralph and his management could take. Ralph's plan would produce a large gain for EG shareholders if it were successfully executed. Exhibits 2.14 and 2.15 show the projected sources of increase in the value of EG's stock and the increment over EG's recent share value in the market. Ralph's restructuring plan would include:

- Making improvements in the Consumerco business aimed at doubling its already high value—increasing prices; investing more in advertising and new products; rationalizing the large direct salesforce to raise productivity; hiring several top-flight marketing executives from leading consumer companies, and cutting staff functions that had been allowed to grow unchecked.

- Accelerating the consolidation of the Woodco companies and focusing on increasing returns in basic furniture markets rather than expanding into upscale segments.

- Stopping further expansion in Foodco and putting the company up for sale.

- Putting the finance company portfolio up for sale, and taking steps to wind down the rest of its business activities.

- Selling the newspaper and property development companies—valuable properties, but needless distractions for EG.

- Undertaking a review of corporate overhead, starting from the premise that EG could operate with only a handful of people by moving to a holding-company structure, with staff functions pushed down into the divisions.

- Recapitalizing the company by borrowing $500 million and aiming for a BBB rating for EG, rather than its historically conservative AA rating.

Exhibit 2.13   EG Corporation—Summary of Restructuring Actions

Area	Action
Consumerco	Cut costs of sales
	Reorganize sales force
	Increase advertising and R&D
	Build marketing skills
Foodco	Sell
Woodco	Keep and consolidate; sell if in two years management cannot reach next level of performance
Propco	Sell
Finco	Liquidate
Newsco	Sell
Corporate	Cut by 50%; decentralize remainder
New growth opportunities	To be determined
Financing	Increase leverage to maintain BBB rating and capture tax benefits

Exhibit 2.14   EG Corporation—Value Created through Restructuring

	Historical extrapolation ($ million)	Restructuring plan ($ million)	Difference (percent)
Consumerco	1,750	2,900	+66 improvements
Foodco	300	350	+17 sale
Woodco	200	800	+300 consolidation/sale
Newsco	175	190	+9 sale
Propco	125	160	+28 sale
Finco	25	45	+80 liquidation
Corporate overhead	(425)	(225)	+47 cuts
Debt tax benefit	NA	200	NA
Total	2,150	4,420	+106
Debt	(300)	(300)	
Equity value	**1,850**	**4,120**	**+123**
New growth opportunities	0	800+	
Equity value with new growth opportunities	**1,850**	**4,920**	**+166**

- Finding growth opportunities, to build off EG's strong brand name and to develop new skills, although this would probably have to wait until everything else was under way.
- Developing a strategy for communicating with investors about the restructuring plan and its potential impact on the value of EG.

Ralph and his team were confident that their plan would work well. Since they could take immediate steps, they also expected to get a quick and favorable response to the program.

Exhibit 2.15   EG Corporation—Value Buildup

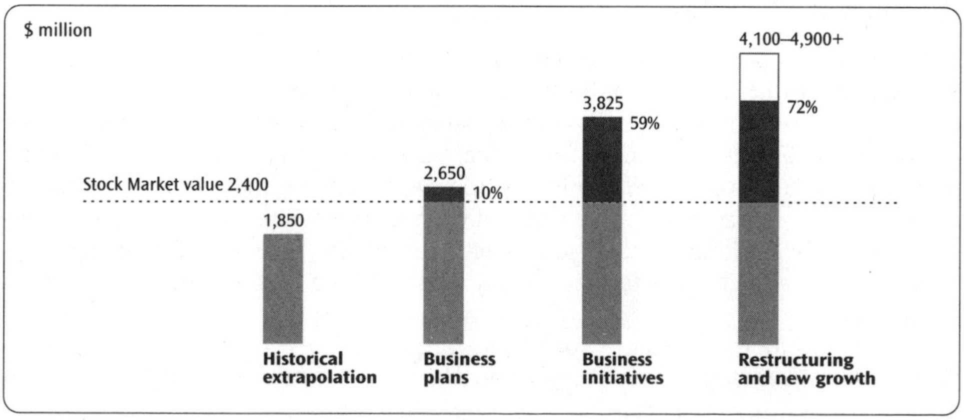

$ million

Stock Market value 2,400

			4,100–4,900+
1,850	2,650 10%	3,825 59%	72%
Historical extrapolation	Business plans	Business initiatives	Restructuring and new growth

PART 3: RALPH AS VALUE MANAGER

EG's restructuring plan resulted in an increase in the price of the company's shares. EG's price jumped immediately when the plan was announced. Then, when investors saw that EG was taking the actions it had promised, the stock price rose further. Over the first six months of 1999, EG's shares increased more than 40 percentage points above the stock market average increase. The analysts who followed EG stopped talking about takeovers and applauded the "transformation" of the company.

Needless to say, Ralph and his team were pleased with the results. Ralph regretted having had to reduce the corporate staff and sell some of EG's businesses, but took some comfort from the knowledge that he did it in a more orderly and humane way than an outsider would have. Despite the successes, Ralph knew he had a lot more work ahead to see the restructuring plan through to completion, and needed to begin building an orientation toward managing value into the company. Otherwise, he feared that employees would become complacent about EG's performance, and the accumulation of untapped value potential would begin anew. He wanted to build on the fragile momentum he had established.

Ralph planned to take six steps to build EG's ability to manage value:

1. Focus planning and business performance reviews around value creation.
2. Develop value-oriented targets and performance measurement.
3. Restructure EG's compensation system to foster an emphasis on creating shareholder value.
4. Evaluate strategic investment decisions explicitly in terms of impact on value.
5. Begin communication with investors and analysts more clearly about the value of EG's plans.
6. Reshape the role of EG's CFO.

Ralph's plans and thinking in each of these areas are set out next. (Chapter 6, *Making Value Happen*, provides a systematic approach to carrying out these ideas.)

Put Value into Planning

Ralph was convinced that one of the main reasons EG had gotten into trouble was a lack of focus on value creation in developing corporate-level and business-unit plans. Likewise, evaluations of the performance of the businesses had only a vague focus on value. Ralph firmly believed that it was the responsibility of all senior managers to focus on value creation. Ralph would ensure that company plans included a thorough analysis of the value of each of the businesses under alternative scenarios. He would also make sure that EG used the restructuring hexagon approach on an annual basis to identify any restructuring opportunities within EG's portfolio.

This new focus on value would also require some changes in the way EG thought about its corporate strategy. For the next year or so, EG had to focus on restructuring. In the longer term, Ralph would need to develop a plan for sustaining EG's advantage in the market for corporate control. To do this, he would need to better understand the company's skills and assets and in which businesses they would be most valuable. Most important, he would have to ensure that the value of these skills could be identified in terms of higher margins, growth rates, and the like before building action plans around them. Too often, Ralph was convinced, EG had done a perfunctory analysis of its capabilities and entered businesses without a clear idea of how and why EG would be a better owner and able to create value for its shareholders. As a first step, later in the year Ralph would establish a task force to compile an inventory and do an analysis of EG's skills and assets compared with its competition, as well as ideas for new businesses EG might enter.

At the business level, EG's new focus on value would require some changes too. The restructuring review had pointed out a number of specific strategic and operating actions that the various business managers would need to take. Beyond this, management in the business units would need to think differently about their operations. They would need to focus on what was driving the value of their businesses—whether it was volume growth, margins, or capital utilization. Everyone was accustomed to focusing on growth in earnings, but what would matter in the future would be growth in value and economic returns on investment. Sometimes this would mean foregoing growth in the business that would have been accepted in years gone by. At other times, managers would have to get more comfortable with the idea of reporting lower earnings when investment in research and development or advertising with a longer term payoff made economic sense. Ralph knew that these changes would be difficult for his management group, because it had not been encouraged to think this way in the past. To help bring about change, he decided to share with the management group the results of the corporate restructuring analysis and to develop a series of training seminars for senior division management about shareholder value.

Develop Value-Oriented Targets and Performance Measures

Ralph knew that his managers needed clear targets and performance measures to track their progress. While the stock price performance was the ultimate measure, he needed something more concrete and directly manageable by his managers, particularly his business unit managers. He also knew that traditional accounting measures like net income ignored the opportunity cost of the capital tied up to generate earnings. Return on invested capital (ROIC), on the other hand, ignored value-creating growth. So he turned to a measure that incorporated both growth and return on invested capital, called economic profit (EP). EP is the spread between the return on capital and its opportunity cost times the quantity of invested capital:

$$EP = \text{Invested capital} \times (\text{ROIC} - \text{Opportunity cost of capital})$$

Ralph chose this measure because he knew that the discounted value of future economic profit (plus the current amount of invested capital) would equal the discounted cash flow (DCF) value (see Chapters 3 and 4 for a more complete description). In other words, EG could maximize DCF value by maximizing economic profit. Ralph asked that all strategic plans and budgets include economic profit targets for each of the business units.

Knowing that lower level managers also needed targets and performance measures that they could directly influence, he asked his business unit managers to translate economic profit targets into specific operational performance measures for their operating managers. For example, the manufacturing manager might be measured by cost per unit, quality, and meeting delivery schedules. Sales might be measured by sales growth, price discounts of list prices, and selling costs as a percent of revenues.

This integrated system of target setting and performance measurement required a new mindset for Ralph's accounting group, which was accustomed to dealing with accounting results. The accounting group resisted but Ralph convinced it of the benefits of integrating financial results with operating measures and with moving toward more economically relevant financial measures.

Tie Compensation to Value

Ralph believed that one of the most powerful levers he could use in building a value-creation focus throughout EG was the compensation system. At present, the package contained relatively little performance-based incentive for top managers. They did receive a bonus, but it was a relatively modest proportion of total compensation. They also received stock options, but few viewed these as significant in terms of their ability to build capital for doing a good job. It was clear to Ralph that the top-management incentives did not focus on value creation. Bonus payouts were geared toward achievement of earnings-per-share targets, which as he knew did not always correlate well with creating value. In addition, the compensation of business-unit managers was tied more closely to the performance of EG as a whole than it was to the fortunes of their particular business unit.

Ralph figured that several schemes were capable of meeting his objectives. He asked his human resources executives to consider phantom stock for each of the divisions; a deferred compensation program structured around the economic profit targets that the businesses were adopting, and using the attainment of goals on particular value drivers as a basis for compensation awards.

Assess Value of Strategic Investments

Injecting a value-creation focus into EG's planning and performance review process would make a big difference. Ralph also knew he needed to make changes in the way the company looked at major spending proposals.

To evaluate capital spending, EG had been using discounted cash flow analysis for at least five years, as had most other companies. This was fine, but Ralph saw two problems. First, capital spending was not linked tightly enough to the strategic and operating plans for the businesses. Because of this, capital spending proposals were out of context and difficult to evaluate. Second, EG had been using a corporatewide hurdle rate to assess capital investment proposals. From the restructuring review of EG, Ralph knew that each of the EG businesses involved a different degree of risk, so the hurdle rates for assessing capital investments should be different, too. To make matters worse, the hurdle rate was too high, having been set in an attempt to smoke out unrealistic operating projections. The result was an ineffective capital spending process. Ralph figured that many investments that earned about the cost of capital were being passed up because they did not meet EG's extremely high hurdle rate. On the other hand, major capital investments were not evaluated as closely as they should be since the whole process had degenerated into a numbers game about assumptions. Ralph intended to tie capital spending closely to strategic and operating plans to ensure that its evaluation was realistic and fact-based. He would also ensure that the finance staff developed appropriate hurdle rates that would differ by division to reflect the relevant opportunity cost of capital.

Ralph knew that one of EG's biggest problems had been the evaluation of acquisitions. He knew they had paid too much for the Woodco acquisitions in the 1980s. In the restructuring review, he had seen the impact of paying too much on the company's share price. Fortunately, as CEO he would have direct control over the decision to pursue acquisitions. He would insist that when proposing an acquisition, the relevant operating manager and CFO do a thorough valuation analysis based on cash flow returns for the transaction. He would not make the mistake his predecessor had of believing that just because he could make the accounting earnings and dilution figures look good in the first year or two of an acquisition, it made sense from a value standpoint.

To Ralph it was really quite simple. Either the cash flow value to EG's shareholders of an acquisition would be higher than the price EG would have to pay, or Ralph would not make the acquisition. And he believed that value could be assessed much more systematically than in the past.

First, EG management would evaluate the target's business on an "as is" basis, just as the team had done for EG. Next, management would use the restructuring hexagon approach to identify improvements that could be made to the value of the company on a stand-alone basis. The management of the target company might or might not be capable of making these improvements on its own. Third, EG management would evaluate the potential for synergies with other EG businesses on a systematic basis. These synergies would be evaluated in concrete terms for their impact on value. Finally, EG management would think about the strategic options the acquisition would create. These would be difficult to evaluate and value, but could nevertheless be important. For example, an acquisition might give EG an option on a new technology in one of its businesses, or access to a new market, both of which could have substantial value under the right conditions.

Armed with this information, Ralph would be much better able to evaluate the logic of any acquisition, certainly much clearer than EG management had ever been. He would know how much EG could afford to pay. Equally important, he would know more specifically what to do with the business after it had been acquired. Before entering negotiations, Ralph would also have his team assess the value of the target to other potential acquirers; in this way he could be sure that he would not enter into a fruitless bidding contest or end up buying the company at a price higher than he needed to. He certainly did not want to fall into the trap of giving all the potential value of the candidate to the selling shareholders. After all, why should EG do all the work and the sellers receive all the rewards?

Acquisition proposals would be subjected to a new test. EG management would no longer presume that the best way to pursue a new business idea was by acquisition. Ralph would ensure that management considered entering a business in other ways, such as through a joint venture. Such approaches might be alternatives to the "big bang" acquisitions that seem like easy solutions at the time, but afterward cause endless problems for the company's stock market performance.

Develop Investor Communications Strategy

Ralph planned to continue working hard to build the company's credibility with Wall Street analysts and investors. It would be essential for EG to track analyst views on its performance and prospects on a regular basis. Ralph wanted to do this for two reasons. First, he would be able to ensure that the market had sufficient information to evaluate the company at all times. Second, Ralph knew that the market was smart. He could learn a lot about the direction of his industry and competitors from the way investors evaluated his shares and those of other companies. He did not believe that he could, nor would he try, to fool the market about EG. He was convinced that it was sound strategy to treat investors and the investing community with the same care that the company showed its customers and employees. Had previous management taken the time to understand what the market was saying about EG, the company might have avoided the difficult position in which it found itself.

In addition to tracking the analysts' opinions and meeting with them regularly, Ralph thought EG should be more active and clearer in communicating with investors. Henceforth, communications with the market at securities analyst meetings and in press releases would focus on what EG was doing to build value for shareholders. He even thought it might be a good idea to have a section in the annual report entitled "Perspective on the Value of Your Company" that would discuss the company's strategy for creating value.

He thought that EG could go as far as publishing estimates of the value of the company, as long as the assumptions were spelled out clearly. Ralph knew that this communications strategy would be a break with the practices of many companies and with EG's recent past. However, Ralph did not really think investors got much benefit from the mechanical—and usually vague—explanations of changes in year-to-year performance typically found in annual reports. Likewise, the glossy photographs and glowing language in the front sections of many annual reports did little to give investors a clear sense of where a company was going and what the status of their investment was.

Reshape CFO's Role

Critical to the success of Ralph's efforts to build a value-creation focus into EG was the need to upgrade the role of the CFO. It was clear to Ralph that the link between business strategy and financial strategy was becoming tighter. Corporate strategies, which are designed to create an advantage in the market for corporate control and financial markets, are by definition intertwined with financial considerations. Furthermore, it was going to take a lot of work to make managing value an important element of EG's strategy and management approaches. Ralph would need a strong executive who would be able to help him push this through.

EG financial officers had been focused on running the treasury operation, producing financial reports, and negotiating the occasional deal. Ralph needed much more, and since his current CFO was due to retire at the end of the year, he felt this was a perfect opportunity to redefine the role. Ralph's concept was to create a position that would blend corporate strategy and finance responsibilities. The officer would act as a bridge between the strategic/operating focus of the division heads and the financial requirements of the corporation and its investors. Ralph drafted a job description for this position, which in EG's case would carry the title of executive vice president (EVP) for corporate strategy and finance (Exhibit 2.16). The EVP would act as a kind of "super CFO" and take the lead in developing a value-creating corporate strategy for EG, as well as to work with Ralph and the division heads to build a value-management capability throughout the organization.

Exhibit 2.16   Job Description: Executive Vice President for Corporate Strategy and Finance, EG Corporation

---

Job Concept

The EVP will act as key advisor to the CEO and division heads on major strategic and operational issues and will manage EG's financial and planning functions. Responsibilities will include:

- Corporate strategy.
- Financial strategy.
- Budgeting and management control.
- Financial management.

Corporate strategy   The EVP will take the lead role in coordinating the development of a value-maximizing overall corporate strategy for EG:

- Ensuring that plans are in place to create maximum value for EG from its current businesses.
  - Assessing the value creation potential of plans on an ongoing basis.
  - Ensuring that plans focus on key issues by challenging important assumptions and the rationale for changes in performance, and providing external reference points for value-creation opportunities (for example, value of the businesses to alternative owners).
  - Acting as a sounding board for the CEO and division heads on critical proposals.
  - Establishing financial measurement standards and developing systems to monitor performance against goals.

(continued)

Exhibit 2.16   Continued

- Supporting the development of corporate expansion strategies to create additional shareholder value.
  - Developing perspectives on market opportunities in businesses closely related to current businesses.
  - Assessing EG's skills and assets in place for pursuing opportunities and suggesting programs to build skills to fill gaps.
  - Conducting business and financial evaluations of specific proposals.
- Planning and executing major transactions required to carry out EG's strategies.

Financial strategy   The EVP will have responsibility for developing, recommending, and executing an overall financial strategy for EG that supports its business strategies and captures maximum value for its shareholders:

- Developing value-creating capital structure and dividend policy recommendations.
- Designing and managing a strategy for communicating the key elements of EG's plans and performance to investors and the financial community.
- Negotiating and executing all major financial transactions, including borrowing, share issuance, and share repurchases.

Budgeting and management control   The EVP will design and carry out processes to ensure that EG managers have the right information to set goals, make decisions, and monitor performance:

- Coordinating preparation of short-term operating budgets.
- Developing key performance measures for each business unit.
- Ensuring that business units have adequate management controls in place.
- Evaluating business-unit performance in conjunction with the CEO and division heads.

Financial management   The EVP will ensure the effective and efficient management of EG's financial operations:

- Ensuring that all external reporting and compliance obligations are fulfilled.
- Establishing controls to safeguard EG's assets.
- Ensuring the integrity and efficiency of cash, receivables, and payables management.
- Filing and paying all tax obligations.
- Pursuing opportunities to reduce EG's tax burden.
- Maintaining strong day-to-day relationships with EG's banks.
- Managing EG's pension fund.
- Managing EG's risk management programs.

Exhibit 2.16 Continued

Success Criteria

If the EVP is successful:

One year from now:

- A well-defined corporate strategy will have been created, and early phases of execution will have been completed.
- A clearly articulated financial strategy will have been developed and implementation will have begun.
- Division heads and key managers will think in terms of shareholder value creation when developing their plans and evaluating proposals.
- The financial management functions will be operating smoothly.
- Securities analysts wll understand EG's strategy and evaluate it as a strong operating company rather than a breakup candidate.

Three years from now:

- EG will have provided shareholders with superior returns.
- EG will have begun pursuing several value-creating expansion initiatives (most likely through internal investments).
- Securities analysts will view EG as a leading-edge value manager of its businesses.

Major Resources

The EVP's staff will include the treasury, controller, planning, and tax departments. In addition, the financial staffs of the operating units will have dotted-line reporting relationships to the EVP. The EVP will have broad discretion in organizing the staff.

Key Organizational Relationships

The EVP's integrating role will require close working relationships with all the other key executives at EG:

- *CEO:* The EVP will provide recommendations and analyses to the CEO on all major issues. The EVP will carry out the financial policy decisions made by the CEO.
- *Operating-Unit Heads:* The EVP will work with the operating-unit heads to ensure the smooth functioning of the planning, reporting, and control systems, and to resolve conflicts between corporate and business-unit priorities. The EVP will also counsel the operating-unit heads on finance-related issues and provide analytical support for special projects.

(continued)

Exhibit 2.16   Continued

The EVP and staff will manage the relationships with important outside groups, including:

- Investors, securities analysts, rating agencies, and the financial press.
- Financial institutions (banks and investment banks).
- External auditors.
- Regulators and tax authorities.

Critical Skills/Requirements for the Job

The EVP should bring a broad business perspective and should possess the following characteristics:

- Seasoned business judgment and superior analytical abilities, particularly in strategic business and financial analysis.
- Ability to take an independent stance and challenge the ideas of the CEO and operating managers while maintaining their respect and confidence.
- Presence to deal with the financial community.
- Ability to lead/orchestrate negotiations in major transactions.
- Strong administrative and people management skills.

In addition, the EVP should have familiarity with the following:

- Financial markets.
- Financial and managerial accounting.
- Treasury operations.
- Taxation.

The EVP would also be responsible for managing the normal financial affairs and financial reporting of the corporation. But his or her success would be measured mainly by how well EG made the transition to a corporation that managed value in a superior way. If the EVP were successful, in a year or so EG would have a first-draft corporate strategy in place, a clearly articulated financial strategy that supported it, and leading managers who were acting in terms of value creation when submitting plans and proposals. Securities analysts would also have a much clearer understanding of EG's strategy and the reason why it would not make sense to view the company as a breakup candidate. Longer term, the EVP's success would be measured as part of a team that would provide shareholders with superior returns, assist in launching value-creating expansion opportunities, and establish EG with a reputation in the financial community as a leading-edge, value-managing company.

Ralph Demsky expected that his six-part plan for building a sharper focus on value into EG could take as long as two years. It would require the recruitment of the new EVP and substantial time and attention from Ralph himself. Focusing planning and performance measurement on value creation, evaluating all major decisions in terms of impact on value, redesigning the compensation system for senior management, and communicating more clearly and consistently with the stock market would help to ensure that EG maintained an advantage in the market for corporate control and produced outstanding value for shareholders. Moreover, by following this much more integrated approach, it would be easier for EG to set corporate priorities, since major decisions would be brought back to the common benchmark of their impact on the value of the company.

SUMMARY

The ability to manage value is an essential part of developing sound corporate and business strategies—strategies that create value for shareholders and maintain an advantage in the market for corporate control. As the case of EG Corporation shows, managing value is not a mysterious process. Valuation techniques and approaches can be complex in their details, but are relatively straightforward in their objectives and applications. Our objective in the balance of this book is to demystify the approaches needed to carry out value management in most companies.

As in the EG case, managing value consists of three broad steps: *taking stock* of the value-creation situation within the company and identifying restructuring opportunities; *acting* on those opportunities, which usually involves major transactions such as divestitures and acquisitions as well as reorganization of the company, and *instilling* a value-creation philosophy in the company.

A managing-value focus does not create value through financial manipulations. Rather, it creates value through developing sound strategic and operating plans for a company's businesses. The link between sound strategy and value creation is a tight one. As many CEOs have learned, financial manipulation on its own seldom works.

Many companies are not in as desperate a condition as we outlined for EG. Most companies, however, would benefit from a thorough review of restructuring opportunities. Perhaps it is because many companies that have gone through massive restructuring believe that it will only happen once. As we discussed in Chapter 1, we believe that restructuring and an active market for corporate control are now facts of corporate life. Consequently, managers need to ensure that they identify and act on value-creation opportunities regularly—not just once when they are a takeover target. This is best done through fundamental changes in the way their businesses are structured and operated. By acting now, value managers can avoid the need to react under duress.

3

Fundamental Principles of Value Creation

To effectively measure and manage the value of a company, you need to understand the fundamental principles of value creation. Before immersing you in the details in Chapter 4, we want to make sure that these fundamentals are clear. This chapter illustrates the basics of value creation with the story of Fred's Hardware.

Fred's business goes through a remarkable transformation. Fred starts out as the owner of a small chain of hardware stores. Then he develops the idea of Fred's Superhardware and converts his stores to the new concept. To expand, Fred goes public to raise additional capital. His success leads Fred to develop additional retail concepts, such as Fred's Furniture and Fred's Garden Supplies. In the end, Fred is faced with the complexity of managing a retail conglomerate.

THE EARLY YEARS

In the early years, Fred owned a small chain of hardware stores. Not being a finance person, he asked us how he would know if he was achieving attractive financial results. To keep things simple, we told Fred that he should measure the return on invested capital (after-tax operating profits divided by the capital invested in working capital and property, plant, and equipment) and compare it with what he could earn if he invested his capital elsewhere (say the stock market).

Fred calculated his return on invested capital as 18 percent. We suggested that he could earn 10 percent by investing his capital in the stock market, so Fred was pretty satisfied, since his investment was earning more than he could earn elsewhere.

Exhibit 3.1   Fred's Hardware—Low Return Store Analysis

	ROIC (percent)	WACC (percent)	Spread (percent)	Invested capital ($ thousand)	Economic profit ($ thousand)
Entire company	18	10	8	10,000	800
Without low return store	19	10	9	8,000	720

Fred then asked if he should try to maximize return on invested capital. One of his stores was earning only a 14 percent return on invested capital and if he closed it, he could increase average return on invested capital. We told him that what he should care about is not the ROIC itself, but the combination of ROIC (versus cost of capital) and the amount of capital, expressed as economic profit. We showed him a simple example (Exhibit 3.1).

Economic profit can be expressed as the spread between ROIC less the cost of capital, multiplied by the amount of invested capital. In Fred's case, economic profit was $800,000. If he closed down his low returning store, average ROIC would increase, but economic profit would decline. Even though the store earns a lower ROIC than the other stores, it still earns more than its cost of capital. The objective is to maximize economic profit over the long-term, not ROIC. Fred was convinced. He set out to maximize economic profit.

Almost immediately, Fred came back very unhappy. His sister Sally, who owned Sally's Stores, had just told him about her aggressive expansion plans. Exhibit 3.2 shows the projected growth of Sally's Stores' operating profit next to Fred's. As you can see, Sally's operating profit was projected to grow much faster. Fred didn't like the idea of his sister bettering him.

Exhibit 3.2   Fred and Sally—Projected Operating Profit

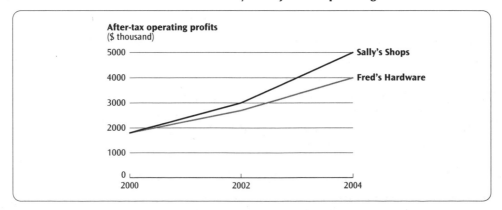

Exhibit 3.3   Fred and Sally—Projected Economic Profit

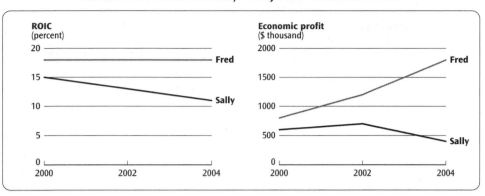

Wait a minute, we said. How is Sally getting all that growth? What about her economic profit? Fred went back to check and came back with Exhibit 3.3. Yes, indeed, the way Sally was achieving her growth was by investing lots of capital. Her company's ROIC was declining significantly, leading to a decrease in economic profit despite the growth in operating profit. Fred was relieved and went off to explain it all to Sally.

FRED'S NEW CONCEPT

Fred was happy with the economic profit framework for a number of years. Then he came back to us. He wanted to develop a new concept called Fred's Superhardware. But when he looked at the projected results (he now had a financial analysis department), he found that economic profit would decline in the next few years if he converted his stores to the new format because of the new capital investment required (Exhibit 3.4). After four years, economic profit would be greater, but he didn't know how to trade off the short-term decline in economic profit against the long-term improvement.

We said, yes, Fred, you're right. You need some more sophisticated financial tools. We were trying to keep it simple. But now Fred was faced with a decision where the straightforward rule of increasing or maximizing economic profit doesn't offer a clear answer. You need discounted cash flows (DCF), also known as present value.

Fred said that he knew about DCF. This is a way of collapsing the future performance of the company into a single number. You forecast the future cash flow of the company and discount it to the present at the same opportunity cost of capital that we discussed above. We helped Fred apply DCF to his new store concept. We discounted the projected cash flows at 10 percent.

Exhibit 3.4   Fred's New Concept

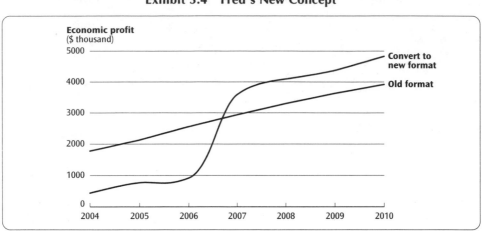

The DCF value of his company without the new concept was $53 million. With the new concept, the DCF value increased to $62 million. He was relieved that he could pursue the new concept.

But, said Fred, what is confusing to me is when do I use economic profit and when do I use DCF? And why aren't they the same?

Good question, we said. In fact, they are the same. Let's discount the future economic profit at the same cost of capital. If we add the discounted

Exhibit 3.5   Equivalence of DCF and Economic Profit Valuation

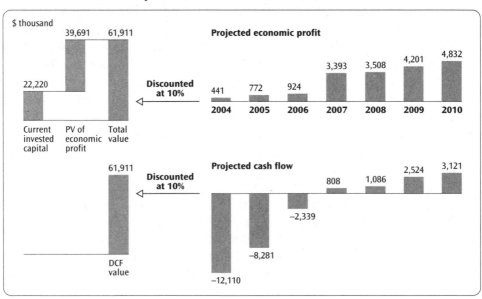

economic profit to the amount of capital you have invested today you get the same result as the DCF approach (exactly, to the penny, not just an approximation) (Exhibit 3.5).[1]

FRED GOES PUBLIC

So now Fred had a way of making important strategic decisions over multiple time periods. His Superhardware concept was very successful and he came to us again with great ambitions. I need to build more stores, so I need more capital, Fred said. Besides, I want to provide an opportunity for some of my employees to become owners. So I have decided to go public. What's going to happen?

Well, we said, now you need to learn the distinction between financial markets and real markets and how they are related to each other. We need to teach you that good performance in one market does not necessarily mean good performance in another.

Until now, we have been talking about the real market: How much profit and cash flow are you earning relative to the investments you have to make? Are you maximizing your economic profit and cash flow? In the real market your decision rule is simple: Choose strategies or make operational decisions that maximize the present value of future cash flow or future economic profit.

When a company enters the financial (or capital market), the real market decision rules are essentially unchanged, but life gets more complicated because management must simultaneously deal with the financial market.

When a company goes public (sells shares to a wide range of investors who can trade those shares in an organized market), the interaction (or trading activity) between investors and speculators sets a price for those shares. The price of the shares is based on what investors *think* those shares are worth. Each investor decides what he thinks the value of the shares should be and trades based on whether the current price is above or below his estimate of the intrinsic value.

This intrinsic value is based on the future cash flows or earnings power of the company. This means, essentially, that investors are paying for the performance that they expect the company to achieve in the future, not what the company has done in the past and certainly not the cost of the assets in the company.

Fred then asked the question, "How much will we get when we sell our shares?" Let's assume that the market's overall assessment of your company's future performance is similar to what you think your company will do. So the first step is to forecast your company's performance and discount

---

[1] See Chapter 8 for a detailed discussion of the DCF and economic profit valuation approaches.

the future expected cash flows. Based on this analysis, the intrinsic value of your shares is $20 per share.

That's interesting, Fred said, because the amount of capital I have invested is only $7 per share. We responded, that means the market should be willing to pay you a premium of $13 over the invested capital for the future economic profit that you will earn. But if they pay me this premium up front, he asked, how will the investors make any money?

They may not, we said. Let's see what happens if your company performs exactly as expected by you and the market. Let's value the company in five years.

The value of the company in five years will be $32 per share, if you perform exactly as you anticipate and expectations beyond five years don't change. Let's assume that you have not paid any dividends. So an investor who bought a share for $20 per share today could sell the share for $32 in five years. The annualized return would be 10 percent, exactly the same as the discount rate we used to discount your future performance. The interesting thing is that as long as you perform as expected, the return for your shareholders will be equal to their opportunity cost.

If, on the other hand, you did better then expected, your shareholders would earn more than 10 percent. If you did worse than expected, your shareholders would earn less than 10 percent.

Investing in the stock market is like betting on sports teams. When you bet on American football, you bet based on a market-determined point spread. If you bet on the favorite, they not only have to win the game for your bet to pay off, they have to win by more points than the spread. In other words, the favorite has to win by more points than expected for their supporters to win their bets.

So, Fred said, the return that investors earn is driven not by the performance of my company but by the performance relative to expectations. Exactly, we said. That means I have to manage my company's performance in the real markets and the financial markets at the same time? Exactly, we said. If you create lots of value in the real market (by earning more than your cost of capital and growing fast) but don't do as well as investors expect, they will be disappointed. Your task as manager is to maximize the intrinsic value of the company and to properly manage the expectations of the financial market.

Managing the expectations of the market is tricky. You don't want their expectations to be too high or too low. We have seen companies convince the market that they will deliver great performance and then not deliver on those promises. Not only does the share price drop when the market realizes that the company will not be able to deliver, but it may take years for the company to regain credibility with the market. On the other hand, if the market's expectations are too low and you have a low share price relative to the opportunities the company faces, you may be subject to a hostile takeover.

Okay, said Fred, I'm ready to go public. Fred initiated an IPO and raised the capital he needed for the company.

FRED EXPANDS INTO RELATED FORMATS

Fred's Hardware grew quickly and regularly beat the expectations of the market, so his share price was a top performer in the market. Fred was comfortable that his management team would be able to achieve high growth in the Superhardware stores so he decided to try some new concepts: Fred's Furniture and Fred's Garden Supplies. But he was a little concerned about how to manage the business as it became more and more complex. He had always had a good feel for the business. As the business grew and he had to delegate more decision making, he wasn't so confident that things would be managed well.

He told us that his financial people had put in place a planning and control system to closely monitor the economic profit of every store and each division overall. Economic profit targets were set annually for the next three years, progress monitored monthly and managers' compensation tied to economic profit against these targets. Yet, he wasn't sure that the company was on track for the long-term performance that he and the market were expecting.

You need a planning and control system that incorporates forward-looking financial measures, not just backward-looking ones, we told Fred. Tell me more, said Fred.

As you pointed out, Fred, the problem with financial measures is that they can't tell you how your managers are doing at building the business for the future. For example, in the short term, managers could improve their financial results by cutting back on customer service (the number of employees available in the store at any time to help customers, or employee training), or deferring maintenance or brand-building spending. You must also incorporate measures related to customer satisfaction or brand awareness that can give you an idea about the future, not just the current performance.

Finally, Fred was satisfied. He came back to see us, but only for social visits.

SUMMARIZING FRED'S LESSONS

While Fred's story may be simplistic, it highlights the core ideas around value creation and its measurement. Here are five key lessons of value creation:

1. In the real market, you create value by earning a return on your invested capital greater than the opportunity cost of capital.

2. The more you can invest at returns above the cost of capital the more value you create (i.e., growth creates more value as long as the return on capital exceeds the cost of capital).

3. You should select strategies that maximize the present value of expected cash flows or economic profit (you get the same answer regardless of which you choose).

4. The value of a company's shares in the stock market equals the intrinsic value based on the market's expectations of future performance, but the market expectations of future performance may not be an unbiased estimate of performance.

5. The returns that shareholders earn depend primarily on changes in expectations more than actual performance of the company.

4

Metrics Mania:
Surviving the Barrage
of Value Metrics

We saw through Fred's story in Chapter 3 how companies create value and how it can be measured. In the real world, managers have been bombarded with advice about performance measures: TRS, DCF, economic profit,[1] EVA™, CFROI, ROIC, EPS, profit margin, and many others. But we think that the debate over which metric to use has come unstuck from the real purpose of metrics: to help managers make value-creating decisions and to orient all company employees toward value creation.

Attempts to compare metrics that have different goals just lead to confusion. DCF and economic profit, for example, are not alternatives. DCF collapses performance across time into a single result and is used for strategic analysis. Economic profit is a short-term financial indicator.

Some metrics are indeed better than others. We prefer economic measures (such as economic profit) to accounting-based measures (such as earnings per share). First, empirical research suggests that cash flow, not accounting earnings, is what drives share price performance. Second, it's easier to understand short versus long-term tradeoffs when you use an economic measure. Finally, you can better understand the sources of value if you use economic measures.

However, there is no perfect performance measure. As a result, we use a framework that links various economic measures to describe different aspects of performance (Exhibit 4.1). The framework describes which combinations of measures are useful for each aspect and also explains how different measures relate to each other.

---

[1] Economic profit is a generic term synonymous with Stern Stewart's metric EVA™.

Exhibit 4.1   Comprehensive Value Metrics Framework

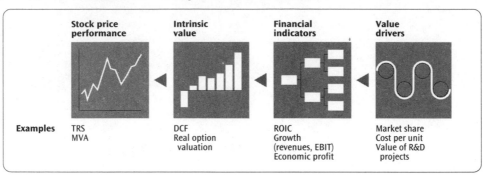

	Stock price performance	Intrinsic value	Financial indicators	Value drivers
Examples	TRS MVA	DCF Real option valuation	ROIC Growth (revenues, EBIT) Economic profit	Market share Cost per unit Value of R&D projects

Reviewing Exhibit 4.1 starting from the left, the ultimate output measure is shareholder value creation in the stock market. Since it is an output measure, managers cannot use it for decision making, but they can set shareholder value creation targets.

Shareholder value creation in the stock market must be linked to some measure of intrinsic value. Intrinsic value is ultimately driven by the long-term cash-flow-generating ability of the company. Hence, intrinsic value can be measured by discounted cash flow (DCF). Intrinsic value based on DCF can be used to evaluate specific investment opportunities or the strategy of a business unit or an entire company.

While a valuable tool for strategic analysis, DCF values cannot be used to evaluate historical performance because they are based on projections. Another drawback of DCF values is that they are difficult to assess in the abstract. But DCF value can be linked to important financial indicators. The financial drivers of cash flow and DCF value are growth (in revenues and profits) and return on invested capital (relative to a company's cost of capital).

Because short-term financial measures may signal changes in value creation too late, we also need to use operating and strategic measures, called value drivers. Monitoring these drivers helps avoid sacrificing long-term value creation for short-term financial results. The value drivers are also helpful in identifying value creation opportunities and focusing the organization on these high priority areas.

Referring again to Exhibit 4.1, each class of measure has a role in management decision making and performance management:

- Corporate management can set long-term value creation targets in terms of the market value of the company or total returns to shareholders (TRS).
- Alternative strategies and opportunities and the value of the business units or the entire company can be evaluated in terms of intrinsic value (DCF or option value).

- Intrinsic values can be translated into short- and medium-term financial targets and targets for operating and strategic value drivers.

- Performance can be assessed by comparing results with targets on both financial indicators and key value drivers. Managerial rewards (compensation and others) can be linked to performance on both financial measures and key value drivers.

A MORE DETAILED LOOK AT THE FRAMEWORK

Let's look in more detail at the elements of the overall metrics framework. We will focus on four core issues:

1. What is the best way to understand the performance of a company from a stock market perspective?
2. What is the logic of the DCF approach to valuing companies compared with other valuation approaches, particularly multiples?
3. If DCF is the best way to value companies, why do we need to look at ROIC and growth?
4. What are the shortcomings of all financial measures, and why must they be supplemented by nonfinancial measures?

PERFORMANCE IN THE STOCK MARKET: THE EXPECTATIONS TREADMILL[2]

Many financial analysts believe that TRS—that is, share price appreciation plus dividends—is the best way to measure performance. Though TRS has many merits, incorrectly used, it can give rise to misunderstandings about performance that in turn distort management incentives, and lead to bad decisions. A comprehensive way of looking at corporate performance is required.

Issues with TRS

A performance measure must do more than simply record how much a stock goes up or down. It must cut through the noise of the market and provide an accurate picture of exactly how and why managers are creating value. Seen from this perspective, TRS has limitations.

Many factors other than management performance drive share prices. During the one to three years that TRS is usually measured for the purpose of evaluating performance, the market as a whole or the industry sector in

[2] This section is based on the following article: R. Dobbs and T. Koller, "The Expectations Treadmill," *McKinsey Quarterly*, no. 3 (1998), pp. 32–43.

which a company operates will drive the share-price movements. Analysis of total shareholder returns for a sample of nearly 400 companies showed that market and sector movements explained on average more than 40 percent of the returns during any one- or three-year period.

It follows that if performance is measured on the basis of TRS alone, managers are in effect being partially rewarded or penalized for events outside their control (this can be alleviated by using TRS relative to a market or sector index). Yet traditional share option schemes do just that, and the bull market of the 1990s rewarded option-holding employees in all but the most woefully underperforming companies. The other side of the coin is a growing problem for the volatile high-technology industry. When a sector re-rating made share prices plummet, companies found they had to reprice employee share-option packages to retain important staff.

In fact, in the short term, differences between actual performance and market expectations and changes in these expectations drive share prices more than the level of performance per se. It is the delivery of surprises that produces higher or lower total shareholder returns compared to the market. As a result, companies that consistently meet high performance expectations can find it hard to deliver high TRS. The market may believe that management is doing an outstanding job, but its approval has already been factored into the share price.

One way to understand the problem is by analogy to a treadmill. The speed of the treadmill represents the expectations for future financial performance implicit in the share price. If managers are able to beat these expectations, they accelerate the treadmill and so deliver above-average shareholder returns. As performance improves, the expectations treadmill turns more quickly. The better managers perform, the more the market expects from them; they have to pound the treadmill ever faster just to keep up.

For outstanding companies, the treadmill is moving faster than for anyone else. It is difficult for management to deliver at the expected level without faltering. Accelerating the treadmill will be hard. Continuing to accelerate the treadmill will eventually become impossible.

This explains why extraordinary managers may deliver only ordinary share price increases in the short run. If their compensation is based significantly on TRS through stock options, they are likely to be insufficiently rewarded. This predicament illustrates the old saw about the difference between a good company and a good investment: In the short term, good companies may not be good investments, and vice versa.

In the case of companies of which less is expected, TRS-driven measures may overcompensate managers. During the early years of a turnaround, for example, beating expectations may be relatively easy because the expectations treadmill is not moving fast. Since the market reflects changes in the performance expected in all future years, the net effect is that managers can deliver high TRS even when they have improved performance only marginally.

There is a considerable multiplier effect when the market re-rates a company to reflect higher expectations. The movement in share price reflects the present value of all the changes in expectations for all future years' cash flows. As a result, TRS could be well over 50 percent. Merely to announce a new chief executive officer can be enough to shift a share price by more than 10 percent before the new manager has even arrived, and certainly long before there has been any improvement in performance. On the day in 1996 that Credit Suisse announced the appointment of Lukas Muehlemann as CEO, the bank's share price rose by about 20 percent, causing shareholder value to soar by $3 billion.

Market Value Added: A Complementary Measure

An alternative market-based performance measure, market value added (MVA), has gained popularity, especially with the publication of the financial consultant Stern Stewart's MVA rankings in *Fortune* magazine in the United States and in other financial publications around the world. MVA is calculated as the difference between the market value of a company's debt and equity and the amount of capital invested. The market to capital ratio, a variation on MVA expressed as a ratio rather than a dollar amount, is the market capitalization of a company's debt and equity divided by the amount of capital invested.

MVA and market-to-capital ratio pose definition and measurement problems because they use accounting data. They are also subject to some of the same criticisms as TRS, namely that important elements of the valuation are outside of management's control. But they provide a worthy complement to TRS by measuring different aspects of a company's performance.

TRS can be likened to the speeding up or slowing down of the treadmill. It measures performance against the expectations of financial markets and changes in these expectations. TRS is a measure of how well a company beats the target set by market expectations—a measure of improvement, in other words. MVA and market-to-capital, on the other hand, can be likened to the current speed of the treadmill. They measure the financial market's view of future performance relative to the capital invested in the business. In this way, they assess a company's absolute level of performance.

To understand the difference between MVA and TRS, consider the example of the U.S. retailers Sears and Wal-Mart. In the five years ending December 31, 1997, Sears achieved an average TRS of 22 percent a year, while Wal-Mart managed 5 percent a year. Is Sears creating more value? Is it performing better?

The MVAs and market-to-capital for Sears and Wal-Mart are shown in Exhibit 4.2. On December 31, 1997, Wal-Mart's market capitalization (debt and equity) was $101.3 billion and its invested capital $32.1 billion. This resulted

Exhibit 4.2   MVA for Sears and Wal-Mart

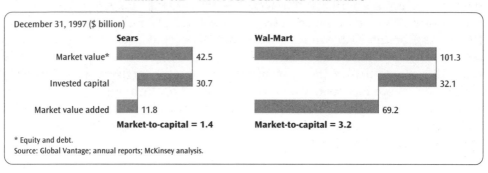

December 31, 1997 ($ billion)

	Sears	Wal-Mart
Market value*	42.5	101.3
Invested capital	30.7	32.1
Market value added	11.8	69.2
	Market-to-capital = 1.4	**Market-to-capital = 3.2**

* Equity and debt.
Source: Global Vantage; annual reports; McKinsey analysis.

in an MVA of $69.2 billion, one of the highest in the world. Sears' MVA was $11.8 billion, based on a market value of $42.5 billion and invested capital of $30.7 billion. If we then look at the market-to-capital ratios, Wal-Mart scored 3.2, Sears 1.4. In other words, every dollar that Wal-Mart had invested was valued by the market at $3.20, while every dollar Sears had invested was valued at $1.40.

Wal-Mart creates more value, so it has a high market-to-capital. It was not able, however, to exceed the market's performance expectations because its treadmill was already moving fast. Sears does not create as much value, so it has a lower market-to-capital. But during its restructuring, it has beaten market expectations. Its treadmill was moving slowly, and has speeded up. It could be argued that both companies have performed well over the five years, given their different starting points.

Combining TRS and market-to-capital can provide interesting insights into the dynamics of a company's performance, especially when the period examined is less than 10 years. To illustrate, Exhibit 4.3 plots a number of leading retailers in terms of market-to-capital ratio and TRS. The companies fall into four quadrants.

Quadrant 1 companies are the corporate elite. They include the U.S. clothing retailer The Gap, the U.S. supermarket chain Kroger, and the French supermarket chain Carrefour. These companies have earned exceptionally high TRS in the five years to December 1997 and have high market values in relation to the amount of capital invested in them. Quadrant 3 companies are the opposite; they face a considerable performance challenge. They include the U.S. supermarket Great Atlantic and Pacific, the U.S. discount retailer Kmart, and the German retailer Karstadt. In each case, TRS is low or negative, and market-to-capital is lower than for most retailers. Companies in this quadrant (and in quadrant 1) are easy to evaluate because both measures are low (or high).

Evaluating companies in quadrants 2 and 4 is more difficult. Quadrant 2 companies are recovering underperformers. This group includes Sears, the

Exhibit 4.3   Market Capitalization and TRS for Leading Retailers

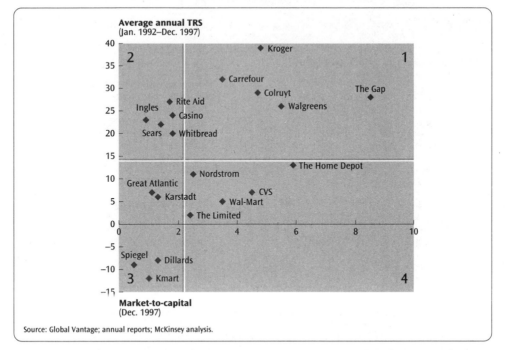

Source: Global Vantage; annual reports; McKinsey analysis.

U.S. drugstore chain Rite Aid, and the U.K. brewer, pub, and restaurant chain Whitbread. These companies have high TRS but low relative market-to-capital. Five years ago, when expectations of their performance were low, their market-to-capital was even poorer. They have since performed better than expected, accelerating the treadmill, but their market-to-capital ratios are still nowhere near those of excellent competitors.

Companies in quadrant 4 may have suffered from unrealistic market expectations, or they may be underachievers. They include Wal-Mart and Nordstrom. These companies have high relative market-to-capital but low TRS. You might think of them as emerging underperformers. Although highly valued, they have not exceeded—indeed, in some cases have not met—market expectations. Without detailed analysis, it is impossible to say whether this is the result of unrealistic performance expectations by the market at the beginning of the period, or of managers' inability to realize their companies' potential. The treadmills were simply moving too fast, and the companies have been unable to keep running at the required pace.

In these assessments, we used the relative measure of market-to-capital, but we can also use the absolute measure of MVA. Exhibit 4.4 shows the performance of the same retail companies using both absolute and size-adjusted measures. Relative to the amount of capital invested, the top retailer in our sample is The Gap. On an absolute basis, the winner is Wal-Mart. The

Exhibit 4.4   MVA and Market-to-Capital: Absolute and Relative Measures

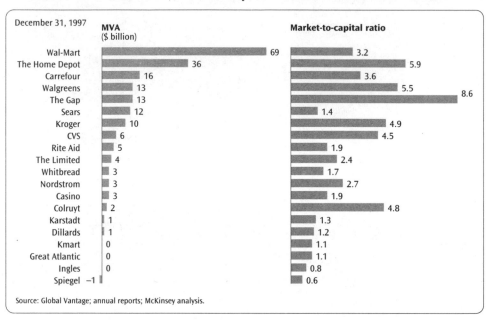

December 31, 1997	MVA ($ billion)	Market-to-capital ratio
Wal-Mart	69	3.2
The Home Depot	36	5.9
Carrefour	16	3.6
Walgreens	13	5.5
The Gap	13	8.6
Sears	12	1.4
Kroger	10	4.9
CVS	6	4.5
Rite Aid	5	1.9
The Limited	4	2.4
Whitbread	3	1.7
Nordstrom	3	2.7
Casino	3	1.9
Colruyt	2	4.8
Karstadt	1	1.3
Dillards	1	1.2
Kmart	0	1.1
Great Atlantic	0	1.1
Ingles	0	0.8
Spiegel	−1	0.6

Source: Global Vantage; annual reports; McKinsey analysis.

Gap creates more value for each dollar invested, but Wal-Mart creates more absolute wealth. Which is better? It is impossible to say, and probably irrelevant. Both are star performers.

MARKET VALUE DRIVEN BY INTRINSIC DCF

The second issue to address in detailing our metrics framework is what drives the market value of companies. To make the problem tractable, we will compare the DCF approach to the earnings-multiple approach. The DCF approach provides a more sophisticated and reliable picture of a company's value than an earnings-multiple approach. In the next chapter, *Cash Is King*, we provide evidence that market behavior is consistent with the theory.

We begin by defining the two competing approaches:

1. In the earnings-multiple approach, companies are valued based on a multiple of accounting earnings. In its extreme form, the earnings-multiple approach says that only this year's or next year's earnings matter. A more complex form might discount the future stream of earnings at some rate or some form of "normalized" earnings.[3]

---

[3] A variation on earnings multiples is the use of multiples of operating parameters as a shorthand when comparing companies. For example, asset managers are often valued as a percentage of

Exhibit 4.5   Projected Income of Long Life and Short Life Companies

Income statements						
$	**Year 1**	**Year 2**	**Year 3**	**Year 4**	**Year 5**	**Year 6**
Long Life Company						
Sales	1,000	1,050	1,100	1,200	1,300	1,450
Cash expenses	(700)	(745)	(790)	(880)	(970)	(1,105)
Depreciation	(200)	(200)	(200)	(200)	(200)	(200)
Net income	100	105	110	120	130	145
Short Life Company						
Sales	1,000	1,050	1,100	1,200	1,300	1,450
Cash expenses	(700)	(745)	(790)	(880)	(970)	(1,105)
Depreciation	(200)	(200)	(200)	(200)	(200)	(200)
Net income	100	105	110	120	130	145

2. In the DCF approach, the value of a business is the expected cash flow discounted at a rate that reflects the riskiness of the cash flow.

The essential problem with the earnings-multiple valuation approach is that it does not value directly what matters to investors. Investors cannot buy a house or car with earnings. Only the cash flow generated by the business can be used for consumption or additional investment. Exhibit 4.5 shows the projected income statements of two companies. Based on this accounting information, would you pay more for Longlife Company or Shortlife Company? Both the level and expected growth rates of earnings are identical, so most people would be inclined to pay the same multiple of earnings (say 10 times) and therefore the same price for both companies. As we shall see, however, this is the wrong conclusion because earnings alone is inadequate without understanding the investment required to generate the earnings.

Exhibit 4.6 shows the projected cash flow statements for the two companies, where cash flow equals the operating profits of the companies less the net investment in working capital and fixed assets required to support the company's growth. Longlife Company uses manufacturing equipment that must be replaced every three years, while Shortlife Company uses equipment that must be replaced every year but costs one-third what

---

assets under management. In November 1999, Allianz bought 70 percent of PIMCO Advisors, a large asset manager, for $3.3 billion. News accounts about the transaction commented that Allianz paid an amount equal to 1.8 percent of the assets under management, while Merrill Lynch paid 3 percent of assets under management for Mercury Asset Management in 1997. That is a large difference, but is it good or bad? Who got a better deal? If you dig deep you will find that PIMCO and Mercury are quite different. PIMCO manages more fixed income funds that earn lower profits than the equity funds that Mercury focuses on. Their growth prospects are also very different. The price paid relative to assets might be an interesting benchmark for conversation, but it certainly isn't good enough for a manager to make an important acquisition decision.

Exhibit 4.6 Projected Cash Flow of Long Life and Short Life Companies

Cash flow statements

$	Year 1	Year 2	Year 3	Year 4	Year 5	Year 6	Cumulative
Long Life Company							
Net income	100	105	110	120	130	145	710
Depreciation	200	200	200	200	200	200	1,200
Capital expenditures	(600)	0	0	(600)	0	0	(1,200)
Increase in receivables	(250)	(13)	(13)	35	45	(23)	(219)
Cash to (from) shareholders	(550)	292	297	(245)	375	322	491
Short Life Company							
Net income	100	105	110	120	130	145	710
Depreciation	200	200	200	200	200	200	1,200
Capital expenditures	(200)	(200)	(200)	(200)	(200)	(200)	(1,200)
Increase in receivables	(150)	(8)	(8)	(15)	(15)	(23)	(219)
Cash to (from) shareholders	(50)	97	102	105	115	122	491

Longlife's equipment costs. In addition, Shortlife does a better job of collecting its receivables.

Which one would you pay more for? Most people would pay more for Shortlife, because most people prefer to have cash now rather than later. Note that the total cash flow over the entire six-year period is the same for both companies, though Shortlife shareholders get their cash earlier. In fact, if you discounted these cash flows to the beginning of year 1 at 10 percent, you would see that the present value of Shortlife's cash flow ($323) is about 50 percent larger than the present value of Longlife's cash flows ($212). This example illustrates the earnings-multiple approach's main weakness. If you look only at earnings, and ignore the capital required to generate the earnings, you cannot see that Shortlife should be valued at a higher earnings multiple than Longlife. It does not consider the investment required to generate earnings or its timing. Longlife Company has less value than Shortlife because it invests more capital (or the same amount of capital earlier) to generate the same level of sales and earnings.

The DCF model, however, accounts for the difference in value by factoring in the capital spending and other cash flows required to generate the earnings. This approach is widely used by companies to evaluate capital spending proposals. The DCF model applies this approach to entire businesses, which are effectively just collections of individual projects.

The DCF approach is based on the simple concept that an investment adds value if it generates a return on investment above the return that can be earned on investments of similar risk. In other words, for a given level of earnings, a company with higher returns on investment will need to invest less capital in the business and will, in turn, generate higher cash flows and higher value.

So why has the earnings-multiple approach endured? Like most things that stand the test of time, it works well in certain situations. When earnings reflect cash flow (e.g., businesses with little capital such as software companies), the approach provides a good proxy for discounted cash flow. It is when earnings and cash flow diverge that earnings multiples come up short.

Suppose Longlife Company has figured out a way to increase its earnings each year by 10 percent by increasing invested capital at the same rate. The earnings-multiple approach and DCF analysis would suggest that the value of Longlife should increase by 10 percent as well, because both earnings and cash flow increase by 10 percent each year. So the earnings-multiple approach would appear to value Longlife correctly.

Now suppose that Longlife's controller can increase the first year's earnings by 10 percent by recording some revenues in year one that would otherwise appear in year two (but without actually changing the timing of cash flows). The increase in year one's earnings is exactly offset by the decrease in year two's. The most extreme accounting approach would say that the value of Longlife has increased by 10 percent. The DCF model would not be fooled. Cash flow has not changed, so Longlife's value would be unchanged in the DCF model.

Before maligning the earnings-multiple approach too much, we should show how to develop a more sophisticated model that mimics the DCF model well under some circumstances. This entails finding a way to incorporate the quality of earnings into the P/E ratio so that we can differentiate between companies with identical earnings but different cash flows or risks.

Let's construct another simple example, using Value Inc. and Volume Inc., as shown in Exhibit 4.7. Both companies have identical earnings once again, but Value Inc. has a larger cash flow. Then we value the companies using DCF analysis.

If we assume that both companies have identical risk, we can discount their cash flows at the same discount rate, say 10 percent. Both companies

---

Exhibit 4.7   Cash Flows of Value Inc. and Volume Inc.

$ Value Inc.	Year 1	Year 2	Year 3	Year 4	Year 5
Net income	100	105	110	116	122
Net investment	(25)	(26)	(27)	(29)	(31)
Cash to shareholders	75	79	83	87	91

Volume Inc.	Year 1	Year 2	Year 3	Year 4	Year 5
Net income	100	105	110	116	122
Net investment	(50)	(52)	(55)	(58)	(61)
Cash to shareholders	50	53	55	58	61

also continue their respective earnings and cash flow growth rates forever. Using some algebra that helps us deal with growing perpetuities, we can compute the value of Value Inc. to be $1,500 and Volume Inc. to be $1,000. This also means that Value Inc. has a P/E ratio of 15 and Volume Inc. of 10.

The key to Value Inc.'s larger cash flow and higher value is that it does not invest as much capital to generate additional earnings. For example, Value Inc. invests only $25 in the first year to generate $5 additional earnings the next year, while Volume Inc. invests $50 to generate the same incremental earnings. Value Inc. earns a return of 20 percent on its new capital, while Volume Inc. earns a return of only 10 percent on its new capital.

We can develop a simple formula that allows us to predict the P/E ratios of the two companies.[4] That formula is:

$$P/E = \frac{1 - g/r}{k - g}$$

Where g = The long-term growth rate in earnings and cash flow
   r = The rate of return earned on new investment
   k = The discount rate

This formula correctly calculates the P/E ratios for Value Inc. and Volume Inc.

For Value Inc.:

$$P/E = \frac{1 - 5\%/20\%}{10\% - 5\%} = 15$$

For Volume Inc.:

$$P/E = \frac{1 - 5\%/10\%}{10\% - 5\%} = 10$$

The formula also improves the performance of the earnings-multiple approach by adding investment and risk to the equation. But it also highlights the shortcomings of the naive model. For example, what is the impact on Value Inc. if it can increase its growth rate from 5 percent to 8 percent, while the return on incremental capital declines from 20 percent to 10 percent? The basic accounting model suggests that Value Inc.'s value will increase as a result of the higher earnings growth. Our formula, however, tells us that the new P/E ratio should be 10 and the resulting value should be $1,000, a

---

[4] See Chapter 12 for the derivation of this formula.

substantial decline in value. So higher growth in this situation will yield a decline in value. Only the cash flow enhanced earnings-multiple model leads us to the right conclusion.

While the enhanced earnings-multiple approach works in a simplified world, it begins to break down once we add real-world complications:

- Varying accounting treatments for inventories, depreciation, and other items make it difficult to measure the incremental return on investment consistently across companies.
- Inflation distorts the relationship of accounting earnings to cash flow.
- Cyclicality is not dealt with by the accounting model, which attempts to capture an entire cycle in a single P/E ratio.
- The pattern of investments and their returns is not so simple that investments are made in one year and earn constant returns in all succeeding years.
- The base level of earnings must be normalized to eliminate any nonrecurring items.

We could develop a complex version of the earnings-multiple approach to handle these and other considerations. But in most cases the DCF model is simpler to work with since it already explicitly incorporates important valuation parameters like investment and risk.

BEYOND CASH FLOW: GROWTH AND ROIC

Discounted cash flows drive the value of a company. Unfortunately, short-term cash flows themselves are not good performance measures. The cash flow in any year (or short period of years) is meaningless and easy to manipulate. A company can delay capital spending or cut back on advertising or research to improve short-term cash flow. Large negative cash flow is not a bad thing if the company is investing to generate even larger cash flows.

Most importantly, cash flows are not intuitive. You can't look at a series of historical or projected cash flows and say what that means. What drives cash flow, as we commented earlier, is the growth of the company (revenues and earnings) and return on invested capital. This is the third issue in our metrics framework.

Using ROIC and growth helps to understand how the levers of value creation may have different impact depending on the current position of businesses. Exhibit 4.8 illustrates how this works for a hypothetical company. The exhibit shows the value of a company with different combinations of projected growth and ROIC. The exhibit assumes a 10 percent cost of capital. A

Exhibit 4.8   How ROIC and Growth Drive Value[1]

DCF value	Operating profit (annual growth)	ROIC				
		7.5%	10.0%	12.5%	15.0%	20.0%
	3%	887	1,000	1,058	1,113	1,170
	6%	708	1,000	1,117	1,295	1,442
	9%	410	1,000	1,354	1,591	1,886

◀ Value destruction   Value neutral   Value ▶ creation

1 Assumes starting operating profit = 100, cost of capital = 10%, and a 25-year horizon after which ROIC = cost of capital.

company with an already high ROIC creates more value by increasing growth rather than earning ever higher ROICs. Companies earning less than their cost of capital can't create value by growing unless their ROIC moves up above the cost of capital. In fact, additional growth at current ROIC levels actually destroys value.

Here is the historical and projected free cash flow for Heineken, the Dutch brewer:

	Historical free cash flow (NLG millions)		Projected free cash flow (NLG millions)
1994	238	1999	446
1995	618	2000	754
1996	(1,035)	2001	800
1997	560	2002	526
1998	364	2003	910

There is not much interesting to say about this series of numbers. But now look at Heineken's performance from the perspective of growth and ROIC.

	Actual 1994–98 (percent)	Projected 1999–2003 (percent)
Revenue growth	8.5	5.6
EBITA growth	12.9	6.6
ROIC (after goodwill)	12.3	12.3

With this information, we can understand intuitively how Heineken is performing. We can assess its growth relative to the industry. We can evaluate whether its ROIC is improving or deteriorating and how it compares with other branded consumer products companies. Companies need to be cautioned, however, about shifting their focus entirely to ROIC and ignoring growth. An unbalanced focus on ROIC can lead to harvesting behavior, leaving a company out of the race for long-term growth.

Returning to the Sears and Wal-Mart comparison, Exhibit 4.9 plots the revenue growth and return on invested capital for Sears and Wal-Mart between 1995 and 1997. (Before 1995, Sears' performance was distorted by its ownership of Dean Witter Discover and Allstate Insurance.) Over the period, Wal-Mart's revenue growth averaged 12.6 percent a year compared with 7.7 percent for Sears, and its return on capital averaged 14.2 percent against Sears' 10.4 percent. Both companies' cost of capital was about 9 percent. Wal-Mart achieved higher growth and higher returns on capital.

How can it be that Sears earned higher TRS than Wal-Mart when its underlying performance was so much poorer? The answer goes back to the treadmill. Sears was not expected to do well, but did better than expected. Wal-Mart, on the other hand, was the victim of high expectations. It probably earned more economic profit than any other retailer in the world, while sustaining high growth. But the market expected even better.

We can also compare historical performance to the expected performance implied by the market. Exhibit 4.10 shows both the historical results of the two companies as well as a line showing the combinations of future growth and return on invested capital that are consistent with today's market value. These lines represent the level of performance needed to meet market expectations. If a company delivers this level of performance, its share price should rise in line with its cost of equity less the dividend yield (assuming the market as a whole moves in line with expectations). If it exceeds expectations, its share price should rise more quickly. Wal-Mart is expected to perform considerably better than Sears, and even better than it has done in the years to 1998. For Sears, the opposite is true. The market does not appear to expect it to perform as well as it has in recent years.

In addition to providing better insights into the economics of a business than cash flow, growth and ROIC can also be used to set short-term

Exhibit 4.9   Underlying Financial Performance of Sears and Wal-Mart

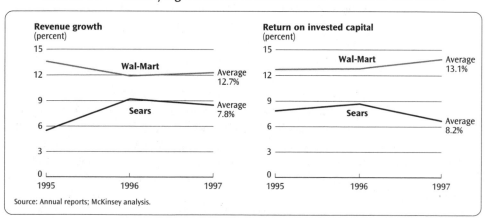

Source: Annual reports; McKinsey analysis.

Exhibit 4.10   Market Expectations of Sears and Wal-Mart

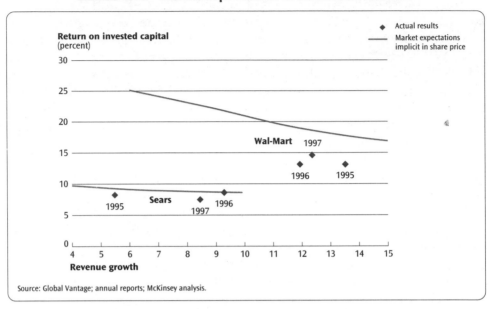

Source: Global Vantage; annual reports; McKinsey analysis.

performance targets for a company or business unit. Looking back at the figures for Heineken, management can compare actual ROIC and growth to projections to see if its progress is on track. It can't do the same with free cash flow.

VALUE DRIVERS: LEADING INDICATORS

The fourth issue that our framework raises is that market measures and financial measures are not sufficient to understand why a business performs the way it does. Short-term financial measures can be especially misleading. One could even argue that financial measures are inadequate by themselves because they can be manipulated.

Take the example of a packaged foods division of a major consumer products company as related by its chief financial officer. The division was a market leader and had shown steadily improving financial performance for years. Since its numbers were so good, no one at headquarters asked too many questions about the results. In fact, the division had achieved its stellar performance by raising prices. This encouraged new entrants and led to steady erosion of market share. As the competition got stronger, the business could no longer sustain its financial performance. A major restructuring was needed.

The important point is that companies should be as concerned about how a business achieves its financial results as about whether it meets its financial targets. Value drivers help companies to understand the reasons for their current performance and how their future performance will likely develop.

In addition, value drivers can serve as leading indicators of performance. Financial results (ROIC and growth) tell what a company has achieved in the past; they are "lagging indicators." Management needs performance measures that tell it where it is going in the future, "leading indicators." Market share might be a leading indicator for a packaged food company. The R&D pipeline could be a leading indicator for a pharmaceutical company. As companies and the financial markets get more sophisticated, the emphasis is shifting to these leading indicators. The high valuations of Internet stocks and their behavior is important evidence of this shift.

SUMMARY

In this chapter we discussed a comprehensive framework to cut through the confusion of proliferating metrics. Shareholder value in the stock market is the ultimate output measure of a company's performance. Shareholder value tracks a company's intrinsic value based on discounted cash flows. While valuable for strategic analysis, DCF cannot be used to assess historical performance or set short-term targets. Financial indicators like revenue growth and ROIC drive DCF values and can be used to set targets and track performance. Financial indicators, however, must be supplemented with strategic and operating value drivers that provide insights about where a company's performance is heading.

5

Cash Is King

On October 1, 1974, the *Wall Street Journal* published an editorial lamenting the widespread focus on earnings per share as an indicator of value:

> A lot of executives apparently believe that if they can figure out a way to boost reported earnings, their stock prices will go up even if the higher earnings do not represent any underlying economic change. In other words, the executives think they are smart and the market is dumb. . . . The market is smart. Apparently, the dumb one is the corporate executive caught up in the earnings-per-share mystique.

When we excerpted this editorial in the first edition of *Valuation* in 1990, we observed that many corporate managers still worshiped earnings per share, and thus were still betting that the market was dumb. The story has been changing since we wrote those words. Many managers have accepted that the market is much more sophisticated than they had given it credit for and doesn't fall for earnings-per-share tricks.

This change in attitude is also reflected on Wall Street. Alfred Jackson, the former head of equity research at CS First Boston, described how he introduced more of a cash flow and economic profit approach at his bank:

> In October of 1994, I assumed the role of Global Director of Equity Research at CS First Boston. . . . I had long been dissatisfied with the quality and type of analysis done by our and other firms in the investment community. The almost obsessive focus on earnings per share—in particular, the amount of time and effort spent on estimating the next quarter's EPS down to the penny—appeared foolish to me. Such practices seemed a gross contradiction of the discounted cash flow concept of valuation that I had learned years ago in business school. The DCF method, for all its logical superiority, appeared

Special thanks to Irina Grigorenko and Kim Vogel for supporting the research on this chapter.

to me to be largely ignored in the real world of investing—or at least in the sell side part of it.[1]

We are encouraged by the trends in the investment world and Main Street, but still believe that there is a long way to go. In this chapter, we present evidence that the market does indeed work the way the theory suggests.

The evidence falls into four categories:

1. Changes in value (i.e., total returns to shareholders) are linked more closely to changes in expectations than to absolute performance.
2. Valuation levels (i.e., market/book) are linked to return on invested capital and growth.
3. The market sees through cosmetic earnings effects and focuses on underlying economic results.
4. The market puts great weight on long-term results, not just short-term performance.

At the end of this chapter, we discuss the running debate about whether the stock market is efficient and the implications for management behavior. We conclude that even if the market does demonstrate inefficiencies, they are mostly small and short term. As a result, managers should behave as if the markets were quite efficient.

TRS LINKED TO CHANGES IN EXPECTATIONS

In Chapter 4, we made the case that total returns to shareholders are linked more to performance against expectations than absolute levels of performance. For example, on October 15, 1997, Intel reported that its earnings were up 19 percent compared with the previous year. Intel's share price declined 6.3 percent on the announcement because analysts had forecast a 23 percent increase in earnings. Over horizons of at least 15 years, TRS will be linked to earnings because earnings growth will track cash flow and returns on capital. Over shorter periods, however, we would expect performance against expectations to be more important for TRS than the level of earnings growth.

We conducted a statistical analysis of TRS against various performance measures. We correlated TRS with traditional earnings and earnings growth measures, as well as economic profit and economic profit growth. We also

---

[1] A. Jackson, "The How and Why of EVA® at CS First Boston," *Journal of Applied Corporate Finance*, vol. 9, no. 1 (spring 1996), pp. 98–103.

Exhibit 5.1   TRS Linked to Performance against Expectations

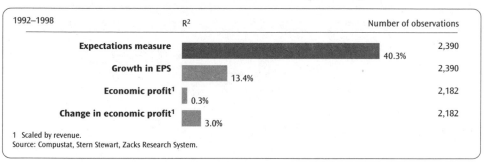

1 Scaled by revenue.
Source: Compustat, Stern Stewart, Zacks Research System.

correlated TRS with the difference between actual economic profit and expected economic profit using consensus earnings forecasts from the Zacks Research System database.

As the theory would suggest, there is a strong relationship between TRS and deviations from expected performance but almost no relationship between TRS and the various earnings measures. Exhibit 5.1 summarizes the results of the analysis. The R^2 (in this instance, a measure of how much of TRS is explained by each of the tested measures) for the deviation from expectations measure is 40 percent, high for such a regression.

VALUATION LEVEL LINKED TO ROIC/GROWTH

It is clear from the above analysis that changes in value (TRS) over short periods are more linked to performance compared with expectations than to absolute performance. A company's value at a point in time, on the other hand, is more linked to the absolute level of performance (i.e., expected sales and earnings growth and ROIC).

As you will see next, the evidence from the market supports this idea. We compared the market value of 340 of the largest U.S. companies with their five-year growth in sales and five-year average spread (in percentage points) between return on invested capital and opportunity cost of capital. The companies' market values were divided by their book values to adjust for size differences.

We then grouped the companies into cohorts with similar sales growth and spread (for example, all companies with average sales growth between 9 percent and 13 percent and spread between 2 percent and 6 percent). We then calculated the average market/book value for each cohort. Exhibit 5.2 shows the results of this analysis. You can see that for any level of growth, higher spread leads to a higher market/book. You can also see that higher levels of sales growth are associated with higher market/book, except for

Exhibit 5.2   Relationship between Market Values, Spread, and Growth

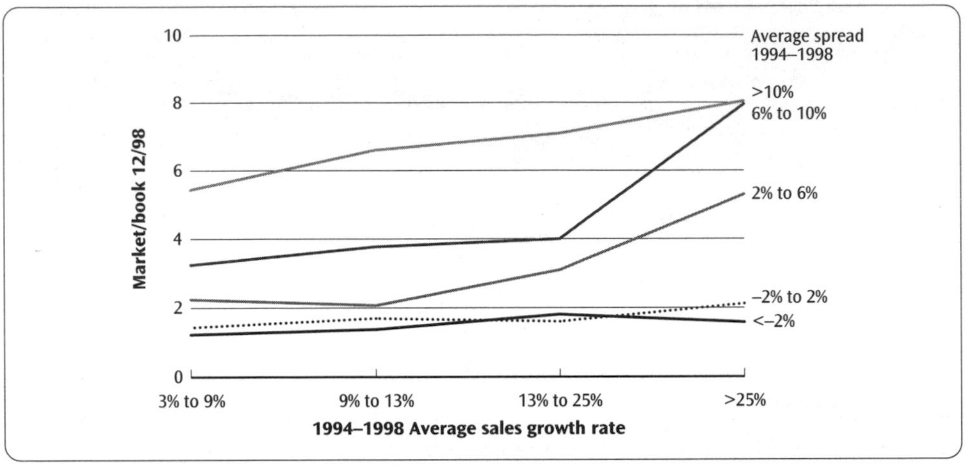

low or negative spread companies. This analysis lends support to our argument that the market values companies based on sales growth and spread.

To test the significance of these relationships statistically, we conducted a regression of market-to-book values against various measures, including spread and various growth measures. The results are summarized on Exhibit 5.3. The regression of market-to-book versus sales growth and spread resulted in an R^2 of 46 percent, which is very high for such a test. The results were similar whether we used operating profit growth rates or sales growth.

Analyzing Exhibit 5.3 indicated that spread was more important than sales growth and that perhaps growth was not important at all. The theory suggests that growth should matter most when spread is high. (This is apparent from Exhibit 5.2.) We next separated the sample of 340 companies

Exhibit 5.3   Market-to-Book Regressions

Dependent variable	Variable 1	Variable 2	R^2 (percent)
12/98 Market-to-book	Spread 94-98	Revenue growth 94-98	46
12/98 Market-to-book	Spread 94-98	N/A	45
12/93 Market-to-book	Spread 94-98	Revenue growth 94-98	40
12/93 Market-to-book	Spread 94-98	N/A	35
12/93 Market-to-book	Revenue growth 94-98	N/A	10
12/98 Market-to-book	Revenue growth 94-98	N/A	9
12/98 Market-to-book	EBITA growth 94-98	N/A	8
12/93 Market-to-book	EBITA growth 94-98	N/A	4

Exhibit 5.4   Market-to-Book Regressions for Spread Cohorts

Spread cohort	Number of companies	Slope	R^2	T–statistic
>10%	70	5.8	0.03	1.5
6–10%	61	11.9	0.21	4.0
2–6%	87	10.7	0.36	6.9
−2 −+2%	96	2.4	0.08	2.9
<−2%	26	2.0	0.16	2.1

into different spread cohorts and conducted separate regressions of market-to-book against growth. As the theory would predict, growth is much more important for high spread companies as shown on Exhibit 5.4. The slope of the regression line for high spread companies is significantly positive; for low spread companies it is relatively flat and not statistically different than zero.

In another test, we applied the DCF approach to the valuation of 31 companies. We developed cash-flow forecasts based on projections from the Value Line Investment Survey and discounted the cash flows at the weighted average cost of capital (WACC). As Exhibit 5.5 shows, we found a strong correlation with the companies' market values.

These results are not scientific proof, and we cannot test our hypothesis more directly by measuring expected future growth and returns. But these

Exhibit 5.5   Correlation between Market Value and DCF Value for 31 Large U.S. Companies, 1999

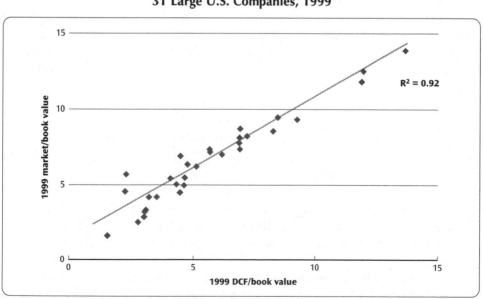

tests do provide more evidence that cash flow, led by the combination of revenue growth and spreads, drives the value of companies.

MARKET SEES THROUGH COSMETIC EARNINGS EFFECTS

Does the market respond naively to accounting numbers or does it look deeper? Many managers seem obsessed with reported earnings. Yet, the evidence is clear: The market looks much deeper than reported earnings.

The simplest piece of evidence comes from companies that use different accounting methods depending on the market in which they are reporting financial results. Hoechst was one of the largest German industrial companies, with over DM 50 billion in revenues in 1997. Hoechst listed its shares on the New York Stock Exchange in 1996, and was required to report financial results using U.S. accounting standards. Until then, it had only reported results under German accounting rules. Here is a comparison of its reported net income under the two standards:

Year	German accounting (DM million)	U.S. accounting (DM million)	Difference (percent)
1995	1,709	(57)	NM
1996	2,114	1,324	−37
1997	1,343	377	−72

If the market just looked at reported earnings, which would it use? It wouldn't use either one, it would have to look deeper than reported earnings.

A classic area of research on this topic is inventory accounting. U.S. tax authorities require that the method used for financial reporting also be used for calculating taxable income. As a result, the choice of accounting method affects both earnings and cash flow, but in opposite directions. In periods of rising prices, the last-in, first-out (LIFO) inventory method results in lower earnings than the first-in, first-out (FIFO) method, because the cost of goods sold is based on more recent, higher costs. Lower earnings mean lower income taxes. Since the pretax cash flow is the same regardless of the accounting method, LIFO accounting leads to a higher after-tax cash flow than FIFO accounting, despite the lower reported earnings.

A number of researchers have looked at the stock price reaction of companies that have switched from one accounting method to the other. The accounting model suggests that switching from FIFO to LIFO should result in a lower share price because investors would anticipate lower reported earnings.

While the evidence is not conclusive, some researchers have found that switching from FIFO to LIFO results in a higher share price. This is attributed

Exhibit 5.6 Effect of Inventory Accounting Change on Share Value

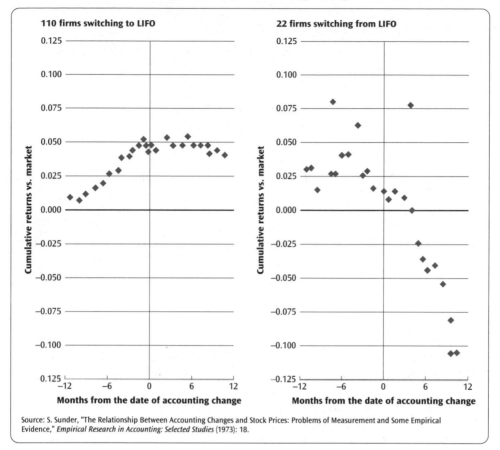

Source: S. Sunder, "The Relationship Between Accounting Changes and Stock Prices: Problems of Measurement and Some Empirical Evidence," *Empirical Research in Accounting: Selected Studies* (1973): 18.

to increased cash flow, which is what the DCF model predicts. After adjusting for movements in the broad market and other contemporaneous effects, companies switching to LIFO experienced significant share price increases, while firms switching to FIFO saw share price declines (see Exhibit 5.6). In fact, Biddle and Lindahl[2] (1982) found that the larger the reduction in taxes resulting from the switch to LIFO, the greater the share price increase attributed to the change.

Much more topical than the LIFO-FIFO debate are accounting standards for mergers and acquisitions. In the United States, a transaction accounted for as a purchase requires that the difference between the price paid for the target and the book value of its assets (with some adjustment) be recorded as goodwill, and amortized over a period of up to 40 years.

[2] G. Biddle and F. Lindahl, "Stock Price Reactions to LIFO Adoptions: The Association Between Excess Returns and LIFO Tax Savings," *Journal of Accounting Research*, vol. 53 (1982), pp. 548–551.

Exhibit 5.7 Market Reaction to Purchase and Pooling Transactions

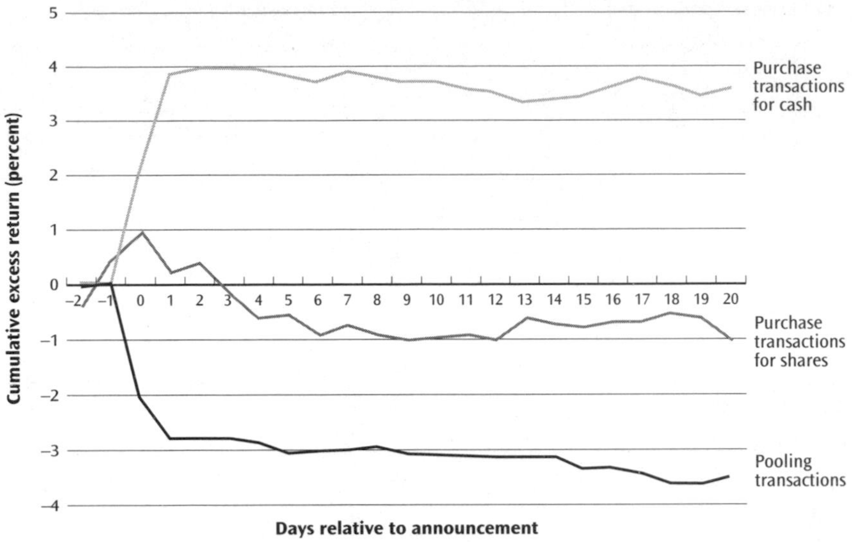

Source: E. Lindenberg and M. Ross, Financial Strategy Group of Salomon Smith Barney.

Under pooling-of-interests accounting, the acquisition is reported at book value with no goodwill or amortization. Goodwill is generally not deductible for tax purposes so the acquiring company's cash flow will be the same regardless of the accounting method. Reported earnings will be higher under pooling accounting because there is no goodwill to amortize.[3]

There is a common perception that the market mechanically accepts the earnings impact of transactions. So investors should view more favorably deals treated as a pooling of interests. But Lindenberg and Ross[4] have shown that the reverse is true. Analyzing more than 1,400 transactions, they found that the market responded positively to the purchase transactions paid for in cash, negatively to the pooling transactions, and was neutral about purchase transactions paid in shares, as shown on Exhibit 5.7. The authors hypothesize that the negative reaction to pooling may reflect the following:

- The market's view that pooling acquirers have less purchase price discipline than do purchase acquirers.

---

[3] The Financial Accounting Standards Board has proposed eliminating pooling of interests accounting for transactions completed after December 31, 2000.

[4] E. Lindenberg and M. Ross, "To Purchase or to Pool: Does It Matter?" *Journal of Applied Corporate Finance*, vol. 12, no. 2 (summer 1999), pp. 32–47.

- The market's realization that the pooling acquirer will be unable to implement value creating activities, such as spinoffs or asset sales, or to conduct nonroutine stock buybacks in the near future.[5]

- The revelation that the management of the acquirer cares more about accounting cosmetics than financial flexibility.

Lindenberg and Ross go one step further and test whether companies with goodwill amortization are valued differently than other companies. If the market sees through goodwill, then price-earnings multiples should be much higher for companies with lots of goodwill amortization relative to other companies. This is because goodwill amortization reduces earnings, yet is not a cash charge. On the other hand, valuation multiples based on a cash flow measure like EBITDA (earnings before interest, taxes, depreciation, and amortization) should be in the same range as other companies in the same industry. The authors examined 3,633 companies and found that, as expected, companies with goodwill had higher PE ratios but not higher EBITDA multiples.

An interesting example of the goodwill issue was the 1995 acquisition of First Interstate Bank by Wells Fargo.[6] One analyst was quoted as saying that the "Wells offer was futile" because it would be accounted for as a purchase, while a competing bid from First Bank System had the advantage of a pooling of interests. But the market ignored the conventional view of the analyst and chose Wells Fargo's bid despite $400 million per year of goodwill amortization. In fact, Wells Fargo's share price went up 3 percent on the day it was announced that its bid had prevailed and more than 20 percent during the next 10 trading days.

The other side of the coin is the story of AT&T's acquisition of NCR in 1991. Lys and Vincent concluded that AT&T incurred additional costs of $500 million to get NCR to agree to terms that would allow the telephone giant to do pooling accounting (primarily by agreeing to pay a higher price in exchange for NCR's removing obstacles to pooling). The authors estimated that the market value of AT&T fell by $4 billion to $6 billion during the merger negotiations.[7] You could infer that AT&T's insistence on pooling made the market even more skeptical about the value creation potential of the transaction.

---

[5] These actions are prohibited for several years under pooling accounting.
[6] M. Davis, "The Purchase vs. Pooling Controversy: How the Stock Market Responds to Goodwill," *Journal of Applied Corporate Finance,* vol. 9, no. 1 (spring 1996), pp. 50–59.
[7] T. Lys and L. Vincent, "An Analysis of Value Destruction in AT&T's Acquisition of NCR," *Journal of Financial Economics,* vol. 39 (1995), pp. 353–378.

MARKET FOCUSES ON LONG TERM

A lot of confusion about how the market evaluates accounting earnings has to do with the time frame of investors. Many managers believe that the stock market focuses too narrowly on near-term earnings. They believe that the market does not give credit for long-term investments. A quick look at the high values the stock market has placed on emerging Internet companies, without any earnings or even any products to sell in many cases, should be evidence enough that the market takes a long view. In October 1999, Amazon.com's stock market capitalization was $23 billion. Yet, as of that date, Amazon was still reporting accounting losses. (See Chapter 15 for a discussion of the valuation of very high growth companies.)

In this section, we summarize research showing that the market does take a long-term perspective. You may note that some of the research is more than 10 years old. In the academic community, this issue has been settled for some time, so academics have no more interest in pursuing it.

A simple test of the stock market's time horizon is to examine how much of a company's current share price can be accounted for by expected

Exhibit 5.8   Present Value of Expected Dividends for 20 Fortune 500 Companies, December 1997

Company	Present value of dividends expected over the next five years	Share price	Dividends as percentage of stock price (percent)
American General	5.78	54.06	10.7
BankBoston	9.60	46.97	20.4
BellAtlantic	5.70	45.50	12.5
Comerica	5.51	60.17	9.2
DuPont	5.36	60.06	8.9
Exxon	6.30	61.19	10.3
Ford	9.08	48.56	18.7
Gillette	2.35	50.22	4.7
Hasbro	1.73	31.50	5.5
Hewlett-Packard	3.03	62.38	4.9
Kellogg	3.67	49.63	7.4
Lockheed Martin	7.18	98.50	7.3
McGraw-Hill	5.92	74.00	8.0
Nordstrom	2.46	30.19	8.2
PPG Industries	5.51	57.13	9.6
Procter & Gamble	4.31	79.81	5.4
Reynolds Metals	5.50	60.00	9.2
United Technologies	5.36	72.81	7.4
Wachovia Corporation	7.67	81.13	9.5
Xerox	5.11	73.88	6.9
			Average = 9.2

Note: 12% discount rate assumed.
Source: Compustat.

Exhibit 5.9 Evidence That the Market Reacts Favorably to Increases in Investment

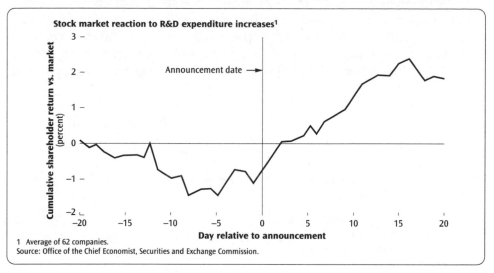

Stock market reaction to R&D expenditure increases[1]

Announcement date →

Cumulative shareholder return vs. market (percent)

Day relative to announcement

1 Average of 62 companies.
Source: Office of the Chief Economist, Securities and Exchange Commission.

dividends over the next several years. For a random sample of 20 Fortune 500 companies, as shown in Exhibit 5.8, an average of only 9.2 percent of the total share value could be accounted for by dividends expected in the next five years. The largest percentage of value that the next five years' dividends could explain was 20.4 percent for BankBoston. From this test, the market appears to take a long view. More rigorous analyses described next support this view.

We showed earlier that pure accounting manipulation does not fool the market. But managers can take other actions to improve earnings at the expense of long-term cash flow. They can reduce spending on research and development or capital goods. Cutting spending on research and development will increase earnings and cash flow in the short run, potentially at the expense of developing profitable products in the long run. Similarly, cutting back on capital spending will increase short-term profits because new capital projects often earn low profits in their early years.

Securities and Exchange Commission economists examined the stock price reaction to announcements by 62 companies that they were embarking on R&D projects.[8] As Exhibit 5.9 shows, the market had a significant positive reaction to these announcements.

[8] Office of the Chief Economist, "Institutional Owners, Tender Offers, and Long-Term Investment," Washington, DC: Securities and Exchange Commission, 1985.

The evidence on capital spending supports the DCF model as well. McConnell and Muscarella examined the stock market's reaction to announcements of increased capital spending.[9] For a sample of 349 such announcements (containing no other company-specific information) by industrial companies from 1975 to 1981, the stock market on average reacted positively to spending increases and negatively to spending decreases:

	Sample size	Market adjusted return (percent)
Industrial companies		
• Budget increases	273	+1.3
• Budget decreases	76	−1.8
Public utility companies		
• Budget increases	39	+0.4
• Budget decreases	17	−0.8

The authors also found that these results held for all industries except oil and gas exploration and development. Apparently, the market did not believe that oil and gas exploration was a profitable investment at the time. Given the subsequent decline in oil prices and the high cost of exploration in the United States relative to other parts of the world, the market was probably right. In any case, it is clear that the market does not arbitrarily penalize companies for making long-term investments.

Another supporting piece of research on long-term investments comes from Woolridge.[10] He examined the two-day stock market reaction (market-adjusted) to strategic investment announcements by 634 companies. He found a significant positive reaction for all the categories of investments he studied:

Type of investment	Sample size	Cumulative 2-day market adjusted return (percent)
Capital expenditures	260	+0.35
Product strategies	168	+0.84
R&D expenditures	45	+1.20
Joint venture formations	161	+0.78
Total sample	634	+0.71

[9] J. McConnell and C. Muscarella, "Corporate Capital Expenditure Decisions and the Market Value of the Firm," *Journal of Financial Economics* (March 1985), pp. 399–422.

[10] J.R. Woolridge, "Competitive Decline and Corporate Restructuring: Is a Myopic Stock Market to Blame?" *Journal of Applied Corporate Finance*, vol. 1, no. 1 (spring 1988), pp. 26–36.

Conversely, the market also reacts favorably when companies write off bad investments, despite the negative short-term earnings impact. While the complex nature of write-offs prohibits comprehensive statistical analysis, Mercer looked at 40 major write-offs from 1984 to 1986 and found that 60 percent of them resulted in share price increases.[11] Furthermore, 75 percent of write-downs resulting from abandonment of entire businesses were associated with share price increases.

More evidence supporting the view that the market values cash, not earnings, emerges from changes in leverage and their impact on share prices and earnings per share. Copeland and Lee (1988) studied 161 exchange offers and stock swaps from 1962 to 1984.[12] The study showed that the earnings-per-share impact of the transaction did not matter. What mattered was whether the transaction was leverage-increasing or leverage-decreasing. Following are the average percentage changes in share value upon the announcement of the transactions relative to the changes in the market average:

	EPS increasing transactions (percent)	EPS-decreasing transactions (percent)
Leverage-increasing transactions	3.77	8.41
Leverage-decreasing transactions	−1.18	−0.41

On average, leverage-decreasing transactions resulted in negative share price reactions, regardless of the earnings-per-share impact. Copeland and Lee also concluded that the most likely explanation for the direction of the share price movements was that investors interpret leverage-changing transactions as management signals of the direction of cash flow. Such transactions could signal strong cash flows in the future, leading corporate insiders to increase their share holdings in the company.

IMPLICATIONS OF MARKET INEFFICIENCY FOR CORPORATE MANAGERS

Sometimes managers point to evidence of inefficiency in the stock market to justify their belief that the market behaves irrationally. These managers would argue that even academics are finding inefficiencies in the market, so any argument supporting the discounted cash flow approach would not

---

[11] G. Mercer, "A Review of Major Corporate Writeoffs, 1984–86" (McKinsey & Co., 1987).
[12] T. Copeland and W.H. Lee, "Exchange Offers and Stock Swaps—New Evidence," *Financial Management*, vol. 20, no. 3 (autumn 1991), pp. 34–48.

square with the real world. We would argue that even if the market is occasionally inefficient, managers should make business decisions as if the market were efficient.

It has been more than 30 years since the concept of efficient markets was proposed. It is one of the most debated and researched ideas in economics, if not all the social sciences. Yet it is also one of the most misunderstood. Many business people believe that the theory of efficient markets means that the stock market always "gets it right." The ambitions of efficient markets theory are much more modest. In layman's terms, a market is efficient if new information is quickly or instantaneously reflected in share prices. Essentially, this means that it is hard for investors to beat the market unless they have better information than the market as a whole. Trading-oriented strategies, such as momentum trading, are unlikely to generate market-beating returns.[13]

Ever since academics suggested that the stock market behaves efficiently, researchers have been looking for anomalies to refute the thesis. While the debate is unresolved, it is fair to say that some anomalies have been identified. The question relevant for us is what are the implications of market inefficiencies for investors and corporate managers.

For investors, it is clear that this represents an opportunity to make money. To exploit these inefficiencies, however, requires massive computing power and the ability to execute stock trades instantly. As with most market inefficiencies, only the biggest and quickest investors are likely to benefit. In any case, once these inefficiencies become known, they usually disappear and the search is on for new ones.

What are the implications for corporate managers? As long as your company's share price returns to its long-run DCF value, you might as well use the DCF approach for strategic decisions. What should matter is the long-term behavior of the company's share price, not whether it is 5 percent undervalued this week.

If you can systematically identify when your company's stock is misvalued, you could try to use that information to determine when to sell more shares (or use shares to pay for an acquisition) or buy back shares. But for strategic business decisions, the evidence strongly suggests that the market acts more like it is using the DCF approach than the accounting approach.

---

[13] For an excellent summary of the history and current debate, see R. Ball, "The Theory of Stock Market Efficiency: Accomplishments and Limitations," *The New Corporate Finance*, ed. D. Chew, Jr. (New York: Irwin McGraw-Hill, 1999), pp. 35–48.

SUMMARY

Managers who use the DCF approach to valuation, focusing on increasing long-term free cash flow, ultimately will be rewarded by higher share prices. The evidence from the market is conclusive. Naive attention to accounting earnings will often lead to value-destroying decisions.

6

Making Value Happen

Most publicly traded companies today have a stated aim of creating value for their shareholders. The question for many managers is not "Why should we create value?" but "How can we create value?" This question translates into issues in a number of areas, such as:

- How can we set targets that reinforce our overall goal of creating shareholder value?
- How can we align our management processes with the goal of value creation?
- How should we structure our incentive programs?
- How can we promote a value emphasis throughout our corporate culture?

Various approaches have been proposed for companies to carry out value-based management. Some are strictly metrics focused; others take a wide scope, including strategic, financial, and organizational issues. Some promise almost immediate impact, while others ask managers to commit to multiyear improvement programs. Some are highly data- and systems-intensive, almost reminiscent of planning programs of the 1960s, whereas others try to get by with a minimum of paperwork.

Regardless of the approach, not all companies have had success with such programs. We looked at the total returns to shareholders of a sample of companies that announced they would undertake value-based management. Only one-third outperformed their sector index by more than 5 percent

Special thanks to Susan Nolen who co-wrote this chapter. Material in this chapter draws upon the work of McKinsey's working group on "Making Value Happen," including Petri Allas, Steve Bear, Richard Benson-Armer, Parke Boneysteele, Richard Dobbs, John Hall, Johanne Lavoie, Susan Nolen, Neville Salkeld, Bas van der Brugge, and Kristina Wollschlaeger. The "Performance Ethic" initiative headed by Warren Strickland has also provided considerable insight.

following the announcement; this pattern was consistent over 3-, 5-, and 10-year intervals. Our hypothesis is that in many companies, value-based management is taken up as a one-time project and not translated into long-term changes, with the effect that results are limited.

The central issue isn't whether companies have a special program called value-based management; rather, value results from a set of interrelated activities that most companies already have in place. The point is to what extent these activities are done in ways that lead to value creation, and to what extent values and behaviors that promote value creation are a part of "how we do things around here." This chapter describes what a company that actively manages for value would look and feel like, as well as how a company interested in achieving a high level of performance can get started.

The prerequisite for making value happen is that a company's actions build on a foundation of value thinking. Value thinking in turn has two dimensions—value metrics and value mindset.

The central question of *value metrics* is whether management really understands how companies create value and how the stock market values companies. Does management balance long- and short-term results, or focus on short-term results only? Is the opportunity cost of capital included in the measurement? Are the metrics based on economic results or on accounting results? Chapters 3 and 4 detailed an economics-based view of value creation metrics.

Value mindset refers to how much management cares about shareholder value creation. This mindset expresses itself in several crucial areas of the CEO's thinking and behavior. One aspect is whether the CEO truly seeks to create as much shareholder value as possible, as opposed to creating as much as is needed to quiet restive shareholders. Another aspect is whether the CEO sees managing for shareholder value as a way of life or just as a short-term project. Sir Brian Pitman, chairman of Lloyds TSB Group, introduced the target of doubling the bank's share price every three years in the 1980s, and was quoted in 1998 as saying, "We are willing to go on changing in order to double the value of the company—to stretch ourselves beyond the things that we are doing at the moment."[1]

Finally, the value-driven CEO is willing to make unpopular decisions if these are the choices that will maximize shareholder value in the long run. Pfizer, for example, was strongly criticized by analysts in the late 1980s for its high level of research and development spending. When this R&D spending translated into blockbuster drug sales in the 1990s, the market rewarded Pfizer's patience with one of the highest valuations of any pharmaceutical company. In almost all companies that have successfully done

[1] A. Morgan and P. Bose, "Banking on Shareholder Value: An Interview with Sir Brian Pitman, Chairman of Lloyds TSB," *McKinsey Quarterly*, vol. 2 (1998), pp. 96–105.

value-based management, the CEO's commitment to shareholder value is a crucial first element.

Building on the foundation of value thinking, there are six areas where a company must act to reinforce a shareholder value focus, as presented in Exhibit 6.1:

1. It must combine an inspiring aspiration with tough quantitative targets linked to value creation.
2. It should adopt a rigorous approach to managing its portfolio of businesses for maximum value creation, including radical restructuring if necessary.
3. It must ensure that its organizational design and culture reinforce the value creation imperative.
4. It must develop superior insights into the key value drivers of each of its businesses.
5. It must establish an effective approach to managing the performance of its business units through sophisticated target setting and rigorous performance reviews.
6. It must find ways to motivate managers and employees to work toward value creation through financial rewards and other incentives.

Most of these are grounded in basic management common sense. Yet we find that most companies don't systematically evaluate their performance in each area. The remainder of the chapter discusses each in greater detail.

Exhibit 6.1 Areas of Activity for Making Value Happen

SETTING ASPIRATIONS AND TARGETS

The principles of making value happen can be powerful tools to help a company achieve its goals—provided it knows what these goals are and how they link to value creation. All too often, a company's externally communicated goals represent just an incremental increase over historical performance, and may link more to accounting measures such as earnings per share than to more economically based measures. Equally, its internally communicated goals, as embodied in a mission or vision statement, may have nothing to do with what people actually try to achieve on a day-to-day basis.

A company wishing to make value happen needs to develop an aspiration that combines two dimensions: an inspirational statement of intent and value-linked quantitative targets.

An Inspirational Statement of Intent

For most companies, stating that their goal is to maximize shareholder value is not enough to excite employees, focus organizational energy, or direct their long-term ambitions. Thus, companies often develop broader statements of purpose. A good example is Disney, whose mission is "To offer quality entertainment that people will seek out" and whose vision is "To create shareholder value by continuing to be the world's premier entertainment company from a creative, strategic, and financial standpoint."

A statement of intent will only excite and unite stakeholders if it is perceived to reflect how management actually acts day-to-day. Otherwise it may even be counterproductive, if employees then suspect the other elements of making value happen to be equally insincere. Therefore it is important for companies' statements to reflect a raison d'être that the entire organization can identify with and support. Examples of causes that can really inspire passionate support are to save the company from an imminent crisis; to defeat another competitor; to build something new; to serve a noble purpose, or to create wealth. To be practical, the aspiration should also answer the questions: What business(es) are we in and what do we aspire to be known for? Finally, the aspiration should be written in a language that people can relate to, avoiding lofty or abstract phrasings.

A Value-Linked Quantitative Target

Companies need to mark the milestones toward their aspiration with value-linked targets. Some companies target their share price, promising to double it in three, four, or five years. Others target key value drivers, whether these are expressed in financial terms (e.g., EBIT) or operational terms (e.g., number of customers).

How should companies set their overall targets? There is no one deductive method that will tell management "how much is enough." However, there are three kinds of analysis that will help provide a fact base:

1. Targets should be calibrated against *financial market expectations.* Reverse-engineering the expectations of future growth and return on invested capital implicit in a company's share price can provide a perspective on this topic, as can reviewing equity analysts' reports.[2]

2. Targets should also take the *industry context* into account, both to get a fact base for what opportunities exist in the relevant markets and to understand what competitors are likely to achieve.

3. Finally, great companies can serve as *role models*, both in terms of the kinds of targets they set and the records that they have achieved.

Building on these analyses, the CEO and other top managers need to examine their own goals for the company, being sure to challenge any limiting beliefs in their current thinking. The top team also needs to calibrate the proposed targets against historical performance to observe how large a gap needs to be closed. Ideally, targets should provide some degree of stretch, but not so much as to undermine morale.

By combining the hard dimension of hitting financial numbers with the softer dimension of appealing to people's hearts and minds, aspirations can provide an overarching motivation for making value happen.

MANAGING THE CORPORATE PORTFOLIO

To maximize value, a company must determine to what extent its current portfolio of businesses will help it meet its aspirations. Building a portfolio is not just a financial exercise, since shareholders can buy and sell shares of various companies to get the reward/risk tradeoff they prefer. Instead, it is a combination of exploiting the strategic advantages of the corporation, relentlessly looking for performance improvement opportunities, and managing a growth pipeline. Three perspectives on portfolio management follow.

Strategy: Corporate Theme Analysis

As spin-offs and divestitures become more common, companies have to justify why they retain ownership of their component businesses. Researchers still debate whether the majority of multibusiness companies add value

---

[2] For more on how to reverse-engineer a company's share price, see T. Koller and R. Dobbs, "The Expectations Treadmill," *McKinsey Quarterly,* vol. 3 (1998), pp. 32–43.

Exhibit 6.2   Seven Recurring Corporate Themes

The Industry Shaper repeatedly spots discontinuities in industries and acts pre-emptively to shape the emerging new industry to its own advantage.

The Deal Maker systematically beats the market through its superior skill at spotting and executing deals. This could either be through superior insight into the inherent value of companies or through superior insight into specific industries.

The Scarce Asset Allocator efficiently allocates capital, cash, time, and talent across multiple business units.

The Skill Replicator repeatedly transfers particular skills across business units. The skill of lateral transfer is a distinct skill from the functional skill itself.

The Performance Manager has proven skills at instilling a high performance ethic with matching incentives and MIS processes across multiple business units.

The Talent Agency institutionalizes a model for attracting, retaining. and developing talent that is truly distinctive relative to all others in the industry.

The Growth Asset Attractor possesses a proven and sustained record of consistently leading in innovation in multiple businesses.

---

above the sum of their parts. Yet there are some multibusiness companies where the corporate center consistently brings out the best from a diverse set of businesses. We have identified seven corporate themes, or ways in which the corporate center can add value, as listed in Exhibit 6.2. Successful multibusiness companies create value across their component businesses by being distinctive in at least one or two of these themes. A company analyzing its portfolio should examine how well it executes each theme, and if it is distinctive in none, determine which theme is most appropriate for its businesses and develop the relevant skills.

Performance: Outside-In Restructuring Analysis

In Chapter 2, Ralph Demsky used a hexagon framework to examine potential value improvements at the EG Corporation. The hexagon helps quantify the impact of value creation levers: investor communication; internal improvements; disposals; growth opportunities (whether organic or through acquisitions), and financial engineering. Using the hexagon can help management understand how much value to expect from restructuring and where the biggest opportunities lie.

Growth: Three Horizon Analysis

An analysis of companies with sustained above-average growth indicates that they manage their business portfolios across three horizons.[3] These

---

[3] M. Baghai, S. Coley, and D. White, *The Alchemy of Growth: Kickstarting and Sustaining Growth in Your Company* (London: Orion Business, 1999).

Exhibit 6.3   Three Horizons of Growth

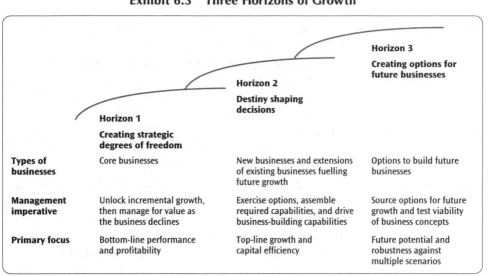

	Horizon 1 Creating strategic degrees of freedom	Horizon 2 Destiny shaping decisions	Horizon 3 Creating options for future businesses
Types of businesses	Core businesses	New businesses and extensions of existing businesses fuelling future growth	Options to build future businesses
Management imperative	Unlock incremental growth, then manage for value as the business declines	Exercise options, assemble required capabilities, and drive business-building capabilities	Source options for future growth and test viability of business concepts
Primary focus	Bottom-line performance and profitability	Top-line growth and capital efficiency	Future potential and robustness against multiple scenarios

companies ensure that their portfolios always include businesses in all three of the stages of development depicted in Exhibit 6.3:

1. Horizon 1 includes current core businesses, which generally account for the greatest part of current profits and cash flow.

2. Horizon 2 includes emerging opportunities, the "rising star" businesses of the company that already have customers and revenues, even if they do not yet generate positive cash flow.

3. Horizon 3 includes future options, which are opportunities where initial activity has already begun, be it a pilot project, minority stake, or memorandum of understanding.

Since value-based management is sometimes faulted for placing too little stress on profitable growth, doing a growth horizon analysis will ensure a balanced viewpoint on potential sources of value creation.

Combining these three perspectives helps managers put traditional value-based management activities into the broader context of creating value for the firm. Sometimes restructuring the portfolio to realign it with the overarching corporate strategy or to begin building growth businesses has much greater potential than improving the performance in any one business. If the portfolio is in reasonably good shape, then it is useful to look into the organizational and performance management dimensions of making value happen.

ORIENTING THE ORGANIZATION TOWARD VALUE

Having the "right" organization in place is critical to making value happen because it ensures that the company's value creation aspirations and strategy are translated into disciplined execution. There is no one right approach to organization, nor must a company seeking to make value happen necessarily embark on a major organizational redesign. Work with our clients indicates that both hard and soft elements of organizational design can greatly influence the effectiveness of value-based management. The important hard areas are structure (who reports to whom), decision rights (who can make decisions), people (who holds key jobs), and coordination mechanisms (how do things get communicated or done). The soft areas include beliefs (how much potential people believe exists in a market) and values (what people think is important) as well as leadership style.

One essential organizational question is, "Does our organization have clearly defined performance units and individual accountabilities?" If not, the company will have difficulty setting targets, measuring performance, and rewarding success either for a unit or for an individual. In general, we recommend that performance units be defined according to scope (coherence of products and of customers), control (profit-and-loss accountability), and materiality (big enough that top management wants to spend time on performance discussions with its managers).

Within a unit, the overall performance responsibilities for each individual or work team should also be defined. Generally a flat, decentralized organization structure is recommended for making value happen, as this enables transparency and clear communication. But in keeping with the belief, "There is no one 'right' organization," if a company finds that accountability and decision rights are clear in a centralized organization structure, there is no need to change for change's sake.

Structure can impede or enhance performance in other ways. For example, the dominant axis along which a company is organized should reflect its sources of advantage (e.g., a company that thrives on being close to the market might best be organized along a regional axis). However, changing an organizational structure is a major intervention into the daily life of a company. So less intrusive moves, such as changes in decision rights, putting new people in key positions, or improving coordination mechanisms, may also be able to resolve organizational problems.

Soft issues can be equally important blockers or enablers of performance within an organization. As an example, if engineers hold the belief, "Every power plant we build must be customized," this may entail extra design and production expenses that cut into overall profitability, when in fact customers might be willing to accept standardized models. Leadership style can impede if managers' actions send out different messages about what they value than their words do. To make value happen, managers need to address these psychological and mental blocks to higher performance.

It is difficult to work directly on changing beliefs and values. One approach that we have taken is to survey managers anonymously about how much they agree with a series of statements related to a certain belief or value. The survey asks not only about the headline belief ("We need to grow") but about degree of commitment ("I really believe this is an important goal"), feasibility ("I think we can achieve the target on schedule"), skills ("I know what to do in order to create growth"), and other logically consistent beliefs. Although many participants may say they agree with the headline statement, a surprising degree of dissension may appear in the other areas. When people are confronted with these mixed results, this can provide a platform for open discussion and building a new consensus. Delving deep into issues of organizational mindset may fall outside the boundaries of value-based management as narrowly defined, but a company trying to carry out major changes as part of making value happen may find that mindset issues are critical.

UNDERSTANDING THE DRIVERS OF VALUE

A company that has made a top-level decision to make value happen needs to understand what elements in its day-to-day operations, as well as in its major investment decisions, have the most impact on value. Properly done, the process of defining value drivers can help managers in three ways. First, it can help both business unit managers and their staff understand how value is created and maximized in the business. Second, it can help in prioritizing these drivers and thus in determining where resources should be placed (or removed). Third, it can align business unit managers and employees around a common understanding of top priorities.

As we will use the term here, a *value driver* is a performance variable that has impact on the results of a business, such as production effectiveness or customer satisfaction. The metrics associated with the value drivers are called *key performance indicators* (KPIs). Such metrics might be capacity utilization or customer retention rates. KPIs are used both for target setting and for performance measurement. Three principles are central to defining value drivers well:

1. *Value drivers should be directly linked to shareholder value creation and cascade down throughout the organization.* Linking value drivers to the overall objective of shareholder value creation has two benefits. First, it aligns different levels of the organization to a single objective. When front-line staff and business unit management agree on how

front-line actions affect overall value creation, they can harmonize their goals and measures, instead of working at cross-purposes. Second, it allows management to objectively balance and prioritize different value drivers as well as short-term and long-term actions. When difficult decisions must be made, management can use long-term value creation as the criterion for the decision—and as a rationale to communicate the decision to a skeptical stock market.

Note that a shareholder value focus does not exclude other important objectives for a company, such as safety or environmental concerns. These constraints can also be included in the value driver definition and in performance scorecards. What is important is that there are clear rules about how and when these objectives take precedence over shareholder value maximization, so that the value focus isn't diluted.

2. *Value drivers should be targeted and measured by both financial and operational KPIs.* Companies frequently undertake value driver analysis by breaking down return on invested capital into its component financial measures (as discussed in Chapter 9 on return-on-invested-capital trees). This is a good beginning, but by itself doesn't provide a full understanding of value drivers. For one thing, management has no way to affect financial ratios directly; it can only do so by affecting operating factors. So management must go one step further. For example, if a hard goods retailer wants to analyze how it can increase the earnings-before-income-taxes (EBIT) margin, it needs to break down the EBIT margin into its components—gross margin, warehouse costs, delivery costs, and other selling, general, and administrative costs. It can then disaggregate the factors driving each kind of cost, so that delivery costs can be broken down into trips per transaction, the cost per trip, and number of transactions. This level of operating detail allows managers to analyze concrete improvement actions.

Operational numbers are particularly useful as leading indicators. Financial ratios alone can fail to alert managers that there are problems ahead. For example, a business unit's return on invested capital may improve on a short-term basis because the management team is failing to maintain assets or make needed investments. Asking managers to report on operational measures such as maintenance expense, uptime of machines, or plans to expand or replace assets would reveal that the improvement in return on invested capital is not sustainable.

3. *Value drivers should cover long-term growth as well as operating performance.* Although many companies focus their attention on current performance, as businesses mature and decline, successful companies

must invent ways to grow. Therefore, value driver analysis should highlight drivers to grow at a return above the cost of capital as well as drivers to improve today's return on invested capital. For a retailer, this might include the number of stores to be opened in a given year or the number of new product categories introduced. Sometimes, though, growth does not come in easily measured units such as new stores. For some cases, the right answer is to use project-based measures. In a metals company, the source of growth might be the introduction of a new process, for which milestones in implementation might serve as the value drivers. In other cases, using qualitative measures is more appropriate. A consumer goods company may need to rate its own understanding of market trends as excellent, good, fair, or poor.

As a natural outcome of these principles, note that each business unit should have its own set of key value drivers and KPIs. Although a corporate center may be tempted to impose the same template on all business units in a company, this is often not meaningful for any measures beyond high-level financial numbers. Even when two business units are in the same industry, it may be best for them to focus on separate value drivers if their current performance is different. For example, a business unit with superior operating performance and margins should focus on growth-related KPIs while a low margin unit should focus on cost-related KPIs.

Also note that a business unit should limit the number of performance indicators. Managers should monitor these numbers regularly to obtain an overview of business performance, with other value drivers used as supplemental diagnostic indicators to understand underlying issues. Experience suggests that 5 to 10 KPIs are sufficient to provide a good overview, with 20 an upper bound. If a company tries to use more than 20, it will probably have difficulty deciding which numbers to focus on.

The process of value driver definition has three phases (which are described here sequentially, although in practice there is significant iteration): identification, prioritization, and institutionalization, as illustrated in Exhibit 6.4.

1. *Identification.* The first task is creating value trees that systematically link the operating elements of the business to value creation. While mathematical links are desirable, it is better to include a nonquantifiable link than to omit it. It is also helpful to draw trees in at least three different ways (see Exhibit 6.5) to provoke creativity and thoroughness. Management can then integrate these into a single tree that best reflects its understanding of the business. For this exercise to succeed, managers within the business unit must be directly involved in the brainstorming and debate.

Exhibit 6.4   Overview of Value Driver Analysis

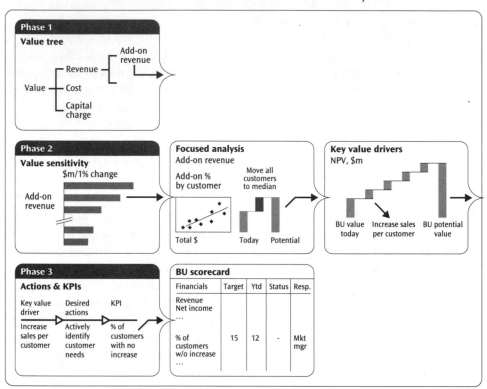

2. *Prioritization.* Once managers have agreed upon an integrated tree, the next step is to determine which drivers could have the greatest impact on the value. The first part of prioritization is building a discounted cash flow model for testing the sensitivity of the business unit's value to changes in each of the value drivers, looking one by one at the effect that a small change in each driver could bring. The second part is analyzing a limited number of value drivers to determine the "real life" potential and ease of capture for each improvement action. The end of this phase is a list of key value drivers and the potential associated with each one.

3. *Institutionalization.* Value drivers are incorporated into the targets and scorecards of on-going business performance management, as described in the next section. Note that value drivers should be reviewed periodically, as the highest-priority levers may change as market conditions or the company's skills evolve.

Exhibit 6.5   Value Driver Trees from Different Perspectives

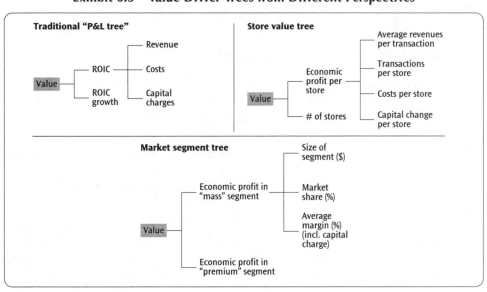

MANAGING BUSINESS PERFORMANCE

Once a company understands how to create value in each business by influencing the value drivers, the next challenge is managing each business to attain results consistent with the top-down aspirations. Business performance management is the process of setting targets for a performance unit and regularly reviewing progress against them, with the goal that different layers of the company will work together for enhanced performance. Business performance management is often the crux of managing for value, as this is where value metrics, value drivers, and targets must translate into everyday actions and decision making.

When business performance management is working well, it helps different layers of the organization communicate frankly and effectively. In particular, effective business performance management greatly improves the dialogue between the corporate center and the business units. It gives managers space to manage, while assuring their bosses that the agreed-upon level of performance will be achieved. But when business performance management is done poorly, it can degenerate into piles of paperwork and much wasted time.

There are several components of successful business performance management. First, a business unit must have a clear strategy for creating value. Second, it should set targets with a clear link to specific value drivers.

Third, it needs a structured calendar of performance reviews to discuss results against value-linked KPIs.

Crafting Business Unit Strategy to Create Value

Crafting business unit strategy is a prerequisite for effective business performance management, even though it is not part of the process itself. We will not give a full description of strategic planning here, but rather point out how discounted cash flow analyses, such as those developed in value driver analysis, can greatly assist management in choosing a business unit strategy.

Applying valuation to strategy can produce significant insights:

- The retail banking division of a money center bank had been following a "harvest" strategy and taking cash out of the business. The division's new chief operating officer wanted to switch to an aggressive growth strategy to regain market share. This strategy had a price tag of $100 million for refurbishing branch bank facilities, installing automatic teller machines, better training for tellers, and a new advertising campaign. While the bank's CEO originally rejected the new strategy because it would lead to reduced return on equity in the first year, he changed his mind when a DCF valuation showed that the value of the aggressive growth strategy was 124 percent higher than that of the harvest strategy.

- A consumer products company determined that pursuing accelerated category growth had twice the potential value increase and a fraction of the downside compared with expanding the brand into new products.

Another benefit of making a direct link between strategy and valuation is that this explicitly links the strategy development process with other efforts to make value happen. If the business unit strategy process is not set up with a value creation focus, then performance management will be less meaningful, as its goals may not be congruent with the chosen strategy.

Setting Value-Linked Targets

Translating strategy into specific quantitative goals requires management to set value-linked targets. In this section, we will focus on the target-setting process for a business unit, but the principles can be applied to more specific targets such as those used for frontline performance.

A starting point is deciding what principles to use in setting targets. Typical approaches are to set targets on the basis of history ("we can get 3 percent more than last year") or a degree of stretch that has no basis in the underlying business ("everybody in this corporation has to get 15 percent growth"). We recommend looking at the actual opportunities available along each of the key performance indicators. Opportunities can be gauged by benchmarking competitors; industry analysis; theoretical limits such as capacity utilization, and, where appropriate, benchmarking against comparable business units within the same company. This process will generally create operating stretch, but one with a basis in reality.

A related issue is deciding how to deal with externalities. This is particularly important for businesses where one or more of the key drivers—commodity prices, for example—is influenced by factors outside of management's control. Generally the best approach is to adjust the targets to reflect the changing environment. The rules should be clearly stated ahead of the performance measurement period so that all parties can agree that they are fair.

Once the corporate center and business unit management agree on principles, they must also decide how to interact in setting targets. Getting a fit between top-down and bottom-up targets requires negotiation between the center and the business unit, which makes the target setting process an iterative one. While this demands more time and energy than simply dictating targets from the top, the iterative approach draws more deeply on the business unit managers' expertise and is more likely to gain their true commitment.

A well-informed corporate center is the most important prerequisite for this dialogue. Top management, particularly the CEO, needs a good understanding of the economics and operating environment of each business, independent of the information provided by the business itself. Various approaches can make this happen, including having the corporate center operate as a kind of principal investing firm, or having an "equity analysis" function within the corporate center. When these approaches work well, they can provide useful support for the business unit as well as insight for the CEO.

After agreeing on a target, the corporate center and business unit can formalize this commitment in a performance contract. The contract should contain the milestones and quantitative and qualitative goals that the business unit intends to achieve throughout the performance period. The goals should be explicit enough to avoid ambiguities in expectations, but not so constraining as to hamper the manager's legitimate scope of action. Having the CEO and the business unit manager sign the contract gives symbolic weight to the commitment.

While we have focused on setting targets at the overall business unit level, targets should cascade throughout the organization just as the value drivers do. The CEO and the business unit head might discuss a few high-level operational and financial indicators. The business unit head would then discuss the key performance indicators at the next level of detail with his or her direct reports. On the frontline, managers and staff will discuss operational levers such as inventory turnover. If a company has organized into performance units and done a thorough value driver analysis, then creating cascading targets should be straightforward.

Regularly Reviewing Performance

To periodically check performance against targets, a company needs a structured calendar of performance reviews. These provide a series of forums throughout the year for managers and employees to evaluate and discuss performance and look for ways to improve. Some factors for success in performance reviews are the information used in the reviews, the timing of the overall calendar, and the tone of the discussions.

The best information base for the reviews is a scorecard incorporating value metrics and KPIs from the value driver analysis. It is tempting for managers to think that financial reports alone can serve as the basis for performance discussions. Accounting inputs are only part of the picture. A scorecard also should contain value metrics grounded in economic results and KPIs that reveal underlying performance. As a measure of value creation over a period of time, economic profit is widely used. For the drivers of value creation, historical KPIs show the operating performance behind the financial results. For example, if revenue is dropping, is the cause lower market share, more discounts than usual, or other factors? Additionally, leading indicators give a sense of future developments and may head off any negative trends. A sample of a scorecard that contains these elements is included in Exhibit 6.6.

While it can be tempting for the corporate center to impose one scorecard on all its business units, this is shortsighted. Any gains in comparability across businesses are more than offset by the losses in understanding the unique drivers of value in each unit. The ideal model is to have custom-tailored scorecards cascading down in each business, so that each manager can monitor the key value drivers most important to him or her. Once managers know what data they want to review in the scorecards, they need to establish how they will get the data in a timely, complete, and accurate way for each review. Companies differ in the degree to which they decide to automate this process. Some choose elaborate software solutions, whereas others get by with more informal systems. In either case, the process should be as streamlined as possible so that reviews do not precipitate a data collection crisis each time they occur. Accuracy of the data in the scorecards is critical so that people feel they are being measured fairly. Further, management must figure out how it will capture qualitative data on a continual basis.

Exhibit 6.6   Sample Performance Scorecard for a Business Unit

	Month			YTD			Status	
	Actual	Target	Last year	Actual	Target	Last year		
Value creation								
Economic profit	30	35	25	150	160	140	○	
Financial results								
Gross margin							◉	
Selling expense							◉	
General & admin. expense							○	
Net income							○	
ROIC							○	
Operating results								
Sales per square meter							◉	
Inventory turnover							○	
Staff turnover							◉	
Leading indicators								
Store opening milestone							◉	
New category launch							○	
Customer satisfaction							◉	

Legend:
◉ At least 95% of projected
○ 80-95% of projected
● Less than 80% of projected

Scorecards are the "what" of performance reviews; the calendar is the "when." Reviews need to happen as part of a structured, repeating cycle, as this makes them an on-going part of management's agenda for the business. The length of the cycle should be chosen with care. While the default choice for most companies is one year, crucial KPIs may be best measured over a longer or shorter cycle depending upon their lead times. Finally, managers should coordinate the performance review calendar with other important events, such as capital budgeting and individual performance reviews. Carrying out business performance management apart from the normal flow of events often leads to a corresponding loss of impact.

The style and tone of performance reviews also affects their success. In some companies, performance reviews don't have any real impact because they are only "show and tell" presentations where no challenging questions are asked and no underlying issues addressed. One approach to enable true problem solving in performance reviews is to have peer groups meet on a regular basis. In such meetings, managers with similar degrees of responsibility in different areas of the business unit or of the corporation can share experiences.

If done well, business performance management is not an added burden on already busy managers. Instead, it can save time and effort by providing managers with clear objectives, motivation to achieve them, and support along the way.

MANAGING INDIVIDUAL PERFORMANCE

In individual performance management, two value creation imperatives meet. One imperative is making managers think like owners by linking managers' rewards to behavior that creates overall shareholder value. The other is that in an increasingly knowledge-based economy, management talent is itself an important source of value, and therefore companies must attract and retain talent by offering attractive incentives. Companies need a process that will link individuals' behavior to overall value creation activities and incentives that will motivate and reward strong individual performance.

Just as in business performance management, the process of people performance management should include target-setting and performance reviews. Targets for an individual should link to the KPIs for which he or she is accountable, so that there is consistency between what the business is asked to achieve and what the individual is asked to achieve. Exhibit 6.7 shows how different layers of management within the company can be reviewed using measures that cascade down the organization, ranging from total returns to shareholders for top management to operational value drivers for mid-level managers. Targets related to accountability for group performance should also be included when collaboration is important to a given job.

Performance reviews for individuals should be held regularly and feature challenging, candid feedback. High-performing companies tend to move swiftly when they find that people are underperforming, either retraining them, moving them, firing them, or pushing them to leave through peer pressure. Making the consequences of low performance visible is important so that everyone in the organization realizes the seriousness of living up to targets.

When employees' performance meets or exceeds expectations, visible rewards are equally appropriate. Companies need to craft their reward

Exhibit 6.7   Matching Performance Measures with Managerial Roles

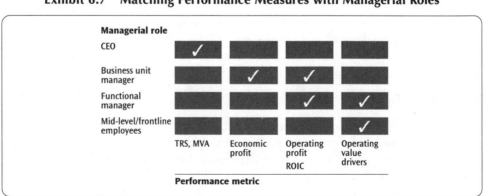

systems to tap into the real sources of motivation for their employees. High-performing companies tend to combine the following three types of motivation levers, with a distinctive emphasis on one type of lever:

1. *Financial incentives,* such as a high percentage of compensation at risk through bonus schemes or stock options.
2. *Opportunities,* such as fast-track career paths that rotate strong performers through positions of increasing responsibility.
3. *Values and beliefs,* in which employees gain inherent satisfaction from living up to a distinctive "XYZ Way" of doing business.

Most companies that want to make value happen will use at least some financial incentives to reward value creation and to retain top performers. The following principles can be useful in designing a financial incentive system:

- Consider setting the base level of compensation higher than the median in comparable companies. Our research shows that high-performing companies tend to offer a higher base level of compensation than their competitors, which combined with incentive pay means that their employees also receive a higher total overall compensation package.
- Variable pay should include a meaningful level of differentiation based on performance. Meaningful differentiation is more important to many executives than total pay, particularly to high performers.
- Bonus caps can lead to managers' ceasing to give their all once they have attained the results needed for their maximum compensation.
- Make clear what constraints (e.g., safety or environmental) people must not ignore as they seek to achieve their targets and what the consequences will be for doing so. Link at least some of the incentives to long-term value creation by using mechanisms to defer compensation (e.g., bonus banks).

Ideally, the individual performance management process personalizes the overall value creation goals of the company. In so doing, it should align the interests of owners and managers and thus enhance long-term performance of the company.

STARTING TO MAKE VALUE HAPPEN

If you are interested in making value happen at your company, you will want to know several things: where to get started, what steps to take, and what will create lasting success. Be aware in advance that there is no one recipe or master plan that will make value happen at all companies. The examples below, taken from two companies that have successfully moved to a shareholder value focus, illustrate two different paths:

1. An industrial products company began with a full-scale organizational redesign focusing on restructuring into performance units. The corporate center then set aggressive targets for each of those units. To give business unit managers direction on how to achieve these targets, the company embarked on detailed value driver analysis and instituted business performance management in various units.

2. A conglomerate began at the corporate center, reviewing its aspirations and portfolio and deciding on its overall framework for business performance management. The center then rolled out the system to each business unit in turn.

Each company will need to develop its own timeline tailored to specific needs. Most companies can benefit by beginning with certain diagnostic analyses. On the financial dimension, we recommend that companies do a valuation and economic profit calculation for each business unit to determine where value is being created or destroyed. Reverse-engineering expectations in the share price helps management understand where the market thinks that the company should be in the future. Management can then review companywide aspirations and targets in light of both "what is" and "where we might be."

On the organizational dimension, management needs to develop a fact base on how well current organizational structure and performance management processes are working. Often companies do this by having staff at various levels answer questionnaires about how the current state of the company compares with the value-creating best practices described above. (Note that these need to be anonymous so that people will answer freely.) To supplement the questionnaires, management workshops can provide a forum for discussing what is working and what isn't.

Once you have done this initial diagnostic, you need to prioritize the areas that most need attention. While there's no one order in which you must proceed, working effectively in some areas requires that others be in good order first; for example, you can't do business performance management effectively until you know what the key value drivers are. Also realize that looking systematically at all aspects of making value happen is generally a process that takes several years if it is to have lasting impact in a company.

What separates the companies that have succeeded in making value happen from others that have tried with less success? We have observed the following factors for success:

- Visible top management commitment is needed so that employees realize that this is not just the latest fad, but an effort to change fundamental attitudes and behaviors.

- Extensive participation by business unit managers, particularly in value driver analysis, is critical, both to capture their insights and to ensure that they have a feeling of ownership.

- Links to existing processes are essential to ensure that the efforts to make value happen can have impact on the strategic planning, capital allocation, and promotion and compensation decisions of the company. Ideally, an assessment of shareholder value impact is included in all major management decisions.

- A pragmatic, action-oriented approach ensures that making value happen is inspiring, rather than paper-generating and bureaucratic.

SUMMARY

While all public companies must face the challenge of creating shareholder value, each company will have to choose its own path, based on its starting position and its unique aspirations. In this chapter we have outlined the aspects of finance, strategy, and organization that we have found most important in making value happen. By addressing these areas, companies can create lasting improvement in performance.

7

Mergers, Acquisitions, and Joint Ventures

Most senior executives will be involved in at least one major strategic transaction during their careers, and perhaps many. Even if they never complete a transaction, they can expect at a minimum to receive an overture from another company, bid on a business offered for sale by a persuasive investment banker, or debate with business colleagues the merits of a deal.

Mergers, acquisitions, divestitures, joint ventures, and the like have long been features of the corporate landscape. They became notorious in the late 1800s in the United States with the activity of the "robber barons" and the consolidating activities of J.P. Morgan and others in the early 1900s. Since then, there have been several waves of activity in the United States—first in the booming economy of the late 1960s, then in the controversial restructuring wave of the 1980s, and most recently with the mega-deals at the close of the 1990s. Europe is also experiencing drastically increased merger and acquisition activity driven by the introduction of the Euro, overcapacity in many industries, and steps (albeit halting) to make its capital markets shareholder-friendly. European acquirers have also been active in international transactions. Asian markets have seen less mergers and acquisitions for a variety of reasons; Japan, however, is likely to witness increasing activity as it begins to recover from a decade-long economic slump.

Mergers and acquisitions (M&A) have become an increasingly important means of reallocating resources in the global economy and for executing corporate strategies. For some firms, such as private equity shops and publicly traded industry consolidators like Starwood, pursuing acquisitions and divestitures *is* the corporate strategy. A large—and seemingly insatiable—infrastructure has grown up to facilitate such transactions, including investment bankers, lawyers, consultants, public relations firms, accountants, deal magazines, private investors and private investigators. Considering that most investment banks did not even have M&A departments in the late 1970s, the transformation is remarkable.

In this chapter we focus mainly on the buy side—mergers and acquisitions—because an understanding of how to buy a company provides a foundation for the related activities of divesting and arranging joint ventures. We attempt to provide a general perspective and share our thoughts about some of the lessons we have learned.

WINNERS AND LOSERS

Whether M&A activity benefits the economy is often debated by economists, politicians, journalists, and people in the street. The reality is that there are as many answers as there are deals and vantage points from which to argue. A merger may be good for shareholders of both the acquiring and acquired companies but bad for the economy if it creates a monopoly position detrimental to consumers. An individual who loses his or her job or a town that loses its main plant to merger cutbacks are not immediately (and may never be) better off than they were. Conversely, real improvements in efficiency can lead to higher quality and less costly products. The economy overall is likely to be more vibrant, opportunity-rich, and create more jobs if resources are continuously moved out of lower value uses into more profitable ones.

That said, our main concern is creation of value for shareholders. Anyone considering an acquisition needs to understand the basic fact that many corporate acquisitions fail to increase shareholder value. The market for corporate control is fairly efficient: easy, good deals are hard to come by, if they exist at all. Most successful deals result from highly disciplined deal making—and sometimes just good luck.

Two broad types of research provide this warning. Academic studies typically look at the *ex ante* market reaction to the announcement of a deal, taking into account not only expected costs and benefits of the deal, but also the market's expectation of whether the deal will actually be consummated. This approach assumes the market is smart and able to size up the price paid, potential synergies, and integration ability of the managements involved to arrive at an unbiased estimate of the likelihood of a deal adding to the value of a company. Another analytical approach is *ex post*, assessing merger programs after their completion—looking back to see how what did happen compares with what had been hoped for.

Ex Ante Market Reactions

Exhibit 7.1 summarizes the results of dozens of academic studies of transactions involving public companies. Shareholders of acquired companies are the big winners, receiving on average a 20 percent premium in a

Exhibit 7.1   Empirical Studies of M&A Activity

Type of event		Average return to shareholders (percent)
Merger	Acquired company	20
	Acquiring company	2–3[1]
Tender offer for takeover	Acquired company	35
	Acquiring company	3–5
Sell-off	Spin-off	2–5
	Divestiture	
	• Seller	0.5–1.0
	• Buyer	0.34
	Equity carve-out	2

1 Not statistically significant.
Source: Copeland and Weston 1988, 754.

friendly merger and a 35 percent premium in a hostile takeover. Shareholders of acquiring companies, on average, earned small returns that are not even statistically different from zero. The shareholders of acquired companies receive most of the benefit, because competition among acquirers forces the target's price up to the point where little or no expected benefit to acquiring shareholders is left.

This does not mean that acquirers never succeed after the fact nor that the market's reaction to a deal is always lukewarm or unfavorable. However, it does serve to point out how skeptical investors are about the likelihood of acquirers getting more than they pay for in a deal. Likewise, a favorable initial reaction by the market is merely an expectation that the deal will create value—whether it will is revealed over time.

To know that overall the market is unimpressed with acquirers' deals, despite undoubtedly glowing promises when the deals were announced, is certainly interesting and sobering. But it masks additional information about what types of deals the market might expect to create value. To probe this, several colleagues analyzed the market's ex ante reaction to all transactions with a deal size greater than $500 million among publicly traded U.S. companies from January 1996 to September 1998. The results are consistent with prior academic findings—acquirers on average were not expected to earn exceptional profits from their deals, while selling shareholders gained significantly 90 percent of the time.

Peering beneath the surface of the results reveals that there were many transactions the market thought were good deals for the acquiring shareholders. The problem is that there are also many that were expected to be poor deals—leading to an insignificant overall effect. For acquirers whose stock moved significantly one way or the other near the announcement of a deal, 42 percent were winners and 58 percent losers.

What types of deal were expected to be good ones? The research suggests the following factors at work, all of which comport with common sense:

- *Bigger value creation overall.* An acquirer can increase its chance of success significantly if there is seen to be substantial value creation in the whole deal. If the deal is judged a marginal or losing proposition overall, acquirers' share prices dropped 98 percent of the time. If there is seen to be substantial juice—believable, unique synergies—in a deal, it's much more likely that the acquirer will be able to capture a portion for its shareholders, while paying a "fair" price to the sellers.

- *Lower premiums paid.* Acquirers who pay lower premiums (less than 10 percent or no premiums) are three times as likely to see their stock prices affected favorably by the announcement. Moreover, acquirers who buy subsidiaries or divisions of other companies are more likely to have deals seen as favorable than buyers of entire publicly traded companies. This could be due to lack of a publicly traded price to anchor price negotiations, the desire of sellers to complete a transaction so management can rid itself of a problem division, or perhaps the ability of the acquiring company to integrate the business more rapidly and effectively.

- *Better-run acquirers.* Below-average operators fared less well than acquirers whose financial performance was above average for their industries. Acquirers whose five-year returns on invested capital (ROIC) were above average for their industries were statistically more likely to see their stock price rise upon announcement of a deal—whereas below-average performers were more likely to see their prices drop.

Ex Post Results

So much for the stock market's prognostications—what really happens? In the late 1980s, McKinsey's Corporate Leadership Center studied 116 acquisition programs, usually involving multiple acquisitions in the United States and the United Kingdom, between 1972 and 1983. They started with companies in either the Fortune 200 largest U.S. industrials or the *Financial Times* top 150 U.K. industrials. A program was judged successful if it earned its cost of capital or better on funds invested in it, after giving the programs at least three years to season. Programs usually involved multiple acquisitions such as General Mills' 47 acquisitions of small, high-growth, consumer-oriented companies. Unfortunately, sixty-one percent of the programs ended in failure, only 23 percent in success. For the 97 programs that were clear winners or losers, the greatest chance of success (at 45 percent) was for those programs where acquirers bought smaller companies in related businesses.[1] If

---

[1] The acquired company was judged to be small if the purchase price was less than 10 percent of the acquiring company's market value. It was classified as related if the target's markets were similar to those of the acquiring company.

the target was large and in an unrelated line of business, then the success rate fell to only 14 percent.

Consistent with the ex ante results, the probability of success is also heavily influenced by the strength of the core business of the acquirer. Of the 23 percent of U.S. programs that were successful, 92 percent had high performing core businesses.

In another study, Anslinger and Copeland looked at the results achieved by 13 leveraged buyout firms and 8 U.S. corporate buyers of businesses that seemed not to have synergies with the acquirer.[2] Overall, these 21 companies were very successful. They made 829 acquisitions and 80 percent believed they had earned more than the cost of capital invested in their deals. The U.S. corporate acquirers averaged more than 18 percent return to shareholders over a 10-year period, outperforming the S&P 500 during the period. The buyout firms reported that return to investors exceeded 35 percent in the period. The results provide a sharp contrast to those obtained by the typical large corporate buyer described earlier.

How did the buyout firms do it? They focused on quickly improving operating performance at acquired companies. They identified and created big incentives for the top leaders at the companies—and replaced them if their performance did not make the grade. They focused on the cash flow generated by the business, rather than accounting earnings, and used an active and interactive involvement among owners, board members, and management to push the pace of change and create a sense of urgency. Finally, many of the acquirers had their personal wealth involved in each deal. They concentrated on buying at reasonable prices, identifying concrete operating improvements, and extracting their investment within five years. This is quite a contrast to the typical large company, where management has little direct stake in a business it buys and can be easily deluded into accepting "strategic" arguments for paying more.

Overall, the record suggests that profitable growth by acquisition is not easy, although some management teams and buyers have been successful. More often, management finds that its acquisition proposals are met with skepticism and worse by investors and by poor returns afterwards.

REASONS FOR FAILURE

Why are so many acquisitions failures? Setting luck aside, most acquisitions turn out badly because purchasers have paid too much—a situation from which it is hard to recover since it happens upfront. Another basic reason is poor post-acquisition management.

---

[2] P. Anslinger and T. Copeland, "Growth through Acquisitions: A Fresh Look," *Harvard Business Review* (January/February 1996).

Why do companies overpay? Four reasons we have seen are: (1) overoptimistic appraisal of market potential, (2) overestimation of synergies, (3) poor due diligence, and (4) overbidding. No executive sets out deliberately to overpay. However, once the deal process begins, events and rationalizations prey upon even the most disciplined acquirers. The more time and effort that has gone into a deal, the harder it is to admit that it won't create value for shareholders at a given price or on particular terms, regardless of sheer business logic.

Overoptimistic Appraisal of Market Potential

Acquisition is a dangerous enterprise if based on the assumption that a market will rebound from a cyclical slump or that a company will turn around. No less problematic or uncommon is the assumption that rapid growth will continue indefinitely. Remember, if you pay a premium to acquire a company you will either need to capture synergies, improve the company's operations, or both. If you cannot do either, then you are betting against the market and the seller, and both are likely to know more about the business than you do.

We can't rule out the possibility that a company's actual value is higher than its market value. But one should be skeptical and be sure to understand where and why the market's assumptions about the future are different than yours. In fact, it is less unusual for a company's traded market value to exceed its underlying value, since at times many companies have some expectation of a takeover reflected in their stock prices. This points out the need for an independent assessment of the value of a company on a standalone basis as the essential underpinning of any deal.

Overestimation of Synergies

Synergy is a peculiar word—depending on the context it either stands for the pipe dreams of management or a hard-nosed rationale for a deal. Often it is a little of both. Consider the following example: A large health services company paid several billion dollars for a more profitable company in a related industry segment. Given its stepped-up investment base, the target's post acquisition after-tax earnings would have had to be about $500 million for the acquirer's return on its investment to approach its cost of capital. The year before the transaction was consummated, the target's earnings were about $225 million. Therefore, it needed to close an earnings gap of more than $275 million through "operating synergies." That meant more than doubling the earnings base. The acquirer's inability to make improvements of this magnitude resulted in destruction of significant shareholder value. In the ensuing three years, market indices rose while the acquirer's returns to its shareholders were actually negative. Clearly in the foregoing case, the estimation of deal benefits became disconnected from reality somewhere along the way. "The Vision Thing" often underlies such situations, where a visionary CEO's idea of an industry-transforming deal runs straight into the reality of day-to-day business.

Overlooking Problems

Due diligence is a difficult process from which to get good business results. It has an intensive legal and accounting aspect to it that involves large numbers of accountants and lawyers working long hours in unpleasant conditions. There is also a need for secrecy and speed, since leaks can prompt problems with securities regulators, customers, suppliers, and employees. Beyond this, many participants are either inexperienced or not sure what they are looking for. And many people do not want to be the bearer of bad news, especially as the process becomes more frenetic and the CEO and others get more excited about doing the deal. Put it all together and sometimes even major problems, including accounting and legal problems that should have been caught, slip through and blow up, usually in the year after closing.

Overbidding

In the heat of a deal, the acquirer may bid up the price beyond the limits of reasonable valuations. It is all too easy to find benchmarks that justify a higher price or bargain away important nonprice terms that restrict the ability of the acquirer to achieve planned-for savings and growth. Remember the winner's curse: If you are the winner in a bidding war, why did your competitors drop out (bearing in mind that they too may have scratched to find the last penny for their bid!)?

Poor Post-Acquisition Integration

Assuming that the price paid would allow for an acquirer to create value from a deal, there is still another hurdle to clear: implementation. It goes almost without saying that poor implementation can ruin even the best strategy. In M&A situations, the execution of a sound business strategy is made especially difficult by the complex task of integrating two different organizations. Relationships with customers, employers, and suppliers are often disrupted during the process; this disruption may cause damage to the value of the business. Aggressive acquirers often believe they can improve the target's performance by injecting better management talent, but end up chasing much of the talent out. Yet it is this very integration that should yield the returns to make the acquisition pay off. Failure to integrate can be as costly as integrating poorly. Exhibit 7.2 shows a typical losing pattern for unsuccessful merger programs. This death spiral, unfortunately, is all too common.

Exhibit 7.2   Typical Losing Pattern for Acquisitions

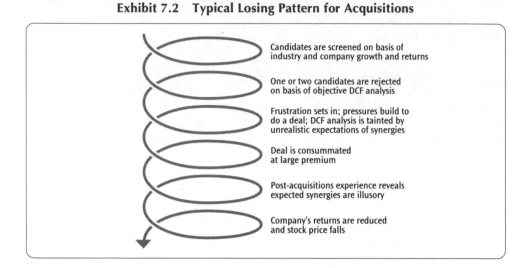

Candidates are screened on basis of
industry and company growth and returns

One or two candidates are rejected
on basis of objective DCF analysis

Frustration sets in; pressures build to
do a deal; DCF analysis is tainted by
unrealistic expectations of synergies

Deal is consummated
at large premium

Post-acquisitions experience reveals
expected synergies are illusory

Company's returns are reduced
and stock price falls

STEPS IN SUCCESSFUL MERGERS AND ACQUISITIONS

We can break an acquisition program into the five distinct steps. The process begins with a pre-acquisition phase that involves a self-examination of your company and its industries. And the process ends with a carefully planned post-merger integration that is executed as quickly as possible to capture the premium that was paid for the acquisition.

Step 1: Do Your Homework

If you have valued your own company and understand the changing structure of your industry and the players in it, then you should have a clear vision of the value-adding approach that will work best. Three avenues to consider are:

1. Strengthen or leverage your core business by gaining access to new customers or customer segments and to complementary or better products and services.
2. Capitalize on functional economies of scale (e.g., in distribution or manufacturing) to cut costs and improve product and service quality.
3. Benefit from technology or skills transfer. Some companies are better at doing certain things than others or have developed unique technologies. If these skills can be applied to larger volumes of business or opportunity, then they can be a source of real value.

When it comes to thinking through synergies, companies at times fail to focus on how revenues will increase or costs will fall. For example, it is tempting to assume that revenues for a new combined company will be the sum of the predecessor companies' sales plus a boost from cross-selling additional products. The reality can be quite different. First, the fact of a merger itself will disrupt customer relationships, leading to loss of business. Second, smart competitors use mergers as a prime opportunity to break into new accounts—including recruiting star salespeople or product specialists. Finally, customers are not shy about asking for price and other concessions in the midst of a merger, which salespeople will be eager to offer for fear of losing the business and getting bad publicity. It is hard to overestimate how much effort is required to deal with such issues, and to underestimate the impact if you do not.

Likewise, on paper, salesforces might be integrated to move more product through the same number of salespeople. Reality in the field might be quite different if the salesforces of the merging companies do not make exactly the same customer calls. For example, it is unlikely that two college textbook companies, one specializing in liberal arts books and the other in scientific texts, can profit from salesforce savings. Salespeople in the two companies actually visit different parts of campus, with little redundancy.

Sometimes value can be gained from skills or technology transfer through the merger. But this approach, while often touted, can be fraught with problems. More often than not, managerial hubris creates overly optimistic self-assessments of skills that can be leveraged. It pays to be skeptical. Probe for the specifics on everything and sort the benefits of possible deals into two categories—the measurable and eminently believable and the conceivable and possibly ephemeral. This way you will at least avoid mixing the two and know what you're counting on to make a deal work.

In parallel with understanding your business strategy and how it may be aided by acquisitions, there are a number of housekeeping/homework tasks that should be addressed before getting involved in a deal.

Housekeeping/homework means identifying the details that are necessary for getting a transaction evaluated and approved (or not) ahead of time. Concretely, this means knowing who in the organization needs to approve a deal as a formal matter. What must go to the board of directors and when? Which types of deals must shareholders approve? Are there any restrictions on types of consideration, issuance of options to an acquired company's employees, or changes to benefit plans? Which regulators will need to be consulted and what are the criteria for deal approval? Are there customer, supplier, employee, or other contracts that contain provisions that would be affected by various types of transactions? What is the company's tax profile—how would it be affected by possible transactions?

Step 2: Identify and Screen Candidates

Successful acquirers actively screen and cultivate candidates. It may make sense to explain your acquisition criteria to selected investment banks and others that may have special insight or access into potential candidates. However, it is best not to sit back and passively react to investment banking proposals for acquisition candidates. It is much better to develop and actively cultivate your own. Often, if a banker approaches you with a company for sale, odds are that the company is being widely shopped. In this event, you will likely end up paying top dollar to acquire it after a time-pressured evaluation and due diligence process—hardly a prescription for success.

The best approach is to develop a database and set of files on all prospective candidates in your areas of interest. It is likely that you will track many candidates for several years and will want to update your information periodically. You will want to consider publicly held companies, divisions of companies, privately held companies, and foreign as well as domestic companies. You will be aware of many candidates as a result of business strategy work. At this point you may find it useful to winnow the universe of candidates by employing a list of knock-out criteria. Targets that are too large, too small, or heavily connected with unrelated businesses can be quickly eliminated. The end product of this stage should be a set of candidates that have solid businesses; offer potential for revenue and cost synergies; fit culturally so they can be integrated with least disruption; are affordable, and are available (at least possibly) for purchase.

Step 3: Assess High Potential Candidates in Depth

Once you have narrowed your list of candidates to a handful of realistic possibilities, you will begin the detailed work of valuing each candidate and identifying your strategy for creating value. You will need a plan that more than earns back the purchase price, including a premium that you would have to pay to complete a deal. With takeover premiums running 30 percent to 40 percent and more above the pre-acquisition market values, you will want to be sure the synergies are both large and clearly identified.

When undertaking a detailed evaluation of the remaining candidates, keep in mind the distinction between the value to you and the price you will need to pay. Your obvious objective should be to maximize the former while minimizing the latter. The essential starting point is a clear understanding of the value of the company to you under your ownership. This consists of its standalone value, as operated by current management; likely net synergies from the combination, after taking into account potential lost business from disruption, and transactions costs, such as restructuring charges and deal fees. The more specific you can be in assessing each of these areas, the better prepared you will be for negotiations and subsequent integration.

Standalone value should be looked at from multiple perspectives, including average securities analyst estimates, past performance, and management pronouncements. Likewise, synergies should be categorized and quantified wherever possible. You should also assess how long it will take to capture the synergies. And don't forget about the impact of competitor reactions to your deal that could have a financial impact on the combined firm.

When valuing synergies, you will need to identify not only the synergies that you can obtain, but also those that may accrue to other potential acquirers. If the synergies that you can capture are less than those that can be captured by a competitor, you are likely to lose in a bidding war. Synergies fall into one of three broad categories, as detailed by Bill Pursche:[3]

1. *Universal.* Generally available to any logical acquirer with capable management and adequate resources. Examples are economies of scale (such as leveraging the fixed cost of a management information systems department or eliminating redundant senior management) and some exploitable opportunities (raising prices, cutting corporate overhead, and eliminating waste).

2. *Endemic.* Available to only a few acquirers, typically those in the same industry as the seller. These include economies of scope (broadened geographic coverage) and most exploitable opportunities (redundant sales forces).

3. *Unique.* Opportunities that can be exploited only by a specific buyer (or seller).

The value to the buyer and seller depends on the type of synergy and who controls it. Universal synergies, since they are widely accessible, usually accrue to the sellers as do unique synergies, if under control of the seller. If the buyer possesses the unique synergy, it may pay a lower price (because there is no competing buyer) and keep most of the value. This is especially the case where the buyer has alternate means of "monetizing" the capability that does not depend on acquiring a specific target company.

Endemic synergies fall in between, with the buyer and seller potentially sharing the value created as a result of who brings what to the table and the parties' respective negotiating skills and power.

When analyzing synergies, consider restructuring and financial engineering. Assets that are worth more to other owners can be profitably redeployed through liquidations, divestitures, spin-offs, or leveraged buyouts. Hidden asset values, such as overfunded pension plans or underused real

[3] W. Pursche, "Building Better Bids: Synergies and Acquisition Prices," *Chief Financial Officer USA* (1988), pp. 63–64.

estate, can be captured. Finally, alternative financing arrangements, including sale/leaseback arrangements, royalty trusts, partial equity offerings, tracking stock, and contingency payment units, can also create value by better use of tax shelters, reducing the capital base without cutting earnings, or raising funds in an optimal way.

The tax treatment of an M&A transaction can be vitally important to its economics. Moreover, the field is constantly changing, complex, and specific to each jurisdiction and to a company's circumstances. Almost anything that we could write would soon be outdated and incorrect. Our recommendation is that anyone working on M&A transactions establish a good working relationship with tax experts and keep them involved every step of the way.

It is also important to understand the accounting treatment of potential acquisitions, because managements are required to present their results to external parties in accordance with an elaborate set of rules. In Chapter 5, we discussed some of the issues surrounding M&A accounting methods.

Step 4: Contact, Court, and Negotiate

Eventually, you will be ready to begin contacting your top priority acquisition candidates. This courtship process can be delicate, and may require years until actual combination discussions take place. Many sellers do not want to sell—they have their own plans they believe in and prefer to remain independent. If the target company's financial situation allows it, then there is little that can be done until circumstances change. If the company is publicly traded and has weak defenses, you may want to consider a hostile bid, but this will make the job of finalizing your assessment of the target very difficult and set a poor tone for effective integration after the deal.

The purpose of a discreet courtship process is threefold: to learn more about whether there is a good fit between the companies, to convince the sellers to sell, and, to convince them to sell to *you*, preferably through exclusive negotiations where you can achieve better price and terms than in a competitive situation.

Once the sellers are at the table, the negotiations begin in earnest. Negotiating carefully and purposefully will help you avoid overpaying and boxing yourself into terms that will make successful post-merger management difficult. Acquirers who fail in an acquisition because they overbid, or because they could not make the acquisition work, often become targets themselves.[4]

---

[4] See Mark Mitchell and Ken Lehn, "Do Bad Bidders Become Good Targets?" Working Paper (Washington, DC: Office of Economic Analysis, Securities and Exchange Commission, 1985).

It is important to realize that negotiation is really an art. It depends on your ability to keep your eye calmly on your objectives and interests, while reading and dealing effectively with the other side. Acting and histrionics can play a role. Knowing how and when to leave the table, how to identify and trade off various terms, how to enlarge the total pie—these all matter.

You will also want to be on the lookout for creative ways to handle stumbling blocks. Some of these arise from different perceptions about future prospects and others simply get down to arguing over who will bear risk. In purchases of private companies and divisions, contingent payment structures such as "earnouts" keyed to achieving profit targets can help bridge the gap. At other times, payments tied to customer retention work well. Employee retention can also be an issue, particularly in service businesses; stay-put payments, stock plans and the like can help ensure key staff remain long enough to give the new company a chance to work and be seen as an attractive employer in its own right.

It is easy to be blinded by the "fog of war" and concessions already made can be nearly impossible to reclaim. If you have followed the steps described above, you will be in a good position. You will know clearly what the logic is for a deal, how the companies fit together, and what the economics might look like. You will also know a lot about the target company and its management.

Step 5: Manage Post-Merger Integration

From a shareholder's perspective, post-merger management (PMM) is a fancy phrase for figuring out how to recoup your investment in a deal. As we discussed earlier, poor post-deal execution causes many mergers to fail. Exhibit 7.3 sets out three broad must-do action areas for top management involved in a merger integration. The approach to executing against each will vary by circumstance.

Exhibit 7.3   Management Must Execute Quickly in Three Areas

	Must-do actions
Define the new business model	1. Unify strategic direction 2. Develop new operating model 3. Set clear targets, accountability, and performance incentives
Resolve uncertainty and conflicts	4. Decide top management 5. Embrace top performers 6. Communicate to get employee buy-in
Respond to external pressures	7. Sell deal to key customers 8. Communicate with external stakeholders 9. Keep regulators satisfied

1. *Define the new business model.* At a high level this entails ensuring that the rationale for creating value in the deal translates into a game plan that the combined business can pursue quickly. It should identify how the businesses will come together and how each of the main synergies can be realized. Ideally, this planning will begin as part of the deal negotiations, be firmed up between signing and closing, and be ready for implementation immediately after the close.

2. *Resolve uncertainty and conflicts.* Mergers generate tremendous excitement and stress within an organization. Many employees fear they will lose jobs and will have little say about how the operation will be run. Not much can be done to dispel this anxiety, because the fact is that some people usually *will* lose their jobs. Moreover, for the deal to be a success, something must change and change can be scary.

   Usually the passage of time will lead to a calmer state of affairs, but there are some actions management can take to minimize disruption. Setting the top-level organization quickly is important, so that factions do not develop and people down the line do not have the experience of "watching their parents fight." Senior management also needs to identify and handhold top performers throughout the organization. They are usually well known to competitors and recruiters and vulnerable to being lured away. Do not underestimate the depth of anxiety even star producers may feel in the midst of a merger. Once convinced of the benefits of a deal, however, they can be very helpful advocates throughout the organization. Finally, communicate as candidly and often as possible with the employee base at large. They may not like everything that happens, but it will go a long way toward reducing the fear and resentment that a feeling of secrecy can engender. Remember, too, that employees are a key source of information for customers and suppliers—poor morale internally can end up creating problems externally.

3. *Respond to external pressures.* Regulators, shareholders, and creditors will need to be kept informed as a merger proceeds. Indeed, they will likely demand it. If you've done your homework you know about all the regulatory requirements and legal notices required.

   If your company is publicly traded you will want to make a presentation to securities analysts on the day of the announcement about the deal, if it is a significant one for the company. You may also be required by securities laws to file disclosure statements. Keep in mind that these materials will have a wider audience, including your own employees and customers.

   The CEO and others down the line should contact important customers early in the process—perhaps right after the deal is announced on the news wires—to explain the benefits of the combination and how they will be affected. Competitors will miss few chances to do so on your behalf, so you want to get your story out first. Few things can be more demoralizing than the loss of an important customer shortly after a deal is completed. Conversely, early wins with existing or new customers can be a tremendous source of energy.

Overall, speed of action in merger integration is crucial. Moving quickly dispels uncertainty. And, of course, the sooner cash flow improvements can be realized the better from a value perspective.

JOINT VENTURES

Joint ventures differ from acquisitions in several ways. First, they are effectively partnerships and their creation does not usually involve a takeover premium to either party. Second, to be successful they must be structured to allow effective control. As a form of alliance, joint ventures are particularly important. Many alliance options are available, as can be seen in Exhibit 7.4. Mergers and acquisitions tend to deal with the entire business system of a company and are more permanent in nature. Joint ventures can be focused on pieces of the business system (a sales joint venture or a production or development joint venture) and can be dissolved after a period of time.

Exhibit 7.4   Alliance Options

Alliances	Develop new product markets	Share upstream risks	Share development costs	Leapfrog product technology	Increase capacity utilization	Exploit economies of scale	Fill product line gaps	Penetrate new geographic market
Acquisition				✓	✓	✓	✓	✓
Merger				✓	✓	✓	✓	
Core business JV				✓	✓	✓	✓	✓
Sales JV				✓	✓		✓	✓
Production JV				✓	✓	✓		✓
Development JV			✓		✓		✓	✓
Product swap			✓	✓		✓	✓	
Production license	✓		✓	✓	✓	✓		
Technology alliance	✓	✓						
Development license	✓	✓	✓					

In their study of joint ventures, Bleeke and Ernst examined the partner-ships of 150 companies ranked by market value—the 50 largest in the United States, Europe, and Japan.[5] Their findings were:

- Both cross-border acquisitions and cross-border alliances have roughly the same success rate (about 50 percent).
- Acquisitions work well for core businesses and existing geographical areas. Alliances are more effective for edging into related businesses or new geographic areas.
- Alliances between strong and weak rarely work.
- Successful alliances must be able to evolve beyond their initial objec-tives. This requires autonomy and flexibility.
- More than 75 percent of the alliances that are terminated end with an acquisition by one of the parents.

To be considered a success in the study, an alliance had to pass two tests. First, both partners had to achieve their on-going strategic objectives. Second, they both had to recover their financial cost of capital. For acquisitions ex-ceeding 20 percent of the acquirer's market value, the deal was judged to be a financial success if the acquirer was able to maintain or improve its return on equity and return on assets. For smaller acquisition programs, interviews were conducted to assess financial success. A comparison of cross-border mergers and acquisitions with cross-border alliances shows the same success rate—about 50 percent.

The motivation for cross-border mergers and acquisitions, however, seems to be different than for joint ventures. Mergers and acquisitions seem to benefit from geographical overlap, perhaps because synergies such as consolidation of production facilities, integration of distribution net-works, and reorganization of sales forces are more easily achieved by high geographical proximity. Alliances, on the other hand, are usually intended to expand the geographical reach of the partners. There are fewer alliances with high geographical overlap and they have a much lower success rate for both partners.

Ownership structure is also important for the success of joint ven-tures. When the ownership of the joint venture was evenly split, the prob-ability of success for both was 60 percent compared with only 31 percent when the ownership split was uneven. Alliances work best when both par-ents are strong. When one partner or the other is weak, the "weak link" becomes a drag on the venture's competitiveness and hinders successful management. When one parent has a majority stake, it tends to dominate decision-making and puts its own interests above those of the partner, or the joint venture itself.

---

[5] J. Bleeke and D. Ernst, eds., *Collaborating to Compete* (New York: Wiley, 1993).

Joint ventures work best when they have autonomy and flexibility. Flexibility is important because the relative power of the parents will inevitably change, because markets and customer needs will shift, and new technologies arise. During interviews with the top companies that have alliances, Bleeke and Ernst found that of those alliances that evolved, 79 percent were successful and 89 percent were still surviving at the end of the sample period. Of those alliances whose scope had remained unchanged, only 33 percent were successful and more than half had ended.

Flexibility and autonomy can be built by giving the joint venture a strong, independent president and a full business system of its own (R&D, sales, manufacturing, marketing, and distribution) and providing it with an independent, powerful board of directors.

Joint ventures have a limited life span. More than 75 percent of the terminated partnerships were acquired by one of the partners. This does not necessarily imply that the joint venture failed. Alliances often end after meeting the partner's goals. It does mean that it is useful to prepare for the break-up of the alliance. If the eventual seller does not anticipate such an outcome the sale can compromise its long-term strategic interests. Often the natural buyer is the company that is the most willing to invest to build the joint venture.

SUMMARY

An active market for corporate control drastically reduces the chances of success for acquiring companies. Even in situations where the acquired company is in the same line of business as the acquirer and is small enough to allow easy post-merger integration, the likelihood of success is only about 50 percent.

A disciplined acquisition program is essential. You must have control of the process. Don't rely on the deals brought to you by third parties. Find your own targets, starting with a self-analysis that leads to a value-adding approach.

Identify useful knockout criteria in the screening process. Before bidding on a candidate, understand exactly how you intend to recoup a takeover premium. Try to find synergies that are unique—those that cannot be captured by another bidder. Decide on your maximum price and stick to it as part of a carefully planned negotiation strategy. Finally, move as quickly as possible during post-merger integration and carefully manage the process.

Joint ventures are a form of alliance that permit temporary relationships that focus more specifically on parts of the business system. Although they are successful for both partners only about half of the time, their success rate is improved if there is a low geographical overlap, and if the alliance is provided with autonomy and flexibility between two strong parents with equal ownership.

Part Two

Cash Flow Valuation: A Practitioner's Guide

8

Frameworks for Valuation

In Part One, we described an overall framework for understanding what drives value and how managers can use these concepts to create value in their companies. In particular, we made the case that a company's value is driven by its ability to generate cash flow over the long term. Furthermore, a company's cash-flow generating ability (and hence its value creation ability) is driven by long-term growth and the returns that the company earns on invested capital relative to its cost of capital.

Part Two provides a step-by-step guide to analyzing and valuing a company, including technical details on how to get the numbers right and guidelines for interpreting the results. The first chapter of Part Two provides a high-level summary of how to value a company using the discounted cash flow approach and describes some of the alternatives to this method. Chapters 9 to 13 detail each step in the valuation process.

While there are a number of ways to apply the discounted cash flow (DCF) approach, over the next five chapters we will describe two in detail: the enterprise DCF model and the economic profit model. The enterprise DCF model is the most widely used in practice. The economic profit model is gaining in popularity. Its advantage is that it highlights whether a company is earning its cost of capital. It is important to point out that both models result in exactly the same value, so the choice is mostly driven by the instincts of the user. At the end of this chapter, we discuss two other models: the adjusted present value (APV) model and the equity DCF model. These models are particularly useful in special situations. For example, the equity DCF model is best suited for financial institutions such as banks and insurance companies. The APV model is helpful for valuing companies with changing capital structures, such as leveraged buyout targets. These two models also give the same result as the enterprise DCF and equity DCF models.

THE ENTERPRISE DISCOUNTED CASH FLOW MODEL

The enterprise DCF model values the equity of a company as the value of a company's operations (the enterprise value that is available to all investors) less the value of debt and other investor claims that are superior to common equity (such as preferred stock). The values of operations and debt are equal to their respective cash flows discounted at rates that reflect the riskiness of these cash flows. Exhibit 8.1 illustrates this model. As long as the discount rates are selected properly to reflect the riskiness of each cash flow stream, the enterprise approach will result in exactly the same equity value as if we directly discounted the cash flow to the shareholders at the cost of equity.

The enterprise DCF model is especially useful when extended to a multibusiness company, as shown in Exhibit 8.2. The equity value of the company equals the sum of the values of the individual operating units, plus cash-generating corporate assets, less the present value of the cost of operating the corporate center and the value of the company's debt and

---

Exhibit 8.1 Enterprise Valuation of a Single-Business Company

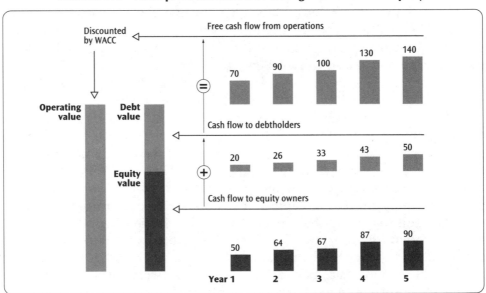

Exhibit 8.2   Enterprise Valuation of a Multibusiness Company

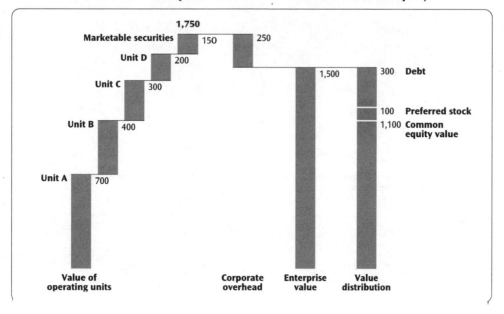

preferred stock. The exhibit helps highlight the reasons for recommending the enterprise DCF model:

- The model values the components of the business that add up to the enterprise value, instead of just the equity. This helps in identifying and understanding the separate investment and financing sources of value for the equity holders.
- This approach helps pinpoint key leverage areas and therefore aids the search for value-creating ideas.
- It can be applied consistently at different levels of aggregation (i.e., the company as a whole or individual business units) and is consistent with the capital budgeting process most companies are already familiar with.
- It is sophisticated enough to deal with the complexity of most situations, while at the same time easy to carry out with simple personal computer tools.

Exhibit 8.3 is a basic valuation summary for the Hershey Foods Corporation.

Exhibit 8.3   Hershey Foods—Free Cash Flow Valuation Summary

Year	Free cash flow (FCF) ($ million)	Discount factor (7.5%)	Present value of FCF ($ million[1])
1999	331	0.930	308
2000	349	0.865	302
2001	364	0.805	293
2002	379	0.749	284
2003	395	0.697	275
2004	412	0.648	267
2005	429	0.603	258
2006	447	0.561	251
2007	466	0.522	243
2008	485	0.485	235
Continuing value	14,710	0.485	7,138
			9,855
Mid-year adjustment factor[2]			1.037
Value of operations			10,217
Value of non-operating investments			450
Total enterprise value			10,667
Less : Value of debt			1,282
Equity value			**9,385**
Equity value per share			**62.78**

1 Except per share.
2 Value adjusted for the average receipt of cash flows half way through the year.

Value of Operations

The value of operations equals the discounted value of expected future free cash flow. Free cash flow is equal to the after-tax operating earnings of the company, plus noncash charges, less investments in operating working capital, property, plant and equipment, and other assets. It does not incorporate any financing-related cash flows such as interest expense or dividends. Exhibit 8.4 shows a summarized free cash flow calculation for the Hershey Foods Corporation. Free cash flow is the correct cash flow for this valuation model because it reflects the cash flow generated by a company's operations that is available to all the company's capital providers, both debt and equity. As you can see in Exhibit 8.4, free cash flow is also equal to the sum of the cash flows paid to or received from all the capital providers (interest, dividends, new borrowing, debt repayments, and so on).

For consistency with the cash flow definition, the discount rate applied to the free cash flow should reflect the opportunity cost to all the capital providers weighted by their relative contribution to the company's total capital. This is called the weighted average cost of capital (WACC). The opportunity cost to a class of investors equals the rate of return the investors could expect to earn on other investments of equivalent risk. The cost to the company equals the investors' costs less any tax benefits received by the

Exhibit 8.4 Hershey Foods—Free Cash Flow Summary

Free cash flow ($ million)	1997	1998	Forecast 1999	Forecast 2000	Forecast 2001
Earnings before interest, taxes, and amortization (EBITA)	646	610	648	671	700
Cash taxes on EBITA	(204)	(177)	(227)	(236)	(246)
Net operating profits less adjusted taxes (NOPLAT)	442	434	420	436	454
Depreciation	137	142	139	151	159
Gross cash flow	579	576	559	586	613
Change in working capital	(18)	(195)	35	(26)	(27)
Capital expenditures	(183)	(142)	(275)	(223)	(235)
Increase in net other assets	(18)	(47)	12	12	13
Gross investment	(219)	(384)	(228)	(237)	(249)
Operating free cash flow	**360**	**192**	**331**	**349**	**364**
Cash flow from non-operating investments	(0)	25	450	0	0
After-tax interest income	2	0	0	0	0
Decrease/(increase) in marketable securities	0	0	(40)	(170)	210
Cash flow available to investors	**362**	**217**	**741**	**179**	**574**
Financing flow					
Net interest expense after tax	48	52	43	42	36
Decrease/(increase) in net debt	(322)	36	3	0	(108)
Common dividends	122	129	195	137	146
Share repurchases	514	0	500	0	500
Financing flow	**362**	**217**	**741**	**179**	**574**

company (for example, the tax shield provided by interest expense). Exhibit 8.5 shows a sample WACC calculation for Hershey Foods.

An additional issue in valuing a business is its indefinite life. One approach is to forecast the free cash flow for one hundred years and not worry about what comes after, because its discounted value at that point will be insignificant. However, this approach suffers from the difficulty of explicitly forecasting decades of performance. Alternatively, the problem can be

Exhibit 8.5 Hershey Foods—WACC Summary

Percent

Source of capital	Proportion of total capital	Opportunity cost	Tax rate	After-tax cost	Contribution to weighted average
Debt	12.1	5.5	39.0	3.4	0.4
Equity	87.9	8.1		8.1	7.1
WACC					**7.5**

solved by separating the value of the business into two periods, during and after an explicit forecast period. In this case,

$$\text{Value} = \frac{\text{Present value of cash flow}}{\text{\textit{during} explicit forecast period}} + \frac{\text{Present value of cash flow}}{\text{\textit{after} explicit forecast period}}$$

The value after the explicit forecast period is referred to as the continuing value. Formulas derived from discounted cash flows using several simplifying assumptions can be used to estimate continuing value. One such formula that we recommend is as follows (Chapter 12 contains a more detailed look at continuing value approaches):

$$\text{Continuing value} = \frac{\text{NOPLAT}\,(1 - g/\text{ROIC}_\text{I})}{\text{WACC} - g}$$

Where NOPLAT = Net operating profits less adjusted taxes (in the year after the explicit forecast period)

ROIC_I = Incremental return on new invested capital

g = Expected perpetual growth in the company's NOPLAT

WACC = Weighted average cost of capital

Exhibit 8.6 shows the continuing value calculation for Hershey.

Value of Debt

The value of the company's debt equals the present value of the cash flow to debt holders discounted at a rate that reflects the riskiness of that flow. The discount rate should equal the current market rate on similar-risk debt with comparable terms. In most cases, only the company's debt outstanding on the valuation date must be valued. Future borrowing can be assumed to have zero net present value because the cash inflows from these borrowings will exactly equal the present value of the future repayments discounted at the opportunity cost of the debt.

Exhibit 8.6   Hershey Foods—Continuing Value

NOPLAT $_{2009}$	634
Return on incremental invested capital (ROIC$_\text{I}$)	21.3%
NOPLAT growth rate in perpetuity (g)	4.0%
Weighted average cost of capital (WACC)	7.5%

$$\text{Continuing value} = \frac{\text{NOPLAT}_{t+1}\,(1 - g/\text{ROIC}_\text{I})}{\text{WACC} - g}$$

$$= 14{,}710$$

Value of Equity

The value of the company's equity is the value of its operations plus non-operating assets, such as investments in unrelated, unconsolidated businesses, less the value of its debt and any nonoperating liabilities. The valuation of Hershey's equity (as illustrated in Exhibit 8.3) is $9.4 billion, including $450 million representing the value of its pasta business, which was sold in early 1999.

WHAT DRIVES CASH FLOW AND VALUE

You could stop right here and say that once you have projected free cash flow and discounted it at the WACC, the valuation is complete. This would not be satisfying, however, because you have not evaluated the free cash flow projection upon which the valuation was based. How does the projection compare to past performance? How does the projection compare with other companies? What are the economics of the business? Are they expressed in a way that managers and others can understand? What are the important factors that could increase or decrease the value of the company? You need to step back and understand the underlying economic value drivers of the business.

Since value is based on discounted free cash flow, the underlying value drivers of the business must also be the drivers of free cash flow. As we explained in Chapters 3 and 4, there are two key drivers of free cash flow and ultimately value: the rate at which the company is growing its revenues, profits, and capital base, and the return on invested capital (relative to the cost of capital). These value drivers make common sense. A company that earns higher profit for every dollar invested in the business will be worth more than a similar company that earns less profit for every dollar of invested capital. Similarly, a faster growing company will be worth more than a slower growing company if they are both earning the same return on invested capital (and this return is high enough to satisfy the investors).

A simple model will demonstrate how growth and return on invested capital actually drive free cash flow. First, some definitions are needed. Return on invested capital (ROIC) equals the operating profits of the company divided by the amount of capital invested in the company.

$$ROIC = \frac{NOPLAT}{Invested\ capital}$$

Where, NOPLAT = Net operating profits less adjusted taxes
Invested capital = Operating working capital + Net property, plant, and equipment + Other assets

Earlier in this chapter (see Exhibit 8.4), we defined free cash flow as equal to gross cash flow (NOPLAT plus depreciation) minus gross investment (increases in working capital plus capital expenditures). To simplify the following examples, we will show free cash flow as NOPLAT less net investment, having subtracted depreciation from both gross cash flow and gross investment. In year 1, Company A's NOPLAT equals $100 and net investment equals $25, so free cash flow must equal $75.

Company A	Year 1
NOPLAT	$100.0
Net investment	25.0
Free cash flow	$ 75.0

Company A invested $25 over and above depreciation to earn additional profits in future years. Assume Company A earns a 20 percent return on its new investment in year 2 and every subsequent year. Year 2's NOPLAT would equal year 1's NOPLAT ($100) plus 20 percent of year 1's investment or $5 ($25 × 20%) for a total of $105. (We have also assumed that the operating profit on the base level of capital in place at the beginning of year 1 does not change.) Suppose the company reinvests the same percentage of its operating profits each year and earns the same return on new capital. Company A's free cash flow would look as follows:

	Year				
Company A	1	2	3	4	5
NOPLAT	$100.0	$105.0	$110.3	$115.8	$121.6
Net investment	25.0	26.2	27.6	39.0	30.4
Free cash flow	$ 75.0	$ 78.8	$ 82.7	$ 86.8	$ 91.2

Each year the company's operating profits and free cash flow grow at 5 percent and each year the company reinvests 25 percent of its cash flows in order to achieve future growth at a return of 20 percent. We can say that in this simple world, a company's growth rate is the product of its return on new capital and its investment rate (net investment divided by operating profits):

$$\text{Growth rate} = \text{Return on new invested capital} \times \text{Investment rate}$$

For Company A,

$$\text{Growth rate} = 20\% \times 25\% = 5\%$$

Now suppose that Company B wants to generate the same profit growth as company A. It, too, earns $100 in year 1. However, company B earns only a 10 percent return on its capital. For company B to increase its profits in year 2 by $5, it must invest $50 in year 1. Company B's free cash flow would look as follows:

Company B	Year				
	1	2	3	4	5
NOPLAT	$100.0	$105.0	$110.3	$115.8	$121.6
Net investment	50.0	52.5	55.2	57.9	63.8
Free cash flow	$ 50.0	$ 52.5	$ 55.1	$ 57.9	$ 63.8

A greater return on invested capital results in more free cash flow given the same desired growth rate in operating profits. As would be expected, Company A is worth more than Company B despite identical operating profits and growth rates.

Now let's look at how growth drives cash flow and value. Suppose Company A wants to increase its growth rate (and it can invest more capital at the same return). If A wants to grow at 8 percent instead of 5 percent, it must now invest 40 percent of its operating profits each year, as shown next. (We can use the formula developed above to calculate the required investment rate.)

Company A	Year				
	1	2	3	4	5
NOPLAT	$100.0	$108.0	$116.6	$126.0	$136.0
Net investment	40.0	43.2	46.6	50.4	54.4
Free cash flow	$ 60.0	$ 64.8	$ 70.0	$ 75.6	$ 81.6

Note that Company A's free cash flow is lower each year than it had been. At this new higher growth rate, Company A's free cash flow is lower than the first scenario until year 9, but from then on the free cash flow becomes much larger (as shown on Exhibit 8.7). Which scenario results in a higher value? It turns out that as long as the return on new invested capital is greater than the WACC used to discount the cash flow, higher growth will generate greater value. In these two scenarios, if we assume that the growth and return patterns continue forever and that Company A's WACC is 12 percent, then the present value of the 5 percent growth scenario is $1,071 and the present value of the 8 percent growth scenario is $1,500. This means that it is worthwhile for the investors to accept lower free cash flow in the earlier years.

Exhibit 8.7   Proving a Point on Company A

5% Growth rate ($ millions)												
	Year 1	2	3	4	5	6	7	8	9	10	11	12
NOPLAT	100	105	110	116	122	128	134	141	148	155	163	171
Net investment	25	26	27	29	31	32	33	35	37	39	41	43
Free cash flow	75	79	83	87	91	96	101	106	111	116	122	128

8% Growth rate ($ millions)												
	Year 1	2	3	4	5	6	7	8	9	10	11	12
NOPLAT	100	108	117	126	136	147	159	171	185	200	216	233
Net investment	40	43	47	50	54	59	64	68	74	80	86	93
Free cash flow	60	65	70	76	82	88	95	103	111	120	130	140

Exhibit 8.8 shows a matrix of values for a hypothetical company over a range of projected growth rates and returns on invested capital. A given value can result from different combinations of growth and return. Assuming companies cannot always have more of both, a table like this helps managers set targets for long-term performance improvement. This table also demonstrates what happens when the return on new invested capital does not exceed the cost of capital. If the return exactly equals the WACC, then additional growth neither creates nor destroys value. This makes sense as investors will not pay more for additional growth if they can earn the same returns elsewhere. If the return on new invested capital is less than WACC then additional growth actually destroys value. Investors would be better off investing their capital elsewhere.

These examples are quite simplistic. Companies do not grow at constant rates, they do not invest the same proportion of their profits, and they do not earn the same return on capital every year. However, the core idea that

Exhibit 8.8   How ROIC and Growth Drive Value[1]

DCF value	Operating profit (annual growth)	ROIC				
		7.5%	10.0%	12.5%	15.0%	20.0%
	3%	$887	$1,000	$1,058	$1,113	$1,170
	6%	708	1,000	1,117	1,295	1,442
	9%	410	1,000	1,354	1,591	1,886

◄ Value   Value   Value ►
destruction   neutral   creation

1 Assumes starting NOPLAT = 100, WACC = 10%, and a 25-year horizon after which ROIC = WACC.

Exhibit 8.9   Hershey Foods—Return on Invested Capital Calculation

$ million	1997	1998	Forecast 1999	Forecast 2000	Forecast 2001
NOPLAT					
Revenues	4,302	4,063	4,245	4,436	4,636
Operating expenses	(3,656)	(3,452)	(3,598)	(3,765)	(3,936)
Earnings before interest, taxes, and amortization (EBITA)	646	610	648	671	700
Cash taxes on EBITA	(204)	(177)	(227)	(236)	(246)
NOPLAT	**442**	**434**	**420**	**436**	**454**
Invested Capital					
Operating current assets	1,035	1,020	1,074	1,122	1,173
Noninterest-bearing current liabilities	(508)	(412)	(501)	(523)	(547)
Operating working capital	527	608	573	599	626
Net property, plant, and equipment	1,648	1,477	1,613	1,686	1,762
Other assets net of other liabilities	(290)	(255)	(267)	(279)	(292)
Operating invested capital	**1,885**	**1,830**	**1,919**	**2,005**	**2,096**
ROIC					
Return on invested capital (beginning of year)	24.3%	23.0%	23.0%	22.7%	22.6%
WACC	8.3%	7.5%	7.5%	7.5%	7.5%
Spread	16.0%	15.5%	15.5%	15.2%	15.1%

the key drivers of value are return on invested capital (relative to WACC) and growth is generally applicable for all companies. Exhibit 8.9 shows the calculation of Hershey's return on invested capital. Exhibit 8.10 shows Hershey's historical and projected performance in terms of growth and return on invested capital. These results are summarized below:

Hershey Foods Corporation	1989–93 (percent)	1994–98 (percent)	Forecast 1999–2008 (percent)
Average spread			
ROIC	19.0	21.5	22.7
WACC	9.7	8.7	7.5
Spread	9.3	12.8	15.2
Average annual growth			
Revenues	9.4	3.1	4.5
NOPLAT	7.3	12.3	2.7
Invested capital	9.9	2.3	4.6

Exhibit 8.10   Hershey Foods—ROIC and Growth Trends

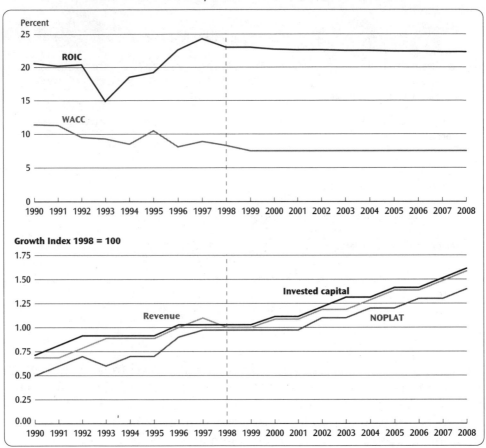

Hershey has consistently earned a return on invested capital of about 20 percent, even while interest rates and its WACC have declined. Thus, Hershey's spread has increased to an average of 12.8 percent over the five years from 1994 to 1998. Returns on invested capital in this scenario are projected to remain essentially constant. Revenue growth is projected to be somewhat higher than in recent years and NOPLAT is projected to grow in line with revenues (in other words, margins are expected to remain constant). Managers can use information like this to assess the projection and to set long-term performance targets.

In summary, return on invested capital (relative to WACC) and growth are the fundamental drivers of a company's value. To increase its value, a company must do one or more of the following:

- Increase the level of profits it earns on its existing capital in place (earn a higher return on invested capital on legacy assets).
- Ensure that the return on new capital investment exceeds WACC.
- Increase its growth rate, but only as long as the return on new capital exceeds WACC.
- Reduce its cost of capital.

THE ECONOMIC PROFIT MODEL

The second valuation framework that we will use throughout this book is the economic profit (EP) model. In this model, the value of a company equals the amount of capital invested, plus a premium equal to the present value of the value created each year. The concept of economic profit dates to at least 1890, when the economist Alfred Marshall wrote: "What remains of his [the owner or manager's] profits after deducting interest on his capital at the current rate may be called his earnings of undertaking or management."[1]

Marshall said that the value created by a company during any time period (its economic profit) must take into account not only the expenses recorded in its accounting records but also the opportunity cost of the capital employed in the business.

An advantage of the economic profit model over the DCF model is that economic profit is a useful measure for understanding a company's performance in any single year, while free cash flow is not. For example, you would not track a company's progress by comparing actual and projected free cash flow because free cash flow in any year is determined by discretionary investments in fixed assets and working capital. Management could easily improve free cash flow in a given year at the expense of long-term value creation by simply delaying investments.

Economic profit measures the value created in a company in a single period and is defined as follows:

$$\text{Economic profit} = \text{Invested capital} \times (\text{ROIC} - \text{WACC})$$

In other words, economic profit equals the spread between the return on invested capital and the cost of capital times the amount of invested capital. Company C has invested capital of $1,000, return on invested capital of 10 percent, and WACC of 8 percent. Its economic profit for the year is $20:

$$
\begin{aligned}
\text{Economic profit} &= \$1{,}000 \times (10\% - 8\%) \\
&= \$1{,}000 \times 2\% \\
&= \$20
\end{aligned}
$$

[1] Alfred Marshall, *Principles of Economics*, vol. 1 (New York: MacMillan, 1890), p. 142.

Economic profit translates the two value drivers discussed earlier, return on invested capital and growth, into a single dollar figure (growth is ultimately related to the amount of invested capital or the size of the company). Another way to define economic profit is as after-tax operating profits less a charge for the capital used by the company.

$$\text{Economic profit} = \text{NOPLAT} - \text{Capital charge}$$
$$= \text{NOPLAT} - (\text{Invested capital} \times \text{WACC})$$

This alternative calculation generates the same value for economic profit:

$$\text{Economic profit} = \$100 - (\$1{,}000 \times 8\%)$$
$$= \$100 - \$80$$
$$= \$20$$

This approach shows that economic profit is similar in concept to accounting net income, but it explicitly charges a company for all its capital, not just the interest on its debt.

A simple example will illustrate how economic profit can be used for valuations. Assume that Company C from above invested $1,000 in working capital and fixed assets at the beginning of period 1. Each year after that it earns $100 of NOPLAT (a 10 percent ROIC). Its net investment is zero, so its free cash flow is also $100. Company C's economic profit is $20 a year as calculated above.

The economic profit approach says that the value of a company equals the amount of capital invested plus a premium or discount equal to the present value of its projected economic profit:

$$\text{Value} = \text{Invested capital} + \text{Present value of projected economic profit}$$

The logic behind this is straightforward. If a company earned exactly its WACC every period, then the discounted value of its projected free cash flow should exactly equal its invested capital. The company is worth exactly what was originally invested. A company is worth more or less than its invested capital only to the extent that it earns more or less than its WACC. Therefore, the premium or discount relative to invested capital must equal the present value of the company's future economic profit.

Company C earns $20 a year more than investors demand (its economic profit). So the value of company C should equal $1,000 (its invested capital at the time of the valuation) plus the present value of its economic profit. In this case since economic profit remains forever at $20 a year, we can use a perpetuity formula to calculate the present value of its economic profit.

$$\text{Present value of economic profit} = \frac{\$20}{8\%}$$
$$= \$250$$

Company C's value is $1,250. If you were to discount company C's free cash flow you would also end up with a value for company C of $1,250. Company C's projected free cash flow is $100 a year.

$$\text{Present value of FCF} = \frac{\$100}{8\%}$$
$$= \$1,250$$

Exhibits 8.11 and 8.12 show the economic profit and economic profit valuation of Hershey Foods. In 1998, Hershey generated economic profit of $293 million. In other words, Hershey made $293 million of operating profit more than required by investors based on the returns available from alternative investments. Note that the economic profit value of Hershey exactly equals the discounted free cash flow value that we calculated earlier in this chapter. Furthermore, as would be expected, the value of operations, $10.2 billion, exceeds the amount of invested capital (at the end of 1998) of $1.8 billion. In present value terms, Hershey has created $8.4 billion of value ($10.2 billion less $1.8 billion).

Exhibit 8.11   Hershey Foods—Economic Profit Calculation

$ million	1997	1998	Forecast 1999	Forecast 2000	Forecast 2001
Return on invested capital	24.3%	23.0%	23.0%	22.7%	22.6%
WACC	8.3%	7.5%	7.5%	7.5%	7.5%
Spread	16.0%	15.5%	15.5%	15.2%	15.1%
Invested capital (beginning of year)	1,815	1,885	1,830	1,919	2,005
Economic profit	**291**	**293**	**283**	**292**	**304**
NOPLAT	442	434	420	436	454
Capital charge	(151)	(141)	(137)	(144)	(150)
Economic profit	**291**	**293**	**283**	**292**	**304**

Exhibit 8.12 Hershey Foods—Economic Profit Valuation Summary

Year	Economic profit ($ million)	Discount factor (7.5%)	Present value of economic profit ($ million[1])
1999	283	0.930	263
2000	292	0.865	252
2001	304	0.805	245
2002	316	0.749	237
2003	329	0.697	229
2004	343	0.648	222
2005	357	0.603	215
2006	372	0.561	209
2007	387	0.522	202
2008	403	0.485	196
Continuing value	11,858	0.485	5,754
Present value of economic profit			8,024
Invested capital (beginning of year)			1,830
			9,854
Mid-year adjustment factor			1.037
Value of operations			10,217
Value of non-operating investments			450
Total enterprise value			10,667
Less : Value of debt			1,282
Equity value			**9,385**

1 Except per share.

THE ADJUSTED PRESENT VALUE (APV) MODEL

The adjusted present value (APV) model is similar to the enterprise DCF model. As with enterprise DCF, the APV model discounts free cash flows to estimate the value of operations, and ultimately the enterprise value, once non-operating assets are added. From this enterprise value, the value of debt is deducted to arrive at an equity value. The difference is that the APV model separates the value of operations into two components: the value of operations as if the company were entirely equity-financed and the value of the tax benefit arising from debt financing.[2]

This valuation model reflects the conclusions from the Modigliani-Miller propositions on capital structure developed in the late 1950s and early 1960s. The MM propositions showed that in a world with no taxes, the enterprise value of a company (the sum of its debt plus equity) is independent of capital structure (or the amount of debt relative to equity). The intuitive logic here is that the value of a company should not be affected by how

[2] For more information on the Miller-Modigliani propositions and the APV approach, see Thomas E. Copeland and J. Fred Weston, *Financial Theory and Corporate Policy*, 3rd ed. (Reading, MA: Addison-Wesley, 1988), pp. 439–451, and Richard A. Brealey and Stewart C. Myers, *Principles of Corporate Finance*, 5th ed. (New York: McGraw-Hill, 1996), pp. 525–541.

you slice it up (between debt and equity or any other claims). Professor Clifford Smith of the University of Rochester illustrates this with the story of the former American baseball player Yogi Berra at a pizza parlor. Berra is asked whether he would like his pizza cut into six or eight pieces. Berra replies: "Six please, I am not hungry enough to eat eight." Of course, the pizza is the same size no matter how many pieces you cut it into.

The implication of MM for valuation in a world without taxes is that the weighted average cost of capital must be constant regardless of the company's capital structure. This must be so if the total value is constant and the free cash flows are by definition independent of the capital structure. The result is that capital structure can only affect value through taxes and other market imperfections and distortions.

The APV model uses these concepts to highlight the impact of taxes on valuation. The APV model first values a company at the cost of capital if the company had no debt in its capital structure (referred to as the unlevered cost of equity). It then adds the impact of taxes from leverage to this value. In most countries, interest payments made by a company are deductible for tax purposes. Therefore, the overall taxes paid by a company and its investors are lower if the company employs debt in its capital structure.

In the enterprise DCF model, this tax benefit is taken into consideration in the calculation of the weighted average cost of capital by adjusting the cost of debt by its tax benefit. In the APV model, the tax benefit from the company's interest payments is estimated by discounting the projected tax savings. If done correctly and with identical assumptions about capital structure, both models will result in the same value.

Key to reconciling the two approaches is the calculation of the weighted average cost of capital. The following equation is one approach to relating WACC to the unlevered cost of equity assuming that the tax benefit of debt is discounted at the unlevered cost of equity. (See Appendix A for alternative approaches.)

$$\text{WACC} = k_u - k_b \left(\frac{B}{B+S} \right) T$$

Where k_u = Unlevered cost of equity
k_b = Cost of debt
T = Marginal tax rate on interest expense
B = Market value of debt
S = Market value of equity

Let's illustrate the APV model with the Hershey case. Estimate Hershey's k_u from its WACC. Turning around the above equation, k_u can be expressed in terms of WACC:

$$k_u = \text{WACC} + k_b\left(\frac{B}{B+S}\right)T$$
$$= 7.5\% + (5.5\% \times 13.8\% \times 39.0\%) = 7.8\%$$

Discounting Hershey's projected free cash flow at k_u results in an un-levered value of operations of $9,390 million, as shown in Exhibit 8.13. The value of Hershey's debt tax shields is $642 million, as shown in Exhibit 8.14. The result gives an equity value for Hershey of $9,200 million, as follows:

	(in millions)
Value of operating free cash flow	$ 9,390
Value of debt tax shield	642
Non-operating assets	450
Total enterprise value	$10,482
Less: Value of debt	1,282
Equity value	$ 9,200

You may have noted that the enterprise DCF value of operations does not exactly match that given by the APV approach. The difference is about 2 percent. The enterprise DCF model assumes that the capital structure (the ratio of debt to debt plus equity in market values) and WACC would be constant every period. Actually, the capital structure changes every year. If we go back to the enterprise DCF model and estimate a separate capital structure

Exhibit 8.13   Hershey Foods—APV Free Cash Flow Valuation Summary

Year	Free cash flow ($ million)	Unlevered cost of equity ($ million)	Discount factor	Present value of cash flow at k_u ($ million)
1999	331	7.80%	0.928	307
2000	349	7.80%	0.860	301
2001	364	7.80%	0.798	290
2002	379	7.80% .	0.740	281
2003	395	7.80%	0.687	271
2004	412	7.80%	0.637	262
2005	429	7.80%	0.591	253
2006	447	7.80%	0.548	245
2007	466	7.80%	0.508	237
2008	485	7.80%	0.472	229
Continuing value	13,526	7.80%	0.472	6,380
				9,056
Mid-year adjustment				1.037
APV value of FCF				9,390

Exhibit 8.14   Hershey Foods—Interest Tax Shield Valuation Summary

Year	Interest tax shields ($ million)	Discount factor at 7.80% k_u	Present value of tax shields at k_u ($ million)
1999	27.5	0.928	26
2000	26.6	0.860	23
2001	22.9	0.798	18
2002	29.8	0.740	22
2003	25.8	0.687	18
2004	33.4	0.637	21
2005	29.2	0.591	17
2006	36.5	0.548	20
2007	31.9	0.508	16
2008	38.9	0.472	18
Continuing value	890.0	0.472	420
			619
Mid-year adjustment			1.037
APV value of tax shields			642

**Exhibit 8.15   Hershey Foods—Enterprise DCF
Adjusted for Changing Capital Structure**

Year	Free cash flow ($ million)	Debt/total value (percent)	WACC (percent)	Discount factor	Present value of cash flow at WACC ($ million)
1999	331	13.3	7.52	0.930	308
2000	349	12.3	7.54	0.865	302
2001	364	10.2	7.59	0.804	293
2002	379	12.7	7.53	0.748	283
2003	395	10.6	7.58	0.695	274
2004	412	13.2	7.52	0.646	266
2005	429	11.1	7.57	0.601	258
2006	447	13.3	7.52	0.559	250
2007	466	11.2	7.56	0.520	242
2008	485	13.1	7.52	0.483	234
Continuing value	14,416	13.1	7.52	0.483	6,965
					9,675
Mid-year adjustment					1.037
Value of operations					10,032
Value of non-operating investments					450
Enterprise value					10,482
Debt					1,282
WACC equity value					9,200

Exhibit 8.16   Hershey Foods—Equity DCF Valuation Summary

Year	Equity cash flow ($ million)	Discount factor at 8.1% k_s	Present value of cash flow at k_s ($ million)
1999	245	0.925	227
2000	137	0.856	118
2001	644	0.792	512
2002	149	0.733	109
2003	708	0.678	481
2004	162	0.628	102
2005	723	0.581	420
2006	176	0.537	95
2007	738	0.497	367
2008	193	0.460	89
Continuing value	12,895	0.460	5,934
Discounted equity cash flow			8,454
Mid-year discount adjustment			357
Value of non-operating investments			450
Equity value			9,261

and WACC for each period, we get an equity value of $9,200 million, identical to that given by the APV model (Exhibit 8.15).[3]

The APV model is easier to use than the enterprise DCF model when the capital structure is changing significantly over the projection period. For this reason it is particularly helpful for leveraged buyouts and distressed company valuations. It is also useful when a company has significant tax loss carry-forwards that are difficult to factor into the WACC.

THE EQUITY DCF MODEL

The equity DCF model is the simplest model in theory, but is actually difficult to carry out in practice. The equity DCF model discounts the cash flows to the equity owners of the company at the cost of equity. Exhibit 8.16 shows the equity DCF valuation for Hershey using the 8.1 percent cost of equity as the discount rate that we derived earlier in this chapter. The value is $9,261 million, or less than 1 percent off of the APV model value. This is because, once again, we have not adjusted for the changing capital structure. To

---

[3] To be technically correct when using the enterprise DCF model, you should assume that the unlevered cost of equity is constant and the levered cost of equity and WACC change each year to reflect the capital structure for that year. You can do this by working back from the future and iterating a solution. Starting with the last year, you solve iteratively for a capital structure and WACC, which results in values for debt and equity consistent with the capital structure. Next, work back one year at a time until you get to your starting point.

adjust for the changing capital structure, we need to recalculate the cost of equity every period. Use the following formula or one of the approaches discussed in Appendix A.

$$k_s = k_u + (k_u - k_b)\frac{B}{S}$$

Where k_s = levered cost of equity

Once we adjusted the cost of equity, the value using the equity DCF approach is $9,200 million (Exhibit 8.17), the same as the APV approach and the enterprise DCF model with WACC adjusted every period.

While the equity DCF model is intuitively the most straightforward valuation technique, it is not as useful as the enterprise model, except for financial institutions (as described in Chapters 21 and 22). Discounting equity cash flow provides less information about the sources of value creation and is not as useful for identifying value-creation opportunities. Furthermore, it requires careful adjustments to ensure that changes in projected financing do not incorrectly affect the company's value.

A common error in discounted equity valuations is an inconsistency between the company's dividend policy and the discount rate used. Suppose you construct a valuation that results in a value of, say, $15 a share. Next, you

---

Exhibit 8.17   Hershey Foods—Adjusted Equity DCF Valuation Summary

Year	Equity[1] cash flow ($ million)	Debt/total value (percent)	Levered k_s (percent)	Discount factor	Present value of cash flow at k_s ($ million)
1999	245	13.3	8.16	0.925	227
2000	137	12.3	8.13	0.855	117
2001	646	10.2	8.07	0.791	511
2002	149	12.7	8.14	0.732	109
2003	709	10.6	8.08	0.677	480
2004	162	13.2	8.16	0.626	101
2005	723	11.1	8.09	0.579	418
2006	177	13.3	8.16	0.535	95
2007	738	11.2	8.09	0.495	366
2008	193	13.1	8.15	0.458	88
Continuing value[2]	12,838	13.1	8.15	0.458	5,880

Discounted equity cash flows	8,393
Mid-year discounting adjustment[3]	357
Value of non-operating investments	450
Equity value	**9,200**

1 Dividends plus share repurchases; excludes proceeds from sale of business in 1999 ($450), which are added separately below.
2 Assumes 2009 net income 580.9 (before goodwill); 4% growth and incremental ROE of 41.44% (ROIC of 21.27% from WACC approach adjusted for leverage).
3 From WACC approach.

increase the dividend payout ratio while holding the projected operating performance constant (in other words, no changes in revenues or margins). Presto! The equity value has just increased because of the higher dividend payments despite the constant operating performance. The error here is that the discount rate was not changed. Increasing the dividend payout ratio requires more use of debt. More debt means riskier equity and a higher discount rate for the equity.

Another shortcoming of the direct equity approach appears when valuing business units. The direct equity approach requires allocating debt and interest expense to each unit. This creates extra work without any extra information being provided.

OPTION VALUATION MODELS

Option-pricing models are variations on standard discounted cash flow models that adjust for management's ability to modify decisions as more information becomes available. Option models hold particular promise for valuing strategic and operating flexibility such as opening and closing plants, abandoning operations, or natural resource exploration and development. Chapter 20 discusses how option valuation approaches can be used.

OTHER APPROACHES

You may also come across three other DCF variations:

1. Using real instead of nominal cash flows and discount rates.
2. Discounting pretax cash flows instead of after-tax cash flows.
3. Using formula-based approaches instead of explicitly forecasting cash flows.

We would not typically recommend these approaches except in limited circumstances.

Using Real Instead of Nominal Cash Flows and Discount Rates

Companies can be valued by projecting cash flow in real terms (for example, in constant 1999 dollars) and discounting this cash flow at a real discount rate (for example, the nominal rate less expected inflation). Most managers think in terms of nominal rather than real measures, so nominal measures are often easier to communicate. Interest rates are generally quoted nominally rather than in real terms (excluding expected inflation). Moreover, since historical financial statements are stated in nominal terms, projecting future statements in real terms is difficult and confusing.

An important difficulty occurs when calculating rates of return on invested capital. The historical statements are nominal, so historical returns on invested capital are nominal. But if the projections for the company are real rather than nominal, returns on new capital are also real. Projected returns on total capital (new and old) are a combination of nominal and real, which are impossible to interpret. The only way around this is to restate historical performance on a real basis, a complex and time-consuming task. We have generally found that the extra insights from this effort are insignificant for most companies, except in high inflation environments as described in Chapter 19.

Discounting Pretax Cash Flow Instead of After-Tax Cash Flow

The enterprise model we recommend uses after-tax cash flow and an after-tax discount rate. It is conceptually valid to use pretax cash flow and a pretax discount rate, as the following example illustrates:

$$Value = \frac{After\text{-}tax\ cash\ flow}{After\text{-}tax\ discount\ rate}$$

$$After\text{-}tax\ cash\ flow = Pretax\ cash\ flow \times (1 - tax\ rate)$$

$$After\text{-}tax\ discount\ rate = Pretax\ discount\ rate \times (1 - tax\ rate)$$

Substituting into the initial equation gives:

$$Value = \frac{Pretax\ cash\ flow \times (1 - tax\ rate)}{Pretax\ discount\ rate \times (1 - tax\ rate)}$$

$$= \frac{Pretax\ cash\ flow}{Pretax\ discount\ rate}$$

Real-world after-tax cash flow is not simply pretax cash flow adjusted by the tax rate. Taxes are based on accrual accounting (for example, the tax benefit of purchasing a machine is received in a different period from when the machine is paid for), not cash flow. Therefore, after-tax free cash flow is not equal to pretax free cash flow times a tax rate. You cannot simply gross up the discount rate to a pretax rate and discount the pretax cash flow and get the same result as the recommended approach. It is virtually impossible to perform a real-world discounted cash flow analysis using the pretax approach.

Formula-Based DCF Approaches

Formula-based DCF approaches make simplifying assumptions about a business and its cash flow stream (for example, constant revenue growth and margins) so that the entire discounted cash flow can be captured in a concise formula. These formulas are most often too simple for real problem solving, though they may serve as valuable communication tools.

The Miller-Modigliani (MM) formula is useful for communicating the sources of a company's value. The MM formula (1963) values a company as the sum of the value of the cash flow of its assets currently in place plus the value of its growth opportunities.[4] The formula is based on sound economic analysis, so it can be used to illustrate the factors that will affect the value of the company. Its simplifying assumptions (at least in the version given below) render it too inaccurate for precise valuations.

The MM formula is defined as follows:

$$\text{Value of enterprise} = \text{Value of assets in place} + \text{Value of growth}$$

$$= \frac{\text{NOPLAT}}{\text{WACC}} + \text{K(NOPLAT)N} \frac{\text{ROIC} - \text{WACC}}{\text{WACC}(1 + \text{WACC})}$$

Where NOPLAT = Expected level of net operating profits less adjusted taxes in the first projected period

WACC = Weighted average cost of capital

ROIC = Expected rate of return on invested capital

K = Investment rate, the percentage of NOPLAT invested for growth in new projects

N = Expected number of years that the company will continue to invest in new projects and earn the projected ROIC, also called the interval of competitive advantage

SUMMARY

This chapter described the most common DCF valuation models, with particular focus on the enterprise DCF model and the economic profit model. We explained the rationale for each model and discussed the economic drivers of a company's value. The remaining chapters in Part Two describe a step-by-step approach to valuing a company:

- Chapter 9—Analyzing Historical Performance.
- Chapter 10—Estimating the Cost of Capital.

[4] M. Miller and F. Modigliani, "Dividend Policy, Growth, and the Valuation of Shares," *Journal of Business* (September 1961), pp. 411–433.

- Chapter 11—Forecasting Performance.
- Chapter 12—Estimating Continuing Value.
- Chapter 13—Calculating and Interpreting Results.

These chapters explain both the technical details, such as calculating free cash flow from complex accounting statements, and interpreting the valuation through careful financial analysis.

9

Analyzing Historical Performance

This chapter begins the step-by-step valuation process. While we present this process sequentially, valuation is typically more of an iterative process. As you learn more, you develop new questions and insights that require re-visiting earlier work.

The first step in valuing a business is analyzing its historical performance. A sound understanding of the company's past performance provides an essential perspective for developing and evaluating forecasts of future performance. (This assumes that the company has a history, which is not always the case. See the discussion on valuing Internet stocks in Chapter 15, when you don't have historical information.)

Historical performance analysis should focus on the key value drivers discussed in Chapter 8: namely, return on invested capital and growth. The rate of return on invested capital (ROIC) is the single most important value driver. A company creates value for its shareholders only when it earns rates of return on new invested capital that exceed its cost of capital. Return on invested capital and the proportion of its profits that the company invests for growth drive free cash flow, which in turn drives value.

Historical analysis, done well, is an integrated process. ROIC and growth are broken down into their component drivers (for example, ROIC is driven by capital turnover and operating profit margins). Financial ratios that do not contribute to understanding ROIC and growth or that largely duplicate other ratios need not be used. For example, the return on total assets (ROA) is not used because everything that can be learned from ROA is incorporated into the ROIC analysis.

In addition to analyzing the value drivers, you should analyze the company from a credit or liquidity perspective. Is the company generating or consuming cash? How much debt does the company employ relative to equity? What margin of safety does the company have with respect to its debt financing? The organization of this chapter follows:

- Reorganizing the accounting statements to gain greater analytical insights and to calculate ROIC and economic profit.
- Calculating free cash flow.
- Breaking down ROIC and developing an integrated perspective.
- Analyzing credit health and liquidity.
- Dealing with more advanced issues in analyzing financial performance.

At the end of the chapter, we begin a detailed case study and valuation of Heineken, the Dutch brewer, where we apply the principles described in the chapter. The Heineken case is extended at the end of each of the next four chapters.

REORGANIZING THE ACCOUNTING STATEMENTS

To analyze a company, we begin by reorganizing its accounting statements to estimate ROIC, free cash flow, and economic profit. We do this reorganization

Exhibit 9.1 Hershey Foods—Historical Income Statement

$ million	1995	1996	1997	1998
Revenues	3,691	3,989	4,302	4,063
Cost of goods sold	(1,992)	(2,168)	(2,336)	(2,142)
Selling, general, and administrative expenses	(1,054)	(1,124)	(1,183)	(1,168)
Depreciation expense	(119)	(118)	(137)	(142)
Amortization of goodwill	(15)	(16)	(16)	(16)
Interest expense, net	(45)	(48)	(76)	(86)
Total costs and expenses	(3,225)	(3,474)	(3,748)	(3,554)
Income before non-operating items	466	515	554	509
Non-operating income	0	35	0	48
Income before taxes	466	480	554	557
Provision for income taxes	(184)	(207)	(218)	(216)
Net income	282	273	336	341
Reconciliation of equity				
Shareholders equity, beginning of year	1,441	1,083	1,161	853
Net income	282	273	336	341
Dividends	(110)	(115)	(122)	(129)
Share repurchases, net	(525)	(77)	(514)	0
Translation adjustment	(5)	(3)	(8)	(23)
Shareholders equity, end of year	1,083	1,161	853	1,042

so that ROIC and economic profit reflect more of an economic than accounting view of the company. For example, we need to distinguish operating from non-operating assets. We need to determine how various reserves and provisions affect operating capital and operating profits.

The result of this reorganization is the estimation of NOPLAT (net operating profit less adjusted taxes) and operating invested capital, reflecting as much as possible the true economics of the business.

Throughout this chapter, the Hershey Foods Corporation will be used to demonstrate the calculation of the value drivers from Hershey's income statement (Exhibit 9.1) and balance sheet (Exhibit 9.2).

Invested Capital

We reorganize the balance sheet to see how much capital is invested in the company by the shareholders and creditors and how much of the capital has been invested in operating activities and other non-operating activities. Exhibit 9.3 shows the reorganized balance sheet for Hershey.

Exhibit 9.2   Hershey Foods—Historical Balance Sheet

Assets ($ million)	1995	1996	1997	1998
Operating cash	32	61	54	39
Accounts receivable	326	295	361	394
Inventories	398	475	506	436
Other current assets	166	155	114	150
Total current assets	922	986	1,035	1,020
Gross property, plant, and equipment	2,190	2,423	2,587	2,528
Accumulated depreciation	(754)	(821)	(939)	(1,051)
Net property, plant, and equipment	1,436	1,602	1,648	1,477
Goodwill	429	566	552	530
Other assets	44	31	56	92
Discontinued operations	0	0	0	285
Total assets	2,831	3,185	3,291	3,404
Liabilities and equity				
Short-term debt and current portion of long-term debt	438	340	288	403
Accounts payable	102	109	116	100
Accrued liabilities	324	368	391	312
Total current liabilities	864	817	796	815
Long-term debt	357	655	1,029	879
Other long-term liabilities	334	327	347	347
Deferred income taxes	192	224	267	321
Total shareholders' equity	1,083	1,161	853	1,042
Total liabilities and equity	2,831	3,185	3,291	3,404

Exhibit 9.3   Hershey Foods—Invested Capital Calculation

$ million	1995	1996	1997	1998
Operating current assets	922	986	1,035	1,020
Non-interest-bearing current liabilities	(426)	(477)	(507)	(412)
Operating working capital	496	509	527	608
Net property, plant, and equipment	1,436	1,602	1,648	1,477
Other operating assets, net of other liabilities	(290)	(297)	(290)	(255)
Operating invested capital (ex goodwill)	1,642	1,815	1,885	1,830
Goodwill	533	686	688	682
Operating capital (including goodwill)	2,175	2,501	2,573	2,512
Excess cash and securities	0	0	0	0
Non-operating investments	0	0	0	285
Total investor funds	**2,175**	**2,501**	**2,573**	**2,797**
Equity	1,083	1,161	853	1,042
Cumulative goodwill amortization	104	120	136	152
Deferred income taxes	192	224	267	321
Adjusted equity	1,380	1,505	1,256	1,515
All interest-bearing debt	795	995	1,317	1,282
Total investor funds	**2,175**	**2,501**	**2,573**	**2,797**

Operating invested capital represents the amount invested in the
operations of the business. It is the sum of operating working capital; net
property, plant, and equipment, and net other assets (net of noncurrent,
non-interest-bearing liabilities). Invested capital, plus any non-operating
investments, measures the total amount invested by the company's investors, which we will call total investor funds. Total investor funds can
also be calculated from the liability side of the balance sheet as the sum
of all equity (plus quasi-equity items like deferred taxes) and interest-
bearing debt.

From the asset side, specific line items include:

Operating current assets. Operating working capital equals operating
current assets minus non-interest-bearing current liabilities. Operating
current assets comprise all current assets used in or necessary for the operations of the business, including some cash balances, trade accounts receivables, and inventories.

Specifically excluded are cash and marketable securities greater than
the operational needs of the business. This excess cash generally represents

temporary imbalances in the company's cash flow. For example, the company may build up cash while deciding how to invest or distribute it. These excess cash or marketable securities balances are not generally directly related to the company's operations, so we treat them as non-operating or as financing (negative debt).

Considering excess cash as non-operating makes valuation easier. Excess cash is usually much less risky than the operations of the company. As excess cash grows or declines in relation to the size of the company, its overall level of risk and cost of capital should rise or fall. Modeling the change in the cost of capital is complex. It is much easier to consider the value of a company as the sum of the value of its operating free cash flow plus the present value of the cash flow related to its excess cash, where the risk of each component is relatively stable.

Excess cash and marketable securities are the short-term cash and investments that the company holds above its *target* cash balances to support operations. The target balances can be estimated by observing the variability in the company's cash and marketable securities balances and comparing these with similar companies. As a rule of thumb, we often consider any cash and marketable securities balances over 0.5 percent to 2.0 percent of revenues to be excess, depending on the industry. By excluding excess cash, we also can get a better sense of how operating working capital has changed relative to revenues and how the company compares to competitors.

Recognize that the investment of excess cash in short-term marketable securities is a zero-net-present-value investment. (It could also be argued that they are slightly negative NPV investments if the double taxation of corporate income is considered.) The return on this investment just compensates for its risk. Therefore, the present value of the cash flow related to these marketable securities must equal the market value of the excess marketable securities on the company's books at the time of the valuation. Excluding excess cash is important because we have seen companies with cash balances as much as $5 billion to $10 billion that are clearly not needed to run the business. Excluding excess cash and securities gives us a cleaner view of the operations of the business.

Non-interest-bearing current liabilities. Non-interest-bearing current liabilities such as accounts payable and accrued expenses are subtracted to calculate net operating working capital. The reason for subtracting these liabilities is to achieve consistency with the definition of NOPLAT. The implicit financing costs associated with these liabilities are included in the expenses that are deducted in calculating NOPLAT. For example, the implicit interest that companies incur when they pay their bills for goods or services in 30 days rather than paying on delivery is included in the cost of goods sold. By subtracting the non-interest-bearing liabilities in calculating capital, we achieve consistency with NOPLAT. Alternatively, we could add back the estimated financing cost associated with non-interest-bearing liabilities and not subtract the liabilities from capital. This approach adds considerable complexity without providing any additional insight into the economics of the business.

Any interest-bearing current liabilities, such as short-term debt and the current maturities of long-term debt, are not subtracted from operating invested capital since the financing cost associated with these liabilities is explicitly excluded from the NOPLAT calculation.

Net property, plant, and equipment. Net property, plant, and equipment is the book value of the company's fixed assets. Whether fixed assets should be revalued at market values or replacement costs will be discussed later.

Other operating assets, net of other liabilities. Any other assets or non-interest-bearing liabilities that are related to the operations of the business are also included in invested capital. In deciding whether an item is operating or non-operating, make sure that the treatment of the asset is consistent with the treatment of any associated income or expense in calculating NOPLAT. Also, consider industry norms so that the calculation of ROIC is as consistent as possible with the company's peers.

Non-operating assets. Any assets not included in operating invested capital should be added when calculating total investor funds, unless they are netted against equity or debt (e.g., deferred debt issuance costs).

From the liability side, the line items to include in total investor funds are:

Equity. Equity should include the sum of all common equity accounts, such as paid-in-capital and retained earnings, preferred shares, and the minority interest in consolidated subsidiaries (which may not be classified as equity in the company's accounts).

Quasi-equity items. Quasi-equity items are accounts that have been recorded as liabilities for accounting purposes, but should be treated as equity for purposes of determining how much capital the shareholders have invested. In Germany, companies can set aside reserves for unspecified future purposes. They typically use these reserves to smooth out earnings. The reserves do not represent liabilities in the sense of amounts that are known and payable at a certain time. We generally treat these as quasi-equity accounts. (See the section of this chapter on advanced issues in analyzing financial performance for more on how to treat reserves.)

Deferred income taxes are the most typical quasi-equity account for U.S. companies. Until the taxes are paid to the government, the funds belong to the shareholders and the shareholders expect to earn a return on these funds.

Hence, treat them like equity. For consistency, income tax expense is also converted to a cash basis in the calculation of NOPLAT.

Adjusted equity. Adjusted equity is the sum of all the equity accounts plus all quasi-equity accounts.

Interest-bearing debt. The other source of funds is interest-bearing debt. Interest-bearing debt includes long-term debt, short-term debt, current maturities of long-term debt, and capitalized leases.

As you can see from Exhibit 9.3, total investor funds (the sum of operating invested capital and non-operating assets) must be the same whether calculated from the asset perspective or the financing perspective.

NOPLAT

Net operating profit less adjusted taxes (NOPLAT) represents the after-tax operating profits of the company after adjusting the taxes to a cash basis. Exhibit 9.4 shows the reorganization of Hershey's income statement, the

Exhibit 9.4   Hershey Foods—NOPLAT Calculation

NOPLAT ($ million)	1995	1996	1997	1998
Revenues	3,691	3,989	4,302	4,063
Cost of goods sold	(1,992)	(2,169)	(2,336)	(2,142)
Selling, general, and administrative expenses	(1,054)	(1,124)	(1,183)	(1,168)
Depreciation	(119)	(118)	(137)	(142)
Operating earnings before interest, taxes, and amortization (EBITA)	525	579	646	610
Taxes on EBITA	(202)	(239)	(247)	(231)
Changes in deferred taxes	(1)	32	43	54
NOPLAT	323	371	442	434
Taxes on EBITA				
Provision for income taxes (from income statement)	184	207	218	216
Tax shield on interest expense, net	18	18	30	33
Tax on non-operating income	0	14	0	(18)
Taxes on EBITA	202	239	247	231
Reconciliation to net income				
Net income	282	273	336	341
Add: Increase in deferred taxes	(1)	32	43	54
Add: Goodwill amortization	15	16	16	16
Adjusted net income	296	321	395	411
Add: Interest expense after-tax, net	27	30	46	52
Total income available to investors	323	351	442	463
After-tax non-operating income	0	22	0	(29)
NOPLAT	323	371	442	434

calculation of Hershey's NOPLAT, and a reconciliation of NOPLAT to Hershey's accounting net income:

- *Earnings before interest, taxes, and amortization of goodwill (EBITA).* The NOPLAT calculation begins with EBITA, the pretax operating income that a company would have earned if it had no debt and no goodwill amortization. It includes all types of operating income, including most revenues and expenses. Generally excluded are interest income, interest expense, the gain or loss from discontinued items, extraordinary income or loss, and the investment income from non-operating investments. Depreciation of fixed assets should be subtracted in calculating EBITA but goodwill amortization should not. Goodwill and goodwill amortization will be given special treatment below.

- *Taxes on EBITA.* Taxes on EBITA represent the income taxes that are attributable to EBITA. They are the taxes the company would pay if it had no debt, cash above operating needs, or non-operating income or expenses. Taxes on EBITA equal the total income tax provision (current and deferred) adjusted for the income taxes attributed to interest expense, interest income, and non-operating items. For Hershey, 1998 taxes on EBITA are calculated as follows:

Total income tax provision from income statement	$216
Tax shield on interest expense	33
Tax on interest income	(0)
Tax on non-operating income	(18)
Taxes on EBITA	$231

The taxes related to interest expense, interest income, and non-operating items are calculated by multiplying the marginal tax rate by the item (unless more specific tax information is available). The marginal tax rate is generally the statutory marginal rate, including state and local taxes. In Hershey's case, we estimated its marginal tax rate to be 39 percent. For example, the tax shield on interest expense ($33) equals interest expense ($86) times the 39 percent marginal tax rate. (Companies with tax-loss carry-forwards or those subject to the alternative minimum tax may have different marginal rates.)

- *Change in deferred taxes.* For valuation and analytical purposes, income taxes need to be adjusted to a cash basis. Investors expect the company to continue to earn a return on the capital saved as a result of tax deferrals. Putting taxes on a cash basis is consistent with the treatment of deferred tax balances as capital on which investors expect to earn a return, just as they do on all other capital.

The provision for income taxes in the income statement generally does not equal the actual taxes paid in cash by the company because of differences between GAAP and tax accounting. The adjustment to a cash basis generally can be made by calculating the change in accumulated deferred income taxes on the company's balance sheet (the net of long- and short-term deferred tax assets and long- and short-term deferred tax liabilities).

- *Reconciliation to net income.* We generally also reconcile net income to NOPLAT, as shown on the bottom of Exhibit 9.4, to ensure that nothing is missed in the calculation of NOPLAT and to ensure a complete understanding of the company's financial statements.

Return on Invested Capital

Now that NOPLAT and invested capital have been defined, we can calculate return on invested capital. ROIC is defined as follows:

$$ROIC = \frac{\text{Net operating profit less adjusted taxes}}{\text{Invested capital}}$$

Invested capital is generally measured at the beginning of the period or as an average of the beginning and end of the period. The most important aspect of calculating ROIC is to define the numerator and denominator consistently. In other words, if you include an asset in invested capital, the income related to that asset should be in NOPLAT. The definitions of NOPLAT and invested capital that we have developed above should ensure that consistency is achieved. Exhibit 9.5 shows the ROIC calculation for Hershey.

ROIC is a better analytical tool for understanding the company's performance than other return measures such as return on equity or return on assets because it focuses on the true operating performance of the company. Return on equity mixes operating performance with financial structure, making peer group analysis or trend analysis less meaningful because you can't understand the underlying operating performance of the company. The return on total assets (ROA) is inadequate because it includes a number of inconsistencies between the numerator and the

---

Exhibit 9.5   Hershey Foods—ROIC Calculation

$ million	1995	1996	1997	1998
NOPLAT	323	371	442	434
Operating invested capital (beginning of year)	1,686	1,642	1,815	1,885
Return on invested capital	19.2%	22.6%	24.3%	23.0%
ROIC (using average capital)	19.4%	21.5%	23.9%	23.3%
ROIC (average capital and including goodwill)	14.7%	15.9%	17.4%	17.1%

denominator. Non-interest-bearing liabilities are not deducted from the denominator, total assets. Yet the implicit financing cost of these liabilities is included in the expenses of the company and, therefore, deducted from the numerator.

Economic Profit

As we mentioned in Chapter 8, economic profit combines spread and the size of the company into a dollar, as opposed to percentage, measure of performance. It measures the dollars of economic value created by a company in a single year and is defined as follows:

$$\text{Economic profit} = \text{Invested capital} \times (\text{ROIC} - \text{WACC})$$

Recall from Chapter 8 that economic profit can also be defined as follows:

$$\text{Economic profit} = \text{NOPLAT} - \text{Capital charge}$$

where the capital charge equals invested capital times WACC:

$$\text{Economic profit} = \text{NOPLAT} - (\text{Invested capital} \times \text{WACC})$$

As a practical matter, we generally use invested capital measured at the beginning of the period or the average of beginning and ending capital. Technically, for the economic profit valuation to exactly equal the DCF valuation, you must use beginning capital. If you use average capital the variance will generally be small. Exhibit 9.6 shows the economic profit for Hershey.

Economic profit is an important measure because it combines size and ROIC into a single result. Too often companies focus on either size (often measured by earnings) or ROIC. Focusing on size (say earnings or earnings growth) could destroy value if returns on capital are too low. Conversely, earning a high ROIC on a low capital base may mean missed opportunities.

It is important not to confuse economic profit, which measures realized value creation, with the increase in the value of a company during the period. In 1998, Hershey earned economic profit of $293 million. However, during 1998, the market value of Hershey's shares increased by $49 million. Adding the dividends paid to Hershey's shareholders of $129 million in 1998, gives a total shareholder value creation of $178 million, substantially less than economic profit. The two concepts measure different aspects of value. Market value measures future value creation expectations (both short- and long-term); the increase in market value over a year equals economic profit (the short-term realized value creation) plus or minus the change in the value creation expectations. In Hershey's case, expectations were not met, so the value of the company did not increase as much as economic profit. The change in

Exhibit 9.6   Hershey Foods—Economic Profit Calculation[1]

Before goodwill ($ million)	1995	1996	1997	1998
Return on invested capital[1]	19.2%	22.6%	24.3%	23.0%
WACC	8.1%	8.9%	8.3%	7.5%
Spread	11.0%	13.7%	16.0%	15.5%
Invested capital (beginning of year)	1,686	1,642	1,815	1,885
Economic profit (before goodwill)	186	225	291	293
NOPLAT	323	371	442	434
Capital charge	(137)	(147)	(151)	(141)
Economic profit (before goodwill)	186	225	291	293
After goodwill				
Return on invested capital	14.5%	17.1%	17.7%	16.9%
WACC	8.1	8.9	8.3	7.5
Spread	6.4%	8.1%	9.4%	9.4%
Invested capital (beginning of year)	2,229	2,175	2,501	2,573
Economic profit (after goodwill)	142	177	234	242

1 Using beginning of year capital.

market value will equal economic profit only if there is no change in expected future performance and if the WACC remains constant during the year (an unlikely combination of events).

FREE CASH FLOW

We also need to calculate free cash flow to see how the company generates or consumes cash. Free cash flow is a company's true operating cash flow. It is the total after-tax cash flow generated by the company that is available to all providers of the company's capital, both creditors and shareholders. It can be thought of as the after-tax cash flow that would be available to the company's shareholders if the company had no debt. Free cash flow is before financing and therefore not affected by the company's financial structure, even though the financial structure may affect the company's weighted average cost of capital and therefore its value.

It is essential to define free cash flow properly to ensure consistency between the cash flow and the discount rate used to value the company. Free cash flow equals NOPLAT less net investment, where net investment is the change in invested capital. Adding depreciation to NOPLAT and net investment gives us gross cash flow and gross investment, which is how most free cash flow statements are presented:

$$FCF = NOPLAT - Net\ investment$$
$$= [NOPLAT + Depreciation] - [Net\ investment + Depreciation]$$
$$= Gross\ cash\ flow - Gross\ investment$$

Exhibit 9.7 shows the free cash flow calculation for Hershey and its recon-ciliation to total cash flow available to investors. The following defines the components of free cash flow that have not been examined earlier:

- *Depreciation.* Depreciation includes all the noncash charges deducted from EBITA except goodwill amortization (which is not added back to NOPLAT because it was not deducted in calculating NOPLAT). The amortization of other intangible assets such as patents and fran-chises are typically treated the same as goodwill.

- *Gross cash flow.* Gross cash flow represents the total cash flow thrown off by the company's operations. It is the amount available to reinvest in the business for maintenance and growth without relying on additional capital.

- *Change in operating working capital.* The change in operating work-ing capital is the amount the company invested in operating working capital during the period. Use the definition of operating

---

Exhibit 9.7   Hershey Foods—Free Cash Flow Calculation

$ million	1995	1996	1997	1998
NOPLAT	323	371	442	434
Depreciation	119	118	137	142
Gross cash flow	442	489	579	576
(Increase)/decrease in working capital	4	(13)	(18)	(195)
Capital expenditures	(87)	(284)	(183)	(142)
(Increase) in other assets, net of liabilities	8	6	(6)	(35)
Foreign currency translation effect	(5)	(4)	(9)	(18)
Gross investment	(80)	(294)	(217)	(390)
Free cash flow before goodwill	362	195	361	186
Investment in goodwill (and adjustments)	10	(153)	(1)	6
Free cash flow	**372**	**42**	**360**	**192**
Non-operating cash flow	0	(21)	0	25
After-tax interest income	2	2	2	0
Increase/(decrease) in excess marketable securities	0	0	0	0
Cash flow available to investors	**374**	**23**	**362**	**217**
Financing flow				
After-tax interest expense	29	32	48	52
Decrease/(Increase) in debt	(291)	(200)	(322)	36
Dividends	110	115	122	129
Share repurchases/(issues)	525	77	514	0
Total financing flow	**374**	**23**	**362**	**217**

working capital described earlier in this chapter when we calculated invested capital.

- *Capital expenditures.* Capital expenditures include expenditures on new and replacement property, plant, and equipment. Capital expenditures can be calculated from the balance sheet and income statement as the increase in *net* property, plant, and equipment plus depreciation expense for the period. (Technically, this calculation results in capital expenditures less the net book value of retired assets.)

- *Increase in other assets, net of liabilities.* The increase in net other assets equals the expenditure on all other operating assets including deferred expenses, and net of increases in non-current, non-interest-bearing liabilities. These can be calculated directly from the change in the balance sheet accounts plus any amortization included in depreciation.

- *Gross investment.* Gross investment is the sum of a company's spending for new capital, including working capital, capital expenditures, and other assets.

- *Investment in goodwill.* The investment in goodwill equals the expenditures to acquire other companies in excess of the book value of their net assets. In any year, the investment in goodwill is best calculated as the net change in the goodwill account on the balance sheet plus the amortization of goodwill in that period. This ensures that goodwill amortization does not affect free cash flow in either gross cash flow or gross investment.

- *Non-operating cash flow.* Non-operating cash flow represents the after-tax cash flow from items not related to operations. Free cash flow explicitly does not include non-operating cash flow. Caution must be exercised in considering an item to be non-operating. Any non-operating cash flow must be explicitly reflected in the value of the company. We do this by defining the total enterprise value of the company as the discounted present value of the company's free cash flow plus the value of its after-tax non-operating cash flow.

Present value of company's free cash flow	+	Present value of after-tax non-operating cash flow and marketable securities	=	Total value of company

Cash flow items that are sometimes considered non-operating include cash flow from discontinued operations, extraordinary gains or losses, and the cash flow from investments in unrelated subsidiaries. Remember that the present value of any non-operating cash flow must be reflected in the total value of the company.

It is generally not advisable to consider a recurring cash flow as non-operating. The company's risk and, therefore, its cost of capital reflects all its assets and its cash flow. Arbitrarily excluding items from free cash flow may violate the principle of consistency between free cash flow and cost of capital.

- *Change in excess marketable securities and interest income.* Just as excess cash and marketable securities and related interest income were excluded from invested capital and NOPLAT, they should be excluded from free cash flow. The change in excess marketable securities can be treated as non-operating cash flow or as financing cash flows (they can be considered negative debt). The after-tax interest income on excess marketable securities equals the pretax income times 1 minus the appropriate marginal income tax rate.

- *Foreign currency translation effect.* The change in the cumulative foreign currency translation gains or losses account is driven by the changes in translation rates applied to both assets and debt. As a practical matter, you generally cannot separate the asset and debt gains or losses without internal information. Therefore, treat these gains/losses as non-operating cash flow in the free cash flow. If you have the information needed to separate the asset from the debt effects, treat the gains/losses on assets as adjustments to free cash flow and gains/losses on debt as financial cash flow. (See Financial Accounting Standards Board Statement No. 52 for a discussion of foreign currency accounting.)

The sum of free cash flow and the non-operating items enumerated above equals the total funds available to investors (or if negative, the funds the investors must provide). These total funds available must equal the financing cash flows. That is, the total cash generated by the company's operations (plus non-operating cash flow, if any) must equal the net payments to all the company's creditors and shareholders. Conversely, if free cash flow is negative, it must equal the net funds provided by the company's shareholders and creditors (for example, through new issues of debt or equity).

This equality between operating and financial flows helps ensure that the free cash calculation is correct. The complexity of some financial statements often leads to mistakes in free cash flow calculations. Errors can be minimized by always calculating the company's financial flow and ensuring that it equals the funds available to investors. The financing flow line items are described below:

- *Change in debt.* The change in debt represents the net borrowing or repayment on all the company's interest-bearing debt, including short-term debt and capitalized leases.

- *After-tax interest expense.* The after-tax interest expense equals the pretax interest expense times 1 minus the company's marginal income tax rate. The marginal tax rate should be consistent with the rate used for the adjustment of taxes on EBITA.
- *Dividends.* Dividends include all cash dividends on common and preferred shares. Dividends paid in stock have no cash effects and should be ignored.
- *Share issues/repurchases.* Share issues/repurchases include both preferred and common shares and the effects of conversions of debt to equity. This figure can be calculated by taking the change in total equity plus dividends less net income.

DISAGGREGATING ROIC AND DEVELOPING AN INTEGRATED PERSPECTIVE

Now that we have done all the necessary calculations, the next step is to analyze ROIC and other measures to derive an integrated perspective on the company's performance.

A useful way to organize an analysis of the rate of return is to develop a return-on-invested-capital tree. The ROIC tree disaggregates ROIC into its key components to provide more insights into the drivers of ROIC. The tree begins by dividing ROIC into its key components:

$$\text{ROIC} = \frac{\text{NOPLAT}}{\text{Invested capital}}$$

Since NOPLAT can be expressed as EBITA times (1 – Cash tax rate), ROIC can be expressed as a pre-tax ROIC (based on EBITA rather than NOPLAT) adjusted for taxes:

$$\text{ROIC} = \frac{\text{EBITA}}{\text{Invested capital}} \times (1 - \text{Cash tax rate})$$

If we relate EBITA and invested capital to revenues, we get the equation:

$$\frac{\text{EBITA}}{\text{Invested capital}} = \frac{\text{EBITA}}{\text{Revenues}} \times \frac{\text{Revenues}}{\text{Invested capital}}$$

Pre-tax ROIC is thus broken down into two components:

1. Operating margin (EBITA/Revenues) measures how effectively the company converts revenues into profits.

2. Capital turnover (Revenues/Invested capital) measures how effectively the company employs its invested capital.

Each of these components can be further disaggregated into their components where the expense or capital items are compared to revenues. Exhibit 9.8 shows how the components can be organized into an ROIC tree for Hershey.

The component measures of the return on invested capital are industry- and company-specific. For example, wholesalers typically have slim margins and high capital turnover, while telephone companies have high margins and low capital turnover. These ratios may also reflect the company's operating strategy relative to its competitors. Higher margins might compensate for lower capital turnover (although the best companies often outperform their competitors on all measures).

Once you have calculated the historical value drivers, analyze the results by looking for trends and comparing with other companies in the same industry. Try to assemble this into an integrated perspective that combines the financial analysis with an analysis of the industry structure (opportunities for differentiation, entry/exit barriers, etc.) and a qualitative assessment of the company's strengths and vulnerabilities.

Developing this integrated perspective is not a mechanical process, so it is difficult to generalize. But we can provide some examples:

- For consumer products companies with strong brand names, like Hershey Foods, you are likely to find high ROICs. The key issues tend to be about growth (market share, new products, managing the

Exhibit 9.8   Hershey Foods—1998 ROIC Tree[1]

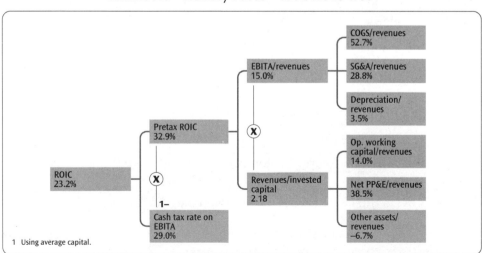

1 Using average capital.

distribution chain) and benchmarking performance against competitors (manufacturing costs, overhead, inventory management).

- For commodity companies, like paper or some chemical companies, you need to understand whether the company and the industry have been able to earn their cost of capital. In many cases they haven't. You then need to understand the short- and long-term supply/demand picture for the industry and evaluate competitor behavior. Try to identify where the industry is in its cycle and whether there are structural changes that will change the cycle permanently. Think about whether the company has any competitive advantages (technology, market access). Has the company been able to turn these advantages into higher returns than the industry average? How good a job has the company done at timing major capital expenditures?

While it is impossible to provide a comprehensive checklist for understanding a company's historical performance, here are some things to keep in mind:

- Look back as far as possible (at least ten years). This will help you to understand whether the company and the industry tend to revert to some normal level of performance and whether short-term trends are likely to be permanent breaks from the past.
- Go as deep into the value drivers as you can, getting as close to operational performance measures as possible.
- If there are any radical changes in performance, identify the source of the change and determine whether it is real or perhaps just an accounting effect and whether any change is likely to be sustained.

CREDIT HEALTH AND LIQUIDITY

The final step in the historical analysis is understanding the financial health of the company from a credit perspective. Here we are not concerned with value creation itself, but how has the company been financing its value creation. Specifically, is the company generating or consuming investors' cash? What proportion of invested capital comes from creditors rather than equity investors? How safe is this capital structure?

The best way to understand a company's financial health is to project its cash flows and develop a financing plan for a number of cash-flow scenarios. As a first step, an analysis of historical performance provides some early insights. Since this book's focus is not credit analysis, we will just touch on some of the important measures we use to analyze financial health. Exhibit 9.9 shows an analysis of Hershey Foods' historical financial health.

Exhibit 9.9   Hershey Foods—Financing Analysis

$ million	1995	1996	1997	1998
Interest coverage				
EBITA	525	579	646	610
Interest expense	48	52	79	86
EBITA/interest expense	10.9	11.1	8.2	7.1
Capital structure				
Total interest-bearing debt	795	995	1,317	1,282
Total investor funds	2,175	2,501	2,573	2,791
Debt/total funds (book value)	36.6%	39.8%	51.2%	45.9%
Debt/total funds (market values)	7.8	9.8%	12.9%	12.6%
Investment rate				
Net investment	(39)	176	80	248
NOPLAT	323	371	442	434
Net investment rate	−12%	47%	18%	57%
Gross investment	80	294	217	390
Gross cash flow	442	489	579	576
Gross investment rate	18%	60%	37%	68%
Dividend payout				
Common dividends	110	115	122	129
Net income available to common	282	273	336	341
Dividend payout ratio	39%	42%	36%	38%

Interest Coverage

Interest coverage, the amount of earnings available to pay interest expense, measures the company's financial cushion. It provides a sense of how far operating profits could fall before the company would have difficulty servicing its debt. We generally measure coverage as EBITA divided by interest expense and required preferred dividends. There are number of variations for this measure such as adding required lease payments to the denominator or adding depreciation back to the numerator. These may be helpful in some circumstances, particularly when you are trying to get a short-term perspective on the ability of the company to pay its creditors. For a long-term perspective, we generally stick with the basic ratio.

Hershey's interest coverage ranged from 7.1 times to 11.1 times during the 1995 to 1998 period, which is extremely safe (thus accounting for Hershey's AA bond rating). Hershey's EBITA could fall to $\frac{1}{7}$ of its 1998 level and its EBITA would still exceed its interest expense. Investment grade companies typically have coverage ratios exceeding about four times interest expense.

Note that Hershey's coverage ratio has declined over the last several years, primarily as a result of significant share repurchases. This is an explicit strategy to capture some of the tax benefits associated with debt financing, while maintaining adequate financial flexibility.

Debt/Total Investor Funds

Debt/investor funds measures the company's reliance on debt capital. While debt has tax advantages that will be outlined in Chapter 10, it also can reduce a company's flexibility because debtholders expect to be paid on a set schedule, whereas the company has great flexibility in paying dividends to shareholders. We generally measure total interest-bearing debt to total investor funds, expressed both at book values and at market values. You may also consider subtracting excess cash and marketable securities from both the numerator and denominator if the excess cash could be used to pay down debt.

At book values, which creditors often use, Hershey's debt-to-total-investor funds ratio was 46 percent in 1998, and has been increasing steadily. On a market basis, the debt-to-total-value is quite low at 13 percent. For companies like Hershey with high returns on capital, book-debt-to-capital ratios are becoming less reliable as indicators of financial capacity. Despite the 46 percent debt-to-investor-funds ratios, coverage is above seven times. More and more creditors are focusing on coverage rather than book-debt-to-capital ratios.

Investment Rate

The investment rate is the ratio of investment to available funds. This can either be expressed on a net basis (Net investment/NOPLAT) or gross basis (Gross investment/Gross cash flow). In either case, this measure tells you whether the company is consuming more funds than it is generating (investment rate greater than one) or generating extra cash flow that can be paid to investors as interest expense, dividends, debt reductions, share repurchases, and so on.

Dividend Payout Ratio

The dividend payout ratio is total common dividends divided by income available to common shareholders. We can better understand the company's financial situation by analyzing the payout ratio in relation to the investment rate. If the company has a high dividend payout ratio and an investment rate greater than one, then it must be borrowing money to fund a negative free cash flow, to pay interest, and to pay dividends. We might be concerned about how sustainable this is. On the other hand, a company with positive free cash flow and low dividend payout is probably paying down debt. If sustained, this company might be passing up the tax benefits of debt.

Hershey's gross investment rate has consistently been far less than 100 percent. Rather than increase its dividend or pay down debt, Hershey has used this cash flow to repurchase shares, thus maintaining the tax benefits of debt without the quasi-permanent commitment to a substantially higher dividend. (It would have to more than double its dividend to a payout ratio over 70 percent to consistently absorb all the cash it is generating.)

ADVANCED ISSUES IN ANALYZING FINANCIAL PERFORMANCE

We have kept the analysis of financial statements relatively simple. Depending on the company, you may come across one or more difficult accounting issues that will affect the estimation of NOPLAT, invested capital, economic profit, and free cash flow. This section discusses the most important of these issues.

Goodwill

We explicitly excluded goodwill, both the asset and the amortization, from the calculation of ROIC. In most cases, ROIC should be calculated both with and without goodwill. ROIC excluding goodwill measures the operating performance of the company and is useful for comparing operating performance across companies and for analyzing trends. It is not distorted by the price premiums paid for acquisitions made in building the company. ROIC including goodwill measures how well the company has used investors' funds. Has the company earned its cost of capital, taking into consideration the premiums it paid for acquisitions?

It is not uncommon for companies to earn high returns on an operating basis while not earning their cost of capital when acquisition premiums are considered. Walt Disney acquired Cap Cities/ABC, the publishing company and television network, in 1996. As a result, it had $18 billion of cumulative goodwill at the end of 1998 compared with operating invested capital of $16 billion. Including goodwill reduces Disney's ROIC by half:

	1995 (percent)	1996 (percent)	1997 (percent)	1998 (percent)
ROIC excluding goodwill	20.9	19.5	33.1	24.7
ROIC including goodwill	20.1	9.6	12.8	11.2

Disney's operating ROIC has actually increased since the acquisition, but it is not yet clear that the company is earning its cost of capital on the total acquisition price.

On a technical note, the proper way to include goodwill in the ROIC calculation is to add to invested capital the total amount of goodwill before cumulative amortization and not to deduct from NOPLAT any goodwill amortization. In effect, this reverses the amortization of goodwill. The reason for not amortizing goodwill for economic analysis is that goodwill, unlike other fixed assets, does not wear out and is not replaced. For other assets, depreciation or amortization is a proxy for the physical deterioration of the asset with the recognition that the asset must be replaced if the company wishes to remain in business.

Operating Leases

Operating leases are any lease obligations that the company has not capitalized. Operating leases represent a type of financing and, if material, should be treated as such in the calculation of the company's value drivers.

To do this, adjust the company's financial statements to treat operating leases as if they were capitalized. First, reclassify the implied interest expense portion of the lease payments from an operating expense (usually in cost of goods sold, or selling, general, and administrative expense) to an interest expense. This increases EBITA by the amount of implied interest. Do not forget to adjust EBITA taxes as well. Second, add the implied principal amount of operating leases to invested capital and to debt. Finally, treat the principal amount as additional debt in the weighted average cost of capital calculation. This mimics the effects that would have occurred had the leases been capitalized.

To estimate the implied principal amount of the operating leases, a rule of thumb is to capitalize this year's or next year's lease payments as a perpetuity using the cost of debt. Another approach is to discount the future minimum lease payments (disclosed in the footnotes to U.S. audited statements) at the company's marginal borrowing rate, although this approach will understate the value of leases that management intends to renew. To estimate the implied interest expense, multiply the implied principal amount by the marginal borrowing rate.

If you capitalize operating leases you also need to ensure that the cost of capital incorporates the impact of the leases as well and you need to subtract the value of the leases from the enterprise value to derive the value of equity.

Pensions

Adjusting for pension plans depends on whether the plan is over- or underfunded and whether any over- or underfunding is recorded on the financial statements. For fully funded plans, no adjustments are necessary. We will describe how to treat unfunded or underfunded plans. (Note that these same principles apply to European companies, where pensions are often unfunded.) The treatment of overfunded plans is the opposite of underfunded plans.

For unfunded or underfunded plans where the liability is recorded in the financial statements, treat the liability the same as interest-bearing debt in calculating invested capital and the cost of capital. For NOPLAT, estimate the implied interest expense on the liability for the year and reclassify a portion of operating expenses equal to this amount as interest expense. The footnotes to the financial statements generally provide enough information to do this. These adjustments ensure consistency between NOPLAT and invested capital by treating them as if the company had borrowed the necessary money to fund the liability.

Exhibit 9.10   Provisions in NOPLAT, Invested Capital, and Cash Flow Calculations

INCOME STATEMENT	Year 2	BALANCE SHEET	Year 1	Year 2
Revenues	147.0	Assets	200.0	247.0
COGS	(20.0)			
SG&A	(20.0)	Debt	72.0	80.0
Increase in provisions	**(23.0)**	**Provision for plant closure**	-	10.0
Depreciation	(20.0)	**General provision**	8.0	16.0
Operating income	64.0	**Retirement-related liabilities**	15.0	20.0
Interest expense	(4.0)	Equity	105.0	121.0
Earnings before taxes	60.0	Liabilities and equity	200.0	247.0
Taxes	(18.0)			
Income before extraordinary items	42.0			
Extraordinary loss	(10.0)			
Net income	32.0			
Marginal tax rate	30.0%			
Interest rate on ret.-rel. liabilities	5.0%			
Dividend payout ratio	50.0%			

NOPLAT		INVESTED CAPITAL		
Operating income	64.0	Operating assets	200.0	247.0
Add: Increase in general provision	**8.0**	Operating invested capital	200.0	247.0
Add: Interest on ret.-rel. liabs	**1.0**			
Adjusted EBITA	73.0	Equity	105.0	121.0
Less: Taxes on EBITA	(19.5)	**Add: Provision for plant closure**	-	**10.0**
NOPLAT	53.5	**Add: General provision**	**8.0**	**16.0**
		Adjusted equity	113.0	147.0
Taxes on EBITA		Debt	72.0	80.0
Taxes on income statement	18.0	**Retirement-related liabilities**	**15.0**	**20.0**
Add: Tax shield on interest expense	1.2	Total investor funds	200.0	247.0
Add: Tax shield on ret.-rel. liabs	**0.3**			
Taxes on EBITA	19.5			
Reconciliation to net income				
Net income	32.0			
Add: Extraordinary items	10.0			
Add: Interest expense after-tax	2.8			
Add: Interest on ret.-rel. liabs after tax	**0.7**			
Add: Increase in general provision	**8.0**			
NOPLAT	53.5			

CASH FLOWS				
NOPLAT	53.5	Interest expense after tax	2.8	
Add: Depreciation	20.0	Interest expense on ret.-rel.	0.7	
Gross cash flow	73.5	liabs after tax		
Less: Gross investment	(67.0)	(Inc)/decrease in debt	(8.0)	
Free cash flow	6.5	(Inc)/decrease in equity	-	
		(Inc)/decrease in ret.-rel. liabs	(5.0)	
		Dividends	16.0	
		Financing flow	6.5	

For unfunded and unrecorded pension liabilities that are material, the proper procedure is to first adjust the financial statements to how they would appear if the liability were recorded. Then follow the procedure above for calculating NOPLAT and invested capital. Adjusting the financial statements involves reclassifying a portion of retained earnings as the pension liability and adjusting each year's earnings by the increase in the unfunded liability. To avoid enormous swings in ROIC attributed to large changes in the unfunded liability, consider smoothing the adjustments. (See the example in Exhibit 9.10 for a comparison with the treatment of other provisions and reserves.)

Provisions and Reserves

Provisions or additions to reserves are noncash expenses that reflect future costs or expected losses.[1] Companies take provisions by reducing income and setting up a corresponding reserve on the liability side of the balance sheet (or deducting the amount from the relevant assets).

The rules for setting up provisions vary by country. Some countries only allow provisions for specifically identifiable future costs or losses, while others allow provisions for unspecified costs. In countries with flexible rules, companies often use provisions to manage their earnings, setting up provisions in good years and drawing them down in bad years. Provisions are also tax deductible in some countries. See Chapter 18 for a summary of the rules for provisions across countries.

The following table classifies provisions into three categories and identifies how they should be treated with regard to invested capital and NOPLAT. (We have included pension reserves for comparison.)

Type of provision	Treatment for NOPLAT calculation	Treatment for invested capital calculation
Restructuring (for specifically identifiable future costs or losses)	No adjustment needed	Equity
On-going nonpension (for unspecified costs)	Add change in the provision back to NOPLAT	Equity
Pension	Add interest on the provision back to NOPLAT	Debt

[1] A note on terminology: In U.S. usage, the word "provision" should refer to an income statement item (a charge against income to reflect decline in the value of an asset or an expected loss). A balance sheet item that reflects funds set aside against future liability should be called a "reserve." In continental Europe, the two words are often used interchangeably.

Each category is discussed further next. Exhibit 9.10 contains a sample treatment of each of the types of provision for a hypothetical company.

Restructuring provisions relate to specific future events that will entail costs or losses (e.g., closure of a plant or shutdown of a business unit). In contrast with provisions that are used to smooth income from year to year, restructuring provisions reflect a nonrecurring drop in earnings. They should be treated as follows:

- NOPLAT does not need to be adjusted for these provisions. This is in keeping with the general rule of excluding extraordinary gains or losses from the calculation of NOPLAT.
- In the calculation of invested capital, treat these provisions as equity.
- These calculations are shown by the treatment of the "Provision for Plant Closure" in Exhibit 9.10.

On-going nonpension provisions that do not relate to specific future losses are often used merely to smooth earnings. For financial analysis and valuation, this practice distorts the true performance of the company. In calculating NOPLAT, invested capital, and ROIC, the impact of these provisions should be reversed. When calculating these measures, adjust them in the following way:

- Add back the increase in the balance sheet reserves to operating profits to calculate NOPLAT.
- For invested capital, treat the balance sheet reserves as equity.
- Then use these adjusted measures to calculate ROIC.
- These calculations are shown in the treatment of the "General Provision" in Exhibit 9.10.

Minority Interest

A minority interest occurs when a third party owns some percentage of one of the company's consolidated subsidiaries. If material, minority interest should be handled as follows:

- Treat the balance sheet amount as a quasi-equity account.
- Treat the earnings attributable to minority interest as a financing cost like interest expense, with an appropriate adjustment for income taxes.
- Treat the associated cash flow to the minority investors as a financing flow. The cash flow can be estimated as the earnings attributable to the minority interest less the increase in the balance sheet

account. This essentially equals the dividends paid to the minority investors less any contributions from them.

Post-Retirement Medical Benefits

Financial Accounting Standards Board Statement No. 106 requires companies to record as a liability the present value of expected post-retirement medical benefits for employees. These are conceptually similar to unfunded pension plans that are recorded on a company's financial statements and should be treated the same way.

Capitalizing Expensed Investments

Accounting rules require the immediate write-off of expenditures for marketing and research and development. Yet clearly these expenditures are investments for the future. A case can be made that, in analyzing the performance of a company, these investments should be capitalized, rather than written off. Suppose we were to capitalize Hershey's advertising spending and then amortize it over a four-year period (other marketing and promotion expenditures are not specifically disclosed). If we did this, Hershey's 1998 NOPLAT would increase by only $6 million (because spending is stable from year to year), and its invested capital would increase by $283 million to $2,113 million, resulting in a decline in Hershey's ROIC from 23.0 percent to 21.0 percent.

While sensible in theory, it is difficult to decide how to capitalize and amortize these expenditures. If spending on these investments varies considerably from year to year, or deviates significantly from peers, then it is probably worth the extra time to make this adjustment, to better understand the trend in performance or performance against peers (despite its inherent inaccuracy).

Adjustment for Property, Plant, and Equipment Lumpiness and Asset Life

For companies with lumpy capital expenditures, ROIC may vary considerably from year to year. In certain situations, it may be helpful to consider a more complex approach to measuring ROIC.

Consider Company R, a restaurant company that invests $1,000 every four years to rebuild its one restaurant (assume zero taxes as well). At the beginning of every four-year period its invested capital is $1,000. But every year, its invested capital declines by $250 of depreciation. Assuming a constant $350 of profits before depreciation every year, its results would look like the following:

	Year				
	0	1	2	3	4
EBITDA		$350	$350	$350	$350
Depreciation		250	250	250	250
NOPLAT		$100	$100	$100	$100
Net PPE	$1,000	750	500	250	0
ROIC (beg. of yr)		10%	13%	20%	40%

Company R's ROIC varies from 10 percent to 40 percent, despite its constant earnings. Assuming a 13 percent cost of capital, Company R would appear to destroy value in the first year, break even in the second year, and create value in years 3 and 4. Ideally, the ROIC each year would equal the internal rate of return on the investment. Using the classic IRR formula, you would find that Company R earns an average ROIC of 15 percent over the life of the restaurant.

To correct for this discrepancy, you could mimic the IRR by employing an approach described in *CFROI Valuation,* by Bartley Madden.[2] Exhibit 9.11 summarizes the approach for Hershey using 1997 results. For any year, set investment equal to the gross property, plant, and equipment (PPE) of the company (before accumulated depreciation) plus any other assets like working capital. Set cash flow equal to NOPLAT plus depreciation. Assume that this cash flow is earned every year for the life of the PPE (estimate the average life by dividing depreciation into gross PPE). For the last year, assume cash flow is the same as the other years plus a return of working capital and other assets. Now solve for the IRR of this stream of cash flows (we

Exhibit 9.11   Hershey Foods—Estimation of CFROI, 1997

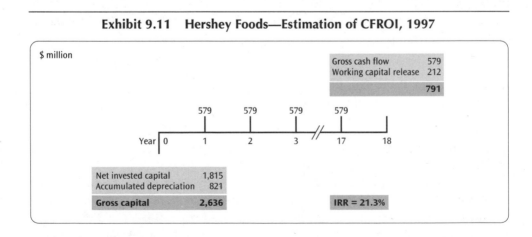

[2] B. Madden, *CFROI Valuation: A Total System Approach to Valuing the Firm* (Oxford, England: Butterworth-Heinemann, 1999).

will call this result cash flow return on investment, or CFROI, as referred to by its originators).

As you can see from Exhibit 9.11, Hershey's CFROI for 1997 is 21.3 percent, compared with an ROIC of 23.9 percent (using average beginning and ending invested capital). Exhibit 9.12 compares Hershey's ROIC and CFROI for the years 1990 to 1998. In most years the difference is within the normal error range for these imprecise calculations. And the trends are similar. One thing you will note is the divergence toward the end of the period attributable to a significant increase in average plant age.

The CFROI captures the lumpiness better than ROIC but is complex to calculate and more difficult to explain to non-finance managers. Weighing the benefits and costs of CFROI versus ROIC, we suggest using CFROI when it makes a big difference in the result. Big differences will occur in the following situations:

- Companies with very long-lived fixed assets (over 15 years on average).
- Companies with large fixed assets relative to working capital.
- Companies whose fixed assets are very old or very new.
- Companies with lumpy capital expenditure patterns.

Inflation Effects

While ROIC is the best single return measure, like other historical cost accounting measures, it can be distorted by inflation. To remedy this

Exhibit 9.12   Hershey Foods—Comparison of Adjusted and Unadjusted ROIC

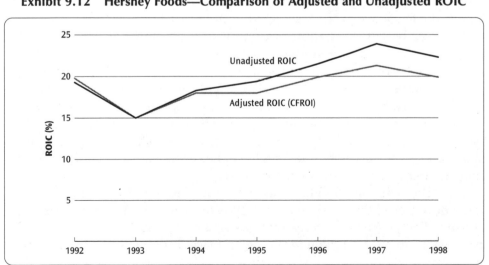

distortion it is sometimes suggested to adjust net property, plant, and equipment using either of three approaches: replacement cost, market values, or inflation-adjusted costs. Let's explore each in turn.

The replacement cost approach values the plants at the cost to replace them today. We disagree with the replacement cost approach for the simple reason that assets do not have to be and may never be replaced. It may be economically justifiable to continue to use an old asset even though the cost of replacing it with new equipment may outweigh the higher profits that the new asset will eventually generate. Furthermore, a company with a plant built several years before its competitors (assuming the same productivity potential) at a lower cost than its competitors' plants has a real competitive advantage that should be reflected in a higher ROIC. This advantage is similar to a company that has lower labor costs because its workers are nonunionized or a company located in a low tax jurisdiction. These advantages must be reflected in a company's returns.

Using the market values of assets is appropriate when the realizable market value of the assets substantially exceeds the historical cost book value. You are only likely to find tangible assets with such high values in the case of assets that have general uses beyond the company's current use of the assets. Real estate and airplanes are good examples where the realizable market values of the assets might exceed the book values. For most assets, such as equipment, computers, and fixtures, the market values for used assets are generally very low. For most companies, the proportion of assets with market values significantly higher than book values is low, so calculating ROIC based on book values does not introduce significant distortions.

If market values are used, NOPLAT must be adjusted to reflect the annual appreciation of the value of the assets. It would be inconsistent to write up the assets without reflecting the appreciation in profits. This is a common error that we see when analysts argue for using market values. They ignore the economic profit associated with the write-up.

It could be argued that the reason for writing up the assets and for not including the appreciation in profits is to get a sense of whether a company's assets would be better used some other way. Consider a retailer that owns valuable real estate. The retailer might earn less than its cost of capital if the market value of the real estate were used instead of its book value. While this is true, remember we are trying to analyze the company's actual performance, not whether it is making the best use of its assets. Companies should do both, measure actual performance and determine whether or not they are making the best use of their assets.

Finally, adjusting assets for inflation is complex. For every year, you must decompose the fixed assets into layers based on when they were purchased. Then each layer is revalued using an appropriate price index. Depreciation must be revalued using a price index. ROIC can then be estimated by dividing the adjusted NOPLAT by the adjusted invested capital. This ROIC is a real ROIC and must be compared to a real cost of capital (excluding inflation). While this approach is sensible in theory it is complex to apply and difficult to work with. It is particularly useful, however, in high inflation environments. See Chapter 19, *Valuation in Emerging Markets,* for an example of how to apply this approach.

HEINEKEN CASE

To wrap up this and each of the next four chapters, we present a case study: Heineken N.V.[3] This case will illustrate the concepts from each of the chapters and provide a comprehensive integration of all the pieces of a valuation.

The Netherlands-based Heineken is one of the largest beer companies in the world, and enjoys the second-largest market share, behind Anheuser-Busch. Its main brands are the popular Heineken and Amstel beers. In 1998, the last year used in our valuation, Heineken had revenues of NLG 13.8 billion[4] and had over 33,500 employees worldwide. It is also the most international brewer: only 9 percent of its revenues comes from the Netherlands. Forty-one percent of revenues originates in the rest of Europe, 6 percent from North America, and the remaining 44 percent from Latin America, Asia, and Africa. In addition, only 25 percent of its sales comes from its flagship brands; the rest is from Heineken-owned regional brands.

In this chapter of our case study, we analyze the historical performance of Heineken and develop an understanding of the beer market and how Heineken has performed relative to the market.

CALCULATE THE VALUE DRIVERS

Exhibits 9.13 through 9.20 detail the historical financial analysis of Heineken. Exhibits 9.13 and 9.14 present Heineken's income statement and balance sheet for the years 1994 through 1998. Exhibits 9.15 through 9.17 detail the calculations of Heineken's NOPLAT, invested capital, and free cash flow for each year. Exhibit 9.18 shows the calculations of Heineken's economic profit. The remainder of the exhibits offer the backup calculations and ratios to be used for forecasting.

In analyzing Heineken's financial statements, several accounting issues merit special attention.

---

[3] The authors would like to thank our colleague, David Krieger, who prepared this analysis of Heineken.
[4] During 1998 and 1999, the Dutch guilder most often traded within a range of 2.0 to 2.1 times the U.S. dollar. The Dutch guilder is also now fixed at 2.20 euros.

Exhibit 9.13   Heineken—Historical Income Statement

NLG million	1993	1994	1995	1996	1997	1998
Revenues	9,049	9,974	10,443	12,189	13,512	13,822
Duties, levies, and trade taxes	(1,198)	(1,359)	(1,387)	(1,621)	(1,849)	(1,806)
COGS - Marketing	(1,219)	(1,418)	(1,580)	(1,436)	(1,642)	(1,741)
COGS - Merchandising	(756)	(989)	(1,028)	(1,466)	(1,637)	(1,597)
COGS - Packaging	(1,014)	(1,070)	(1,151)	(1,393)	(1,409)	(1,448)
COGS - Raw materials	(663)	(567)	(616)	(858)	(876)	(738)
COGS - Other	(1,257)	(1,407)	(1,386)	(1,603)	(1,878)	(1,923)
Personnel costs	(1,643)	(1,684)	(1,734)	(2,174)	(2,274)	(2,295)
Amortization of goodwill	0	0	0	0	0	0
Depreciation expense	(501)	(586)	(556)	(626)	(744)	(822)
Operating income	798	895	1,006	1,012	1,203	1,453
Interest and dividend income	168	158	173	178	159	189
Interest expense	(152)	(103)	(99)	(136)	(123)	(117)
Earnings before taxes	814	950	1,079	1,053	1,239	1,525
Income taxes	(320)	(318)	(384)	(369)	(456)	(518)
Minority interest	24	(28)	(31)	(29)	(21)	(26)
Income before extraordinary items	519	603	664	655	761	981
Extraordinary items (after tax)	0	59	0	0	0	0
Net income	519	662	664	655	761	981
Statement of changes in equity						
Beginning equity		3,973	4,354	4,734	4,514	5,103
Net income		662	664	655	761	981
Common dividends		(140)	(203)	(176)	(176)	(254)
Revaluations		(13)	(9)	139	134	(151)
Goodwill written off		(127)	(72)	(839)	(131)	(612)
Ending equity		4,354	4,734	4,514	5,103	5,066

Acquisitions and Treatment of Goodwill

Heineken has made several acquisitions and has increased stakes in companies in the years to 1998. Most notable are the investments in Birra Moretti in Italy and the French brewers Fischer and Saint-Arnould, all in 1996. Given these large purchases, the pre-1996 data may not be entirely comparable to more recent data. In forecasting, we will give more weight to the latter years' data than to the earlier figures.

Through its various acquisitions, Heineken has taken on more than NLG 2.3 billion in goodwill. In the United States, goodwill must be recorded as an asset and then amortized over a 40-year life. In the Netherlands, goodwill may be written off immediately to equity, which is Heineken's policy. Using this accounting method would distort comparison of Heineken's ROIC with companies such as Anheuser-Busch that

Exhibit 9.14   Heineken—Historical Balance Sheets

NLG million	1993	1994	1995	1996	1997	1998
Operating cash	173	204	210	246	276	283
Excess marketable securities	1,393	1,536	1,945	1,382	1,595	1,806
Accounts receivable	658	792	879	1,220	1,275	1,218
Inventories	690	687	793	985	1,026	996
Other current assets	314	359	361	479	486	490
Total current assets	3,228	3,578	4,189	4,313	4,658	4,793
Gross prop, plant, and equipment	9,946	10,882	11,383	11,672	14,022	14,283
Accum. depreciation	(5,583)	(6,187)	(6,669)	(6,169)	(8,368)	(8,459)
Net property, plant, and equipment	4,363	4,695	4,715	5,503	5,654	5,824
Goodwill	0	0	0	0	0	0
Investments and advances	541	646	738	838	945	1,080
Total assets	8,132	8,919	9,641	10,654	11,257	11,697
Short-term debt	479	433	586	774	476	474
Accounts payable	530	584	701	885	903	907
Dividends payable	86	86	105	106	106	129
Other current liabilities	951	1,123	1,223	1,454	1,564	1,708
Total current liabilities	2,046	2,226	2,615	3,219	3,050	3,218
Long-term debt	462	503	424	792	909	1,151
Deferred income taxes	584	582	624	635	629	601
Investment facilities equalization	130	119	119	100	100	83
Retirement-related provisions	168	164	167	162	157	103
Ongoing provisions	528	616	612	821	909	912
Minority interest	239	354	346	410	401	564
Total common equity	3,973	4,354	4,734	4,514	5,103	5,066
Total liabilities and equity	8,132	8,919	9,641	10,654	11,257	11,697

follow U.S.-style practices. For comparison purposes, then, it is best to look at performance both with and without goodwill.

Revaluation Reserves

Each year, Heineken makes an adjustment to its balance sheet and equity called a "revaluation reserve." The details of this adjustment are not disclosed though they are most likely due to foreign currency translation adjustments and fixed asset revaluations. We have treated these adjustments as non-operating cash flows.

Government Grants

Some governments have agreed to give Heineken favorable financing as an incentive to expand into their countries. The company records these incentives as "investment

Exhibit 9.15   Heineken—Historical NOPLAT

NLG millions	1994	1995	1996	1997	1998
Reported EBITA	895	1,006	1,012	1,203	1,453
Adjustment for retirement-related liability	13	12	11	9	5
Increase in ongoing provisions	88	(4)	209	88	3
Adjusted EBITA	996	1,014	1,231	1,301	1,461
Taxes on EBITA	(304)	(363)	(358)	(447)	(494)
Change in deferred taxes	(2)	42	11	(7)	(28)
NOPLAT	690	693	885	847	939
Taxes on EBITA					
Provision for income taxes	318	384	369	456	518
Tax shield on interest expense	36	35	48	43	41
Tax shield on retirement-related interest	5	4	4	3	2
Tax on interest income	(55)	(61)	(62)	(56)	(66)
Taxes on EBITA	304	363	358	447	494
Reconciliation to net income					
Net income	662	664	655	761	981
Add: Increase in deferred taxes	(2)	42	11	(7)	(28)
Add: Increase in ongoing provisions	88	(4)	209	88	3
Add: Extraordinary items	(59)	0	(0)	0	0
Add: Minority interest	28	31	29	21	26
Adjusted net income	717	733	905	864	983
Add: Interest expense after tax	67	65	89	80	76
Add: Interest expense on retirement-related liab.	9	8	7	6	3
Total income available to investors	792	806	1,001	950	1,062
Less: Interest income after tax	(103)	(112)	(116)	(103)	(123)
NOPLAT	690	693	885	847	939

facilities equalization accounts." We can either treat them as low-cost sources of financing and include any change in financing flows, or as operating liabilities, and include any change in operating cash flow. We chose the latter for simplicity and because we view the government grants as a benefit of doing business in new countries, not as an investor to whom the company owes returns.

Pension Plans

Heineken had an unfunded pension liability at the end of 1998 of about NLG 103 million, primarily related to the company's Spanish operations, the annual report states. This liability represents an effective borrowing from employees. Accordingly, we treat Heineken's pension provision as debt.

The interest expense on this obligation—a 5 percent interest rate, according to the financial statements—was most likely recorded as a personnel expense. As a result, we reclassify the interest expense from an operating cost to interest

Exhibit 9.16   Heineken—Historical Invested Capital

NLG million	1993	1994	1995	1996	1997	1998
Operating current assets	1,835	2,042	2,243	2,931	3,063	2,987
Operating current liabilties	(1,481)	(1,707)	(1,925)	(2,339)	(2,467)	(2,615)
Operating working capital	355	335	319	591	597	372
Net property, plant, and equipment	4,363	4,695	4,715	5,503	5,654	5,824
Other assets net of other liabilities	(130)	(119)	(119)	(100)	(100)	(83)
Oper invested capital (before goodwill)	4,587	4,911	4,914	5,995	6,150	6,113
Cumulative goodwill written off and amortized	522	649	722	1,561	1,692	2,304
Oper invested capital (after goodwill)	5,109	5,561	5,636	7,556	7,842	8,417
Excess marketable securities	1,393	1,536	1,945	1,382	1,595	1,806
Investments and advances	541	646	738	838	945	1,080
Total investor funds	7,043	7,743	8,319	9,776	10,382	11,303
Total common and preferred equity	3,973	4,354	4,734	4,514	5,103	5,066
Cum goodwill written off and amortized	522	649	722	1,561	1,692	2,304
Deferred income taxes	591	583	624	635	629	601
Dividends payable	86	86	105	106	106	129
Ongoing provisions	528	616	612	821	909	912
Adjusted equity	5,694	6,288	6,797	7,637	8,439	9,012
Minority interest	239	354	346	410	401	564
Debt	941	937	1,009	1,567	1,385	1,625
Retirement-related liability	168	164	167	162	157	103
Total investor funds	7,043	7,743	8,319	9,776	10,382	11,303

expense. (We normally would not make an adjustment for such a small amount, but we do here to illustrate the technique.)

Taxes

The marginal tax rate in the Netherlands has been 35 percent in recent years to 1998. This information is useful for calculating taxes related to interest income and expense.

Deferred Taxes and Ongoing Provisions

Heineken has NLG 601 million in deferred taxes and NLG 912 million in "provisions for other personnel schemes" and "other provisions." We assume that both are ongoing rather than one-time restructuring provisions. So we add both deferred taxes and on-going provisions to equity as a "quasi-equity account," and adjust NOPLAT each year for the change in these provisions.

Exhibit 9.17   Heineken—Historical Free Cash Flow

NLG million	1994	1995	1996	1997	1998
Operating cash flows					
NOPLAT	690	693	885	847	939
Depreciation	586	556	626	744	822
Gross cash flow	1,276	1,249	1,510	1,591	1,761
Less: Increase in working capital	19	16	(272)	(5)	225
Less: Capital expenditures	(919)	(575)	(1,414)	(895)	(992)
Less: Increase in other assets	(11)	0	(20)	0	(17)
Gross investment	(911)	(559)	(1,706)	(900)	(784)
Free cash flow before goodwill	365	690	(196)	691	977
Investment in goodwill	(127)	(72)	(839)	(131)	(612)
Free cash flow after goodwill	238	618	(1,035)	560	364
Nonoperating cash flow	(59)	(101)	39	28	(286)
After-tax interest income	103	112	116	103	123
(Increase)/Decrease in excess marketable securities	(144)	(409)	563	(213)	(211)
Cash flow available to investors	138	220	(317)	478	(10)
Financing flows					
After-tax interest expense	67	65	89	80	76
Interest on retirement-related liability	9	8	7	6	3
Decrease/(Increase) in debt	4	(73)	(557)	181	(240)
Decrease/(Increase) in retirement-related liabilities	4	(2)	5	5	54
Minority interest	(86)	38	(34)	30	(136)
Common dividends	140	185	175	175	232
Decrease/(Increase) in share capital	0	0	0	0	0
Total financing flows	138	220	(317)	478	(10)

DEVELOP AN INTEGRATED HISTORICAL PERSPECTIVE

In developing a historical perspective, we first outline the competitive landscape of the beer industry, and then analyze where Heineken fits strategically and financially within this changing environment.

Industry Landscape

The beer industry has always been fragmented, regional and slow growing.[5] Over the five years to 1997, the worldwide market has grown 2.5 percent annually. It is expected to increase by another 2.6 percent per year from 1998 to 2010, most of which will come from growth in emerging markets (Exhibit 9.21).

---

[5] This analysis is based on the following article: R. Benson-Armer, J. Leibowitz, D. Ramachandran; "Global Beer: What's on Tap?" McKinsey Quarterly, no. 1 (1999), pp. 110–121.

Exhibit 9.18   Heineken—Historical Economic Profit

NLG million	1994	1995	1996	1997	1998
Return on invested capital (before goodwill)	15.0%	14.1%	18.0%	14.1%	15.3%
WACC	10.5%	9.6%	8.9%	8.3%	7.3%
Spread	4.5%	4.5%	9.1%	5.8%	7.9%
Invested capital (beginning of year)	4,587	4,911	4,914	5,995	6,150
Economic profit (before goodwill)	206	220	445	347	488
NOPLAT	690	693	885	847	939
Capital charge	(483)	(473)	(439)	(500)	(451)
Economic profit (before goodwill)	206	220	445	347	488
Return on invested capital (after goodwill)	13.5%	12.5%	15.7%	11.2%	12.0%
WACC	10.5%	9.6%	8.9%	8.3%	7.3%
Spread	3.0%	2.8%	6.8%	2.9%	4.6%
Invested capital (beginning of year)	5,109	5,561	5,636	7,556	7,842
Economic profit (after goodwill)	151	157	381	216	364
NOPLAT	690	693	885	847	939
Capital charge	(539)	(536)	(504)	(630)	(576)
Economic profit (after goodwill)	151	157	381	216	364

In 1998, the top four players had just a combined 20 percent of the worldwide market. This fragmentation is due in large part to regional oligopolies. Two or three players with a combined market share of 80 percent or more dominate most countries, though usually not the same players in each country (Exhibit 9.22). In addition, Heineken is one of only six brewers worldwide that in 1997 had at least 50 percent of sales originate outside the home country (Exhibit 9.23). Anheuser-Busch, on the other hand, is a more typical regional brewer with more than 85 percent of its sales coming from the United States.

Even as the major brewers have expanded outside their home markets, competition has remained local. This is largely due to consumer preference for local brands and tastes, high government tariffs, regulations, and limited opportunities for economies of scale or scope across national borders. As a result, when brewers have gone into new markets, they typically focus on transferring skills such as marketing rather than building globally integrated businesses. The dominance of local competition has slowed the pace of industry consolidation, as local brewers don't necessarily feel the need to sell their businesses to the majors to remain competitive.

As tastes converge, technology improves, transportation costs decline, and brewers learn to better leverage their expertise and brand names, the industry will slowly begin to reach consumers on a global scale. Heineken, Carlsberg, and Corona brands are already sold in at least 140 countries. At least 20 percent of the volume growth since 1990 of six of the top 10 breweries has come through

Exhibit 9.19   Heineken—Historical Operating Ratios

	1994	1995	1996	1997	1998
Adjusted EBITA/revenues					
Duties, levies, and trade taxes/revenues	13.6%	13.3%	13.3%	13.7%	13.1%
Cost of goods sold/revenues	54.6%	55.2%	55.4%	55.1%	53.9%
Personnel costs/revenues	16.9%	16.6%	17.8%	16.8%	16.6%
Depreciation/revenues	5.9%	5.3%	5.1%	5.5%	5.9%
Ret-rel liab adj/revenues	–0.1%	–0.1%	–0.1%	–0.1%	0.0%
Increase in provisions/revenues	–0.9%	0.0%	–1.7%	–0.7%	0.0%
Adjusted EBITA/revenues	10.0%	9.7%	10.1%	9.6%	10.6%
Return on invested capital (beg of yr)					
Net PPE/revenues	43.7%	45.0%	38.7%	40.7%	40.9%
Working capital/revenues	3.6%	3.2%	2.6%	4.4%	4.3%
Net other assets/revenues	–1.3%	–1.1%	–1.0%	–0.7%	–0.7%
Revenues/invested capital	2.2	2.1	2.5	2.3	2.2
Pre-tax ROIC	21.7%	20.6%	25.1%	21.7%	23.8%
Cash tax rate	30.8%	31.6%	28.1%	34.9%	35.7%
After-tax ROIC	15.0%	14.1%	18.0%	14.1%	15.3%
After-tax ROIC (incl. goodwill)	13.5%	12.5%	15.7%	11.2%	12.0%
Return on invested cap (avg)					
Net PPE/revenues	45.4%	45.1%	41.9%	41.3%	41.5%
Working capital/revenues	3.5%	3.1%	3.7%	4.4%	3.5%
Net other assets/revenues	–1.3%	–1.1%	–0.9%	–0.7%	–0.7%
Revenues/invested capital	2.1	2.1	2.2	2.2	2.3
Pre-tax ROIC	21.0%	20.6%	22.6%	21.4%	23.8%
After-tax ROIC	14.5%	14.1%	16.2%	13.9%	15.3%
After-tax ROIC (incl. goodwill)	12.9%	12.4%	13.4%	11.0%	11.6%
Growth rates					
Revenue growth rate	10.2%	4.7%	16.7%	10.9%	2.3%
Adjusted EBITA growth rate		1.8%	21.5%	5.6%	12.3%
NOPLAT growth rate		0.5%	27.6%	–4.3%	10.9%
Invested capital growth rate	7.1%	0.1%	22.0%	2.6%	–0.6%
Net income growth rate	27.6%	0.4%	–1.4%	16.2%	28.8%
Investment rates					
Gross investment rate	71.4%	44.7%	113.0%	56.6%	44.5%
Net investment rate	217.1%	160.8%	263.5%	194.2%	171.0%
Financing					
Coverage (adjusted EBITA/interest)	9.7	10.2	9.0	10.6	12.5
Cash coverage (gross CF/interest)	12.4	12.6	11.1	12.9	15.0
Debt/total cap (book)	14.2%	14.3%	11.5%	17.1%	19.4%
Debt/total cap (market)	7.3%	6.1%	8.5%	6.7%	4.2%
Average ROE	15.9%	14.6%	14.2%	15.8%	19.3%
Mkt val op inv cap/BV op inv cap	1.9	2.5	2.3	2.5	5.3
Mkt val op inv cap/adj EBITA	9.2	12.2	11.1	11.9	22.3

Exhibit 9.20   Heineken—Supporting Calculations

NLG million	1994	1995	1996	1997	1998
Change in working capital					
Increase in operating cash	31	5	36	30	6
Increase in accounts receivable	134	88	341	55	(57)
Increase in inventories	(3)	106	192	40	(30)
Increase in other current assets	44	3	118	7	4
(Increase) in accounts payable	(54)	(117)	(184)	(17)	(4)
(Increase) in other current liabilities	(172)	(101)	(230)	(110)	(144)
Net change in working capital	(19)	(16)	272	5	(225)
Capital expenditures					
Increase in net PPE	332	20	788	151	170
Depreciation	586	556	626	744	822
Capital expenditures (net of disposals)	919	575	1,414	895	992
Nonoperating cash flow					
Extraordinary Items	59	0	0	0	0
Change in restructuring provisions	0	0	0	0	0
Revaluation effect	(13)	(9)	139	134	(151)
Change in investments and advances	(105)	(92)	(100)	(107)	(135)
Nonoperating cash flow	(59)	(101)	39	28	(286)

Exhibit 9.21   Worldwide Beer Growth

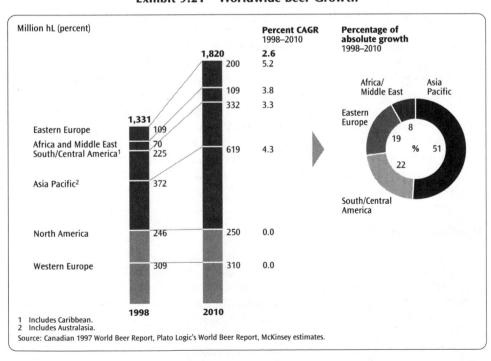

1 Includes Caribbean.
2 Includes Australasia.
Source: Canadian 1997 World Beer Report, Plato Logic's World Beer Report, McKinsey estimates.

Exhibit 9.22   National Market Share

Market Region	Top Players	Market Share (percent)
Netherlands	Heineken	51
	Grolsch	15
	Interbrew	14
United Kingdom	Scottish & Newcastle	27
	Bass	23
	Carlsberg	15
United States	Anheuser-Busch	47
	Miller	22
	Coors	11
Belgium	Interbrew	55
	Alken-Maes	15
Germany	Binding	9
	Brau & Brunnen	8
	Holsten	6
France	Kronenbourg	41
	Heineken	23
	Interbew	8
China	Yanjing	4
	Chocolate Products	3
	Tsingtao	3
South Africa	South African Breweries	98
Brazil	Brahma	48
	Antarctica	25
	Kaiser	17

1997

acquisitions (Exhibit 9.24). Miller, owned by Philip-Morris, started a price war in 1997, and it is continuing. Price competition will force companies to drive down costs, leverage brand names, and rationalize excess capacity.

There are two distinct strategies for brewers: They can specialize by focusing on a specific link in the value chain or become a geographic integrator. The specialization strategy involves breaking the industry business system into product development, brewing, packaging, distribution, and marketing, and subsequently becoming the global leader in one or two of these links. Guinness, for example, has focused on a product with a unique flavor that it exports from its home base with aggressive global marketing. Boston Beer Company runs a "virtual" beer company in which it controls product development and marketing but contracts out most production. Geographic integrators such as Heineken and Interbrew, on the other hand, purchase underperforming breweries or breweries in developing countries and apply best practices in brewing, distribution, and marketing.

Heineken's Financial Performance

To evaluate Heineken's financial performance, we compared its performance to that of other large, publicly traded beer companies using both stock market-based measures and underlying financial indicators. We compared Heineken to companies that produce mostly beer, as opposed to broader consumer goods companies where beer is just one of a host of products: Anheuser-Busch, Carlsberg, and South African Breweries. Exhibit 9.25 shows Heineken's size relative to its peers. Of these companies, Heineken is the second largest in revenues, at $7 billion in 1998. That is

Exhibit 9.23 Domestic/Non-Domestic Split of Sales

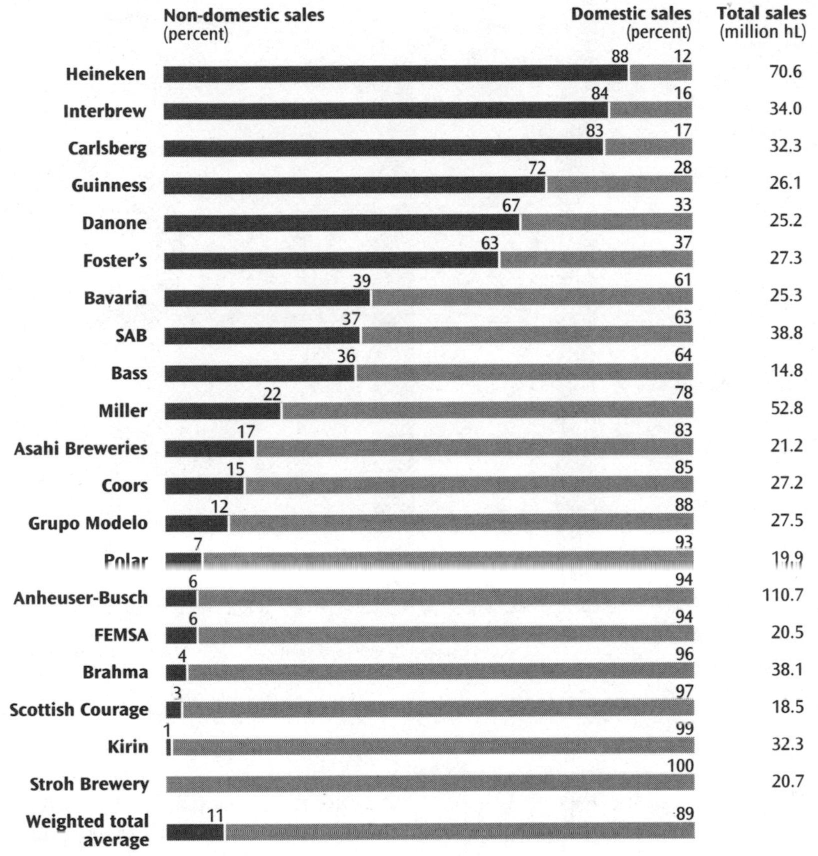

	Non-domestic sales (percent)	Domestic sales (percent)	Total sales (million hL)
Heineken	88	12	70.6
Interbrew	84	16	34.0
Carlsberg	83	17	32.3
Guinness	72	28	26.1
Danone	67	33	25.2
Foster's	63	37	27.3
Bavaria	39	61	25.3
SAB	37	63	38.8
Bass	36	64	14.8
Miller	22	78	52.8
Asahi Breweries	17	83	21.2
Coors	15	85	27.2
Grupo Modelo	12	88	27.5
Polar	7	93	19.9
Anheuser-Busch	6	94	110.7
FEMSA	6	94	20.5
Brahma	4	96	38.1
Scottish Courage	3	97	18.5
Kirin	1	99	32.3
Stroh Brewery		100	20.7
Weighted total average	11	89	

Source: Impact U.S. Beer Industry Report, 1997.

about half as large as Anheuser-Busch and marginally larger than South African Breweries. Heineken's 1998 EBITA is also second largest at $0.7 billion, but in this case only about a third as large as the leader, Anheuser-Busch.

Performance in the stock market We compared these companies using two indicators of stock market performance: total returns to shareholders and market value added. TRS includes share price appreciation and dividends and measures the wealth creation of companies during a specific time period.

Market value added compares the market value of a company (both debt and equity) to the amount of capital that has been invested in the company (fixed assets, working capital, and investments in intangibles from acquisitions) and measures the market's perception of wealth creation capability. Market value added can either be expressed as a ratio or as a dollar amount. We use a ratio to adjust for size differences.

Exhibit 9.24   Beer Industry M&A Activity

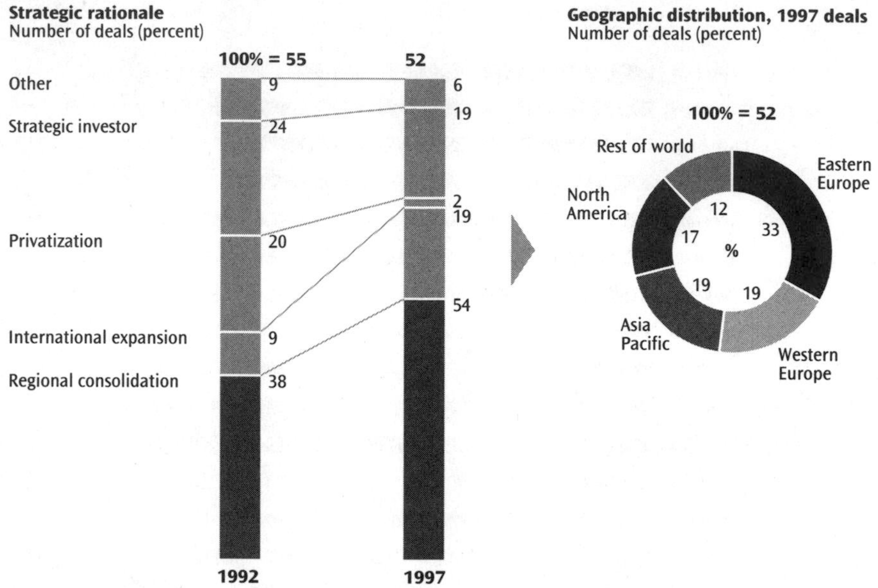

Strategic rationale
Number of deals (percent)

Geographic distribution, 1997 deals
Number of deals (percent)

	1992	1997
	100% = 55	52
Other	9	6
Strategic investor	24	19
Privatization	20	2 / 19
International expansion	9	54
Regional consolidation	38	

Geographic distribution: 100% = 52

- Eastern Europe 33
- Western Europe 19
- Asia Pacific 19
- North America 17
- Rest of world 12

Note: Regional consolidation captures deals in which acquirer purchases or increases stake in a regional competitor.
   International expansion captures deals in which companies pursue M&A as a means to enter a new market.
   Other includes share buy-backs and transactions to comply with legal regulations (e.g., ownership changes for antitrust during mergers, divestitures, etc.).
Source: SDC database; McKinsey analysis.

Heineken was the top performer among its peers in total returns to shareholders (Exhibit 9.26), when measured over the last one, three, and five years to 1998. Over the last five years, Heineken's shareholder returns have averaged 34 percent per year, much higher than Anheuser-Busch, at 25 percent. (These are in local currencies, not in a common currency. We tested total returns in U.S. dollars and found the relative performance to be the same.)

Heineken's market-to-book ratio is 3.3 and its market value added is $13 billion (Exhibit 9.27). This means that the market assigns a value of $3.30 for every dollar invested in the company. Heineken's market-to-book is about the same as that of

Exhibit 9.25   Relative Size of Leading Brewers

1998

Company	Revenues ($ billion)	EBITA	Operating[1] invested capital ($ billion)
Heineken	7.0	0.7	3.1
Anheuser-Busch	13.2	2.1	8.4
Carlsberg	4.4	0.3	1.8
South African Breweries	6.3	0.6	2.4

1 Excludes goodwill.

Exhibit 9.26 Total Returns to Shareholders

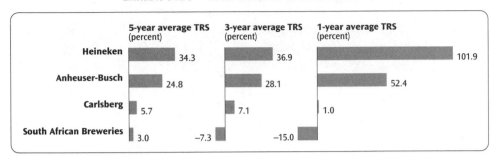

Busch and much higher than Carlsberg or South African Breweries. Heineken's market value added is much less than Busch because it is a smaller company.

Considering both market-to-book and returns to shareholders, we conclude that Heineken is not only perceived as a strong performer, but has been clearly exceeding market expectations. Busch, while valued highly, probably hasn't beaten market expectations in the five years to 1998. Carlsberg is a clear underachiever both in perceived performance and relative to market expectations. South African Breweries is harder to evaluate, given that its performance is heavily influenced by the decline of the South African currency, the rand.

Underlying financial performance   The performance of the companies in the stock market has been consistent with their underlying financial performance. Exhibit 9.28 summarizes the underlying growth and returns on capital. Anheuser-Busch's higher market-to-book is primarily driven by a greater ROIC, 16.1 percent in 1998 versus 11.6 percent for Heineken. (The companies have roughly comparable costs of capital. Our sense is that the market expects future ROICs to be in line with historical performance.) Heineken has grown faster,[6] which is partly due

Exhibit 9.27   Market-to-Book Value

Company	MV of debt and equity ($ billion)	Adjusted BV of investor funds ($ billion)	Market value added ($ billion)	Market to book value ($ billion)
Heineken	19.0	5.7	13.3	3.3
Anheuser-Busch	36.5	10.8	25.7	3.4
Carlsberg	4.8	3.5	1.3	1.4
South African Breweries	7.9	3.5	4.4	2.3

Average exchange rates for 1998 to the US dollar: Guilder – 0.51, Kroner – 0.15, Rand – 0.18.

[6] Anheuser-Busch growth and ROIC figures are for continuing operations only. They are adjusted for 1995 and 1996 restructurings, including the company's sale of Earthgrains Company, Eagle Snacks, and the St. Louis Cardinals baseball team.

Exhibit 9.28   Growth and Returns on Capital

Percent

Company	Average growth 1994–1998		ROIC[1]		
	Revenues	EBITA	Before goodwill 1998	After goodwill 1998	After goodwill 1994–1998
Heineken	8.5	12.9	15.3	11.6	12.3
Anheuser-Busch	3.1	3.2	17.0	16.1	15.2
Carlsberg	14.7	5.2	6.7	5.5	10.0
South African Breweries	10.2	11.1	21.8	21.4	21.0

1 Based on average invested capital.

to acquisitions. Carlsberg has been growing quickly, but its return on capital has been declining, touching 5.5 percent in 1998. South African Breweries is an interesting case. The company has the highest ROIC—21.4 percent in 1998—yet a low market-to-book. This is primarily because high interest rates in South Africa (risk-free rates in the 15 percent to 20 percent range) result in an elevated cost of capital.

Exhibit 9.29 breaks down into its components 1998 ROIC for Heineken and its peers. Heineken underperforms its competitors in operating margin, but

Exhibit 9.29   Decomposition of Return on Invested Capital[1]

1998

Company	Operating expenses/ revenue (percent)	Depreciation/ revenue (percent)	Operating margin (percent)
Heineken	83.6	5.9	10.6
Anheuser-Busch	74.5	6.6	18.9
Carlsberg	85.6	5.9	8.5
South African Breweries	82.4	4.4	12.8
Average	81.5	5.7	12.7

Company	Working capital/ revenue (percent)	Net PPE/ revenue (percent)	Other assets/ revenue (percent)	Capital turnover
Heineken	3.5	41.5	−0.7	2.3
Anheuser-Busch	0.0	69.4	5.3	1.3
Carlsberg	2.0	53.2	(0.8)	1.8
South African Breweries	12.7	29.8	0.1	2.3
Average	4.6	48.5	1.0	1.9

Company	Operating margin (percent)	Capital turnover	1 – Cash tax rate (percent)	After-tax return on invested capital (before goodwill) (percent)
Heineken	10.6	2.3	64.3	15.3
Anheuser-Busch	18.9	1.3	67.3	17.0
Carlsberg	8.5	1.8	43.1	6.7
South African Breweries	11.3	2.3	73.4	21.8
Average	12.7	1.9	62.0	15.2

1 ROIC before goodwill.

Exhibit 9.30   Heineken N.V. Historical ROIC versus WACC, 1994–1998[1]

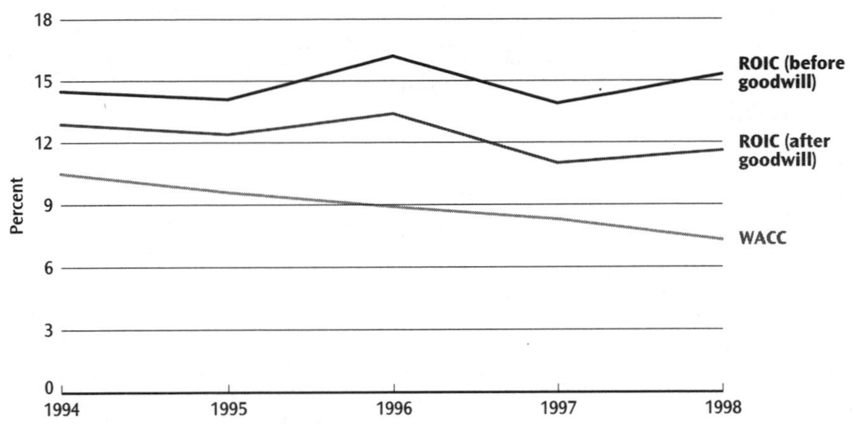

1 Based on average capital.

outperforms them in capital turnover. We hypothesize that Heineken's operating margin is less than Busch's because it is spending more on marketing, which in turn has contributed to a higher growth rate.

In the five years to 1998, Heineken's spread between ROIC and WACC increased from 4.5 percent in 1994 to 7.9 percent, as shown on Exhibit 9.30. This has been primarily due to declining interest rates and the resulting reduction in WACC.

Financial health from a credit perspective   Heineken has a conservative capital structure policy. While it took on significant debt in 1996 to fund acquisitions, its debt-to-total capital has remained low at 19 percent on an accounting basis and 4 percent in market value terms (Exhibit 9.31). At 12.5 times interest, Heineken is substantially less leveraged than its competitors in interest coverage (adjusted EBITA/interest expense). Heineken's interest coverage has been increasing and will continue to do so as it generates much more cash flow than it can reinvest. One could speculate that Heineken is significantly under-leveraged, resulting in a higher cost of capital than necessary.

Exhibit 9.31   Credit Ratios

1998 ($ million)

Company	Adjusted EBITA	Interest expense	Adjusted EBITA/ interest expense	Gross cash flow/ interest expense	Debt to market value of investor funds
Heineken	741	59	12.5	15.1	4.4%
Anheuser-Busch	2,125	266	8.0	8.2	14.3%
Carlsberg	280	87	3.2	3.6	22.9%
South African Breweries	635	112	5.7	6.2	13.3%

10

Estimating the
Cost of Capital

Both creditors and shareholders expect to be compensated for the opportunity cost of investing their funds in one particular business instead of others with equivalent risk. The weighted average cost of capital (WACC) is the discount rate, or time value of money, used to convert expected future free cash flow into present value for all investors.[1] The bull market of the late 1990s directed attention to the importance of estimating an appropriate cost of capital.

The most important general principle to recognize when estimating a WACC is that it must be consistent with the overall valuation approach and with the definition of the cash flow to be discounted. To be consistent with the enterprise DCF approach, the estimate of the cost of capital must:

- Comprise a weighted average of the costs of all sources of capital— debt, equity, and so on—since the free cash flow represents cash available to all providers of capital.
- Be computed after corporate taxes, since the free cash flow is stated after taxes.
- Use nominal rates of return built up from real rates and expected inflation, because the expected free cash flow is expressed in nominal terms (or real rates if inflationary effects are appropriately removed from the cash flows that are being forecasted).

---

[1] In Chapter 8, we described the adjusted present value model, where free cash flow is discounted at the unlevered cost of equity to arrive at an enterprise value before the tax benefit of debt. You can use the principles described in this chapter to estimate a levered cost of equity and convert it to an unlevered cost of equity using the formulas in Chapter 8 and the appendix at the end of the book.

- Adjust for the systematic risk borne by each provider of capital, since each expects a return that compensates for the risk taken.
- Employ market value weights for each financing element, because market values reflect the true economic claim of each type of financing outstanding, whereas book values usually do not.
- Be subject to change across the cash flow forecast period, because of expected changes in inflation, systematic risk, or capital structure.

FORMULA FOR ESTIMATING THE WACC

The general formula for estimating the after-tax WACC is simply the weighted average of the marginal after-tax cost of each source of capital:

$$\text{WACC} = k_b\,(1-T_c)\,(B/V) + k_p\,(P/V) + k_s\,(S/V)$$

where k_b = The pretax market expected yield to maturity on noncallable, nonconvertible debt

T_c = The marginal tax rate for the entity being valued[2]

B = The market value of interest-bearing debt

V = The market value of the enterprise being valued ($V = B + P + S$)

k_p = The after-tax cost of capital for noncallable, nonconvertible preferred stock (which equals the pretax cost of preferred stock when no deduction is made from corporate taxes for preferred dividends)

P = The market value of the preferred stock

k_s = The market-determined opportunity cost of equity capital

S = The market value of equity

We have included only three types of capital (nonconvertible, noncallable debt; nonconvertible, noncallable preferred stock; and equity) in this formula. The actual weighting scheme may be more complex, because a separate market value weight is required for each source of capital that involves cash payments, now or in the future. Other possible items include leases (operating and capital), subsidized debt (for example, industrial revenue bonds), convertible or callable debt, convertible or callable preferred stock, minority interests, and/or warrants and executive stock options. A wide variety of unusual securities—for example, income bonds, bonds with

---

[2] The marginal tax rate is the rate applied to a marginal dollar of interest expense. It is usually the statutory rate. If the company has substantial tax loss carry-forwards or carry-backs, or faces bankruptcy so that its tax shields may never be used, the marginal rate can be lower than the statutory rate—even zero.

payments tied to commodity indexes, and bonds that are extendable, put-table, or retractable—may also be included.[3]

The approach we describe in this chapter provides a technically correct estimation of WACC. Estimating the costs for many sources of capital is not very precise and the specific instruments used by the company will change. In practice, we often make simplifying assumptions. For example, we rarely distinguish between callable and noncallable debt in a company's capital structure because the cost differences are small and it is impossible to say what the mix of these instruments will be.

Non-interest-bearing liabilities, such as accounts payable, are excluded from the calculation of WACC to avoid inconsistencies and simplify the valuation. Non-interest-bearing liabilities have a cost of capital, just like other forms of debt, but this cost is implicit in the price paid for the goods generating the liability and shows up in the company's operating costs and free cash flow. Separating the implied financing costs of these liabilities from operating costs and free cash flow would be complex and time-consuming without improving the valuation.

The balance of this chapter describes the three related steps involved in developing the discount rate, or WACC:

1. Developing market value weights for the capital structure.
2. Estimating the opportunity cost of nonequity financing.
3. Estimating the opportunity cost of equity financing.

As a practical matter, the three are performed simultaneously.

STEP 1: DEVELOP MARKET VALUE WEIGHTS

The first step in developing an estimate of the WACC is to determine a capital structure for the company you are valuing. This provides the market value weights for the WACC formula.

The theoretically correct approach to capital structure is to use a different WACC for each year that reflects the capital structure for the year. In practice, we usually use one WACC for the entire forecast.[4] We also think in terms of a target capital structure rather than the current capital structure because at any point a company's capital structure may not reflect the capital structure expected to prevail over the life of the business. Capital structure

---

[3] See Chapter 20 on "option pricing" for a discussion of the cost of capital for callable, convertible debt.

[4] If anticipated changes in capital structure are expected to significantly affect the value of the company, you should consider using the APV approach described in Chapter 8 or adjust the WACC each year.

might be affected by recent changes in the market value of the securities out-standing and the "lumpiness" of financing activities, particularly those in-volving securities offerings. Moreover, management may have plans to change the capital mix as an active policy decision. All these factors mean that future financing levels could be different from current or past levels.

The second reason for using a target capital structure is that it solves the problem of circularity involved in estimating the WACC. This circularity arises because we need to know market value weights to determine the WACC, but we cannot know the market value weights without knowing what the market value is in the first place—especially the market value of equity. To determine the value of equity, which is the objective of the valua-tion process itself, we must discount the expected free cash flow at the WACC. In essence, we cannot know the WACC without knowing the market value of equity, and we cannot know the market value of equity without knowing the WACC.

One way out of this circularity problem is to simply iterate between the weights used in the WACC and the resulting value of equity. The second ap-proach is to work with the idea of a target capital structure, which will not be affected by changes in the value of the company and which also avoids incorrect conclusions about the impact of capital structure on value.

To develop a target capital structure for a company, we suggest using a combination of three approaches:

1. Estimate the current market value-based capital structure of the company.
2. Review the capital structure of comparable companies.
3. Review management's explicit or implicit approach to financing the business and its implications for the target capital structure.

Estimating Current Capital Structure

Where possible, you should estimate market values of the elements of the current capital structure and review how they have changed. The best ap-proach is to identify the values of the capital structure elements directly from their prices in the marketplace. If a company's common stock and debt are publicly traded, simply multiply the number of each type of outstanding se-curity by its respective price in the marketplace. Most of the difficulty arises because sources of funds often are not traded in a marketplace where we can observe their prices directly.

Be prepared to deal with these categories of financing: debt-type fi-nancing; equity-linked/hybrid financing; minority interests, and preferred and common equity financing. In the paragraphs that follow, we provide guidance on how to estimate values when market prices for the specific fi-nancing sources of the company are not available.

Debt-type financing   Financing forms in this category normally obligate the company to make a series of payments to the holders of the outstanding instruments, according to a payment schedule stipulated in the financing documents. Interest, coupon, or dividend payments may be fixed or variable. In this category fall short-term and long-term debt, leases, and some preferred stock. Their value depends on three factors: the agreed-upon payment schedule, the likelihood the borrower will make the payments as promised, and the market interest rates for securities with a similar pattern of expected payments.

Generally, their market value can be approximated without difficulty. The process is as follows:

1. Identify the contractually promised payments. Is the financing instrument a variable-rate note with interest determined each six months at a fixed spread over the prime rate, or a 20-year zero-coupon bond?

2. Determine the credit quality of the instrument to be valued. Credit ratings are often available for even illiquid issues, or can be estimated from ratings on other company borrowings (adjusting for the security of the specific instrument in bankruptcy) or from bond rating models that attempt to mimic the behavior of the rating agencies.[5] Estimate the yield to maturity for which the instrument would trade were it publicly traded, by reference to market yields on securities with equivalent coupons, maturities, and ratings.

3. Calculate the present value of the stream of financing payments, using the yield to maturity on an equivalent issue as the discount rate. The resulting present value should approximate the market value. (This is equivalent to discounting expected payments at the expected market equilibrium rate of return.)

This approach will work well in most cases, but a few special situations might call for a different approach.

- *Option features.* Interest rate option features such as "caps," "floors," and call provisions have an effect on future payments, depending on the level of interest rates. They therefore affect the value of the security that contains them. There are two approaches to adjust for these features. The first is to find a comparable security with a similar feature and use it as a proxy. The second is to use an option-pricing approach to estimate the value of the option feature separately (see Chapter 20).

---

[5] The Alcar Group markets a software package and database service that estimates bond ratings using standard financial ratios.

- *Swaps.* Many companies enter into interest-rate and currency swap agreements that change the duration and/or currency profile of their financing. Swaps are off-balance-sheet transactions that are disclosed in the footnotes to the financial statements. They are also sometimes used by corporations to speculate on interest rates. A company could have a debt swap outstanding even though it is financed entirely with common equity.

  For valuation purposes, swaps should be treated in the same way as any other financing instruments, with the promised cash flow in the agreement valued at the prevailing market rate. This can be a complicated and nearly impossible to do without specific information about the swap instruments themselves.

  If you can associate a swap with a specific outstanding instrument, you should estimate the value of the "synthetic" security that the combination of the security plus swap creates. A company may have issued floating-rate debt and entered into an interest-rate swap that converts it to a five-year fixed-rate instrument. In this case, estimate the value of the five-year instrument using the standard procedure noted earlier.

- *Foreign currency obligations.* If a company has financing outstanding in a currency other than its home currency, the value of this financing will need to be stated in terms of the company's home currency. This involves a two-step process. First, value the debt in foreign currency terms according to the standard procedure. Second, translate the resulting foreign currency market value into the home currency by using the spot foreign exchange rate. If a U.S. company has issued 10-year Swiss franc bonds, it would determine the market value of the bonds in Swiss francs, using Swiss interest rates for equivalent issues (if necessary), and then translate the result into current U.S. dollars.

- *Leases.* Leases substitute for other forms of debt and can therefore be treated like debt. Standard accounting principles divide leases into two classes: capital leases and operating leases. Capital leases, as defined by the Financial Accounting Standards Board, are essentially those that transfer most of the ownership risk of the asset to the lessee. All other leases are considered operating leases.

  Capital leases are accounted for as if the lessee had purchased the asset and borrowed the funds. The present value of the lease payments is added to the company's assets with other fixed assets and to the liability side of the balance sheet alongside other debt. Operating leases do not appear on the balance sheet, and the lease payments are included with other operating costs. While the accounting treatment of capital and operating leases differs, the economics of the two types of leases is often similar. Some companies carefully structure leases to keep them off the balance sheet, but the accounting treatment should not drive your valuation analysis.

Since capital leases are already shown as debt on the balance sheet, their market value can be estimated just like other debt. Operating leases may also be treated like other forms of debt. The market value of an operating lease is the present value of the required future lease payments (excluding the portion of the lease payment for maintenance) discounted at a rate that reflects the riskiness to the lessee of the particular lease. (Required future lease payments on both capital and operating leases are disclosed in the financial statement footnotes if they are significant.)

If operating leases are not significant, don't bother to treat them as debt. Leave them out of the capital structure and keep the lease payments as an operating cost.

Equity-linked/hybrid financing   Companies commonly have, in addition to fixed-income obligations, financing that has all or part of its return linked to the value of all or part of the business. These financing forms include warrants, employee stock options, convertible debt, and convertible preferred stock. When these securities are traded, their market value should be determined from their current market prices. When they are not traded, estimating their market value is more difficult than is the case with the fixed-income obligations.

- *Warrants and employee stock options.* Usually warrants represent the right to buy a set number of shares of the company's equity at a predetermined price. They can also be warrants to purchase other types of securities, such as preferred stock or additional debt. Warrants are essentially long-term options having an original issue exercise period of five to ten years, with a strike price equal to the price the holder would pay, on exercise, to acquire the underlying security. Since they are options, warrants should be valued using option-pricing approaches. If the company you are valuing has a large number of warrants or employee stock options outstanding, their cost should be included in the company's WACC.

- *Convertible securities.* Convertible securities represent a combination of straight, nonconvertible financing and a specified number of warrants that comprise the conversion feature. Their value and true opportunity cost cannot be determined properly without recognizing the value of the conversion feature (warrant). The stated interest rate on these issues is lower than on straight-debt equivalents because the conversion feature has value. Investors are willing to pay for this value by foregoing the higher yield available on nonconvertible securities. The deeper in the money it is, the lower the traded yield, and vice versa. Since each convertible bond is a portfolio of straight debt and warrants, the true opportunity cost is higher than for straight debt but lower than for equity. To deal with convertible securities in a company's capital structure, follow an approach similar to the one used for warrants.

Minority interests   Minority interests represent claims by outside shareholders on a portion of a company's business. Minority interests usually arise after an acquisition when the acquiring company does not purchase all of the target company's shares outstanding. They can also arise if the company sells a minority stake in one of its subsidiaries to a third party.

The treatment of minority interests depends on the information available. If the minority shares are publicly traded, then their approximate value can be determined directly from the market prices for the shares. If, as is more often the case, the shares are not traded, then theoretically we should value the subsidiary separately using the discounted free cash flow valuation approach and compute the value of the minority stake according to the percentage of the subsidiary's shares the minority shareholders own.

If information about the subsidiary's free cash flow cannot be developed, then the value of the minority stake could be approximated by applying price-to-earnings or market-to-book ratios for similar companies to the minority's share of income or net assets. Both of these items are disclosed in the financial statements—sometimes separately for each subsidiary in which a minority interest exists.

Preferred stock   Holders of preferred stock receive preferred dividends perpetually. In bankruptcy, payments to preferred shareholders are subordinate to those of bondholders, but senior to payments to equity holders. Preferred stock is riskier than debt but less risky than equity, and its cost of capital will be between these two extremes. If the preferred stock is not callable or convertible then the cost of preferred can be estimated by dividing the annual dividends by the current stock price.

Common equity   If a traded market for the company's common shares exists, follow the familiar approach of using current market price multiplied by the number of shares outstanding.

If a traded market does not exist, you can develop an implied equity value by testing alternative values for the equity and the implications they would have for the market value weights in the WACC computation. These alternative weights can be used to develop estimates of the cost of capital, and can be refined through iterations. When the value of equity used in the WACC formula is approximately equal to the discounted cash flow value of equity produced by applying the discount rate to the free cash flows and the continuing value, then you have an implied economic capital structure for the business.

Review the Capital Structure of Comparable Companies

In addition to estimating the market-value-based capital structure of the company, also review the capital structures of comparable companies. The benefits are:

- It will help you understand whether your current estimate of capital structure is unusual. For the company's capital structure to be different is perfectly acceptable, but you should understand the reasons why it is or is not. For instance, is the company by philosophy more aggressive or innovative in the use of nonequity financing, or is the current capital structure only a temporary deviation from a more conservative target? Often, companies finance acquisitions with debt that they plan to pay down rapidly or refinance with a stock offering in the next year. Alternatively, is there anything different about the company's cash flow or asset intensity that means that its target capital structure can or should be fundamentally different from those of comparable companies?

- Another reason for reviewing comparable companies is a more practical one. In some cases you cannot directly estimate the current financing mix for the company. For privately held or thinly traded companies, or for divisions of a publicly traded company, a market-based estimate of the current value of equity many not be available. In these situations, use comparables to help assess the reasonableness of the estimate of the target proportion of equity development through the iterative process described in the previous section.

Review Management's Financing Philosophy

Where possible, try to determine whether the company's managers have an explicit or implicit target capital structure that is different from the current capital structure. If the managers' target is different than the current capital structure, use it if you believe that it is realistic and achievable within the next few years.

STEP 2: ESTIMATE THE COST OF NONEQUITY FINANCING

In this section we discuss approaches to estimating market opportunity costs for financing forms that do not have explicit equity features. These include the following:

- Straight investment-grade debt (fixed and variable rate).
- Below-investment-grade debt (for example, junk bonds).
- Subsidized debt (for example, industrial revenue bonds).
- Foreign-currency-denominated debt.
- Leases (capital leases, operating leases).
- Straight preferred stock.

Straight Investment-Grade Debt

If the company has straight debt that is not convertible into other securities—like common stock—and that is not callable, then we can use discounted cash flow analysis to estimate the market rate of return and the market value of the debt. For investment-grade debt, the risk of bankruptcy is low. Therefore, yield to maturity is usually a reasonable estimate of the opportunity cost.

The coupon rate—that is, the historical (or imbedded) cost of debt—is irrelevant for determining the current cost of capital. Always use the most current market rate on debt of equivalent risk. A reasonable proxy for the risk of debt is Moody's or Standard & Poor's bond rating. If the bond rating is not available, calculate traditional financial ratios—times-interest-earned, debt-to-equity, and so on—to compare the entity you are valuing with known firms.

Most companies have variable-rate debt, either acquired through swaps, as an original security issue, or in the form of revolving bank loans. If the variable-rate loan has no cap or floor, then use the long-term rate, because the short-term rate will be rolled over and the geometric average of the expected short-term rates is equal to the long-term rate. If the variable-rate debt has a cap or floor, or if the interest payment is determined as a moving average of past rates, then an option is involved and the problem becomes more complicated. For example, if market rates have risen and a variable rate loan is "capped out," then it becomes a subsidized form of financing that adds value to the company.

Below-Investment-Grade Debt

When dealing with debt that is less than investment grade, be aware of the difference between the expected yield to maturity and the promised yield to maturity. The promised yield to maturity assumes that all payments (coupons and principal) will be made as promised by the issuer. Consider the following simple example: A three-year bond promises to pay a 10 percent coupon at the end of each year, plus a face value of $1,000 at the end of the third year. The current market value of the bond is $951.96. What is the yield to maturity? It can be computed by solving the following formula:

$$B_0 = \sum_{t=1}^{3} \frac{Coupon_t}{(1+y)^t} + \frac{Face}{(1+y)^3}$$

Where B_0 = The current market value of noncallable, nonconvertible debt
Coupon = The promised coupon paid at the end of time period t
Face = The face value of the bond, promised at maturity
y = The promised yield to maturity

The solution is $y = 12$ percent. This promised yield to maturity assumes that the debt is default-free. Suppose that there is a 5 percent chance that the bond will default and pay only $400.

If we were to rewrite the formula, putting the bond's expected payments rather than its promised payments in the numerator, we could calculate the market's expected rate of return as opposed to the promised rate of return implicit in the yield to maturity. As recomputed, the market expected rate of return on the risky debt would be 11.09 percent. The rate of return that the market expects to earn is 91 basis points lower than the promised yield to maturity. The promised yields on junk bonds are very different (frequently much higher) from the expected yields that the market anticipates on these risky securities.

Our problem is that we need to compute the expected yield to maturity, not the quoted, promised yield. We can do this if we have the current market price of the low-grade bond and estimates of its expected default rate and value in default. The necessary data are usually unavailable. Default rates on original issue corporate bonds in the United States are given in Exhibit 10.1. Original issue junk bonds (those with the lowest rating of CCC) have large default rates after a period of time (26.7 percent after 5 years, and 37.7 percent after 10 years).

Exhibit 10.1   Mortality Losses by Original Rating

1971–1999 (% of principal)	Years after issuance									
	1	2	3	4	5	6	7	8	9	10
AAA	0.00	0.00	0.00	0.00	0.01	0.01	0.01	0.01	0.01	0.01
AA	0.00	0.00	0.07	0.15	0.15	0.15	0.15	0.15	0.17	0.19
A	0.00	0.00	0.02	0.08	0.12	0.19	0.21	0.28	0.32	0.32
BBB	0.02	0.19	0.33	0.66	0.76	1.01	1.15	1.19	1.24	1.44
BB	0.25	0.70	2.68	3.91	5.05	5.92	6.98	7.12	7.90	9.52
B	0.67	2.65	6.97	10.91	13.90	15.72	17.24	18.39	19.05	19.60
CCC	1.02	12.00	21.39	25.30	26.68	31.52	33.98	35.75	35.75	37.73

Source: E. Altman, *Defaults & Returns on High Yield Bonds: Analysis Through 1998 & Default Outlook for 1999-2000*, New York University Salomon Center, January 1999.

If the necessary data are not available, use the yield to maturity on BBB-rated debt, which reduces most of the effects of the difference between promised and expected yields.

Although the promised yield to maturity is not equivalent to the opportunity cost of capital for debt with high default risk, it can serve as a useful proxy for the market's estimate of default risk. Exhibit 10.2 shows the relationship between promised yields to maturity and maturity periods for portfolios of bonds varying in risk from default-free U.S. government obligations (U.S. Treasury strips) to CCC-rated corporate debentures.

Subsidized Debt

The coupon rate on subsidized debt such as industrial revenue bonds is below the market rate for taxable bonds of equivalent risk because they are tax-free to investors. The cost of capital for this type of debt is their current market yield to maturity, where known. If the bonds are not traded, their yield can be estimated by reference to similarly rated tax-free issues that are actively traded (or from similar new issues of tax-exempt debt).

Foreign-Currency-Denominated Debt

When an obligation is denominated in a foreign currency, the local currency nominal rate of return is usually an inappropriate measure of the actual cost of capital to the issuer in its home currency. This is due to the foreign exchange exposure inherent in the financing.

When a company issues foreign-currency-denominated debt, its effective cost equals the after-tax cost of repaying the principal and interest in

Exhibit 10.2   Promised Yields versus Bond Ratings

June 1999 (percent)

	Risk-free rate	AAA	AA	A	BBB	BB	B
3 months	4.90	5.18	5.21	5.32	5.70	6.18	7.39
6 months	5.00	5.53	5.56	5.70	6.04	6.64	7.78
1 year	5.34	5.74	5.78	5.90	6.30	6.86	7.99
2 years	5.67	6.03	6.06	6.18	6.66	7.47	8.43
5 years	5.92	6.39	6.43	6.61	7.03	8.00	8.83
10 years	6.19	6.64	6.73	6.82	7.33	8.74	9.86
15 years	6.36	6.92	6.97	7.12	7.65	8.87	10.07
20 years	6.37	6.99	7.05	7.29	7.73	8.88	10.30
25 years	6.29	7.03	7.09	7.34	7.81	9.02	10.39
30 years	6.22	6.96	7.07	7.31	7.80	9.01	10.28

Source: Bloomberg Business News.

terms of the company's local currency. Usually the all-in cost of borrowing in foreign currency will be close to the cost of borrowing in domestic markets because of the interest-rate parity relationship enforced by the active arbitrage of issuers, investors, and intermediaries in the cash, forward exchange, and currency swap markets.

The interest-rate parity relationship (leaving minor transaction costs and temporary, small arbitrage opportunities aside) generally guarantees the following relationship (further explained in Chapter 17):

$$1 + k_b = (X_o / X_f)(1 + r_o)$$

where k_b = The domestic pretax cost of N-year debt
X_o = The spot foreign exchange rate (units of foreign currency per dollar)
X_f = The N-year forward foreign exchange rate (units of foreign currency per dollar)
r_o = The foreign interest rate on an N-year bond

To illustrate, suppose that your domestic borrowing rate is 7.25 percent and that the rate on a one-year loan denominated in Swiss francs is 4 percent. How would these rates compare? If the spot exchange rate is 1.543 francs per dollar, and the one-year forward rate is 1.4977 francs per dollar, then the equivalent domestic one-year borrowing rate is 7.15 percent for the Swiss franc loan.

$$1 + k_b = [1.543 / 1.4977] \; (1 + 0.04)$$
$$= 1.0715 \text{ or } k_b = 7.15\%$$

Although we can use forward-rate contracts to estimate equivalent domestic rates for relatively short-term debt (less than 18 months), no easily referenced forward markets exist farther out. For longer-term borrowing, we recommend that you assume the domestic equivalent rate is roughly equal to the actual domestic rate.

Leases

Leases, both capital and operating, are substitutes for other types of debt. It is reasonable in most cases to assume that their opportunity cost is the same as for the company's other long-term debt.

Straight Preferred Stock

The cost of preferred stock that is perpetual, noncallable, and nonconvertible can be calculated as follows:

$$k_p = \frac{\text{div}}{P}$$

where k_p = The cost of preferred stock
    div = The promised dividend on the preferred stock
     P = The market price of the preferred stock

If the current market price is not available, use yields on similar-quality issues as an estimate. For a fixed-life or callable preferred stock issue, estimate the opportunity cost by using the same approach as for a comparable debt instrument. In other words, estimate the yield that equates the expected stream of payments with the market value. For convertible preferred issues, option-pricing approaches are necessary.

STEP 3: ESTIMATE THE COST OF EQUITY FINANCING

The opportunity cost of equity financing is the most difficult to estimate because we can't directly observe it in the market. We recommend using the capital asset pricing model (CAPM) or the arbitrage pricing model (APM). Both approaches have problems associated with their application, including measurement difficulty. Many other approaches to estimating the cost of equity are conceptually flawed. The dividend yield model (defined as the dividend per share divided by the stock price) and the earnings-to-price ratio model substantially understate the cost of equity by ignoring expected growth.

The Capital Asset Pricing Model

The CAPM is discussed at length in all modern finance texts (for example, see Brealey and Myers, 1999, or Copeland and Weston, 1992).[6] These detailed discussions will not be reproduced here. (In this section, we assume that you are generally familiar with the principles that underlie the approach.) The CAPM postulates that the opportunity cost of equity is equal to the return on risk-free securities plus the company's systematic risk (beta) multiplied by the market price of risk (market risk premium). The equation for the cost of equity (k_s) is as follows:

---

[6] T. Copeland and J. Weston, *Financial Theory and Corporate Policy*, 3rd ed. (Reading, MA: Addison-Wesley, 1992); and R. Brealey and S. Myers, *Principles of Corporate Finance*, 5th ed. (New York: McGraw-Hill, 1999).

$$k_s = r_f + [E(r_m) - r_f]\,(\text{beta})$$

where r_f = The risk-free rate of return
$\quad E(r_m)$ = The expected rate of return on the overall market portfolio
$E(r_m) - r_f$ = The market risk premium
$\quad\quad$ beta = The systematic risk of the equity

The CAPM is illustrated in Exhibit 10.3. The cost of equity, k_s, increases linearly as a function of the measured undiversifiable risk, beta. The beta for the entire market portfolio is 1.0. This means that the average company's equity beta will also be about 1.0. It is very unusual to observe a beta greater than 2.0 or less than 0.3. The market risk premium (the price of risk) is measured as the slope of the CAPM line in Exhibit 10.3, that is, the slope is $E(r_m) - r_f$.

To carry out the CAPM approach, we need to estimate the three factors that determine the CAPM line: the risk-free rate, the market risk premium, and the systematic risk (beta). The balance of this section describes a recommended approach for estimating each.

Determining the risk-free rate Hypothetically, the risk-free rate is the return on a security or portfolio of securities that has no default risk and is completely uncorrelated with returns on anything else in the economy. In theory, the best estimate of the risk-free rate would be the return on a zero-beta portfolio, constructed of long and short positions in equities in a way that produces the minimum variance zero-beta portfolio. Because of the cost and complexity of constructing minimum variance zero-beta portfolios, they are not practical for estimating the risk-free rate.

We have three reasonable alternatives that use government securities: the rate for Treasury bills, the rate for 10-year Treasury bonds, and the rate

Exhibit 10.3   The Capital Asset Pricing Model

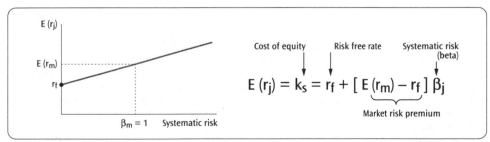

for 30-year Treasury bonds. We recommend using a 10-year Treasury-bond rate for several reasons:[7]

- It is a long-term rate that usually comes close to matching the duration of the cash flow of the company being valued. Since the current Treasury-bill rate is a short-term rate, it does not match duration properly. If we were to use short-term rates, the appropriate choice would be the short-term rates that are expected to apply in each future period, not today's short-term interest rate. The 10-year rate is a geometric weighted average estimate of the expected short-term Treasury-bill rates.

- The 10-year rate approximates the duration of the stock market index portfolio—for example, the S&P 500—and its use is therefore consistent with the betas and market risk premiums estimated relative to these market portfolios.[8]

- The 10-year rate is less susceptible to two problems involved in using a longer-term rate, such as the 30-year Treasury-bond rate. Its price is less sensitive to unexpected changes in inflation, and so has a smaller beta than the 30-year rate. Also, the liquidity premium built into 10-year rates may be slightly lower than that of 30-year bonds. These are technical details, with a minor impact in normal circumstances. But they do argue for using a 10-year bond rate.[9]

Determining the market risk premium   The market risk premium (the price of risk) is the difference between the expected rate of return on the market portfolio and the risk-free rate, $E(r_m) - r_f$. The market risk premium is one of the most vexing issues in finance. It can be based on either historical data, assuming that the future will be like the past, or on ex ante estimates that attempt to forecast the future. Both approaches have their proponents and critics.

In early 2000, we were recommending using a 4½ percent to 5 percent historically estimated market risk premium for U.S. companies. Depending on the period chosen and the type of average, historically based estimates of the market risk premium can vary from about 3 percent to almost 8 percent,

---

[7] Theoretically, you should use a distinct WACC for each year's projected cash flows based on the yield curve for risk-free securities. This is rarely done in practice, but should be considered when the cash flows are heavily front-end or back-end loaded or when the yield curve is unusually steep.

[8] For an economic rationale of this argument, with supporting evidence, see J. Campbell and L. Viceira, "Who Should Buy Long-Term Bonds?" Working Paper, National Bureau of Economic Research (November 1998).

[9] The market for 30-year U.S. Treasury bonds was in flux in early 2000 because of the federal government's declining borrowing needs.

as shown on Exhibit 10.4. Following is the series of choices that we make to arrive at our estimate:

- We measure the risk premium over as long a period as possible.
- We use an arithmetic average of rates of return because the CAPM is based on *expected* returns, which are forward-looking.
- We adjust the historical arithmetic rate of return downward by 1½ percent to 2 percent because the historical rate is biased upward by survivorship bias.
- We calculate the premium over long-term government bond returns to be consistent with the risk-free rate we use to calculate the cost of equity.

Historical period   Since the market risk premium is a random variable, a longer time frame (which encompasses a stock market crash, expansions, recessions, two wars, and stagflation) is probably the better estimate of the future than a short, but more recent time frame. An example of the problematic nature of choosing a short interval to estimate arithmetic average returns occurred during the summer of 1987. Many analysts were using the relatively low 2.5 percent to 3.5 percent risk premium taken from the 1962–1985 period. This estimate helped to justify the extraordinarily high prices observed in the stock market. After all, the argument went, it does not make sense to use long-term rates because extraordinary events like a stock market crash will not be repeated. Yet in October 1987, the market crashed again, falling by 25 percent.

Are there any historical data to suggest a systematic decline in the market risk premium? Exhibit 10.5 plots five-year rolling averages of the market equity risk premium from 1930 to 1995. The volatility of the market risk premium has decreased, but what about the average market risk premium? A regression of the rolling five-year market risk premium versus time indicates that there is no statistically significant change in the risk premium between 1926 and 1995. The slope of the regression is not significantly different from zero.

Exhibit 10.4   Average Market Risk Premiums

	1926–1998	1974–1998	1964–1998
Risk premium based on:[1]			
Arithmetic average returns	7.5%	5.5%	4.1%
Geometric average returns	5.9%	4.9%	3.6%

1 Excess U.S. market return over 20-year U.S. Treasury bond.
Source: Ibbotson Associates (1999).

Exhibit 10.5   Five-Year Rolling Average of Market Risk Premia

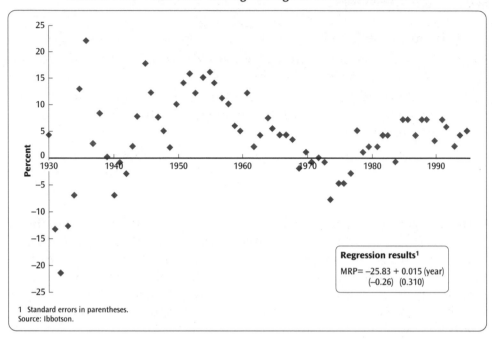

Regression results[1]

MRP= −25.83 + 0.015 (year)
     (−0.26) (0.310)

1 Standard errors in parentheses.
Source: Ibbotson.

Geometric versus arithmetic average   Let's turn to the question of geometric versus arithmetic average rates of return. An arithmetic average of rates of return is the simple average of the single period rates of return. Suppose you buy a share of a non-dividend-paying stock for $50. After one year the stock is worth $100. After two years the stock falls to $50 once again. The first period return is 100 percent; the second period return is −50 percent. The arithmetic average return is 25 percent—100 percent −50 percent divided by 2. The geometric average is the compound rate of return that equates the beginning and ending value, zero in our example.

What can we infer from these data? If we are willing to make the strong assumption that each return is an independent observation from a stationary underlying probability distribution, then we can infer that four equally likely return paths actually exist: 100 percent followed by 100 percent, 100 percent followed by −50 percent, −50 percent followed by 100 percent, and −50 percent followed by −50 percent. These possibilities are illustrated in Exhibit 10.6. The shaded area represents what we have actually observed, and the remainder of the binomial tree is what we have inferred by assuming independence.

The difference between the arithmetic and geometric averages is that the former infers expected returns by assuming independence, and the latter treats the observed historical path as the single best estimate of the

Exhibit 10.6   Arithmetic versus Geometric Return

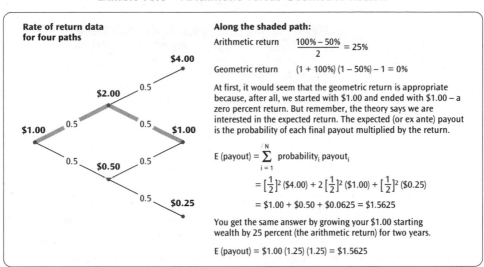

Rate of return data for four paths

Along the shaded path:

Arithmetic return $\dfrac{100\% - 50\%}{2} = 25\%$

Geometric return $(1 + 100\%)\,(1 - 50\%) - 1 = 0\%$

At first, it would seem that the geometric return is appropriate because, after all, we started with $1.00 and ended with $1.00 – a zero percent return. But remember, the theory says we are interested in the expected return. The expected (or ex ante) payout is the probability of each final payout multiplied by the return.

$$E\,(\text{payout}) = \sum_{i=1}^{N} \text{probability}_i\ \text{payout}_i$$

$$= \left[\tfrac{1}{2}\right]^2 (\$4.00) + 2\left[\tfrac{1}{2}\right]^2 (\$1.00) + \left[\tfrac{1}{2}\right]^2 (\$0.25)$$

$$= \$1.00 + \$0.50 + \$0.0625 = \$1.5625$$

You get the same answer by growing your $1.00 starting wealth by 25 percent (the arithmetic return) for two years.

$$E\,(\text{payout}) = \$1.00\,(1.25)\,(1.25) = \$1.5625$$

future. If you believe that it is proper to apply equal weighting to all branches in the binomial tree, and if your starting position is $50, then your expected wealth is as follows:

$$1/4\ (\$200) + 1/2\ (\$50) + 1/4\ (\$12.50) = \$78.125$$

Exactly the same value can be obtained by computing the arithmetic average return and applying it to the starting wealth as follows:

$$\$50\ (1.25)\ (1.25) = \$78.125$$

The arithmetic average is the best estimate of future *expected* returns because all possible paths are given equal weighting. The single geometric average return is 0 percent, but this is the historical return along a single path that was realized by chance. Although the geometric return is the correct measure of historical performance, it is not forward looking.

The arithmetic return is always higher than the geometric return. The difference between them becomes greater as the variance of returns increases. Also, the arithmetic average depends on the interval chosen. For example, an average of monthly returns will be higher than an average of annual returns. The geometric average, being a single estimate for the entire time interval, is the same regardless of the interval chosen.

Exhibit 10.7 shows illustrative returns during 10 periods, and their arithmetic and geometric average during various intervals. The geometric average is independent of the time interval that is chosen for averaging, but the arithmetic average declines as a function of the time interval.

Exhibit 10.7   The Interval Effect

Percent

Year	Return		Arithmetic average	Geometric average
1	5	10 one-year intervals	4.70	4.17
2	−10	5 two-year intervals	4.51	4.17
3	8	2 five-year intervals	4.19	4.17
4	16	1 ten-year interval	4.17	4.17
5	−6			
6	−10			
7	20			
8	4			
9	18			
10	2			

Exhibit 10.8 shows the market risk premium for U.S. large capitalization stocks using the arithmetic mean for different return periods. For example, for the three-year periodicity, we calculated the three-year returns for 24 periods and then took the arithmetic average of the three-year returns (annualized to one year). The results show that the estimated arithmetic average declines as you average over longer intervals. There is no guidance or intuition that would lead us to conclude that the CAPM, a one-period model, is necessarily a one-year model. Note that the arithmetic risk premium, based on two-year intervals, is a full one percent less than the premium based on one-year intervals. Given the large gap between one- and two-year intervals compared with the gap between two years and all other intervals, we chose to base our market risk premium estimate on the two-year interval.

Our choice of a two-year or greater interval is supported by evidence that historical returns are not independent draws from a stationary distribution. Empirical research by Fama and French (1988), Lo and MacKinlay (1988), and Poterba and Summers (1988)[10] indicates that a significant long-term negative

Exhibit 10.8   Arithmetic Average for Various Intervals

Percent

1926–1998	Large company stocks	Long-term government bonds	Market risk premium
Arithmetic mean of 1-year returns	13.2	5.7	7.5
Arithmetic mean of 2-year returns	11.9	5.4	6.5
Arithmetic mean of 3-year returns	11.6	5.3	6.3
Arithmetic mean of 4-year returns	11.4	5.3	6.1
Geometric mean	11.2	5.3	5.9

autocorrelation exists in stock returns. The implication is that the true market risk premium lies between the arithmetic and geometric averages.

Survivorship bias   Brown, Goetzmann, and Ross first raised survivorship bias as an issue (1995), claiming that survival imparts a bias to ex post returns.[11] If the market risk premium were zero, a substantial upward bias would be imparted on markets that survive over a century without going under. Jorion and Goetzmann (1999) have attempted to estimate the survivorship bias by collecting monthly rate of return data from 1921 to 1996 for 39 stock market indices.[12] If one looks at geometric returns, the United States outperformed all others during the twentieth century, averaging 6.9 percent in nominal terms annually, or 4.3 percent in real terms (deflating by the wholesale price index) between January 1926 and December 1996. Of the group of 24 markets that existed in 1931, only seven experienced no interruption in trading (the United States, Canada, the United Kingdom, Australia, New Zealand, Sweden, and Switzerland), seven suspended trading for less than a year, and the remaining 10 suffered long-term closure. The breaks were not favorable events. Over World War II the Japanese market fell 95 percent in real terms, and the German market fell 84 percent.

It is unlikely that the U.S. market index will do as well over the next century as it has in the past, so we adjust downward the historical arithmetic average market risk premium. Using the tables in Jorion and Goetzmann, we find that between 1926 and 1996, the U.S. arithmetic annual return exceeded the median return on a set of 11 countries with continuous histories dating to the 1920s by 1.9 percent in real terms, or 1.4 percent in nominal terms. If we subtract a 1½ percent to 2 percent survivorship bias from the long-term arithmetic average of 6.5 percent, we conclude that the market risk premium should be in the 4½ percent to 5 percent range.

Ex ante estimates of the market risk premium   An alternative to the historically estimated market risk premium is an ex ante estimate, one based on the current value of the share market relative to projections of earnings or cash flows. One approach estimates the expected rate of return on the market portfolio, $E(r_m)$, by adding the analysts' consensus estimate of

---

[10] E. Fama and K. French, "Dividend Yields and Expected Stock Returns," *Journal of Financial Economics* (October 1988), pp. 3–26; A. Lo and C. MacKinlay, "Stock Prices Do Not Follow Random Walks: Evidence from a Simple Specification Test," *Review of Financial Studies* (1988), pp. 41–66; J. Poterba and L. Summers, "Mean Reversion in Stock Prices," *Journal of Financial Economics* (October 1988), pp. 27–60.

[11] S. Brown, W. Goetzmann, and S. Ross, "Survivorship Bias," *Journal of Finance* (July 1995), pp. 853–873.

[12] P. Jorion and W. Goetzmann, "Global Stock Markets in the Twentieth Century," Working Paper (New Haven, CT: Yale School of Management, 1999).

growth in the dividend of the S&P 500 Index, g, to the dividend yield for the index, Div/S:

$$E(r_m) = \frac{\text{Div}}{S} + g$$

The risk-free rate is then subtracted from the expected return on the market to obtain the forecast of the market risk premium. Analysts have shown limited skill in forecasting price changes in the S&P 500. In addition, the formula that provides the basis for this approach implicitly assumes perpetual growth at a constant rate, g. This is a particularly stringent assumption.

There is a growing literature that uses either the above-mentioned dividend discount model, or an equity free cash flow model and observed stock prices, to impute the equity discount rate (and the market risk premium) as an internal rate of return. A typical example is the work of Gebhardt, Lee, and Swaminathan.[13] They estimate the cost of equity at the individual company level using a residual income model to value the equity of a company (this is the same approach in principle as the economic profit model described in Chapter 8). Assume a flat term structure and that the firm uses clean surplus accounting (implying that all gains and losses affecting the book value of equity are also run through the income statement). Then the value of the stock, S_t, is equal to the book value of equity, B_t, plus the discounted expected economic profit (defined as the spread between the return on equity, ROE, and the cost of equity, r_e, multiplied by the book value of equity). An ex ante estimate of the cost of equity for

$$S_t = B_t + \sum_{i=1}^{\infty} \frac{E_t[(ROE_{t+i} - r_e)\, B_{t+i-1}]}{(1+r_e)^i}$$

a company is estimated through the following process: plug in the current stock price and the book value of equity; use I/B/E/S estimates of expected earnings per share to estimate net income as ($ROE \times B_{t+i-1}$) for the next three years; implicitly forecast economic profit to year 12 by assuming that the company return on equity fades to equal the industry median return on equity by year 12; assume that economic profit during the terminal value period is a perpetuity, and then solve the above equation for the cost of equity.

Both the Gebhardt, Lee, and Swaminathan paper and a paper by Claus and Thomas find similar results.[14] The ex-ante market risk premium

[13] W. Gebhardt, C. Lee, and B. Swaminathan, "Toward an Ex-Ante Cost of Capital," Working Paper (Ithaca, NY: Cornell University, 1999).

[14] J. Claus and J. Thomas, *The Equity Risk Premium Is Much Lower than You Think It Is: Empirical Estimates from a New Approach,* Working Paper (New York: Columbia University, 1998).

(estimated by subtracting the yield on 10-year U.S. Treasury bonds from the cost of equity) is in the two to three percent range while the historical risk premium is about 5 percent. We prefer not to use the ex ante approach because it always fits the data. Even if one makes an error forecasting future cash flows, the ex ante approach will produce an internal rate of return that is consistent with the observed stock price.

Exhibit 10.9 shows the valuation of 31 companies in August 1999. It duplicates the results of Exhibit 5.5, which showed a 92 percent r-squared between the market value and the DCF estimate of the value of these companies—except for one thing. In Exhibit 10.9, the free cash flows are discounted at a WACC that assumes a market risk premium of 3 percent (based on published ex ante estimates of the market risk premium). The results show that the r-squared falls to 79 percent, the slope of the line is significantly below unity, and so the DCF model vastly overvalues companies. Clearly, the 3-percent market risk premium assumption worsened the results. The higher market risk premium that we used in Exhibit 5.5 better fits the actual market values than the ex ante premium.

A number of investment banks have begun publishing estimates of the market risk premium, several using ex ante approaches. In early 2000, most of these estimates were 3½ percent to 5 percent.

Estimating the systematic risk (beta)   For listed companies, using published estimates of beta is the easiest approach. BARRA publishes betas for more than 10,000 companies around the world, but we recommend checking several reliable sources because beta estimates vary considerably. You should also compare the beta with the industry average beta. If the betas

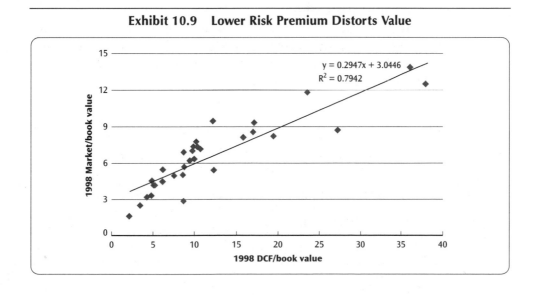

Exhibit 10.9   Lower Risk Premium Distorts Value

from several sources vary by more than .2 or the beta for a company is more than .3 from the industry average, consider using the industry average. An industry average beta is typically more stable and reliable than an individual company beta because measurement errors tend to cancel out. When constructing the industry average, unlever the betas to estimate the average. The average unlevered beta can then be relevered using the company's capital structure.

For unlisted companies and business units, you should generally use industry averages as well. See Chapter 14 for a more detailed discussion.

Is Beta Dead? Criticism of the CAPM

In June 1992, Eugene Fama and Ken French of the University of Chicago published a paper in *The Journal of Finance* that received a great deal of attention because they concluded:

> In short, our tests do not support the most basic prediction of the SLB model [The Sharpe-Lintner-Black Capital Asset Pricing Model] that average stock returns are positively related to market betas.[15]

At that time, theirs was the most recent in a long line of empirical studies that questioned the usefulness of measured betas in explaining the risk premium (above the riskless rate) on equities. Banz (1981) and Reinganum (1981) found a prominent size effect that added to the explanation of cross-sectional returns, in addition to beta. Basu (1983) found a seasonal (January) effect. Bhandari (1988) demonstrated that the degree of financial leverage was important. And Stattman (1980) as well as Rosenberg, Reid, and Lanstein (1985) found that average returns are positively related to the firm's equity book-to-market ratio.[16]

If beta is not dead, then surely it's wounded. Fama and French concluded that equity returns are inversely related to the size of a company measured by the value of its equity capitalization, and positively related to the ratio of the book value of the company's equity to its market value.

[15] E. Fama and K. French, "The Cross-Section of Expected Stock Returns," *Journal of Finance* (June 1992), pp. 427–465.

[16] R. Blanz, "The Relationship between Return and the Market Value of Common Stocks," *Journal of Financial Economics* (March 1981), pp. 3–18; M. Reinganum, "Misspecification of Capital Asset Pricing: Empirical Anomalies Based on Earnings Yields and Market Values," *Journal of Financial Economics* (March 1981), pp. 19–46; S. Basu, "The Relationship between Earnings Yield, Market Value and Return for NYSE Common Stocks: Further Evidence," *Journal of Financial Economics* (June 1983), pp. 129–156; L. Bhandari, "Debt/Equity Ratio and Expected Common Stock Returns: Empirical Evidence," *Journal of Finance* (April 1988), pp. 507–528; D. Stattman, "Book Values and Stock Returns," *The Chicago MBA: A Journal of Selected Papers* (1980), pp. 25–45; and B. Rosenberg, K. Reid, and R. Lanstein, "Persuasive Evidence of Market Inefficiency," *Journal of Portfolio Management* (1985), pp. 9–17.

When these variables were taken into account, beta added nothing to the ability to explain the returns on equity.

A practical implication is that one might estimate the required return on the equity of a company by looking up its size and market-to-book ratio in a table of average risk premia over the risk free rate. This might give better results than using estimates of beta and the CAPM. Another possible implication, and one that Fama and French hint at, is the need to use a multifactor approach like the arbitrage pricing model, which is discussed in the next section.

There have been some papers that add to the debate and give practitioners some reasons to stick with the CAPM. In particular, the work of Kothari, Shanken, and Sloan (1995) is worth reading.[17] They have five major conclusions. First, and most important:

> Our examination of the cross-section of expected returns reveals economically and statistically significant compensation (about 6 to 9 percent per annum) for beta risk . . .

Second, they point out that the Fama and French statistical tests were of sufficiently low power that they could not reject a non-trivial (beta-related) risk premium of 6 percent over the post-1940 period. Third, if annual returns are used to estimate beta (to avoid seasonality in returns) there is a statistically significant linear relationship between beta and returns over the 1941 to 1990 period. Fourth, size is also significantly related to returns; however, the incremental economic contribution is not large (less than 1 percent). Finally, the relationship between return and the book/market ratio is the result of survivorship bias in the Compustat database, and is not economically significant.

To explain this last, important conclusion, let's go back to the history of the Compustat database. In 1978 it was expanded from 2,700 to 6,000 companies by adding small companies that had survived until 1978. By definition their rates of return were higher than their failed peers and that were not included in the database. Consequently, the returns on small Compustat companies are biased upward. The Center for Research and Securities Prices returns database do not have this bias because it includes all companies ever listed on the exchange and does not remove them should they fail. Kothari, Shanken, and Sloan found that the returns for the set of companies that were on CRSP but not on Compustat were, in fact, lower than the set of companies that were on both data sets.

What's the bottom line? It takes a better theory to kill an existing theory, and we have not seen the better theory yet. Therefore, we continue to

---

[17] S. Kothari, J. Shanken, and R. Sloan, "Another Look at the Cross-Section of Expected Returns," *Journal of Finance* (December 1995).

use the CAPM (and sometimes the arbitrage pricing model), being wary of all of the problems with estimating it.

The Arbitrage Pricing Model

The APM can be thought of as a multifactor analogue to the CAPM. The CAPM explains securities returns as a function of one factor, which is called the market index, and is usually measured as the rate of return on a well-diversified portfolio. The APM cost of equity is defined as follows:

$$k_s = r_f + [E\,(F_1) - r_f]\,\text{beta}_1 + [E\,(F_2) - r_f]\,\text{beta}_2 + \cdots + [E\,(F_k) - r_f]\,\text{beta}_k$$

where $E(F_k)$ = The expected rate of return on a portfolio that mimics the kth
factor and is independent of all others
beta_k = The sensitivity of the stock return to the kth factor

Instead of one measure of systematic risk, the APM includes many. Each beta measures the sensitivity of a company's stock return to a separate underlying factor in the economy. Empirical work has suggested that five fundamental factors are changes in:

- The industrial production index, a measure of how well the economy is doing in terms of actual physical output.
- The short-term real interest rate, measured by the difference between the yield on Treasury bills and the Consumer Price Index.
- Short-term inflation, measured by unexpected changes in the Consumer Price Index.
- Long-term inflation, measured as the difference between the yield to maturity on long- and short-term U.S. government bonds.
- Default risk, measured by the difference between the yield to maturity on Aaa- and Baa-rated long-term corporate bonds.

Empirical evidence also confirms that the APM explains expected returns better than the single-factor CAPM (for example, see Chen 1983; Chen, Ross, and Roll 1986; or Berry, Burmeister, and McElroy 1988).[18] In addition, the APM can add insight into the type of risk that is relevant. This is illustrated in Exhibit 10.10. The axes are two of the fundamental factors, the industrial production index and short-term inflation. The diagonal dotted lines

[18] N. Chen, R. Roll, and S. Ross, "Economic Forces and the Stock Market," *Journal of Business* (July 1986), pp. 383–403; and M. Berry, E. Burmeister, and M. McElroy, "Sorting Out Risks Using Known APT Factors," *Financial Analysts Journal*, vol. 44 (March/April 1988), pp. 29–42.

Exhibit 10.10   The Arbitrage Pricing Model

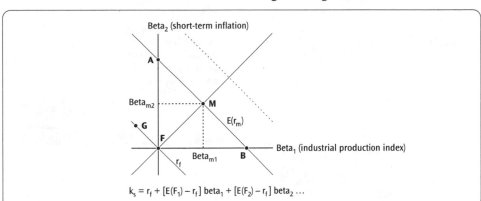

$$k_s = r_f + [E(F_1) - r_f]\, beta_1 + [E(F_2) - r_f]\, beta_2 \ldots$$

represent constant returns with different combinations of risk. Any portfolio at the origin (point F) has no exposure to either factor, and therefore earns the riskless rate, r_f.

For a portfolio at point G, exposure to the systematic risk of unexpected inflation has increased but is offset by decreased risk relative to the industrial production index. The net result is that point G earns the riskless rate, just like point F, but is exposed to a different bundle of risks. A similar story can be told about points A, M, and B. All earn the same expected return as the CAPM market portfolio, $E(r_m)$, but have varying exposures to the risk of unexpected inflation and changes in the industrial production index.

Exhibit 10.11 shows the difference in risk premiums as calculated by the APM and the CAPM for five industries. Oil and money center banks are riskier in every dimension. Forest products are less risky, and electric utilities have much less default risk. A larger risk premium means that the industry is more sensitive to a given type of risk than would be predicted by the CAPM. Banks and other financial institutions are more sensitive to unexpected changes in long-term inflation, and the market charges a risk premium—that is, it requires a higher cost of equity.

Exhibit 10.12 shows the net effect of using the CAPM versus the APM to estimate the cost of equity for nine industries. The importance of these differences for valuation of an all-equity perpetual stream of cash flows is reflected in the last column. The 4.7 percent higher APM cost-of-equity estimate in the oil industry means that equity cash flows discounted using the CAPM would be overvalued by 25 percent. Cost-of-equity estimates using the APM are significantly lower for forest products and electric utilities and significantly higher for money center banks and for oil companies with more than 50 percent of their assets in oil reserves.

Exhibit 10.11 Differences in Risk Premiums between APM and CAPM

Source: Alcar APT!, McKinsey analysis.

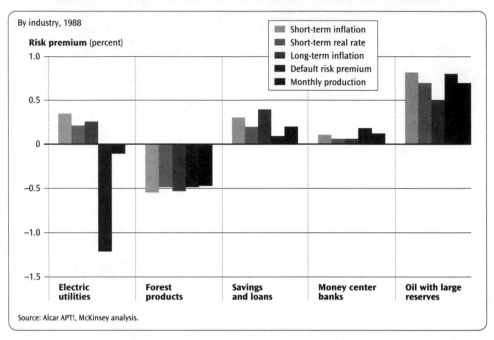

Exhibit 10.12 Comparison of CAPM and APM Cost of Equity Estimates

Industry	Number of companies	Cost-of-equity estimate CAPM (percent)	APM (percent)	Difference (percent)	Change in value (percent)
Brokerage	10	17.1	17.4	–0.3	–1.7
Electric utilities	39	12.7	11.8	0.9	7.6
Food and beverage	11	14.4	14.3	0.1	0.7
Forest products	7	16.8	15.0	1.8[1]	12.0
Large savings and loans	18	15.8	19.6	–3.8[1]	–17.7
Mining	15	14.7	14.2	0.5	3.5
Money center banks	12	15.9	16.9	–1.0[1]	–5.9
Oil with large reserves	12	14.4	19.1	–4.7[1]	–24.6
Property and casualty insurance	13	14.6	13.7	0.9	6.6

1 Statistically significant at the 5% confidence level.
Source: Alcar's APT!, McKinsey analysis.

HEINEKEN CASE

We estimated Heineken's WACC as 6.7 percent, as of December 31, 1998, calculated as shown on Exhibit 10.13. We assumed that Heineken would maintain its capital structure at 1998 levels, so the target weights are based on the market values on December 31, 1998 (Exhibit 10.14). The following sections describe how we estimated the cost of each capital source and its market value.

SHORT-TERM DEBT

Short-term debt matures within one year, so in most cases book value approximates market value. The cost of Heineken's debt was assumed to equal the cost of its long-term debt, 4.3 percent, since the short-term debt is most likely a revolving loan that will be continuously rolled over. Applying Heineken's marginal tax rate of 35 percent resulted in an after-tax cost of 2.8 percent.

LONG-TERM DEBT

None of Heineken's debt is publicly traded, so market quotes were unavailable. Heineken supplied the interest costs of each of its long-term debt issues. Given the current face value, years to maturity, coupon rate, and opportunity cost of debt, we can estimate the market value of the debt by discounting the future expected cash flows to the present (see Exhibit 10.15). To determine the opportunity cost, we assumed that Heineken's opportunity cost of debt would equal that of similarly rated companies (as expressed as a premium over the risk free rate). Although Heineken has not been rated by S&P or Moody's, we have assumed that its rating would be similar to or better than the highest rated beer companies. In the Netherlands, the market risk premium for investment-grade companies comparable to Heineken was about 30 basis points at the end of 1998. Since the risk-free rate in December was 4

Exhibit 10.13   Heineken—Weighted Average Cost of Capital

12/31/98 (percent) Source of financing	Target weight	Cost of capital	After-tax cost	Contribution to WACC
Short-term debt	1.2	4.3	2.8	0.0
Long-term debt	3.0	4.3	2.8	0.1
Retirement-related liabilities	0.3	4.3	2.8	0.0
Total debt	4.5			0.1
Market value of equity	89.9	6.9	6.9	6.2
Minority interest	5.6	6.9	6.9	0.4
Total equity	95.5			6.6
			WACC	6.7

Exhibit 10.14　Heineken—Target Capital Structure

12/31/98 (NLG million) Source of financing	Book value	Estimated market value	Percent of total capitalization
Short-term debt	474	474	1.2%
Long-term debt[1]	1,151	1,187	3.0%
Retirement-related liabilities	103	100	0.3%
Total debt	1,728	1,760	4.5%
Common equity	9,012	35,435	89.9%
Minority interest	564	2,218	5.6%
Total equity	9,576	37,652	95.5%
Total capitalization	**11,304**	**39,413**	**100.0%**

1　Includes current portion of long-term debt.

percent (in guilders), the opportunity cost of debt is 4.3 percent before-tax, or 2.8 percent after-tax.

RETIREMENT-RELATED LIABILITIES

While the Netherlands requires that companies fully fund their pension liabilities by making contributions to an independent fund, Heineken has unfunded liabilities in Spain, according to the annual report. We generally assume the market value for such a liability is equal to the book value since the company calculates the liability by discounting the future liabilities to the fund to the present by an appropriate cost of debt. Heineken used a 4 percent rate, which is at a discount to the company's current opportunity cost of debt (4.3 percent). We therefore calculate the market value of the pension liability as if it were a bond with a 15-year maturity.

Exhibit 10.15　Heineken—Market Value of Debt Instruments

(12/31/98 NLG million) Debt instrument	Original pre-tax cost	Amount	Maturity	Market value
Loans from Dutch credit institutions	5.6%	250	2006	272
Loans from Dutch credit institutions	5.3%	250	2008	270
Loans from French credit institutions	3.5%	258	2001	253
Private contract loans	6.8%	150	2000	157
Other debts and private loans	6.5%	151	2013	187
Other debts, interest free	0.0%	92	2013	49
Total long-term debt **(not including current portion)**		**1,151**		**1,187**
Retirement-related liabilities	4.0%	103	2013	100

COMMON EQUITY, ONGOING PROVISIONS, MINORITY INTEREST, AND DEFERRED INCOME TAXES

On December 31, 1998, the market value of Heineken's equity was NLG 35.4 billion, based on a share price of NLG 113 and a total of 313.6 million shares outstanding. To estimate a market value for minority interest, we assume that the market-to-book of the minority interest would be similar to that of the shareholders of the entire enterprise (as a first-order approximation). Given an equity market-to-book value of 3.9 (slightly higher than the enterprise market-to-book value) and NLG 564 million in minority interest, we obtain a market value of minority interest of about NLG 2.2 billion.

Using the CAPM, we estimated Heineken's cost of equity to be 6.9 percent:

$$k_s = r_f + [E(r_m) - r_f]\,(\text{beta})$$
$$k_s = 4.0\% + (5.0\% \times 0.58) = 6.9\%$$

The following assumptions were used:

- A risk-free rate of 4.0 percent, the yield to maturity of ten-year Dutch Treasury bonds.
- A market risk premium of 5.0 percent.
- A levered beta of 0.58, based on the average unlevered beta for a sample of brewers (.56) adjusted for Heineken's leverage (debt/capital of 4.5 percent).

We used the average unlevered beta for the industry (Exhibit 10.16), rather than Heineken's beta (.32), because it better reflects true market risk. We sometimes find that individual company betas vary randomly from their industry average. Most of the competitors in the sample have unlevered betas between 0.4 and 0.7, with Heineken as the low statistical outlier and two high outliers with betas near 0.8. We are more confident using the industry sample average, given how close the betas of

---

Exhibit 10.16   Beer Industry Unlevered Betas

Company name	Unlevered beta
Anheuser-Busch	0.64
Brau-Union	0.44
Carlsberg	0.46
Coors	0.51
Foster's Brewing Group	0.82
Heineken	0.32
Oesterreichische	0.43
Scottish & Newcastle	0.62
South African Breweries	0.82
Average	**0.56**

Source: Barra.

most of the companies in the sample are to each other and no other special information about the company.

GOVERNMENT GRANTS

Heineken is receiving inexpensive financing because some governments subsidize its investments in new markets. In the value drivers section we account for these subsidies as operating liabilities. As such, they have no impact on WACC.

11

Forecasting Performance

Now that you've analyzed the company's historical performance and estimated its cost of capital, you can move on to forecasting future performance. The key is developing a point of view on how the company will perform on the most important value drivers: growth and return on invested capital.

None of us can predict the future. However, careful analysis can yield insights into how a company may develop. That should be your objective. This chapter is organized around the basic steps needed to develop a financial forecast. These steps are often iterative rather than sequential:

1. Determine the length and level of detail for the forecast. We favor a two-stage approach, a detailed forecast in the near term followed by a summary forecast for the longer term.

2. Develop a strategic perspective on future company performance, considering both the industry characteristics as well as the company's competitive advantages or disadvantages.

3. Translate the strategic perspective into financial forecasts: the income statement, balance sheet, free cash flow, and key value drivers.

4. Develop alternative performance scenarios to the base case you developed in steps 2 and 3.

5. Check the overall forecasts (the resulting ROIC and sales and profit growth) for internal consistency and alignment with your strategic perspective.

To help guide your analysis, we include data on the long-term performance of companies. We close this chapter with the next section of the Heineken case study.

DETERMINE LENGTH AND DETAIL OF THE FORECAST

The first step is to determine how many years to forecast and how detailed your forecast should be. As we described in Chapter 8, you typically develop an explicit forecast for a number of years, followed by a simplified formulaic approach to valuing the remaining life of the company, the *continuing value*, as explained in detail in Chapter 12. All continuing value approaches are based on an assumption of steady state performance. The explicit forecast period must be long enough so that the company has reached a steady state by the end of this period. This steady state can be characterized as follows:

- The company earns a constant rate of return on all new capital invested during the continuing value period.
- The company earns a constant return on its base level of invested capital.
- The company grows at a constant rate and reinvests a constant proportion of its operating profits in the business each year.

The forecast should be long enough so that you are comfortable projecting growth in the continuing value period close to the rate of growth in the economy. Much higher growth would lead to companies becoming unrealistically large relative to the economy. We recommend using a forecast period of 10 to 15 years for most companies. Very high growth or cyclical companies may need an even longer time to reach a relatively mature stage. Using a short forecast period (3 to 5 years) will typically result in the significant undervaluation of a company or require heroic long-term growth assumptions in the continuing value.

Such a long forecast period raises its own issues. Forecasting is predicting the future, which most of us can't do, especially not 10 to 15 years removed. To simplify the problem and avoid the error of false precision, we often split the forecast into two periods:

1. A detailed forecast for 3 to 5 years, where complete balance sheets and income statements are developed with as much linkage to real variables as possible (e.g., unit volumes, cost per unit).
2. A simplified forecast for the remaining years, focusing on a few important variables, such as revenue growth, margins, and capital turnover.

In addition to simplifying the forecast, this approach also forces you to focus on the long-term economics of the business, not just the individual line items of the forecast. The Heineken example at the end of the chapter shows how this works.

DEVELOP STRATEGIC PERSPECTIVE

Developing a strategic perspective essentially means crafting a plausible story about the company's future performance. One such story might be summarized as follows:

> Demand is increasing rapidly because of changing demographics, yet prices will remain stable because of the competitive structure of the industry. Given the company's competitive position, it should be able to increase its market share somewhat, although profitability will remain constant.

This story provides the context for the financial forecast. This story should be based on a thoughtful strategic analysis of the company and its industry. There is an extensive strategy literature to help you develop these stories; in this chapter, we will describe some of the analytical frameworks that you could use.

Keep in mind that what ultimately drives the value of the company is your assessment of whether and for how long a company can earn returns in excess of its opportunity cost of capital. To do this, companies must develop and exploit a competitive advantage. Without a competitive advantage, competition would force all the companies in the industry to earn only their cost of capital (or even less).

Competitive advantages that translate into a positive ROIC versus WACC spread can be categorized as:

1. Providing superior value to the customer through a combination of price and product attributes that cannot be replicated by competitors. These attributes can be tangible (the fastest computer) or intangible (brands, copyrights, patents).
2. Achieving lower costs than competitors.
3. Using capital more productively than competitors.

A competitive advantage must ultimately be expressed in terms of one or more of these characteristics. Describing competitive advantages this way also helps to begin to shape the financial forecast.

The four analytical frameworks that we will touch on are the classical industry structure analysis based on work by Michael Porter; customer segmentation analysis; competitive business system analysis, and a more recent analytical framework by two colleagues, Kevin Coyne and Somu Subramaniam.

Industry Structure Analysis (Porter Model)

Industry structure analysis looks at the forces that will shape an industry's profitability. Michael Porter of Harvard is best known for having formalized

Exhibit 11.1   Porter Industry Structure Model

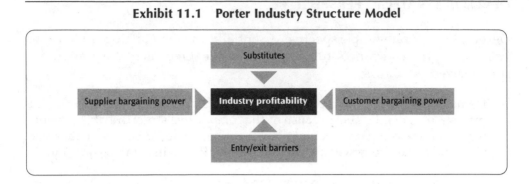

industry structure models.[1] An approach to industry structure analysis is shown on Exhibit 11.1. In this model, four forces drive an industry's profit potential: substitute products, supplier bargaining power, customer bargaining power, and entry/exit barriers.

The existence of substitute products can place significant limits on an industry. For example, railroads and trucks compete for the movement of freight. Rail movement is relatively cheap for large, long hauls but is not as flexible and inexpensive as truck movement for small, short hauls. For some shipments between the very long and very short, a shipper could use either rail or truck transportation and could try to create bidding competitions between them.

Entry and exit barriers determine the likelihood of competitors entering and leaving the industry. Entry barriers arise when there are skills or assets that only a few competitors can obtain. Access to capital is rarely an entry barrier because it is easy to obtain. On the other hand, access to new technology and patents can shut out new competitors. Exit barriers exist when competitors are better off staying in the industry, even though they are not earning their cost of capital. Exit barriers often arise in capital intensive industries where companies may be earning more than their marginal cost so they do not wish to exit, but the returns on capital are low. Furthermore, management may continue to invest capital in low-return industries for long periods because they do not wish to dismantle their organization or they are hoping other competitors will leave first.

The bargaining power of suppliers determines what share of the total pool of customer revenues can be retained by the industry. If a company can increase its bargaining power, its share of the revenue will increase. Wal-Mart, the discount retailer, has successfully exploited its purchasing power and information technology about customer wants to obtain from vendors

[1] M. Porter, *Competitive Strategy: Techniques for Analyzing Industries and Competitors* (New York: Free Press, 1980).

lower prices and better service than its competitors. But attempts to extract value from suppliers do not always work. Many department stores have attempted to cut out the manufacturers altogether by developing their own house brands for which they design the products and contract out the manufacturing. Some of these retailers have found that costs for design and manufacturing are not low enough to make up for the lower prices they generally have to charge for their non-name-brand goods.

The bargaining power of customers also affects the industry's share of revenues. In carpet manufacturing, for example, the major competitors have found ways to skip the wholesalers—who traditionally distributed their products to retailers—and deal directly with the retail stores. They have thus been able to take a significant share of the total revenue pool away from the wholesalers.

The Porter model is static. The Structure-Conduct-Performance model, developed by McKinsey consultants in the 1980s, adds a dynamic element to industry structure analysis as illustrated in Exhibit 11.2. The S-C-P model adds external shocks to the system to analyze how they will affect the structure, how competitors are likely to respond, and how the performance of the industry and competitors will be affected.

Customer Segmentation Analysis

The purpose of customer segmentation analysis is to help estimate potential market share by explicitly identifying why customers will choose one company's products over others. It also tells us how difficult it will be for a competitor to differentiate itself and helps to identify how profitable each type of customer is likely to be, based on their needs and cost to serve.

Customer segmentation analysis works from two perspectives: the customer and the producer. From the customer perspective, product attributes have different importance to different groups of customers. After-sale service may be more important to a small manufacturing customer than a large customer with its own in-house maintenance staff. In addition, competitors may include different attributes in their product offering and, in this way, deliver different benefits to customer groups.

Exhibit 11.2   Structure-Conduct-Performance Model

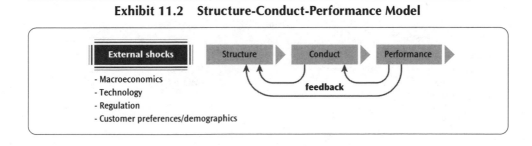

A customer segment is a group of customers to whom similar product attributes provide similar benefits. Segmenting customers forces the analyst to understand why customers prefer one product over another, often despite the fact that the products appear similar. This helps to identify why competitive market share may differ across customer groups and to find opportunities for segment differentiation. In the overnight package delivery business, for example, detailed billing information on each package is important to some customers, while others are content with summary data. Some customers want to know instantaneously where a package is, while other customers can wait for the information. So while all customers receive the same overnight delivery, other less apparent attributes may be important.

From the producer perspective, different customers have different costs to serve. In the salt industry, distance to the customer has a major impact on the costs to serve because of salt's low value-to-weight characteristics. Some customers may be simply too far away to serve if competitors are much closer. It follows that customers close by may be important to lock up because their proximity creates a major competitive advantage.

By segmenting customers according to both the customer and producer attributes, and then comparing a company's ability to satisfy those customers relative to competitors, you can begin to identify current or potential competitive advantages.

Competitive Business System Analysis

The business system is the way that a company provides product attributes to the customer, as illustrated in Exhibit 11.3. The business system extends from product design to after-sales service. Analysis of the business system provides insight into how a company can achieve a competitive advantage through lower costs, better capital use, or superior customer value. To do this, the analyst needs to lay out the business systems of the major competitors and identify:

- What product attributes does each competitor provide with its business system?

Exhibit 11.3   Business System Analysis

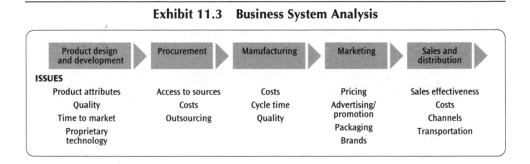

Product design and development	Procurement	Manufacturing	Marketing	Sales and distribution
ISSUES				
Product attributes	Access to sources	Costs	Pricing	Sales effectiveness
Quality	Costs	Cycle time	Advertising/ promotion	Costs
Time to market	Outsourcing	Quality	Packaging	Channels
Proprietary technology			Brands	Transportation

Exhibit 11.4   Coyne/Subramaniam Model

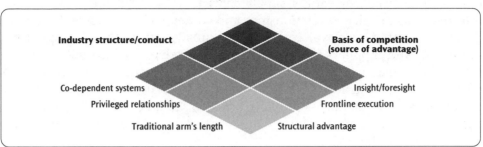

- What costs and capital are associated with providing these attributes? Ideally, this should be done for each component of the business system. In addition, linkages between the components should be considered.

- What are the reasons for differences in performance among competitors?

A competitor may have a manufacturing cost advantage because its labor force is not unionized. To overcome this labor cost advantage, other competitors must achieve greater labor productivity or cost savings elsewhere in the business system or provide a superior product to their customers.

A variation on this business system analysis focuses on core processes rather than the functional orientation of the traditional business system. A core process for a fast-food chain might be site development (including site selection and construction), which might cut across many traditional functional areas, including marketing, real estate, construction, and finance. The advantage of this perspective is that it highlights the competitive advantages that can be gained from better cross-functional management.

Coyne/Subramaniam Industry Model

Kevin Coyne and Somu Subramaniam have developed a strategy model that adds several important dimensions to the Porter model.[2] Exhibit 11.4 summarizes this approach. You can see two of the dimensions: industry structure/conduct and the basis of competition. The Porter model inhabits the large box on the bottom of the exhibit, where companies compete on an arm's-length basis and structural advantage is the basis of competition. Coyne and Subramaniam add additional structures and bases of competition.

[2] K. Coyne and S. Subramaniam, "Bringing Discipline to Strategy," *McKinsey Quarterly*, no. 4 (1996), pp. 14–25.

Along the industry structure dimension, the traditional arm's-length relationship between players is supplemented by two additional structures, referred to as privileged relationships and co-dependent systems. In the traditional model, each player competes at arm's length with its competitors, customers, and suppliers for a share of the total value. Co-dependent systems refer to industries where alliances, networks, and economic webs are critical elements of competition. Industries based on privileged relationships are characterized by companies providing special "non-economic" treatment of each other because of common financial interests, friendship, political connections, or ethnic loyalty.

Along the basis-of-competition axis, the traditional model assumes that structural advantages provide the source of extraordinary returns. Coyne and Subramaniam add two other sources of advantage: front-line execution and insight/foresight. Some companies can beat the competition simply by better execution of day-to-day tasks. This can sometimes overwhelm any structural advantage. Other companies can create value by consistently developing insights or knowledge ahead of the competition.

Bringing together the three industry structures and the three sources of advantage provides a more complete picture of how a company can create value.

TRANSLATE THE STRATEGIC PERSPECTIVE INTO FINANCIAL FORECAST

Now that you have your story about the company's future performance, you can translate it into a financial forecast. It is best to begin with an integrated income statement and balance sheet forecast. Free cash flow and ROIC can then be derived from the income statement and balance sheet.

It is possible to forecast free cash flow directly rather than going through the income statement and balance sheet, but we do not recommend it. If you do not construct the balance sheet, it is easy to lose sight of how all the pieces fit together. An analyst doing a valuation tried to simplify the forecasting process by ignoring the balance sheet. The company's history showed that it usually generated about two dollars in sales for each dollar of net fixed assets. By the end of the analyst's forecast, however, the company was generating five dollars in sales for each dollar of net fixed assets. The analyst had not intended this result and did not even know it was happening, because a balance sheet and supporting ratios had not been constructed. The balance sheet also helps to identify the financing implications of the forecast. It shows how much capital must be raised or how much excess cash will be available.

The most common approach to forecasting the income statement and balance sheet for nonfinancial companies is a demand-driven forecast. A demand-driven forecast starts with sales. Most other variables (expenses, working capital) are driven off the sales forecast. Such a forecast typically works as follows:

1. Build the revenue forecast. This should be based on volume growth and price changes.
2. Forecast operational items, such as operating costs, working capital, property, plant, and equipment, by linking them to revenues or volume. (Working capital and PPE are discussed in more detail next.)
3. Project non-operating items, such as investments in unconsolidated subsidiaries and related income as well as interest expense and interest income.
4. Project the equity accounts. Equity should equal last year's equity plus net income and new share issues less dividends and share repurchases.
5. Use the cash and/or debt accounts to balance the cash flows and balance sheet.
6. Calculate the ROIC tree and key ratios to pull the elements together and check for consistency.

While we will not discuss every line in the income statement and balance sheet, two issues merit further discussion: stocks versus flows and inflation.

Stocks versus Flows

When forecasting balance sheet items, one of the first issues you will face is whether to forecast the balance sheet directly (stocks) or indirectly through changes in the balance sheet (flows). The stock approach would forecast end-of-year inventories as a function of the year's revenues. The flow approach would forecast the change in inventories as a function of the growth in revenues. We favor the stock approach. The relationship between the balance sheet accounts and revenues (or other volume measures) is more stable than the relationship between balance changes and changes in revenues.

Consider the example on Exhibit 11.5. The ratio of inventories to revenues remains within a small band of 9.6 percent to 10.4 percent, while the ratio of changes in inventories to changes in revenues ranges from 5 percent to 18 percent. Moreover, forecasting changes in inventories to be 15 percent to 18 percent of changes in revenues would lead to a substantial increase in inventories to revenues.

This issue is particularly acute for property, plant, and equipment. A common method for forecasting PPE is to forecast capital spending as a percent of revenues. This will often lead to significant increases or decreases in capital turnover (the ratio of net PPE to revenues). Yet when you examine

Exhibit 11.5   Stock versus Flow Example

	Year 1	Year 2	Year 3	Year 4
Revenues	1,000	1,100	1,200	1,300
Inventories	100	105	117	135
Inventories as percent of sales	10%	9.6%	9.8%	10.4%
Change in inventories as percent of change in sales		5%	12%	18%

companies over long periods, you find that the ratio of net PPE to revenues is often stable. We favor the following approach for PPE:

1. Forecast net PPE as a percentage of revenues.
2. Forecast depreciation, typically a percent of gross or net PPE.
3. Capital spending is then a "plug," equal to change in net PPE plus depreciation.

When forecasting PPE don't forget to build in some retirements of assets, otherwise gross PPE and accumulated depreciation will be quite large even though net PPE may be reasonable. See the Heineken case at the end of the chapter for a detailed example of this approach.

Inflation

We recommended in Chapter 8 that forecasts and costs of capital be estimated in nominal rather than real currency units. For consistency, both the financial forecast and the cost of capital must be based on the same expected general inflation rate. This means that the inflation rate built into the forecast must be derived from an inflation rate implicit in the cost of capital.[3]

The expected general inflation rate implicit in the cost of capital can generally be derived from the term structure of government bond rates. The nominal interest rate on government bonds reflects investor demands for both a real return plus a premium for expected inflation. Expected

---

[3] Individual line items, however, could have specific inflation rates that are higher or lower than the general rate, but they should still derive from the general rate. For example, the revenue forecast should reflect the growth in units sold and the expected increase in unit prices. The increase in unit prices, in turn, should reflect the general expected level of inflation in the economy plus or minus an inflation rate differential for that specific product. Suppose that general inflation is expected to be 4.0 percent and that unit prices for the company's products were expected to increase at 1 percent lower than general inflation. Overall, the company's prices would be expected to increase at 3.0 percent per year. Assuming a 3 percent annual increase in units sold would lead to a forecast of 6.1 percent annual revenue growth ($1.03 \times 1.03 - 1.00$).

inflation can be estimated as the nominal rate of interest less an estimate of the real rate of interest using the following formula:

$$\text{Expected inflation} = \frac{(1 + \text{Nominal rate})}{(1 + \text{Real rate})} - 1$$

For example, if the nominal rate on 10-year government bonds is 6 percent and your estimate of the real rate is 2.5 percent, then expected inflation over the time period would be 3.4 percent.

Why not use all the readily available economists' forecasts of inflation? First, these forecasts rarely extend beyond a couple of years. Second, they may not be consistent with the market's forecast embedded in the term structure of interest rates. Third, empirical analysis suggests that market-based estimates are the least biased.[4]

Estimating the real rate of interest is not easy. Here are three approaches:

1. Over the years 1926 through 1998, long-term government bonds in the United States returned 5.3 percent compounded annually, while inflation averaged 3.0 percent. Thus the real return from investing in long-term government bonds was 2.2 percent.[5]

2. Another historical approach is to examine yields (the income portion of the total return) on government bonds versus realized inflation. Exhibit 11.6 shows the yield on 20-year government bonds less next year's inflation. The average real yield has increased significantly from about 2.0 percent from 1958 to 1972 to about 4.1 percent from 1987 to 1998 (ignoring the turbulent period from 1973 to 1986, when inflation and interest rates fluctuated wildly).

3. The U.S. government recently began issuing inflation-indexed bonds. In September 1999, the real yield on these bonds was about 4 percent (these were fairly stable over the prior year). For technical and tax reasons, some credit market analysts have suggested that these bonds are not liquid enough to represent a fair estimate of market expectations of real returns. As the market for these bonds develops, these concerns may diminish.

Each of these approaches has its drawbacks. In our experience, most valuations assume a real risk-free rate of 3 percent to 4 percent.

---

[4] See E. Fama and M. Gibbons, "A Comparison of Inflation Forecasts," *Journal of Monetary Economics* (May 1984), 327–348; or G. Hardouvelis, "The Predictive Power of the Term Structure during Recent Monetary Regimes," *Journal of Finance* (June 1988), 339–356.

[5] Ibbotson Associates, *Stocks, Bonds, Bills, and Inflation 1999 Yearbook* (Chicago: Ibbotson, 1999).

Exhibit 11.6   Yield on U.S. Government Bonds Less Inflation

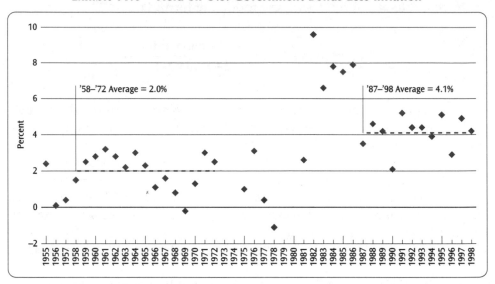

DEVELOP PERFORMANCE SCENARIOS

To this point you will have developed a single forecast for your company, probably the most likely case. Most of us would not have much confidence that our forecast is the only route to the future. Using scenarios is a way to acknowledge that forecasting financial performance is an educated guess. The best we can do is narrow the range of likely future performance. Consider a high-tech company that is developing a proprietary product. If the company successfully develops it, its competitive advantage will be a product that delivers superior value to customers. Its growth and returns on capital are likely to be huge. If the company fails to develop the product, it will likely go out of business. A scenario that projects moderate growth and returns is highly unlikely, even though it could be considered most likely from a statistical perspective. While this situation may be extreme, we strongly believe that it is better to develop a number of scenarios for a company, and to understand the company's value under each scenario, than to build a single most likely forecast and value.

Once the scenarios are developed, an overall value of the company can be estimated. This will involve a weighted average of the values of the independent scenarios, assigning probabilities to each scenario. Exhibit 11.7 shows how we valued a steel company.

Developing scenarios does not mean mechanically changing the sales growth rate by 10 percent. Instead, it means developing a comprehensive set of assumptions about how the future may evolve and how that is likely to

Exhibit 11.7   Valuation of a Steel Company

Scenario ($ million)	Enterprise value ($ million)	Debt ($ million)	Equity value ($ million)	Probability (percent)	Weighted equity value ($ million)
Business as usual	2,662	2,520	142	15	
Industry behavior improves slightly	3,694	2,520	1,174	65	1,228
Sustained improvement in industry behavior	4,736	2,520	2,216	20	

affect industry profitability and the company's financial performance. (See the Heineken case for an example.)

CHECKING FOR CONSISTENCY AND ALIGNMENT

The final step in the forecasting process is to construct the free cash flow and key value drivers from the income statements and balance sheets and to eval uate the forecast. The forecast should be evaluated the same way the company's historical performance was analyzed. To understand how the value drivers are expected to behave, ask:

- Is the company's performance on the value drivers consistent with the company's economics and the industry competitive dynamics?
- Is revenue growth consistent with industry growth? If the company's revenue is growing faster than the industry's, which competitors are losing share? Will they retaliate? Does the company have the resources to manage that rate of growth?
- Is the return on capital consistent with the industry's competitive structure? If entry barriers are coming down, shouldn't expected returns decline? If customers are becoming more powerful, will margins decline? Conversely, if the company's position in the industry is becoming much stronger, should you expect returns to increase? How will returns and growth look relative to the competition?
- How will technology changes affect returns? Will they affect risk?
- Can the company manage all the investment it is undertaking?

Finally, you must understand the financing implications of the forecast. Will the company have to raise large amounts of capital? If so, can it obtain the financing? Should it be debt or equity? If the company is generating excess cash, what options does it have for investing the cash or returning it to shareholders?

SOME DATA TO GUIDE YOUR FORECASTS

Long-term ROIC and growth are the key drivers of value. So how have companies performed on these parameters? Several colleagues gathered long-term performance data for companies in a number of industries.

- *Companies rarely outperform their peers for long periods of time.* Exhibits 11.8 and 11.9 show the percentage of companies in selected industries that are able to achieve top third performance relative to their peers in terms of ROIC and revenue growth over 10 or 15 years (measured in 5-year periods). In terms of ROIC, less than a quarter of top-performing companies can beat their peers consistently for 10 years and less than 10 percent can beat their peers for 15 years. The numbers are slightly higher for revenue growth—less than 40 percent of top-performing companies can beat their peers for 10 years and less than 20 percent for 15 years.

  The implication for valuation is that you should not assume that the company you are evaluating will always outperform the industry. (Some do; the trick is to figure out which ones.) As theory suggests, competition works at reducing returns.

- *Company performance varies widely from industry averages.* Exhibit 11.10 shows that in terms of revenue growth, more that 70 percent of companies are more than plus or minus 20 percent from the industry average. (If the industry average is 10 percent in a year, more than 70 percent of the companies in the industry have growth less than 8 percent or more than 12 percent.) Similarly for unregulated industries,

Exhibit 11.8   Few Companies Maintain High ROIC Relative to Industry

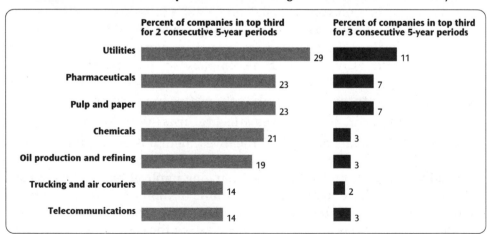

Exhibit 11.9   Few Companies Maintain High Revenue Growth Relative to Industry

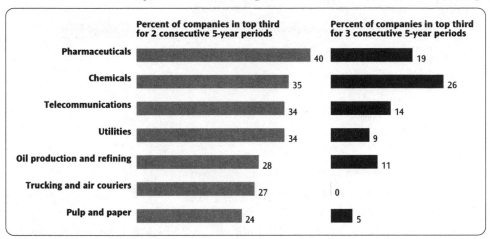

Exhibit 11.10   Company Performance Varies Widely from Industry Average

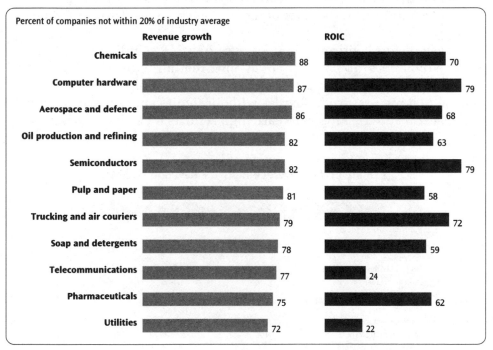

Exhibit 11.11   Average Industry ROIC

Percent	Average 1966–1975	Average 1976–1985	Average 1986–1995
Pharmaceuticals	25	17	27
Chemicals	13	14	14
Trucking and air courier	13	13	8
Oil production and refining	12	12	6
Pulp and paper	10	11	10
Telecommunications	7	9	9
Utilities	7	8	7

more than about 60 percent of companies earn ROICs more than 20 percent from their industry average.

- *Industry average ROICs and growth rates are linked to economic fundamentals.* Exhibit 11.11 shows the average ROICs for selected industries over 10-year intervals from 1966 to 1995. An industry such as pharmaceuticals consistently earns high returns because of patent protection on new drugs. Trucking shows a marked decline in ROIC after deregulation. Oil production and refining shows a large decline after the end of the oil crisis and the inability of OPEC to keep prices high. The other industries in the sample are quite stable, though utilities and telecommunications earned significantly lower returns than the other industries (because of regulation and lower costs of capital).

These results confirm the importance of understanding industry competitive dynamics. You should not assume that all industries will eventually earn just the cost of capital (see pharmaceuticals). You should also not assume that high-return industries without significant barriers to competition (e.g., oil and trucking) will earn high returns if barriers are removed.

Exhibit 11.12   Average Industry Revenue Growth

Percent	Average 1966–1975	Average 1976–1985	Average 1986–1995
Pharmaceuticals	10	3	12
Chemicals	9	2	4
Trucking and air courier	7	8	10
Oil production and refining	14	6	−2
Pulp and paper	9	5	6
Telecommunications	12	11	5
Utilities	7	6	2
Semiconductors	N/A	34	20
Computer hardware	N/A	25	14
Aerospace and defence	4	5	−1

Exhibit 11.12 shows the average revenue growth rates for companies in selected industries. (These are average growth rates for a sample of companies in the industry, not total industry growth.) These numbers will tend to be higher than the industry growth because of survivorship bias (only surviving companies are in the sample) and because they include the effect of mergers and acquisitions. Nevertheless, they do provide some clues about long-term performance.

With few exceptions, growth rates will decline as the industry matures. Exceptions always make this interesting. Trucking and air couriers growth increased because of deregulation and innovation (overnight delivery). Pharmaceuticals growth increased because of innovative new drugs. In most industries, though, growth tends to slow to rates not much greater than overall economic growth. Once again, you can see how fundamental analysis can help you predict how growth rates will behave.

You are now ready to put the finishing touch on your valuation, by adding the continuing value.

HEINEKEN CASE

In this section, we develop a forecast for Heineken's financial performance, following the approach laid out in the chapter. First, we offer a strategic perspective on Heineken and describe several scenarios. We then translate the base case scenario into a financial forecast.

For this case, we use a five-year detailed forecast, followed by a summary forecast for the next 10 years. The continuing value follows after the 15-year forecast (discussed in the next chapter).

DEVELOP STRATEGIC PERSPECTIVE

Heineken's recent success can be linked to its globalization strategy (as described in the last chapter), where it seeks to leverage its brand and manufacturing skills worldwide. A business system analysis provides a useful framework for describing how Heineken blends global brand consistency and use of best practices in manufacturing and marketing with catering to local markets (Exhibit 11.13).

- *Product development.* Heineken adopts a global standard for the recipe of its main brands. In doing so, the company not only minimizes product development costs, but also ensures consistent quality worldwide.
- *Brewing.* Heineken controls quality by using a roving staff of brew masters, who employ best practices in production sites worldwide. This helps to lower brewing costs in developed markets and to add value to sites purchased or

Exhibit 11.13   Heineken—Business System Analysis

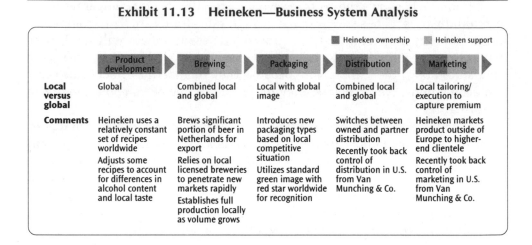

	Product development	Brewing	Packaging	Distribution	Marketing
				■ Heineken ownership ■ Heineken support	
Local versus global	Global	Combined local and global	Local with global image	Combined local and global	Local tailoring/ execution to capture premium
Comments	Heineken uses a relatively constant set of recipes worldwide Adjusts some recipes to account for differences in alcohol content and local taste	Brews significant portion of beer in Netherlands for export Relies on local licensed breweries to penetrate new markets rapidly Establishes full production locally as volume grows	Introduces new packaging types based on local competitive situation Utilizes standard green image with red star worldwide for recognition	Switches between owned and partner distribution Recently took back control of distribution in U.S. from Van Munching & Co.	Heineken markets product outside of Europe to higher-end clientele Recently took back control of marketing in U.S. from Van Munching & Co.

developed in new markets. To maximize penetration into new markets, Heineken combines exports, licensed brewing, and acquiring production capacity and local brands.

- *Packaging.* Although Heineken standardizes images on beer labels to support brand awareness, it also tailors packaging to satisfy local customers' tastes. This may add variable costs, but the impact is more than offset by the success it enjoys penetrating markets.

- *Distribution.* The ownership of distribution varies by country, depending on market maturity and Heineken's strategy there.

- *Marketing.* Leveraging its brand is an important part of Heineken's success. Heineken is the most global player in the market; its beer can be found in over 170 countries. Heineken bills its major brands (Heineken and Amstel) as premium products in non-European markets, and as mainstream products in European markets. It segments marketing and advertising campaigns to capture as much premium as possible. Finally, it reinvests much of its retained earnings in advertising and brand development in each country.

Heineken enhances this business strategy with an aggressive acquisition program. The company has purchased various producers and distributors since its major expansion in Europe during the 1980s. Its acquisitions since Van Munching & Co. (its U.S. distributor and marketer) in 1991 include Sorgyar (Hungarian brewer), Interbrew Italia, Zalty Bazant (Slovakia), Birra Moretti (Italy), Fischer and Saint-Arnould (France), and Zywiec (Poland). It has enjoyed more growth through acquisition than any other major brewer except Interbrew (Exhibit 11.14).

Exhibit 11.15 shows that this globalization and acquisition strategy has helped cement Heineken's place as a solid competitor in all major regions around the world, though it enjoys top market share only in Europe (1997 market shares).

Given that two or three players usually dominate each regional market (or country), we can see that Heineken is strongly positioned in Europe and Africa, and

Exhibit 11.14   Percentage of Current Volume Achieved through Acquisition Since 1990[1]

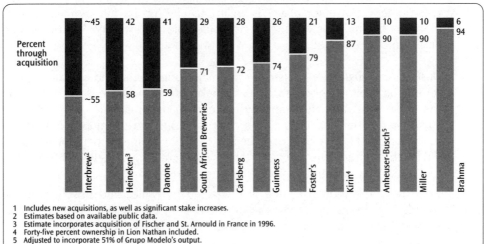

1 Includes new acquisitions, as well as significant stake increases.
2 Estimates based on available public data.
3 Estimate incorporates acquisition of Fischer and St. Arnould in France in 1996.
4 Forty-five percent ownership in Lion Nathan included.
5 Adjusted to incorporate 51% of Grupo Modelo's output.
Source: McKinsey estimates based on literature search.

more weakly positioned in the Americas and Asia-Pacific. Although Heineken has enjoyed faster growth than its domestic U.S. competitors, it is still far behind the big three: Anheuser-Busch, Miller, and Coors. In addition, in 1999, the Mexican import Corona surpassed Heineken's position as the leading imported beer in the United States.

DEVELOP PERFORMANCE SCENARIOS

The beer industry is slow growing, fragmented on a global basis, and concentrated on a regional (or country) basis. Growth opportunities in the emerging markets outpace those of Europe and North America. We also observe that there are two strategies in the offing: global integrator and value chain specialist. It seems from the size and reach of the largest players that many of them, including Heineken,

Exhibit 11.15   Market Share and Position by Geographic Region

1997

Region	Top players	Heineken market share (percent)	Heineken market position
Europe	Heineken, Carlsberg, Danone, Bass	8.1	#1
Western Hemisphere	AB, Miller, Brahma, Interbrew	4.2	#9
USA	AB, Miller, Coors, Busch	3–4	#12
Asia-Pacific	Kirin, Asahi, San Miguel, Fosters	2.7	#7
Africa	SAB, Heineken, BGI, Guinness	14.3	#2

have chosen the global integrator approach. Most markets have consolidated, so apart from a megamerger, all the integrators can look forward to is the relatively slow growth that can be squeezed out organically or through minor acquisitions.

At the moment, no major player is willing to give up its independence. That may not always be the case, so there is considerable uncertainty. We developed three performance scenarios:

1. *Business as usual.* The industry avoids major price wars, and overall industry returns on capital slightly improve. Heineken's performance is the same as in the late 1990s, and the company makes two major acquisitions and some small ones in the near future. The company continues to globalize and captures a market share of 6.6 percent by 2003 versus 6.1 percent in 1998. Given this picture, we forecast stable, value-creating growth, with margins and returns on invested capital remaining relatively flat.

2. *Price war.* The industry price wars started by Miller and Busch continue worldwide, dropping returns toward the cost of capital. Heineken's performance is stable, but with weaker margins and no new acquisitions.

3. *Market discipline/industry consolidation.* The industry consolidates and avoids price wars. Heineken improves gross and EBITA margins through an aggressive mergers-and-acquisitions program. It becomes a leader in the drive for industry consolidation.

For the remainder of this chapter and in Chapter 12 (Continuing Value), we will only analyze in detail the Business as Usual scenario. The resulting valuations of the other two scenarios will be covered in Chapter 13.

FORECAST INDIVIDUAL LINE ITEMS FOR THE SHORT-TERM HORIZON

We offer a 15-year forecast to allow a sufficient period for the industry strategic game to play out and for Heineken to reach a steady-state financial performance. A detailed forecast was prepared for the first five years, and a condensed forecast is used for the remaining 10 years. This forecast is driven by demand; in other words, most income statement and balance sheet line items are derived from the sales forecast. The detailed projections for the first five years are laid out in Exhibits 11.16 and 11.17.

Revenues

There are several ways to model revenue growth that allow it to be broken down into its major parts. A Merrill Lynch investment report in December 1998 provided one such model, which we adapted for forecasting purposes. In this model, revenue growth is a function of volume growth, average price changes (price per unit or changing product mix), and acquisitions.

For the Business-as-Usual scenario, we forecast Heineken's underlying volume growth to average 1.5 percent per year (excluding acquisitions), somewhat lower

Exhibit 11.16   Heineken—Short-Term Financial Forecast

Business as usual case (NLG million)	1994	1995	1996	1997	1998	Forecast 1999	Forecast 2000	Forecast 2001	Forecast 2002	Forecast 2003
Revenues										
Volume growth	4.0%	1.0%	−1.0%	1.0%	4.0%	2.0%	1.5%	1.5%	1.5%	1.5%
Price increase/Mix change	1.0%	3.0%	3.0%	3.0%	3.0%	2.8%	2.6%	2.4%	2.2%	2.0%
Underlying growth/Organic growth	5.0%	4.0%	2.0%	4.0%	7.0%	4.8%	4.1%	3.9%	3.7%	3.5%
Excise duty increase	0.0%	1.0%	1.0%	1.0%	0.0%	0.0%	0.0%	0.0%	0.0%	0.0%
Acquisitions	5.0%	4.0%	15.0%	3.0%	2.0%	3.0%	1.0%	1.0%	3.0%	1.0%
Currency changes	0.0%	−4.0%	−1.0%	3.0%	−2.0%	−1.0%	0.0%	0.0%	0.0%	0.0%
Revenue growth–modeled	10.0%	5.0%	17.0%	11.0%	7.0%	6.8%	5.1%	4.9%	6.7%	4.5%
Base business revenues (NLG)	9,522	9,573	9,736	10,595	10,431	10,827	11,271	11,711	12,144	12,569
Revenues from acquisitions	452	870	2,453	2,917	3,392	3,969	4,280	4,602	5,262	5,620
Worldwide market growth	3.7%	2.5%	1.2%	2.7%	2.6%	2.0%	2.0%	1.5%	1.5%	1.5%
Worldwide market size (MM HL)	1,196	1,226	1,240	1,273	1,306	1,333	1,359	1,380	1,401	1,422
Market share (%)	4.9%	5.2%	5.7%	5.8%	6.1%	6.2%	6.3%	6.3%	6.5%	6.6%
Total volume sales (MM HL)	59.1	64.3	70.7	73.8	79.1	83.1	85.1	87.3	91.2	93.5
Operating costs as percent of revenues										
Duties, levies, and trade taxes	13.6%	13.3%	13.3%	13.7%	13.1%	13.1%	13.1%	13.1%	13.1%	13.1%
Marketing	14.2%	15.1%	11.8%	12.2%	12.6%	12.6%	12.6%	12.6%	12.6%	12.6%
Merchandising	0.0%	0.0%	12.0%	12.1%	11.6%	11.6%	11.6%	11.6%	11.6%	11.6%
Packaging	10.7%	11.0%	11.4%	10.4%	10.5%	10.5%	10.5%	10.5%	10.5%	10.5%
Raw materials	5.7%	5.9%	7.0%	6.5%	5.3%	5.3%	5.3%	5.3%	5.3%	5.3%
Other costs of goods sold	14.1%	13.3%	13.2%	13.9%	13.9%	13.9%	13.9%	13.9%	13.9%	13.9%
Personnel costs	16.9%	16.6%	17.8%	16.8%	16.6%	16.6%	16.6%	16.6%	16.6%	16.6%
Interest rates										
Int rate on excess mkt secs						3.3%	3.3%	3.3%	3.3%	3.3%
Int rate on existing debt	11.0%	10.6%	13.5%	7.8%	8.5%	8.5%	8.5%	8.5%	8.5%	8.5%
Int rate on new long-term debt						4.3%	4.3%	4.3%	4.3%	4.3%
Taxes										
EBITA tax rate	30.5%	35.8%	29.1%	34.4%	33.8%	33.8%	33.8%	33.8%	33.8%	33.8%
Marginal tax rate	35.0%	35.0%	35.0%	35.0%	35.0%	35.0%	35.0%	35.0%	35.0%	35.0%
Incr def tax/Tax on EBITA	−0.8%	11.7%	3.1%	−1.5%	−5.6%	3.0%	3.0%	3.0%	3.0%	3.0%
Minority interest										
Min int/income after tax	4.4%	4.4%	4.3%	2.7%	2.6%	4.3%	4.3%	4.3%	4.3%	4.3%
Minority int payout ratio	−308.9%	125.1%	−116.7%	142.0%	−513.5%	60.0%	60.0%	60.0%	60.0%	60.0%

than the industry because of Heineken's stronger presence in the slower growing developed markets. Adding 1 percent to 3 percent per year additional volume from acquisitions pushes volume growth slightly above the market. As a result, Heineken's market share increases from 6.1 percent to 6.6 percent by 2003.

Geographic mix of sales affects price increases, since prices are lower in emerging markets. We have forecast effective price increases to level out at 2 percent per year as more sales shifts to developing markets. This is somewhat lower than historical price increases. Overall revenue growth, including volume, price changes and acquisitions, is forecast at about 6 percent per year.

Exhibit 11.17   Heineken—Balance Sheet Forecast Assumptions

Business as usual case (NLG million)	1994	1995	1996	1997	1998	Forecast 1999	Forecast 2000	Forecast 2001	Forecast 2002	Forecast 2003
Capital expenditures and depreciation										
Net PP&E/revenues	45.4%	45.1%	41.9%	41.3%	41.5%	41.5%	41.5%	41.5%	41.5%	41.5%
Depreciation/net PP&E (EOY)	12.5%	11.8%	11.4%	13.2%	14.1%	14.1%	14.1%	14.1%	14.1%	14.1%
Depr on retirements/gross PPE	−0.2%	0.7%	9.9%	−12.5%	5.2%	1.0%	1.0%	1.0%	1.0%	1.0%
Other assets										
Investment facilities/revenues	1.2%	1.1%	0.8%	0.7%	0.6%	0.6%	0.5%	0.5%	0.4%	0.4%
Investments & advances growth	19.3%	14.3%	13.6%	12.7%	14.3%	5.0%	5.0%	5.0%	5.0%	5.0%
Working capital										
Inventories/revenues	6.9%	7.6%	8.1%	7.6%	7.2%	7.2%	7.2%	7.2%	7.2%	7.2%
Accounts receivable/revenues	7.9%	8.4%	10.0%	9.4%	8.8%	8.8%	8.8%	8.8%	8.8%	8.8%
Other current assets/revenues	3.6%	3.5%	3.9%	3.6%	3.5%	3.5%	3.5%	3.5%	3.5%	3.5%
Operating cash/revenues	2.0%	2.0%	2.0%	2.0%	2.0%	2.0%	2.0%	2.0%	2.0%	2.0%
Accounts payable/revenues	5.9%	6.7%	7.3%	6.7%	6.6%	6.6%	6.6%	6.6%	6.6%	6.6%
Other current liabilities/revenues	11.3%	11.7%	11.9%	11.6%	12.4%	11.8%	11.8%	11.8%	11.8%	11.8%
Net working capital/revenues	3.4%	3.1%	4.9%	4.4%	2.7%	3.3%	3.3%	3.3%	3.3%	3.3%
Equity										
Dividend payout ratio	21.2%	30.6%	26.8%	23.1%	25.9%	25.9%	100.0%	25.9%	26.5%	100.0%
Issue of new shares	0	0	0	0	0	0	0	0	0	0
Revaluation adjustment	(13)	(9)	139	134	(151)	0	0	0	0	0
Goodwill written off	(127)	(72)	(839)	(131)	(612)	(253)	(91)	(95)	(299)	(108)
Other liabilities										
Short-term debt (NLG)	433	586	774	476	474	218	150	257	0	0
Long-term debt (NLG)	503	424	792	909	1,151	933	783	526	526	526
Retirement-related liability (NLG)	164	167	162	157	103	103	103	103	103	103

Operating Expenses

Heineken's operating expenses (not including depreciation) as a percentage of revenues have fluctuated between 83.5 percent and 86.6 percent during 1994 to 1998, with the lowest figure recorded in 1998. Only the years 1996 to 1998 are comparable because of the acquisitions of Fischer Group, Saint-Arnould, and Birra Moretti in 1996. We can see clear trends in a few of the cost categories. Marketing and merchandising expenses combined have been the largest portion of the operating costs (33.8 percent–34.3 percent of revenues), and have been relatively constant. This fits with the company's strategy of global marketing and branding. Raw material costs have decreased. The company partially attributes the decline to cost-saving programs and the appreciation of the dollar against other currencies, including the euro. Other costs including packaging and personnel have remained constant, slightly decreasing from 1996. The dip from 1996 could best be explained by the full integration of the newly acquired operations. Without any other sources of information, we forecast operating expenses to remain constant as a percentage of revenues (compared to 1998) during the next several years.

Depreciation

Most of the depreciable assets purchased by Heineken are related to the company's breweries, including buildings and large machinery. In the years 1994 to 1998, depreciation was between 11 percent and 14 percent of net plant, property, and equipment. We assume that depreciation remains constant as a percentage of net property, plant, and equipment, given the slow growth and industrial nature of the business.

Financing Costs

The annual report provides the amortization schedule for Heineken's existing debt. We create new debt or marketable securities in our forecast to balance the sources and uses of cash. For simplicity, we estimate interest expense based on the level of debt at the beginning of that year, rather than on the average level of debt. We forecast the interest rate on existing debt as 8.5 percent, the same as the effective rate in 1998. The rate on new debt and retirement-related liability is the opportunity cost of borrowing, 4.3 percent. We use the interest rate on short-term treasury bills in the Netherlands to estimate the interest rate on excess marketable securities.

Taxes

We estimate Heineken's marginal tax rate as 35 percent, the statutory tax rate in the Netherlands. Heineken's EBITA effective tax rate has historically been close to the marginal tax rate, between 33 percent and 36 percent, with the exception of the heavy acquisition years. So we use 1998's effective tax rate of 33.8 percent to forecast effective cash taxes.

Working Capital

Operating working capital is comprised of operating cash, accounts receivable, inventories, and other current assets (such as prepaid expenses) less accounts payable, and other current liabilities (such as taxes payable). It does not include short-term sources of funds such as short-term debt or dividends payable. Between 1994 and 1998, net working capital was about 3 percent of revenues, with the exception of 1996 and 1997 (which were acquisition years). The only significant change in any single line item seems to be other current liabilities. We believe this will revert to a normal level of about 11.8 percent of revenues, generating a forecasted level of working capital of 3.3 percent of revenues.

In general, consider the following when forecasting working capital:

- Does the company's acquisition (or other growth) strategy affect its need for working capital?
- How much working cash does this company generally need to operate (we assume 2 percent of revenue in this case; for most industrial companies it is between 1 percent and 2 percent of revenue)?

- Does the company plan to reduce working capital in the near future? If there is a clear trend in working capital, will this trend continue or stabilize?

Year-end working capital can be volatile simply because it is measured on the last day of the year. Average measures are probably more stable, yet generally not available. So do not give too much weight to minor year-to-year fluctuations. Focus instead on major trends.

Net Property, Plant, and Equipment

Property, plant, and equipment are more difficult to forecast than other line items because revenues, costs, and working capital are generally equally affected by inflation. PPE are not. The bottom-up approach of forecasting individual expenditures (new and replacement) may be the most accurate approach, but can usually only be done from within the company.

We use a simpler approach to forecasting PPE. We make an assumption about the steady-state amount of net PPE it takes to generate each dollar of sales. This is supported by the observation that Heineken's net PPE-to-revenues have remained flat. The only major change in this ratio occurred when the company made acquisitions in 1996. (Before 1996, it was 45 percent; since the acquisitions it has been 41 percent.) We forecast that net PPE will remain the same as in 1998, which is about the same as the average for 1996 to 1998. These assumptions probably would not hold for a high growth company or in an inflationary environment.

We will also assume that fixed assets are used until they are fully depreciated and that they have no material scrap value. So the amount of assets retired from gross plant, property, and equipment each year will equal the amount of the reduction in accumulated depreciation. We have set this level at 1 percent.

Dividends

Let's assume that dividends remain the same percentage of net income as in 1998. As a result, Heineken would build up large amounts of excess cash, given its high cash flow and little debt. To avoid this, we have projected that Heineken will eventually distribute excess cash to shareholders. If Heineken were a U.S. company, we would assume that it would repurchase shares. As a Dutch company, Heineken's ability to repurchase shares is limited. Instead we assume that Heineken periodically pays out a large special dividend. (Unilever, a major Anglo-Dutch company, began paying out a similar special dividend in 1998.) These dividends are declared in the second and fifth years of the forecast.

Other

Dutch companies can write off goodwill as it is incurred, rather than amortizing it, as is the case in the United States. Thus, we forecast that Heineken will write off goodwill immediately upon acquiring another company. We assume that Heineken will pay a market-to-book value of 2 for acquisitions, and thus would incur goodwill equal to the book value of assets taken on. We assume that growth in revenues is proportional to growth in book value of acquisitions. If that is the case, then goodwill that is written off will be equal to our forecasted revenue growth rate through acquisitions multiplied by the invested capital at the beginning of the year.

We model the existing debt to be paid off as given in the notes to the accounting items in the annual report. We assume that the short-term debt is the amount paid off in the year of a given debt's maturity.

Pension liabilities declined in 1998 as a result of a substantial payout to retirees. Without additional information from the company, we expect this level to remain about the same.

Exhibits 11.18 to 11.24 contain the resulting projected income statements, balance sheets, and calculations of NOPLAT, invested capital, free cash flow, and economic profit for the years 1999 to 2003.

Exhibit 11.18   Heineken—Forecast Income Statements

Business as usual case (NLG million)	1998	Forecast 1999	Forecast 2000	Forecast 2001	Forecast 2002	Forecast 2003
Revenues	13,822	14,796	15,551	16,313	17,406	18,189
Duties, levies, and trade taxes	(1,806)	(1,933)	(2,032)	(2,131)	(2,274)	(2,376)
COGS–Marketing	(1,741)	(1,864)	(1,959)	(2,055)	(2,193)	(2,291)
COGS–Merchandising	(1,597)	(1,709)	(1,796)	(1,885)	(2,011)	(2,101)
COGS–Packaging	(1,448)	(1,550)	(1,629)	(1,708)	(1,823)	(1,905)
COGS–Raw materials	(738)	(790)	(830)	(871)	(929)	(971)
COGS–Other	(1,923)	(2,059)	(2,164)	(2,270)	(2,422)	(2,531)
Personnel costs	(2,295)	(2,457)	(2,582)	(2,709)	(2,890)	(3,020)
Amortization of goodwill	0	0	0	0	0	0
Depreciation expense	(822)	(867)	(911)	(956)	(1,020)	(1,065)
Operating income	1,453	1,568	1,648	1,729	1,844	1,927
Interest and dividend income	189	59	46	27	35	30
Interest expense	(117)	(138)	(97)	(79)	(66)	(45)
Earnings before taxes	1,525	1,489	1,596	1,676	1,813	1,913
Income taxes	(518)	(503)	(539)	(566)	(613)	(647)
Minority interest	(26)	(42)	(45)	(48)	(52)	(54)
Income before extraordinary items	981	944	1,011	1,062	1,149	1,212
Extraordinary items (after tax)	0	0	0	0	0	0
Net income	981	944	1,011	1,062	1,149	1,212
Statement of changes in equity						
Beginning equity	5,103	5,066	5,512	5,421	6,112	6,657
Net income	981	944	1,011	1,062	1,149	1,212
Common dividends and repurchases	(254)	(245)	(1,011)	(275)	(304)	(1,212)
Revaluations	(151)	0	0	0	0	0
Goodwill written off	(612)	(253)	(91)	(95)	(299)	(108)
Ending equity	5,066	5,512	5,421	6,112	6,657	6,550

Exhibit 11.19   Heineken—Forecast Balance Sheets

Business as usual case (NLG million)	1998	Forecast 1999	Forecast 2000	Forecast 2001	Forecast 2002	Forecast 2003
Operating cash	283	302	318	333	356	372
Excess marketable securities	1,806	1,409	820	1,077	935	530
Accounts receivable	1,218	1,304	1,371	1,438	1,534	1,603
Inventories	996	1,066	1,120	1,175	1,254	1,310
Other current assets	490	524	551	578	617	645
Total current assets	4,793	4,606	4,181	4,602	4,696	4,460
Gross property, plant, and equipment	14,283	15,326	16,397	17,505	18,804	20,006
Accum. depreciation	(8,459)	(9,183)	(9,941)	(10,733)	(11,577)	(12,454)
Net property, plant, and equipment	5,824	6,143	6,456	6,773	7,227	7,552
Goodwill	0	0	0	0	0	0
Investments and advances	1,080	1,134	1,190	1,250	1,312	1,378
Total assets	11,697	11,883	11,827	12,624	13,235	13,390
Short-term debt	474	218	150	257	0	0
Accounts payable	907	971	1,020	1,070	1,142	1,193
Dividends payable	129	138	145	152	162	169
Other current liabilities	1,708	1,741	1,830	1,919	2,048	2,140
Total current liabilities	3,218	3,068	3,145	3,399	3,352	3,503
Long-term debt	1,151	933	783	526	526	526
New long-term debt	0	0	0	0	0	0
Deferred income taxes	601	617	634	651	670	690
Investment facilities equalization	83	82	78	74	70	64
Retirement-related provisions	103	103	103	103	103	103
Ongoing provisions	912	989	1,065	1,142	1,219	1,295
Minority interest	564	581	599	618	638	660
Total common equity	5,066	5,512	5,421	6,112	6,657	6,550
Total liabilities and equity	11,697	11,883	11,827	12,624	13,235	13,390

Exhibit 11.20   Heineken—Forecast NOPLAT

Business as usual case (NLG million)	1998	Forecast 1999	Forecast 2000	Forecast 2001	Forecast 2002	Forecast 2003
Reported EBITA	1,453	1,568	1,648	1,729	1,844	1,927
Adjustment for retirement liability	5	4	4	4	4	4
Increase in ongoing provisions	3	77	77	77	77	77
Adjusted EBITA	1,461	1,649	1,729	1,810	1,925	2,008
Taxes on EBITA	(494)	(532)	(559)	(586)	(625)	(654)
Change in deferred taxes	(28)	16	17	18	19	20
NOPLAT	939	1,133	1,187	1,241	1,319	1,375
Taxes on EBITA						
Provision for income taxes	518	503	539	566	613	647
Tax shield on interest expense	41	48	34	28	23	16
Tax shield on retirement-related interest	2	2	2	2	2	2
Tax on interest income	(66)	(21)	(16)	(9)	(12)	(11)
Taxes on EBITA	494	532	559	586	625	654
Reconciliation to net income						
Net income	981	944	1,011	1,062	1,149	1,212
Add: Increase in deferred taxes	(28)	16	17	18	19	20
Add: Increase in other provisions	3	77	77	77	77	77
Add: Extraordinary items	0	0	0	0	0	0
Add: Minority interest	26	42	45	48	52	54
Adjusted net income	983	1,079	1,150	1,204	1,296	1,363
Add: Interest expense after tax	76	89	63	51	43	29
Add: Interest exp on retirement liab	3	3	3	3	3	3
Total income available to investors	1,062	1,171	1,216	1,258	1,342	1,394
Less: Interest income after tax	(123)	(38)	(30)	(17)	(23)	(20)
NOPLAT	939	1,133	1,187	1,241	1,319	1,375

Exhibit 11.21   Heineken—Forecast Invested Capital

Business as usual case (NLG million)	1998	Forecast 1999	Forecast 2000	Forecast 2001	Forecast 2002	Forecast 2003
Operating current assets	2,987	3,197	3,360	3,525	3,761	3,930
Operating current liabilities	(2,615)	(2,712)	(2,850)	(2,990)	(3,190)	(3,333)
Operating working capital	372	485	510	535	571	597
Net property, plant, and equipment	5,824	6,143	6,456	6,773	7,227	7,552
Other assets net of other liabilities	(83)	(82)	(78)	(74)	(70)	(64)
Oper invested capital (before goodwill)	6,113	6,547	6,889	7,234	7,728	8,084
Cumulative goodwill written off and amortized	2,304	2,557	2,648	2,743	3,042	3,150
Oper invested capital (after goodwill)	8,417	9,104	9,536	9,977	10,770	11,235
Excess marketable securities	1,806	1,409	820	1,077	935	530
Investments and advances	1,080	1,134	1,190	1,250	1,312	1,378
Total investor funds	11,303	11,646	11,547	12,304	13,017	13,143
Total common and preferred equity	5,066	5,512	5,421	6,112	6,657	6,550
Cum goodwill written off and amortized	2,304	2,557	2,648	2,743	3,042	3,150
Deferred income taxes	601	617	634	651	670	690
Dividends payable	129	138	145	152	162	169
Ongoing provisions	912	989	1,065	1,142	1,219	1,295
Adjusted equity	9,012	9,812	9,913	10,801	11,751	11,854
Minority interest	564	581	599	618	638	660
Debt	1,625	1,151	933	783	526	526
Retirement-related liability	103	103	103	103	103	103
Total investor funds	11,303	11,646	11,547	12,304	13,017	13,143

Exhibit 11.22   Heineken—Forecast Free Cash Flow

Business as usual case (NLG millions)	1998	Forecast 1999	Forecast 2000	Forecast 2001	Forecast 2002	Forecast 2003
Operating cash flows						
NOPLAT	939	1,133	1,187	1,241	1,319	1,375
Depreciation	822	867	911	956	1,020	1,065
Gross cash flow	1,761	2,000	2,098	2,196	2,338	2,440
Less: Increase in working capital	225	(114)	(25)	(25)	(36)	(26)
Less: Capital expenditures	(992)	(1,186)	(1,224)	(1,272)	(1,473)	(1,391)
Less: Increase in other assets	(17)	(2)	(4)	(4)	(4)	(6)
Gross investment	(784)	(1,301)	(1,253)	(1,301)	(1,513)	(1,422)
Free cash flow before goodwill	977	699	845	895	825	1,018
Investment in goodwill	(612)	(253)	(91)	(95)	(299)	(108)
Free cash flow after goodwill	364	446	754	800	526	910
Nonoperating cash flow	(286)	(54)	(57)	(60)	(62)	(66)
After-tax interest income	123	38	30	17	23	20
(Incr)/decr in excess mktble securities	(211)	397	589	(257)	142	405
Cash flow available to investors	(10)	828	1,316	501	628	1,269
Financing Flows						
After-tax interest expense	76	89	63	51	43	29
Interest on retirement-related liability	3	3	3	3	3	3
Decrease/(increase) in debt	(240)	474	218	150	257	0
Decrease/(increase) in retirement-related liabilities	54	0	0	0	0	0
Minority interest	(136)	25	27	29	31	33
Common dividends	232	236	1,004	268	294	1,204
Decrease/(increase) in share capital	0	0	0	0	0	0
Total financing flows	(10)	828	1,316	501	628	1,269

Exhibit 11.23 Heineken—Forecast Economic Profit

Business as usual case (NLG million)	1998	Forecast 1999	Forecast 2000	Forecast 2001	Forecast 2002	Forecast 2003
ROIC (before goodwill)	15.3%	18.5%	18.1%	18.0%	18.2%	17.8%
WACC	7.3%	6.7%	6.7%	6.7%	6.7%	6.7%
Spread	7.9%	11.8%	11.4%	11.3%	11.5%	11.0%
Invested capital (beginning of year)	6,150	6,113	6,547	6,889	7,234	7,728
Economic profit (before goodwill)	488	721	745	777	831	854
NOPLAT	939	1,133	1,187	1,241	1,319	1,375
Capital charge	(451)	(412)	(441)	(464)	(488)	(521)
Economic profit (before goodwill)	488	721	745	777	831	854
ROIC (after goodwill)	12.0%	13.5%	13.0%	13.0%	13.2%	12.8%
WACC	7.3%	6.7%	6.7%	6.7%	6.7%	6.7%
Spread	4.6%	6.7%	6.3%	6.3%	6.5%	6.0%
Invested capital (beginning of year)	7,842	8,417	9,104	9,536	9,977	10,770
Economic profit (after goodwill)	364	566	573	598	646	649
NOPLAT	939	1,133	1,187	1,241	1,319	1,375
Capital charge	(576)	(567)	(614)	(643)	(672)	(726)
Economic profit (after goodwill)	364	566	573	598	646	649

Exhibit 11.24 Heineken—Supporting Calculations

Business as usual case (NLG million)	1998	Forecast 1999	Forecast 2000	Forecast 2001	Forecast 2002	Forecast 2003
Change in working capital						
Increase in operating cash	6	20	15	16	22	16
Increase in accounts receivable	(57)	86	67	67	96	69
Increase in inventories	(30)	70	54	55	79	56
Increase in other current assets	4	35	27	27	39	28
(Increase) in accounts payable	(4)	(64)	(50)	(50)	(72)	(51)
(Increase) in other current liabilities	(144)	(33)	(89)	(90)	(129)	(92)
Net change in working capital	(225)	114	25	25	36	26
Capital expenditures						
Increase in net property, plant, and equipment	170	319	313	316	454	325
Depreciation	822	867	911	956	1,020	1,065
Capital expenditures (net of disposals)	992	1,186	1,224	1,272	1,473	1,391
Nonoperating cash flow						
Extraordinary items	0	0	0	0	0	0
Change in restructuring provisions	0	0	0	0	0	0
Revaluation effect	(151)	0	0	0	0	0
Change in investments and advances	(135)	(54)	(57)	(60)	(62)	(66)
Nonoperating cash flow	(286)	(54)	(57)	(60)	(62)	(66)

Exhibit 11.25 Heineken—Forecast Medium Term Operating Ratios

Business as usual case	1999	2000	2001	2002	2003	2004	2005	2006	2007	2008	2009	2010	2011	2012	2013	2014
Revenues																
Volume growth	2.0%	1.5%	1.5%	1.5%	1.5%	1.5%	1.5%	1.5%	1.5%	1.5%	1.5%	1.5%	1.5%	1.5%	1.5%	1.5%
Price/mix	2.8%	2.6%	2.4%	2.2%	2.0%	1.9%	1.8%	1.7%	1.6%	1.5%	1.5%	1.5%	1.5%	1.5%	1.5%	1.5%
Underlying growth	4.8%	4.1%	3.9%	3.7%	3.5%	3.4%	3.3%	3.2%	3.1%	3.0%	3.0%	3.0%	3.0%	3.0%	3.0%	3.0%
Excise duty	0.0%	0.0%	0.0%	0.0%	0.0%	0.0%	0.0%	0.0%	0.0%	0.0%	0.0%	0.0%	0.0%	0.0%	0.0%	0.0%
Acquisitions	3.0%	1.0%	1.0%	3.0%	1.0%	1.0%	1.0%	1.0%	1.0%	1.0%	1.0%	1.0%	1.0%	1.0%	1.0%	1.0%
Currency changes	–1.0%	0.0%	0.0%	0.0%	0.0%	0.0%	0.0%	0.0%	0.0%	0.0%	0.0%	0.0%	0.0%	0.0%	0.0%	0.0%
Revenue growth–modeled	6.8%	5.1%	4.9%	6.7%	4.5%	4.4%	4.3%	4.2%	4.1%	4.0%	4.0%	4.0%	4.0%	4.0%	4.0%	4.0%
Revenues (NLG)	14,796	15,551	16,313	17,406	18,189	18,989	19,806	20,638	21,484	22,343	23,237	24,167	25,133	26,139	27,184	28,271
Worldwide market growth	2.0%	2.0%	1.5%	1.5%	1.5%	1.5%	1.5%	1.5%	1.5%	1.5%	1.5%	1.5%	1.5%	1.5%	1.5%	1.5%
Worldwide market size (MM HL)	1,333	1,359	1,380	1,401	1,422	1,444	1,466	1,489	1,511	1,534	1,557	1,580	1,604	1,628	1,653	1,677
Market share (%)	6.2%	6.3%	6.3%	6.5%	6.6%	6.6%	6.6%	6.6%	6.6%	6.6%	6.6%	6.6%	6.6%	6.6%	6.6%	6.6%
Volume sales (MM HL)	83.1	85.1	87.3	91.2	93.5	94.9	96.3	97.7	99.2	100.7	102.2	103.7	105.3	106.9	108.5	110.1
Adjusted EBITA margin	11.1%	11.1%	11.1%	11.1%	11.0%	11.0%	11.0%	11.0%	11.0%	11.0%	11.0%	11.0%	11.0%	11.0%	11.0%	11.0%
Cash tax rate	31.3%	31.4%	31.4%	31.5%	31.6%	31.6%	31.6%	31.6%	31.6%	31.6%	31.6%	31.6%	31.6%	31.6%	31.6%	31.6%
Working capital/revenues	2.7%	2.8%	2.8%	2.9%	2.9%	2.9%	2.9%	2.9%	2.9%	2.9%	2.9%	2.9%	2.9%	2.9%	2.9%	2.9%
Net PP&E/revenues	41.5%	41.5%	41.5%	41.5%	41.5%	41.5%	41.5%	41.5%	41.5%	41.5%	41.5%	41.5%	41.5%	41.5%	41.5%	41.5%
Revenues/inv capital	2.3	2.3	2.3	2.3	2.3	2.3	2.3	2.3	2.3	2.3	2.3	2.3	2.3	2.3	2.3	2.3
Pre-tax ROIC	26.1%	25.7%	25.6%	25.7%	25.4%	25.4%	25.4%	25.4%	25.3%	25.3%	25.3%	25.3%	25.3%	25.3%	25.3%	25.3%
ROIC	17.9%	17.7%	17.6%	17.6%	17.4%	17.4%	17.4%	17.4%	17.3%	17.3%	17.3%	17.3%	17.3%	17.3%	17.3%	17.3%
ROIC–including goodwill	12.9%	12.7%	12.7%	12.7%	12.5%	12.6%	12.7%	12.8%	13.0%	13.1%	13.2%	13.3%	13.5%	13.6%	13.7%	13.8%
Invested capital growth	7.1%	5.2%	5.0%	6.8%	4.6%	4.4%	4.3%	4.2%	4.1%	4.0%	4.0%	4.0%	4.0%	4.0%	4.0%	4.0%
EBITA growth	12.9%	4.8%	4.7%	6.4%	4.3%	4.4%	4.3%	4.2%	4.1%	4.0%	4.0%	4.0%	4.0%	4.0%	4.0%	4.0%
NOPLAT growth	20.6%	4.7%	4.6%	6.3%	4.2%	4.4%	4.3%	4.2%	4.1%	4.0%	4.0%	4.0%	4.0%	4.0%	4.0%	4.0%
Continuing value																
ROIC				17.0%												
NOPLAT growth:				4.0%												

Exhibit 11.26 Heineken—Medium-Term Financial Forecast

Business as usual case (NLG million)	1999	2000	2001	2002	2003	2004	2005	2006	2007	2008	2009	2010	2011	2012	2013	2014
Invested capital																
Net property, plant, and equipment	6,143	6,456	6,773	7,227	7,552	7,884	8,223	8,568	8,920	9,277	9,648	10,034	10,435	10,852	11,286	11,738
Operating working capital	404	432	461	501	533	556	580	604	629	654	681	708	736	765	796	828
Invested capital	6,547	6,889	7,234	7,728	8,084	8,440	8,803	9,173	9,549	9,931	10,328	10,741	11,171	11,618	12,082	12,566
Cum gw. written off and amort	2,557	2,648	2,743	3,042	3,150	3,150	3,150	3,150	3,150	3,150	3,150	3,150	3,150	3,150	3,150	3,150
Invested capital (inc goodwill)	9,104	9,536	9,977	10,770	11,235	11,590	11,953	12,323	12,699	13,081	13,478	13,891	14,321	14,768	15,233	15,716
NOPLAT																
Revenues	14,796	15,551	16,313	17,406	18,189	18,989	19,806	20,638	21,484	22,343	23,237	24,167	25,133	26,139	27,184	28,271
Operating costs	(13,147)	(13,822)	(14,503)	(15,480)	(16,181)	(16,893)	(17,619)	(18,359)	(19,112)	(19,876)	(20,671)	(21,498)	(22,358)	(23,252)	(24,182)	(25,150)
Adjusted EBITA	1,649	1,729	1,810	1,925	2,008	2,097	2,187	2,279	2,372	2,467	2,566	2,668	2,775	2,886	3,002	3,122
Cash taxes	(516)	(542)	(569)	(607)	(634)	(662)	(690)	(719)	(749)	(779)	(810)	(842)	(876)	(911)	(947)	(985)
NOPLAT	1,133	1,187	1,241	1,319	1,375	1,435	1,497	1,560	1,624	1,688	1,756	1,826	1,899	1,975	2,054	2,136
Free cash flows																
NOPLAT	1,133	1,187	1,241	1,319	1,375	1,435	1,497	1,560	1,624	1,688	1,756	1,826	1,899	1,975	2,054	2,136
Increase oper invested capital	(687)	(433)	(441)	(793)	(465)	(356)	(363)	(370)	(376)	(382)	(397)	(413)	(430)	(447)	(465)	(483)
Free cash flow	446	754	800	526	910	1,079	1,134	1,190	1,247	1,307	1,359	1,413	1,470	1,528	1,590	1,653
Economic profit																
Invested capital (beg of yr)	6,113	6,547	6,889	7,234	7,728	8,084	8,440	8,803	9,173	9,549	9,931	10,328	10,741	11,171	11,618	12,082
WACC	6.7%	6.7%	6.7%	6.7%	6.7%	6.7%	6.7%	6.7%	6.7%	6.7%	6.7%	6.7%	6.7%	6.7%	6.7%	6.7%
Annual capital charge	412	441	464	488	521	545	569	593	618	644	669	696	724	753	783	814
NOPLAT	1,133	1,187	1,241	1,319	1,375	1,435	1,497	1,560	1,624	1,688	1,756	1,826	1,899	1,975	2,054	2,136
Annual capital charge	(412)	(441)	(464)	(488)	(521)	(545)	(569)	(593)	(618)	(644)	(669)	(696)	(724)	(753)	(783)	(814)
Economic profit	721	745	777	831	854	890	928	966	1,005	1,045	1,087	1,130	1,175	1,222	1,271	1,322

FORECAST MEDIUM-TERM HORIZON

For the years 2004 to 2013, we use a streamlined model, focusing only on core value drivers such as revenue growth, EBITA margin, and the ratio of working capital to revenues. The assumptions are laid out in Exhibit 11.25 on page 263 and the resulting summary financial statements are in Exhibit 11.26.

This forecast is also driven by sales, and only its components are forecast individually; cost and capital items are not separately forecast. We forecast revenue growth to drop from 4.5 percent to 4 percent as growth in emerging markets slows (keeping Heineken's market share at a constant 6.6 percent), and assume a constant adjusted EBITA margin of 11 percent, working capital to revenues of 2.9 percent, and net PPE to revenues at its current 41.5 percent. The result is an after-tax ROIC of about 17 percent, compared with the ROIC Heineken earned in 1998 of 15.3 percent.

CHECK FOR REASONABLENESS

Exhibit 11.27 summarizes Heineken's performance in the Business-as-Usual scenario. Heineken's growth and ROIC do not change drastically in the forecast. While the company's growth does slow, its market share does not decrease. There is a slight dip in capital turnover from 2004 to 2008, corresponding to the increases in capital spending associated with its strategy of purchasing small breweries and consolidating them into the Heineken network. Overall, the results are consistent with the scenario and current strategy we have described.

Exhibit 11.27 Heineken—Business as Usual Case

Check for reasonableness of assumptions

Percent	1994–1998	Short-term forecast 1999–2003	Medium-term forecast 2004–2008	Medium-term forecast 2009–2013
Revenue growth	9.0	5.6	4.2	4.0
EBITA growth[1]	10.3	6.6	4.2	4.0
Invested capital growth	6.2	5.8	4.2	4.0
EBITA/revenues	10.0	11.1	11.0	11.0
Revenues/invested capital	2.2	2.3	2.3	2.3
Cash tax rate	32.2	31.4	31.6	31.6
ROIC (after tax, before goodwill)	14.8	17.6	17.4	17.3
WACC	9.0	6.7	6.7	6.7
Average economic profit	341.1	785.6	966.9	1,177.2

1 For the historical period, revenue and EBITA growth are only calculated for the first four years.

12

Estimating
Continuing Value

Chapter 8 introduced the continuing value concept as a method for simplifying company valuations. This chapter explains how to estimate continuing values. As we stated earlier, a company's expected cash flow can be
separated into two periods and the company's value defined as follows:

$$\text{Value} = \begin{array}{c} \text{Present value of cash} \\ \text{flow } during \text{ explicit} \\ \text{forecast period} \end{array} + \begin{array}{c} \text{Present value of cash} \\ \text{flow } after \text{ explicit} \\ \text{forecast period} \end{array}$$

The second term is the *continuing value*. It is the value of the company's expected cash flow beyond the explicit forecast period. Using simplifying assumptions about the company's performance during this period—for
example, assuming a constant rate of growth—permits us to estimate continuing value with one of several formulas. Using a continuing value formula
eliminates the need to forecast in detail the company's cash flow over an extended period.

A high-quality estimate of continuing value is essential to any valuation,
because continuing value often accounts for a large percentage of the total
value of the company. Exhibit 12.1 shows continuing value as a percentage of
total value for companies in four industries (given an eight-year explicit forecast). In these examples, continuing value accounts for 56 percent to 125 percent of total value. Although these continuing values are large, this does not
mean that most of a company's value will be realized in the continuing value
period. It often just means that the cash inflow in the early years is offset by
outflows for capital spending and working capital investment—investments
that should generate higher cash flow in later years. The proper interpretation of continuing value will be discussed in more detail later in this chapter.

Exhibit 12.1   Continuing Value as a Percentage of Total Value

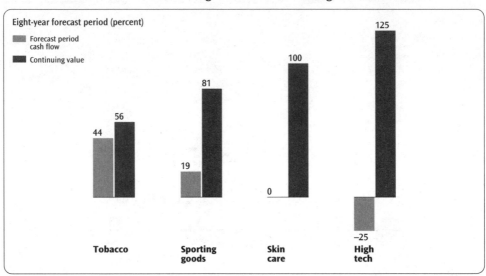

The continuing value approaches outlined in the following pages are consistent with the overall discounted cash flow and economic profit frameworks. This is important because we often see continuing value treated as though it is different from the DCF valuation of the explicit forecast period. Some acquirers estimate continuing value by applying a price-earnings multiple five years in the future equal to the multiple they are considering paying for the company. They are assuming that the target company is worth what they are willing to pay for it (adjusted for growth during the intervening five years), regardless of its economics, and that someone else would be willing to pay the same price. This type of circular reasoning leads to inaccurate valuations. Instead, they should try to estimate what the multiple should be at the end of the forecast period, given the industry conditions at that time.

The approaches we recommend not only provide consistency with the company's economic performance, they also offer insight into the underlying forces driving the value of the company.

We begin with recommended formulas for DCF and economic profit valuation. We discuss some of the issues commonly raised about interpreting continuing value and suggest some best practices in estimating continuing value parameters such as growth and return on invested capital. Finally, we compare the recommended formulas with other continuing value techniques and discuss more advanced formulas.

RECOMMENDED CONTINUING VALUE FORMULA FOR DCF VALUATION

If you are using the enterprise DCF model, we recommend the value-driver formula for estimating continuing value.

$$\text{Continuing value} = \frac{\text{NOPLAT}_{T+1}\,(1 - g/\text{ROIC}_I)}{\text{WACC} - g}$$

where NOPLAT_{T+1} = The normalized level of NOPLAT in the first year after the explicit forecast period.
g = The expected growth rate in NOPLAT in perpetuity.
ROIC_I = The expected rate of return on net new investment.
WACC = The weighted average cost of capital.

We call this the value-driver formula because the input variables (growth, ROIC, and WACC) are the key drivers of value discussed throughout this book. The formula is derived by projecting cash flows into perpetuity and discounting them at WACC while making the following simplifying assumptions:

- The company earns constant margins, maintains a constant capital turnover, and thus earns a constant return on existing invested capital.
- The company's revenues and NOPLAT grow at a constant rate and the company invests the same proportion of its gross cash flow in its business each year.
- The company earns a constant return on all new investments.

We start with the simple formula for a cash flow perpetuity that grows at a constant rate:

$$\text{Continuing value} = \frac{\text{FCF}_{T+1}}{\text{WACC} - g}$$

where FCF_{T+1} = The normalized level of free cash flow in the first year after the explicit forecast period.

This formula is well established in the finance and mathematics literature.[1] Next, define free cash flow in terms of NOPLAT and the investment rate:

---

[1] For the derivation, see T. Copeland and J.F. Fred Weston, *Financial Theory and Corporate Policy*, 3rd ed. (Reading, MA: Addison-Wesley, 1988), Appendix A.

$$\text{Free cash flow} = \text{NOPLAT} \times (1 - \text{IR})$$

where IR = The investment rate, or the percentage of NOPLAT reinvested in the business each year.

In Chapter 8 we developed the relationship between the investment rate (IR), the company's projected growth in NOPLAT (g), and the return on new investment:

$$g = \text{ROIC}_I \times \text{IR}$$

Turning this equation around gives:

$$\text{IR} = \frac{g}{\text{ROIC}_I}$$

Now build this into the free cash flow (FCF) definition:

$$\text{FCF} = \text{NOPLAT} \times \left(1 - \frac{g}{\text{ROIC}_I} \right)$$

Substituting for free cash flow gives the value driver formula:

$$\text{Continuing value} = \frac{\text{NOPLAT}_{T+1}(1 - g/\text{ROIC}_I)}{\text{WACC} - g}$$

Many readers will be tempted to use the FCF perpetuity formula, rather than the value driver formula. After all, aren't they the same? Technically, yes, but applying the FCF perpetuity is tricky and most analysts get it wrong. The common error is to incorrectly estimate the level of free cash flow that is consistent with the growth rate you are forecasting. If growth in the continuing value period is forecast to be less than the growth in the explicit forecast period (as is normally the case), then the proportion of NOPLAT that needs to be invested to achieve growth is likely to be less as well. In the continuing value period more of each dollar of NOPLAT becomes free cash flow available for the investors. If this transition is not taken into consideration, the continuing value could be significantly understated. Later in this chapter, we give an example that illustrates what can go wrong when using this formula.

A simple example demonstrates that the value driver formula does, in fact, replicate the process of projecting the cash flows and discounting them to the present. Begin with the following cash flow projections:

			Year		
	1	2	3	4	5
NOPLAT	100	106	112	120	126
Net investment	50	53	56	60	63
Free cash flow	50	53	56	60	63

The above pattern continues after the first five years presented. In this example, the growth rate in NOPLAT and free cash flow each period is 6 percent. The rate of return on net new investment is 12 percent, calculated as the increase in NOPLAT from one year to the next, divided by the net investment in the prior year. The WACC is assumed to be 11 percent. First, use a long forecast, say 150 years:

$$CV = \frac{50}{1.11} + \frac{53}{(1.11)^2} + \frac{56}{(1.11)^3} + \cdots + \frac{50(1.06)^{149}}{(1.11)^{150}}$$

$$= 999$$

Next, use the growing free cash flow perpetuity formula:

$$CV = \frac{50}{11\% - 6\%}$$

$$= 1,000$$

Finally, use the value-driver formula:

$$CV = \frac{100(1 - 6\%/12\%)}{11\% - 6\%}$$

$$= 1,000$$

All three approaches yield the same result. (If we had carried out the discounted cash flow beyond 150 years, the result would have been the same.)

RECOMMENDED CONTINUING VALUE FORMULA FOR ECONOMIC PROFIT VALUATION

With the economic profit approach, the continuing value does not represent the value of the company after the explicit forecast period. Instead, it is the incremental value over the company's invested capital at the end of the explicit forecast period.

The total value of the company is as follows:

$$
\text{Value} = \begin{matrix} \text{Invested} \\ \text{capital at} \\ \text{beginning of} \\ \text{forecast} \end{matrix} + \begin{matrix} \text{Present value of} \\ \text{forecasted economic} \\ \text{profit } during \text{ explicit} \\ \text{forecast period} \end{matrix} + \begin{matrix} \text{Present value of} \\ \text{forecasted economic} \\ \text{profit } after \text{ the explicit} \\ \text{forecast period} \end{matrix}
$$

While the economic profit continuing value (the last term in the preceding equation) is different from the DCF continuing value, the value of the company will be the same given the same projected financial performance.

The recommended economic profit formula is:

$$
\text{CV} = \frac{\text{Economic profit}_{T+1}}{\text{WACC}} + \frac{(\text{NOPLAT}_{T+1})(g/\text{ROIC}_{I})(\text{ROIC}_{I} - \text{WACC})}{\text{WACC}(\text{WACC} - g)}
$$

where, Economic profit$_{T+1}$ = The normalized economic profit in the first year after the explicit forecast period.

NOPLAT$_{T+1}$ = The normalized NOPLAT in the first year after the explicit forecast period.

g = The expected growth rate in NOPLAT in perpetuity.

ROIC$_{I}$ = The expected rate of return on net new investment.

WACC = The weighted average cost of capital.

This formula says that the value of economic profit after the explicit forecast equals the present value of economic profit in the first year after the explicit forecast in perpetuity, plus any incremental economic profit after that year created by additional growth at returns exceeding the cost of capital. If expected ROIC$_{I}$ equals WACC, the second half of the equation equals zero and the continuing economic profit value is the value of the first year's economic profit in perpetuity.

The continuing value using a discounted cash flow approach will equal the sum of the economic profit continuing value plus the amount of invested capital in place at the end of the explicit forecast period.

ISSUES IN THE INTERPRETATION OF CONTINUING VALUE

In this section, we address three common misunderstandings about continuing value. First is the perception that the length of the forecast affects the value of a company. Second, there is often confusion about the ROIC assumption in the continuing value period. Third, some incorrectly infer that a large continuing value relative to the total value of a company means that all the company's value is created after the explicit forecast period.

Does the Length of Forecast Affect the Value of a Company?

While the length of the explicit forecast period you choose is important, it does not affect the value of the company, only the distribution of value of the company between the explicit forecast period and the years that follow. In the examples in Exhibits 12.2 and 12.3, no matter what the length of the forecast period, the company value is $893. With a forecast horizon of five years, the present value of the continuing value accounts for 79 percent of total value, while with a 10-year horizon, the present value of continuing value accounts for only 60 percent of total value.

The choice of forecast horizon can have an indirect impact on value if it is associated with changes in the economic assumptions underlying the continuing value estimate. Analysts often unknowingly change their performance forecasts when they change their forecast horizon. Many forecasters assume that the rate of return on new invested capital equals the cost of capital in the continuing value period, but that the company will earn returns exceeding the cost of capital during the explicit forecast period. When they extend the explicit forecast period, they also extend the time period during which returns on new capital are expected to exceed the cost of capital. Therefore, extending the forecast period leads to an increase in value, attributable to the increase in the rate-of-return assumptions.

As we explained earlier in this chapter, the explicit forecast should be long enough so that the business will have reached a steady state of operations by the end of the period. Suppose you expect the company's margins to decline as its customers become more powerful. Margins are currently 12 percent and you forecast they will fall to 9 percent over the next seven years.

Exhibit 12.2   Comparison of Total Value Estimates Based on Different Forecast Horizons

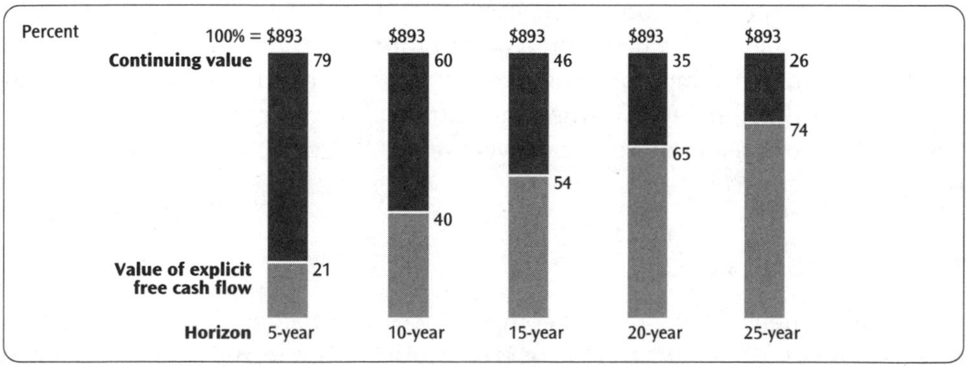

Exhibit 12.3 Comparison of Total Value Calculations for Five-Year and Ten-Year Horizons

$ million

Overall assumptions (percent)	Years 1–5	Years 6+
Return on investment (r)	16	12
Growth rate (g)	9	6
WACC	12	12

5-year horizon	1	2	3	4	5	Base for CV
NOPLAT	$100.0	109.0	118.8	129.5	141.2	149.6
Depreciation	20.0	21.8	23.8	25.9	28.2	
Gross cash flow	120.0	130.8	146.6	155.4	169.4	
Gross investment	76.3	83.1	90.6	98.7	107.6	
FCF	43.8	47.7	52.0	56.7	61.8	
Discount factor	0.893	0.797	0.712	0.636	0.567	
Present value of cash flow	39.1	38.0	37.0	36.0	35.0	

$$\text{Present value of continuing value} = \frac{\text{NOPLAT}\,(1 - g/\text{ROIC})}{\text{WACC} - g}\,[1/(1 + \text{WACC})]^5 = \frac{\$149.6\,(1 - 6\% / 12\%)}{12\% - 6\%}\,(0.5674)$$
$$= \$707.5$$

Present value of FCF 1 – 5	185.1
Continuing value	707.5
Total value	892.6

10-year horizon	1	2	3	4	5	6	7	8	9	10	Base for CV
NOPLAT	100.0	109.0	118.8	129.5	141.2	149.6	158.6	168.6	178.2	188.9	200.2
Depreciation	20.0	21.8	23.8	25.9	28.2	29.9	31.7	33.6	35.6	37.8	
Gross cash flow	120.0	130.8	142.6	155.4	169.4	179.6	190.3	201.7	213.9	226.7	
Gross investment	76.3	83.1	90.6	98.7	107.6	104.7	111.0	117.7	124.7	132.2	
FCF	43.8	47.7	52.0	56.7	61.8	74.8	79.3	84.1	89.1	94.5	
Discount factor	0.893	0.797	0.712	0.636	0.567	0.507	0.452	0.404	0.361	0.322	
Present value of cash flow	39.1	38.0	37.0	36.0	35.0	37.9	35.9	34.0	32.1	30.4	

$$\text{Present value of continuing value} = \frac{\text{NOPLAT}\,(1 - g/r)}{\text{WACC} - g}\,[1/(1 + \text{WACC})]^{10} = \frac{\$200.21\,(1 - 6\% / 12\%)}{12\% - 6\%}\,(0.322)$$
$$= \$537.2$$

Present value of CF 1–10	355.4
Continuing value	537.2
Total value	892.6

The explicit forecast period in this case must be at least seven years, because continuing value approaches cannot account for the declining margin (at least not without much computational complexity). The business must be operating at an equilibrium level for the continuing value approaches to be useful. If the explicit forecast is more than seven years, there will be no effect on the total value of the company.

Confusion about ROIC

A related issue is the concept of competitive advantage period or the period of super-normal returns. This is the notion that companies will earn returns above the cost of capital for a period of time, followed by a decline to the cost of capital. While this is clearly a useful concept, it is dangerous to link it to the length of the forecast. One reason is simply that, as we just showed, there is no necessary connection between the length of the forecast and the value of the company.

More important is that we have seen the concept of competitive advantage period inappropriately linked to the continuing value formula. Remember, the value-driver formula is based on incremental returns on capital, not companywide average returns. If you assume that incremental returns in the continuing value period will just equal the cost of capital, you are not assuming that the return on total capital (old and new) will equal the cost of capital. The return on the old capital will continue to earn the returns it is projected to earn in the last forecast period. In other words, the company's competitive advantage period has not come to an end once you reach the continuing value period. Exhibit 12.4 shows the implied average ROIC assuming that projected continuing value growth is 4.5 percent, the return on base capital is 18 percent, the return on incremental capital is 10 percent, and the WACC is 10 percent. The average return on all capital declines gradually. From its starting point at 10 percent, it declines to 14 percent (the halfway point to the incremental ROIC) after 11 years. It reaches 12 percent after 23 years and 11 percent after 37 years.

When Is Value Created?

Managers are sometimes uncomfortable that "all the value is in the continuing value." Exhibit 12.5 illustrates the problem for Innovation Inc. It appears that 85 percent of Innovation's value comes from the continuing value. Exhibit 12.6 suggests an alternative interpretation of where value is coming

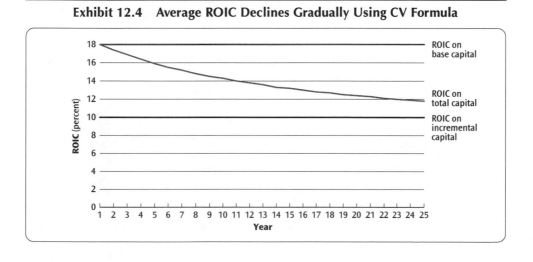

Exhibit 12.4 Average ROIC Declines Gradually Using CV Formula

Exhibit 12.5   Innovation Inc., Free Cash Flow Forecast and Valuation

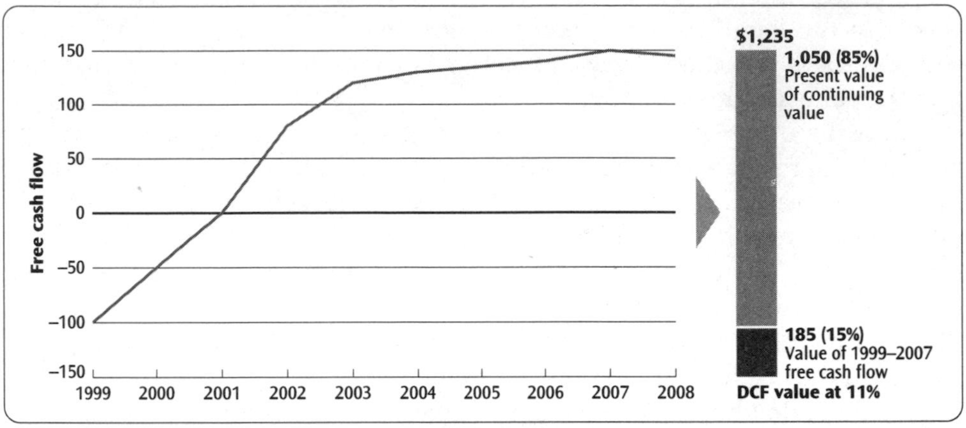

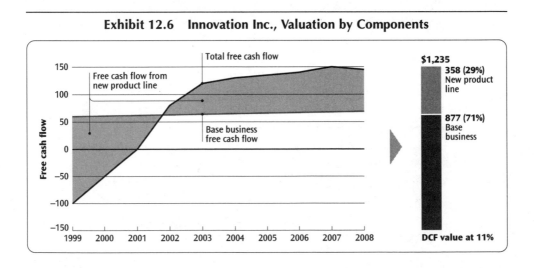

from—a business components approach. Innovation Inc. has a base business that earns a steady 12 percent return on capital and is growing at 4 percent per year. It also has developed a new product line that will require several years of negative cash flow because of construction of a new plant. Exhibit 12.6 shows that the base business has a value of $877, or 71 percent of Innovation's total value. So 71 percent of the company's value comes from operations that are currently generating strong cash flow. But the company has decided to reinvest this cash flow in a profitable new product line. This does not mean that 85 percent of the value is more than eight years out. It just means that the cash flow pattern mechanically results in the *appearance* that most of the value is a long way off.

Exhibit 12.6   Innovation Inc., Valuation by Components

Exhibit 12.7   Innovation Inc., Comparison of Continuing Values

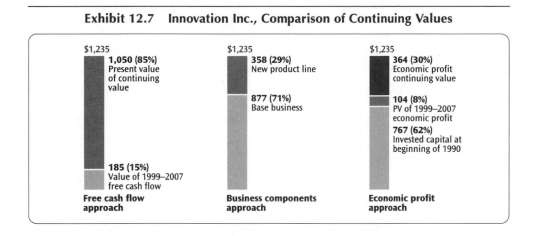

We can also use the economic profit model for another interpretation on continuing value. Exhibit 12.7 compares the components of value for Innovation Inc. using the two interpretations discussed earlier as well as the economic profit model. Under the economic profit model 62 percent of Innovation's value is simply its invested capital. The rest of the value is the present value of projected economic profit (8 percent for economic profit before 2007 and 30 percent for economic profit after 2007).

ESTIMATING PARAMETERS FOR CONTINUING VALUE VARIABLES

The parameters that must be defined to estimate continuing value are net operating profits less adjusted taxes (NOPLAT), free cash flow (FCF), rate of return on new investment (ROIC), rate of growth in NOPLAT (g), and weighted average cost of capital (WACC). Careful estimation of these parameters is critical because continuing value is sensitive to their value, particularly the growth assumption. Exhibit 12.8 shows how continuing value (calculated using the value driver formula) is affected by various combinations of growth rate and rate of return on new investment. The example assumes a $100 base level of NOPLAT and a 10 percent WACC. Notice that at a 14 percent expected rate of return on new capital, changing the growth rate from 6 percent to 8 percent increases the continuing value by 50 percent, from about $1,400 to about $2,100.

Estimating the continuing value parameters should be an integral part of the forecasting process. The continuing value parameters should reflect a coherent forecast for the long-term economic situation of the company and its industry. Specifically, the continuing value parameters should be based on the expected steady state condition to which the company will migrate in the scenario you are valuing.

Exhibit 12.8   Impact of Continuing-Value Assumptions

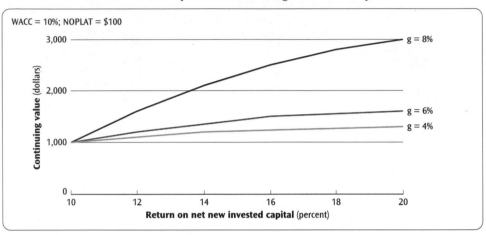

Some suggestions follow regarding continuing value parameters for the value-driver and the free cash flow perpetuity formulas:

- *NOPLAT.* The base level of NOPLAT should reflect a normalized level of earnings for the company at the midpoint of its business cycle. Revenues should generally reflect the continuation of the trends in the last forecast year adjusted to the midpoint of the business cycle. Operating costs should be based on sustainable margin levels, and taxes should be based on long-term expected rates.

- *Free cash flow.* First, estimate the base level of NOPLAT as described above. Although NOPLAT is usually based on the last forecast year's results, the prior year's level of investment is probably not a good indicator of the sustainable amount of investment needed for growth in the continuing value period. Carefully estimate how much investment will be required to sustain the forecasted growth rate. Often the forecasted growth in the continuing value period is lower than in the explicit forecast period, so the amount of investment should be a proportionately smaller amount of NOPLAT.

- *Incremental ROIC.* The expected rate of return on new investment should be consistent with expected competitive conditions. Economic theory suggests that competition will eventually eliminate abnormal returns, so for many companies, set ROIC = WACC. If you expect that the company will be able to continue its growth and to maintain its competitive advantage, then you might consider setting ROIC equal to the return the company is forecasted to earn during the explicit forecast period.

Exhibit 12.9 Potential Positioning on Continuing Value Parameters

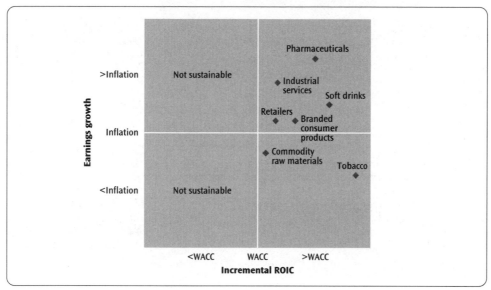

- *Growth rate.* Few companies can be expected to grow faster than the economy for long periods. The best estimate is probably the expected long-term rate of consumption growth for the industry's products, plus inflation. We also suggest that sensitivity analyses be done to understand how the growth rate affects value estimates.

- *WACC.* The weighted average cost of capital should incorporate a sustainable capital structure and an underlying estimate of business risk consistent with expected industry conditions.

- *Investment rate.* The investment rate is not explicitly in the formula, but it equals ROIC divided by growth. Make sure that the investment rate can be explained in light of industry economics.

Exhibit 12.9 suggests where companies in different industries may lie relative to each other in terms of long-term growth and ROIC. This is merely a suggestion; each company will have unique characteristics.

COMMON PITFALLS

Some of the mistakes made in estimating continuing values include naive base-year extrapolation and overconservatism:

Naive base-year extrapolation. Exhibit 12.10 illustrates a common error in forecasting the base level of free cash flow. From Year 9 to Year 10 (the

Exhibit 12.10   Right and Wrong Ways to Forecast the Base Free Cash Flow

	Year 9	Year 10	Year 11 (5% growth)	
			Incorrect	Correct
Sales	1,000	1,000	1,155	1,155
Operating expenses	(850)	(935)	(982)	(982)
EBIT	150	165	173	173
Cash taxes	(60)	(66)	(69)	(69)
NOPLAT	90	99	104	104
Depreciation	27	30	32	32
Gross cash flow	117	129	136	136
Capital expenditures	30	33	35	35
Increase in working capital	27	30	32	17
Gross investment	57	63	67	52
Free cash flow	60	66	69	84
Memo: Year-end working capital	300	330	362	347
Working capital/sales	30%	30%	31%	30%
Increase in working capital/sales	2.7%	2.7%	2.7%	1.5%

last forecast year), the company's earnings and cash flow grew by 10 percent. The forecast suggests that growth in the continuing value period will be 5 percent per year. A naive, and incorrect, forecast for Year 11 (the continuing value base year) simply increases every cash flow from Year 10 by 5 percent, as shown in the third column. This forecast is wrong because the increase in working capital is far too large for the increase in sales. Since sales are growing more slowly, the proportion of gross cash flow devoted to increasing working capital should decline significantly, as shown in the last column. In the last column, the increase in working capital is the amount necessary to maintain the year-end working capital at a constant percentage of sales. The naive approach results in a continual increase in working capital as a percentage of sales and will significantly understate the value of the company. Note that in the third column, free cash flow is 18 percent lower than it should be.

Naive overconservatism. Many analysts always assume the incremental return on capital in the continuing value period will equal the cost of capital. This also relieves them of having to forecast a growth rate, since growth in this case neither adds nor destroys value. For some businesses, this is obviously wrong. For example, both Coca-Cola's and PepsiCo's soft drink businesses earn high returns on invested capital, and their returns are unlikely to fall substantially as they continue to grow. Assuming that ROIC = WACC for these businesses would substantially understate their values. This applies equally to almost any business that sells something proprietary that is unlikely to be duplicated, including many pharmaceutical companies, consumer products companies, and some software companies.

Purposeful overconservatism. Analysts sometimes are overly conservative because of the uncertainty and size of the continuing value. If continuing value is estimated properly, the uncertainty cuts both ways: The results are just as likely to be higher than the estimate as they are to be lower. So conservatism overcompensates for the uncertainty. This is not to say that you should not be concerned about the uncertainty. That is why careful development of scenarios is a critical element of any valuation.

EVALUATING OTHER APPROACHES

A number of continuing value approaches are used in practice, often with misleading results. Some of these are acceptable if used carefully, but we prefer the approaches just recommended because they explicitly rely on the underlying economic assumptions embodied in the company analysis. The other approaches tend to hide the underlying economic assumptions. Exhibit 12.11 illustrates, for a sporting goods company, the wide dispersion of continuing value estimates arrived at by different techniques. This section explains why we prefer the recommended approaches. We classify the most common techniques into two categories: (1) other DCF approaches, and (2) non-cash flow approaches.

Other DCF Approaches

The recommended DCF formulas can be modified to derive additional continuing value formulas with more restrictive (and sometimes unreasonable) assumptions.

The first variation is the *convergence* formula. For many companies in competitive industries, the return on net new investment can be expected to

---

Exhibit 12.11   Continuing-Value Estimates for a Sporting Goods Company

Technique	Assumptions	Continuing value ($ million)
Book value	Per accounting records	268
Liquidation value	80% of working capital 70% of net fixed assets	186
Price-to-earnings ratio	Industry average of 15X	624
Market-to-book ratio	Industry average of 1.4X	375
Replacement cost	Book value adjusted for inflation	275
Perpetuity based on final year's cash flow	Normalized FCF growing at inflation rate	428

eventually converge to the cost of capital as all the excess profits are competed away. This assumption allows a simpler version of the value-driver formula, as follows:

$$CV = \frac{NOPLAT_{T+1}}{WACC}$$

The derivation begins with the value-driver formula:

$$CV = \frac{NOPLAT_{T+1}(1 - g/ROIC_I)}{WACC - g}$$

Assume that $ROIC_I = WACC$. In other words, the return on incremental invested capital equals the cost of capital.

$$CV = \frac{NOPLAT_{T+1}(1 - g/WACC)}{WACC - g}$$

$$= \frac{NOPLAT_{T+1}\dfrac{(WACC - g)}{(WACC)}}{WACC - g}$$

Canceling the term $WACC - g$ leaves a simple formula:

$$CV = \frac{NOPLAT_{T+1}}{WACC}$$

The growth term has disappeared from the equation. This does not mean that the nominal growth in NOPLAT will be zero. It means that growth will add nothing to value, because the return associated with growth just equals the cost of capital. This formula is sometimes interpreted as implying zero growth (not even with inflation), even though this is clearly not the case.

Misinterpretation of the convergence formula has led to another variant: the *aggressive* formula. This formula assumes that earnings in the continuing value period will grow at some rate, most often the inflation rate. The conclusion is then drawn that earnings should be discounted at the real WACC rather than the nominal WACC. The resulting formula is:

$$CV = \frac{NOPLAT_{T+1}}{WACC - g}$$

Here, g is the inflation rate. This formula can substantially overstate continuing value because it assumes that NOPLAT can grow without any incremental capital investment. This is unlikely (or impossible), because any growth will probably require additional working capital and fixed assets.

To show how this formula relates to the value-driver formula, let us assume that the return on incremental capital investment (ROIC) approaches infinity.

$$CV = \frac{NOPLAT_{T+1}(1 - g/ROIC_I)}{WACC - g}$$

$$ROIC_I \to \infty \quad \text{therefore } g/ROIC_I \to 0$$

$$CV = \frac{NOPLAT_{T+1}(1 - 0)}{WACC - g}$$

$$= \frac{NOPLAT_{T+1}}{WACC - g}$$

Exhibit 12.12 compares the two variations of the DCF formulas. This exhibit shows how the average return on invested capital (both existing and new investment) behaves under the two assumptions. In the aggressive case, NOPLAT grows without any new investment, so the return on invested capital eventually approaches infinity. In the convergence case, the average return on invested capital moves toward the weighted average cost of capital (WACC) as new capital becomes a larger portion of the total capital base.

Non-Cash Flow Approaches

In addition to DCF techniques, non-cash flow approaches to continuing value are sometimes used. Four common approaches are liquidation value, replacement cost, price-to-earnings ratio, and market-to-book ratio.

The liquidation-value approach sets the continuing value equal to an estimate of the proceeds from the sale of the assets of the business, after paying

Exhibit 12.12   Rates of Return Implied by Alternative Continuing Value Formulas

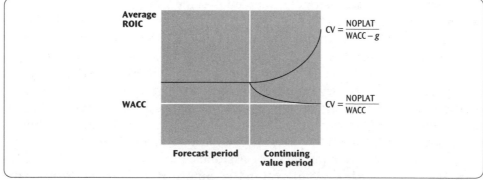

off liabilities at the end of the explicit forecast period. Liquidation value is often far different from the value of the company as a going concern. In a growing, profitable industry, a company's liquidation value is probably far below the going-concern value. In a dying industry, liquidation value may exceed going-concern value. Do not use this approach unless liquidation is likely at the end of the forecast period.

The replacement-cost approach sets the continuing value equal to the expected cost to replace the company's assets. This approach has a number of drawbacks. First, only tangible assets are replaceable. The company's "organizational capital" can be valued only on the basis of the cash flow the company generates. The replacement cost of the company's tangible assets may greatly understate the value of the company.

Second, not all the company's assets will ever be replaced. Consider a machine used only by this particular industry. The replacement cost of the asset may be so high that it is not economical to replace it. As long as it generates a positive cash flow, the asset is valuable to the ongoing business of the company. Here, the replacement cost may exceed the value of the business as an ongoing entity.

The price-to-earnings (P/E) ratio approach assumes the company will be worth some multiple of its future earnings in the continuing period. Of course, this will be true; the difficulty arises in trying to estimate an appropriate P/E ratio.

Suppose today's current industry average P/E ratio is chosen. Today's P/E ratio reflects the economic prospects of the industry during the explicit forecast period as well as the continuing value period. However, prospects at the end of the explicit forecast period are likely to be very different from today's. We need a different P/E ratio that reflects the company's prospects at the end of the forecast period. What factors will determine that ratio? As we discussed in Chapter 8, the company's expected growth, the rate of return on new capital, and the cost of capital are the primary determinants of its P/E ratio. These are the same factors that are in the value driver formula. So unless you are comfortable using an arbitrary P/E ratio, you are much better off with the value driver formula.

When valuing acquisitions, companies sometimes fall into the circular reasoning that the P/E ratio for the continuing value will equal the P/E ratio paid for the acquisition. In other words, if I pay 18 times earnings, I should be able to sell the business for 18 times earnings. In most cases, the reason a company is willing to pay a high P/E for an acquisition is that it believes it can take actions to greatly improve earnings. So the effective P/E it is paying on the improved level of earnings will be much less than 18. Once the improvements are in place and earnings are higher, buyers will not be willing to pay the same P/E unless they can make additional improvements.

The market-to-book ratio approach assumes the company will be worth some multiple of its book value, often the same as its current multiple or the multiples of comparable companies. This approach is conceptually similar to the P/E approach and faces the same problems. In addition to the complexity of deriving an appropriate multiple, the book value itself is distorted by inflation and important accounting assumptions. Once again, the DCF approaches are easier to use.

ADVANCED FORMULAS FOR CONTINUING VALUE

A variation of the value driver formula for DCF valuations is the two-stage value driver formula. This formula allows you to break up the continuing value period into two periods with different growth and ROIC assumptions. You might assume that during the first eight years after the explicit forecast period that the company would grow at 8 percent per year and earn an incremental ROIC of 15 percent. After those eight years, the company's growth would slow to 5 percent and incremental ROIC would drop to 11 percent:

$$CV = \left[\frac{NOPLAT_{T+1}(1 - g_A/ROIC_A)}{WACC - g_A} \right] \left[1 - \left(\frac{1 + g_A}{1 + WACC} \right)^{N-1} \right]$$
$$+ \left[\frac{NOPLAT_{T+1}(1 + g_A)^{N-1}(1 - g_B/ROIC_B)}{(WACC - g_B)(1 + WACC)^{N-1}} \right]$$

where N = The number of years in the first stage of the continuing value period.

g_A = The expected growth rate in the first stage of the CV period.

g_B = The expected growth in the second stage of the CV period.

$ROIC_A$ = The expected incremental ROIC during the first stage of the CV period.

$ROIC_B$ = The expected incremental ROIC during the second stage of the CV period.

Note that g_B must be less than WACC for this formula to be valid (otherwise the company would eventually take over the entire world economy).

A two-stage economic profit continuing value formula follows:[2]

$$CV = \frac{Economic\ profit_{T+1}}{WACC}$$
$$+ \left[\frac{NOPLAT_{T+1}(g_A/ROIC_A)(ROIC_A - WACC)}{WACC(WACC - g_A)} \right] \left[1 - \left(\frac{1 + g_A}{1 + WACC} \right)^{N-1} \right]$$
$$+ \frac{NOPLAT(1 + g_A)^{N-1}(g_B/ROIC_B)(ROIC_B - WACC)}{WACC(WACC - g_B)(1 + WACC)^{N-1}}$$

where all the variables are defined as in the earlier equations.

[2] Thanks to Pieter de Wit and David Krieger for deriving this formula.

Here is a two-stage formula that builds in a decline in incremental ROIC during the first stage:[3]

$$
\begin{aligned}
CV = &[NOPLAT_{T+1} \times (1 - g_A/ROIC_A)/(WACC - g_A)] \\
&\times [1 + \alpha \times ((1 + g_A)/(WACC - g_A)) \times (((1 + g_A)/(1 + WACC))^{N-1} - 1)] \\
&+ NOPLAT_{T+1} \times ((1 + g_A)/(1 + WACC))^N \times (((1 - g_B/ROIC_B)/(WACC - g_B)) \\
&- ((1 - g_A/ROIC_B)/(WACC - g_A)))
\end{aligned}
$$

Where α is the rate of decrease in ROIC and is given by the following formula:

$$
\alpha = (1/(N-1)) \times (1 - g_A/ROIC_B)/(1 - g_A/ROIC_A)))
$$

In all these formulas, the ROIC referred to is the incremental ROIC on net new investment. The assumption is always made in these formulas that the return on the base level of capital remains constant at the level of the last year of the explicit forecast.

If you want to model a decline in ROIC for all capital, including the base level of capital, it is best to model that into the explicit forecast. This is difficult to model with formulas because the growth rate in revenues and NOPLAT will not equal the growth rate in FCF and there are multiple ways for the ROIC to decline. ROIC could decline by setting the growth rate for capital and reducing NOPLAT over time (in which case NOPLAT will grow much slower than capital). Or you could set the growth rate for NOPLAT and adjust FCF each period (once again FCF growth will be slower than NOPLAT growth). The dynamics of these relationships are complex and we do not recommend embedding them in continuing value formulas, where the key value drivers will become less transparent.

HEINEKEN CASE

We used the value-driver model to estimate Heineken's DCF continuing value. The values of the parameters for the Business as Usual case are estimated as follows:

- The NOPLAT at the beginning of the continuing value period (one year after the last forecasted year) is 2014's NOPLAT. In Chapter 10, we forecasted Heineken's 2014 NOPLAT to be NLG 2,136 million.

---

[3] Thanks to Olivier Berlage for deriving this formula.

- Heineken's WACC is forecasted to remain at 6.7 percent. We do not foresee any significant change in Heineken's capital structure or business risk.

- Heineken's return on new invested capital before goodwill beyond 2013 is forecasted to be 17 percent. This is consistent with the forecast performance in the years leading up to 2013 in this scenario. This implies that Heineken has a basis for sustainable long-term advantage. Like Coca-Cola or Procter & Gamble, Heineken has created a brand that will allow it to achieve returns superior to what a company would normally earn if it were perfectly competitive in the long run (i.e., returns on invested capital equaling cost of capital).

- We expect that Heineken's NOPLAT will grow at 4 percent, based on 2 percent real growth and 2 percent price increases.

Using these parameters in the recommended continuing value formula results in an estimated continuing value of NLG 59.6 billion in 2013.

$$CV = \frac{NOPLAT_{2014}\left(1 - \frac{g}{ROIC_1}\right)}{WACC - g}$$

$$= \frac{2,136\left(1 - \frac{4.0\%}{17\%}\right)}{6.7\% - 4.0\%}$$

$$= NLG\ 59.6\ billion$$

Using the economic profit approach and the same parameter's results in a continuing value of economic profit after 2013 equal to NLG 47.5 billion, calculated as:

$$CV\ of\ economic\ profit = \frac{Economic\ profit_{2014}}{WACC} + \frac{NOPLAT_{2014}\left(\frac{g}{ROIC}\right)(ROIC - WACC)}{WACC(WACC - g)}$$

$$= \frac{1,322}{6.7\%} + \frac{2,136\left(\frac{4.0\%}{17\%}\right)(17\% - 6.7\%)}{6.7\%(6.7\% - 4.0\%)}$$

CV of economic profit $= 19.6 + 27.9 = $ NLG 47.5 billion

The continuing value is nontrivial because Heineken is expected to earn more than its cost of capital during and after the explicit forecast. However, the economic profit continuing value is not as large as the DCF continuing value. Adding the amount of invested capital at the end of 2013 to the continuing value of economic profit gives a total continuing value of NLG 59.6 billion, the same value calculated using the DCF approach.

$$CV = Invested\ capital_{2014} + CV\ of\ economic\ profit$$
$$= 12.1 + 47.5$$
$$= NLG\ 59.6\ billion$$

13

Calculating and
Interpreting the Results

The final phase of the valuation process involves calculating and testing the company's value, then interpreting the results in terms of the specific decision at hand.

CALCULATE AND TEST RESULTS

You are now ready to complete the valuation and calculate the company's equity value. Here are the steps:

1. Discount the forecasted free cash flow or economic profit to the present at the WACC.

2. Discount the continuing value to the present at the WACC. Note that the continuing value will already be expressed as a value at the end of the explicit forecast period, so you should discount it by the number of years in the explicit forecast. For example, if the forecast has 10 years, discount the continuing value by 10 years, not 11 years.

3. Calculate the value of operations by adding the present value of the explicit period to the present value of the continuing value. (In the economic profit approach, also add the invested capital at the beginning of the forecast period.) Adjust for mid-year discounting. We often assume that the cash flows occur continuously throughout the year rather than at the end of the year. Thus, we increase the value by growing it at WACC for the number of months we need to add (typically six months or more, if we are doing the forecast late in the year).

4. Add the value of any nonoperating assets whose cash flows were excluded from free cash flow and economic profit to estimate the value of the total enterprise. Such items might include excess marketable securities and investments in unrelated subsidiaries. The value of these assets should be estimated on the basis of their respective expected cash flows and appropriate discount rates, or by reference to their market values. For example, because excess marketable securities are zero-net-present-value investments, the present value of all future cash flow related to marketable securities equals their current market value (which for most money market instruments also equals their book value).

5. Subtract the market value of all debt, hybrid securities, minority interest, or other claims to estimate the equity value. (The estimation of market values of these instruments was explained in Chapter 10.) Do not subtract the value of accounting liabilities such as reserves that are quasi-equity. The key is consistency with cash flow. If the cash flows from an item are excluded from free cash flow (e.g., interest-bearing debt and related interest expense), then subtract the value of the liability. If the cash flows are not excluded (e.g., reserves for deferred taxes), do not subtract the value to estimate the equity value.[1]

Exhibit 13.1 illustrates a typical equity-value calculation. After estimating the equity value for each scenario, perform several checks to test the logic of the results, minimize the possibility of errors, and ensure that you have a good understanding of the forces driving the valuation. You might start by ensuring that the value is consistent with the forecast. A company that has been projected to earn rates of return on invested capital far above its WACC should have a value far above such benchmarks as book value. If the resulting value is low, a computational error has probably been made.

Next, compare the resulting value to the company's market value. If your estimate of value is far from the market value, try to identify the causes of the difference as concretely as possible. Do you expect higher revenue growth than the market? Higher margins? Lower capital spending?

Evaluate the financial aspects of the forecast (amount of debt and marketable securities). If debt or excess marketable securities are excessive relative to the company's targets, how should the company resolve the imbalance? Should it raise equity if too much debt is projected? Should the company be willing to raise equity at its current market price?

---

[1] Employee stock options can be treated in two ways. One approach is to estimate their value and subtract them, like other liabilities. The other approach, which is best for in-the-money options, is to assume that the options are exercised and so the number of shares outstanding is increased accordingly.

Exhibit 13.1   Sample Valuation Summary

	$ million
Value of operations (PV of FCF)	5,000
Excess cash and marketable securities	50
Investments in unconsolidated subsidiaries	300
Other non-operating assets	100
Enterprise value	**5,450**
Interest-bearing debt	(1,000)
Capitalized value of operating leases	(400)
Minority interest	(100)
Preferred shares	(200)
Employee stock options	(200)
Equity value	**3,550**

As you begin to synthesize the results of your valuation, we suggest that you compare the value of each scenario against its value drivers and any critical assumptions like gross margins, capital spending, new product development, and expected competitive response. This should help provide an overall perspective on each scenario and the relationships among them.

The final step is to estimate a most likely value based on the probability of each scenario. Assign probabilities to each scenario, multiply the probabilities by the value of each scenario and add the resulting values to find the most likely value. This last step may not be necessary. Just having the scenario values may provide enough information to make whatever decisions are necessary.

INTERPRET THE RESULTS

The purpose of valuing a company is always to help guide some management or investment decision, be it acquisition, divestiture, or adoption of internal strategic initiatives. The results must be analyzed from the perspective of the decision at hand. Since uncertainty and risk are involved in most business decisions, think of value in terms of scenarios and ranges of value that reflect this uncertainty.

The decision based on any one scenario will generally be obvious, given its estimated impact on shareholder value. But interpreting multiple scenarios and having confidence in your results are considerably more complex. At a minimum, we would suggest a number of additional analyses.

Understand how much the variables underlying the results of each scenario could change without calling into question your decision. This provides a sense of the margin for error. A large margin gives greater comfort in the decision, but too large an error margin is suspicious. Reconsider your assumptions by asking if the decision is clearly to go ahead with the contemplated action, what would have to go wrong to invalidate the decision? How likely is that to occur? If the decision is negative, what are the upside possibilities that are being passed up?

Assess the likelihood of change in the important assumptions underlying each scenario (assigning each a probability of occurrence). Consider:

- The impact and likelihood of change in the broad assumptions underlying the scenario. How critical are these assumptions to the results? Some industries are more dependent on basic economic conditions than others. Home building, for example, is highly correlated with the overall health of the economy. Branded food processing, on the other hand, is less affected by broad economic trends.

- Assumptions about the competitive structure of the industry. A scenario that assumes substantial market share increases is probably less likely in a highly competitive and concentrated market than in an industry with fragmented and inefficient competition.

- Assumptions about the company's internal capabilities to achieve the results predicted in the scenario. Can the company develop the products on time and manufacture them within the expected range of costs?

Develop alternative scenarios suggested by the preceding analyses. The process of examining initial results may well uncover unanticipated questions that are best resolved through evaluating additional scenarios. This implies that the valuation process is inherently circular. Doing the valuation itself often provides insights that lead to additional scenarios and analyses.

THE ART OF VALUATION

Valuation depends mainly on understanding the business, its industry, and the general economic environment, and then doing a prudent job of forecasting. Careful thought and hard work leads to foresight. Correct methodology is only a small, but necessary, part of the valuation process.

We would like to close Part Two with two important messages. First, avoid shortcuts: They will usually cost you time in the long term. Invest the time to build an appropriate valuation model before trying to draw conclusions. The investment in a complete model always pays off:

- Your model should include complete income statements and balance sheets as well as cash flow statements and key performance ratios such as return on invested capital, operating margins, and capital turnover. A cash flow statement with no balance sheet is not sufficient.

- Ground the model in historical financial statements. The model should include 5 to 10 years of historical financial data so that the forecast can be analyzed in light of historical performance and to ensure that the forecast is anchored in fact.

- Understand the accounting and tax complications of the company's financial statements. Understanding the accounting is often critical to understanding the economics of the business.

Second, keep in mind that valuation is as much art as science and is inherently imprecise. Valuation is highly sensitive to small changes in assumptions about the future. Take a look at the sensitivity of a typical company with a forward-looking P/E ratio of 20. Changing the cost of capital for this company by 0.5 percentage points will change the value by about 12 percent to 14 percent. Changing the growth rate for the next 15 years by 1 percent per year will change the value by about 7 percent. For high-growth companies, the sensitivity is even greater. The sensitivity is also highest when interest rates are low, as they were at the end of the 1990s.

In light of this sensitivity it should be no surprise that the value of a typical company will fluctuate by 15 percent or more during any three-month period. Exhibit 13.2 shows the distribution of the quarterly share price volatility for 2,117 companies during the 10 years ended June 20, 1999

Exhibit 13.2   Quarterly Volatility of U.S. Companies

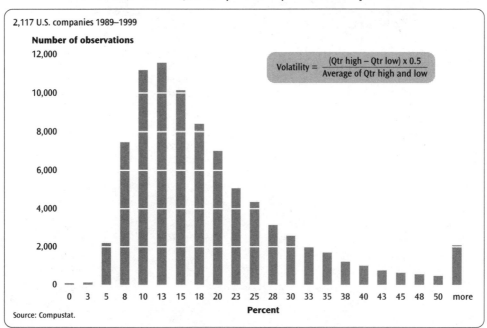

Source: Compustat.

(where volatility is defined as one-half the distance between the quarterly high and low divided by the average price for the quarter).

We typically aim for a valuation range of plus or minus 15 percent, which is similar to the range used by investment bankers. Even professionals who do valuations for a living aren't always accurate. In other words, keep your aspirations for precision in check.

HEINEKEN CASE

We will now complete and analyze the Heineken valuation. First, we will calculate the equity value of Heineken for the Business as Usual scenario. Exhibits 13.3 and 13.4 show the calculation of the value of Heineken's operations using the DCF and economic profit approaches, respectively. The value of Heineken's operations in both methods is NLG 33 billion.

Note that there is a mid-year adjustment factor equal to one-half of a year's value discounted at Heineken's WACC. This is to adjust for the fact that we conservatively discounted the free cash flows and economic profits as if they were entirely realized at the end of each year, when, in fact, cash flows occur (cycles

Exhibit 13.3   Heineken—DCF Valuation

Business as usual case

	Free cash flow after goodwill (NLG million)	Discount factor	Present value of FCF (NLG million)
1999	446	0.937	418
2000	754	0.878	662
2001	800	0.822	658
2002	526	0.770	405
2003	910	0.722	657
2004	1,079	0.676	730
2005	1,134	0.633	718
2006	1,190	0.593	706
2007	1,247	0.556	694
2008	1,307	0.521	681
2009	1,359	0.488	663
2010	1,413	0.457	646
2011	1,470	0.428	629
2012	1,528	0.401	613
2013	1,590	0.376	598
Continuing value	59,629	0.376	22,416
Operating value			31,893
Mid-year adjustment factor			1.033
Operating value (discounted to current month)			**32,950**

Exhibit 13.4   Heineken—Economic Profit Valuation

Business as usual case

	Economic profit before goodwill (NLG million)	Discount factor	Present value of economic profit (NLG million)
1999	721	0.937	675
2000	745	0.878	654
2001	777	0.822	639
2002	831	0.770	640
2003	854	0.722	616
2004	890	0.676	602
2005	928	0.633	588
2006	966	0.593	573
2007	1,005	0.556	559
2008	1,045	0.521	544
2009	1,087	0.488	530
2010	1,130	0.457	517
2011	1,175	0.428	503
2012	1,222	0.401	490
2013	1,271	0.376	478
Continuing value	47,547	0.376	17,874
Present value of economic profit			26,483
Inv capital (beg. of forecast excluding goodwill)			6,113
Less: PV of investments in goodwill			(703)
Operating value			31,893
Mid-year adjustment factor			1.033
Operating value (discounted to current month)			**32,950**

notwithstanding) evenly throughout the year. We take a six-month factor because we are valuing the company as of January 1, 1999; if we had chosen another month we would have to offset the discount factor by one-half year, plus the number of months.

Under the Business as Usual scenario, Heineken's equity value is NLG 33.5 billion, or NLG 107 per share, as shown in Exhibit 13.5. To calculate the market equity value, we add the market value of nonoperating assets such as excess cash, marketable securities, and investments in unconsolidated subsidiaries to the value of operations to obtain the enterprise value. We then subtract debt, minority interest, and other non-equity sources of financing to obtain the equity value.

The value of Heineken's operations is about four times that of its beginning invested capital (including goodwill). Our results seem consistent with the Business as Usual scenario, given that returns on invested capital are about twice that of its WACC.

We also valued the other two scenarios for Heineken. The results are summarized in Exhibit 13.6. In the Price War scenario, we made two adjustments to the assumptions. We assumed that revenue growth would be 0 percent nominally, or negative 1 percent to 2 percent in real terms, because of changes in price mix. We

Exhibit 13.5   Heineken—Value of Equity

Business as usual case

	NLG million
Operating value	32,950
Excess market securities	1,806
Financial fixed assets	1,080
Enterprise value	**35,836**
Debt	1,661
Capitalized operating leases	0
Retirement-related liability	103
Preferred stock	0
Minority interest	564
Restructuring provision	0
Equity value	**33,509**
Most recent shares outstanding	313.6
Value per share	107

also assumed that consolidation would be minimal; only 1 percent (rather than 3 percent) of revenue growth would come from acquisitions. This scenario yields a value of NLG 87.6 per share, an 18 percent discount to the Business as Usual scenario. While a price war could result in even lower prices, it couldn't be sustained for the entire 15-year scenario. Our forecast reflects this outlook.

For the Market Discipline/Industry Consolidation scenario, we allowed prices to rise at the same rate as in the base scenario. But we increased the amount of growth through acquisitions so that by the end of the short-term forecast, Heineken would have a 7 percent market share. This resulted in an equity value of NLG 147.4, a 38 percent premium over the Business as Usual case.

We assigned a higher probability to the upside scenario because we think Heineken's aggressive acquisition strategy will continue to bear fruit. We also believe

Exhibit 13.6   Heineken—Summary of Scenario Values

		Scenario		
		"Price war"	"Business as usual"	"Discipline/ consolidation"
Average revenue growth, 1999–2003	Percent	2.4	5.6	7.0
Average ROIC (including goodwill), 1999–2003	Percent	13.0	13.1	14.2
Company value	NLG billion	29.8	35.8	48.5
Equity value	NLG billion	27.5	33.5	46.2
Equity value per share	Guilders	87.6	106.9	147.4
Probability	Percent	15.0	60.0	25.0
Expected value per share			114.1	

Exhibit 13.7 Heineken—Sensitivity Analysis

	Base value 1999–2003 (percent)	Change (percent)	Change in equity value (NLG billion)	(percent)
Revenue growth	5.6	1.0	3.3	9.8
EBITA margin	11.1	1.0	3.8	11.4
Capital turnover	2.4	0.1	2.4	7.2
WACC	6.7	−0.5	7.5	22.5

that market barriers such as government intervention in emerging markets and local oligopolies will slow globalization and tend to keep prices stable. When we weight the scenario values by their probabilities, we arrive at an equity value of NLG 114 per share, about the same as Heineken's market value in December 1998. Thus, our view of Heineken's prospects is basically the same as what the market sees. This is not surprising given the stability of the beer industry and the company's strategy.

SENSITIVITY ANALYSIS

It is important to understand how the model is affected by changes in growth and ROIC. We first performed a sensitivity analysis on growth, EBITA margin, capital turnover, and WACC. Exhibit 13.7 summarizes the results. We see that, aside from changing WACC, a change in EBITA margin and growth has greater relative impact on the equity value of Heineken than capital turnover. The impact of WACC on the model is especially curious given the current capital structure; it seems that taking on debt can create the greatest value.

The result of the sensitivity analysis is not surprising. Given the already relatively high return on invested capital (above 10 percent), Heineken's best bet would be to increase its growth rate.

OUTLOOK

Heineken is a healthy company that the market expects to maintain its attractive return on capital with moderate growth (slightly better than the beer market overall). Since these expectations are already built into the market value, Heineken will have to come up with something new to increase shareholder returns.

Part Three

Applying Valuation

14

Multibusiness Valuation

Many valuations involve multibusiness companies whose futures depend on successful management of the portfolio of business units under their control. Multibusiness valuation is useful for several purposes, not the least of which is simply understanding the business. Strategic decisions for most multibusiness companies take place at the business-unit level. Thorough understanding of the company requires careful analysis of the threats and opportunities faced by each business unit. A company valuation built from separate valuations of business units provides much deeper insight than a company valuation that looks at the organization as a whole. The separate valuation of business units is at the heart of value-based management.

Multibusiness valuation is also useful for determining whether a company is more valuable as a combination of businesses or whether it is more valuable if the units are operated as stand-alone entities. It helps to create a clearer picture of headquarters costs and benefits since headquarters can be valued as if it were a separate cost center. The central question is usually whether the benefits of headquarters exceed the costs or if some of the extra layers of overhead can be trimmed.

The burden of proof is on management. The most current evidence suggests that conglomerates are valued lower by the market than comparable pure play companies. In the study most often cited on the subject, Berger and Ofek[1] estimated the conglomerate discount to be about 15 percent, based on a study of more than 3,500 companies from 1986 to 1991. In a 1996 study, they also found that companies with larger conglomerate discounts were more likely to be taken over and broken up.[2]

---

[1] P. Berger, and E. Ofek, "Diversification's Effect on Firm Value," *Journal of Financial Economics,* vol. 37 (1995), pp. 39–65.
[2] P. Berger, and E. Ofek, "Bustup Takeovers of Value-Destroying Diversified Firms," *The Journal of Finance,* vol. 51, no. 4 (1996), pp. 1175–1200.

VALUING THE MULTIBUSINESS COMPANY

Valuing a multibusiness company is fundamentally the same as valuing a single-business company. What makes multibusiness valuation more complex is that each business unit has its own cash flows, capital structure, and cost of capital. In addition, business units may have shared cash flows and it may be hard to separate the costs and benefits of corporate headquarters.

Valuing a multibusiness company is somewhat like putting together building blocks. The value of the entire corporation is the sum of the value of the business units, plus nonoperating assets, less the unallocated costs of corporate headquarters. Unique issues in valuing a multibusiness company that were not discussed earlier in this book include:

- Defining business units and their cash flows.
- Determining cash flow costs and benefits of corporate headquarters.
- Estimating business-unit tax rates.
- Estimating business-unit capital structure and cost of capital.
- Estimating a discount rate for headquarters costs.
- Adding up the pieces to value the entire corporation.

Defining Business Units and Their Cash Flows

In principle, a distinct business unit could be split off as a stand-alone business or sold to another company. A good rule of thumb is to define business units at the smallest practical level of aggregation. For example, a company may have a consumer products division that can be broken down into soap, toiletries, and detergents units. These are logically separable business units if they do not have interdependent means of production, distribution, or marketing.

Identifying business units and allocating cash flows among them is not always easy. Exhibit 14.1 illustrates a hypothetical company that markets

---

Exhibit 14.1   Business Units for a Hypothetical Company

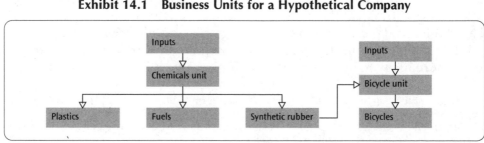

three products: plastics, fuels, and bicycles. Plastics and fuels are joint products from a single chemical plant. This same plant produces synthetic rubber as a by-product that is used for the manufacture of bicycle tires. How should business units be defined? How shall we handle the joint product and by-product problems?

As Exhibit 14.1 suggests, the easiest solution is to create two business units. The first combines the joint products—plastics and fuels—under a single roof. This is advisable because they are produced in a single facility and because their production is interdependent. Management of the business unit must maximize value by choosing the best output mix of plastics and fuels given market demand, production constraints for the two products, and the cost of their inputs. The general principle is to combine joint products (interdependent or contingent products) into a single business unit.

The second business unit produces bicycles. It is clearly independent of business unit 1 except for the fact that a by-product of business unit 1, synthetic rubber, is an input for the bicycle division. However, synthetic rubber could be acquired from another supplier. Hence, the bicycle division is logically separable as a business unit. Synthetic rubber can be sold, at a market-determined transfer price, by business unit 1 to business unit 2. If the transfer price is not acceptable to business unit 2, it should be allowed to purchase synthetic rubber from a third party.

To identify business-unit cash flows, we deal with two typical problems: transfer pricing and corporate overhead. Transfer pricing arises when the output of one business unit is the input of another. A high price will increase profits of the supplier at the expense of the user, and vice versa. The recommended solution is to establish a transfer price as close as possible to the market price of close substitutes. This can be a difficult task if substitutes are hard to find. The main idea is to approximate market prices so that profit is appropriately allocated to the supplier or to the user of the goods or service.

Taxation often complicates transfer pricing. One of the benefits of the corporate umbrella (that is, of headquarters) is that it can establish a transfer-pricing system that keeps profits in the jurisdiction that has the lowest tax burden. As a result, one set of artificial transfer prices may be used for tax purposes and another set of market-determined prices for determining business-unit cash flows (although tax authorities may not permit this). This topic is covered in Chapter 17, where we discuss valuing foreign subsidiaries.

Allocating corporate overhead is a problem closely related to transfer pricing. The central issue is whether business units would use corporate services if they were spun off as separate entities. Many services would be used; for example, accounting, legal, computer, and internal consulting services. Whenever possible, the cost of these services should be allocated to business units on a usage basis or, failing that, on the basis of a reasonable proxy for usage, such as operating income, revenues, capital employed, or number of employees.

In theory, market prices should be used for allocation purposes. For example, one hour of a headquarters accountant's time should be billed to a division based on the market price of accountants' time in general—that is, at the opportunity cost to the division. Any difference between the market price and the actual salary paid to the accountant by headquarters is a benefit or a cost to headquarters. As a practical matter, cost-based pricing is more often used because of the extra administrative costs of a market-based system. However, the basic principle remains—headquarters costs that would not be borne by the business units were they separate should not be allocated.

Determining Cash Flow Costs and Benefits of Corporate Headquarters

Attributable to headquarters are the costs and benefits that arise from combining business units under a single corporate umbrella rather than running them as separate entities. Determining these costs and benefits is a difficult exercise. At one extreme, headquarters is merely an extra level of expense, and great value can be obtained by breaking up the business units, selling them, and demolishing corporate headquarters. At the opposite extreme, headquarters can be too lean for its optimal role as agent for the capital markets in getting the highest performance from the business units, as well as capital allocation, risk management, and tax planning. Headquarters costs that should not be allocated to business units include:

- Headquarters' executive salaries, wages, bonuses, and benefits.
- Directors' fees and insurance.
- Corporate office space (buildings and land) and equipment.
- Support staff and related costs (accounting, legal, planning, personnel, communications, transportation, and administrative).
- Corporate-level advertising.
- Corporate-level research and development.

The portion of each cost to be retained at headquarters is subjective. Consider the cost of running the tax department. Each business unit would have to have its own tax department if it were an independent company. Therefore, some portion of these costs should be allocated to the business units. The relevant consideration is: What would business-unit costs be were the companies separate? To illustrate headquarters costs from an outsider's point of view, we reviewed the 25 largest companies in the Fortune

Exhibit 14.2   1986 Headquarters Cost for 21 of the 25 Largest Industrials

Company	HQ cost ($ millions)	HQ cost as percentage of market equity (percent)	Capitalized HQ cost as percentage of total equity value (percent)	HQ cost as a percentage of sales (percent)
General Motors	1,015	4.8	58	1.0
Allied Signal	249	3.6	34	2.1
Mobil	456	2.8	35	1.0
Chrysler	121	2.3	15	0.5
Atlantic Richfield	213	2.0	31	1.5
Procter & Gamble	257	2.0	15	1.7
Chevron	306	2.0	23	1.3
Occidental Petroleum	82	1.8	155	0.5
Tenneco	92	1.6	130	0.6
DuPont	304	1.5	11	1.1
Shell Oil	334	1.3	16	2.0
Boeing	100	1.3	6	0.6
RJR Nabisco	139	1.1	11	0.8
General Electric	389	1.0	5	1.1
USX	54	1.0	22	0.4
Rockwell International	58	0.9	4	0.5
Exxon	406	0.8	8	0.6
Philip Morris	126	0.7	6	0.6
Amoco Corporation	113	0.7	7	0.6
United Technology	25	0.4	3	0.2
McDonnell Douglas	11	0.4	3	0.1
Average		**1.6**	**30**	**0.9**

500 industrial list using fiscal 1986 publicly available data (Exhibit 14.2). We have not updated the data because segment-based reporting changed and it has become difficult to obtain the needed information—even for estimates.[3]

Headquarters costs averaged 1.6 percent of the 1986 year-end market value of their equity. Managers of mutual funds usually receives an average of 0.5 percent of assets under management. As a percentage of sales, headquarters costs averaged 0.9 percent in 1986.

To compare the present value of headquarters costs with the market value of equity, we capitalized the after-tax cost stream by assuming it would grow at a real rate of 2.5 percent per year and that it had the same risk as the business as a whole. The results shown in column 3 of Exhibit 14.2 are amazing.

---

[3] To compute corporate headquarters expenses, we used the business segment exhibit in the annual report and looked up the corporate expense number located there. No guarantee exists that this number is defined in the same way from company to company because of differences in the way headquarters expenses are allocated to business units. We used the corporate expense number as reported if taxes and financing costs were not included. When they were, and when we knew the tax and financing figures, we made adjustments to estimate the pretax, prefinancing corporate expense. Occasionally, the pretax corporate expense number had to be estimated, when tax and financing expenses were unknown, by assuming interest income of 7 percent on marketable securities, a 10 percent interest expense rate on debt, and a 46 percent corporate income tax rate.

For most of the companies in the sample, headquarters costs absorbed more than 10 percent of the equity value of the company.

Headquarters benefits are usually more difficult to identify than costs. We have divided them into two broad categories: those that are quantifiable, and others that, while important, are extremely difficult to measure.

Benefits that can be quantified (with difficulty) are tax advantages and greater debt capacity. Tax advantages attributable to headquarters arise primarily from the lack of an adequate secondary market for tax shields. A group of business units with highly variable year-to-year taxable earnings can share tax shields by operating under a corporate umbrella. The losses of unit A can be used immediately to shelter the gains of unit B, so the business unit does not have to wait for tax carry-forwards or carry-backs. Conglomerates constructed from business units with low taxable-income variability are likely to benefit less from a corporate tax umbrella than conglomerates built from diverse business units with highly variable income.

Headquarters also provides the benefit of the present value of tax shelters that arise from corporate-level tax planning. In addition to the ability to use tax losses immediately, corporate headquarters is often able to undertake international tax planning (for example, transfer pricing) that might not be available were the business units operating separately.

Finally, greater debt capacity is created because business-unit cash flows are not perfectly correlated. Once the capital structure for each business unit has been developed and business-unit debt has been totaled, a portion attributable to headquarters might yet remain. (See the discussion of determining business-unit capital structure and cost of capital that follows for more on how to allocate debt to business units.) The present value of the tax shield arising from this debt is a benefit of headquarters. If the company owes no corporate-level taxes, this benefit evaporates.

Benefits that are not easily measured include prospective synergies and information advantages. Operating synergies are an obvious benefit of combining business units. If the company makes an acquisition that allows the existing salesforce to assume the duties of the target's salesforce, the present value of the realized savings is a benefit due, at least initially, to headquarters if headquarters recommended the acquisition and subsequent combination of the two businesses. The vision of headquarters is not part of continuing operations and, although valuable, impossible to forecast as part of cash flows.

Information and communications advantages complete the list of headquarter's benefits. Although difficult to quantify, they can be important. Nobel laureate Kenneth Arrow contends that informational advantages of vertical integration can be valuable because they reduce uncertainty. For example, a manufacturer may decide that it is optimal to own production facilities to eliminate variability in supplies that might disrupt production.

Estimating Business-Unit Tax Rates

The relevant tax rate for valuing a business unit depends on the taxes it would be paying were it not under a corporate umbrella. As mentioned earlier, when a business unit is separated from the parent, it loses its ability to shelter taxable income with losses elsewhere in the parent and must resort to tax carry-forwards and tax carry-back provisions of the tax code. This consideration is also relevant when deciding whether to spin off a unit or to sell it to another company. A simple spin-off may increase the unit's tax rate, whereas sale to another company that can shelter the unit's earnings may be preferable. Effective tax rates may change for less obvious reasons. For example, tax advantages of transfer pricing or multinational taxation may be different if a business unit is separated from the parent.

Since we are treating corporate headquarters as a separate business unit for valuation purposes, its effect on taxes must also be estimated. In most cases, headquarters (the corporate umbrella) is a means for generating tax shelters; hence, its implied tax rate is negative. The present value of headquarters tax shelters is a benefit to the company.

Estimating Business-Unit Capital Structure and Cost of Capital

The capital structure of each business unit should be consistent with that of comparable companies in its industry and with the overall philosophy of its parent. If the parent is aggressive and chooses a Baa bond rating, then business units will normally have capital structures that bring them a Baa rating within their industry. At that rating, different business units may be able to borrow varying amounts of debt. An insurance subsidiary may be able to carry an 80 percent debt-to-capital ratio, while a manufacturing subsidiary might only have a 25 percent debt-to-capital ratio. The basis for determining business-unit capital structure will usually depend on cash flow or capital employed at the business unit. Debt-to-capital ratios or interest-coverage ratios for comparable companies are a useful starting point.

The difference between the sum of all business-unit debt and total companywide debt should be attributed to corporate headquarters. Any remaining debt results from the fact that the debt capacity of a portfolio of business-unit cash flows that are not perfectly correlated has less variance than the sum of the separate cash flows. Consequently, the combination of separate business units under a corporate umbrella provides greater debt capacity. The present value of the interest tax shield is a benefit of headquarters.

Having determined the target capital structure and tax rate of each business unit, you still need to estimate the cost of equity to establish its weighted average cost of capital. In the case of a division of a company or a nonpublic company, no betas are published. To estimate a beta, we recommend using one of three approaches: management comparisons; comparison companies, or a multiple regression.

Management comparisons A crude but often effective way of estimating betas is to elicit the help of management. Have three to five managers sit down and position the division or project being analyzed relative to a list of industries and their betas (see Exhibit 14.3 for example). You do not need to show managers the actual betas, or even to explain the concept. Just have a few of them suggest the industry with risk closest to their division. If they all agree (and they usually do), you will have a reasonable estimate of the levered beta of the division.

Comparison companies A second approach is to identify the publicly traded competitors most similar to the division. You can then look up the betas for these companies, which are *presumed* to have similar risk. But there is a catch. Beta is a measure of the systematic risk of the levered equity of the comparison companies, and these companies may employ leverage differently from that used by the division you are attempting to value. To get around this problem, you have to unlever the betas of the comparison companies to obtain their business risk, then relever using the target capital structure of the division you are analyzing.

The unlevered beta measures the business risk of a company by removing the effect of financial leverage. The observed equity beta computed from market return data presents a picture of the risk of equity given the company's existing leverage. To unlever the beta, you need data on the company's levered beta, its target capital structure, and its marginal tax rate.

Exhibit 14.3   Average Industry Betas, August 1998

Industry	Number of companies	Lowest Beta	Highest Beta	Average Beta
Brokerage	9	0.52	1.75	1.40
Retail	12	1.03	1.51	1.21
Banking	9	0.87	1.28	1.06
Chemicals	9	0.83	1.25	0.95
Steel	8	0.53	1.33	0.93
Automotive assembly	8	0.55	1.24	0.90
Forest products	8	0.62	1.07	0.83
Non-alcoholic beverages	8	0.43	1.09	0.81
Food processing	8	0.65	1.07	0.76
Oil	8	0.58	0.81	0.67
Electric utilities	9	0.27	0.60	0.39

Source: BARRA.

Suppose that the levered beta of Comparison Corporation is 1.2 and that it has a debt-to-equity ratio of 1.3. The division you are valuing has a target debt-to-equity ratio of 0.8. To estimate the unlevered equity beta of the division, the following formula will prove useful. (Levering and unlevering betas is a conceptually tricky business, especially for extreme leverage situations. The following formula assumes that debt is risk free. In addition, the corporate marginal tax rate may change as a function of leverage, and the formula assumes that it does not. See Appendix A for alternative formulas.)

$$beta_L = \left[1 + (1 - T_c)\frac{B}{S}\right]beta_u$$

Where $beta_L$ = The levered equity beta
T_c = The corporate marginal tax rate
B/S = The debt-to-equity ratio for the division, estimated in terms of market value
$beta_u$ = The unlevered equity beta (a measure of the business risk of the division)

To use this formula, you also need to know the marginal tax rate of both Comparison Corporation and of the division you are studying. Suppose the tax rate of Comparison Corporation is 25 percent and your tax rate will be 34 percent. The unlevered beta (the operating risk) of Comparison Corporation is:

$$beta_u = \frac{beta_L}{\left[1 + (1 - T_c)\frac{B}{S}\right]}$$

$$= \frac{1.2}{\left[1 + (1 - 0.25)1.3\right]}$$

$$= 0.61$$

Relying on the assumption that Comparison Corporation has the same business risk as your division, you can now estimate the levered beta of your division as follows:

$$beta_L = \left[1 + (1 - 0.34).8\right].61 = 0.93$$

Multiple regression approach   One of the most difficult problems with estimating the cost of equity for business units is that good comparisons can rarely be found because most companies have multiple lines of business and different percentages of their assets in each. A way around this problem is to recognize that the business risk (that is, the unlevered beta) of a multidivisional company is a weighted average of the risks of each line of business. Note also that business risk, on the assets side of the balance sheet, equals the weighted average of all risks on the liabilities side. This is a demonstration of the principle of the conservation of risk.

In the United States, it is possible to use line-of-business data to estimate the percentages of assets that companies have tied up in their separate lines of business. If you have data on two companies, each with two lines of business, and know the company's unlevered betas as well as the asset weights, then you can construct two equations with two unknowns:

$$beta_{u1} = W_{A1}beta_{UA} + W_{B1} beta_{UB}$$
$$beta_{u2} = W_{A2}beta_{UA} + W_{B2} beta_{UB}$$

It is then easy to solve for the unlevered line-of-business betas, $beta_{UA}$, and $beta_{UB}$.

If there are more companies than lines of business, the unlevered business-unit betas can be estimated by running a linear regression of the unlevered company betas against the weights for the lines of business, being careful to suppress the constant term. The coefficients from the regression are unbiased estimates of the business-unit betas.

Exhibit 14.4 illustrates data for forest products companies. Our regression results based on these data indicated the following:

Unlevered beta for building products = 1.08

Unlevered beta for paper products = 0.88

The unlevered beta represents an estimate of the operating risk of the business unit. Next, the actual tax rate and leverage of the business unit, along with the estimated unlevered beta, can be used to compute an estimate of its levered beta. Given the levered beta of a business unit, the capital asset

Exhibit 14.4   Forest Products Betas

Company	Levered beta	Unlevered beta	Market debt/equity (percent)	Asset weights Building	Paper
Champion International	1.23	0.86	70.4	0.15	0.85
Chesapeake Corporation	0.88	0.59	82.5	0.06	0.94
Great Northern Nekoosa	1.21	1.10	16.9	0.04	0.96
Louisiana-Pacific	1.32	0.98	57.9	0.79	0.21
Pope and Talbot	1.18	1.06	18.9	0.51	0.49
Longview Fibre	1.16	1.01	24.6	0.26	0.74
Temple Inland	1.16	0.99	28.4	0.19	0.81

pricing model, as discussed in Chapter 10, can be used to compute the cost of equity, k_s.

When changes in risk are expected, be prepared to re-estimate an equity beta. Sometimes a company's strategic plan implies that risk is expected to change. A young company, recently gone public, is risky now (high beta), but is expected to have declining risk across time. Although we cannot suggest foolproof steps for estimating changing risk, it will change. This implies that the weighted average cost of capital may also change (decline) as the company matures. Consequently, it becomes necessary to discount year-N cash flows at a risk-adjusted rate approximate for the risk in year N, not other years when the risk might be higher or lower.

The last step is to compute the weighted average cost of capital for each business unit, to be used as a discount rate for the business-unit after-tax cash flows:

$$WACC = k_b(1-T)\frac{B}{B+S} + k_s\frac{S}{B+S}$$

The cost of debt, k_b, is the long-term rate, consistent with the target bond rating of the business unit. The tax rate (T) is the business-unit effective tax rate. The percentage of debt in the capital structure, $B/(B+S,)$ is the target market-value capital structure. The cost of equity, k_s, uses the relevered beta estimated earlier and the percentage of equity is 1 minus the percentage of debt.

Estimating a Discount Rate for Headquarters Costs

You can determine the discount rates of the headquarters by breaking down headquarters cash flows into three categories, each to be discounted at a rate appropriate for its risk: tax shields provided by debt, non-interest tax shields, and headquarters costs.

Tax shields provided by debt have the same risk as corporate debt and are typically discounted at the pretax cost of debt, k_b. The present value of these tax shields (assuming they will be available perpetually) is the marginal tax rate, T_c, times the market value of debt, B.

Non-interest tax shields (from transfer pricing or the fact that losses of one division can shelter gains at another) depend on the probability of realizing them. Thus, cash flows must be defined as expected cash flows from non-interest tax shields. The appropriate discount rate for transfer-pricing tax shields depends on the business risk of the company. Financial leverage is irrelevant because transfer-pricing schemes are expenses before interest. For these reasons, expected transfer-pricing tax shields should be discounted at the unlevered cost of equity for the company as a whole. Tax shields based on the fact that losses in one business unit can shelter gains in another should be discounted at the levered cost of equity, because they can be realized only on income after interest expenses.

Headquarters costs should be discounted at a rate somewhere between the risk-free rate and the unlevered cost of equity, depending on their co-variance with general business conditions (as measured by the market port-folio). For most companies headquarters costs tend to rise in good business conditions (as executives and staff receive higher compensation) and fall during recessions. If the changes correlate well with operating profits, then the discount rate could be as high as the unlevered cost of equity. Changes in headquarters costs that are not correlated with business conditions (for example, one-time cutbacks) do not affect the discount rate.

Adding Up the Pieces to Value the Entire Corporation

The final step in multibusiness valuation is to combine headquarters costs and benefits with business unit values. Exhibit 14.5 shows how the values of two hypothetical divisions can be added. From these, you subtract head-quarters costs and add headquarters benefits and the value of excess mar-ketable securities. The result is the aggregated value of the company. When the market value of corporate debt has been subtracted, the result should be the value of equity for the company.

A few special situations need to be discussed. How should unconsoli-dated subsidiaries be handled? How can double counting be avoided? What should be done with excess debt and marketable securities?

Unconsolidated subsidiaries are often an important part of a company. They are clearly separable business units, but how should we think about the cash flows they provide to the parent? Assuming they are not foreign subsidiaries, the best approach is to value them separately, then multiply their equity value by the fraction that the parent owns, and add their result to your estimate of the parent's equity value. An alternative approach is to

Exhibit 14.5   Summary Multi-Business Valuation

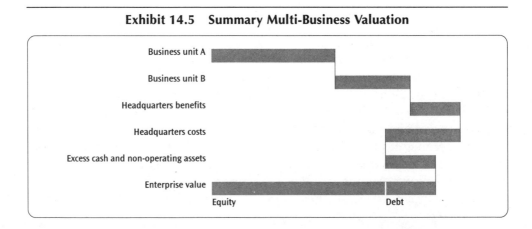

discount expected dividends paid from the subsidiary to the parent at a cost of equity appropriate for the riskiness of the dividend stream. This method is difficult to use because dividends are discretionary and, therefore, difficult to forecast.

Double counting can occur when an undervalued asset is carried on the books of a business unit. For example, paper companies sometimes own thousands of acres of timberland that is carried on the books at low value. An almost irresistible temptation is to estimate the market value of the forest and add it to the present value of cash flow. To do so would be double counting because expected cash flow already assumes that harvested trees will be used to produce lumber. They are, in every sense, an inventory. As with inventory, their value is not added, because it is already included in future cash flow as an input to production.

Another common example of double counting is corporate headquarters or other real estate carried at low book value. The rental opportunity cost of the buildings is already reflected in a cash flow that is higher than it might otherwise be if the company were to sell its headquarters, then lease the office space. You cannot have it both ways. Either discount the cash flow as it is, or subtract the expected rental cost from the cash flow and add the market value of the headquarters building.

Excess marketable securities build up in the projected balance sheet of a business unit if it is doing well or, alternately, if debt is increased. This effect is a normal part of the forecasting process and, as discussed in Chapter 11, it has no effect on the present value of a business unit. Excess cash held by the company at the start of the valuation period is a different matter. It should not be allocated to business units. Its value should simply be kept separate and added to the other corporate level values during the aggregation stage.

CONCLUSION

Valuing a multibusiness company by components often leads to a critical rethinking about what business units really belong as part of the company, as we described in Chapter 2. Frequently managers will decide to restructure the company and focus on a smaller scope of activities. Managers are then faced with how to dispose of units that no longer fit. Over the past decade or so, the choice of restructuring techniques has widened as different techniques have been perfected and accepted by the stock markets. In addition to selling a business unit to another company, managers can now choose among spin-offs, equity carve-outs, tracking stock, and management buyouts.[4] Valuation is a key tool for managers to use to determine what is best for their shareholders among all the options.

---

[4] For a discussion of the various breakup techniques, see P. Anslinger, S. Klepper, and S. Subramaniam, "Breaking Up Is Good to Do," *McKinsey Quarterly*, no. 1 (1999), pp. 16–27.

15

Valuing Dot.coms

In early 2000, Internet entrepreneurs had succeeded in quickly transforming their business ideas into billion-dollar valuations that seemed to defy common wisdom about profits, multiples, and the short-term focus of capital markets. Valuing these high-growth, high-uncertainty, high-loss firms is a challenge, to say the least; some practitioners have even described it as hopeless.

We respond to that challenge by asserting that the principles described in this book work well in understanding the value of these companies. Using a classic discounted-cash-flow (DCF) approach to valuation, buttressed by microeconomic analysis and probability-weighted scenarios, is the best way to value Internet companies. Although DCF may sound suspiciously retro, we believe that it works where other methods fail, reinforcing the continued importance of basic economics and finance, even in uncharted Internet territory. Yet it is important to bear in mind that while the valuation techniques we sketch out can help bound and quantify uncertainty, they won't make it disappear. Internet stocks are highly volatile for sound and logical reasons.

DCF ANALYSIS WHEN THERE IS NO *CF* TO *D*

The most common critique one hears about the valuation of Internet companies is that their values balloon as their losses balloon. The perceived correlation between ever high stock prices and ever higher losses has become a rich source of jokes for stand-up comics and cartoonists, even though the phenomenon is not that difficult to explain.

This relationship is driven by two factors: supernormal growth and investments running through the income statement. Many Internet-related start-ups experience annual growth rates exceeding 100 percent. Only five years ago, a company was considered high growth if it managed to generate revenue growth of 15 percent. This hypergrowth, when fueled by investments that have to be expensed (through the income statement) rather than capitalized (on the balance sheet), will create ever increasing losses until growth rates slow.

Internet companies typically don't require heavy investments of the type that get capitalized, such as factories. Indeed, total investment for a full-featured, e-commerce-enabled Web site runs somewhere between $3 million and $5 million. That is not to say that e-commerce start-ups don't need heavy investment, but their investment is in customer acquisition, which has to be expensed through the income statement. For example, if the acquisition cost per customer, through advertising and direct mail of CD-ROMs, is about $40 per customer and a company successfully builds its customer base from one million in year one, to three million in year two, to six million in year three, its acquisition costs will rise from $40 million in year one to $120 million in year three.

Another way to illustrate this phenomenon is by comparing a "bricks-and-mortar" retailer with an e-commerce retailer. In the bricks and mortar case, much of the customer acquisition cost consists of securing the store location, construction, and furniture and fixtures. These items are largely capitalized and expensed over their useful life. In the case of the virtual retailer, almost all customer acquisition costs are expensed. The physical retailer will break even many years earlier than the virtual retailer, even if they have identical cash flows! Provided the virtual retailer will earn a positive net present value on its customer acquisition investments, increasing losses because of accelerating customer acquisition will raise the value of the company.

One thing is certain, though. These conditions of supernormal growth and investment through the income statement render short-hand valuation approaches, including price-to-earnings and revenue multiples, meaningless. Some analysts have suggested benchmarks such as price per customer or multiples of revenues three or five years out. These approaches are fundamentally flawed as high growth, if the company succeeds, is likely to continue for another 5 to 10 years. More important, these short-hand methods can't account for the uniqueness of each company in this rapidly evolving space. Indeed, one of the key reasons for skepticism about Internet valuations is the tendency to apply these types of valuation shortcuts.

The best way of valuing Internet companies is to return to economic fundamentals with the DCF approach, which makes the distinction between expensed and capitalized investment unimportant because accounting treatments don't affect cash flows. The absence of meaningful historical data and positive earnings to serve as the basis for price-to-earning multiples also doesn't matter, because the DCF approach relies solely on forecasts of performance and can easily capture the worth of value-creating businesses that have several years of initial losses. The DCF approach can't eliminate the need to make difficult forecasts, but it does address the problems of ultrahigh growth rates and uncertainty in a coherent way.

We focus on the three twists required to make DCF more useful for valuing Internet companies: starting from a fixed point in the future and working back to the present, using probability-weighted scenarios to address high uncertainty in an explicit way, and exploiting classic analytical techniques to understand the underlying economics of these companies and to forecast their future performance.

We will illustrate this approach with a valuation of Amazon.com, the archetypal Internet company, as of November 1999. In the four years from its launch to October 1999, it built a customer base of 10 million and expanded its offerings from books to compact discs, videos, digital video discs, toys, consumer electronics goods, and auctions. In addition, Amazon.com invested in branded Internet players such as pets.com and drugstore.com, and beginning in September 1999 it allowed other retailers to sell their wares on its Web site through an associates program. The company has become a symbol of the new economy; market research showed that in 1999 101 million people in the United States recognized the Amazon.com brand name.

All this activity was rewarded with a high market capitalization: $25 billion as of mid-November 1999. Yet Amazon.com had never made a profit and lost $390 million in 1999. The company became the focus of a debate about whether Internet stocks were greatly overvalued.

START FROM THE FUTURE

In forecasting the performance of high-growth companies like Amazon.com, don't be constrained by current performance. Instead of starting from the present—the usual practice in DCF valuations—start by thinking about what the industry and the company could look like when they evolve from today's very high-growth, unstable condition to a sustainable, moderate growth state in the future, and then extrapolate back to current performance. The future growth state should be defined by metrics such as the penetration rate, average revenue per customer, and sustainable gross margins. Just as important as the characteristics of the industry and company in this future state is the point when it actually begins. Since Internet-related companies are new, more stable economics probably lie at least 10 to 15 years in the future.

But consider what Amazon.com had already achieved. Its ability to enter and dominate categories is unprecedented, both in the off- and the online worlds. In 1998, for example, it took the company just three months to banish CDNow to second place among online purveyors of music. In early 1999, it assumed the leadership among online sellers of videos in 45 days; later that year, it became the leading online consumer electronics seller in 10 days.

Let us create an optimistic scenario based on this record. Suppose that Amazon.com were the next Wal-Mart, another retailer that has radically changed its industry and taken a significant share of sales in its target markets. Say that by 2010, Amazon.com continues to be the leading online retailer and has established itself as the overall leading retailer, both off- and online, in certain markets. If the company could take a 13 percent and 12 percent share of the total U.S. book and music markets, respectively, and captured a roughly comparable share of some other markets, it would have revenues of $60 billion in 2010, when Wal-Mart's revenues will probably have exceeded $300 billion.

What operating profit margin could Amazon.com earn on that $60 billion? The superior market share of the company is likely to give it significant purchasing power. Remember, too, that Amazon.com will earn revenues and incur few associated costs from other retailers using its site. In this optimistic scenario, Amazon.com, with an average operating margin in the 11 percent range, would most likely do a bit better than most other retailers.

And what about capital? In the optimistic scenario, Amazon.com may well need less working capital and fewer fixed assets than traditional retailers do. In almost any scenario, it should need less inventory because it can consolidate its stock-in-trade in a few warehouses, and it won't need retail stores at all. We assume that Amazon.com's 2010 capital turnover (revenues divided by the sum of working capital and fixed assets) will be 3.4, compared with 2.5 for typical retailers.

Combining these assumptions gives us the following financial forecast for 2010: revenues, $60 billion; operating profit, $7 billion; total capital, $18 billion. We also assume that Amazon.com will continue to grow by about 12 percent a year for the next 15 years after 2010 and that its growth will decline to 5.5 percent a year in perpetuity after 2025, slightly exceeding the nominal growth rate of the gross domestic product.[1] To estimate Amazon.com's current value, we discount the projected free cash flows back to the present. Their present value, including the estimated value of cash flows beyond 2025, is $37 billion.

How can we credibly forecast 10 or more years of cash flows for a company like Amazon.com? We can't. But our goal is not to define precisely what *will* happen but to offer a rigorous description of what could.

---

[1] Real GDP growth has averaged about 3 percent a year for the past 40 years, and the long-term expected inflation rate built into current interest levels is probably about 2 to 2.5 percent a year.

WEIGHTING FOR PROBABILITY

Uncertainty is the hardest part of valuing high-growth technology companies, and the use of probability-weighted scenarios is a simple and straightforward way to deal with it. This approach also makes critical assumptions and interactions far more transparent than other modeling approaches, such as Monte Carlo simulation. The use of probability-weighted scenarios requires us to repeat the process of estimating a future set of financials for a full range of scenarios—some more, some less optimistic. For Amazon.com, we have developed four of them (Exhibit 15.1).

In Scenario A, Amazon.com becomes the second-largest retailer (off- or online) based in the United States. It uses much less capital than traditional retailers because it is primarily an online operation. It captures much higher operating margins because it is the online retailer of choice, even if its prices are comparable to those of other online retailers, it has more purchasing clout, and lower operating costs. This scenario implies that Amazon.com was worth $79 billion in the fourth quarter of 1999.

Scenario B has Amazon.com capturing revenues almost as large as it does in Scenario A, but its margins and need for capital fall in the range between those of that first scenario and the margins and capital requirements of a traditional retailer. This second scenario implies that Amazon.com had a value of $37 billion as of the fourth quarter of 1999.

Amazon.com becomes quite a large retailer in Scenario C, though not as large as it does in Scenario B, and the company's economics are closer to those of traditional retailers. This third scenario implies a value for Amazon.com of $15 billion.

Exhibit 15.1   Amazon.com—Potential Outcomes

	U.S. book sales	U.S. music sales	Other sales[1]	Total sales	Margin of earnings before interest, taxes, and amortization	Discounted cash-flow value
	($ billion)	($ billion)	($ billion)	($ billion)	(percent)	($ billion)
Scenario A: 15% market share in U.S. books, 18% in U.S. music	24	13	48	85	14	79
Scenario B: 13% market share in U.S. books, 12% in U.S. music	20	9	31	60	11	37
Scenario C: 10% market share in U.S. books, 8% in U.S. music	16	6	19	41	8	15
Scenario D: 5% market share in U.S. books, 6% in U.S. music	7	5	5	17	7	3

1 Books and music sold outside the United States, as well as sales of videos, digital video discs, toys, and consumer electronics goods in any market

---

Exhibit 15.2   Amazon.com—Expected Value

	Discounted cash-flow value ($ billion)	×	Probability (percent)	=	Expected value ($ billion)
Scenario A	79		5		3.9
Scenario B	37		35		13.0
Scenario C	15		35		5.3
Scenario D	3		25		0.8
					23.0

Finally, in Scenario D, Amazon.com becomes a fair-sized retailer with traditional retailer economics. Online retailing mimics most other forms of the business, with many competitors in each field. Competition transfers most of the value of going online to consumers. This scenario implies that Amazon.com was worth only $3 billion.

We now have four scenarios in which the company's value ranges from $3 billion to $79 billion. Although the spread is quite large, each scenario is plausible.[2] Now comes the critical phase of assigning probabilities and generating the resulting values for Amazon.com (Exhibit 15.2). We assign a low probability, 5 percent, to Scenario A. Although the company might achieve outrageously high returns, competition is likely to prevent this. Amazon.com's current lead over its competitors suggests that Scenario D, too, is improbable. Scenarios B and C—both assuming attractive growth rates and reasonable returns—are therefore the most likely.

When we weight the value of each scenario, depending on its probability, and add all four of these values, we end up with $23 billion, which happened to be the company's market value on October 31, 1999. It therefore appears that Amazon.com's market valuation can be explained by plausible forecasts and probabilities.

Now, however, look at the sensitivity of this valuation to changing probabilities. As Exhibit 15.3 shows, relatively small variations lead to big swings in value. The share prices of companies like Amazon.com are extremely volatile because small changes in the market's view of the likelihood of different outcomes affect the current value of these shares quite significantly. Nothing can be done about this volatility.

---

[2] We capture cash-flow risk through the probability-weighting of scenarios, so the cost of equity applied to each of them shouldn't include any extra premium; it can consist of the risk-free rate, an industry-average beta, and a general market-risk premium.

Exhibit 15.3   Amazon.com—Volatility of Expected Values

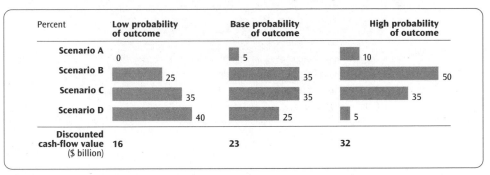

Percent	Low probability of outcome	Base probability of outcome	High probability of outcome
Scenario A	0	5	10
Scenario B	25	35	50
Scenario C	35	35	35
Scenario D	40	25	5
Discounted cash-flow value ($ billion)	16	23	32

CUSTOMER VALUE ANALYSIS

The last difficult aspect of valuing very high-growth companies is relating future scenarios to current performance. How can you tell a soon-to-be successful Internet play from a soon-to-be-bankrupt one? Here, classic microeconomic and strategic skills play a critical role because building sound scenarios for a business requires knowledge of what actually drives the creation of value. For Amazon.com and many other Internet companies, customer-value analysis is a useful approach. Five factors drive the customer-value analysis of a retailer like Amazon.com:

1. The average revenue per customer per year from purchases by its customers, as well as revenues from advertisements on its site and from retailers that rent space on it to sell their own products.
2. The total number of customers.
3. The contribution margin per customer (before the cost of acquiring customers).
4. The average cost of acquiring a customer.
5. The customer churn rate (that is, the proportion of customers lost each year).

Let us see how Amazon.com could achieve the financial performance predicted by Scenario B and compare this with the company's current performance. As Exhibit 15.4 shows, the biggest changes over the next 10 years involve the number of Amazon.com's customers and the average revenue for each. In Scenario B, Amazon.com's customer base increases from 9 million a

Exhibit 15.4   Amazon.com—Customer Economics, Scenario B

		1999	2010
Average revenue per customer	$	140	500
Customers	Million	9	120
Contribution margin	Percent	14	14
Acquisition cost per customer	$	29	50
Customer churn rate	Percent	25	25

year in 1999 to about 120 million worldwide by 2010—84 million in the United States and 36 million outside it. We assume that Amazon.com will remain the number one U.S. online retailer and achieve an attractive position abroad.

Scenario B also calls for Amazon.com's average revenue per customer to rise to $500 by 2010, from $140 in 1999. That $500 could be accounted for by two CDs at $15 each, three books at $20 each, two bottles of perfume at $30 each, and one personal organizer at $350. Amazon.com will probably continue to dominate its core book and music markets. It will probably enter adjacent categories and may come to dominate them.

In Scenario B, Amazon.com's 2010 contribution margin per customer before the cost of acquiring customers is 14 percent, a figure in line with that of current top-notch large-scale retailers—Wal-Mart, for instance. Despite competition, this seems rational in view of Amazon.com's likely ability to gain offsetting economies of scale, for example, by renting other retailers space to market their products on Amazon.com's Web sites.

Scenario B predicts that Amazon.com will have acquisition costs per customer of $50. Despite the argument that these costs will rise once all online customers have been claimed, this is a reasonable figure if the company can achieve brand dominance and advertising economies of scale. The cost of acquiring new customers is closely linked to the customer churn rate, which at 25 percent suggests that once Amazon.com acquires customers it will keep them four years. This implies a truly world-class (or addictive) customer offer and a deeply loyal (or lazy) customer base.

Looking at customer economics in this way makes it possible to generate the kind of information needed to assess the probabilities assigned to various scenarios. Consider how two hypothetical young companies, Loyalty.com and Turnover.com, with different customer economics might evolve (Exhibit 15.5). Each had $100 million in revenues in 1999 and an operating loss of $3 million. On traditional financial statements, the two companies look the

Exhibit 15.5   Customer Economics

An example		Loyalty.com	Turnover.com[1]
Average revenue per customer	$	250	342
Contribution margin	Percent	15	15
Acquisition cost per customer	$	75	93
Churn rate	Percent	20	46

1 Assumes discount rate of 12% in Year 2.

same. Deeper analysis, using the customer economics model, reveals striking differences.

The lifetime value of a typical Loyalty.com customer is $50 over an average of five years; the typical Turnover.com customer is worth –$1 over two years. The difference in the value of a customer reflects the churn rate (20 percent attrition each year for Loyalty.com versus 46 percent for Turnover.com) and Turnover.com's higher acquisition costs.

Even though Turnover.com earns higher revenues per customer than Loyalty.com does with similar contribution margins, its economic model is not sustainable. Loyalty.com will find it much easier to grow because it doesn't have to find as many new customers each year. Since Loyalty.com will have substantially lower customer acquisition costs than Turnover.com, Loyalty.com's figures for earnings before income tax (EBIT) will turn positive

Exhibit 15.6   Long-Term Performance

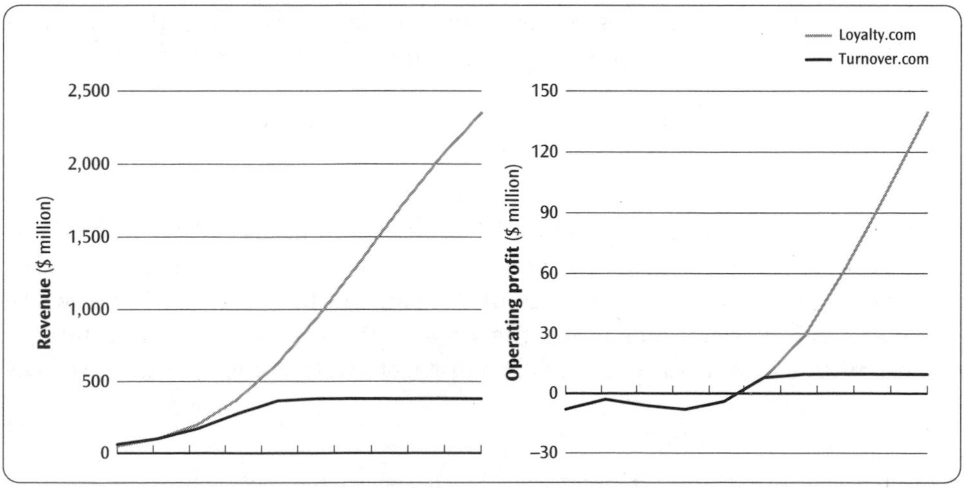

more quickly. If Loyalty.com and Turnover.com invested the same amount of money in efforts to acquire customers over the next 10 years, and other factors remained the same, the revenue growth and EBIT patterns of the two companies would vary a good deal (Exhibit 15.6 on page 323). This in turn means that their DCF values would differ radically, despite similar short-term financial results.

UNCERTAINTY IS HERE TO STAY

By using this adapted DCF approach, we can generate reasonable valuations for seemingly unreasonable businesses. But investors and companies entering fast-growth markets like those related to the Internet face huge uncertainties. Look at what could happen under our four scenarios to an investor who holds a share of Amazon.com stock for 10 years after buying it in 1999.

If Scenario A plays out, the investor will earn a 23 percent annual return, and it will seem that in 1999 the market significantly undervalued Amazon.com. If Scenario C plays out, the investor will earn about 7 percent a year, and it will seem that the company was substantially overvalued in 1999. These high or low returns should not, however, be interpreted as implying that its 1999 share price was irrational; they reflect uncertainty about the future.

A great deal of this uncertainty is associated with the problem of identifying the winner in a large competitive field: even in the world of high-tech initial public offerings, not every Internet company can become the next Microsoft. History shows that a small number of players will win big while the vast majority will toil away amid obscurity and worthless options, and it is hard to predict which companies will prosper and which will not.[3] Neither investors nor companies can do anything about this uncertainty, and that is why investors are always told to diversify their portfolios—and why companies don't pay cash when acquiring Internet firms.

SUMMARY

As the emergence of the Internet and related technologies led to tremendous value creation for select entrepreneurs at the end of the twentieth century, it also raised questions about the sanity of a stock market that appeared to value companies more, the greater the losses they generated. In this chapter, we showed that the DCF approach, with some adaptations, was

---

[3] Morgan Stanley research on 1,243 technology IPOs has shown that more than 86 percent of the value created in them during the past decade came from only 5 percent of the companies.

an essential tool for understanding the value of these companies. When valuing dot.coms, you need to start from the future rather than today when making your forecast, you need to think in terms of probabilities, and you need to understand the economics of the business model compared to peers. You cannot do anything to reduce the volatility of these companies, but at least you can understand it.

16

Valuing Cyclical
Companies

Volatile earnings introduce additional complexity into the valuation of cyclical companies. In this chapter, we explore how the share prices of cyclical companies behave. This leads to a suggested approach to valuing those companies and potential implications for managers.

SHARE PRICE BEHAVIOR OF CYCLICAL COMPANIES

Cyclical companies are characterized by significant fluctuations in earnings over a number of years. Earnings of such companies, including those in the steel, airline, paper, and chemical industries, fluctuate because of big changes in the prices of their products. In the airline industry, for example, cyclicality of earnings is linked to broader macroeconomic trends. In the paper industry, cyclicality is largely driven by industry factors, typically related to capacity.

The share prices of companies with cyclical earnings are often more volatile than less cyclical companies. Is this consistent with the DCF valuation approach? At first glance, theory and reality don't coincide.

When Theory and Reality Conflict

Let's explore the theory. Suppose that you were valuing a cyclical company using the DCF approach and you had perfect foresight about the industry cycle. Would the value of the company behave similar to the earnings? No, the DCF value would exhibit much lower volatility than the

This chapter is based on an analysis for a dissertation, *Underestimating Change* (Rotterdam: Erasmus University, August 1999), by Marco de Heer under the supervision of one of the co-authors.

earnings or cash flows. DCF reduces future expected cash flows to a single value. As a result, any single year is not important. For a cyclical company, the high cash flows cancel out the low cash flows. Only the long-term trend really matters.

An example will clarify how this works. The business cycle of Company A is 10 years. Exhibit 16.1, part 1, shows its hypothetical cash flow pattern. It is highly volatile, containing both positive and negative cash flows. Discounting the free cash flows at 10 percent produces the DCF values in Exhibit 16.1, part 2.

Exhibit 16.1, part 3, which brings together the cash flows and the DCF value (the values are indexed for comparability), shows that the DCF value is far less volatile than the underlying cash flow. In fact, there is almost no volatility in the value. This is because no single year's performance has a significant impact on the value of the company.

In the real world, of course, the share prices of cyclical companies are less stable. Exhibit 16.2 shows the earnings and share values (indexed) for 15 companies with a four-year cycle. The share prices are more volatile than the DCF approach would predict—suggesting that theory and reality conflict.

Exhibit 16.1 The Long-Term View: Free Cash Flow and DCF Volatility

1 Free cash flow pattern, Company A ($ million)

Period (years)	0	1	2	3	4	5	6	7	8	9	10
After-tax operating profit	10	9	6	3	0	−2	3	18	7	6	10
Net investment	3	3	2	2	1	3	5	3	3	3	3
Free cash flow	7	6	4	1	−1	5	−3	15	4	3	7

Cash flows valued from any one year forward

2 DCF value

			34	33	27	28	30	35	40	33	33	34	31

3 Free cash flow and DCF value patterns

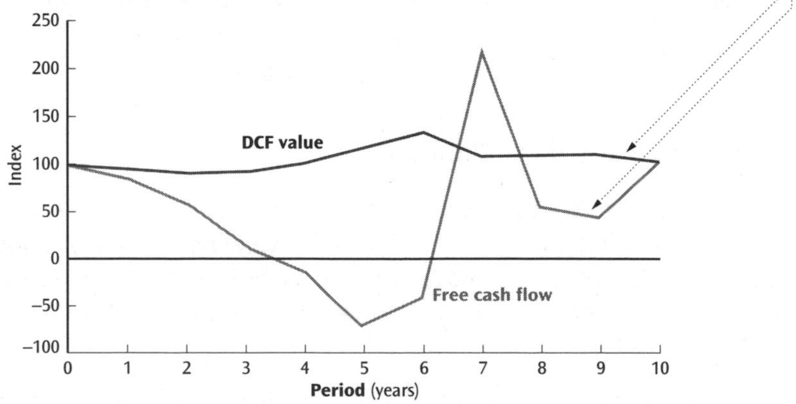

Exhibit 16.2   Share Prices and EPS for 15 Cyclical Companies

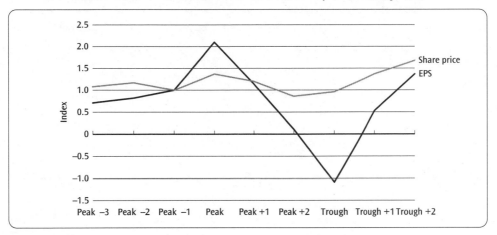

Are Earnings Forecasts the Culprit?

How can we reconcile theory and reality? We examined the earnings forecasts for cyclical companies to see if they provided any clues on the assumption that the market values of the companies would be linked to consensus earnings forecasts.

What we found was quite surprising. Consensus earnings forecasts for cyclical companies appeared to ignore cyclicality entirely. The forecasts invariably showed an upward sloping trend, regardless of whether the companies were at the peak or trough of the cycle. It appeared not that the DCF model was inconsistent with the facts but that the earnings and cash flow projections of the market (assuming the market followed the analysts' consensus) were to blame.

The conclusion was based on an analysis of 36 U.S. cyclical companies during the years 1985–1997. We divided them into groups with similar cycles (e.g., three, four, or five years from peak to trough), and calculated scaled average earnings and earnings forecasts. We then compared actual earnings with consensus earnings forecasts over the cycle.[1]

Exhibit 16.3 plots the actual earnings and consensus earnings forecast for the set of 15 companies with four-year cycles in primary metals and manufacturing transportation equipment. The consensus forecasts do not predict the earnings cycle at all. In fact, except for the "next-year forecasts" in the years beginning from the trough, the earnings-per-share are forecasted to

---

[1] Note that we have already adjusted downward the normal positive bias of analyst forecasts to focus just on the cyclicality issue. V.K. Chopra, "Why So Much Error in Analysts' Earnings Forecasts?" *Financial Analysts Journal* (November/December 1998), pp. 35–42.

Exhibit 16.3   Actual EPS and Consensus EPS Forecasts for Cyclical Companies

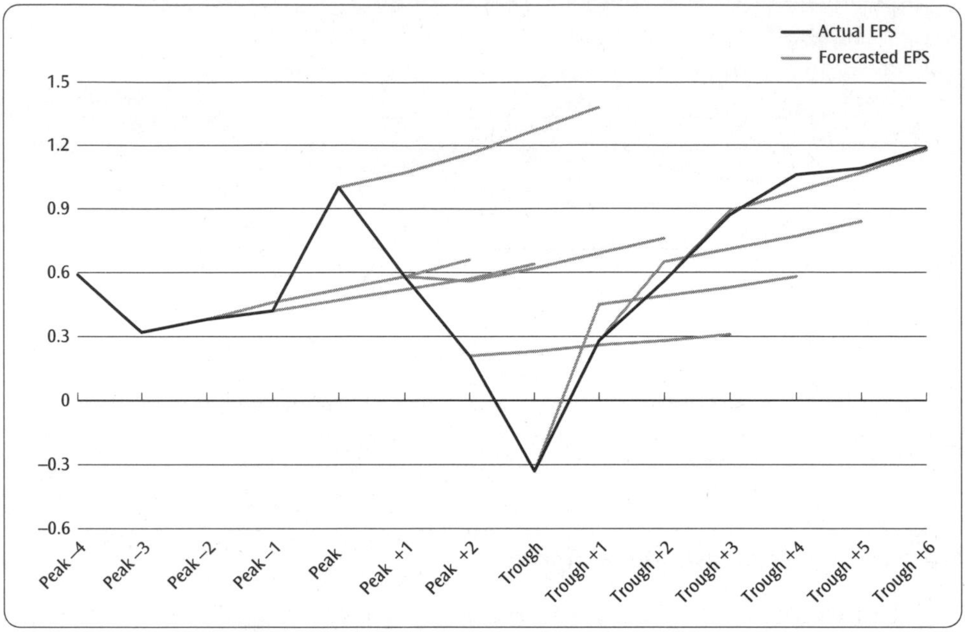

follow an upward sloping path with no future variation. You might say that the forecast doesn't even acknowledge the existence of a cycle.[2]

One explanation could be that equity analysts have incentives not to predict the cycle, particularly the down part. Academic research has shown that earnings forecasts have a general positive bias that is sometimes attributed to the incentives facing equity analysts at investment banks.[3] For example, pessimistic earnings forecasts may damage relations between an analyst's employer—an investment bank—and a particular company. In addition, companies that are the target of negative commentary might cut off an analyst's lines of communication. From this evidence, we could conclude that analysts as a group are unable or unwilling to predict the cycle for these

---

[2] Similar results were found for companies with three- and five-year cycles.

[3] The following articles discuss this hypothesis: M.R. Clayman, and R.A. Schwartz, "Falling in Love Again—Analysts' Estimates and Reality," *Financial Analysts Journal* (September/October 1994), pp. 66–68; J. Francis, and D, Philbrick, "Analysts' Decisions as Products of a Multi-Task Environment," *Journal of Accounting Research*, vol. 31, no. 2 (autumn 1993), pp. 216–230; K. Schipper, "Commentary on Analysts' Forecasts," *Accounting Horizons* (December 1991), pp. 105–121; B. Trueman, "On the Incentives for Security Analysts to Revise Their Earnings Forecasts," *Contemporary Accounting Research*, vol. 7, no. 1, pp. 203–222.

companies. If the market followed analyst forecasts, that could account for the high volatility of cyclical companies' share prices.

Market Appears Smarter Than Consensus Forecast

We know that cycles are hard to predict, particularly their inflection points. So it is not surprising that the market doesn't get it exactly right. However, we would be disappointed if the market entirely missed the cycle as the consensus earnings analysis seems to suggest. We went back to the question, how should the market behave? Should it be able to predict the cycle and therefore exhibit little share price volatility? That would probably be asking too much. At any point, the company or industry could break out of its cycle and move to one that is higher or lower, as illustrated on Exhibit 16.4.

Suppose you are valuing a company that is apparently at a peak in its earnings cycle. Based on past cycles, you would expect the industry to turn down soon. However, there are signs that the industry is about to break out of the old cycle. A reasonable valuation approach might be to build two scenarios and weight their values. You could assume with a 50 percent probability that the cycle will follow the past, and that the industry will turn down in the next year or so. The second scenario, also with 50 percent probability, would be that the industry breaks out of the cycle and follows a new long-term trend based on current improved performance. The value of the company would

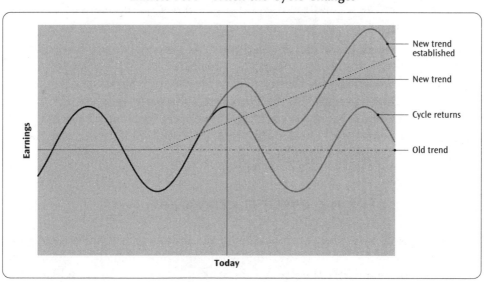

Exhibit 16.4 When the Cycle Changes

Exhibit 16.5   The Market Is Smarter

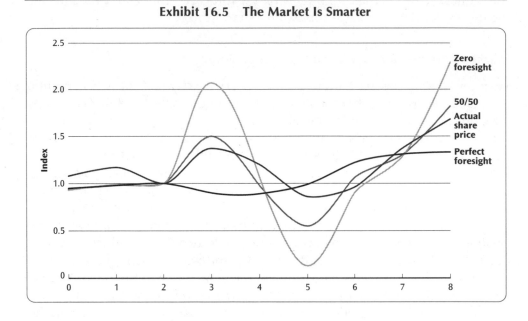

then be the weighted average of these two values. We found evidence that this is in fact the way the market behaves.

We valued the four-year cyclical companies three ways:

1. With perfect foresight about the upcoming cycle.
2. With zero foresight, assuming that current performance represents a point on a new long-term trend (essentially the consensus earnings forecast).
3. Fifty percent of perfect foresight and 50 percent of zero foresight.

Exhibit 16.5 summarizes the results. As shown, the market doesn't follow either the perfect foresight or the zero foresight path; it follows a middle path, much closer to the 50/50 path. So the market has neither perfect foresight, not zero foresight. One could argue that this 50/50 valuation is the right place for the market to be.

APPROACH TO VALUING CYCLICAL COMPANIES

No one can precisely predict the cycle for an industry, and any single forecast of performance must be wrong. Managers and investors can benefit from following explicitly the probabilistic approach to valuing cyclical companies as outlined earlier, just as we saw in the last chapter the benefit of the probabilistic approach for valuing Internet companies. The probabilistic approach avoids the traps of the single forecast and allows the exploration of a wider range of outcomes and their implications.

Here is a two-scenario approach for valuing cyclical companies (of course, you could always have more than two scenarios):

1. Construct and value the "normal cycle" scenario using information about past cycles. Pay particular attention to the long-term trend line of operating profits, cash flow, and ROIC because it will have a major impact on the valuation. Make sure the continuing value is based on a "normalized" level of profits (i.e., a point on the company's long-term cash flow trend line).

2. Construct and value a new trend-line scenario based on the recent performance of the company. Once again, focus most on the long-term trend line, because it will have the largest impact on value. Don't worry too much about modeling future cyclicality (although future cyclicality will be important for financial solvency).

3. Develop the economic rationale for each of the two scenarios, considering factors such as demand growth, companies entering or exiting the industry, and technology changes that will affect the supply and demand balance.

4. Assign probabilities to the scenarios and calculate a weighted value of the scenarios. Use the economic rationale and its likelihood to estimate the weights assigned to each scenario.

This approach provides an estimate of the value as well as scenarios that put boundaries on the valuation. Managers can use these boundaries to think about ways to modify their strategy and how to respond to signals about which scenario is likely to come true.

Is there anything managers can do to reduce or take advantage of the cyclicality of their industry? In our experience, managers often miss opportunities and even cause greater cyclicality. For example, cyclical companies often commit to major capital spending projects just when prices are high and the cycle is hitting its peak, presumably on the assumption that prices will remain high. Conversely, cyclical companies retrench when prices are low. Sometimes companies develop forecasts similar to the equity analysts, upward sloping regardless of where the company is in the cycle. Managers, who have detailed information about their markets, should be able to do a better job than the financial market in figuring out the cycle and take appropriate actions.

One further consequence of this behavior is that cyclical companies often send the wrong signals to the market. Expanding when prices are high tells the financial market that the future looks great (often just before

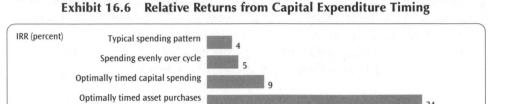

Exhibit 16.6   Relative Returns from Capital Expenditure Timing

the cycle turns down). Signalling pessimism just before an upturn also confuses the market. Perhaps it should be no surprise that the stock market has difficult valuing cyclical companies.

How could managers exploit their superior knowledge? The most obvious action would be better timing of capital spending. Companies could also pursue financial strategies, such as issuing shares at the peak of the cycle or repurchasing shares at the cycle's trough. The most aggressive managers could take this one step further by adopting a trading approach, making acquisitions at the bottom of the cycle and selling assets at the top. Exhibit 16.6 shows the results of a simulation of optimal cycle timing. The typical company's returns could more than double.

Can companies really behave this way? It's actually very difficult for a company to take the contrarian view. The chief executive officer has to convince the board and the company's bankers to expand when the industry outlook is gloomy and competitors are retrenching. Or the CEO has to hold back while competitors build at the top of the cycle. Often, the companies in the industry exacerbate the cycle. Breaking out of the cycle may be possible, but it is a rare CEO who can do it.

SUMMARY

After first glance, the share prices of cyclical companies appear too volatile to be consistent with the DCF valuation approach. We showed in this chapter, however, that the share price volatility can be explained by the uncertainty over the direction of the industry cycle. A systematic DCF approach, using scenarios and probabilities, can be used by managers and investors to value and analyze cyclical companies. Unfortunately, managers of cyclical companies are rarely willing to use the insights from this approach to break the cycle and create value for their shareholders.

17

Valuing Foreign Subsidiaries

Valuing foreign subsidiaries of multinational companies follows the same basic approach and employs the same principles as valuing business units of domestic companies. However, several wrinkles need to be considered.

- Translation of foreign currency accounts.
- Differences in foreign tax and accounting regulations.
- Interrelationship between transfer pricing and foreign taxes.
- Determining the appropriate cost of capital.
- The effect of foreign exchange hedging on value.
- Dealing with political risks.

This chapter is organized around a step-by-step process for valuing a foreign subsidiary and covers the first four issues above. Foreign exchange hedging is discussed at the end of the chapter. Dealing with political risk is covered in Chapter 19, "Valuation in Emerging Markets."

Exhibit 17.1 illustrates the cash-flow pattern for a hypothetical U.S.-based parent company with a wholly owned subsidiary domiciled in England that receives revenues from France (as well as from England), pays for raw materials supplied from Denmark (in addition to labor and raw material costs in England), and borrows in Switzerland (as well as in England). The English subsidiary receives capital and materials from its U.S. parent and returns cash flow in the form of dividends and license fees. Taxes are paid by the parent in the United States and by the subsidiary in England. This example is sufficiently rich to show most of the complexities of valuing a foreign subsidiary, and we will follow it throughout this chapter. We assume that this valuation is from inside the parent company—that is, that we have full access to internal financial and planning data.

Exhibit 17.1   Cash Flow for a U.S. Company's Foreign Subsidiary

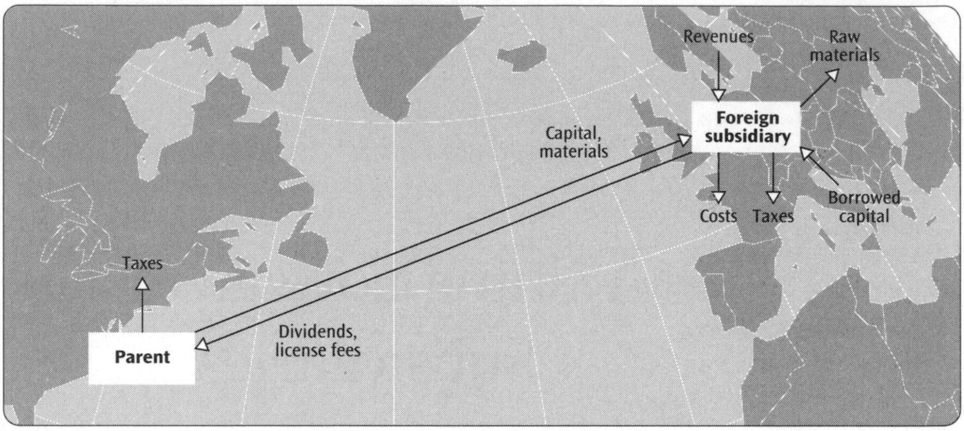

The steps for valuing a foreign subsidiary are summarized in Exhibit 17.2. The starting point is to understand the historical performance of the subsidiary. Second, forecast free cash flow in the currency of the foreign subsidiary. For our example company, we forecast English revenues in pounds sterling and French revenues in Euros. Third, we convert nonpound cash flow into pounds by using forward foreign exchange rates. Once we have converted all expected cash flow to pounds, the fourth step is to discount it at the English subsidiary's cost of capital, and convert the resulting value to dollars, the home currency, by using the spot foreign exchange rate.[1]

Exhibit 17.2   Steps in Valuing a Foreign Subsidiary

	Issues specific to foreign subsidiaries
1. Analyze historical performance	Foreign currency translation accounting
	Cross country taxation
	Tax minimization and transfer pricing
2. Forecast cash flow in subsidiary's home currency	Forecasting future exchange rates
3. Estimate foreign currency discount rate	Local cost of equity and debt
	Country risk
	Capital structure
4. Discount FCF and translate to parent currency	

[1] An equivalent approach would be to use dollars as the currency for the English subsidiary—dollar-forecasted cash flows and a dollar discount rate. Given this approach, it becomes unnecessary to convert the value of the English subsidiary from pounds sterling to dollars at the spot foreign exchange rate (in the last step).

STEP 1: ANALYZE THE HISTORICAL PERFORMANCE

Before beginning the forecast, you need to understand the current situation of the foreign subsidiary. You can follow the approach laid out in Chapter 9, "Analyzing Historical Performance." This section highlights some of the issues you will encounter when dealing with a foreign subsidiary: foreign currency translation accounting, cross-country taxation, and understanding the interaction of transfer prices and taxation. The next chapter describes additional accounting issues when dealing with financial statements prepared in different countries.

Foreign Currency Translation Accounting

To avoid potential distortions caused by foreign currency translation accounting, it is best to conduct the entire analysis and valuation in the currency of the foreign subsidiary. Sometimes, financial statements of the foreign subsidiary have already been converted by the parent company using U.S. accounting standards, and it may (on occasion) be necessary to adjust them back to the foreign currency to avoid distorting cash-flow forecasts.

To understand the performance of the subsidiary and, if necessary, to reverse-engineer the U.S. statements, you must understand the accounting principles involved. The Financial Accounting Standards Board's Statement No. 52 describes the methods for translating foreign currency transactions and statements.

Transactions in currencies other than the home currency of the subsidiary are translated into the home currency at the exchange rate on the date of the transaction. For example, a sale by the English subsidiary in Euros will be recorded by the English subsidiary in pounds at the exchange rate on the day of the sale. Similarly, the English subsidiary will record a receivable in pounds for the sale at the same rate. Whenever the English subsidiary prepares financial statements, assets such as receivables in Euros or cash accounts in Euros are presented at the exchange rate for the balance sheet date. Gains or losses on these assets or liabilities flow through the income statement.

Translation of subsidiaries' financial statements into the currency of its parent is more complex. For moderate inflation economies, the *current* method is used. All balance sheet items except equity are translated at the year-end exchange rate. Translation gains and losses on the balance sheet are carried directly to the equity account and do not affect net income. The average exchange rate for the period is used for translating the income statement.

For high inflation economies, the *temporal* method is used. Historical exchange rates are applied to physical assets such as property, plant, and equipment and inventories. Year-end rates are applied to monetary assets and liabilities like cash, receivables, and payables.

Both methods are illustrated in the example set out in Exhibit 17.3. The foreign subsidiary is assumed to have acquired fixed assets at the beginning of the year when the foreign currency was at $0.95 per unit. By year's end, the exchange rate was $0.85, and the average during the year was $0.90. The subsidiary used last-in-first-out (LIFO) inventory accounting with an applicable historical exchange rate of $0.91.

The current method starts with the income statement, converting all items at the average exchange rate during the year. Net income is transferred as retained earnings to the balance sheet; all assets and liabilities are translated at the spot exchange rate; common stock is translated at the historical rate, and the equity adjustment from foreign currency translation is a plug figure.

The temporal method begins by estimating the dollar equivalent for all assets and liabilities and computing retained earnings, $85, as a residual. Since no dividends are paid, retained earnings (or the change in retained earnings) must equal net income. Once all income statement items have been determined, the foreign exchange gain of $70 is computed as a plug figure.

Exhibit 17.3   Example of Translating Financial Statements

Balance sheet	Foreign currency	Temporal method		Current method	
		Rates used	U.S. dollars	Rates used	U.S. dollars
Cash and receivables	100	0.85	85	0.85	85
Inventory	300	0.91	273	0.85	255
Net fixed assets	600	0.95	570	0.85	510
	1,000		928		850
Current liabilities	180	0.85	153	0.85	153
Long-term debt	700	0.85	595	0.85	595
Equity					
Common stock	100	0.95	95	0.95	95
Retained earnings	20		85		18
Equity adjustment from foreign currency translation	–		–		(11)
	1,000		928		850
Income statement					
Revenue	130	0.90	117	0.90	117
Cost of goods sold	(60)	0.93[1]	(56)	0.90	(54)
Depreciation	(20)	0.95[1]	(19)	0.90	(18)
Other expenses, net	(10)	0.90	(9)	0.90	(9)
Foreign exchange gain / (loss)	–		70		–
Income before taxes	40	0	103		36
Income taxes	(20)	0.90	(18)	0.90	(18)
Net income	20		85		18

1 Historical rates for cost of goods sold and depreciation of fixed assets.
Source: Peat, Marwick, Mitchell and Company, Statement of Financial Accounting Standards, No. 52, Foreign Currency Translation (1981), p. 52.

Cross-Country Taxation

The taxation of multinational corporations is complex and constantly changing. The Internet further complicates matters because it becomes harder to define where income is earned. Any valuation requires understanding at least two perspectives: the domestic tax code applicable to the parent and the tax code of the foreign country where the subsidiary is located. In most cases, it also requires understanding of tax codes (and their enforcement) in every country where the parent company and its subsidiaries do business.

One technical issue relevant to valuing subsidiaries of multinational companies is the treatment of foreign tax credits. Exhibit 17.4 provides examples of U.S. tax treatment of foreign tax credits. The local tax rates are 34 percent on U.S. income, 20 percent on income in country E, and 60 percent on income in country M. U.S. taxes are computed as 34 percent of consolidated pretax income less foreign tax credits that may not exceed 34 percent of foreign

Exhibit 17.4   Tax Calculation for a U.S. Company with and without Excess Foreign Tax Credits

1. With excess foreign tax credits	U.S.	Country E ops.	Country M ops.	Consolidated
Pretax income	$1,000	$200[1]	$300[1]	$1,500
Local tax rate	X 34%	X 20%	X 60%	–
Local taxes	340	40	180	
U.S. tax rate				X 34%
Preliminary U.S. taxes				510
Less: Foreign tax credits[2]				(170)
Net U.S. taxes				340
Foreign taxes				220
Consolidated income taxes				560
Less: Total local taxes				(560)
Corporate tax penalty				0

2. Without excess foreign tax credits	U.S.	Country E ops.	Country M ops.	U.S., E, and M consolidated	U.S. and M consolidated
Pretax income	$1,000	$400[1]	$100[1]	$1,500	$1,100
Local tax rate	X 34%	X 20%	X 60%		
Local taxes	310	80	60		
U.S. tax rate				X 34%	X 34%
Preliminary U.S. taxes				510	374
Less: Foreign tax credits[2]				(140)	(34)
Net U.S. taxes				370	340
Foreign taxes				140	60
Consolidated income taxes				510	400
Less: Total local taxes				(480)	(400)
Corporate tax penalty				30	0

1 Includes only income subject to U.S. tax rates.
2 Foreign tax credit is the foreign taxes paid or the foreign income times U.S. tax rate ($500 X 34% = $170), whichever is lower.

income. Whenever foreign tax credits reach the maximum allowable under U.S. law, as in the first example in Exhibit 17.4, consolidated taxes paid equal the total of local taxes, and no corporate tax penalty is levied. When tax credits are below the maximum allowable, as in the second example in Exhibit 17.4, consolidated taxes exceed the total of local taxes, and a U.S. corporate tax penalty is levied. In effect, the U.S. tax code may raise the effective tax rate for subsidiaries located in lower-tax countries.

For the second example in Exhibit 17.4, the U.S. tax code has raised the average effective tax rate to the parent company on income in country E from 20 percent to $(30 + 80)/400 = 27.5$ percent. The marginal effective tax rate on country E income is 34 percent, the U.S. tax rate. The effective tax rate in a foreign country may not be its domestic statutory rate, because, given the specific circumstances, it may depend on the parent company's tax rate. Looking at the second example in Exhibit 17.4, if this situation were expected to persist, it might be advisable for the parent to sell company E to an owner from country E. The reason is that the after-tax cash flow would be higher from the perspective of a country E owner.

These examples are simplified. The U.S. government typically only imposes taxes on the income of foreign subsidiaries when that income is brought back to the United States as dividends. If dividends can be deferred, so can the extra burden of U.S. taxes.

Tax Minimization and Transfer Pricing

Companies always try to reduce profits in high-tax jurisdictions. They may charge out as many headquarters functions as possible; charge subsidiaries for research and development expenses, borrow at the subsidiary level; consolidate same-country profitable subsidiaries with unprofitable subsidiaries to take advantage of tax-loss carryforwards; bill back employee stock options to other countries; use cost-plus accounting to reduce foreign profit; increase royalty charges to a foreign subsidiary; establish management-fee arrangements; consider leaving high-tax jurisdictions; and take advantage of transfer pricing. All of these maneuvers are subject to scrutiny by tax authorities. Nevertheless, tax planning can have a major impact on the value of multinational corporations.

Transfer pricing between business units of a multinational company is one of the most important tax minimization methods and determines where profits are reported.[2] The interrelationship between transfer pricing

---

[2] Actually, foreign income is separated into ten "income baskets" by the 1986 U.S. Tax Reform Act. Baskets are categorized by type of income—for example, passive interest, DISC dividends, foreign-trade income of foreign sales corporations, and foreign oil and gas extraction income. Income that generates high foreign tax credits can be combined with low-foreign-tax-credit income within but not across baskets.

and effective tax rates is complex. Suppose that the profits reflected in the first example in Exhibit 17.4 are based on market prices. The economics textbooks usually recommend that, tax considerations aside, all decision making should be based on market prices. In this example, however, tax considerations cannot be ignored. Suppose transfer pricing enables the parent company to shift $200 of pretax income from its subsidiary in country M, the high-domestic-tax country, to country E, the low-tax environment. The results are shown in the next-to-last column of the second example. Consolidated income taxes have declined from $560 to $510, but a corporate tax penalty of $30 emerges.

The $30 corporate tax penalty under the transfer-pricing scheme makes it tempting to consider selling subsidiary E to a foreign company also domiciled in country E. But from the perspective of the buyer, the subsidiary can earn only $200 of pretax profits, calculated using market prices, not the parent's artificial transfer prices. Therefore, the value of business unit E depends on your point of view. From the parent's point of view, using artificial transfer prices, it is worth $3,200, given the assumptions in Exhibit 17.5.

$$(\$100 - \$00) \div 10\% = \$3,200$$

But from the point of view of an owner domiciled in country E and using market prices, it is worth only

$$(\$200 - \$40) \div 10\% = \$1,600$$

After considering the interaction of transfer pricing and the U.S. tax code for multinationals, the optimum decision for the U.S. parent is to employ transfer pricing to minimize taxes and to retain both of its foreign subsidiaries. As shown in Exhibit 17.5, the value of this combination is the pretax profit, $1,500, less consolidated taxes of $510, discounted at 10 percent in perpetuity, for a total of $9,900. If subsidiary E were sold for $1,600 (after taxes), the total value (including the value of the U.S. operation and the subsidiary in M) would be only $8,600.

Exhibit 17.5   Value of Various Business Combinations to the Parent[1]

Business combination	Using example 1 in Exhibit 17.4, which assumes market pricing	Using example 2 in Exhibit 17.4, which assumes transfer pricing
Combined U.S. + M + E	$9,400	$9,900
Sell E, keep U.S. and M	9,400	8,600
Sell M, keep U.S. and E	9,120	9,640
All three separate	9,400	8,600

1 Values are estimated by assuming the businesses have no debt, cash flows are perpetuities, and the cost of capital is 10 percent.

The answer would change if the situation in example two of Exhibit 17.4 were to reflect market prices. Then, it would be best to sell subsidiary E. The resulting value (not shown in Exhibit 17.5) would be $3,200 from selling subsidiary E plus $7,000 for the remaining U.S. and country M operations. The alternative of keeping all three operations would be worth only $9,900.

STEP 2: FORECAST CASH FLOW IN THE SUBSIDIARY'S HOME CURRENCY

As mentioned at the beginning of this chapter, it is best to value a foreign subsidiary in its home currency. But first, you should forecast the components of cash flow in their *most relevant* currency. This means forecasting the British pound cash flows in British pounds, the Swiss franc cash flows in Swiss francs, and so on, before combining them into a set of financials for the foreign subsidiary. In practice, this is an iterative process: you cannot forecast the individual line items without considering how they affect the other line items in the forecast. You need a coherent integrated forecast that reflects the competitive dynamics of the business unit.

Once all cash flow has been forecasted in terms of its most relevant currency, it should be converted into the currency of the subsidiary before discounting using the forward-rate method. In our example, forward foreign exchange rates are used to convert forecasted French Euro revenues to British pound cash flow on a year-by-year basis. Then it combines this with other pound-equivalent cash flow received by the English subsidiary, and discounts it at the English subsidiary's weighted average cost of capital. As a practical matter, for most currencies forward exchange rates are not available beyond 18 months. Using this method means forecasting long-term foreign exchange rates, a task that will be explained shortly.

A mathematically equivalent alternative to the forward-rate method is the spot-rate method. We will employ it in step 3 to discount all of the subsidiary's cash flow that has been restated in pounds sterling at the English subsidiary's cost of capital to translate its present value to U.S. dollars at the spot exchange rate.

The spot-rate method is not generally used to convert partial cash flow, such as a revenue stream denominated in Euros, because no practical way exists to estimate a risk-adjusted Euro discount rate for the revenue stream alone. Estimating the appropriate discount rate for total cash flow from operations is difficult enough.

To do the forward-rate method, you must use interest-rate parity to forecast future spot foreign exchange rates, and then use the future spot foreign exchange rates to convert predicted foreign currency cash flow into the subsidiary's domestic currency. We will focus on a stream of revenue

Exhibit 17.6   English Subsidiary's Forecasted French Revenues

Year	French Euro revenue (Euro, million)	Forecasted future spot FX rate, (£/Euro)	£ equivalent cash revenue (£ million)
1	106	.5821 next year	£ 61.70
2	114	.5882 2 years ahead	67.05
3	123	.5948 3 years ahead	73.16
4	119	.6016 4 years ahead	71.59
5	125	.6055 5 years ahead	75.69

received from France by the English subsidiary. The forecasted Euro revenues are shown in Exhibit 17.6.

The interest-rate parity theory is based on the idea that changes in foreign exchange rates are related to the ratio of expected inflation rates between two countries. Exhibit 17.7 plots the relationship between domestic inflation and domestic interest rates for 47 countries from 1977 to 1981. Inflation often explains most of the difference in nominal interest rates

Across countries, the interest-rate parity theory is expressed as follows: the expected spot foreign exchange rate in year t, X_{ft}, is equal to the current

Exhibit 17.7   Relationship between Inflation and Interest Rates

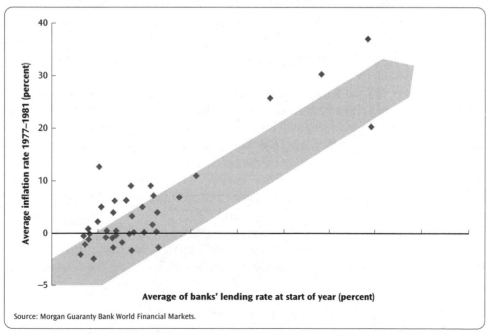

Source: Morgan Guaranty Bank World Financial Markets.

spot rate, X_0, multiplied by the ratio of nominal rates of return in the two countries over the forecast interval, t (for a derivation, see Copeland and Weston, pp. 790–803[3]):

$$X_{ft} = X_0 \left[\frac{1+N_f}{1+N_d} \right]^t$$

Where, f = The foreign currency
         d = The domestic currency

To illustrate the theory for a single year, suppose that our English subsidiary can borrow one-year money in Switzerland at a 4 percent nominal interest rate, N_f, while the borrowing rate in England is 7.1 percent. The spot exchange rate, X_0, is 2.673 Swiss francs per pound sterling and the one-year forward rate, X_f, is 2.5944 Swiss francs per dollar. We can use interest-rate parity to estimate what English borrowing rate a 4 percent borrowing rate in Switzerland is equivalent to:

$$
\begin{aligned}
1 + N_d &= (1 + N_f)(X_0/X_{ft}) \\
&= (1.04)(2.673 \text{ fr./pounds} \div 2.594 \text{ fr./pounds}) \\
&= 7.15\%
\end{aligned}
$$

No practical difference exists between borrowing in England at 7.15 percent or in Switzerland at 4 percent, because the Swiss rate is equivalent to 7.15 percent in England. The foreign borrowing rate, when converted to a domestic equivalent rate, is usually close to the domestic rate (unless there are tax implications).

Next, we show how to use interest-rate parity to forecast future spot rates and use that information to convert the French Euro revenues in Exhibit 17.6 to English pounds. Exhibit 17.8 uses U.K. and French data to illustrate. The first two rows are the term structures of interest rates on government debt for England and France. The third row is the ratio of nominal rates. We know from the interest-rate parity theory that the ratio of nominal rates multiplied by the current spot rate (pounds/Euros) provides an estimate of the forward exchange rate.

As indicated in the fifth row, the market is forecasting that the pound will strengthen versus the Euro. The French Euro revenues in line 6 of Exhibit 17.8 are converted to pound revenues (line 7) by using the interest-rate

[3] T.E. Copeland and J.F. Weston, *Financial Theory and Corporate Policy*, 3rd ed. (Reading, MA: Addison-Wesley, 1988).

Exhibit 17.8   Example of Forecasting Forward Exchange Rates

	1-year	2-year	3-year	4-year	5-year
1. British gilts, N_d	6.5%	6.6	6.7	6.8	6.8
2. French Euros, N_f	5.2%	5.4	5.5	5.6	5.7
3. $[(1+N_d)/(1+N_f)]^t$	1.0124	1.02291	1.0345	1.0462	1.0531
4. Spot rate £/Euro, X_0	0.5750	0.5750	0.5750	0.5750	0.5750
5. Forecasted forward exchange rate, £/Euro, X_f	0.5821	0.5882	0.5948	0.6016	0.6055
6. Revenues in Euros	106.00	114.00	123.00	119.00	125.00
7. Revenues in £	61.70	67.05	73.16	71.59	75.69

parity relationship. Once all revenues and costs of the English subsidiary have been converted to pounds sterling, the result is a complete forecast of the subsidiary income statement and balance sheet in pounds sterling.

STEP 3: ESTIMATE FOREIGN CURRENCY DISCOUNT RATE

To estimate the foreign currency discount rate, the general principle is to discount foreign cash flow at foreign risk-adjusted rates. The fact that a subsidiary is located in a foreign country does not change the definition of the weighted average cost of capital. The two most common errors in setting the WACC are making ad hoc adjustments for risk and using the parent country WACC to discount foreign currency cash flow. Regarding the first point, ad hoc adjustments to the discount rate to reflect political risk, foreign investment risk, or foreign currency risk are entirely inappropriate. As we will explain in Chapter 19, political risk is best handled by adjusting expected cash flow, weighting it by the probability of various scenarios. Foreign currency or foreign investment risk is handled by the spot exchange rate, and is perfectly symmetrical. An equal chance of a gain or a loss of purchasing power exists. It should be clear that if cash flow is predicted in units of the foreign currency, it should be discounted at the foreign country discount rate because this rate reflects the opportunity cost of capital in the foreign country, including expected inflation and the market risk premium.

The target capital structure for a subsidiary is the mix of financing, stated in market values, that it would maintain in the long run on a standalone basis. The actual capital structure imposed on the subsidiary by its parent may depart widely from the subsidiary's target. For tax reasons, the subsidiary may be loaded up with debt. The tax effect of this type of transfer-pricing arrangement is captured when expected cash flow is estimated and should not be double counted when estimating the discount rate.

STEP 4: DISCOUNT FREE CASH FLOW

Having determined the subsidiary's weighted average cost of capital, you are ready to discount the free cash flow forecasted in step 2 and convert it to your domestic currency. Exhibit 17.9 shows the expected free cash flow to our example subsidiary in England. It is discounted to the present at the subsidiary's WACC, assumed to be 11.8 percent, and then converted to dollars by multiplying the present value in pounds sterling by the spot exchange rate, 0.63 pounds/dollar.

One caveat is in order: Because we have discounted cash flow to the subsidiary, its present value in the domestic currency (dollars in our example) to the parent may be different if a country has restrictions that limit the expatriation of cash flow to the parent. Although ways around these constraints can sometimes be found—for example, barter or transfer pricing—keep in mind that the value to the parent depends on the quantity and timing of free cash flow (or cash equivalents) that can actually be paid out.

THE EFFECTS OF FOREIGN EXCHANGE HEDGING

Hedging is a conceptually difficult topic mainly because it is hard to justify on theoretical grounds as beneficial to shareholders. It is not unusual for multinational companies to take large positions in foreign exchange forward contracts to hedge against unexpected changes in exchange rates. Though designed to reduce currency risk, this practice is often risky in itself. It has

Exhibit 17.9   English Subsidiary Valuation

	Free cash flow (£)	Present value factor at 11.8% foreign rate	Present value (£)
2000	100	0.8945	89.45
2001	115	0.8000	92.01
2002	130	0.7156	93.03
2003	142	0.6401	90.89
2004	160	0.5725	91.60
2005	180	0.5121	92.18
2006	196	0.4580	89.78
2007	225	0.4097	92.18
2006	252	0.3665	92.35
2009	280	0.3278	91.78
Continuing value	2,653	0.3278	869.61
		PV in £	£1,784.86
		Spot rate £/$	÷0.63
		PV in $	$2,833.3

Exhibit 17.10   Use of Derivatives

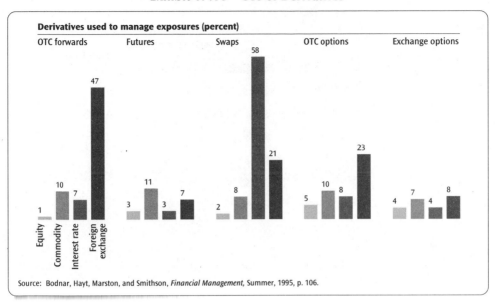

Source: Bodnar, Hayt, Marston, and Smithson, *Financial Management,* Summer, 1995, p. 106.

resulted in many well-publicized disasters. Volkswagen lost $200 million and Spectra Physics had an entire year's profits wiped out by inappropriate foreign exchange trading positions. Management either hedged the wrong exposure, or forgot that hedge positions that are too large are actually speculation. Also, other ways of hedging exist. If the local currency might decline in value, a company can reduce holdings of local currency cash and marketable securities, delay accounts payable, invoice exports in the foreign currency and imports in the domestic currency, tighten trade credit in the foreign currency, and borrow more in the foreign currency.

Until the 1990s, the literature on hedging was sparse and relatively incomplete. Most authors wrote about hedging individual transactions (such as the sale of a product with a deferred payment) or reducing the variance of cash flows (variance reduction). Recently, these approaches have been superceded by value maximization approaches that compare the benefits and costs of hedging programs. The implication is that not every company should hedge. Not every company does. The problem to which we now turn our attention is how do you decide whether or not your company should hedge, what approach should be used, and if so, what hedge ratio is appropriate? Exhibit 17.10 shows the results of a survey of 530 nonfinancial firms by Bodnar, Hayt, Marston, and Smithson[4] regarding their use of financial

[4] Bodnar, Hayt, Marston, and Smithson, "Wharton Survey of Derivatives Usage by U.S. Nonfinancial Firms," *Financial Management* (summer 1995), pp. 104–114.

Exhibit 17.11   Reasons for Using Derivatives

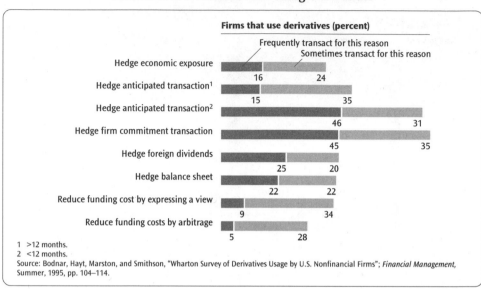

Firms that use derivatives (percent)

Frequently transact for this reason
Sometimes transact for this reason

Reason	Frequently	Sometimes
Hedge economic exposure	16	24
Hedge anticipated transaction[1]	15	35
Hedge anticipated transaction[2]	46	31
Hedge firm commitment transaction	45	35
Hedge foreign dividends	25	20
Hedge balance sheet	22	22
Reduce funding cost by expressing a view	9	34
Reduce funding costs by arbitrage	5	28

1 >12 months.
2 <12 months.
Source: Bodnar, Hayt, Marston, and Smithson, "Wharton Survey of Derivatives Usage by U.S. Nonfinancial Firms"; *Financial Management*, Summer, 1995, pp. 104–114.

derivatives for hedging. Thirty-five percent of the responding companies used derivatives for hedging, and given that they hedged, 47 percent used over-the-counter forward contracts. The prevalence of transaction hedging is shown in Exhibit 17.11. The common practice is to identify a specific source of risk in a foreign currency, then take an offsetting position in forward contracts or options. The problem with this approach is that it does not take all cash flows into account (and may actually unhedge the company). Even if it does consider all cash flows, these cash flows, usually payables and receivables, cannot be forecasted with a high degree of accuracy. Therefore, the hedge may be ineffective.

If we look at pure risk (or variance) reduction, the efficiency of the hedge is the percentage reduction in the variance of the hedged variable (usually the operating cash flows of a company). The math for this type of problem is important. Suppose that we define the hedged position of a company as the change in operating cash flows minus a hedge ratio, h, times the change in the value of a forward position:

$$\text{Operating profit} = (P_1 - P_0) - h(F_1 - F_0)$$

The expected hedged operating cash flows and their variance can therefore be written as:

$$E(\text{Operating profit}) = [E(P_1 - P_0) - hE(F_1 - F_0)]$$
$$\text{VAR}(\text{Operating profit}) = \text{VAR}(P) - 2rh\sigma_p\sigma_F + h^2\text{VAR}(F)$$

Where $P_1 - P_0$ = The change in operating profit.
   $F_1 - F_0$ = The change in the price of a forward or futures contract.
      h = The variance minimizing hedge ratio.
VAR(P) = The variance of operating cash flows.
VAR(F) = The variance of dollar returns of a forward or futures contract.
      r = The correlation between operating cash flows and dollar returns on a forward or futures contact.

Taking the derivative of the variance of operating profit with respect to the hedging ratio h, and setting the result equal to zero gives the optimal hedge ratio for the minimum variance portfolio:

$$h^* = \frac{r\sigma_p}{\sigma_F}$$

Note that this is the slope of a linear regression of the operating profits against the gains (or losses) on the forward contracts. By substituting the optimal hedge ratio into the variance equation, we see that the standard deviation of the minimum variance hedge portfolio depends on the correlation between the operating profit and the gains or losses on the forward contracts:

$$\sigma_{h(min)} = \sigma_p \sqrt{1 - r^2}$$

For example, the r-squared must be 60 percent in order to reduce the variance of the unhedged operating profits by 37 percent. An r-squared of 90 percent will reduce the variance roughly 68 percent. This demonstrates that regardless of the optimal hedge ratio, one must have a very high correlation between the operating profits and the forward contracts in order to have an efficient hedge. In practice, the inability to accurately forecast receivables and payables makes it difficult to have highly efficient hedges.

Even though your company hedges at the optimal hedge ratio, the cost of hedging may exceed the benefits (Exhibit 17.12). In the exhibit, the firm's operating cash flows are characterized as a random walk (a Gauss Wiener process) through time, starting at level P_0, with a positive drift to reflect expected growth. If this line should happen to touch a lower boundary, illustrated by the upward sloping straight line starting at h_0, the firm experiences business disruption costs such as the loss of customers and talented management, missed investment opportunities, or even a trip to the bankruptcy courts.

Hedging has two effects on operating cash flows. The desirable effect is to reduce the volatility of cash flows. The line representing hedged cash flows has lower volatility. The undesirable effect is that the cost of hedging reduces the slope of the line. Thus, a value-maximizing approach to hedging examines the expected benefit versus the expected cost. An article by

Exhibit 17.12   Cash Flows and a Boundary Condition Over Time

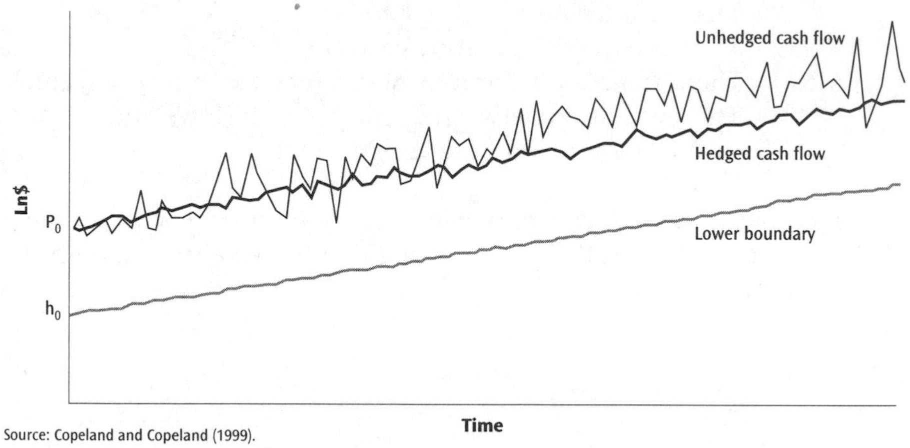

Source: Copeland and Copeland (1999).

Copeland and Copeland discusses this approach in greater depth.[5] The implication for a value-maximizing firm is that the expected benefit is the present value of the change in the probability of crossing the lower boundary multiplied by the cost of touching it—the expected business disruption costs (e.g., 15 percent of the value of the firm). The cost is the present value of the expected total cost of the hedge (e.g., 50 basis points per year) from now until the expected time to touching the boundary condition, given the hedge. A possible, and even common, outcome is that the expected time before the unhedged cash flows will touch the boundary is so long that even though the cost of hedging is low (50 basis points per year), the expected cost of hedging exceeds the expected benefit. The decision to hedge depends on the volatility and rate of growth in unhedged cash flows; the initial coverage ratio measured as the distance between the starting cash flows and the starting boundary condition; the efficiency of the hedge (how much it reduces volatility); the cost of business disruption, and the cost of hedging.

Once it has been determined that the firm should hedge, Copeland and Copeland provide the optimal hedge ratio. This is the original hedge ratio, h^*, based on the slope of a linear regression between the unhedged operating profit and the gains or losses on the forward position, minus an adjustment equal to the cost of the hedge per year, μ_x, divided by the variance of the forward contract value, σ_x.

[5] T. Copeland and M. Copeland, "Managing Corporate FX Risk: A Value-Maximizing Approach," *Financial Management*, vol. 28, no. 3 (autumn 1999), pp. 68–75.

$$h = h^* - \frac{\mu_x}{\sigma_x^2}$$

This value-maximizing approach predicts that very profitable firms, with adequate liquidity, are less likely to hedge than other firms in the same industry that have lower coverage ratios, lower growth in operating profits, or higher business disruption costs. It reaches the conclusion that hedging is not necessarily the best thing to do.

SUMMARY

This chapter has focused primarily on the example of valuing the English subsidiary of a U.S. parent multinational corporation. After analyzing historical performance, we forecasted all cash flow, wherever it occurred, in the most relevant currency. Next, this cash flow was translated year-by-year into pounds, the subsidiary's currency, by using forecasts of the future spot foreign exchange rates. Once all free cash flow was stated in pounds, it was discounted at the weighted average cost of capital for the subsidiary. The resulting pound value of the company was then converted to dollars at the spot exchange rate.

Along the way, we covered a number of difficult issues: the need to understand foreign (and U.S.) accounting standards, the transfer-pricing problem, forecasting forward foreign exchange rates, and understanding the effect of hedging on value.

18

Valuation Outside the United States

Does everything that we have described about valuation apply outside the United States? Absolutely. This does not mean that all capital markets are as efficient as the U.S. market or that all managers outside the United States are as focused on shareholder value creation. But our ideas about valuation can help managers everywhere make better strategic and financial decisions.

In Chapter 5, we showed that in the United States, the market value of companies supports the discounted cash flow approach. The evidence from other countries also lends credence to the DCF method. Exhibit 18.1 shows how the market values of European companies relate to ROIC and growth. Companies with higher ROIC have larger market-to-capital

Exhibit 18.1 Relationship between Market Values, ROIC, and Growth in Europe

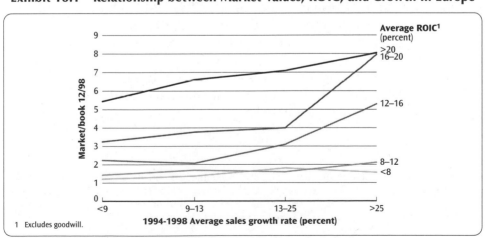

1 Excludes goodwill.

ratios. Companies that are growing faster have higher market-to-capital ratios when ROIC exceeds WACC.

In this chapter, we describe some of the differences in valuation analysis outside the United States. These differences fall into three categories: accounting, taxes, and cost of capital. The information in this chapter is primarily relevant for Europe, Japan, Canada, and other developed countries. Chapter 19 deals with special valuation issues in emerging markets.

ACCOUNTING DIFFERENCES

Major differences in world accounting standards are likely to continue for some time, although harmonization efforts are under way as more companies list shares outside home markets. Furthermore, more countries are permitting the use of International Accounting Standards (IAS) for companies domiciled in their country.[1] In any case, the calculation of free cash flow— and thus valuations—is unaffected by accounting rules. Regardless of the accounting system, if you follow the approach in Chapter 9, free cash flow will be the same. When developing cash-flow projections, however, we typically use financial ratios like margin and ROIC as benchmarks for the projections. Following the approach in Chapter 9, we can eliminate some but not all of the accounting differences that show up in ratios like margin and ROIC.

In 1996, Hoechst, the German chemicals and life sciences company, translated its 1996 financial statements, prepared under German accounting standards, to U.S. generally accepted accounting principles (GAAP) to list its shares on the New York Stock Exchange. Under German accounting standards, Hoechst reported net income of DM 2.1 billion. Under U.S. GAAP, Hoechst's net income was only DM 1.1 billion, a difference of DM 1.0 billion (Exhibit 18.2). When both sets of books are translated into NOPLAT, invested capital, and ROIC, the gap is narrowed but not eliminated. Based on the German books, NOPLAT is DM 2.3 billion, while it is DM 2.0 billion based on the U.S. books. It is not possible to reconcile the accounting methods because estimations have been made, but using NOPLAT narrows the gap to 13 percent, from 100 percent.

The major accounting differences that warrant discussion include provisions, pensions, goodwill, fixed asset revaluation, deferred taxation, consolidation, and foreign currency translation.

---

[1] In early 2000, the United States Securities and Exchange Commission was considering allowing non-U.S. companies to list their shares in the United States if they reported their results using IAS. We expect that over the next 5 to 10 years, IAS will become the de facto accounting standard for major companies around the world (except the United States).

Exhibit 18.2 Comparison of Hoechst AG Results, 1996

Dm, million

Accounting results	German GAAP	US GAAP	Difference
EBIT	4,013	3,119	(894)
Net income	2,114	1,090	(1,024)
Total assets	55,125	55,827	702
Total equity	14,508	15,091	583

Economic results	German GAAP	US GAAP	Difference
Adjusted EBIT	4,520	4,411	(109)
NOPLAT	2,378	2,039	(339)
Invested capital[1]	37,143	37,669	526
Invested capital[2]	46,178	46,880	702
ROIC[1]	6.4%	5.4%	1.0%
ROIC[2]	5.1%	4.3%	0.8%

1 Excluding goodwill.
2 Including goodwill.

Provisions

Additions to provisions are noncash expenses that reflect future costs or expected losses. Companies make provisions by reducing income and setting up a corresponding reserve on the liability side of the balance sheet (or deducting the amount from the relevant assets).

The rules for setting up provisions vary by country. Some countries only allow provisions for specifically identifiable future costs or losses, while others allow provisions for unspecified costs. In countries with flexible rules, companies often use provisions to manage earnings, increasing them in good years and drawing them down in bad years. Provisions are also tax deductible in some countries. Provisions often are the single largest difference between U.S. GAAP accounting and the local accounting statements. Exhibit 18.3 summarizes the rules for provisions across countries. In Chapter 9, we explained how the various types of provisions should be treated in calculating NOPLAT, invested capital, and free cash flow.

Pensions

Pension systems differ greatly by country, as summarized in Exhibit 18.4. European countries such as the United Kingdom and the Netherlands require companies to have pension plans independently managed by pension fund managers or insurance companies. In countries such as Germany, pension obligations are simply recorded as liabilities on the financial statements (called provisions) to be eventually paid out of the operating cash of

Exhibit 18.3   Non-Pension Provisions

Country	Can provisions be made for expected liabilities related to uncertain events? If yes, are they likely to be material?	Which are the most common provisions?	Are provisions tax deductible?
Belgium	Provisions can be made for uncertain liabilities related to specific events and need to be documented	Expected maintenance costs, restructuring costs, losses from uncompleted business transactions	Yes, if correctly documented
Denmark	Only for specific events	Losses for uncompleted business transactions, warranty. All mentioned in notes to the accounts	Yes, if specific
Finland	No	Not applicable	Not applicable
France	Yes	Expected charges, bad debts	Yes, if justified
Germany	Yes	Expected maintenance costs, restructuring costs, losses for uncompleted business transactions	Yes, most of them
Italy	Yes, they could be material, especially in non-listed or non-international companies	Expected maintenance costs, restructuring costs, losses for uncompleted business transactions, unspecified "risk provisions"	Yes
Japan	No	Not applicable	Not applicable
Netherlands	No, provisions can only be made for specific risks and obligations at balance sheet date	Bad debts, inventory obsolescence, reorganization schemes, warranty, major repairs	No (major exception: pension provisions)
Norway	Yes	Expected charges, bad debts	Yes, most of them
Portugal	Yes	Doubtful debts, inventory obsolescence, contingencies and future obligations, renovation of mineral or petroleum sites	Yes, in some cases and within limits
Spain	Yes	Likely expenses or obligations, pending litigations, major repairs/maintenance	Yes, in some cases and within limits
Sweden	Yes	Only for specific events, e.g. restructuring cost, contingencies	No
Switzerland	Yes, they could be material, especially in non-listed or non-international companies	Bad debts, restructuring costs, losses for uncompleted business transactions, unspecified "risk provisions"	Yes, but limited by tax authorities
United Kingdom	No	Not applicable	Not applicable
United States	No	Not applicable	Not applicable
IAS	No	Not applicable	Not applicable

Source: McKinsey research; information from 1998.

the company.[2] Countries' approaches to funding pension plans also vary. A plan is fully funded when, according to the actuarial standards prescribed in the country, the cumulative contributions to the pension fund are equal to cumulative payments due employees. In most countries, companies are required to disclose underfunding in the main body of the financial statements or in the notes. The principles described in Chapter 9 for dealing with unfunded or underfunded pensions apply here as well.

---

[2] Companies based in countries with one system may consolidate in their accounts the retirement-related liabilities of subsidiaries operating in countries with different rules. As a result, pension provisions may be significant even for companies in countries where all pensions are state-funded.

Exhibit 18.4 Pensions and Related Provisions

Country	Are pensions required to be fully funded?	If yes, how are temporary under/over fundings treated?	If not, how are unfunded pensions treated?	Which rules are used to calculate the annual provision?
Belgium	Normally pensions paid by the state	Not applicable	Not applicable	Cash basis
Denmark	No		Shown as liabilities	Actuarial calculation
Finland	No		Shown as liabilities	
France	Normally pensions paid by the state		Not applicable	
Germany	No		Shown as liabilities (internal provisions since 1987). Those existing before 1987 are shown as contingent liabilities	Standard actuarial calculation from tax law (usually underestimated)
Italy	Not applicable: pensions paid by the state	Not applicable	Not applicable	
Japan	Certain pensions must be funded	Recognized as liabilities/assets	Shown as liabilities	Actuarial calculation
Netherlands	Yes, with a few exceptions these have to be deposited in an independent fund	Overfundings are deducted from employee's contribution, underfundings have to be paid for by the company in the year they arise	Not applicable	Actuarial calculation
Norway	No		Shown as contingent liabilities in the notes	Cash basis
Portugal	No		Shown as other liabilities	Actuarial calculation
Spain	Yes (since 1990)	Shown as other liabilities		Actuarial calculation
Sweden	Not applicable: pensions paid by the state	Not applicable	Not applicable	Not applicable
Switzerland	Yes	Shown as liabilities when not transferred to a pension fund		Actuarial calculation
United Kingdom	No		Shown as liabilities and recognized over the expected working life of the employee	Actuarial calculation
United States	Yes	Shown as liabilities when not transferred to a pension fund		Actuarial calculation
IAS	Not applicable	Not applicable	Shown as liabilities	Actuarial calculation

Source: McKinsey research; information from 1998.

Goodwill

In some countries, goodwill can be written off directly against equity at the time of the acquisition.[3] In other countries, it is capitalized and amortized. Exhibit 18.5 summarizes the accounting treatment of goodwill.

In most cases, ROIC should be calculated both with and without goodwill. ROIC excluding goodwill measures the operating performance of the company and is useful for comparing operating performance across companies and analyzing trends. ROIC including goodwill measures how well

[3] The United Kingdom before 1998, and Germany, Switzerland, and Italy before 1994.

Exhibit 18.5   Goodwill

Country	Written off or capitalized?	If choice available, which is the common practice?	Amortization period when capitalized (max. number of years)
Belgium	Capitalized		10–12
Denmark	Company's choice	Capitalization	5
Finland	Capitalized		20
France	Capitalized (written off only if non-cash transaction)	Capitalized (written off only if non-cash transaction)	Useful economic life
Germany	Capitalized		15 (for fiscal purposes) or arbitrarily up to 25% p.a. (for legal purposes)
Italy	Company's choice until 1994; capitalized after 1994	Often written off	5
Japan	Capitalized		5 (20 in some cases)
Netherlands	Company's choice	Capitalization is becoming more frequent	5, in special cases longer useful life
Norway	Capitalized		5
Portugal	Capitalized		Generally 5 (20 in some cases)
Spain	Capitalized		10
Sweden	Capitalized		10–20
Switzerland	Company's choice	Often written off	"Reasonable period," normally 5 years
United Kingdom	Capitalized		"Useful economic life," usually no more than 20 years
United States	Capitalized		Up to 40
IAS	Capitalized		"Useful economic life," usually no more than 20 years

Source: McKinsey research; information from 1998.

the company has used its investors' funds. Specifically, has the company earned its cost of capital, taking into consideration the premiums it paid for acquisitions?

The proper way to include goodwill in the ROIC calculation is to add to invested capital the total amount of goodwill before cumulative amortization and not to deduct from NOPLAT any goodwill amortization. In effect, this reverses the amortization of goodwill. The reason for not amortizing goodwill for economic analysis is that goodwill, unlike other fixed assets, does not wear out and does not have to be replaced. For other assets, depreciation is a proxy for the physical deterioration of the asset, recognizing that the asset must be replaced eventually.

For companies that have written off goodwill against equity, simply add the cumulative goodwill written off to invested capital to calculate ROIC including goodwill. This information is generally available in the notes to the company's financial statements.

Fixed-Asset Revaluation

In some countries, assets can be revalued to take into account the impact of inflation or other price changes. The revaluation takes the form of an increase in fixed assets and a corresponding increase in an equity account. The rationale for this is to show the results of the company on the basis of current costs. In the Netherlands, assets can be revalued every year to reflect net realizable value. In Italy, Spain, and Portugal, assets can be revalued only under special circumstances. In the United States and Germany, on the other hand, they cannot be revalued; assets always reflect historical cost (Exhibit 18.6).

As in the case of goodwill, ROIC should be calculated both with and without revaluation. ROIC including revaluation measures the operating performance of the company irrespective of when the assets have been bought and is useful for comparing operating performance across companies. ROIC excluding revaluation measures how well the company has employed its investors' funds. It shows whether the company has earned its cost of capital, taking into consideration the actual cost paid for fixed assets.

Exhibit 18.6   Fixed Asset Revaluation

Country	Is it allowed?	Which criteria are used?	Is revaluation tax free?	Is depreciation tax deductible?
Belgium	Only if the value has clearly and permanently risen. Usually done only with respect to real estate assets	Market prices, as estimated by authorized experts	No: revaluation reserves are taxable at the corporate tax rate. They are accounted for as "exceptional profits"	Yes
Denmark	Yes	Market value	No	Yes
Finland	Yes, if there is permanent increase in value			
France	Yes, since 1984, under certain conditions	Market value	No	Yes
Germany	No			
Italy	Only according to government decree (most recent in 1983, 1990, and 1991)	Using government price indices	1991 revaluation was subject to a 16% tax	Yes
Japan	No, except that land can be revalued if special permission granted by government (March 31, 1998 to March 31, 2001)	Market value	Yes	Not applicable
Netherlands	Yes, every year	Replacement cost or market value	Yes	No
Portugal	Only according to government decree (usually every two years)	Using government price indices	Yes	Yes, partially (60% of additional depreciation)
Spain	Only according to government decree (most recent in 1983)	Using government price indices	Yes	Yes
Sweden	Yes, if there is permanent increase in value	Market value	Yes	Yes
Switzerland	No			
United Kingdom	Occasionally (land and buildings)	Market value	Yes	Partially, according to tax rules
United States	No			
IAS	Yes	Up-to-date fair value	Not applicable	Not applicable

Source: McKinsey research; information from 1998.

The most appropriate way to take revaluation into account is to annually adjust NOPLAT and invested capital to reflect the annual increase of market values. In countries where revaluation is done over longer periods, the revaluation reserve should be spread over the period in question. In any case, when calculating free cash flow, capital spending should be determined as the increase in net fixed assets plus depreciation, less the increase in the revaluation reserve. Otherwise, investments would be overstated.

Deferred Taxation

Deferred taxes arise from differences between a company's published financial statements and its tax accounts. In Germany, Switzerland, and Italy, deferred taxes normally do not arise in the accounts of individual companies because financial statements are the same as tax accounts. However, deferred taxes may arise in consolidated accounts. In other countries, deferred taxes could be substantial because of items such as asset revaluation and accelerated depreciation.

To calculate NOPLAT, invested capital, and ROIC, income taxes should be stated on a cash basis. For NOPLAT, the increase in deferred taxes (as a balance sheet item) should be subtracted from the amount of taxes on the income statement to calculate taxes on earnings before interest and taxes (EBIT). For invested capital, deferred taxes should be treated as an equity item as described in Chapter 9.

Consolidation

As summarized in Exhibit 18.7, most countries require consolidation of accounts when a subsidiary is more than 50 percent owned, or when there is a controlling interest. In some cases, these consolidation principles were adopted only recently; consequently, historical accounts may not be entirely comparable. The footnotes to a company's accounts should be reviewed to ensure comparability across companies and time.

Foreign Currency Translation

The translation of the accounts for foreign subsidiaries into the parent company's currency for consolidation purposes follows either the current or temporal method.

The current method translates foreign-currency balance sheet items into the parent currency at the end-of-period exchange rate, except for equity accounts. Equity is converted at historical rates, for example, at the exchange rate on the day of a share issue. The income statement is translated at an average rate for the period. An equity account called translation adjustment is credited or debited with the amount necessary to balance the balance sheet.

Exhibit 18.7 Consolidation

Country	When do subsidiaries have to be consolidated?	Consolidation method for affiliates and joint ventures
Belgium	When ownership exceeds 50%	Equity method for affiliates (>20%), proportional consolidation for joint ventures
Denmark	When voting rights exceed 50%	Equity method for affiliates, proportional consolidation for joint ventures
Finland	When ownership exceeds 50% or controlling interest	Equity method for affiliates, proportional consolidation for joint ventures
France	When ownership exceeds 50%, or 40% for two consecutive years, or one parent designated more than half of the directors, or parent has a control on subsidiary through special contracts or clauses	Equity method for affiliates (>20%), proportional consolidation for joint ventures
Germany	When ownership exceeds 50% or the subsidiary is managed by the parent company	Equity method for affiliates (>10%), proportional consolidation for joint ventures is possible but rare
Italy	When ownership exceeds 50% or controlling interest (before 1994 only for listed companies)	Equity method for affiliates (>10%), proportional consolidation for joint ventures is possible but rare
Japan	When ownership exceeds 50% or the subsidiary is effectively controlled by the parent	Equity method for affiliates (>20%) or when parent has substantial influence over management
Netherlands	"Group companies": companies in which the parent executes the rights associated with a controlling interest	Equity method or proportional consolidation for non-"group companies" (A minority interest can be a group company in the case of special voting rights)
Norway	When ownership exceeds 50%	Equity method for affiliates, proportional consolidation for joint ventures
Portugal	When voting rights exceed 50%	Equity method for affiliates (>20%), proportional consolidation for joint ventures is possible but rare
Spain	When ownership exceeds 50% or control majority of board seats	Equity method for affiliates, proportional consolidation for joint ventures is possible but rare
Sweden	When ownership exceeds 50%	Equity method and proportional consolidation can be found for both affiliates and joint ventures
Switzerland	When voting rights exceed 50%	Equity method for affiliates (>20%), proportional consolidation for joint ventures is possible but rare
United Kingdom	When voting rights exceed 50% or controlling interest	Equity method is common, proportional consolidation is only allowed for unincorporated joint ventures
United States	When voting rights exceed 50% or effective management control	Equity method is common
IAS	When voting rights exceed 50% or controlling interest	Equity method for associates (>20%), proportional consolidation for joint ventures

Source: McKinsey research; information from 1998.

Under the temporal method, assets carried at cost, such as fixed assets and inventory, are translated at historical exchange rates (the rate that applied when the asset was acquired). Other assets, and most liabilities, are translated at end-of-period exchange rates. Any gain or loss related to the translation of assets or liabilities at end-of-period rates is shown as an exchange gain or loss on the income statement. In the income statement, all items are translated at the rate in effect on the date of the transaction.

In European countries, the current method is more common. When the current method is used, we recommend that the change in the equity account for foreign translation be treated as an operating cash flow since in most cases it corrects operating assets or liabilities. This should be assessed

Exhibit 18.8   Valuation of a Japanese Electronics Company, 1992

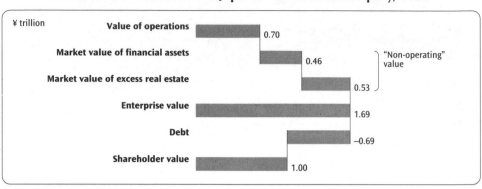

on a case-by-case basis. When the temporal method is used, no adjustments are necessary.

Nonoperating Assets

In some countries, nonoperating assets can be significant. Exhibit 18.8 shows the disguised valuation of a Japanese electronics company. Less than half of the total value is the operations of the business. The remainder is shares of other companies and excess real estate investments. Japanese companies customarily own minority interests in the common stock of their business partners (customers and suppliers). These securities are rarely traded and remain on the books at their historical purchase price, often a small fraction of the current worth. Their current market value should be captured in your valuation.

Real estate is another example of a nonoperating asset whose book value is often far below the market value. Estimate the market value and add it to the valuation as a nonoperating asset if the real estate is being held for eventual resale. If the real estate is used by the company's operations, however, the market value is irrelevant for valuation purposes because it cannot be sold without being replaced or rented.

TAXATION

Taxation systems vary widely and are constantly changing. In Europe, corporate statutory tax rates run from as low as 12 percent in Switzerland to 53 percent in Italy. Effective tax rates may differ from statutory rates because of the way taxable income is calculated. We can't do justice to this subject, but many guides are available summarizing tax rules across countries. We will highlight one conceptual issue that particularly affects company valuation: how to deal with corporate and personal tax integration.

Many European countries have integrated corporate and personal tax systems to eliminate some or all of the double taxation on dividends to shareholders. Where mechanisms to reduce double taxation are present, they may affect companies' value.

Some countries use a dividend imputation system that provides a tax credit to shareholders for some or all of the corporate taxes already paid by the company. Dividend imputation effectively increases cash flow to shareholders by decreasing the amount of taxes received by the government. This cash flow may take the form of a reduction of tax owed or of a tax refund, depending on the overall tax liability of the shareholder. An example is given in Exhibit 18.9, which shows the calculation of tax credits under a dividend imputation system and the resulting differences in net cash flows to investors. Different countries' approaches to the double taxation issue are detailed in Exhibit 18.10.

Dividend imputation has two implications for value. First, because of the higher prepersonal-tax cash flows to shareholders, a company fiscally based in a country using a dividend imputation mechanism should be valued more highly than an identical company fiscally based in a country with double taxation of dividends. Second, in a dividend imputation system, what dividend policy a company chooses will have an impact on the overall

---

Exhibit 18.9   How Dividend Imputation Works

Billion Lire

	Double taxation			Dividend imputation		
Corporate tax rate	37%	37%	37%	37%	37%	37%
Tax credit (rate on net dividend)	0%	0%	0%	56%	56%	56%
Dividend payout ratio	40%	40%	40%	40%	40%	40%
Shareholder tax rate	0%	20%	35%	0%	20%	35%
Company cash flows						
Earnings before taxes	100.0	100.0	100.0	100.0	100.0	100.0
Corporate taxes	(37.0)	(37.0)	(37.0)	(37.0)	(37.0)	(37.0)
Net income	63.0	63.0	63.0	63.0	63.0	63.0
Cash dividend paid	25.2	25.2	25.2	25.2	25.2	25.2
Shareholder taxation						
Shareholder taxable base	25.2	25.2	25.2	39.4[1]	39.4	39.4
Shareholder taxes	-	(5.0)	(8.8)	-	(7.9)	(13.8)
Tax credit	-	-	-	14.2	14.2	14.2
Taxes (paid) received	-	(5.0)	(8.8)	14.2	6.3	0.4
Shareholder cash flows						
Cash dividend received	25.2	25.2	25.2	25.2	25.2	25.2
Taxes (paid) received	-	(5.0)	(8.8)	14.2	16.3	0.4
Net cash to investor	25.2	20.2	16.4	39.4	31.5	25.6

1 Actual cash dividend paid grossed up by the tax credit rate.

Exhibit 18.10   Approaches to Taxation of Dividends

Country	How are dividends taxed?	If there is dividend imputation, what is the tax credit rate on net dividends?
Australia	Dividend imputation	Full imputation.
Belgium	Classical tax (double taxation)	
Denmark	Classical tax with lower personal tax rates on dividends	
Finland	Dividend imputation	7/18 tax credit on net dividends (full imputation of 28% corporation tax).
France	Dividend imputation	Tax credit of 50% on net dividends (full imputation of basic 33% corporate tax rate, but excludes 10% corporate tax surcharge).
Germany[1]	Dividend imputation	Tax credit of 3/7 of the net dividend (full imputation of 30% corporate tax on dividends). Note that taxes on retained earnings are 45%, while on dividends they are 30%.
Italy	Dividend imputation	Tax credit of 56.25% of net dividend (almost full imputation of 37% corporate tax).
Netherlands	Classical tax (double taxation)	
Norway	Dividend imputation	Dividend imputation equivalent to tax credit on net dividends of 7/18 (full refund of corporate tax at 28%) for resident shareholders. The tax credit is implicit rather than explicit, since dividends are considered tax-free.
Portugal	Dividend imputation	Partial imputation with a 33.75% tax credit on net dividends (a refund of 60% of the 36% corporate tax rate).
Spain	Dividend imputation	Partial imputation: Resident individuals receive 40% tax credit on net dividends; resident corporations receive 27% (50% refund of corporate tax at 35%).
Sweden	Classical tax (double taxation)	
Switzerland	Classical tax (double taxation)	
United Kingdom[2]	Classical tax (double taxation)	

1 The German government proposed significant changes to its tax code in early 2000, including eliminating the dividend tax credit.
2 United Kingdom had a dividend imputation system until 1999.
Source: European Tax Handbook, 1997; *Financial Times.*

value of the company: in choosing how much of retained earnings to distribute as dividends, management also determines how much of the potential tax credit shareholders will receive.

How to deal with dividend imputation in valuations is controversial. The debate centers on whether personal tax credits should be taken into consideration in the valuation. As a practical matter, dividend imputation may be irrelevant if the key stock price-setting investors are institutional investors or foreign investors who do not benefit from the dividend tax credit. One approach effectively says that no adjustments should be made to the cash flows or discount rate of companies in countries with dividend imputation. An alternative approach includes the impact of dividend imputation by adjusting the company's cash flows to take into account the dividend tax credit. Here are the steps to follow:

- *Size of tax credit.* The tax credit is equal to the amount of dividend paid in the year multiplied by the tax credit rate on net dividends. The relation between the corporate tax rate (t_c) and the tax credit rate on net dividends (t_i) for countries with full imputation is:

$$t_i = \frac{t_c}{1 - t_c}$$

For countries without full imputation, the government defines the tax credit rate (as shown in the Italian example in Exhibit 18.9).

- *NOPLAT.* As part of the calculation of taxes on EBIT, subtract the tax credit from the income tax provision in the income statement. When NOPLAT is calculated starting from net income, the tax credit should be added back to net income. See Exhibit 18.11 for an example.

- *Cash flows.* There is no need to change the calculation of free cash flow, since the tax credit has already been included in NOPLAT. In the financing flows, include the tax credit on cash dividends paid out. Even though the government pays this, not the company, it should be included to accurately represent the actual cash flow to the shareholder before individual taxation.

- *Cost of capital.* No changes in the WACC formula are necessary.

Exhibit 18.11   Impact on NOPLAT of Dividend Imputation

Billion Lire

NOPLAT		Reconciliation to net income	
Total revenues	31,006	Net income	444
Cost of goods sold	(30,192)	Add: Tax credit on dividends	25
		Add: Interest expense after tax	92
EBIT	814	Total income available to investors	561
Taxes on EBIT	(277)	Less: Nonoperating income after tax	(24)
NOPLAT	537	NOPLAT	537

Taxes on EBIT	
Provision for income taxes	261
Add: Tax shield on interest expense	54
Less: Tax on nonoperating income	(14)
Less: Tax credit on dividends	**(25)** ← 56.25% (tax credit rate) x 44 (dividends)
Taxes on EBIT	277

Corporate tax rate	37%
Partial dividend imputation	
Tax credit on gross dividends	36%
Tax credit on net dividends	56.25%
Dividends paid out	44

Exhibit 18.12   Effect of Changes in Dividend Payout Ration on Valuation

Based on corporate tax rate = 37% (billion lire)	Tax credit on net dividend	Dividend payout ratio				
		0%	20%	40%	70%	100%
Double taxation	0%	5,474	5,474	5,474	5,474	5,474
Dividend imputation	56.25%	5,474	6,507	7,443	8,683	9,747

When dividend imputation is included in a valuation model, the dividend payout ratio can have a significant effect on value. The effects of changing the payout ratio in one model are shown in Exhibit 18.12. Where dividend imputation is not present, dividend policy has no impact on value. Where imputation is used, all other factors being equal, the higher the payout ratio, the higher the value of the firm.

COST OF CAPITAL

The basic approach for estimating the weighted average cost of capital is identical to that described in Chapter 10. The weighted average cost of capital for a company is a weighted average of the costs of its equity, debt, and other financing sources. The cost of capital should be consistent with and expressed in the same currency as the cash flows being discounted.

Most of the components of the cost of capital do not require special discussion here. For example, it is common practice around the world to use the CAPM for estimating the cost of equity. Two issues merit detailed discussion: what market risk premium and beta to use.

As in the United States, the choice of market risk premium is vexing. For countries that are developed and reasonably integrated into the global capital market, we favor using a worldwide risk premium, based on the U.S. risk premium of 4.5 percent to 5 percent.

Our reasoning is based on the globalization of capital markets. In the late 1990s, about 25 percent of all equity trades were considered international—in other words, the shareholder and the company were domiciled in different countries. These global traders, primarily large institutional investors, draw their capital from and invest it all over the world. If expected premiums were significantly different across countries (on a risk-adjusted basis), you would expect to see significant flows to countries with higher-than-average premiums and away from lower-than-average premiums. Such a movement would tend to reequalize premiums.

This makes intuitive sense. Consider the consumer goods companies Procter & Gamble and Unilever. Both sell their household products globally with roughly the same geographic spread. The shares of both are traded in

Exhibit 18.13   Measured Risk Premiums Vary Widely

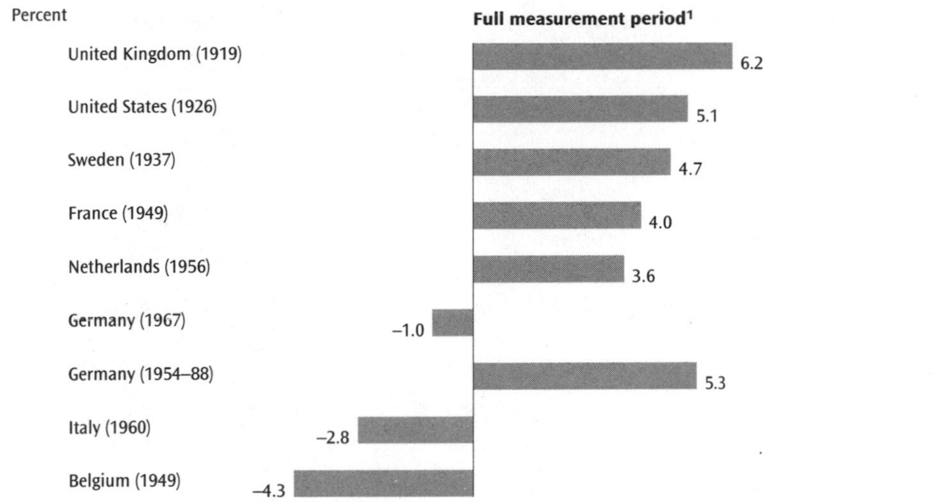

Percent

Full measurement period[1]

United Kingdom (1919) 6.2
United States (1926) 5.1
Sweden (1937) 4.7
France (1949) 4.0
Netherlands (1956) 3.6
Germany (1967) −1.0
Germany (1954–88) 5.3
Italy (1960) −2.8
Belgium (1949) −4.3

1 The starting year is indicated in brackets; 1994 is ending year.
Source: Local market stock and bond returns; McKinsey analysis; Ibbotson Associates 1995 yearbook; BZW Equity-Gilt Study 1994.

the United States and Europe. The primary difference is that Procter & Gamble is domiciled in the United States and Unilever is domiciled in the United Kingdom and the Netherlands. With similar investor bases, it would be odd if the two companies had different costs of capital.

Given this reasoning, how do we account for different realized premiums? Exhibit 18.13 shows the realized premiums on stock market indexes compared with government bond returns for a number of European countries. The realized returns vary considerably. In fact, some of the premiums are negative (Italy and Belgium). Certainly negative premiums don't make any sense.

We would argue that in many cases, these European markets have only recently opened up to the global market. Therefore, the historical data may not properly represent the current situation. More important is the argument that these market indexes do not represent large diversified portfolios. A study by Roll showed that most European stock market indexes had less than 100 stocks and had high industry concentrations.[4] Exhibit 18.14 shows the number of stocks in each index and the Herfindahl index, which is a measure of the dominance of a small number of industries on the index. You can see that the Herfindahl index is much larger than in the United States or United Kingdom. Roll took the analysis one step further and measured the portion

[4] R. Roll, "Industrial Structure and the Comparative Behavior of International Stock Market Indices," *Journal of Finance* (March 1992).

Exhibit 18.14 Index Characteristics

Source: Roll, *Journal of Finance*, March 1992.

of equity returns for a particular country index that could be accounted for by the industry composition of the index. As shown in Exhibit 18.15, on average, 50 percent of the equity returns could be explained by the industry composition of the index. While not reflected in this data, an extreme case would be Nokia, the consumer electronics company that alone accounted for more than two-thirds of the Finnish index in 1999.

An ideal global market risk premium would be based on a global index measured over a long time. Unfortunately, global indexes don't go back very far. As a fallback, we resort to the U.S. market, which is the most diversified and has the longest history. As we explained in Chapter 10, we recommend a 4.5 percent to 5 percent premium for the U.S. market. The U.K. market actually has a longer history than the U.S. market, but it is not as diversified. A study by the securities firm BZW gives a market risk premium for the United Kingdom in the same range as the United States.

Since we are using a global market risk premium, we should also use beta relative to a global stock market index. Company betas measured against a global market index are now available. These global indexes are usually measured in U.S. dollars. Accordingly, currency fluctuations will affect a company's beta.

This discussion raises an important issue about the comparability of market risk premiums around the world. In addition to industry concentration,

Exhibit 18.15 Share of Equity Returns Explained by Industry Composition of Index

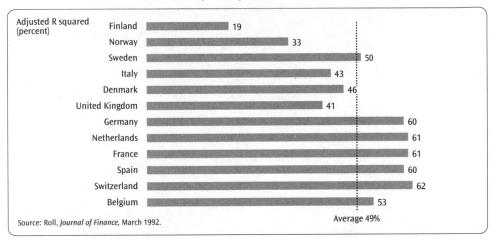

Adjusted R squared (percent)	
Finland	19
Norway	33
Sweden	50
Italy	43
Denmark	46
United Kingdom	41
Germany	60
Netherlands	61
France	61
Spain	60
Switzerland	62
Belgium	53

Average 49%

Source: Roll, *Journal of Finance*, March 1992.

there is theoretical support for the equalization of the cost of capital around the world and a related caveat about how to estimate the cost of capital. This theory is based on the fact that smaller companies have higher returns than larger companies (Exhibit 18.16) and that the average company size in many markets is smaller than in the United States (Exhibit 18.17).[5]

Use Exhibit 18.18 to follow the logic. Start with the CAPM expressed in U.S. dollars, the solid line that begins at the risk-free rate in the United States and goes through the point where beta equals one. Next, plot the U.S.

Exhibit 18.16 Long-Term Returns by Size Decile

U.S. Decile	Arithmetic average return 1926–97 (percent)	Premium over average (percent)
Largest	11.9	−0.3
90th percentile	13.7	0.4
80th percentile	14.3	0.7
70th percentile	15.0	1.0
60th percentile	15.8	1.6
50th percentile	15.8	1.5
40th percentile	16.4	1.6
30th percentile	17.5	2.4
20th percentile	18.2	2.6
Smallest	21.8	5.4

Source: Ibbotson Assoc, Stocks, Bonds, Bills and Inflation: 1998 Yearbook.

[5] See Chapter 10 for a discussion of the relationship between size, beta, and cross-sectional returns.

Exhibit 18.17   Comparison of Company Size Across Countries

August 1998	U.S. equity decile	Size by decile ($ billion)	Median size foreign company (country)	($ billion)
	Largest	77.6		
	90th percentile	33.8		
	80th percentile	16.7		
	70th percentile	10.0		
	60th percentile	7.0	U.K.	5.1
	50th percentile	4.9		
	40th percentile	3.4	Mexico	3.2
	30th percentile	2.7		
	20th percentile	2.0		
	Smallest	1.4	Brazil	1.7
			Indonesia	0.7

Source: Dow Jones Global Indices.

dollar-based CAPM line for a country such as Denmark, which has a much smaller average company size than is found in the United States. The CAPM line (the dashed line) in the exhibit will have a steeper slope because the average company size is smaller.

Now consider an average Danish company. This company has a beta of 1.0 against the Danish CAPM line. Because the company is smaller than a typical U.S. company, it will have a higher beta relative to the U.S. index, say 1.3.

The cost of capital in dollars for this company can be calculated in two ways. Let's assume a U.S. risk-free rate of 6 percent and a U.S. market risk premium of 5 percent. One method would be to calculate the cost of equity

Exhibit 18.18   Global vs Local CAPM

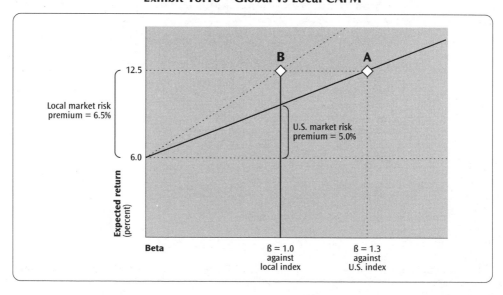

relative to the U.S. market. The cost of equity would be 12.5 percent (6% + 5% × 1.3). The second method is to calculate the cost of capital relative to the Danish market. The cost of equity must again be 12.5 percent, according to the line on Exhibit 18.18. This implies that the market risk premium for the Danish market is 6.5 percent (when expressed in U.S. dollars). We assumed earlier that the company's beta relative to the Danish market is 1.0. Hence its cost of capital of 12.5 percent (6% + 6.5% × 1.0).

This means that if you use a beta relative to the local market, you should use a market risk premium that reflects the size of the local market. If you use a beta relative to the U.S. market or a global market, use a U.S. or global market risk premium. In theory, you should get the same cost of equity. You would rarely get such logical results using actual market data from countries with small illiquid markets and a short history. But in most cases, you are likely to have better data—both market risk premiums and betas for the global or U.S. market—so most often that is the approach to use. Don't forget to adjust for differences in the risk-free rate if you are using different currencies.

SUMMARY

This chapter showed how to apply the DCF valuation approach to companies outside the United States. The approach is the same as in the United States. As expected, you need to understand and reflect local accounting and tax in your analysis, but the adjustments are straightforward. The cost of capital approach is also the same around the world, although estimation of some of the parameters (particularly market risk premium) can be controversial. We recommend using a common market risk premium around the world as the capital markets were substantially integrated by the end of the twentieth century.

19

Valuation in Emerging Markets

As the world economy globalizes and capital becomes more mobile, valuation is gaining in importance in emerging markets for privatization, joint ventures, mergers and acquisitions, restructuring, and value-based management. Yet valuation is much more difficult in these environments because the risks and obstacles that companies face are greater than in developed markets. Major risks and challenges include high levels of macroeconomic uncertainty, illiquid capital markets, controls on the flow of capital in and out of the country, and high levels of political risk.

There is no agreement on how to address these challenges among academics, investment bankers, and industry practitioners. Methods vary considerably and often involve making arbitrary adjustments based on limited empirical evidence and gut feel. In the face of this lack of consensus, we recommend a pragmatic approach of comparing estimates of the value from three methods as summarized in Exhibit 19.1. Our primary approach is to use discounted cash flows with probability-weighted scenarios that explicitly model the risks that the business faces. The value obtained from this approach is then compared to a DCF approach with a country-risk premium built into the cost of capital and a valuation based on comparable trading multiples.[1]

Special thanks to our colleague Mimi James, who co-wrote this chapter.

[1] Note that when using the DCF approach with a country-risk premium built into the discount rate, cash flows should not be reduced by the country risk already in the discount rate. We sometimes refer to this approach as discounting "promised" or "hoped for" cash flows rather than "expected" cash flows.

Exhibit 19.1   Compare Alternative Methods

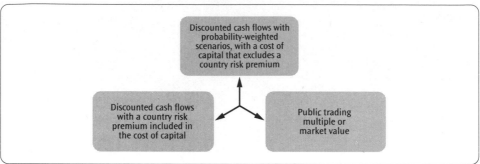

The basics of estimating a DCF value are the same in emerging markets as elsewhere, so we will focus in this chapter on four issues specific to emerging markets:

1. How to factor inflation into the financial analysis and cash flow forecasts.
2. How to deal with exchange rate and inflation rate gaps.
3. How to incorporate special emerging market risks into the valuation.
4. How to calculate the cost of capital in emerging markets.

EFFECTS OF INFLATION ON FINANCIAL ANALYSIS IN EMERGING MARKETS

High and unpredictable levels of inflation are often an important feature of emerging markets. Inflation distorts the financial statements, making year-to-year comparisons and ratio analysis difficult. Forecasting is also complicated.

In most countries, financial statements are not adjusted to reflect the effects of inflation. This means that assets and liabilities are recorded at historical cost and are not revalued to current currency units. This creates distortions in net property, plant, and equipment, and inventories (so-called nonmonetary assets) relative to other balance sheet items and the income statement. Other assets and liabilities (various types of receivables and payables) do not need restating. Some countries (for example, Colombia, Mexico, and Venezuela as of the end of 1999) require adjusting reported financial statements for inflation. At the end of this section, we briefly discuss this issue.

For companies operating in high inflation environments, we strongly recommend that valuations be done in both nominal and real (constant currency) terms. When done properly, the resulting value should be identical. (Nominal cash flows discounted at a nominal rate should equal the corresponding real cash flows discounted at the corresponding real rate.) By applying both methods, you know that you have properly handled the effects of inflation.

Rationale for Valuing in Both Real and Nominal Terms

The major differences and shortcomings of doing a valuation in nominal and real terms are summarized in Exhibit 19.2. In short, doing the valuation in real terms makes it virtually impossible to calculate taxes correctly (taxes are calculated based on nominal financial statements) and also can lead to errors in the cash-flow effects of working capital changes. The downside of using the nominal cash flows is that ratios, such as the ROIC and property, plant, and equipment to revenues are often meaningless in high inflationary environments. Another downside of the nominal DCF valuation is that the continuing value formula needs to incorporate the real growth and expected returns to reflect the true economics of the business in the continuing value period.

The example in Exhibit 19.3 illustrates the need for both nominal and real forecasts. This company does not grow in real terms and the annual inflation rate is 20 percent. The nominal EBITDA grows with inflation and the unadjusted real-cash flows are flat. In the nominal case, the depreciation grows much slower than the EBITDA so that depreciation shelters less and less of the growth of nominal EBITDA from taxes. The working capital requirements in the nominal case, however, continue to grow with inflation, which erodes the cash-flow value. This effect is not reflected in the real cash flows if looked at from changes in the balance sheet. To be accurate, the real cash flows need to reflect the actual tax shields and the working capital requirements. These can only be estimated from the nominal accounts and then translated, as in the third example, where the translations from the nominal accounts are highlighted. If a simple real

---

Exhibit 19.2   Comparing Real vs. Nominal DCF Valuation

	Real	Nominal	Impact on value
Calculates meaningful ratios	+	−	Real allows check on whether forecast is realistic
Captures actual taxes	−	+	Real will overstate value
Captures actual working capital	−	+	Real will overstate value when working capital/revenues >0
No adjustment required to continuing value formula	+	−	Using ordinary CV formula for nominal will overstate value
Enables realistic capital expenditure forecasts	+	−	Nominal approach typically overestimates investment in capital spending

Exhibit 19.3 Inflation Effects on Financial Statements

	Nominal					Unadjusted forecasted real					Real translated from nominal[1]				
	Year 1	Year 2	Year 3	Year 4	Year 5	Year 1	Year 2	Year 3	Year 4	Year 5	Year 1	Year 2	Year 3	Year 4	Year 5
Revenues	1,000	1,200	1,440	1,728	1,901	1,000	1,000	1,000	1,000	1,000	1,000	1,000	1,000	1,000	1,000
EBITDA	300	360	432	518	570	300	300	300	300	300	300	300	300	300	300
Depreciation	(80)	(80)	(83)	(90)	(99)	(80)	(80)	(80)	(80)	(80)	(80)	(80)	(80)	(80)	(80)
EBIT	220	280	349	429	471	220	220	220	220	220	220	220	220	220	220
Taxes at 50%	(110)	(140)	(174)	(214)	(235)	(110)	(110)	(110)	(110)	(110)	(110)	(117)	(121)	(124)	(124)
NOPLAT	110	140	174	214	235	110	110	110	110	110	110	103	99	96	96
Real NOPLAT	110	117	121	124	124	110	110	110	110	110	110	103	99	96	96
Net working capital	200	240	288	346	380	200	200	200	200	200	200	200	200	200	200
Beg net PPE	400	400	416	448	497	400	400	400	400	400	400	400	400	400	400
Depreciation	(80)	(80)	(83)	(90)	(99)	(80)	(80)	(80)	(80)	(80)	(80)	(80)	(80)	(80)	(80)
Capital expenditures	80	96	115	138	152	80	80	80	80	80	80	80	80	80	80
End net PPE	400	416	448	497	549	400	400	400	400	400	400	400	400	400	400
NOPLAT		140	174	214	235		110	110	110	110		103	99	96	96
Plus: depreciation		80	83	90	99		80	80	80	80		80	80	80	80
Less: capital expenditures		(96)	(115)	(138)	(152)		(80)	(80)	(80)	(80)		(80)	(80)	(80)	(80)
Less: change in working capital		(40)	(48)	(58)	(35)		-	-	-	-		(33)	(33)	(33)	(18)
Free cash flow		84	94	108	148		110	110	110	110		70	66	63	78
Real cash flow		70	66	63	78		110	110	110	110		70	66	63	78
Average inflation rate/index	20%	20%	20%	20%	10%	1.00	1.20	1.44	1.73	1.90	1.00	1.20	1.44	1.73	1.90
Networking capital/revenues	20%	20%	20%	20%	20%	20%	20%	20%	20%	20%	20%	20%	20%	20%	20%
PPE/revenues	40%	35%	31%	29%	29%	40%	40%	40%	40%	40%	40%	40%	40%	40%	40%
ROIC	18%	21%	24%	25%	25%	18%	18%	18%	18%	18%	18%	17%	17%	16%	16%

1 The change in working capital for these results is translated from the nominal cash flows, not the real balance sheet. These investments in working capital could also be thought of as real losses because of the effects of inflation on working capital.

valuation were calculated without these nominal account adjustments, the value would be overstated.

On the other hand, if only nominal cash flows were estimated, the PP&E/Revenue ratio and the ROIC would be inaccurate indicators of the economics of the business, since capital in a high-inflation environment grows slower than profits. You can observe this in the declining PP&E/Revenue ratio in the nominal case, even though new inflation-adjusted investments are being made. An understanding of the actual capital needs of a business in real terms is fundamental to providing a realistic forecast of capital spending.

Steps for Constructing Forecast and Valuation in Real and Nominal Terms

A step-by-step approach for developing a forecast in both real and nominal terms is:

1. Convert historical nominal balance sheets and income statements into real terms (usually the current year's currency value) so that you can calculate appropriate financial ratios and develop an understanding of the true economics of the business.
2. Forecast the operating performance in real terms. This should include revenues, cash expenses, working capital, property, plant and equipment, and depreciation.
3. Convert the operating performance into nominal terms. For most items this simply means multiplying the item by the inflation index for the year. Net property, plant, and equipment, depreciation, and inventories should not be adjusted; they are the same in real and nominal financial statements.
4. Forecast interest expense and other nonoperating income statement items in nominal terms (based on the prior year's balance sheet).
5. Calculate income taxes based on the nominal income statement. (This requires some knowledge of the local tax laws.)
6. Complete the balance sheet in nominal terms. First, the equity should equal last year's equity plus earnings less dividends and plus or minus any share issues or repurchases. Then, balance the balance sheet with debt or marketable securities.
7. Complete the income statement and balance sheet in real terms. Convert debt, marketable securities, interest expense, income taxes, and nonoperating terms using the inflation index. The equity account is a plug to balance the balance sheet. To make sure you have done this correctly, the real equity account should equal last year's equity

plus earnings less dividends, plus or minus shares issues or repurchases and plus or minus inflationary gains or losses on the monetary assets (such as cash, receivables, and payables).

You now have income statements and balance sheets in both real and nominal terms. From these you can estimate free cash flows. Calculate the nominal free cash flows first using the same approach as described in Chapter 9. Then convert the nominal cash flows to real cash flows using the inflation index.

The last step before discounting the cash flows is to estimate the continuing value. Using real cash flows requires no adjustments to the normal value driver formula described in Chapter 12. The nominal approach, however, needs to be adjusted because the nominal returns on capital are not meaningful. Use the following formula:

$$\text{Continuing value} = \text{NOPLAT}_{n+1} \times \left(\frac{\text{Real NOPLAT margin}}{\text{Nominal NOPLAT margin}} \right)$$

$$\times \frac{\left(\dfrac{1 - \text{Real growth rate}}{\text{Real ROIC}} \right)}{(\text{Nominal WACC} - \text{Nominal growth})}$$

The nominal NOPLAT used as a base for the continuing value calculation must be adjusted to reflect ongoing profitability, which is why it is multiplied by the ratio of the real NOPLAT margin to nominal NOPLAT margin.[2] The nominal NOPLAT margin will overstate the true long-term profitability because inflation will cause depreciation to be understated. The real NOPLAT margin is a better estimate of long-term profitability and the ability of the company to turn revenues into cash flow. Since the NOPLAT has been adjusted to reflect sustainable profitability, the investment required also needs to reflect real investment. Therefore, real growth and real return rates should be used in the calculation of continuing value.

Finally, you are ready to discount the cash flows to the present. Here the key is the relationship between the real and nominal cost of capital. For each year, make sure the following relationship holds:

$$(1 + \text{Nominal WACC}) = (1 + \text{Real WACC}) \times (1 + \text{Expected inflation})$$

Later in this chapter we discuss how to estimate the WACC for companies in emerging markets. Exhibit 19.4 shows a simplified example of a valuation using the steps just explained (using the assumptions from Ex-

---

[2] NOPLAT margin refers to NOPLAT divided by revenues.

Exhibit 19.4   Equivalence of Nominal and Real Valuations

	Nominal				Adjusted real			
	Year 2	3	4	5	Year 2	3	4	5
ROIC	23.3%	26.6%	29.1%	28.0%	17.2%	16.5%	16.0%	16.0%
NOPLAT Margin	11.7%	12.1%	12.4%	12.4%	10.3%	9.9%	9.6%	9.6%
WACC	29.6%	29.6%	29.6%	18.8%	8.0%	8.0%	8.0%	8.0%
CV growth				10.0%				0.0%
CV ROIC (real)				16.0%				16.0%
Free cash flow/CV	84	94	108	2,076	70	66	63	1,202
Discount factor	.772	.595	.459	.459	.926	.857	.794	.794
PV of FCF/CV	65	56	50	954	65	56	50	954
DCF Value			1,125				1,125	

hibit 19.3). The resulting value using the nominal and real approaches is identical. If you don't obtain identical values using the two approaches, you have made an error.

Other Accounting Issues

Emerging markets often have substantially different accounting conventions than developed markets. These can seriously impair your ability to understand the company's economics. A few countries use different forms of inflation accounting to adjust income statements and balance sheets. In addition, many countries have complicated tax credits and adjustments that make the estimation of cash taxes more difficult than in developed markets. While it is not in the scope of this chapter to detail the effects in each country, we highlight some of the most common issues. One point to note is that the large differences in accounting are frequently eliminated when the income statement and the balance sheet are brought together in the cash-flow calculation.

Inflation accounting   A few countries, such as Colombia, Mexico, and Venezuela (and formerly Brazil), require inflation accounting, often called *monetary corrections*. Monetary corrections attempt to revalue assets because of the effects of inflation and exchange rate changes. Monetary corrections typically require revaluation of fixed assets and sometimes inventory, based on the current inflation environment; accounts receivable and payable are not usually adjusted. To make the balance sheet balance, adjustments are made to equity either directly or through the P&L accounts. While monetary corrections do not have a direct effect on cash until they are realized (i.e., inventory or a plant is sold), they often have an impact on cash taxes paid, which needs to be factored into the cash flows.

Hyperinflation   In countries experiencing hyperinflation (an inflation rate of more than 25 percent per year), companies often report in year-end currency.[3] They make adjustments to the income statements to reflect items, such as revenue, in year-end currency. So if the revenue were booked in July at the July currency, the reported revenues in the annual report will be restated at the year-end purchasing power. Otherwise, in high-inflation environments, the income statement items would not really be additive since they would be based on different purchasing power. The balance sheet only has adjustments to fixed assets, inventory, and equity; the accounts payable and receivable are already in year-end terms. As in inflation accounting valuations, revaluations of property, plant, and equipment need to be backed out of capital spending calculations.

Estimating cash taxes   In emerging markets, an accurate assessment of cash taxes can be quite challenging. An example is Brazil, which has had large and frequent changes to the tax code. In 1996, Brazil eliminated inflation accounting and reduced the corporate tax rate to 30.5 percent. In 1997, the government disallowed the deductibility of the social contribution tax, effectively increasing the tax rate to 33 percent. To make up for the loss of the tax shields that inflation accounting had generated, the government allowed companies to deduct interest on equity net of a withholding tax of 15 percent. Many other emerging markets have significant cash tax adjustments that need to be understood before you start a valuation.

DEALING WITH EXCHANGE RATES AND INFLATION RATE GAPS

In many emerging market companies, the individual components of the cash flows are not denominated in the same currency. A substantial portion of a company's revenues and debt may be denominated in dollars, for example, while its expenses are primarily local. Consider an oil exporter. Its revenues are determined by the dollar price of oil while many of its costs (labor and local purchases) are determined by the local currency. Unless foreign exchange rates immediately adjust to inflation differentials (in other words, purchasing power parity holds), the company's operating margins and cash flows will deviate from their long-term trend.

It is important to keep two facts in mind when estimating the impact of changing exchange rates. First, over the long run, purchasing power does hold. In other words, exchange rates ultimately do adjust for differences in inflation between countries. Second, exchange rates can deviate from purchasing power parity by up to 20 to 25 percent for as long as ten or more years (although purchasing power parity adjusted exchange rates are enormously difficult to estimate).

---

[3] Some companies will report in U.S. dollars to avoid this problem.

Exhibit 19.5   Brazilian PPP Adjusted Exchange Rates

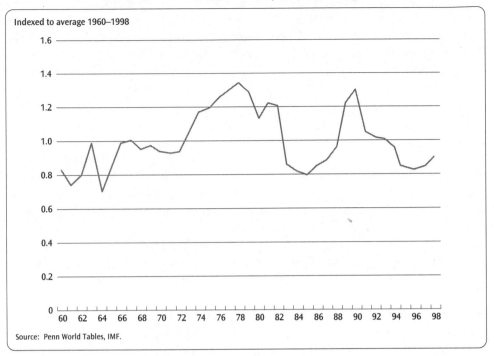

Source: Penn World Tables, IMF.

For example, if you held $100 million of Brazilian currency in 1960, by 1998 it would have been worth less than one cent in U.S. dollars. Yet, on a purchasing power adjusted basis, the value of the currency didn't change as shown on Exhibit 19.5. In other words, if instead of holding $100 million of Brazilian currency, you held $100 million of assets in Brazil whose value increased with inflation, in 1998 your assets would still be worth about $100 million.

When developing your forecast, you first need to develop a perspective on whether the current exchange rate is over- or undervalued on a PPP basis and by how much. You can then estimate the impact of the over- or undervaluation on the profitability of the company. Finally, conduct a sensitivity analysis to assess the impact of the timing of the return to PPP. As you develop your forecast, remember your overall perspective about the economics of the business (in other words, what is the long-term sustainable operating profit margin and ROIC).

INCORPORATING EMERGING MARKET RISKS IN THE VALUATION

The major distinction between valuing companies in developed markets and emerging markets is the increased level of risk. Not only must you account for risks related to the company's strategy, market position, and industry dynamics, as you would in a developed market, but you must also deal with the risks caused by greater volatility in the capital markets, and macroeconomic and political environments. Emerging market risks to consider include inflation, macroeconomic volatility, capital controls, political risk, war or civil disturbances, regulatory changes, poorly defined or enforced contract or investor rights, and corruption.

Pros and Cons of Where to Incorporate Country Risks

There are many opinions on how to incorporate these additional risks in a DCF valuation, and whether to include them in the cash flows (the numerator) or the discount rate (the denominator). Accounting for these risks in the cash flows through probability-weighted scenarios provides a more solid analytical foundation and a more robust understanding of the value than incorporating them in the discount rate.

Four practical arguments support this view. First, most country risks such as expropriation, devaluation, and war are largely diversifiable (though not entirely, as the economic crisis in 1998 demonstrated). Finance theory clearly indicates that the cost of capital should reflect only nondiversifiable risk. Diversifiable risk is better handled in the cash flows. Nonetheless, a recent survey showed that managers generally add some risk premium to the discount rate to adjust for these risks.[4] However, more and more companies are building the risks into the cash flows.

Second, many country risks don't apply equally to all companies in a given country. For example, banks are more likely to be nationalized than retailers; or some companies may benefit from a devaluation (raw materials exporters) while others will be damaged (raw materials importers). Applying the same risk premium to all companies in the country would overstate the risk for some and understate it for others.

Third, country risks tend to be one-sided (only down). It is much easier to build one-sided risks into cash-flow scenarios than discount rates. Most attempts to build risk into the discount rate are ad hoc or based not on equity risk but the credit risk of the country. A common approach is to add a country-risk premium equal to the difference between the interest rate on a local bond denominated in U.S. dollars and a U.S. government bond of similar maturity. In many situations, equity investments in a company in the country will actually be less risky than investing in government bonds. For example, the bonds of YPF (the Argentine oil company) carry lower yields than Argentine government debt. In addition, equity investments carry potential upside risks, while bonds carry only downside risks.

---

[4] T. Keck, E. Levengood, and A. Longfield, "Using Discounted Cash Flow Analysis in an International Setting: A Survey of Issues in Modeling the Cost of Capital," *Journal of Applied Corporate Finance*, Volume 11, number 3, Fall 1998.

Finally, we find that having managers discuss these explicit risks and their effect on cash flow provides more insights for managers than a "black box" addition to the discount rate. By identifying specific factors that have a large impact on value, managers can better plan to mitigate these risks.

In an effort to test whether the equity market actually builds a large risk premium into the valuation of emerging market companies, we valued a small sample of Brazilian companies. In our test, we forecasted cash flows using published investment banking reports that had at least three years of forecasts and were written within one month of the date of our market valuation (April 10, 1999). For the years after the explicit forecast in the reports, we assumed the same performance ratios to drive cash flow and used a perpetuity formula (NOPLAT/WACC) to estimate the continuing value after year 10. We discounted these cash flows using an industry-specific global cost of capital, adjusted for capital structure that included an inflation differential for Brazil versus the United States but no country-risk premium. (The method for estimating the industry-specific global cost of capital will be discussed in the next section.)

We found that the DCF values were extremely close to the market values (Exhibit 19.6). This is not an exhaustive sample and does not definitively prove that there is no country-risk premium in the Brazilian market. But it suggests that additional country-risk premiums in the range of 4 percent to 9 percent are not supported by the market prices for equities. If these

Exhibit 19.6   Market versus DCF Value for Sample of Brazilian Companies

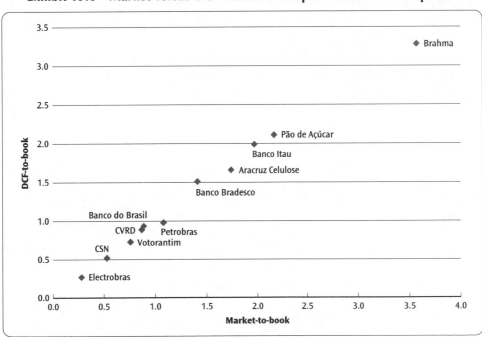

premiums were included in the cost of capital, the DCF values would be 50 percent to 90 percent lower than the market values.

Incorporating Risks in the Cash Flows by Building Integrated Scenarios

When constructing scenarios in emerging markets, company-specific and industry scenarios should be aligned with the macroeconomic scenarios. Start with the macroeconomic scenarios because they influence industry and company performance.

The major macroeconomic variables that need to be forecasted are GDP growth, inflation rates, foreign exchange rates, and interest rates. These items must be linked in a way that reflects economic realities. For instance, GDP growth and inflation are important drivers of foreign exchange rates. When you construct a high-inflation scenario, foreign exchange rates should reflect this inflation in the long run because of purchasing power parity.

Next, determine how each of the components of the cash flow is driven by changes in the macroeconomic variables. Link these items to the macroeconomic variables, so that when the macroeconomic scenario is changed the cash-flow items adjust automatically.

After the macroeconomic variables are linked, think about industry scenarios. Constructing industry scenarios is basically the same in emerging markets as in developed markets, with a few variations. One difference is that industries in emerging markets may be more driven by government actions. Another difference is the dependence on markets outside the company's home country for either revenues or inputs. When constructing the model, make sure that the industry scenarios take the macroeconomic environment into consideration.

An example of a recent outside-in valuation of Pão de Açúcar, a Brazilian retail grocery chain, demonstrates how such scenarios can be built. In this example, Merrill Lynch devised three macroeconomic scenarios in September

Exhibit 19.7   Scenarios—Pão de Açúcar

Macroeconomic assumptions, 1999	Base case International support and fiscal reform	Austerity Protracted higher interest rates and continued volatility with unemployment rising to 14%	Devaluation Dramatic devaluation with results similar to austerity scenario
1999 year end FX rate	1.3	1.3	2.25
Average interest rates	18.0%	20.0%	30.0%
Real GDP growth	0.4%	−3.0%	−5.0%
Inflation	2.2%	0.0%	30.0%
Company assumptions, 1999			
Supermarket sales growth	17.2%	1.7%	42.6%
Nominal same store sales growth	1.2%	−8.2%	33.3%
Consumer lending	Slightly declining balances with higher interest rates in short term	Declining balances but with higher spreads	Credit dries up in short term

Exhibit 19.8   Scenario Values—Pão de Açúcar

Reais (million)	DCF value	Probability	Weighted value
Base case	1,577	33–50%	525–788
Austerity	901	30–33%	270–300
Devaluation	1,145	20–33%	229–381
Probability-weighted value			1,207–1,288
Market value as of September 1998			1,171

1998 (Exhibit 19.7). The base case scenario assumed that Brazil would enact significant fiscal reforms and enjoy continued international support and that as a result, the economy could recover fairly quickly from the Asian crisis. Revenues and margins are quite robust in this scenario.

The second scenario assumes that the Brazilian economy remains in recession for two years with high interest rates and low GDP growth and inflation.

The third scenario assumes a dramatic devaluation (which is what did happen) with inflation rising to 30 percent and the economy shrinking by 5 percent. These scenarios have a significant impact on revenues and margins in the next five years, but in the long run there is convergence to a steady growth path.

Incorporate these scenarios in the cash flows and discount at an industry-specific cost of capital, then adjust for Pão de Açúcar's capital structure and the difference in the Brazilian inflation rate compared with the U.S. inflation rate. Weight the scenarios by probability. Exhibit 19.8 shows the DCF values of the three scenarios and the probability-weighted value. The base case gets a probability of between 33 percent and 50 percent. The others are assigned lower probabilities based on our internal assessments. The DCF value range is about −23 percent to +35 percent of the base case, which is large, because of the uncertain environment at that time.

The resulting value is 1,207 to 1,288 million Reais. The market value at the time of the valuation was 1,171 million Reais. If we use the base-case cash flows with Brazil's country-risk premium, excluding credit risk, at the time of the valuation (September 1998) of 7.8 percent, we find a value of 260 million Reais, far below the market value. If, however, we use a long-term perspective on Brazil's country risk excluding credit risk of 2 percent, the value is a more reasonable 1,044 million Reais.

CALCULATING THE COST OF CAPITAL IN EMERGING MARKETS

While calculating the cost of capital in any country can be challenging, in emerging markets the calculation is an order of magnitude higher. In this section, we provide our basic assumptions, background on the important issues, and a way to estimate the components of the cost of capital that is easy to apply as well as theoretically and empirically correct.

Basic Assumptions

First, we are looking from the perspective of a global investor, either a multinational company or an international investor with a diversified portfolio. Many local markets are not integrated with the global market and frequently there are restraints on the ability of local investors to invest outside their home market. As a result, the cost of capital to a local investor could be considerably different than a global investor. Further, there is not a common framework for estimating the capital cost for local investors.

We assume that the global economy will become fully integrated and that most emerging markets will become open and efficient. This assumption allows application of the CAPM to estimate the cost of equity in emerging markets. We recognize that the degree of integration of emerging markets with developed markets varies significantly and the CAPM is a less robust model for the less-integrated emerging markets. We expect, however, that it will become a better predictor of required equity returns worldwide. We assume that countries with capital controls that restrict local investors' access to a global risk-free rate will eliminate these restrictions in the long run. Since we value cash flows to infinity and assume that it will be a matter of years for most emerging markets to integrate, we believe it is warranted to apply CAPM with minimal adjustments to estimate cost of equity in emerging markets.

A complementary assumption is that most country risks are diversifiable, from the perspective of the global investor. As a result, many of the additional risks encountered in emerging markets should be accounted for in the cash flows rather than the discount rate as discussed in the previous section of this chapter.

Given these assumptions, the cost of capital in emerging markets should generally be close to a global cost of capital adjusted for local inflation and capital structure. Before going on to the methodology itself, we present some overall advice on estimating the cost of capital in emerging markets.

No one "right" answer—be pragmatic   Some ways of estimating the cost of capital in emerging markets, are better than others, but there is room for debate. Moreover, in emerging markets, there are often significant information and data gaps. We recommend a flexible building block approach to assembling the cost of capital.

Cost of capital may change   The cost of capital in an emerging market valuation may change based on evolving inflation expectations (embedded in the risk-free rate and cost of debt), shifts in the openness of the economy, and expected market volatility. There are two ways of incorporating them in the cost of capital: Calculate a year-by-year cost of capital using different assumptions for each period (recommended for high inflation, highly volatile, or restricted countries) or compound the changes and incorporate them as a single addition to the cost of equity and debt to derive one cost of capital for the whole period. The first approach is much more accurate.

Whatever method you choose to calculate the cost of capital—be consistent with how the cash flow is estimated If you are using local nominal cash flows, the cost of capital must reflect the local inflation rate that is embedded in the cash flows. For real cash flows, inflation must be subtracted from the nominal cost of capital. If you are using probability-weighted scenarios, do not double count risk by including a country-risk premium in the cost of capital.

Estimating the Cost of Equity

This section summarizes how to estimate the components of the cost of equity using the standard CAPM model described in Chapter 10.

Risk-free rate In emerging markets, the risk-free rate is not as simple to estimate as it is in developed markets. There are three main problems in determining an appropriate local risk-free rate in emerging markets: Most of the government debt in emerging markets is not, in fact, risk free. The ratings on much of this debt are often well below investment grade. It is difficult to find debt longer than three years in many emerging markets. Finally, the long-term debt that does exist is usually in U.S. dollars, a European currency, or Japanese yen and so is not appropriate to discount local nominal cash flows.

To overcome these obstacles, we recommend a building block approach. Exhibit 19.9 defines three main ways to assemble an emerging market risk-free rate. We make the assumption that cash flows are denominated in local currency.

Exhibit 19.9 Calculating the Risk-Free Rate

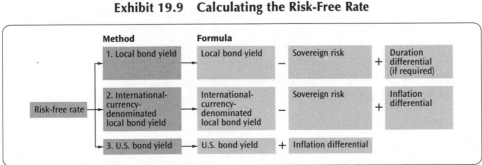

The choice of method depends on which bond instrument is available and liquid. If all instruments are available, it is useful to calculate all three methods to develop an estimate of the risk-free rate. Let's start with some definitions.

- *Local bond yield.* Yield to maturity on a long maturity bond denominated in local currency.
- *Credit-risk premium.* Additional yield demanded by investors to invest in government bonds with lower than AAA rating to cover the risk of default and credit deterioration.
- *Duration differential.* The change in yield between bonds of different maturity.
- *Sovereign-risk premium.* Difference between the yields of a local government bond denominated in U.S. dollars and the equivalent maturity U.S. government bond; includes both country risk and credit risk.
- *Country-risk premium.* Noncredit risks embedded in sovereign-risk premium.
- *Inflation differential.* The compounded difference between the local inflation rate and the U.S. inflation rate over 10 years.

In method one, the starting point is to select the longest maturity local currency denominated debt available and estimate the yield to maturity.[5] The next step is to subtract the sovereign-risk premium, which is the difference between the yield on an international currency-denominated bond like a Brady Bond and its equivalent maturity government bond in the United States or the European Union (EU). The sovereign-risk premium needs to be subtracted because it reflects credit risk and other items that are not part of a risk-free rate. The final step is to adjust the bond so that it is equivalent to a 10-year bond. Usually you can extend the duration by compounding the inflation. In many emerging markets, however, the inflation rates are higher in the early years. As a result, the yield curve is inverted, with the yield declining as the maturity lengthens.

In method two, start with an international currency denominated bond of long duration, and estimate the stripped yield. Then subtract the sovereign-risk premium. If using cash flows denominated in local nominal currency, account for local inflation in the risk-free rate. The international currency bond already has the international currency inflation rate embedded in it, so just add the difference between the international inflation rate and the local rate. You can do this by adding the inflation difference

---

[5] Some emerging markets' country debt is partially guaranteed by international institutions or backed by U.S. Treasury bonds. For these bonds, you need to estimate the yield on the nonguaranteed part of the bond, the "stripped" yield. Stripped yields are available from bond data suppliers.

year by year to develop a separate estimate of the cost of capital by year. You can also compound the inflation difference between the countries and add it as a single number to calculate a single cost of capital for all periods. The level of inflation difference dictates the choice of methods. If it is high, an annual estimate of the cost of capital is preferable.

Method three is the simplest and is available as an option in all countries. It starts with the 10-year U.S. government yield and adds an inflation differential between the U.S. and the local rate to develop a local nominal risk-free rate.

The key assumption in the calculation of the risk-free rate is that most investors, including investors in local markets, have access to an international risk-free rate. In countries such as India or China, however, local investors do not have access to a global risk-free rate. The most risk-free instrument available to them is the local government debt, which has sovereign risk embedded in the yield. This difference in access to a risk-free rate means that foreign investors will have a lower cost of capital than local investors, at least in the short run. As capital controls ease, this difference should disappear. Determining the timing of this is subjective and should be included as part of a scenario.

Country-risk premium   In the previous discussion, we laid out a rationale for excluding country risk. If you do wish to include a country-risk premium, start with the sovereign risk. The sovereign risk can be calculated by subtracting the 10-year U.S. government bond yield from a U.S. dollar-denominated local bond's stripped yield. If there is no U.S. dollar-denominated bond, subtract the inflation differential between the local country and the United States first to calculate the country sovereign-risk premium.

The next step is more controversial—subtracting the credit risk embedded in the yield. This is an attempt to estimate the cost of equity. Again, we do not believe that it is appropriate to include the risk of default and credit deterioration that make up the credit risk of a bond in the cost of equity calculation. The market-risk premium for equity already includes the possibility of losing your investment and so to include that risk again represents double counting.

So how do we eliminate the credit risk? There is no exact way to determine what part of the country-risk premium is associated with credit risk, so we approximate. Assume that since the bond-rating companies have standard criteria for rating bonds worldwide, the premium on bonds with a particular rating is similar across all bonds. The premium associated with a particular rating is readily available for U.S. corporate bonds from the bond rating agencies. The premium for a BB-rated bond can be estimated by taking the difference between the yield to maturity on 10-year BB-rated U.S. corporate bonds and the 10-year U.S. government bonds. This can be used as a proxy for the credit-risk premium included in the country's yield to maturity, whose debt is rated BB. Argentina's debt is rated BB and its country-risk

Exhibit 19.10   How to Calculate the Country Risk Premium—Argentine Example

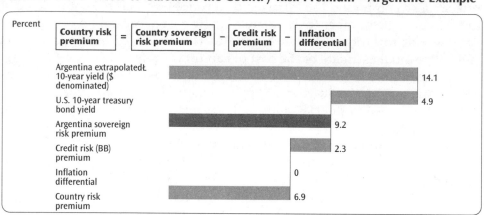

premium is calculated in Exhibit 19.10 as an example. Note that this calculation is for the country-risk premium at a certain point in time. The country-risk premium varies significantly. The question becomes which country-risk premium to use, the current market estimate or a long-run estimate? If a long-run estimate is used, shouldn't the country-risk premium decline to zero, as the country's market becomes more stable and open? In general, we recommend starting with the current estimate and taking it down to zero at least by the end of the explicit forecast period.

Beta   The beta, a measure of a company's systematic risk, is often difficult to calculate accurately in emerging markets, where the equity market is illiquid and often dominated by a small number of stocks. Additionally, historical data do not go back far enough to have appropriately large sample sizes for reliable regressions. Beta estimation through regressions is therefore likely to be flawed.

Since we assume that emerging markets are globalizing, we generally recommend using a global industry beta relevered to the company's target capital structure. Using a comparable global industry beta provides a truer picture of the risk inherent in the company than a regression of the company's returns against the returns of the local market. We also suggest doing a range of value estimates by using several betas. For Pão de Açúcar, a Brazilian supermarket company, we would probably use two estimates of beta; the Barra predicted beta of 1.0 and the comparable industry beta (adjusted for leverage) of .85, as shown in Exhibit 19.11.

Market-risk premium   The market-risk premium in emerging markets is often extremely difficult to calculate. The quality and length of available data on equity and bond market returns are usually unsuitable for making

Exhibit 19.11   Beta Estimation—Pão de Açúcar

	Barra predicted against U.S.	Capital structure (debt/equity) (percent)	Unlevered and relevered to target capital structure with country tax rate
Pão de Açúcar	1.01	65	1.01
Comparable medians	0.66	19	0.85

long-term estimates. In addition, they are not particularly useful as predictors of investors' future expectations about equity returns, since there have been many regulatory changes in these markets. We recommend using a market-risk premium that is consistent with the view that the equity markets are becoming increasingly global. Use a global estimate as discussed in Chapter 10 of 4.5 percent to 5 percent.

In Exhibit 19.12 we summarize the cost of equity calculation by showing an example for Pão de Açúcar.

Estimating the After-Tax Cost of Debt

Although the cost of debt is usually easier to calculate than the cost of equity, it can also be difficult to estimate in emerging markets. The main problem in emerging markets is that a true yield to maturity on debt is difficult to find. The current interest rates in the market are often short term or not public.

Exhibit 19.12   Cost of Equity—Pão de Açúcar

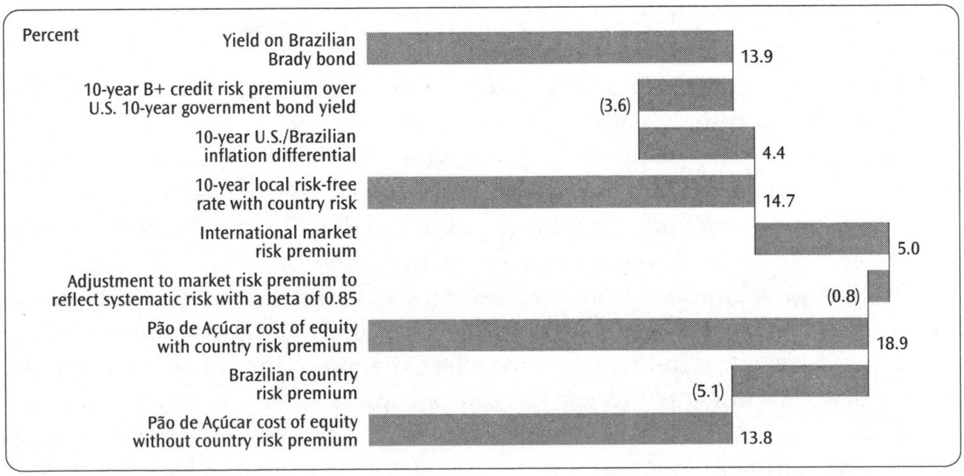

Percent	
Yield on Brazilian Brady bond	13.9
10-year B+ credit risk premium over U.S. 10-year government bond yield	(3.6)
10-year U.S./Brazilian inflation differential	4.4
10-year local risk-free rate with country risk	14.7
International market risk premium	5.0
Adjustment to market risk premium to reflect systematic risk with a beta of 0.85	(0.8)
Pão de Açúcar cost of equity with country risk premium	18.9
Brazilian country risk premium	(5.1)
Pão de Açúcar cost of equity without country risk premium	13.8

The cost of debt for foreign investors is simply the global industry cost of debt adjusted for the company's target capital structure and local inflation. Adding known components, the risk-free rate, the rating premium, and the inflation differential, you can assemble the cost of debt. For global investors, it is important to keep in mind that country risk can be diversified away in a bond portfolio, so no country-risk premium should be included. Coca-Cola and Colgate Palmolive, for example, have costs of debt no higher than their U.S.-focused competitors, even though much of their profits and investments are in emerging markets. Let's set up an example of how the cost of debt could be calculated. Assume that the rating for most global steel companies is BB+ but the capital structure for the local company is more heavily debt laden than the global capital structure, implying that its rating might be BB. You can use the risk-free rate for the country plus the premium required for a U.S. corporate bond rated BB versus the U.S. government bond yield.

Here's how we calculated the cost of debt for Pão de Açúcar:

10-year U.S. government bond yield to maturity	5.2%
Brazilian 10-year inflation differential	4.4
Brazilian risk-free rate	9.6%
Yield differential between 10-year U.S. government debt and B+ 10-year U.S. corporate debt	3.6
Cost of debt for Pão de Açúcar	13.2%

In many emerging markets, the capital markets for debt are even more inefficient than for equity. The cost of financing, if in fact financing can even be obtained, is often substantially different from the cost of debt we are suggesting here. In cases such as these, you may want to consider estimating the tax shields on debt directly as the cost of financing gradually declines to reflect the true cost of debt. The cash flows would be discounted at an unlevered cost of equity and the net present value of the tax shields would be added to the cash-flow value.

The marginal tax rate in emerging markets can be very different from the effective tax rate, which may include investment tax credits, export tax credits, taxes, equity or dividend credits, and operating loss credits. Many of these do not provide a tax shield on interest expense. Only taxes that apply to interest expense should be used in the discount rate. Other taxes or credits should be modeled directly in the cash flows.

In emerging markets, many companies have an unusual capital structure for their industry. Anomalies in the local debt or equity markets often cause the difference. In the long run, when the anomalies are corrected, the companies should expect to converge to a capital structure similar to their global competitors. You may want to forecast the company evolve to a global capital structure.

Exhibit 19.13   Cost of Capital—Pão de Açúcar

Components	Cost	x	Market weight	=	Weighted cost
Cost of equity	13.8%		61%		8.4%
After-tax cost of debt	8.8		39		3.4
Weighted average cost of capital					11.9

Summarizing the Cost of Capital in Emerging Markets

An example of a complete calculation of an emerging markets cost of capital is shown for Pão de Açúcar in Exhibit 19.13. Again, we assume the use of local currency cash flows. Many investment banks and industry practitioners would probably estimate the cost of capital for Pão de Açúcar in the 14 percent to 23 percent range, higher than the cost of capital we find. Note, however, that these results are not directly comparable since they are presumably not using probability-weighted scenarios, as we are.

SUMMARY

In this chapter, we discussed how to value companies in emerging markets. While the valuation concepts applied to developed markets and emerging markets are similar, the application can be somewhat different. Since the value is often more volatile, we recommend comparing multiple approaches and using a range of values based on integrated scenario analysis. An example of the output of this work is summarized for Pão de Açúcar in Exhibit 19.14. The complete value range is actually 0.9 to 1.6 billion Reais, but it has been narrowed using probability weights to 1.0 to 1.3 billion Reais.

Exhibit 19.14   Comparison of Results—Pão de Açúcar

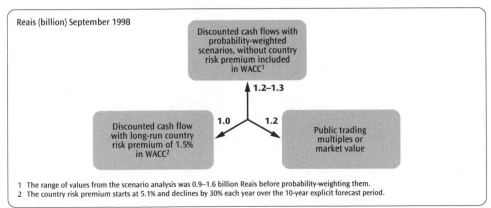

Reais (billion) September 1998

Discounted cash flows with probability-weighted scenarios, without country risk premium included in WACC[1]

1.2–1.3

Discounted cash flow with long-run country risk premium of 1.5% in WACC[2]

1.0   1.2

Public trading multiples or market value

1 The range of values from the scenario analysis was 0.9–1.6 billion Reais before probability-weighting them.
2 The country risk premium starts at 5.1% and declines by 30% each year over the 10-year explicit forecast period.

20

Using Option Pricing Methods to Value Flexibility

Throughout this book we have used discounted cash-flow techniques to value companies. The DCF method was originally applied to project evaluation and later extended to whole companies. Over the past decade or so, theoretical and computational advances have allowed finance practitioners to adapt financial option pricing techniques to the valuation of investment decisions, so-called real options. Option pricing methods are superior to traditional DCF approaches because they explicitly capture the value of flexibility. As a result, we believe that option-pricing techniques will eventually replace traditional DCF methods for investment decisions where there is significant future flexibility. It is not clear that option pricing will replace DCF techniques for valuing whole companies except in limited circumstances. It may be that the bundles of assets and opportunities that companies own cannot be practically valued as options—at least not yet.

To review, the traditional NPV approach for valuing a project assumes the project has an expected life, say 10 years, and that its expected free cash flows should be discounted at a risk-adjusted rate called the cost of capital. From the resulting present value, we subtract the initial investment outlay. The result is a net present value that must be positive to accept the project. This standard approach fails to account for the flexibility that management has. If the project goes badly, its life may be less than 10 years because it will be scaled back or abandoned. If it is highly successful, it may be expanded or extended. Finally, the investment may not be made immediately. It can be deferred until next year or the year after. As we shall see, the real options framework takes these types of managerial flexibility into account, while the NPV approach assumes them away.

An option gives its owner the right (but not the obligation) to buy or sell an asset at a predetermined price (called the strike or exercise price) for a predetermined period of time (called the life of the option). The right to take an action is flexibility. The necessity of taking an action is inflexibility. Call options give the right to buy, and put options the right to sell. Options can be found on both the assets and the liabilities sides of the balance sheet.

Examples of options on the assets side of the balance sheet are primarily related to flexibility. A company that has the option to shut down and restart operations, defer their start, expand, contract, or abandon them, is more flexible and therefore more valuable than the same company without these options. Asset options are important not only because they affect the values of companies that have them but also because they provide explicit criteria for deciding when operations should be opened, closed, or abandoned. An option to open and close a mining operation may add 30 percent to 40 percent to its present value based on expected cash flow. The option provides explicit decision rules; for example, "open the mine when the price of Kryptonite exceeds $100 per ounce."

Options on the liabilities side of the balance sheet are easy to recognize. Convertible debt and preferred stock give their holder the right to exchange them for stock at a predetermined conversion ratio. Therefore, they contain call options. Warrants allow their owner to buy shares at a fixed price— again, a call option. Executive stock options are warrants held by management. Our standard approach to valuation requires that we subtract the market value of these liabilities from the enterprise value to estimate the value of equity.[1] Liability options affect the weighted average cost of capital. A random sample of 100 companies listed on the New York Stock Exchange indicated that 43 had convertible debt or preferred stock outstanding, and these securities contain imbedded call options.

The purpose of this chapter is not to turn you into a rocket scientist. Rather, we show the relation between real option pricing methods and more familiar approaches like net present value (NPV) and decision-tree analysis (DTA), provide examples of asset options and how they have been used in practice, and show how liability options can significantly affect the cost of capital.

REAL OPTION PRICING METHODS

In their book *Investment Under Uncertainty*, Dixit and Pindyck use a simple example to illustrate the difference between NPV and option pricing methods.[2]

---

[1] Empirical evidence indicates that executive stock options are exercised suboptimally. This must be taken into account in their valuation.
[2] A. Dixit and R. Pindyck, *Investment Under Uncertainty* (Princeton, NJ: Princeton University Press, 1994).

Suppose you are deciding whether to invest $1,600 in a new project that makes widgets. The cash flow per widget is $200 but will change to either $300 or $100 at the end of the year with equal probability. After that it will stay at its new level forever. Note that the expected future cash flow is $200, the weighted average of the risky outcomes, $300 and $100. The cost of capital is 10 percent. Assuming that one widget can be sold immediately, and one per year thereafter, the net present value of the project would be estimated as follows:

$$NPV = MAX[-1,600 + \sum_{t=0}^{\infty} \frac{200}{(1.1)^t}, 0]$$

$$= MAX[(-1,600 + 2,200), 0]$$

$$= 600$$

The NPV approach discounts the expected project cash flows at the weighted average cost of capital. The decision rule is to take the maximum of the discounted expected cash flows or zero (meaning don't do the project). The NPV rule is the maximum (determined today) of the expected values. It also makes the implicit assumption that the project should be undertaken immediately or not at all, because the maximum must be decided right now. This assumption rules out the possibility of deferring the investment one year until the uncertainty about the price per widget is resolved. If we look at the project given the option to defer, the economics look better:

$$\text{Option value} = .5\left[MAX\left(\frac{-1,600}{1.1} + \sum_{t=1}^{\infty} \frac{300}{(1.1)^t}, 0 \right) \right] + .5\left[MAX\left(\frac{-1,600}{1.1} + \sum_{t=1}^{\infty} \frac{100}{(1.1)^t}, 0 \right) \right]$$

$$= .5MAX\left[\frac{-1,600 + 3,300}{1.1}, 0 \right] + .5MAX\left[\frac{-1,600 + 1,100}{1.1}, 0 \right]$$

$$= .5\left[\frac{1,700}{1.1} \right] + .5(0)$$

$$= 733$$

With the option to defer you can wait one period to invest, then decide whether to do so, based on the arrival of information about the long-term cash flow per widget. If the cash flow is only 100 per unit you will not exercise the option to invest, but if the cash flow is 300 per unit, you will. Although the NPV of investing immediately is $600, the NPV should you decide to defer is even higher at $733. Therefore, you will defer.

The value of this call option (with an exercise price of 1,600, a one-year life, a variance determined by the cash-flow spread of $200 per unit, and an underlying risky asset that has a value without flexibility of $600) is the difference between the value of the project with flexibility and its value without flexibility, \$733 − \$600 = \$133. Note also that the NPV is the maximum, decided today, of the expected discounted cash flows or zero, while the option value is the expected value of the maximums, decided when information arrives, of the discounted cash flows in each future state of nature, or zero:

$$NPV = \underset{t=0}{MAX} \left[\frac{\text{Expected cash flows}}{\text{Cost of capital}}, 0 \right]$$

$$\text{Option value} = \text{Expected} \left[\underset{t=t}{MAX} \left(\frac{\text{Cash flow given info}}{\text{Cost of capital}}, 0 \right) \right]$$

The two methods use information quite differently. NPV forces a decision based on today's expectation of future information, while option valuation allows the flexibility of making decisions in the future contingent on the arrival of information. Option-pricing methods capture the value of flexibility while NPV does not. The value of a project using option pricing will always be greater than the value of the project using NPV. Sometimes the difference in value between the two approaches is small. This is usually the case when the project has such a high NPV that the flexibility is unlikely to be used, or conversely when the NPV is very negative. The biggest differences (see Exhibit 20.1) occur when the NPV is close to zero, that is, when the decision about whether to undertake the project is a close call. We have found differences in value of more than 100 percent in such situations. These were cases where senior management had often overruled the NPV results and accepted the project for "strategic reasons." As you begin to feel

Exhibit 20.1   When Is Managerial Flexibility Valuable?

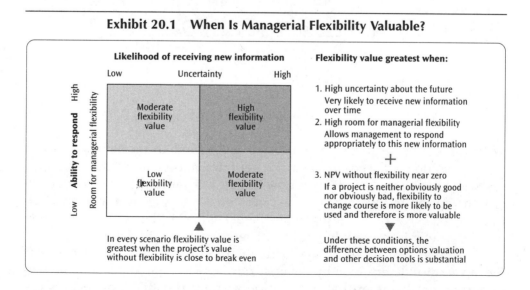

more comfortable with real options, you will see that the concept fits intuition better than the rigid assumptions of NPV.

To extend Dixit and Pindyck's example, let's see what happens if the variability of cash flows per unit increases from $300 versus $100 to $400 versus $0. Notice that the NPV is the same because the expected cash flows remain unchanged and we also assume that the new risk is uncorrelated with the economy, so the capital asset pricing model beta and the cost of capital are unchanged. But the value of the deferral option will increase because it is based on decisions that are contingent on the way that uncertainty is resolved. The algebra looks like this:

$$
\text{Option value} = .5\text{MAX}\left[\frac{-1,600}{1.1} + \sum_{t=1}^{\infty}\frac{400}{(1.1)^t}, 0\right] + .5\text{MAX}\left[\frac{-1,600}{1.1} + \sum_{t=1}^{\infty}\frac{0}{(1.1)^t}, 0\right]
$$

$$
= .5\text{MAX}\left[\frac{(-1,600 + 4,400)}{1.1}, 0\right] + 0
$$

$$
= .5\left[\frac{2,800}{1.1}\right] - 1,273
$$

Now the value of flexibility has increased to $673, because the amount of uncertainty has increased. The value of an option increases as the variability in the value of the underlying risky asset (the cash flow per unit) increases. As with financial options, the value of a real option depends on five parameters: the market value of the underlying asset on which the option is contingent; the exercise price of the option; the time remaining until the maturity of the option; the volatility of the underlying asset, and the risk-free rate of interest. These are all clearly defined for financial options, but require better understanding for real options. A sixth parameter is the amount of dividends paid by the underlying risky asset. We shall come back to it a little later.

The parameters that affect the value of a real option are summarized in Exhibit 20.2. Note that an important difference between financial and real options is that management can affect the value of the underlying risky asset (a physical project under its control) while financial options are side bets owned by third parties that cannot affect the outcome of the underlying asset (e.g., a share of IBM).

Without training, executives often fail to recognize real options and how valuable they can be. One example is a story about the life insurance industry. In the early 1970s, it was common to be able to buy a whole life policy with a clause that allowed you to borrow against the cash value of the policy at, let's say, a 9 percent interest rate, for the life of the policy. At the time, interest rates were about 4 percent on long-term government bonds. No one expected that they would go as high as 9 percent. But the

Exhibit 20.2   Option Value Is Determined by Six Variables

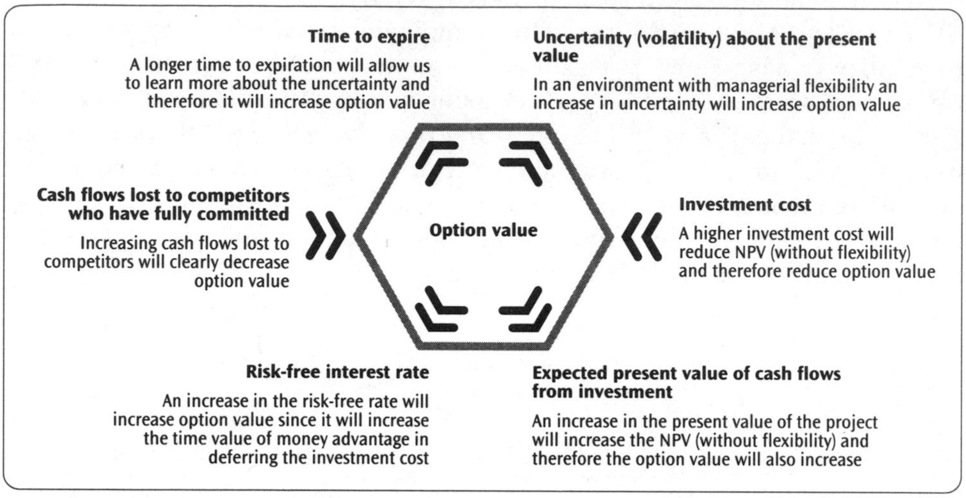

Time to expire

A longer time to expiration will allow us to learn more about the uncertainty and therefore it will increase option value

Uncertainty (volatility) about the present value

In an environment with managerial flexibility an increase in uncertainty will increase option value

Cash flows lost to competitors who have fully committed

Increasing cash flows lost to competitors will clearly decrease option value

Option value

Investment cost

A higher investment cost will reduce NPV (without flexibility) and therefore reduce option value

Risk-free interest rate

An increase in the risk-free rate will increase option value since it will increase the time value of money advantage in deferring the investment cost

Expected present value of cash flows from investment

An increase in the present value of the project will increase the NPV (without flexibility) and therefore the option value will also increase

life of a policy can be long—as long as the life expectancy of the policy-holder. What kind of option was imbedded in the contract, and what were the parameters? The policyholder had a long-term call option on the right to borrow (i.e., on the value of a bond issued by the insurance company) against the cash value (which determines the amount of the loan) of the policy at a fixed rate, for the life of the policy. The underlying uncertainty is the variance of interest rates. In 1981–1982 when interest rates went to double-digit levels, policyholders began to borrow at 9 percent, invest the money in government bonds at double-digit rates, and keep the difference. The losers were the life companies that had to borrow at double-digit rates and receive 9 percent. Several life companies went bankrupt as a result. The executives who originally sold life policies with these valuable options imbedded in them had not clearly understood the value of the options in the life contracts they were writing.

TAXONOMY OF OPTIONS

To identify potential operating flexibility and strategic factors, we can classify asset options into five mutually exclusive (but not exhaustive) categories.

Abandonment option. The option to abandon (or sell) a project—the right to abandon an open pit coal mine—is formally equivalent to an American put option on a stock.[3] If the bad outcome occurs at the end of the first period, the decision maker may abandon the project and realize the expected liquidation value. Then, the expected liquidation (or resale) value of the project may be thought of as the exercise price of the put. When the present value of the asset falls below the liquidation value, the act of abandoning (or selling) the project is equivalent to exercising the put. Because the liquidation value of the project sets a lower bound on the value of the project, the option to liquidate is valuable. A project that can be liquidated is worth more than the same project without the possibility of abandonment.

Option to defer development. The option to defer an investment to develop a property is formally equivalent to an American call option on the stock. The owner of a lease on an undeveloped oil reserve has the right to acquire a developed reserve by paying a lease-on-development cost. The owner can defer the development process until oil prices rise. In other words, the managerial option implicit in holding an undeveloped reserve is a deferral option. The expected development cost may be thought of as the exercise price of the call. The net production revenue less depletion of the developed reserve is the opportunity cost incurred by deferring the investment. If this opportunity cost is too high, the decision maker may want to exercise the option (that is, develop the reserve) before its relinquishment date.

Option to expand or contract. The option to expand the scale of a project is formally equivalent to an American call option on the stock. Management may choose to build capacity in excess of the expected level of output so that it can manufacture at a higher rate if the product is more successful than was anticipated. The expansion option gives management the right, but not the obligation, to make additional follow-on investment (for example, to increase the production rate) if project conditions turn out to be favorable. The option to contract the scale of a project's operation is formally equivalent to an American put option on stock. Many projects can be engineered so that output can be contracted. Foregoing future spending on the project is equivalent to the exercise price of the put.

Option to extend or shorten. It is possible to extend the life of an asset or a contract by paying a fixed amount of money—an exercise price. Conversely, it is possible to shorten the life of an asset or a contract. The option to extend is a call, and the option to shorten is a put. Real estate leases often have clauses that are examples of the option to extend or shorten the lease.

Option to scope up or scope down. Scope is the number of activities covered in a project. Its optionality is expressed in terms of the ability to switch among alternative courses of action at a decision point in the future. Scope is like diversification—it is sometimes preferable to be able, at a

---

[3] An American option can be exercised at any time up to the maturity date of the option. A European option can only be exercised on the maturity date.

higher exercise cost, to chose among a wide range of alternatives. Buying the option to have greater scope is a call.

Switching options. The option to switch project operations is a portfolio of options that consists of both calls and puts. Restarting operations when a project is shut down is equivalent to an American call option. Shutting down operations when unfavorable conditions arise is equivalent to an American put option. The cost of restarting (or shutting down) operations may be thought of as the exercise price of the call (or put). A project whose operation can be turned on and off (or switched between two distinct locations, and so on) is worth more than the same project without the flexibility to switch. A flexible manufacturing system with the ability to produce two products is a good example of this type of option, as is peak-load power generation and the ability to exit and reenter an industry.

Compound options. These are options on options. Phased investments are a good example. You may have a factory that can be built as a sequence of real options, each contingent on those that precede it. The project can be continued at each stage by investing a new amount of money (an exercise price). Alternatively, it might be abandoned for whatever it can fetch. Other examples are research and development programs, new product launches, exploration and development of oil and gas fields, and an acquisition program where the first investment is thought of as a platform for later acquisitions.

Rainbow options. Multiple sources of uncertainty produce a rainbow option. Most research and development programs have at least two sources of uncertainty—technological and product-market uncertainty. The latter is represented by the evolution of the uncertain price of the product from a value that is relatively well known today, to less certain values that are affected by the state of the economy as well as other uncertain influences in the future. Thus, product- market uncertainty increases through time. Technological uncertainty, on the other hand, is reduced over time by conducting research until we learn what the product is and what its capabilities are. A similar type of rainbow option is exploration and development of natural resources like oil reserves.

COMPARING APPROACHES

In this section, we compare three decision methodologies: net present value (NPV), decision tree analysis (DTA), and option pricing methods. We also introduce the fundamental concept behind option pricing. This is that a replicating portfolio of priced securities can be found that has the same payouts as the option and therefore has the same market value. This is also called a zero-arbitrage condition, or the law of one price, because assets with the same payouts should have the same prices in the absence of arbitrage profits.

We use a simple deferral option to illustrate. Suppose that you have the opportunity to invest $115 at the end of the year in a project that has a 50–50 chance of returning either $170 or $65 in cash flows. The risk-free rate, r_f, is 8 percent. You have found a perfectly correlated or twin security that has payouts of $34 and $13 and is trading in the market for a price of $20 per share. Note that the payouts of the twin security are exactly one-fifth of the payouts on our project in each state of nature. There are two ways to use the twin security to help value our project. First, we can estimate the cost of capital for the twin security and apply it to the expected cash flows of our project—a traditional approach. The cost of capital is calculated as the rate that equates the present value of the expected cash flows with the present value of the twin security as follows:

$$PV = \frac{E(FCF)}{(1+k)}$$

$$\$20 = \frac{[.5(\$34) + .5(\$13)]}{(1+k)}$$

$$k = 17.5\%$$

Since the twin security has perfectly correlated payouts, it has the same risk as our project and we can use the same risk-adjusted discount rate, 17.5 percent, to discount the expected cash flows on the project. The value of the project is therefore,

$$PV = \frac{[.5(\$170) + .5(\$65)]}{(1.175)}$$

$$= 100$$

A second approach is to create a replicating portfolio—one that uses the expected cash flows of the priced securities to replicate the cash flows of our project. Suppose we choose N shares of the twin security and B dollars of a risk-free bond to compose our replicating portfolio. In the favorable state of nature this portfolio must yield $170,

$$N \, \$34 + B(1 + r_f) = \$170$$

In the unfavorable state of nature, this portfolio must yield $65:

$$N \, \$13 + B(1 + r_f) = \$65$$

Together, we have two equations and two unknowns. The solution is $N = 5$ and $B = 0$. Using this result plus the fact that one share of the twin security is worth $20, our project must have the same value as the replicating portfolio:

$$PV = 5N + B$$

$$= 5(\$20) + 0 = \$100$$

The net present value of the project, given that we must make the decision to invest today, is the present value of the cash inflows. These have been found to be $100, minus the present value of the cash outflows. This is calculated from the certain outlay of $115 next year, discounted at the riskless rate (8 percent)—a present value of −$106.48:

$$NPV = PV(\text{risky inflows}) - PV(\text{certain outflow})$$

$$= \$100 - \frac{\$115}{(1.08)}$$

$$= \$100 - \$106.48$$

$$= -\$6.48$$

Having maintained the assumption that we must decide now whether to invest at year's end, our decision would be not to invest. But the answer changes if we have a deferral option that allows us to decide next year, after observing which of the two outcomes have occurred. If we were using a decision-tree analysis (DTA), we would observe (from Exhibit 20.3) that the net cash flows in the favorable state are $170 − $115 = $55 because we would decide to invest. In the unfavorable state we would simply not invest,

Exhibit 20.3   Decision Tree Analysis (DTA)—Flexibility "Valued"

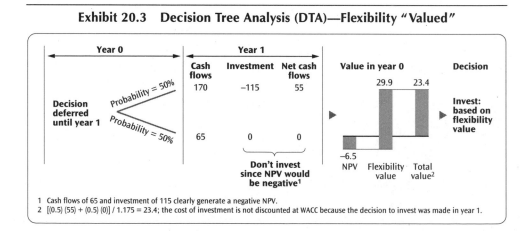

1 Cash flows of 65 and investment of 115 clearly generate a negative NPV.
2 [(0.5) (55) + (0.5) (0)] / 1.175 = 23.4; the cost of investment is not discounted at WACC because the decision to invest was made in year 1.

thereby giving us net cash flows of $0. Discounting the expected cash flows at the cost of capital gives us the result of the DTA approach:

$$DTA = \frac{E(FCF, \text{ given flexibility})}{(1+k)}$$
$$= \frac{[.5(\$55) + .5(\$0)]}{(1.175)}$$
$$= \$23.4$$

The value of the deferral option is the difference between the estimated value of the project with flexibility and its value without flexibility, or $23.4 − (−$6.5) = $29.9.

The problem with this DTA approach is that we used the cost of capital for the underlying project without flexibility to value the deferral option, a real option that has different payouts and therefore different risk than the underlying project. The DTA approach uses an ad hoc discount rate that is incorrect for the riskiness of the cash flows being evaluated.

The option pricing methodology uses the replicating portfolio approach. As before, we construct a portfolio consisting of N shares of the twin security and B dollars of risk-free debt. In the up state, the twin security pays $34 for each of the N shares and the bond pays the face value of the bond, B, plus interest equal to $r_f B$. These payouts must equal $55. A similar construction applies to the down state. The result is two equations and two unknowns:

$$N\, \$34 + B(1 + r_f) = \$55$$
$$N\, \$13 + B(1 + r_f) = \$0$$

The solution is that $N = 2.62$ and $B = -\$31.53$. The value of the project with the flexibility of deferring is:

$$\text{Option value} = N \text{ (Price of twin security)} - B$$
$$= 2.62\, (\$20) - \$31.53 = \$20.86$$

The value of the deferral option itself is the difference between the value of the project with flexibility and its value without flexibility $20.86 − (−$6.48) = $27.4. This is the correct, arbitrage-free solution. If we were using the implied risk-adjusted discount rate, it would be 31.9 percent (not 17.5 percent):

$$\$20.86 = \frac{[.5(\$55) + .5(\$0)]}{(1+k)}$$
$$k = 31.9\%$$

The risk of an option on an underlying risky asset is always greater than the risk of the asset itself. The project has a present value of $100 and a 50–50 chance of going up to $170, a 70 percent increase, or down to $65, a 35 percent decrease. The project with the option is worth $20.86 and has a 50–50 chance of paying off $55, a 164 percent increase, or zero, a 100 percent decrease. This greater risk helps explain why the risk-adjusted discount rate for the project with the option is 31.9 percent.

Exhibit 20.4 summarizes the results. The NPV approach undervalues the project because it does not take into account the value of flexibility. The DTA approach overestimates the value of flexibility because it uses the project risk-adjusted discount rate to discount the cash flows of the deferral option—cash flows that are much riskier.

The option pricing approach gives the correct value because it captures the value of flexibility correctly by using an arbitrage-free replicating portfolio approach. But where does one find the twin security? We can use the project itself (without flexibility) as the twin security, and use its NPV (without flexibility) as an estimate of the price it would have if it were a security traded in the open market. After all, what has better correlation with the project than the project itself? And we know that the DCF value of equities is highly correlated with their market value when optionality is not an issue. We shall use the net present value of the project's expected cash flows (without flexibility) as an estimate of the market value of the twin security. We shall call this the marketed asset disclaimer.

If we use the project itself as the twin security, then the replicating portfolio has the following payouts in the up and down states, given a risk-free rate of 8 percent:

$$N \, \$170 + B(1 + r_f) = \$55$$
$$N \, \$65 + B(1 + r_f) = \$0$$

Exhibit 20.4   Comparison of the Approaches

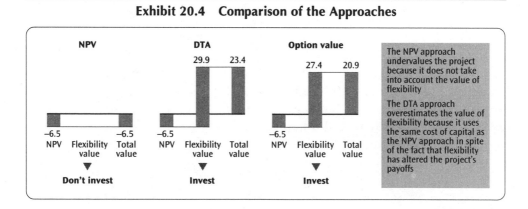

Solving the two equations above for the unknowns, we have

$$N = .524$$
$$B = -31.53$$

Given that the present value of the project without flexibility is $100, the value of the replicating portfolio is also the value of the project with flexibility, namely

$$N \$100 - 31.53 = .524(100) - 31.53 = \$20.86$$

It is no accident that this approach gives the same answer as the twin security approach—the outcomes are perfectly correlated.

NUMERICAL EXAMPLES

For practitioners to use the option pricing approach, it must be relatively transparent and easy to understand. We use a lattice method that requires only basic algebra and which can be solved on an Excel or Lotus spreadsheet. The results are identical to those that use much more complicated branches of mathematics such as stochastic calculus. The objective of the lattice is to model the present value of the project in a simple, but realistic way.

Event Trees

The lattice that models the values of the underlying risky asset is called an event tree. It contains no decision nodes and simply models the evolution of uncertainty in the present value of the underlying risky asset. Suppose we are studying a project that has a present value (*PV*) of $100, volatility of 15 percent per year, and an expected rate of return of 12 percent per year. The risk-free rate is 8 percent per year, and the cash outflow necessary to undertake the project, if we invest in it immediately, is $105. To model a single source of uncertainty (changes in the value of the project) we can chose one of two types of event tree—geometric or arithmetic. A geometric tree has multiplicative up-and-down movements that model a log-normal distribution of outcomes—one that can go to values of plus infinity on the up side and to values of zero on the down side. We chose the geometric event tree because we believe the value of the project can never fall below zero. (Although we will not illustrate it here, an arithmetic tree has additive up and down movements, approaches a normal distribution, and can have values that go to either plus or minus infinity.)

Exhibit 20.5   An Event Tree (No Flexibility)

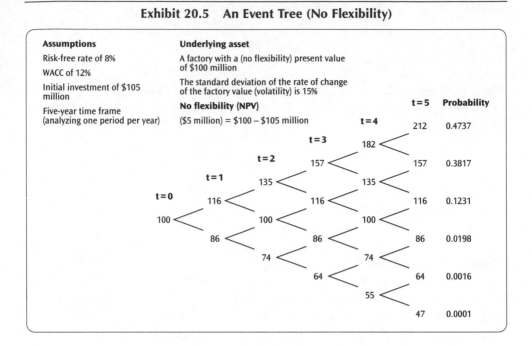

Exhibit 20.5 illustrates the values that our project might take for each of five years, given a geometric event tree. The up-and-down movements are determined by the following formulas:[4]

$$\text{Up movement} = u = e^{\sigma\sqrt{T}}$$

$$u = e^{.15\sqrt{1}} = 1.1618$$

$$\text{Down movement} = d = \frac{1}{u} = \frac{1}{1.1618} = .8607$$

Note that as we trace the down movements, they approach zero:

$$\lim_{n \to \infty} d^n = 0$$

The objective probability of an up movement is 86.12 percent and the objective probability of a down movement is 13.88 percent.[5] Using the tradi-

---

[4] J. Cox, M. Rubinstein, and S. Ross, "Option Pricing: A Simplified Approach," *Journal of Financial Economics* (September 1979), pp. 229–263.

[5] The formula for estimating the objective probability is probability up $= \dfrac{e^{.12} - d}{u - d} = \dfrac{e^{.12} - .8607}{1.16 - .8607} = .8612$; see note 4.

tional NPV rule, we can calculate the present value of any branch in the event tree as the expected payouts discounted at the 12 percent risk-adjusted rate. Let's take the uppermost branch in the fifth time period. Its present value is:

$$PV = \frac{E(\text{Value})}{(1+\text{Risk-adjusted rate})}$$

$$= \frac{[.8612(\$211.70)+.1388(\$156.83)]}{(1+.12)}$$

$$= \frac{[\$182.32+\$21.77]}{1.12}$$

$$= \frac{\$204.08}{1.12}$$

$$= \$182.21$$

A similar calculation will produce any of the values in the event tree. If we have to decide on the project today, we would reject it because the investment required is \$105 and the present value of the project inflows is only \$100.

There is an equivalent approach. Instead of discounting the expected payouts at a risk-adjusted rate, we could first risk-adjust the payouts (by using risk-adjusted probabilities, or as they are often called, risk-neutral probabilities) and then discount them at the risk-free rate. If we define the risk-adjusted probability of an up movement as q and the risk-adjusted probability of a down movement as $1 - q$, then the present value of a branch can be written as:

$$PV = \frac{q(uPV)+(1-q)dPV}{1+r_f}$$

Solving for the risk-adjusted (or risk-neutral) probability, we have:

$$q = \frac{(1+r_f-d)}{(u-d)} = \frac{(1+.08-.8607)}{(1.1618-.8607)}$$

$$= .7283$$

Using the risk-neutral probabilities to calculate a risk-adjusted expected payoff that is then discounted at the risk-free rate gives the same answer. The present value calculation for the uppermost branch in the fifth time period is:

$$PV = \frac{\text{Risk-adjusted expected payouts}}{(1 + \text{Risk-free rate})}$$

$$= \frac{.7283(\$211.70) + .2717(\$156.83)}{(1 + .08)}$$

$$= \frac{\$154.18 + \$42.61}{1.08}$$

$$= \$182.21$$

Next we turn the event tree into a decision tree, and in so doing introduce real options.

Decision Trees

When decision nodes are added to an event tree, it becomes a decision tree. In this section we will illustrate the value of flexibility that is created if it becomes possible to expand, contract, or abandon the project. Suppose that it is possible to expand our simple project and its payouts 20 percent by spending an additional $15, and the expansion is an American option that can be exercised any time during the life of the project. The resulting decision tree is given in Exhibit 20.6. The payouts on the tree have to be solved by working from the final branches backward through time. Take the upward-most branch in period 5. On the upward limb the payout in the absence of expansion would have been $211.70, but with expansion, it is $1.2(\$211.70) - \$15 = \$239.04$. Since the value with expansion is higher, we

Exhibit 20.6   Option to Expand

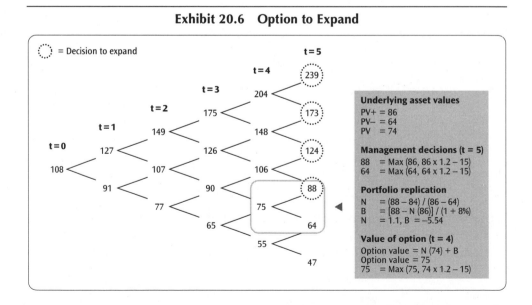

would decide to expand. On the lower limb, the payout with expansion is 1.2($156.83) − $15 = $173.20, versus $156.83 without expansion, so we would expand.

Exhibit 20.7 shows an option to contract. A saving of $25 is generated if the scale and value of the project is decreased by 25 percent. The value of the project with flexibility is determined by working backward through the decision tree, using the replicating portfolio method at each node. If we use the shaded node as an example, the payouts without flexibility are $PV^+ =$ $116 in the up state and $PV^- =$ $86 in the down state. The present value is PV = $100. We can do better if we exercise our option to contract in the down state because the payout becomes 75 percent of $86 plus $25, which is $90 and is higher than $86. We would contract in the down state because $90 is greater than $86.

By choosing a replicating portfolio of N units of the present value type (without flexibility) and a quantity of risk-free bonds, we are able to value the option to expand as follows:

$$N (\$116) + B = \$116$$
$$N (\$86) + B = \$90$$

Solving the two equations for their two unknowns, we find that $N = .8667$ and $B = \$15.46$. The value of the option is:

$$N (PV) + B/(1 + r) = .8667(\$100) + \$15.46/1.08 = \$101.$$

Exhibit 20.7 Option to Contract

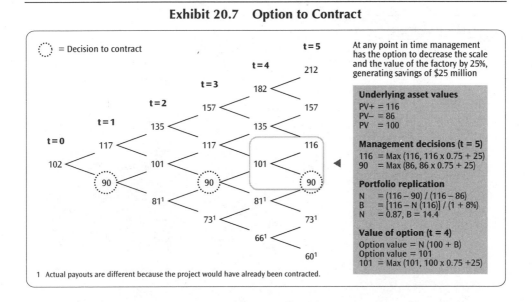

1 Actual payouts are different because the project would have already been contracted.

A replicating portfolio would consist of .8667 units of the present value of the project without flexibility, $100, plus 15.46 bonds worth $1. The value with flexibility is $101 as shown in Exhibit 20.7. We work backward, node by node, to arrive at a present value of $102 with the option to contract. The option increases the net present value of the project from –$5 to $2. So the option is worth $7.

Exhibit 20.8 shows the effect of an option to abandon the project. We assume that if abandoned, the salvage value of the project is $100. We don't abandon immediately because the value of the project and its salvage value are identical, and we do undertake the project because, given the flexibility to abandon, it is worth $106.32 (more than the initial investment of $105). If the project falls in value after the first period, we would abandon it.

To conclude this section, Exhibit 20.9 combines the various sources of flexibility into a single decision tree. If all three types of flexibility were available at once, the value of the project would be $113.49, rather than $100, which is its value without flexibility, and the correct decision would be to accept the project. Note that the value of the combined options, $13.49, is not the simple sum of their individual values, but it is greater than any of them individually. The values of the simple options are not additive because they interact in complex ways.

Exhibit 20.8   Option to Abandon

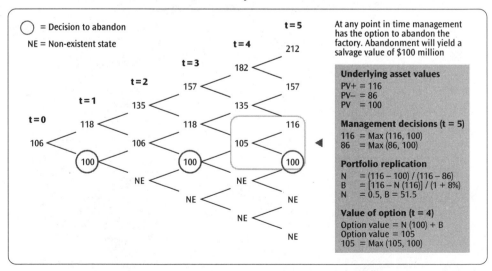

Exhibit 20.9   Option to Expand, Contract or Abandon

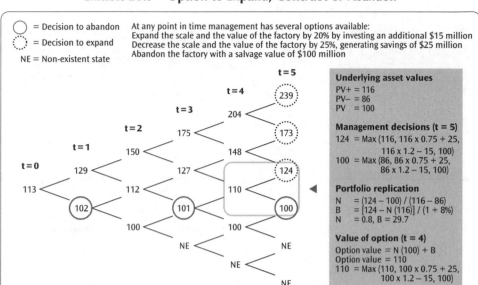

○ = Decision to abandon
⋯○⋯ = Decision to expand
NE = Non-existent state

At any point in time management has several options available:
Expand the scale and the value of the factory by 20% by investing an additional $15 million
Decrease the scale and the value of the factory by 25%, generating savings of $25 million
Abandon the factory with a salvage value of $100 million

Underlying asset values
PV+ = 116
PV− = 86
PV = 100

Management decisions (t = 5)
124 = Max (116, 116 x 0.75 + 25,
                116 x 1.2 – 15, 100)
100 = Max (86, 86 x 0.75 + 25,
                86 x 1.2 – 15, 100)

Portfolio replication
N = (124 – 100) / (116 – 86)
B = [124 – N (116)] / (1 + 8%)
N = 0.8, B = 29.7

Value of option (t = 4)
Option value = N (100) + B
Option value = 110
110 = Max (110, 100 x 0.75 + 25,
                100 x 1.2 – 15, 100)

EVALUATING OPTIONS

The overall approach for option valuation usually is a four-step process as illustrated in Exhibit 20.10. Step one is to calculate the base-case present value without flexibility using a traditional discounted cash flow model. The second step is to expand the DCF model into an event tree, mapping how the value of the project evolves, using explicit values, objective probabilities, and the weighted average cost of capital.[6] It is also necessary at this stage to chose a multiplicative or additive stochastic process and to decide whether to model mean reversion.[7] Since there is still no flexibility in the model, the present value of the project, based on the event tree, should equal the DCF value from the first step.

One of the important considerations in step 2 is that the uncertainty of a project within a company is not the same as the uncertainty of the variable or variables that drive that uncertainty. In one case, we found that the

---

[6] Objective probabilities are estimates of the actual probability that an event will happen. Often experienced managers or scientists supply them. Sometimes they are extracted from historical databases. Occasionally, a forecasting model supplies them.

[7] Mean reversion is a natural property of cyclical businesses. It implies that if prices are currently high, they are more likely to go down toward their long-term trend than to go up even further. When prices are currently low, the opposite is true.

Exhibit 20.10 Overall Approach—Four-Step Process

Steps	1. Compute base case present value without flexibility using DCF	2. Model the uncertainty using event trees	3. Identify and incorporate managerial flexibilities creating a decision tree	4. Calculate option value
Objectives	Compute base case present value without flexibility at t = 0	Understand how the present value develops with respect to the changing uncertainty Choose multiplicative or additive stochastic process	Analyzing the event tree to identify and incorporate managerial flexibility to respond to new information	Value the total project using a simple algebraic methodology and spreadsheet
Comments	Traditional present value without flexibility	Still no flexibility; this value should equal the value from Step 1 Explicitly estimate uncertainty	Flexibility is incorporated into event trees, which transforms them into decision trees The flexibility has altered the risk characteristics of the project, therefore the cost of capital has changed	Option value method will include the base case present value without flexibility plus the option (flexibility) value Under high uncertainty and managerial flexibility option value will be substantial

annualized standard deviation of a world commodity mineral was roughly 6 percent, but the annualized standard deviation of the percentage changes in the value of a mine that produced the commodity was about 35 percent. The mine had higher volatility than the commodity because of the fixed costs of operations that induced operating leverage. In most cases, the annualized volatility of the value of the project is impossible to observe directly. Exogenous effects such as uncertainty in prices, quantity sold, and input costs affect the uncertainty of projects.

We recommend using a Monte Carlo analysis of the variance of the DCF value of the project without flexibility as the best way of combining risks and taking into account the relationships among them. In another case, the price of the final product was an important source of uncertainty, but so too was the price of the major input. Furthermore, they were correlated. We used historical data on the spread between the two to drive the uncertainty in the Monte Carlo model. The spread reduced the two sources of uncertainty to one, and simultaneously took into account the correlation between the input and output prices.

Step 3 turns the event tree into a decision tree by identifying the types of managerial flexibility that are available and building them into the nodes of the tree. As we illustrated earlier, multiple sources of flexibility are possible at a single decision node, but it is important to have clear priority rules among them. Care must be taken on the sequence of decisions regarding flexibility, especially when the decision tree has compound options.

The fourth step is to recognize that the exercise of flexibility alters the risk characteristics of the project. That means the risk-adjusted discount rate is no longer the weighted average cost of capital that was used in step 1.

Instead we must use the replicating portfolio concept of option pricing to value the project with flexibility.

OPTIONS IN PRACTICE

Drawing from our experience, we describe three case histories that illustrate increasingly complex uses of options. Names of corporations and data are disguised to ensure confidentiality. We make explicit comparisons among different valuation approaches to show the usefulness of the option-pricing approach. Finally, we discuss some conclusions and lessons learned from each application.

Most asset option-pricing applications are limited to those situations where the option value depends on the market price of a world commodity, such as oil, coal, copper, nickel, gold, or zinc. By using the marketed asset disclaimer and a lattice approach, however, it is possible to solve a much wider set of problems than ever before, in a way that is fairly easy to understand from a manager's point of view. Exhibit 20.11 shows the progress that has been made applying option-pricing models in a realistic setting.

Kryptonite Mining (Switching Option)

Kryptonite (not the real name of the mineral) is a globally traded commodity product. Kryptonite Mining Limited was the world's leading producer of Kryptonite, supplying over one-third of the Western world's demand. It had four production sites, each with a different layout of operating mines and extraction technology. The random movement of spot Kryptonite prices had been volatile in the past four years. Our study focused on developing a valuation method for each site as well as providing some guidance regarding the shut-down/reopen decision—a switching option. Initial estimates of Kryptonite Mining's NPV based on analysts' forecasts of Kryptonite prices measured only up to 45 percent of Kryptonite Mining's current market value of equity (see Exhibit 20.12). A scenario-based NPV analysis allowing for no explicit operational flexibility increased this estimate to 71

Exhibit 20.11   Recent Advances Bring Wider Applicability

From	To
Uncertainty driven by world commodity product	Source of uncertainty not necessarily market priced
Higher mathematics necessary for application	Algebra and Excel spreadsheets
Single source of uncertainty	Multiple sources of uncertainty (rainbow options)
Simple options	Options on options (compound options, learning options)
Limited application	Many applications

Exhibit 20.12   Valuation of Kryptonite Mining Limited

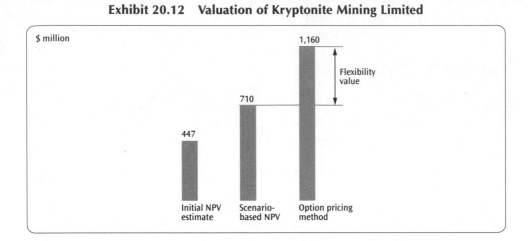

percent of equity value. The option-pricing valuation with shut-down/reopen and abandonment options gave a valuation of Kryptonite Mining's equity of 116 percent of its current market value.

The shut-down, reopen, and abandonment option values, as fractions of the corresponding site option-pricing values, ranged between 5 and 15 percent for a spot price range of $1.75/ounce to $2.25/ounce. These option values were much higher for lower spot prices and much lower for higher spot prices.

A major benefit of the analysis was the insight it provided into the economics of opening and shutting down each site. Given that a mine was open, it was optimal to keep it open even when the marginal revenue from a ton of output was less than the marginal cost of extraction. The intuitive explanation is that the fixed cost of closing an operation might be incurred needlessly if the commodity price rose in the near future. The opposite result applies to a closed mine. The optimal decision might be to keep it closed because of reopening costs until the commodity price rose substantially above the marginal cost of production.

Multiphase Investment (Compound Option)

CHEMCO was considering a $650 million investment in a new chemical plant. Traditional NPV methodology estimated a value of negative $71.2 million. This result was based on a spread between the input and output chemical prices that was volatile, near a high, given current market conditions, and was mean reverting. Mean reversion implied that since the spread was currently high, the probability that it might decrease was deemed to be greater than the probability that it would increase further. Management decided to use an option-pricing approach because it could start the project now, then abandon after an initial design phase, or after a pre-construction phase, if the spread decreased as expected (see Exhibit 20.13).

The project was a compound option because the second phase was conditional on the results of the first phase and on improvement in the spread, and the third phase was contingent on approval of the second phase. It was appropriate to think of the first phase as a platform on which the other phases were contingent. When the additional flexibility was valued, the project's NPV increased from –$71.2 million (without flexibility) to $354.5 (with flexibility).

Compound options are appropriate for a wide range of managerial decisions. They might even be used for distinguishing between a single acquisition and an acquisition program—a sequence of acquisitions. Often the initial deal in an acquisition program is a platform or stepping-stone to other acquisitions. The first deal might be negative NPV when viewed in isolation, but the entire program might have a positive value because it is a compound option.

Compound Rainbow Option (Learning Option)

A compound rainbow option is a sequence of decisions that is affected by two or more sources of uncertainty. The example in Exhibit 20.14 is what we call a learning option. It is applicable to exploration and production decisions, to research and development programs, and to product development programs. Our client was a large integrated oil company that had an extensive natural gas field. The field was 60 percent explored and 40 percent unexplored.

Management was divided about whether to develop the field now or to complete exploration. Those in favor of immediate development argued that

Exhibit 20.13   The Value of Compound Options in a Multiphase Investment

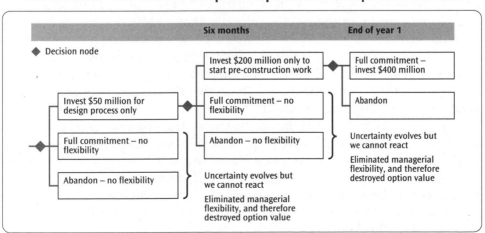

Exhibit 20.14 Compound Rainbow Option

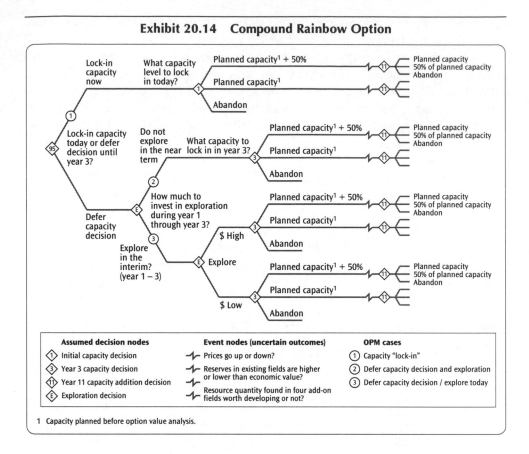

doing so would pull the expected future cash inflows of the project into the present and thereby add cash and value to the company. Others were concerned that early development might result in expensive "wrong sizing" of the billion-dollar investment in refineries, pipelines, and storage facilities. Current development would have to be based on estimates of reserves in the unexplored portion of the field—estimates that had a wide range of error. Once the investment was in place, it would be oversized and have excess capacity if the unexplored part of the field proved to have less natural gas than expected. If it turned out to have more natural gas than expected, the development would be undersized. To resolve the debate, management decided to try a real options approach.

The decision tree in Exhibit 20.14 shows the compound options that were involved. A decision had to be made about whether to start or defer the development of the field. If development were started, another decision had to be made about the scale of investment. If development were deferred, there was the decision about whether to explore, and if so at what level. If exploration took place, should the development decision be made in year 3 or deferred further?

There were two sources of uncertainty. First is the price of natural gas, which is known today, but which becomes more uncertain. Second is the uncertainty about the quantity of natural gas in the ground. It has a wide range of uncertainty today, but the range narrows if the company decides to explore the field.

When the analysis was completed the highest value was obtained by making the decision to explore now, by deferring the development decision until year 3, and making an expansion decision in year 11. The value of this set of decisions was 125 percent higher than the value of the base case, which was to develop the field now and wait for three years before deciding to explore.

It is easy to see from these examples that asset options can substantially alter the value of a business. The fact that the options exist does not mean that they are optimally managed. There are two problems. First, managers are not trained to recognize real options. Second, they are usually not familiar with the methodological advances that have made real options easier to apply and to understand. Understanding asset options can provide insight into managing flexibility as a new approach for dealing with uncertainty.

LIABILITY OPTIONS

We turn to options implicit in various sources of funding. These liability options are important because they affect the company's weighted average cost of capital.

Plain vanilla approaches to valuation describe the weighted average cost of capital as the simple weighted average of the after-tax opportunity costs of debt and equity. But hybrid securities that have option features are often used as sources of capital. We looked at a random sample of 100 companies listed on the New York Stock Exchange and found that 43 of them had convertible securities outstanding. The yield to maturity on convertible securities is usually much lower than on straight debt with the same maturity and quality. But the yield on convertible securities is a particularly bad estimate of their actual cost of capital.

The first part of our analysis will show how to value callable, convertible debt. Then we will discuss how its cost of capital is estimated.

Valuing Callable, Convertible Securities

Convertible bonds allow their owners to convert them into another security at a predetermined exchange ratio for a fixed interval of time. The ABB 2.75s described in Exhibit 20.15 could be converted into common stock at a price of $112.41 per share anytime during their life. The actual common stock price at

Exhibit 20.15   Terms for ABB 2.75s due 2004

Fall 1988			
	Rating	Ba2	
	Amount Authorized	$150.0 million	
	Amount Outstanding	$150.0 million	
	Issued	7/10/97	
	Due	7/10/2004	
	Interest Date	7/10	
	CALL TERMS	Year	Price
		2000	100%
		2004	100%
	Conversion price	$112.41/share	

Source: Remco Bos, Fortis Investment Bank.

the time of data collection was $112.43, almost exactly equal to the conversion price. When exercising conversion rights, the bondholder gives up, as the exercise price, the present value of the expected bond payments. For ABB, the bondholders would give up the bond payments in return for 0.8896 shares (per $100 of face value on the bond). Thus, convertible bonds have a changing exercise price.

To show how to value a callable, convertible bond, let's look at a numerical example. The following set of assumptions details the interest rate environment, the way the value of the company varies, and the provisions of the callable, convertible bond.

- The constant risk-free rate is 8 percent per year.
- The company is worth $400,000 right now (no senior debt).
- There is a 62 percent probability that company value will increase by 35 percent and a 38 percent probability that it will decrease by 26 percent as shown in Exhibit 20.16.
- Two securities are outstanding: 150 shares of stock, and 100 callable, convertible bonds that can be converted at a ratio of one-half share per bond.
- If bonds are converted, bondholders will own $50/(150 + 50) = 25$ percent of the company. If the bondholders decide to convert, they receive the coupon for that period.
- Each $1,000-face-value bond pays $100 per period coupon.
- Anytime before maturity, stockholders can call the bonds for $1,400. (For simplicity, however, we assume the call decision is made only at the end of the first year.)
- The company pays no dividends.
- The first bond coupon has just been paid.

Exhibit 20.16   Value of a Hypothetical Company That Pays a Constant Coupon

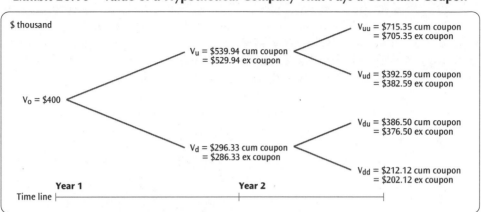

To value the callable, convertible bonds, we start with their final payouts, determine the optimal action, and compute their value at the end of year 1 conditional on the value of the company (illustrated in Exhibit 20.16). Given that the value of the company has gone up the first year, the final value of the company at the end of the second year can be $705,349 or $382,592, ex coupon. If it is $705,349 the bondholders receive $186,337 if they convert and $110,000 otherwise. Obviously, they will convert. If the company value is $382,592, they will not convert, preferring to receive the $1,000 face value per bond plus the last coupon for a total of $110,000 rather than the conversion value of $105,684 (25% of $382,592 plus $10,000). With these facts, we can determine the market value of the bond at the end of year 1. Results of our calculations are given in Exhibit 20.17.

Exhibit 20.17   Valuation of a Callable, Convertible Bond

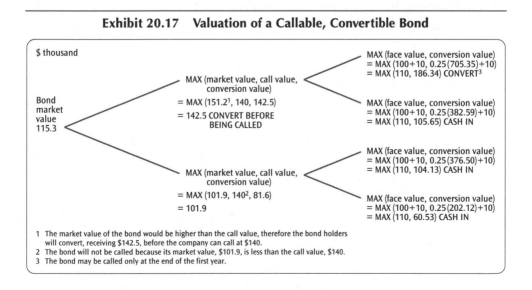

1 The market value of the bond would be higher than the call value, therefore the bond holders will convert, receiving $142.5, before the company can call at $140.
2 The bond will not be called because its market value, $101.9, is less than the call value, $140.
3 The bond may be called only at the end of the first year.

To value the callable, convertible bond at the end of the first year, given that the value of the firm has increased to $539,900 before the coupon and $529,000 ex coupon, we form a replicating portfolio that is composed of "m" units of the company (divided by 4 because the bond holders get ¼th of the company) plus B risk-free bonds. This portfolio will have exactly the same payoffs as the bond in the second year:

Up state payoff $\quad mu(1/4)(529.94) + 1.08B = 186.34$

Down state payoff $\quad \dfrac{-[md(1/4)(529.94) + 1.08B - 110.00]}{m(1/4)(529.94)(u - d) = 76.34}$

Solving, we find that $m = 0.946$, and $B = 15.87$, therefore the market value of the callable, convertible bond is the same as the market value of the replicating portfolio,

$$\text{Market value} = m(1/4)(529.94) + B = 141.25$$

Plus the dividend, $10, for a total of $151.25.

Unfortunately for the bond holders, this market value is higher than the value if called, $140, therefore the firm will call the bonds. As a preventative measure, the bond holders will convert before the firm can call, and will receive 25 percent of $529.90 plus a coupon of $10, a total of $142.50. Thus, their expected payout in this state of nature is $142,500.

To value the bond in other states of nature, we repeat the replicating portfolio approach to estimate the market value of the bond and compare it with the value if converted or called. For example, in the down state in the first year the market value, $101.90, is higher than the value if called or converted. Working backward, we find that the market value today is $115,261 for all of the callable, convertible bonds, or $1,152.61 per bond. Exhibit 20.18

Exhibit 20.18   Values of the Callable Convertible Bond and Implied Interest Rates

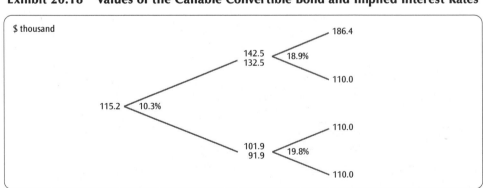

shows the value of the callable, convertible bond in each state of nature, and the discount rates between them. Note that these rates are all greater than the 8 percent risk-free rate.

Whenever the enterprise approach for valuing a company is used, the market value of equity is estimated by first valuing the whole company, the enterprise, and then subtracting the market value of debt to estimate the value of equity. Having a good estimate of the market value of convertible securities is often crucial. In the example, the value of the company, $400,000, less the market value of callable, convertible debt, $115,261, is equal to the value of equity, namely $284,739. Had we used the face value of the debt, $100,000, we would have overestimated the equity value by 5.4 percent.

The Cost of Capital for Callable, Convertible Securities

Professor Eugene Brigham once surveyed the chief financial officers of 22 companies that had issued convertible debt. Of those surveyed, 68 percent said they had used convertible debt because they believed their stock price would rise and that convertibles would provide a way of selling common stock at a price above the existing market. Another 27 percent said that their company had wanted straight debt but had found conditions to be such that a straight bond issue could not be sold at a reasonable rate of interest.

Neither reason makes sense. Convertible bonds are not cheap debt. Because convertible bonds are riskier, their true cost of capital is greater (on a before-tax basis) than the cost of straight debt. Also, convertible bonds are not equal to deferred sale of common stock at an attractive price. The uncertain sale of shares at $28, each at some unknown future date, can hardly be compared directly with a current share price of $25.

The risk of convertible debt is higher than that of straight debt and lower than that of equity, so its true opportunity cost lies between these limits. The yield to maturity on convertible debt (often lower than on the company's senior debt) has nothing to do with its opportunity cost, because convertible debt has an option embedded in it, and options are much riskier than debt. Going back to our numerical example, if we naively estimate the cost of capital on the callable, convertible bond by using the observed price of the bond, $1,152.61, to calculate a yield to maturity, we come up with an estimate of 2.13 percent:

$$B_0 = \$1,152.61 = \$100/(1 + y) + \$1,100/(1 + y)^2$$
$$y = 2.13\%$$

This is obviously wrong because it is less than the risk-free rate of 8 percent. If we use the true risk-adjusted rates in Exhibit 20.18 the implied geometric average required rate of return on the callable, convertible fond is 14.74 percent pretax.

Three broad categories of information are needed to value a callable, convertible bond and to determine its cost of capital:

1. *The interest rate environment.* Ideally, we would capture the entire term structure and its expected variability. But our model can handle only one random variable at a time, and the variability of the company's common stock is the most important element. Consequently, the interest rate environment is captured by the yield to maturity on a Treasury bond with the same maturity as the convertible bond.

2. *Characteristics of the bond.* We need to know the amount outstanding, the face value, the number of months to maturity, the conversion price, the number of months until the first coupon date, the time between coupons, the annual coupon rate, and the call provisions (the call prices and their timing).

3. *Characteristics of the common stock.* Since the bond is convertible into common stock, we need to know the current stock price, the equity beta, the expected dividend per share, the ex dividend dates, the number of shares outstanding, the equity volatility, and the amount of senior debt outstanding.

Exhibit 20.19 shows our estimate of the value and the before-tax cost of capital for a sample of seven callable, convertible bonds. The results were provided by McKinsey's convertible securities pricing model. In every case, the before-tax cost of capital for the callable, convertible bond is higher than the coupon rate, and in all but one case the difference is substantial.

Exhibit 20.19   Valuation and Cost of Capital for Convertible Bonds

March 2000

Company	Theoretical Value[1]	Market Price[1]	Difference (percent)	Coupon Rate (percent)	Cost of Capital (percent)
ABB	106.7	106.4	0.3	2.75	11.1
Ahold	110.5	107.0	3.2	3.00	6.8
America Online	1,044.2	1,036.5	0.7	4.00	16.6
Colt Telecom	113.8	111.3	2.3	2.00	8.3
Hilton	71.9	75.6	−5.1	5.00	10.0
Johnson & Johnson	120.1	120.0	0.1	4.75	10.4
Nestle	88.7	87.5	1.3	1.25	8.0
Texaco	97.3	96.6	0.7	3.50	7.7
Xerox	54.0	53.9	0.3	0.57	8.3

1 Per $100 face value.
Source: Remco Bos, Fortis Investment Bank.

The after-tax cost of the bond depends on the percentage of its opportunity cost that is actually tax-deductible. Thus, an estimate of its after-tax cost is

$$\text{After-tax } K_{cv} = K_{cv}\left[1 - \frac{\text{Coupon rate}}{K_{cv}}(\text{tax-rate})\right]$$

SUMMARY

Option pricing is analogous to flexibility in decision making because the holder of an option can exercise it at his or her discretion. Options can affect every arena of management, and we have illustrated only a few applications. On the assets side of the balance sheet are options to defer, expand, contract, abandon, or switch projects on and off. In addition, these options can appear as compound options, as in phased investments, and may be driven by multiple sources of uncertainty (rainbow options). Net present value analysis, rigidly applied, undervalues assets because it fails to account for the rich set of flexibility options involved in business decisions. On the liabilities side, options can have a significant impact on the cost of capital. We analyzed callable, convertible debt and saw that the true opportunity cost is often substantially higher than the coupon rate. Convertible debt is not a free lunch. It is neither cheap debt nor cheap equity.

21

Valuing Banks

The banking and thrift industries have undergone two decades of change, catalyzed by the globalization of financial markets, privatization, deregulation, the growing popularity of nonbank substitutes, and changes in tax laws. Additionally, the Internet and other technological developments have led to relentless cost reductions by the best banks.

The result has been massive restructuring among financial institutions. This restructuring began in 1988, when the Bank of New York successfully completed its hostile takeover of Irving Trust. In 1991, Chemical Bank and Manufacturers Hanover agreed to merge. The new Chemical Bank merged with Chase Manhattan in 1996. In 1999, Citicorp merged with Travelers to form CitiGroup. In early 2000, the U.S. Congress was in the process of repealing the Glass-Steagall Act, which had kept commercial banks from investment banking activities and certain other financial services. No doubt this repeal will also spur further consolidation in financial services. Valuation is an important tool for helping managers understand and undertake these types of restructuring.

THE DIFFICULTY WITH VALUING BANKS

Valuing banks is conceptually difficult. For an outsider, determining the quality of the loan portfolio, measuring the amount of current accounting profits attributable to interest-rate mismatch (for example, the difference between what is earned on loans with long-term rates and deposits compensated by short-term rates), and understanding which business units are driving the bank's profit potential are all hard to do.

For an insider attempting to value a bank, the major issue is transfer pricing. As illustrated in Exhibit 21.1, most banks can be separated into three basic business units (although most have dozens of distinct businesses): a retail bank that may have only 20 cents in loans for each dollar in deposits, a

Exhibit 21.1   Business Unit Structure of Banks

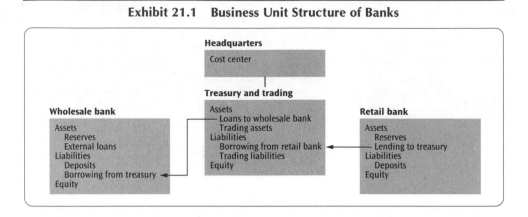

wholesale bank with only 20 cents in deposits for each dollar in loans, and a treasury that stands between them and carries on activities of its own such as securities trading. The excess funds generated by the retail bank can be loaned to the marketplace or to the wholesale bank. If loaned internally, the rate credited to the retail bank and the rate paid by the wholesale bank are crucial transfer prices. If the price credited to the retail bank is set too high, it will appear to be more profitable, and vice versa. It is critical to establish the correct transfer price in order to determine where the bank should allocate its marginal resources—to the retail bank or to the wholesale bank.

This chapter does not present all the answers to bank valuation, but focuses mainly on the issue of how to value banks. First, we discuss the practical reasons why it is easier to use an equity approach than an enterprise approach to valuing banks. Second, we cover the issues involved in an outsider's approach. Finally, we turn to the problems of an insider's approach.

THE EQUITY APPROACH TO VALUING BANKS

Throughout the book we have recommended and used the enterprise DCF approach to valuing companies. (The enterprise approach discounts the after-tax free cash flow from operations at the weighted average cost of capital to first obtain the estimated enterprise value, then subtracts the market value of debt to estimate the equity value.) Although the equity and enterprise approaches are mathematically equivalent, the equity approach to valuing banks is easier to use and reflects the fact that banks can create value from the liability side of the balance sheet. So, we recommend that for banks you forecast free cash flow to equity holders and discount it at the cost of equity.

The enterprise method is more difficult to use for banks because a main source of financing is non-interest-bearing customer deposits raised through the retail bank, not borrowing in capital markets. The cost of capital for these deposits can be difficult to estimate. Furthermore, the retail bank is legitimately a separate business in its own right, unlike the treasury function of most corporations. These facts make it difficult, if not impossible, to value the bank's equity by first valuing its assets (that is, its lending function) by discounting interest income less administrative expenses at the weighted average cost of capital, then subtracting the present value of its deposit business (interest expenses plus consumer bank administrative costs, discounted at the cost of debt). Still another problem with the enterprise approach for banks is that the spread between the interest received on loans and the cost of capital is so low that small errors in estimating the cost of capital can result in huge swings in the value of the bank.

In addition to being easier to use, there is a conceptual reason for using the equity approach for valuing banks. The deposit franchise given by the government to the bank potentially allows the bank to create value on the liabilities side of its balance sheet. If the cost of issuing deposits (e.g., interest expense, check clearing, and tellers) is less than the cost of raising an equivalent amount of funds with equal risk in the open market, then a positive spread is created that creates value for shareholders. Thus, liabilities management is part of the business operations of the bank and is not purely financing. If it were pure financing, there would be no spread. The bank would be paying market rates for funds received and no value would be created for shareholders (aside from the tax shield of interest expense).

To apply the equity DCF method to banks, you need to know how to define free cash flow to shareholders and how to use the "spread" or the "income" model.

Defining Free Cash Flow to Shareholders

Free cash flow to shareholders is net income plus noncash charges less cash flow needed to grow the balance sheet. The value of equity is not simply net income discounted at the cost of equity, because not all of net income can be paid to shareholders. Only dividends can be paid to shareholders.

Exhibit 21.2 shows the definition of free cash flow to shareholders of a bank. The best way to think about it is to keep your eye on actual cash in and cash out. Cash flow from the income statement is reasonably straightforward except for the fact that depreciation and provisions for credit losses are not cash flow. Their only effect is to reduce taxes. We find it easier to treat loan-loss provisions as though they are an actual cash flow. We have little choice in the matter because actual cash flows regarding the nonpayment of loans are not a matter of public record. Balance sheet cash flow starts with cash in as loans are repaid. Actual cash received is gross loans due less provisions (and unearned income) resulting in net loans paid. To this number we must add increases in deposits and external debt, and sale of new equity, all sources of funds. On the uses side, new loans, increases in cash reserves, and securities held represent the main cash outflows.

Exhibit 21.2   Free Cash Flow to Bank Shareholders

Income statement	Balance sheet Sources	Uses
Interest income	Gross loans due	New loans
+ Fee income	– Provisions and unearned income	+ Increase in securities held
– Interest expense	= Net loans paid	+ Increase in accounts receivable
– Provision for credit losses	+ Increase in deposits	+ Increase in net tangible assets
+Non-interest revenue	+ Increase in external debt	+ Increase in other assets
– Non-interest expenses[1]	+ Increase in other liabilities	– Decrease in deposits
+ FX income	+ Increase in accounts payable	– Decrease in external debt
– Taxes		
= Net income		
+ Extraordinary items		
+ Depreciation		
▼	▼	▼
= Cash from operations	**+ Sources**	**– Uses = Free cash flow to equity**

Free cash flow = Dividends paid + Potential dividends + Equity repurchases – Equity issues

1 Includes depreciation.

When cash from operations is combined with sources and uses from the balance sheet, the result is free cash flow to shareholders, which is mathematically identical to dividends that *could* be paid to shareholders. This is usually not the same as actual dividends in a given year because management deliberately smoothes dividend payments across time. This topic is discussed in greater detail later in the chapter when we cover how to value banks from the outside.

Using the Spread or Income Model

The language of banking often expresses income as spreads earned on balances—that is, the difference between the rate paid on borrowings and the

Exhibit 21.3   ABC Bank—Income Model

Balance sheet	$ million	Income statement	$ million
Assets		Interest income, 12% ($933)	112
Cash reserves	120	Interest expense, 5% ($1,000)	(50)
Loans	93	Other expenses	(48)
	1,053	Net profit before tax	14
Liabilities		Taxes at 40%	(6)
Deposits	1,000	Net income	8
Equity	53		
	1,053		

Exhibit 21.4   ABC Bank—Spread Model

Definition	Calculation	$ million
(Spread on loans) x (loan balance)	(12% – 8%) ($933)	37
+ (Spread on deposits) x (deposit balance)	+ (8% – 5%) ($1,000)	30
+ (Equity credit) x (equity)	+ (8%) ($53)	4
– (Reserve debit) x (resources)	– (8%) ($120)	(9)
– Expenses		(48)
= Net profit before tax		14
– Taxes at 40%		(6)
Net income		8

rate received on loans and investments. Consequently, as a first step it is useful to show the equivalence between the traditional computation of earnings as reported in financial statements for nonfinancial companies, which for lack of a better phrase we shall call the income model, and the spread model that is common practice in banking.

The balance sheet and income statement for the hypothetical bank in Exhibit 21.3 show the traditional income model computation of net income. We assume that loans earn 12 percent, cash reserves at the Federal Reserve Bank earn nothing, deposits pay 5 percent, and the tax rate is 40 percent. Note that the income model, based on the financial statements, computes net income as $8.

The spread model is an alternative but equivalent approach for computing net income. It starts with the assumption that an opportunity cost of money (call it the money rate) is charged to the wholesale bank and credited to deposits. In our example, it is 8 percent. The spread model calculates net income by adding spreads times balances. It then adds a credit for the equity component of the bank's financing, since the spreads used assume that investments are 100 percent from borrowings. Likewise, income is reduced for reserves at the Federal Reserve since they do not earn interest. Exhibit 21.4 illustrates the spread-model net income calculation.

The spread model gives the same answer as the income model, but should be used with care. For example, the money rate used in the equity credit is not equivalent to the cost of equity: It is merely an accounting convention necessary to provide the right answer.

VALUING BANKS FROM THE OUTSIDE

Banks remain among the most difficult companies to value despite the multitude of regulatory and reporting requirements imposed on them. It is hard to determine the quality of their loan portfolio, to figure out what percentage of

Exhibit 21.5   Term Structure Slope Creates Mismatch Profits

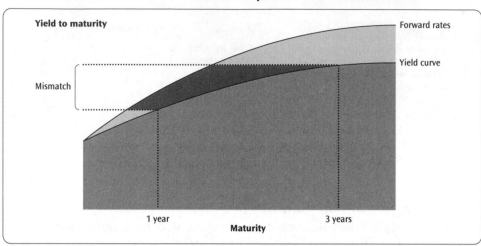

their accounting profits results from interest-rate mismatch gains, and to understand which business units are creating or destroying value.

Understanding Mismatch Gains and Losses

Normally, the term structure of interest rates is upward sloping, as shown in Exhibit 21.5. A bank that lends three-year money and borrows one-year money will earn a mismatch profit equal to the difference between the longer and shorter term rates of interest. Much of this profit is illusory because the one-year funds must be rolled over twice at future one-year spot rates that are expected to be higher than today's one-year rate. The mismatch profit observed in today's market should not, in most circumstances, be forecasted to persist.[1]

To illustrate how spreads would be expected to change, suppose a bank lends $1 million of three-year fixed-rate money and borrows $900,000 of one-year CDs that are rolled over each year for three years. The assumed term structure is as follows:

Maturity (years)	Yield (percent)	1-Year forward rate (percent)
1	8.0	8.0
2	9.0	10.0
3	9.5	10.5

[1] Later in the chapter we will revisit this important issue in greater detail to examine the liquidity premium.

Exhibit 21.6 shows the forecasted income statements and balance sheets for three units of a bank: the wholesale bank that lends $1 million, the retail bank that raises $900,000 in one-year CDs, and the treasury. To keep the example as simple as possible, we have assumed no reserve requirements and no taxes. The wholesale bank is match-funded with three-year money that costs 9.5 percent; it earns 9.5 percent on $1 million and pays 9.5 percent on $950,000, for an annual profit of $4,750. Its spread is 0 percent—not a good deal. The retail bank is forecasted to earn the expected one-year spot rate (8 percent, then 10 percent, and finally 10.5 percent), which is assumed to be equal to the one-year forward rate. The retail bank pays the expected one-year spot rate on CDs. It, too, has a 0 percent spread.

In Exhibit 21.6, both the wholesale and retail banks are perfectly match-funded; all of the mismatch profits appear in the treasury. In the first year, the treasury lends at the three-year rate (to the wholesale bank) and borrows at the one-year rate (from the retail bank) for a net profit of $14,250. In the second and third years, it loses money because it still earns the three-year fixed rate, 9.5 percent, but pays the one-year spot rate, 10 percent in year two and 10.5 percent in year three. The mismatch profits of the treasury are reflected in the bank as a whole.

If you were to build a valuation model that forecasted profits to be $23,000 perpetually (that is, a 23 percent return on equity), the bank would appear profitable. The reality is that the bank return on equity is 5 percent or less in the second year and 0.5 percent or less in the third year. Its high

---

Exhibit 21.6   Financial Statement for Three Units of a Bank

Balance sheets			Income statements			
Wholesale bank				Year 1	Year 2	Year 3
Loans	1,000	Borrowing from treasury 950	Interest income	95	95	95
		Equity 50	Interest expense	(90)	(90)	(90)
	1,000	1,000	Wholesale bank profit	5	5	5
Retail bank						
Lending to treasury	950	Deposits 900	Interest income	76	95	100
		Equity 50	Interest expense	(72)	(90)	(95)
	950	950	Retail bank profit	4	5	5
Treasury (mismatch)						
Lending to wholesale bank	950	Borrowing from 950 retail bank	Interest income	90	90	90
			Interest expense	(76)	(95)	(100)
	950	950	Treasury profit	14	(5)	(10)
Total bank						
Loans	1,000	Deposits 900	Interest income	95	95	95
		Equity 100	Interest expense	(72)	(90)	(95)
	1,000	1,000	Total bank profit	23	5	—

mismatch profits in the first year are an illusion that is discovered only when the forecast of profit takes into account the fact that short-term rates are expected to rise.

The key to handling the problem of mismatch gains or losses is to build a good forecast that takes into account:

- The way spreads are forecasted to change with changing interest rate environments.
- The inflow of funds from loans being paid off and the outflow of funds at new rates as new loans are made.
- The substitution between interest-bearing and non-interest-bearing deposits as interest-rate environments change.
- The portion of mismatch profits that is sustainable because forward rates tend to be higher than their corresponding realized spot rates.

It is not easy to build all of these variables into a forecast. Even if you decide not to do so, it helps to understand the illusion of mismatch profits.

Determining the Quality of Loans

Determining the quality of loans is the most difficult problem for an outsider's valuation, and little information is available to help solve it. Consider loans to emerging market countries or commercial real estate. Although they are sometimes sold in secondary markets for 50 cents on the dollar, this kind of markdown must be viewed with healthy cynicism. The loans that banks keep are probably worth more than those they choose to sell in the secondary market.

The market value of the loan portfolio evolves with changes in interest rates and in the creditworthiness of debt in the bank's loans portfolio. It is possible to find out what percentage of the portfolio is represented by emerging market, leveraged buyout, or commercial real estate lending. These can then be marked to market (at least approximately) as market conditions change.

An Example of Valuing a Bank from the Outside

We valued Citicorp using publicly available 1992 data and Value Line's forecasts of assets, net income, loan loss provisions, and debt balances. We used the income model, and there was no attempt to forecast the effect of the term structure of interest rates on expected cash flows. Our intent is to illustrate how forecasts of the income statement and balance sheet are converted into cash flows to equity—not to provide a detailed (or accurate) forecast. Exhibit 21.7 shows that the total equity value less the market value

Exhibit 21.7   Outside-In Valuation of Citicorp, January 1993

$ billion		
Total equity value		19.0
Value of preferred stock		3.7
DCF estimate of common equity value		15.3
Market value of common stock		13.6
		12% difference

Source: Annual reports; Compustat; Value Line forecasts; McKinsey analysis.

of preferred stock outstanding results in the discounted cash flow value of Citicorp's common stock outstanding. The difference between the DCF estimate and the market value of common is roughly 12 percent. The cost of equity, 12.8 percent, uses a beta of 1.29, an assumed market-risk premium of 5.4 percent, and a 10-year U.S. Treasury bond rate of 5.8 percent. A perpetuity model was used to estimate the continuing value.

Exhibits 21.8, 21.9, and 21.10 show the income statement, the balance sheet, and free cash flow statement, respectively. Exhibit 21.10 also shows a statement of retained earnings, a part of the model that requires more discussion. The discounted cash flow value of equity is the present value of cash flow to equity holders. Normally, one would say that dividends are the same thing as free cash flow, but caution is required. Free cash flow is the cash that *could* be paid as dividends in a given year, not the actual dividends that are paid. The difference between the two is primarily a matter of timing. To build a spreadsheet, one must decide what to do with the cash difference between actual and potential dividends.

There are two ways of handling the problem. One way is to carry surplus cash as "excess marketable securities" and deficits as "unscheduled debt." Under this approach, you must discount actual dividends, not potential dividends, or you will double count earnings on the surplus cash. There is no effect on the value of the company because investments in marketable securities have zero net present value. The other approach is to assume that free cash flow in excess of actual dividends is also disbursed to shareholders. This approach helps keep calculation of key ratios, such as equity as a percent of total assets, as simple as possible You will see that the statement of retained earnings in Exhibit 21.10 starts with the beginning retained earnings, adds net income, subtracts total dividends actually paid, and then subtracts a line called potential dividends to arrive at the end-of-period retained earnings. This process allows us to keep the ratio of equity to total assets at the guideline set by the Bank for International Settlements, and helps to keep the financial statements reasonable to a line manager.

Note that dividend policy has no effect on the company's value in our model. If dividend payout is increased, the potential dividends take up the

Exhibit 21.8 Citicorp—Income Statement

$ millions	1989	1990	1991	1992	Forecast 1993	Forecast 1994	Forecast 1995	Forecast 1996	Forecast 1997	Forecast 1998	Forecast 1999	Forecast 2000	Forecast 2001	Forecast 2002	Forecast 2003
Interest and fees on loans	23,220	24,526	20,440	18,476	17,890	18,256	19,048	20,297	21,626	22,823	23,863	24,950	26,087	27,275	28,518
Other interest income	8,356	6,457	3,914	5,307	6,059	6,689	7,372	7,854	8,386	9,059	9,735	10,410	11,068	11,702	12,298
Total interest revenue	31,576	30,983	24,354	23,783	23,949	24,946	26,420	28,151	30,013	31,883	33,598	35,359	37,155	38,977	40,816
Interest expense	(24,218)	(23,798)	(17,089)	(16,327)	(16,240)	(16,975)	(17,656)	(18,759)	(19,994)	(21,337)	(22,648)	(24,009)	(25,450)	(26,975)	(28,588)
Net interest	7,358	7,185	7,265	7,456	7,709	7,971	8,764	9,392	10,020	10,546	10,950	11,350	11,705	12,002	12,229
Provision for credit losses	(2,521)	(2,662)	(3,890)	(4,146)	(2,637)	(2,182)	(2,200)	(2,264)	(2,326)	(2,455)	(2,566)	(2,683)	(2,806)	(2,933)	(3,067)
Net interest after provisions	4,837	4,523	3,375	3,310	5,072	5,789	6,564	7,129	7,694	8,091	8,383	8,666	8,899	9,069	9,161
Noninterest revenue	5,923	6,745	6,776	7,160	7,281	7,511	7,638	7,926	8,375	8,855	9,365	9,908	10,484	11,096	11,742
Operating expenses	(9,698)	(11,099)	(11,097)	(10,057)	(10,364)	(10,681)	(11,055)	(11,432)	(11,811)	(12,586)	(13,411)	(14,290)	(15,227)	(16,225)	(17,289)
Foreign exchange income/(loss)	471	657	709	1,005	1,136	1,159	1,207	1,283	1,364	1,437	1,501	1,567	1,637	1,709	1,785
Income before taxes	1,533	826	(237)	1,418	3,125	3,778	4,354	4,906	5,622	5,798	5,839	5,851	5,793	5,648	5,400
Income taxes	(1,035)	(508)	(677)	(696)	(1,281)	(1,549)	(1,785)	(2,011)	(2,305)	(2,377)	(2,394)	(2,399)	(2,375)	(2,316)	(2,214)
Income before extraordinary items	498	318	(914)	722	1,844	2,229	2,569	2,894	3,317	3,421	3,445	3,452	3,418	3,332	3,186
Extraordinary items	0	140	457	0	0	0	0	0	0	0	0	0	0	0	0
Net income	498	458	(457)	722	1,844	2,229	2,569	2,894	3,317	3,421	3,445	3,452	3,418	3,332	3,186

Exhibit 21.9 Citicorp—Balance Sheet

$ millions	1989	1990	1991	1992	Forecast 1993	Forecast 1994	Forecast 1995	Forecast 1996	Forecast 1997	Forecast 1998	Forecast 1999	Forecast 2000	Forecast 2001	Forecast 2002	Forecast 2003
Assets															
Excess marketable securities	0	0	0	0	3,085	1,826	0	0	0	0	0	0	0	0	394
Cash and due from banks	6,332	7,098	5,326	5,138	5,241	5,347	5,684	6,044	6,427	6,711	7,008	7,319	7,644	7,983	8,338
Short-term investments	7,659	4,071	4,550	6,381	6,576	6,777	7,221	7,695	8,199	8,737	9,310	9,920	10,570	11,264	12,002
Deposits with banks	13,813	7,546	6,692	6,550	6,615	6,682	6,748	6,816	6,884	6,953	7,022	7,093	7,164	7,235	7,306
Gross loans	162,397	158,571	152,837	141,073	143,974	146,935	156,568	156,834	177,772	185,872	194,341	203,196	212,454	222,134	232,256
Less: provisions and unearned Income	(7,014)	(6,714)	(5,201)	(5,222)	(5,329)	(5,439)	(5,795)	(6,176)	(6,580)	(6,880)	(7,194)	(7,522)	(7,864)	(8,223)	(8,597)
Net loans	155,383	151,857	147,636	135,851	138,645	141,496	150,773	150,658	171,191	178,991	187,147	195,674	204,590	213,912	223,659
Trading securities	9,018	7,518	12,064	17,085	19,897	23,172	26,986	30,428	36,600	42,090	47,983	54,221	60,727	67,407	74,148
Investment securities	14,699	14,075	14,713	15,056	14,820	15,273	15,739	16,771	17,871	19,043	20,291	21,621	23,039	24,550	26,159
Accounts receivable	4,251	3,801	2,917	2,721	2,740	2,854	3,023	3,221	3,434	3,648	3,844	4,045	4,251	4,459	4,670
Investments-permanent	0	501	904	563	593	625	658	693	730	769	810	854	899	947	998
Net tangible fixed assets	3,351	4,010	3,659	3,819	3,846	4,006	4,243	4,520	4,819	5,120	5,395	5,678	5,966	6,259	6,554
Intangible assets	972	910	595	489	489	489	489	489	489	489	489	489	489	489	489
Customer acceptances	3,606	2,165	1,567	1,802	1,838	1,875	1,912	1,951	1,990	2,029	2,070	2,111	2,154	2,197	2,241
Other assets	11,559	13,434	16,297	18,246	18,373	19,138	20,269	21,597	23,026	24,460	25,776	27,127	28,505	29,903	31,314
Total assets	230,643	216,986	216,922	213,701	222,758	229,559	243,746	261,882	281,661	299,040	317,146	336,152	355,998	376,605	398,272
Liabilities and provisions															
Deposits	137,922	142,452	146,475	144,175	148,582	153,123	163,162	173,860	185,259	197,405	210,348	224,139	238,834	254,493	271,179
Short-term borrowing	39,278	22,604	21,566	22,189	24,596	25,091	26,675	28,363	30,160	31,495	32,889	34,347	35,871	37,464	39,129
Long-term borrowing	19,605	19,062	19,221	16,067	15,828	16,499	17,003	18,054	19,397	20,862	22,149	23,490	24,898	26,368	27,894
Additional borrowing	0	0	0	0	0	0	739	4,016	7,611	8,539	9,460	10,252	10,787	10,932	10,932
Acceptances outstanding	3,619	2,276	1,604	1,866	1,903	1,941	1,980	2,020	2,060	2,101	2,143	2,186	2,230	2,275	2,320
Other liabilities	20,103	20,823	18,530	18,187	18,461	18,943	19,332	19,730	20,135	20,550	20,972	21,403	21,844	22,293	22,751
	220,527	207,217	207,396	202,484	209,471	215,597	228,892	246,041	264,623	280,952	297,962	315,818	334,464	353,824	374,205
Shareholders' capital and reserves															
Preferred capital	1,880	1,579	2,177	3,248	3,923	3,923	3,923	3,923	3,923	3,923	3,923	3,923	3,923	3,923	3,923
Common share capital	352	363	372	392	392	392	392	392	392	392	392	392	392	392	392
Share premium	3,016	3,187	3,277	3,598	3,598	3,598	3,598	3,598	3,598	3,598	3,598	3,598	3,598	3,598	3,598
Treasury stock	(421)	(405)	(389)	(389)	(389)	(389)	(389)	(389)	(389)	(389)	(389)	(389)	(389)	(389)	(389)
Retained earnings	5,458	5,204	4,314	4,368	5,764	6,438	7,330	8,317	9,513	10,565	11,660	12,810	14,010	15,257	16,543
Transfers and other movements	(169)	(159)	(225)	0	0	0	0	0	0	0	0	0	0	0	0
Total shareholders' equity	10,116	9,769	9,526	11,217	13,288	13,962	14,854	15,841	17,037	18,089	19,114	20,334	21,534	22,781	24,067
Total liabilities and equity	230,643	216,986	216,922	213,701	222,758	229,559	243,746	261,882	281,661	299,040	317,146	336,152	355,996	376,805	396,272

Exhibit 21.10 Citicorp—Cash Flow

$ millions	1989	1990	1991	1992	Forecast 1993	Forecast 1994	Forecast 1995	Forecast 1996	Forecast 1997	Forecast 1998	Forecast 1999	Forecast 2000	Forecast 2001	Forecast 2002	Forecast 2003
Net income	498	458	(457)	722	1,844	2,229	2,569	2,894	3,317	3,421	3,445	3,452	3,418	3,332	3,186
Increase in assets	(22,977)	13,657	64	3,221	(9,057)	(6,800)	(14,187)	(18,136)	(19,778)	(17,380)	(18,106)	(19,006)	(19,846)	(20,607)	(21,668)
Increase in liabilities	22,765	(13,310)	179	(4,912)	6,987	6,126	13,295	17,150	18,582	16,328	17,010	17,856	18,645	19,360	20,381
Equity cash flow	286	805	(214)	(969)	(227)	1,555	1,676	1,908	2,121	2,370	2,350	2,303	2,218	2,086	1,899
Increase in equity and adjustments	(347)	95	(662)	(1,194)	(675)	0	0	0	0	0	0	0	0	0	0
Dividends paid	633	710	448	225	313	379	617	695	796	821	827	829	820	800	765
Potential dividends	0	0	0	0	134	1,176	1,060	1,213	1,325	1,549	1,523	1,474	1,397	1,286	1,134
Equity cash flow	286	805	(214)	(969)	(227)	1,555	1,676	1,908	2,121	2,370	2,350	2,303	2,218	2,086	1,899
Statement of retained earnings															
Beginning retained earnings	5,593	5,458	5,204	4,314	4,368	5,764	6,438	7,330	8,317	9,513	10,565	11,660	12,810	14,010	15,257
Net income	498	458	(457)	722	1,844	2,229	2,569	2,894	3,317	3,421	3,445	3,452	3,418	3,332	3,186
Dividends paid	(633)	(710)	(448)	(225)	(313)	(379)	(617)	(695)	(796)	(821)	(827)	(829)	(820)	(800)	(765)
Adjustments to retained earnings	0	(2)	15	(443)	0	0	0	0	0	0	0	0	0	0	0
Potential dividends	0	0	0	0	(134)	(1,176)	(1,060)	(1,213)	(1,325)	(1,549)	(1,523)	(1,474)	(1,397)	(1,286)	(1,134)
Ending retained earnings	5,458	5,204	4,314	4,368	5,764	6,438	7,330	8,317	9,513	10,565	11,660	12,810	14,010	15,257	16,543

slack in the statement of retained earnings. Even if actual dividends paid exceed net income, the adjustments line will change sign and the effect will be equivalent to borrowing unscheduled debt. Either way there is no effect on equity free cash flow because it is the sum of actual dividends and potential dividends.

VALUING BANKS FROM THE INSIDE

The main objective of an insider's valuation is to value the bank's business units and to use the results for restructuring or value-based management. Even with complete information, this is a difficult problem because of transfer pricing and shared costs. We will discuss valuation from the inside by focusing on issues concerning the retail bank, the wholesale bank, and the treasury.

The Retail Bank

Most retail banks are in the business of collecting deposits: non-interest bearing demand deposits; interest-bearing demand deposits, money market accounts, and certificates of deposit. For each dollar in deposits, there might be 20 cents in external consumer loans, and the remaining 80 cents is lent to the treasury at a transfer price we call the money rate. The first of several issues central to valuing the retail bank is the correct money rate to use. Next is the value of deposit stability. Conceptual issues concerning capital structure and the cost of equity are also important.

The money rate for the retail bank   The usual economic principle for transfer pricing is to use the market price. But what is the correct opportunity cost for deposits? Logically, it should be the market rate for securities that have the same duration—that is, the same sensitivity of market value to changes in interest rates. Determining the duration of demand deposits and deciding how to match-fund them is tricky. First, most banks confuse the length of time a dollar stays in a demand deposit (that is, its maturity) with the sensitivity of balance values to changes in interest rates (that is, their duration). There is a propensity to choose a money rate that eliminates fluctuations in net interest income rather than to choose a rate that stabilizes shareholder value. Second, you have to decide whether to match-fund to immunize demand deposits or to immunize the entire retail bank against changes in interest rates. In the example in Exhibit 21.11, we have chosen to immunize the entire business unit.

Exhibit 21.11 illustrates how the choice of a money rate affects the stability of net income versus shareholder value. To keep this example simple, we have assumed that the retail bank has deposits that pay no interest but

Exhibit 21.11   Money Rate Affects Stability of Net Income vs. Equity Value

| | Initial situation Interest rate = 10% | | Impact of interest Rate increase to 15% | |
	Book values	Market values	Deposits match-funded with 5yr loan	Deposits match-funded with 3yr loan
Reserves	240	149	119	119
Loans to treasury	1,888	1,888	1,571	1,672
	2,128	2,037	1,691	1,792
Deposits	2,000	1,242	944	944
Equity	128	795	697	798
	2,128	2,037	1,691	1,792
Net income				
Year 1			189	189
Year 2			189	189
Year 3			189	189
Year 4			189	283
Year 5			189	283
			▲	▲
			Net income constant Equity value changes	Net income changes Equity value constant

will be withdrawn in year five. Reserves at the Federal Reserve Bank will be recovered at the same time. The initial situation assumes that the market rate is 10 percent and that loans to the treasury earn 10 percent, so that their market value equals their book value. Reserves and deposits are like zero-coupon notes, so their market value is less than book.

The bank can choose to match-fund deposits at the five-year rate, the time interval equal to their maturity, or the shorter three-year rate. The five-year rate keeps net income constant for five years, but fails to immunize shareholders' wealth. Equity value declines from $795 to $697 when interest rates rise from 10 percent to 15 percent after three years. This happens because the value of assets falls faster than the value of deposits. This problem is alleviated when deposits are match-funded with three-year money, because the interest rate credited to loans to the treasury rises from 10 percent to 15 percent in year four. Consequently, loans to the treasury decline less in value when interest rates rise and the value of equity remains unchanged (immunized against changes in interest rates).

If you wish to centrally manage all interest-rate risk in the treasury, the correct money rate to use for match-funding deposits is the rate that immunizes the value of equity in the retail bank against changes in interest rates. To find this rate, you must take into account the sensitivity of balance levels to changes in interest rates, the ratio of fixed to variable costs into business unit, and the duration of external loans held by the retail bank.

The value of deposit stability   In valuing retail banks, the issue often arises of whether deposit-taking units should receive a credit for deposit stability. The logic for a credit is that depositors understand and value the FDIC insurance attached to demand deposits. When banks get into trouble (for example, when their credit rating is downgraded), customers usually do not withdraw their deposits and place them in safer institutions. As a result, federally insured deposits tend to be stable. Troubled institutions that have fewer insured deposits have to pay higher yields to obtain short-term funding. For example, the Bank of America, with its large deposit base, was able to retain its FDIC-insured deposits during troubled times. But Continental Illinois, without a large deposit base, had to pay relatively higher yields to keep itself funded during a time of crisis.

The benefit of FDIC insurance to a retail bank is directly related to the lower cost of funds that banks have to pay, compared with nonbank institutions, for similar duration liabilities. The lower the credit rating of the bank, the higher the benefit of FDIC insurance to it. The cost of FDIC insurance is deducted directly from the cash flow of the retail bank. The value of FDIC insurance is the difference between the indirect benefit and the direct cost.

FDIC insurance is a put option. In the event of bank default, insured depositors receive the face value of their deposits (up to $100,000) rather than the fraction of the face value they might otherwise receive following bankruptcy or reorganization. The maturity date of the FDIC put option is the interval until completion of the next audit of the bank's assets. Since the FDIC charges a uniform fee, riskier banks receive a subsidy. The value of the subsidy depends primarily on:

- The market value of the bank's assets.
- The variability of the market value of the bank's assets.
- The total debt of the bank.
- The proportion of total debt represented by insured deposits.

Although the procedure is somewhat crude, it is possible to obtain cross-sectional estimates of the per-dollar value of the deposit insurance premium by using a put-option-pricing model. Exhibit 21.12 shows some estimates obtained for a cross-section of banks in 1983.[2] (As you will see, many have since disappeared through mergers and acquisitions, but the example remains valid.) The highest value was 72.41 basis points per dollar of FDIC-insured deposits for the troubled First Pennsylvania Corp., while the average value was 8.08 basis points. Since normal discounted cash flow

[2] E. Ronn and A. Verma, "Pricing Risk-Adjusted Deposit Insurance: An Option-Based Model," *Journal of Finance* (September 1986), pp. 871–895.

Exhibit 21.12   Per-Dollar Value of Federal Deposit Insurance

Bank	Market value of assets ($ million)	Face value of total debt ($ million)	Ratio of assets to debt	Average annual deposit Insurance premium (percent)
First Pennsylvania	3,857	3,866	0.998	0.7241
Crocker National Corp.	15,247	15,195	1.003	0.2666
Continental Illinois	22,287	22,073	1.010	0.1944
Wells Fargo	22,200	21,911	1.013	0.1838
Manufacturers Hanover	34,626	34,313	1.009	0.1269
Bank America	74,642	73,714	1.013	0.1035
First Interstate	37,039	36,405	1.017	0.0856
Chase Manhattan	36,184	35,674	1.014	0.0577
Bankers Trust	20,996	20,266	1.036	0.0568
Citicorp	66,129	63,407	1.143	0.0440
Chemical, New York	32,754	31,718	1.033	0.0270
Security Pacific	29,699	28,682	1.035	0.0162
Mellon	19,864	19,122	1.039	0.0157
NCNB	10,301	9,890	1.042	0.0129
Bank of Boston	10,690	10,231	1.045	0.0106
Morgan, J.P.	28,913	26,981	1.072	0.0001
Average				**0.0808**

Source: Ronn and Verma, 1986.

methods cannot capture the value of deposit stability, the retail bank should be credited with a value equal to its insured deposit balance multiplied by an estimate of the average annual deposit insurance premium.

Capital structure   Exhibit 21.13 shows a simplified balance sheet of a hypothetical retail banking unit. Two broad approaches exist for deciding how much equity should be allocated to the retail banking unit. Since most retail banks have required reserves as a buffer against unanticipated account withdrawals, they would carry less equity than the regulatory requirement. We assume, therefore, that the regulators determine the percentage of equity to be carried on the balance sheet. We could compute

Exhibit 21.13   Balance Sheet of a Retail Banking Unit

Assets	$ million	Liabilities	$ million
Reserves	180	Demand deposits	1,000
Consumer loans	100	Money market accounts	500
Small business loans	100	Certificates of deposit	300
Loans to treasury	+ 1,420	Equity	?
	?		?

equity either as a percentage of total assets, or as a percentage of external assets only (reserves, consumer loans, and small business loan). If we adopt the former approach, then equity is a percentage of a major inter-company account, namely loans to the treasury. This philosophy overallo-cates equity because the total equity of all business units will exceed total equity in the bank. To avoid this aggregation problem, it is better to allo-cate equity to external assets only. Given the numbers in Exhibit 21.13 and assuming that book equity must be 5 percent of external assets, equity in the retail bank would be $19 million and loans to the treasury would be $1.439 billion.

The cost of equity   As always, the cost of equity is the rate of return in-vestors would require for other investments of equivalent risk. Preliminary thinking would indicate that no good market comparable exists for the re-tail banking unit as we have structured it because no stand-alone banks exist with 80 percent of their assets invested in "loans to treasury" (or in government securities that return the money rate, the bank's transfer price). We have deliberately chosen the money rate to immunize the value of share-holders' equity against changes in market rates of interest. Even though in our allocation scheme the book equity of the retail banking unit is only about 1 percent of total assets, it has little interest-rate risk. Reserves serve as a buffer to protect against account withdrawals and loan defaults.

The major risk borne by equity in the retail bank is the portion of loan default risk correlated with the economy, a risk that affects only the exter-nal assets of the retail bank. Since equity is roughly 5 percent of external as-sets (that is, the amount required by regulation in our hypothetical example), equity risk will be roughly the same as for comparable retail banks that have a low ratio of loans to deposits.

The Wholesale Bank

The primary business activity of the wholesale bank is making loans. For each dollar of loans, there might be only 20 cents in deposits; therefore, the wholesale bank funds itself by borrowing from the bank's treasury. The crit-ical issue is how to determine the correct transfer price or money rate the wholesale bank must pay for the funds it uses. Once this issue has been re-solved, we can turn to capital structure and the cost of equity.

The money rate for the wholesale bank   The opportunity cost of funds for a loan portfolio depends on those factors that affect its systematic risk: dura-tion, the sensitivity of its value to changes in interest rates, and the portion of its credit or default risk that cannot be diversified away. Diversifiable credit risk does not affect the opportunity cost of funds; rather, it is reflected in the computation of the expected cash flow to the loan portfolio. Suppose we are

Exhibit 21.14   Expected Payouts for a Low-Quality Loan

Year	Cumulative default rate (percent)	Promised payments ($)	Assumptions
1	1	200	1,000 lent at year 0
2	2	200	When the loan defaults,
3	5	200	nothing can be recovered
4	10	200	
5	20	1,200	

evaluating the opportunity cost of capital for the low-quality loan in Exhibit 21.14. We lend $1,000 in return for promised payments of $200 per year plus repayment of the principal, $1,000, at the end of the fifth year. The promised yield to maturity is 20 percent. However, the cumulative default rate rises each year until only 80 percent of loans of this type reach maturity. Actual cumulative default rates on five- to nine-year-old portfolios of original issue junk bonds were between 19 and 26 percent.[3] We need to figure out the expected yield to maturity, and do this by finding the rate that equates the expected cash flow with the amount we lend out.

$$\$1,000 = \frac{.99(\$200)}{1+y} + \frac{.98(\$200)}{(1+y)^2} + \frac{.95(\$200)}{(1+y)^3} + \frac{.9(\$200)}{(1+y)^4} + \frac{.8(\$1,200)}{(1+y)^5}$$

The expected yield, y, is about 15.8 percent, or 420 basis points lower than the promised yield.

Once the difference between the expected and promised yields has been clarified, you need to decide what money rate to charge the wholesale bank for borrowing from the treasury. If cash-flow estimates forecast charge-offs, then the money rate should be the expected yield for loan portfolios of equivalent credit risk and duration. Alternately, if expected charge-offs are not computed (and by default, all payments are assumed to be made as promised), then the money rate should be the promised yield to maturity for loan portfolios of equivalent credit risk and duration.

A commonly used source of data for yields on loan portfolios of equivalent credit risk and duration is market prices of publicly traded debt issues. Be skeptical when drawing comparisons, because the covenants on publicly held debt issues are often different from bank debt covenants. As a result, a

[3] P. Asquith, D. Mullins Jr., and E. Wolff, "Original Issue High Yield Bonds: Aging Analysis of Defaults, Exchanges, and Calls," *Journal of Finance*, vol. 44, no. 4 (1989), pp. 923–952.

direct comparison of yields may be inappropriate unless they are adjusted for the effect of differences in covenants.

Capital structure   As with the retail bank, the dominant consideration is that the equity for all of the pieces of the bank should equal the total bank equity. We recommend that book equity in the wholesale bank be determined as a percentage of its external assets (usually equal to total assets).

Cost of equity   The cost of equity for the wholesale bank will be less than for the bank as a whole because each loan portfolio is match-funded with a money rate that accounts for both credit risk and interest-rate (duration) risk and the ratio of equity to total assets will be close to the regulatory requirement. Business risk is the primary risk left in the wholesale bank after match-funding. Hence, its cost of equity will be close to the unlevered cost of capital for the entire bank.

Treasury and Headquarters

The bank treasury borrows from the retail bank and lends to the wholesale bank. It also handles the bank's trading business and is responsible for centralized risk management. To organize our discussion of these issues, we cover, in turn, the mismatch problem, centralized risk management, the cost of equity, and the shared-cost problem. We will not discuss the treasury's capital structure except to say that, as before, equity will be allocated to the treasury based on the amount of external assets it holds.

Mismatch profits and losses   The philosophy that we have adopted is to match-fund the retail and wholesale banks as closely as possible for credit and interest-rate (duration) risk. The business reason for doing so is to provide business-unit managers with guidelines that lead directly to positive net present value decisions. For example, a loan officer must earn an all-in rate (fees plus interest) that exceeds a money rate that is adjusted for credit and duration risk. To the extent that the risk and duration of deposits is less than for loans, the treasury unit will record a mismatch profit. We have already illustrated, in Exhibit 21.6 and the accompanying discussion, that mismatch profits can be illusory. Recall that the key to handling mismatch gains or losses is to build a good cash flow forecast that takes into account the way spreads are forecasted to evolve with changing interest-rate environments; the inflow of funds from loans being paid off and the outflow of funds at new rates as new loans are made; the substitution between interest-bearing and non-interest-bearing deposits as interest-rate environments change, and the portion of mismatch profits that are sustainable because forward rates tend to be higher than their corresponding realized rates.

Centralized risk management   Although current mismatch profits or losses may be illusory, the fact that they fluctuate with unexpected changes in the term structure of interest rates means that mismatch creates risk for shareholders. Financial futures positions can be used to offset this mismatch risk. A bank that lends long term and borrows short term can hedge against the risk of an increase in interest rates by taking an offsetting short position in financial futures. This form of risk management is best implemented by the treasury unit, which has a centralized point of view.

The cost of equity   The recommended transfer-pricing mechanism collects interest-rate risks in the treasury unit. If the treasury does nothing to hedge these risks, then the cost of equity will generally be higher for the treasury than for the bank as a whole. To the extent that risks are hedged, the cost of equity will be lower.

The shared-cost problem   Most banks try to use cost accounting systems to push all overhead costs down to the business-unit level. It is better to allocate only those costs that the business units would incur were they standing alone. Unallocated headquarters costs should be kept at headquarters as a cost center. Business units should be encouraged to compare costs of providing services through outsourcing with internal costs. This provides a means of checking that internally provided services are cost-efficient.

The shared-cost problem arises from the fact that multiple business units may use the same resource. For example, a teller may provide services for non-interest-bearing checking, money market accounts, coupon clipping, and mortgage loan payments. If all these activities are within the same business unit—for example, retail banking—no problem results for valuation at the business-unit level. If the costs are shared between business units—for example, retail banking and the trust department—then an effort should be made to allocate the costs on the basis of services used.

SUMMARY

Valuing banks is difficult. From an outsider's point of view, banks are particularly opaque businesses because of blind pool risk in loan portfolios and inadequate information concerning hedging practices. From an insider's perspective, a variety of transfer-pricing schemes are possible. We have discussed an approach that match-funds each business unit for interest rate and credit risk, thereby collecting these risks in a centralized treasury operation where they can be explicitly managed. One of the by-products of this approach is that each match-funded unit, as well as the treasury, has no good market comparables that can be used to estimate the cost of equity. Some guesswork is involved and the answers are soft, requiring the use of ranges rather than point estimates. Nevertheless, the most relevant differences among banking business units are reflected in their expected free cash flow to shareholders, and this is adequately captured in the value process.

22

Valuing Insurance
Companies

In insurance companies, operations and financing are intertwined, as they are in banks. As a result, the equity, rather than enterprise, discounted cash flow approach must be employed to value insurance companies. In addition, insurance companies have unique operating characteristics that warrant further discussion.

INSURANCE COMPANY ACCOUNTING AND ECONOMICS

There are three classes of insurance companies: Life insurance companies offer long-term contracts that pay off in retirement annuities, or as lump sums upon the insured's death, property and casualty companies insure against hazards like worker injuries, automobile accidents, and flood and fire damage, and reinsurance companies take risks from other insurance firms that may be too large for the original underwriters to bear. All three types are heavily regulated and have three accounting systems: statutory accounting for regulatory authorities, generally accepted accounting principles (GAAP) for reports to the public, and a set of accounts for tax authorities. Insurance companies also have two types of ownership. They are either publicly held in the traditional corporate form or held by their policyholders as mutual companies.

Exhibits 22.1 and 22.2 show the balance sheet and income statement for the TransAmerica insurance company prepared under GAAP. We will use the TransAmerica example to talk about the economics and valuation of insurance companies.[1] Any such discussion starts with the fact that insurers

---

[1] We valued TransAmerica as of June 1999, shortly before it was taken over by Aegon.

Exhibit 22.1   TransAmerica—Historical Balance Sheet

$ million	1989	1990	1991	1992	1993	1994	1995	1996	1997	1998
Assets										
Insurance investments	16,444	18,548	20,181	18,294	20,972	22,496	28,027	29,385	32,356	33,656
Cash and short-term investments	74	40	43	22	93	64	68	472	133	159
Excess marketable securities	0	0	0	0	0	0	0	0	0	0
Accounts receivable	1,444	1,535	1,621	885	2,015	2,610	3,130	2,383	2,166	2,254
Net tangible fixed assets	1,230	1,284	1,348	1,388	1,652	2,967	3,274	3,555	3,392	3,527
Intangible assets	570	590	559	511	495	444	402	389	423	423
Deferred policy acquisition costs	1,590	1,724	1,754	1,706	1,929	2,481	1,974	2,138	2,103	2,095
Separate account assets	651	729	867	984	1,367	1,667	2,533	3,528	5,495	9,101
Other assets	7,837	7,333	7,311	8,508	7,527	7,665	8,537	8,024	5,107	7,287
Total assets	29,840	31,784	33,682	32,298	36,051	40,394	47,944	49,875	51,173	58,503
Liabilities and shareholders' equity										
Total debt	8,000	7,528	7,729	7,573	7,704	9,173	10,338	10,328	6,235	8,198
Accounts payable	1,546	1,774	1,800	1,547	1,352	1,628	1,672	1,899	2,097	2,394
Separate account liabilities	651	729	867	984	1,367	1,667	2,533	3,528	5,495	9,101
Other liabilities	164	101	215	277	11	253	116	60	25	0
Total liabilities	10,362	10,132	10,610	10,381	10,434	12,720	14,660	15,816	13,852	19,693
Provisions and reserves	16,550	18,635	20,046	18,616	22,253	24,738	28,785	29,394	31,725	32,388
Minority interest	0	0	0	0	0	200	200	525	715	715
Preferred shares	225	225	225	425	425	316	315	315	0	0
Common shares	76	76	77	79	76	69	68	66	63	62
Share premium	543	559	585	647	475	97	0	83	0	0
Net unrealized capital gains	42	2	101	84	124	(265)	1,080	784	1,534	1,943
Retained earnings	2,047	2,150	2,036	2,100	2,298	2,557	2,866	2,920	3,331	3,746
Transfers and other movements	(4)	5	2	(34)	(35)	(38)	(29)	(28)	(46)	(46)
Total shareholders' equity	2,929	3,017	3,026	3,300	3,363	2,736	4,300	4,141	4,881	5,706
Total liabilities and equity	29,840	31,784	33,682	32,298	36,051	40,394	47,944	49,875	51,173	58,503

receive payments, called premiums, from their customers in advance of paying benefits. So the timing of an insurer's cash flow is reversed from most industrial companies. Industrial companies invest now to capture cash inflows later. Insurance companies may have net cash inflows in the beginning from premium income (although they must pay commissions to their sales force in the first year), followed by a continuous cash stream through most of the life of the policy. Cash payment obligations are concentrated in the latter part of the life of the policy. This is why insurance companies are heavily regulated—to protect policyholders from the threat of an insurer's insolvency. If the company goes bankrupt, policyholders may lose much of their investment in promised insurance benefits. One reason that insurance companies like to maintain high credit ratings (e.g., AAA or Aa) is that policyholder confidence in the insurance company helps to attract business.

The largest liability of insurance companies is provisions and reserves—$32.4 billion for TransAmerica in 1998. This represents the present value of expected future obligations of the company—annuities and death benefits, net of the present value of premiums expected to be paid by policyholders.

Exhibit 22.2   TransAmerica—Historical Income Statement

$ million	1989	1990	1991	1992	1993	1994	1995	1996	1997	1998
Net premium income	3,195	2,903	2,946	1,221	1,256	1,495	1,863	1,848	1,818	1,847
Interest income (investments)	1,434	1,640	1,764	1,578	1,750	1,783	1,990	2,102	2,169	2,274
Realized capital gains	61	20	6	8	39	23	53	39	42	362
Interest income (loans)	1,213	1,173	1,056	1,014	990	1,042	1,165	1,198	503	705
Other revenues	931	967	1,043	1,167	798	1,012	1,030	1,040	1,195	1,241
Total revenues	6,834	6,703	6,815	4,988	4,833	5,354	6,101	6,228	5,726	6,429
Benefits and claims	(3,462)	(3,561)	(3,715)	(2,450)	(2,146)	(2,356)	(2,859)	(2,806)	(2,811)	(2,878)
Amortization of acquisition costs	(459)	(461)	(529)	(135)	(233)	(182)	(191)	(269)	(265)	(269)
Other expense	(1,655)	(1,553)	(1,791)	(1,183)	(1,195)	(1,451)	(1,536)	(1,595)	(1,551)	(1,789)
Total operating expenses	(5,577)	(5,576)	(6,035)	(3,768)	(3,574)	(3,990)	(4,586)	(4,669)	(4,628)	(4,936)
Interest expense	(804)	(758)	(637)	(569)	(512)	(574)	(717)	(690)	(421)	(429)
Income before exceptional provisions	454	369	143	651	748	791	799	868	678	1,063
Exceptional provisions	0	0	0	(91)	(147)	(101)	(94)	(283)	(16)	0
Income before taxes	454	369	143	560	601	690	705	585	662	1,063
Income taxes	(122)	(103)	(44)	(218)	(150)	(262)	(235)	(129)	(130)	(356)
Income before extraordinary items	332	266	99	343	451	428	471	456	532	707
Extraordinary items	0	0	(49)	(100)	(73)	(1)	0	0	262	0
Net income	332	266	50	243	377	427	471	456	794	707
Beginning retained earnings	1,875	2,047	2,150	2,036	2,100	2,298	2,557	2,866	2,920	3,331
Net income	332	266	50	243	377	427	471	456	794	707
Common dividends	(144)	(148)	(152)	(157)	(156)	(143)	(137)	(132)	(128)	(125)
Preferred dividends	(17)	(16)	(12)	(22)	(24)	(25)	(18)	(17)	(3)	0
Potential dividends	0	0	0	0	0	0	0	0	0	0
Adjustments	0	0	(0)	0	(0)	0	(7)	(253)	(253)	(167)
Ending retained earnings	2,047	2,150	2,036	2,100	2,298	2,557	2,866	2,920	3,331	3,746

The following example (not TransAmerica) illustrates how reserves are calculated:

Present value of	Year 0	Year 1	Year 2	Year 3	Year 4	Year 5
Benefits	$3,928	$4,104	$4,284	$4,469	$4,658	$0
Net premiums	3,928	3,209	2,457	1,672	853	0
Reserves	0	895	1,827	2,797	3,805	0

As of year zero, there is a stream of future insurance premiums that are due to the insurance company. In this example, the present value of these net premiums equals the present value of future benefits. At the end of year one, there is one less payment due, so the present value of future premium payments drops. Meanwhile the expected death benefit has come one year closer, so its present value increases. The difference between the present value of the future benefits and the present value of the future premiums is called a reserve. Reserves are liabilities of the insurance company and are added to the liabilities side of the balance sheet. As premiums are paid, the cash is invested on the assets side of the balance sheet. In year five, benefits are paid and the reserve is removed from the liability account. Similarly, the company sustains an equivalent decline in assets as cash is used to pay policyholders.

As this example illustrates, when new insurance business is written, provisions and reserves will increase. This significant liability is undoubtedly part of the operations of the insurance company. Since the net present value of writing new policies is usually positive, reserves are a liability that create value for shareholders. For this reason, it makes sense to use an equity rather than an enterprise approach for valuing insurance companies. The free cash flows to equity holders are discounted at the cost of equity.

The major asset of TransAmerica in 1998 was a portfolio of investments recorded at $33.7 billion on the balance sheet. Roughly 90 percent of these investments were in fixed income securities such as bonds. Insurance companies create value primarily in two ways. First, on the liabilities side of the balance sheet, they try to write policies so that the present value of the expected obligations is less than the present value of the monies flowing from the premiums (net of expenses such as commissions). Second, on the assets side of the balance sheet, they can create value by investing the upfront cash received from policyholders at rates of return higher than required given their risk.

Looking at TransAmerica's 1998 income statement, you will note that net premium income from insurance policies was $1.8 billion pre-tax, and that net interest income, at $2.3 billion, was even higher. Benefits and claims ($2.9 billion) exceed net premium income. However, the bottom-line profit is positive $1.1 billion profit before taxes. It is not uncommon for benefits and claims to exceed premiums. You could say that an insurance company's profit comes from the time value of holding the policyholder's cash until claims are paid. Most insurance companies do not try to create mismatch profits by holding a securities and loan portfolio that is longer in duration than the duration of their liabilities. As mentioned in Chapter 21 on the valuation of banks, duration mismatch is not a source of value. Short-term liabilities have to be rolled over at higher rates, making the near-term mismatch profit illusory because it is offset by expected longer-term losses.

Some of the other assets and liabilities use unusual terminology, and so a few more definitions would be useful. Separate accounts of $5.5 billion appear on both the assets and liabilities side of the balance sheet. These accounts represent other people's money that is managed by the insurance company. Because this money has no net effect on the insurance company's balance sheet, it is carried in equal amounts as both an asset and a liability. Deferred policy acquisition costs are capitalized commission expenses that are not yet written off. Unearned premium reserves are premiums advanced to the insurance company by its policyholders. Provisions are cash set aside to cover potential, but unrealized, credit losses on the loans made by the insurance company, deferred taxes, and pension liabilities. Finally, reserves untaxed represents cumulative allocations set aside as reserves for business contingencies and are used by European and Japanese insurance companies (not usually permitted under U.S. GAAP).

Before discussing the calculation of cash flow, we describe some of the differences between the two accounting methods that insurance companies must employ: Statutory accounting statements are required by state regulatory agencies and GAAP statements are required by the Securities and Exchange Commission. Statutory accounting emphasizes the present solvency of an insurance company, not its potential for profit:

> Statutory accounting principles (SAP) attempt to determine the insurer's ability to satisfy its obligations to policyholders and creditors at all times. Because of the focus on solvency, the statutory balance sheet represents assets and liabilities that generally are valued on a conservative basis. Accordingly, certain illiquid assets, such as furniture and fixtures as well as capitalized contract acquisition costs, are assigned no value (and are referred to as nonadmitted assets). With respect to liabilities, SAP generally require formula-driven reserves relating to invested assets and benefit reserve liabilities using statutory tables or other conservative assumptions.[2]

Generally accepted accounting principles say that financial statements should be prepared on a going-concern basis. GAAP statements are aimed at providing investors with the information they need to make prudent decisions about whether to keep or acquire shares in a particular insurance company. The regulations governing these reports are not designed to secure and demonstrate the company's solvency, but to make clear their potential for increased earnings, larger dividends, and overall growth.[3]

Exhibit 22.3 summarizes the major differences between statutory and GAAP accounting. The first item is contract acquisition costs such as commissions paid to salespersons. Following its conservative nature, statutory accounting expenses all of these costs as incurred. GAAP accounting attempts to match these upfront expenses with the revenue stream that they generate for the insurance company—the premiums paid each year by policyholders. GAAP defers a portion of these acquisition costs and amortizes them relative to the revenue generated.

As mentioned, nonadmitted assets are excluded from the statutory balance sheet and are charged to surplus. This is the equivalent to the book equity that most of us are familiar with in industrial companies. These same nonadmitted assets are capitalized and depreciated under GAAP, similar to industrial companies.

---

[2] American Institute of Certified Public Accountants, *Proposed Audit and Accounting Guide—Life and Health Insurance Entities* (New York, 1998).

[3] S. Mooney and L. Cohen, *Basic Concepts of Accounting and Taxation of Property/Casualty Insurance Companies*, 4th ed., Insurance Information Institute (Addison Shuster, 1995), p. 85.

Exhibit 22.3   Major Differences between Statutory and GAAP Accounting

	Statutory accounting	GAAP accounting
Contract acquisition costs	Charged to expense when incurred	Deferred and amortized in relation to the revenue generated if recoverable from such revenue
Nonadmitted assets, such as furniture and equipment	Excluded from the balance sheet and charged to surplus	Capitalized and depreciated according to FASB rules
Policy reserves — life insurance	Based on actuarial assumptions that are in accordance with or stronger than those called for in policy revisions	Based on actuarial assumptions that are "reasonable and realistic" – generally lower than statutory reserves
Valuation of preferred stock	At cost	Market value
Valuation of bonds not held to maturity	Amortized cost	Market value

The major liability of insurance companies is the present value of their expected future insurance obligations. This liability is called policy reserves, or reserves for future obligations. Usually the reserves on the statutory financial statements are larger than on the GAAP statements because the assumptions used accord with or are stronger than those called for in the policy provisions.

The last two items involve assets held by the insurance company. Under statutory accounting, bonds that the insurance company does not have the intention or ability to hold to maturity are recorded at amortized cost rather than market value. Equity securities are recorded at the value published by the Valuations of Securities manual of statutory accounting. Under GAAP, market values are recorded.

FREE CASH FLOWS TO EQUITY HOLDERS

This section defines free cash flow to the equity holders and demonstrates that identical estimates of free cash flow may be obtained from either statutory or GAAP accounting.

Exhibit 22.4 is the definition of free cash flows for an insurance company. It starts with cash from operations (income statement), then adds sources of funds and subtracts uses of funds resulting from changes in the balance sheet.

Note that when using an equity approach for valuation, liabilities such as debt and reserves are treated as part of the operations of the insurance company, not as part of its financing. Interest expense is deducted from net income before arriving at an estimate of cash from operations, and increases in the amount of debt outstanding are treated as a cash inflow from

Exhibit 22.4   Definition of Free Cash Flows to Equity

From the balance sheet Cash from operations	Sources	Uses
Net premium income	Increase in accounts payable	Increase in investments and cash
− Amortization of deferred acquisition costs	+ Increases in debt	+ Increases in accounts receivable
− Benefits and claims	+ Increase in other liabilities	+ Increases in fixed assets
+ Increase in insurance liabilities and reserves[1]	+ Increase in preferred stock	+ Increases in deferred acquisition costs
= Net insurance income (loss)		+ Increases in other assets
+ Investing income		+ Increase in unearned premium reserve and other provisions
+ Other income		
− Other expense		
− Interest expense		
− Income taxes		
= Net income		
+ Capital gains		
+ Extraordinary items		
− Preferred dividends		
− Minority interest		
= Cash from operations	**+ Sources**	**− Uses**

1 From the balance sheet.

the perspective of equity holders. When using the equity approach, remember that changes in the capital structure affect not only the cost of equity, but also the equity cash flows.

Next, we turn to a comparison of free cash flow estimates that start with either GAAP or statutory financial statements, but end up with the same free cash flow regardless of accounting method.

Exhibit 22.5 gives GAAP and statutory statements for a hypothetical insurance company in 1998 and 1999. The first difference between them is in the line called *investment income.* The two methods of recording investment income differ, both for debt and equity securities. In the example, we assume the company holds only debt securities in its investment portfolio. GAAP subdivides debt into three categories. The first is debt that is held to maturity. The statutory accounting treatment is to value these securities at their estimated value, given amortized cost. In other words, if a five-year bond is purchased at $900 when its face value is $1000, then after one year it would be deemed to be worth about $920 (as the $100 difference is amortized at one-fifth of $100 each year). According to GAAP, both realized and unrealized capital gains are recorded as other income on a pretax basis on the income statement. The second category is called *trading securities.* They are recorded at fair market value at the end of each fiscal year and both realized and unrealized capital gains go to the income statement. The third category is called *available for sale.* In this category, unrealized gains are

Exhibit 22.5 GAAP and Statutory Statements

GAAP statements	1998 ($ millions)	1999 ($ millions)	Statutory statements	1998 ($ millions)	1999 ($ millions)
Income statement			**Statement of operations**		
Premiums		80.0	Earned premium		80.0
Interest income		47.0	Interest income		47.0
Capital gains		5.0	Capital gains		3.0
Total revenues		132.0	Total revenues		130.0
Benefits and claims		(90.0)	Benefits		(50.0)
Amortization of deferred acquisition costs		(27.0)	Increase in policy reserves		(45.0)
			Commissions		(35.0)
Interest expense		(0.0)	Interest expense		(0.0)
Total benefits and expenses		(117.0)	Total costs		(130.0)
Income before tax		15.0	Net gain before tax		0.0
Income tax		(5.3)	Income taxes		0.0
Net income		9.8	Net gain		0.0
Balance sheet			**Balance sheet**		
Assets			**Assets**		
Cash	10.0	25.0	Cash	10.0	25.0
Investments	1000.0	1002.0	Investments	1000.0	1000.0
Deferred policy Acquisition cost	100.0	108.0	Total assets	1010.0	1025.0
Total assets	1110.0	1135.0			
Liabilities			**Liabilities**		
Reserves	800.0	840.0	Reserves	900.0	945.0
Debt	0.0	0.0	Debt	0.0	0.0
Deferred taxes	10.0	15.2			
Total liabilities	810.0	855.2			
Equity			**Capital and surplus**		
Capital stock	50.0	50.0	Capital stock	50.0	50.0
Retained earnings	250.0	229.8	Unassigned surplus	60.0	30.0
Total	250.0	279.8	Capital and surplus	110.0	80.0
Total liabilibies and equity	1110.0	1135.0	Total liabilities and capital	1010.0	1025.0

included (net of applicable deferred taxes) as a separate component of shareholder's equity until the gains or losses are realized.

Statutory accounting practices use the amortized-cost approach for all debt, and report realized capital gains on an amortized basis over the remaining life of the debt asset that was sold. Statutory accounting reporting of capital gains is more conservative than GAAP reporting. This explains why investment income is only $3 on the statutory statements compared with $5 on the GAAP statements. The $2 difference is added to the investment assets on the balance sheet (because the $2 is an unrealized capital gain). This $2 increase in investments becomes a cash outflow in the free cash flow statement, offsetting the higher reported income.

The next major difference between GAAP and statutory accounting is in costs. Under statutory accounting, costs add up to $130 but GAAP totals only $117. The conservatism of statutory practices is again revealed. Commissions of $35 are expensed immediately under statutory conventions, but not under GAAP. Under GAAP, the $35 of new deferred acquisition costs (i.e., commissions) is amortized over five years, at the rate of $7 per year. The $100 of existing deferred acquisition costs is being amortized over five years at the rate of $20 per year. Total amortization of deferred acquisition costs is $27 in 1999 on the GAAP statements. The actual cash paid for commissions is the same and the free cash flow statement will reflect the actual cash paid regardless of the accounting. Tax effects of this and other line-item differences are reflected in the change in deferred taxes item on the free cash flow statement.

Whether we look at GAAP or statutory accounting, the major liability category is called *reserves*. The level of reserves under statutory accounting is higher ($900 compared with $800 at the beginning of the period) and the change in the level of reserves is also higher ($45 compared with $40). The explanation for the differences in reserves between GAAP and statutory accounting is due mainly to the more conservative discount rates used under the latter approach.

The result of these differences is that GAAP reports higher operating income than statutory accounting, but also greater net investment added to the balance sheet (taking into consideration all balance sheet items such as investments, deferred acquisition costs, and deferred taxes). The net is that free cash flow to equity holders is identical—as it must be—regardless of which accounting treatment is used, as shown in Exhibit 22.6.

Dividend policy does not affect either the timing or the value of free cash flow. We assume that all free cash flow in Exhibit 22.6 is paid out. In our example, distributions to shareholders are $30, even though net income is only $9.8 (part of the distribution could be share repurchases). If the company paid only $5 in dividends, the company's cash balance would increase by the $25 and the value of the company would also be $25 higher because the present value of the interest income on the extra cash would equal $25. The shareholders would be indifferent; they either get $25 more in distributions today or shares worth $25 more.

Exhibit 22.6   Free Cash Flow to Equity Holders

GAAP statements	1999 ($ millions)	Statutory statements	1999 ($ millions)
Net income	9.8	Net income	0.0
Change in cash	(15.0)	Change in cash	(15.0)
Change in investments	(2.0)	Change in investments	0.0
Change in deferred policy acquisition costs	(8.0)	Change in reserves	45.0
Change in reserves	40.0	Free cash flow to equity	30.0
Change in deferred taxes	5.3		
Free cash flow to equity	30.0		

AN EXAMPLE: VALUING TRANSAMERICA

The steps in valuing an insurance company are the same as in valuing an industrial company. First, we gather the historical income statement and balance sheets and compute the free cash flows and useful ratios. This enables us to develop an historical perspective, which with an understanding of industry structure and comparable companies, helps to forecast the financial statements.

Exhibit 22.7   TransAmerica—Historical Cash Flow Statement

$ million	1990	1991	1992	1993	1994	1995	1996	1997	1998
Net premium income	2,903	2,946	1,221	1,256	1,495	1,863	1,848	1,818	1,847
Amortization of deferred acquisition costs	(461)	(529)	(135)	(233)	(182)	(191)	(269)	(265)	(269)
Insurance profit before benefits and claims	2,441	2,417	1,087	1,023	1,313	1,672	1,579	1,553	1,578
Benefits and claims	(3,561)	(3,715)	(2,450)	(2,146)	(2,356)	(2,859)	(2,806)	(2,811)	(2,878)
Increase in insurance liabilities and reserves	2,157	1,627	(910)	3,690	2,780	3,162	649	1,599	194
Net cash benefits and claims paid	(1,405)	(2,088)	(3,361)	1,544	423	303	(2,156)	(1,212)	(2,684)
Net insurance cash flow	1,037	329	(2,274)	2,567	1,736	1,974	(577)	341	(1,106)
Net interest income	1,640	1,764	1,578	1,750	1,783	1,990	2,102	2,169	2,274
Other income	2,140	2,099	2,181	1,788	2,054	2,195	2,238	1,697	1,946
Other expense	(1,553)	(1,791)	(1,183)	(1,195)	(1,451)	(1,536)	(1,595)	(1,551)	(1,789)
Exceptional income and provisions	0	0	(91)	(147)	(101)	(94)	(283)	(16)	0
Income taxes	(103)	(44)	(218)	(150)	(262)	(235)	(129)	(130)	(356)
Realized capital gains	20	6	8	39	23	53	39	42	362
Extraordinary items	0	(49)	(100)	(73)	(1)	0	0	262	0
Cash from operations	3,181	2,314	(98)	4,579	3,781	4,349	1,796	2,814	1,330
Other cash sources									
Increase in accounts payable and other liabilities	164	140	(191)	(461)	517	(92)	171	163	272
Increase in unearned premium and other reserves	(72)	(216)	(519)	(53)	(295)	885	(41)	732	469
Total other cash sources	93	(76)	(710)	(513)	222	793	130	894	742
Cash uses									
Increase in investments	2,104	1,633	(1,887)	2,678	1,525	5,530	1,359	2,970	1,301
Increase in cash and short-term investments	(34)	3	(21)	71	(28)	3	404	(339)	27
Increase in accounts receivable	92	86	(736)	1,130	595	520	(747)	(217)	88
Increase in fixed assets	54	63	40	265	1,315	306	282	(163)	135
Increase in intangible and other assets	(484)	(54)	1,149	(996)	86	830	(526)	(2,884)	2,180
Increase in deferred acquisiton costs	134	30	(48)	224	551	(506)	164	(36)	(8)
Total cash uses	1,866	1,761	(1,502)	3,371	4,043	6,684	936	(669)	3,723
Cash flow before financing	1,408	477	694	695	(41)	(1,542)	990	4,377	(1,651)
Increase in debt	(472)	201	(156)	131	1,469	1,165	(9)	(4,093)	1,963
Minority interest	0	0	0	0	200	0	325	190	0
Increase in preferred stock	0	0	200	0	(109)	(1)	0	(315)	0
Interest expense	(758)	(637)	(569)	(512)	(574)	(717)	(690)	(421)	(429)
Equity cash flow	178	41	169	314	946	(1,094)	616	(262)	(118)
Dividends	164	164	179	180	168	155	149	130	125
Increase in common stock and adjustments to retained earnings	14	(123)	(10)	134	778	(1,250)	466	(392)	(243)
Equity cash flow	178	41	169	314	946	(1,094)	616	(262)	(118)

Next, we estimate the cost of equity, which is the appropriate opportunity cost of capital for free cash flows to equity holders. Then we make assumptions about the long-run rate of return on new capital invested in the business and regarding growth in earnings to estimate the continuing value of cash flows beyond the explicit forecast period.

Historical Perspective

Exhibits 22.1 and 22.2 showed the historical income statements and balance sheets for TransAmerica. Exhibits 22.7 and 22.8 show the free cash flow to equity and selected ratios. Net premium income has declined in absolute terms from $3.2 billion in 1989 to $1.8 billion in 1998, and as a percentage of

Exhibit 22.8   TransAmerica—Historical Key Ratios

Percent	1990	1991	1992	1993	1994	1995	1996	1997	1998
Operations									
Net premium growth	(9.1)	1.3	(38.5)	2.8	19.1	24.0	(0.0)	(1.0)	1.0
Investment income/investments	9.9	9.5	7.8	9.6	8.5	8.8	7.5	7.3	7.0
Capital gain/total invested	0.1	0.0	0.0	0.2	0.1	0.2	0.1	0.1	1.1
Capital gain (inc. unrealized gain)/ total invested	(0.1)	0.6	0.0	0.4	(1.7)	6.2	(0.9)	2.7	2.4
Interest (lending) income growth	(3.3)	(10.0)	(4.0)	(2.3)	5.2	11.9	2.8	(58.0)	40.3
Other income growth	3.9	7.9	11.9	(31.6)	26.8	1.7	1.0	14.8	3.9
Total revenue growth	(1.9)	1.7	(26.8)	(3.1)	10.8	13.9	2.1	(8.0)	12.3
Expenses									
Net claims/net premiums	122.7	126.1	200.6	170.9	157.6	153.5	151.8	154.6	155.8
Amortiz of def acq cost/net premiums	15.9	18.0	11.0	18.5	12.2	10.3	14.5	14.6	14.6
Other expense/other revenue	72.6	85.3	54.2	66.8	70.7	70.0	71.2	91.4	91.9
Operating margin	16.8	11.4	24.5	26.1	25.5	24.8	25.0	19.2	23.2
Taxes and financing									
Corporate tax rate	35.0	35.0	35.0	35.0	35.0	35.0	35.0	35.0	35.0
Taxes/pre-tax income	27.8	30.5	38.8	25.0	38.0	33.3	22.0	19.6	33.5
Interest expense/debt	9.5	8.5	7.4	6.8	7.4	7.8	6.7	4.1	6.9
Common dividends/net income	55.6	303.4	64.4	41.4	33.4	29.2	29.0	16.1	17.7
Debt/equity	249.6	255.4	229.5	229.0	335.3	240.4	249.4	127.7	143.7
Working capital									
Operating cash/total revenues	0.6	0.6	0.4	1.9	1.2	1.1	7.6	2.3	2.5
Accounts receivable/net premiums	22.9	23.8	17.7	41.7	48.7	51.3	38.3	37.8	35.1
Net fixed assets/total revenues	19.2	19.8	27.8	34.2	55.4	53.7	57.1	59.2	54.9
Def policy acq cost/net premiums	59.4	59.5	139.6	153.6	165.9	106.0	115.7	115.7	113.4
Growth of separate assets	11.9	18.9	13.6	38.8	22.0	52.0	39.3	55.7	65.6
Interest (lending) income/other assets	16.0	14.4	11.9	13.2	13.6	13.7	14.9	9.8	9.7
Accounts payable/total revenues	26.5	26.4	31.0	28.0	30.4	27.4	30.5	36.6	37.2
Other liabilities/total revenues	1.5	3.2	5.6	0.2	4.7	1.9	1.0	0.4	0.0
Reserves and investments									
Net cash benefits paid/premiums	48.4	70.9	275.1	(122.9)	(28.3)	(16.3)	116.7	66.7	145.3
Net additions to reserves/premiums	197.0	181.3	126.1	464.7	343.5	323.2	187.0	242.6	166.3
Provisions/insurance reserves	2.3	1.3	1.9	1.4	0.0	3.2	3.0	5.3	6.8
Investments/insurance reserves, times	1.06	1.05	1.00	0.96	0.91	1.00	1.03	1.07	1.11

(continued)

Exhibit 22.8 (Continued)

$ million	1990	1991	1992	1993	1994	1995	1996	1997	1998
Equity analysis									
Equity/investment assets	16.3%	15.0%	18.0%	16.0%	12.2%	15.3%	14.1%	15.1%	17.0%
Equity/premiums	103.9%	102.7%	270.2%	267.9%	183.0%	230.8%	224.0%	268.5%	308.9%
Actual equity before adjustments	3,032	3,038	3,322	3,387	2,761	4,318	4,158	4,884	5,872
Required equity	3,017	3,026	3,300	3,363	2,736	4,300	4,141	4,881	5,706
Equity infusion (distribution)	(16)	(12)	(22)	(24)	(25)	(18)	(17)	(3)	(167)
Result Ratios									
ROE	8.8%	1.7%	7.4%	11.2%	15.6%	10.9%	11.0%	16.3%	12.4%
ROA (net income/total assets)	0.8%	0.1%	0.8%	1.0%	1.1%	1.0%	0.9%	1.6%	1.2%
GAAP Loss ratio approximation	122.7%	126.1%	200.6%	170.9%	157.6%	153.5%	151.8%	154.6%	155.8%
GAAP Underwriting expense ratio approximation	15.9%	18.0%	11.0%	18.5%	12.2%	10.3%	14.5%	14.6%	14.6%
GAAP Combined ratio approximation	138.6%	144.0%	211.6%	189.4%	169.8%	163.7%	166.4%	169.2%	170.4%
GAAP Operating ratio approximation	38.8%	26.5%	99.9%	100.3%	91.3%	81.4%	84.3%	60.4%	80.8%
GAAP Premium to surplus approximation	104.0%	105.2%	42.5%	42.7%	61.8%	46.7%	48.3%	37.2%	32.4%
Premiums earned/reserves	16.5%	15.4%	6.7%	5.7%	6.0%	6.7%	6.5%	6.0%	6.1%
Premiums/investment assets	15.7%	14.6%	6.7%	6.0%	6.6%	6.6%	6.3%	5.6%	5.5%
Reserves/total assets	0.6	0.6	0.6	0.6	0.6	0.6	0.6	0.6	0.6
Reserves/premiums	6.4	6.8	15.2	17.7	16.5	15.5	15.9	17.5	17.5
Approx cost of funds (UW loss/avg float)	1.8%	1.8%	1.9%	1.5%	1.2%	1.2%	1.1%	1.1%	1.1%
Cash benefits paid/premiums	48.4%	70.9%	275.1%	–122.9%	–28.3%	–16.3%	116.7%	66.7%	145.3%
Cash acquisition cost/premiums	20.5%	19.0%	7.1%	36.4%	49.1%	–16.9%	23.4%	12.6%	14.1%

total revenues from 47 percent to 29 percent. Expenses also fell, declining from $5.6 billion to $4.9 billion. Net income grew from $332 million to $707 million. The most important measures are total revenue growth, which had been slightly negative, and return on equity, which averaged 10.7 percent per year.

Forecasting Free Cash Flows

We forecasted the income statement and balance sheet for TransAmerica for 1999–2008, based on our historical perspective and analysts' reports. The results are shown in Exhibits 22.9 to 22.12. We forecast that total revenue growth would level out at about 2.6 percent per year in nominal terms. The forecasted return on equity starts at about 12 percent in 1999, but gradually declines to about 8 percent in 2008.

Note that the definition of free cash flows to the equity holders of an insurance company is similar to the definition of the cash flow to shareholders of banks. It is the cash that could be paid to shareholders, but is not necessarily paid out as dividends during the same year that it is earned. If we turn to year 2002 in the forecasted cash-flow statement in Exhibit 22.11, we see that $449 million is the forecasted equity free cash flow, but only $172 million are the actual forecast dividends. The remainder, $277 million, represents potential dividends that we assume are also paid out. These

Exhibit 22.9   TransAmerica—Forecast Balance Sheet

$ million	Forecast 1999	Forecast 2000	Forecast 2001	Forecast 2002	Forecast 2003	Forecast 2004	Forecast 2005	Forecast 2006	Forecast 2007	Perpetuity
Assets										
Insurance investments	32,209	32,481	32,758	33,042	33,332	33,628	33,930	34,240	34,556	35,209
Cash and short-term investments	126	127	129	132	135	138	141	144	147	155
Excess marketable securities	195	0	0	0	0	0	0	0	0	0
Accounts receivable	2,213	2,220	2,263	2,312	2,363	2,415	2,470	2,526	2,585	2,709
Net tangible fixed assets	3,463	3,474	3,540	3,617	3,697	3,779	3,865	3,953	4,045	4,239
Intangible assets	423	423	423	423	423	423	423	423	423	423
Deferred policy acquisition costs	2,127	2,174	2,222	2,271	2,320	2,372	2,424	2,477	2,532	2,644
Separate account assets	10,011	10,512	11,037	11,589	12,169	12,777	13,416	14,087	14,791	16,307
Other assets	7,867	8,339	8,839	9,370	9,932	10,528	11,160	11,829	12,539	14,089
Total assets	58,635	59,749	61,212	62,756	64,370	66,060	67,828	69,680	71,618	75,775
Liabilities and shareholders' equity										
Scheduled debt	8,198	8,198	8,198	8,198	8,198	8,198	8,198	8,198	8,198	8,198
New debt	0	291	861	1,472	2,117	2,799	3,519	4,281	5,086	6,837
Total debt	8,198	8,489	9,059	9,670	10,315	10,997	11,717	12,479	13,284	15,035
Accounts payable	2,351	2,358	2,404	2,456	2,510	2,566	2,624	2,684	2,746	2,877
Separate account liabilities	10,011	10,512	11,037	11,589	12,169	12,777	13,416	14,087	14,791	16,307
Other liabilities	0	0	0	0	0	0	0	0	0	0
Total liabilities	20,560	21,359	22,500	23,715	24,993	26,339	27,757	29,249	30,821	34,219
Provisions and reserves	32,617	32,892	33,173	33,460	33,754	34,054	34,360	34,673	34,994	35,655
Minority interest	715	715	715	715	715	715	715	715	715	715
Preferred shares	0	0	0	0	0	0	0	0	0	0
Common shares	62	62	62	62	62	62	62	62	62	62
Share premium	0	0	0	0	0	0	0	0	0	0
Net unrealized capital gains	1,943	1,943	1,943	1,943	1,943	1,943	1,943	1,943	1,943	1,943
Retained earnings	2,784	2,824	2,864	2,906	2,949	2,993	3,037	3,083	3,129	3,225
Transfers and other movements	(46)	(46)	(46)	(46)	(46)	(46)	(46)	(46)	(46)	(46)
Total shareholders' equity	4,743	4,783	4,824	4,866	4,909	4,952	4,997	5,042	5,089	5,185
Total liabilities and equity	58,635	59,749	61,212	62,756	64,370	66,060	67,828	69,680	71,618	75,775

could have been reinvested in cash or debt reduction with no effect on value because the present value of the interest income or expense associated with the change would equal the change in cash or debt.

Determining the Cost of Equity

The beta for TransAmerica was 0.78 at the time of valuation, June 1999. Using the Capital Asset Pricing Model, a rate of return on 10-year U.S. Treasury bonds of 5.1 percent, and a market risk premium of 5.5 percent, we estimate the cost of equity at 9.4 percent:

$$k_s = r_f + [E(r_m) - r_f] Beta$$
$$= 5.1\% + [5.5\%].78 = 9.4\%$$

Exhibit 22.10 TransAmerica—Forecast Income Statement

$ million	Forecast 1999	Forecast 2000	Forecast 2001	Forecast 2002	Forecast 2003	Forecast 2004	Forecast 2005	Forecast 2006	Forecast 2007	Perpetuity
Revenues										
Net premium income	1,888	1,929	1,972	2,015	2,059	2,105	2,151	2,198	2,247	2,346
Interest income (investments)	2,367	2,277	2,283	2,302	2,322	2,343	2,364	2,385	2,407	2,452
Realized capital gains	44	42	42	42	43	43	44	44	44	45
Interest income (loans)	747	792	840	890	944	1,000	1,060	1,124	1,191	1,338
Other revenues	1,266	1,291	1,317	1,343	1,370	1,398	1,426	1,454	1,483	1,543
Total revenues	6,312	6,331	6,453	6,593	6,738	6,888	7,044	7,205	7,372	7,725
Expenses										
Benefits and claims	(2,926)	(2,952)	(3,016)	(3,083)	(3,151)	(3,220)	(3,291)	(3,363)	(3,437)	(3,590)
Amortization of acquisition costs	(275)	(281)	(287)	(294)	(300)	(307)	(313)	(320)	(327)	(342)
Other expense	(1,851)	(1,813)	(1,844)	(1,876)	(1,920)	(1,966)	(2,013)	(2,062)	(2,113)	(2,219)
Total operating expenses	(5,052)	(5,045)	(5,148)	(5,253)	(5,371)	(5,493)	(5,618)	(5,746)	(5,877)	(6,151)
Interest expense	(530)	(530)	(549)	(586)	(626)	(667)	(711)	(758)	(807)	(915)
Income before exceptional provisions	730	756	756	754	741	728	715	701	688	660
Exceptional provisions	0	0	0	0	0	0	0	0	0	0
Income before taxes	730	756	756	754	741	728	715	701	688	660
Income taxes	(255)	(265)	(265)	(264)	(259)	(255)	(250)	(245)	(241)	(231)
Income before extraordinary items	474	491	491	490	482	473	465	456	447	429
Extraordinary items	0	0	0	0	0	0	0	0	0	0
Net income	474	491	491	490	482	473	465	456	447	429
Beginning retained earnings	3,746	2,784	2,824	2,864	2,906	2,949	2,993	3,037	3,083	3,177
Net income	474	491	491	490	482	473	465	456	447	429
Common dividends	(166)	(172)	(172)	(172)	(169)	(166)	(163)	(160)	(156)	(150)
Preferred dividends	0	0	0	0	0	0	0	0	0	0
Potential dividends	(1,271)	(279)	(279)	(277)	(270)	(264)	(257)	(251)	(244)	(230)
Adjustments	0	0	0	0	0	0	0	0	0	0
Ending retained earnings	2,784	2,824	2,864	2,906	2,949	2,993	3,037	3,083	3,129	3,225

This cost of equity is then used to discount all free cash flows to equity in our valuation.

The Continuing Value Estimate

As with the industrial valuation model, we use a value-driver formula for estimating the present value of all free cash flows to equity beyond the explicit forecast period. For the TransAmerica example, this includes all free cash flows from 2008 to infinity. The value-driver formula for the continuing value (CV) within the equity approach is:

$$CV = \frac{NI(1+g)\left(1-\dfrac{g}{r}\right)}{(k_s - g)}$$

Exhibit 22.11   TransAmerica—Forecast Cash Flow Statement

$ million	Forecast 1999	Forecast 2000	Forecast 2001	Forecast 2002	Forecast 2003	Forecast 2004	Forecast 2005	Forecast 2006	Perpetuity
Net premium income	1,888	1,929	1,972	2,015	2,059	2,105	2,151	2,198	2,346
Amortization of deferred acquisition costs	(275)	(281)	(287)	(294)	(300)	(307)	(313)	(320)	(342)
Insurance profit before benefits and claims	1,613	1,648	1,684	1,721	1,759	1,798	1,837	1,878	2,005
Benefits and claims	(2,926)	(2,952)	(3,016)	(3,083)	(3,151)	(3,220)	(3,291)	(3,363)	(3,590)
Increase in insurance liabilities and reserves	214	258	263	269	275	281	287	293	313
Net cash benefits and claims paid	(2,712)	(2,694)	(2,753)	(2,814)	(2,876)	(2,939)	(3,004)	(3,070)	(3,277)
Net insurance cash flow	(1,099)	(1,046)	(1,069)	(1,093)	(1,117)	(1,141)	(1,166)	(1,192)	(1,272)
Net interest income	2,367	2,277	2,283	2,302	2,322	2,343	2,364	2,385	2,452
Other income	2,013	2,083	2,157	2,233	2,314	2,398	2,486	2,578	2,882
Other expense	(1,851)	(1,813)	(1,844)	(1,876)	(1,920)	(1,966)	(2,013)	(2,062)	(2,219)
Exceptional income and provisions	0	0	0	0	0	0	0	0	0
Income taxes	(255)	(265)	(265)	(264)	(259)	(255)	(250)	(245)	(231)
Realized capital gains	44	42	42	42	43	43	44	44	45
Extraordinary items	0	0	0	0	0	0	0	0	0
Cash from operations	1,219	1,279	1,304	1,345	1,382	1,422	1,463	1,507	1,657
Other cash sources									
Increase in accounts payable and other liabilities	(44)	7	45	52	54	56	58	60	67
Increase in unearned premium and other reserves	14	17	18	18	19	19	19	20	21
Total other cash sources	(29)	25	63	70	73	75	77	80	88
Cash uses									
Increase in investments	(1,447)	271	277	284	290	296	303	309	330
Increas in cash and short-term investments	(33)	0	2	3	3	3	3	3	4
Increase in accounts receivable	(41)	7	43	49	51	53	55	57	63
Increase in fixed assets	(64)	11	67	77	80	82	85	88	99
Increase in intangible and other assets	581	472	500	530	562	596	632	670	797
Increase in deferred acquisiton costs	32	47	48	49	50	51	52	53	57
Total cash uses	(973)	809	937	992	1,035	1,081	1,130	1,180	1,350
Cash flow before financing	2,162	495	429	424	420	415	411	407	395
Increase in debt	0	291	570	610	645	682	721	762	900
(Increase) in excess marketable securities	(195)	195	0	0	0	0	0	0	0
Interest expense	(530)	(530)	(549)	(586)	(626)	(667)	(711)	(758)	(915)
Equity cash flow	1,437	451	450	449	439	430	420	410	380
Dividends	166	172	172	172	169	166	163	160	150
Increase in common and adjustments to retained earnings	0	0	0	0	0	0	0	0	0
Potential dividends	1,271	279	279	277	270	264	257	251	230
Equity cash flow	1,437	451	450	449	439	430	420	410	380

where NI = The net income from the last year of the explicit forecast period
= $485 million.

g = The long-term growth rate in net income, assumed to be 0 percent.

r = The long-term expected return on new equity capital invested in the company, assumed to be 12 percent.

k_s = The opportunity cost of equity capital = 9.4 percent.

Exhibit 22.12   TransAmerica—Forecast Key Ratios

Percent	Forecast 1999	Forecast 2000	Forecast 2001	Forecast 2002	Forecast 2003	Forecast 2004	Forecast 2005	Forecast 2006	Perpetuity
Operations									
Net premium growth	2.2	2.2	2.2	2.2	2.2	2.2	2.2	2.2	2.2
Investment income/investments	7.0	7.0	7.0	7.0	7.0	7.0	7.0	7.0	7.0
Capital gain/total invested	0.1	0.1	0.1	0.1	0.1	0.1	0.1	0.1	0.1
Capital gain (inc. unrealized gain)/ total invested	0.1	0.1	0.1	0.1	0.1	0.1	0.1	0.1	0.1
Interest (lending) income growth	6.0	6.0	6.0	6.0	6.0	6.0	6.0	6.0	6.0
Other income growth	2.0	2.0	2.0	2.0	2.0	2.0	2.0	2.0	2.0
Total revenue growth	(1.8)	0.3	1.9	2.2	2.2	2.2	2.3	2.3	2.4
Expenses									
Net claims/net premiums	155.0	153.0	153.0	153.0	153.0	153.0	153.0	153.0	153.0
Amortiz of def acq cost/net premiums	14.6	14.6	14.6	14.6	14.6	14.6	14.6	14.6	14.6
Other expense/other revenue	91.9	87.0	85.5	84.0	83.0	82.0	81.0	80.0	77.0
Operating margin	20.0	20.3	20.2	20.3	20.3	20.3	20.2	20.3	20.4
Taxes and financing									
Corporate tax rate	35.0	35.0	35.0	35.0	35.0	35.0	35.0	35.0	35.0
Taxes/pre-tax income	35.0	35.0	35.0	35.0	35.0	35.0	35.0	35.0	35.0
Interest expense/debt	6.5	6.5	6.5	6.5	6.5	6.5	6.5	6.5	6.5
Common dividends/net income	35.0	35.0	35.0	35.0	35.0	35.0	35.0	35.0	35.0
Debt/equity	172.8	177.5	187.8	198.7	210.1	222.0	234.5	247.5	290.0
Working capital									
Operating cash/total revenues	2.0	2.0	2.0	2.0	2.0	2.0	2.0	2.0	2.0
Accounts receivable/net premiums	35.1	35.1	35.1	35.1	35.1	35.1	35.1	35.1	35.1
Net fixed assets/total revenues	54.9	54.9	54.9	54.9	54.9	54.9	54.9	54.9	54.9
Def policy acq cost/net premiums	112.7	112.7	112.7	112.7	112.7	112.7	112.7	112.7	112.7
Growth of separate assets	10.0	5.0	5.0	5.0	5.0	5.0	5.0	5.0	5.0
Interest (lending) income/other assets	9.5	9.5	9.5	9.5	9.5	9.5	9.5	9.5	9.5
Accounts payable/total revenues	37.2	37.2	37.2	37.2	37.2	37.2	37.2	37.2	37.2
Other liabilities/total revenues	0.0	0.0	0.0	0.0	0.0	0.0	0.0	0.0	0.0
Reserves and investments									
Net cash benefits paid/premiums	143.7	139.7	139.7	139.7	139.7	139.7	139.7	139.7	139.7
Net additions to reserves/premiums	166.3	166.3	166.3	166.3	166.3	166.3	166.3	166.3	166.3
Provisions/insurance reserves	6.8	6.8	6.8	6.8	6.8	6.8	6.8	6.8	6.8
Investments/insurance reserves	1.05	1.05	1.05	1.05	1.05	1.05	1.05	1.05	1.05

(continued)

Plugging in the numbers from the TransAmerica example, we find that the continuing value estimate is:

$$CV = \frac{NI\left(1 - \dfrac{g}{r}\right)}{(k_s - g)}$$

$$= \frac{485\left(\dfrac{1 - 0.0\%}{12.0\%}\right)}{(9.4\% - 0.0\%)}$$

$$= \$5,156 \text{ million}$$

Exhibit 22.12   (Continued)

$ million	Forecast 1999	Forecast 2000	Forecast 2001	Forecast 2002	Forecast 2003	Forecast 2004	Forecast 2005	Forecast 2006	Perpetuity
Equity analysis									
Equity/investment assets	14.7%	14.7%	14.7%	14.7%	14.7%	14.7%	14.7%	14.7%	14.7%
Equity/premiums	251.3%	248.0%	244.7%	241.5%	238.4%	235.3%	232.3%	229.4%	221.0%
Actual equity before adjustments	6,014	5,063	5,103	5,143	5,179	5,216	5,254	5,293	5,415
Required equity	4,743	4,783	4,824	4,866	4,909	4,952	4,997	5,042	5,185
Equity infusion (distribution)	(1,271)	(279)	(279)	(277)	(270)	(264)	(257)	(251)	(230)
Economic profit									
Beginning equity	5,706	4,743	4,783	4,824	4,866	4,909	4,952	4,997	5,137
Return on beginning equity	8.3%	10.4%	10.3%	10.2%	9.9%	9.6%	9.4%	9.1%	8.4%
Cost of equity	9.4%	9.4%	9.4%	9.4%	9.4%	9.4%	9.4%	9.4%	9.4%
Spread	−1.1%	1.0%	0.9%	0.8%	0.5%	0.2%	0.0%	−0.3%	−1.0%
Economic profit	(62)	45	42	37	24	12	(1)	(14)	(54)
Economic profit (adjusted for unrealized capital gains)									
Beginning equity (less unrealized capital gains)	3,762	2,800	2,840	2,881	2,923	2,965	3,009	3,053	3,193
Return on beginning equity	12.6%	17.5%	17.3%	17.0%	16.5%	16.0%	15.4%	14.9%	13.4%
Cost of equity	9.4%	9.4%	9.4%	9.4%	9.4%	9.4%	9.4%	9.4%	9.4%
Spread	3.2%	8.1%	7.9%	7.6%	7.1%	6.6%	6.0%	5.5%	4.0%
Economic profit	121	228	224	219	207	194	182	169	129
Result ratios									
ROE	10.0%	10.3%	10.2%	10.1%	9.8%	9.6%	9.3%	9.0%	8.3%
ROA (net income/total assets)	0.8%	0.8%	0.8%	0.8%	0.7%	0.7%	0.7%	0.7%	0.6%
GAAP loss ratio approximation	155.0%	153.0%	153.0%	153.0%	153.0%	153.0%	153.0%	153.0%	153.0%
GAAP underwriting expense ratio approximation	14.6%	14.6%	14.6%	14.6%	14.6%	14.6%	14.6%	14.6%	14.6%
GAAP combined ratio approximation	169.6%	167.6%	167.6%	167.6%	167.6%	167.6%	167.6%	167.6%	167.6%
GAAP operating ratio approximation	66.8%	66.7%	66.2%	66.5%	66.4%	66.3%	66.3%	66.4%	67.1%
GAAP premium to surplus approximation	39.8%	40.3%	40.9%	41.4%	42.0%	42.5%	43.0%	43.6%	45.3%
Premiums earned/reserves	6.2%	6.3%	6.3%	6.4%	6.5%	6.6%	6.7%	6.8%	7.0%
Premiums/investment assets	5.9%	5.9%	6.0%	6.1%	6.2%	6.3%	6.3%	6.4%	6.7%
Reserves/total assets	0.6	0.6	0.5	0.5	0.5	0.5	0.5	0.5	0.5
Reserves/premiums	17.3	17.1	16.8	16.6	16.4	16.2	16	15.8	15.2
Approx cost of funds (UW loss/avg float)	1.1%	1.1%	1.1%	1.1%	1.1%	1.1%	1.1%	1.2%	1.2%
Cash benefits paid/premiums	143.7%	139.7%	139.7%	139.7%	139.7%	139.7%	139.7%	139.7%	139.7%
Cash acquisition cost/premiums	16.3%	17.0%	17.0%	17.0%	17.0%	17.0%	17.0%	17.0%	17.0%

Finally, we discount this result for 10 years at the cost of equity to obtain its present value, $2,297 million.

Exhibit 22.13 shows the discounted cash flow estimate of the equity value of TransAmerica, as well as the value estimated by using discounted economic profit plus the book value of equity at the beginning of the forecast period. By definition, both the DCF and the economic profit approaches give the same value.

Exhibit 22.13   Estimated Equity Value of TransAmerica

	Cash flow	Economic profit	PV factor	PV of CF	PV of EP
1999	1,437	121	0.9141	1,313	110
2000	451	228	0.8355	377	191
2001	450	224	0.7637	344	171
2002	449	219	0.6981	313	153
2003	439	207	0.6381	280	132
2004	430	194	0.5832	251	113
2005	420	182	0.5331	224	97
2006	410	169	0.4873	200	82
2007	400	156	0.4454	178	69
2008	390	142	0.4071	159	58
Continuing value	4,637	1,444	0.4071	1,888	588
Operating value				5,527	1,765
Beginning of period equity, less unrealized capital gains					3,762
Equity value (less capital gains)				5,527	5,527
Mid-year adjustment factor				1.04	1.04
Total equity				5,738	5,738
Plus: Unrealized capital gains				1,943	1,943
Less: Market value of preferred stock				0	0
Estimated total equity value				7,681	7,681
Market value of equity				7,045	7,045
Percent difference between market and estimated value				9.0%	9.0%

VALUE-BASED MANAGEMENT AT INSURANCE COMPANIES

This section summarizes some of the insights that a shareholder value perspective and DCF valuation approach have brought to insurance companies.

Separating Asset Management from Insurance Operations

Insurance companies are organized most often by product line. A property and casualty company may have a worker's compensation division, an auto insurance division, a homeowner's division, and so forth. Each will have its own profit and loss statement and balance sheet and will handle its own asset management. In this sense, the organization seems logical because it is customer facing, by type of coverage. But a further breakdown may help.

There are really two kinds of business within each of these divisions: insuring risks and investing the cash from premiums until claims are paid. Insurance companies have traditionally not separated value creation into these two parts. Yet, with advanced portfolio performance techniques it is possible to determine whether the investment management side of the business is creating or destroying value. When companies have consolidated these investment activities under one chief investment officer with clear accountability, they have often been able to increase their portfolio return by 10 to 50 basis points without changing the level of risk.

To consolidate investment management activities, the company needs some way of providing the various lines of business with a fair return on their investment portfolio. Companies can do this by paying a market return based on a fixed income portfolio matched to the duration of their reserves. In this way, the product line managers can focus on the insurance aspects of their business and the asset manager can focus on the investment management side of the business.

Tax and Earnings Management

Insurance companies bolster income by realizing capital gains when the results from the rest of their business have turned down. But the maneuver may reduce the value of the company because the effect of realizing capital gains is to pull the company's cash outflows for tax into the present.

The opposite situation—the realization of capital losses—is also worth discussing. In early 1982, one of the authors met with the chief investment officer of a major West Coast Insurance company. The executive's company had roughly $50 million in unrealized capital losses in its bond portfolio because interest rates had risen dramatically in the past year. He also said that the company had about $50 million in realized capital gains elsewhere in its business. An immediate reaction was to suggest a tax offset by taking the losses on the bond portfolio to shelter the taxes on the gains. The executive rejected the idea "because our profits would be lower if we realize the capital losses." And, he continued, "our share price depends on our profitability." We protested, asking whether he would change his mind if we produced evidence that the marketplace values companies on cash flows, not profits. "That's irrelevant because our CEO believes that the market follows earnings," he replied. And that was more or less the end of the conversation. Even today beliefs have not changed much. But don't forget the lesson of Chapter 5: The empirical evidence heavily supports the conclusion that stock prices depend on cash flows, not earnings.

Using Value Driver Analysis to Change Strategies

A large property and casualty company studied three value drivers: combined ratio, pricing policy, and potential divestiture of selected business units. The total value impact was estimated at $798 million. Exhibit 22.14 shows Company X's combined ratio relative to its peers during a three-year period.

The company decided that it would try to achieve performance in the first quartile of its peer group, meaning a 7 percent combined ratio

Exhibit 22.14   Company X Combined Ratio Relative to Peer Group

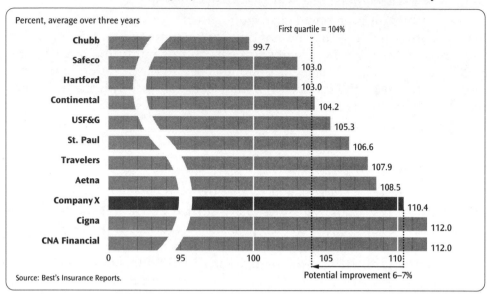

improvement. As shown in Exhibit 22.15, the total company value would increase by $602 million if the improvements could be made.

Next, preliminary analysis of pricing policy suggested that even at improved underwriting performance levels, Company X could maximize the value of its worker's compensation line by raising prices by 7 percent and accepting an expected 30 percent reduction in premium volume. When a similar analysis was applied across the board, aggregate premium volume was expected to decline 13 percent, but the higher prices more than offset this decline, and the total company's value was estimated to increase by $44 million.

Another example of how value drivers shape management thinking is taken from a life insurance company. Let's call it Long Life. Before experimenting with value-based management, Long Life had identified three important value drivers: expense ratio, mortality, and the new premium growth rate. The puzzle was that two of its top competitors had higher profit margins despite the fact that Long Life had superior results in the three levers that management thought were most critical. Something was missing. Through a valuation analysis, the company identified three new value drivers, namely the policy lapse rate, volume of reinsured policies, and investment yield. To everyone's surprise, the investment yield was as important as the expense ratio. Long Life's management decided to track investment yield regularly, and to study opportunities to increase it through improved cash management and portfolio optimization techniques.

Exhibit 22.15 Potential DCF Improvement from Reduction of
Combined Ratio to Upper Quartile by Line

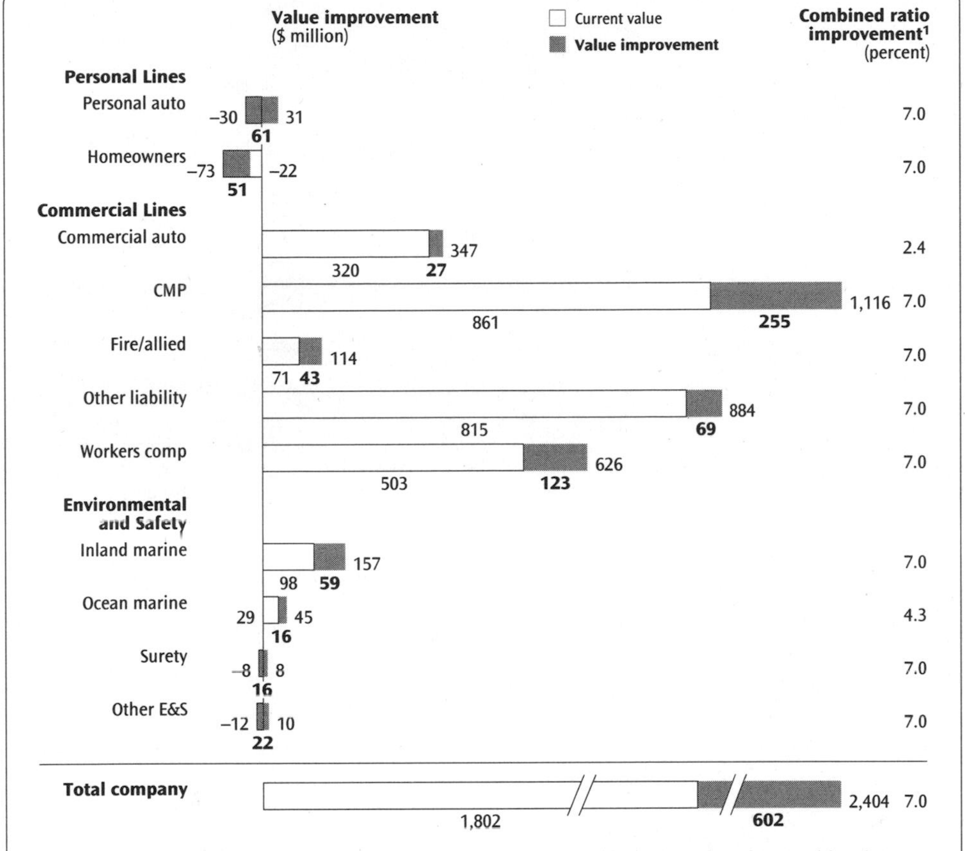

1 7% combined ratio improvement, except in lines where performance is already competitive (ocean marine and commercial auto).

SUMMARY

Insurance companies are financial institutions that provide value for their shareholders (or their policyholders, if they are mutual companies) by writing insurance and investing money. We recommend valuing insurance companies by discounting free cash flow to equity at the cost of equity (we used GAAP accounting but we also demonstrated that free cash flows are the same whether one uses GAAP or statutory accounting). We demonstrated our approach by valuing TransAmerica. Finally, we illustrated some of the value drivers of insurance companies as applied in practice.

More on the Adjusted
Present Value Model

In Chapter 8, we described the adjusted present value model and demonstrated, using the Hershey Foods case, that the value of a company using the adjusted present value (APV) approach was identical to the enterprise DCF and equity DCF approaches. The key to this identity was choosing discount rates that consistently adjusted for the tax benefit of interest expense. We provided formulas for linking the unlevered cost of equity, WACC, and the levered cost of equity to achieve this identity.

The formulas that we provided in Chapter 8 were based on the assumption that the tax benefit of interest expense would be discounted at the unlevered cost of equity. Unfortunately, finance theory doesn't tell us unequivocally that this is the correct rate to use. Some would argue that the tax benefit of interest expense should be discounted at the cost of debt or some rate between the cost of debt and the unlevered cost of equity. In this appendix, we explore the relationship between the APV and enterprise DCF approaches and discuss the arguments for choosing which rate to discount the tax benefit of interest expense.

A SIMPLE EXAMPLE

A simple example illustrates the APV and enterprise DCF approaches. Company K earns $100 per year of NOPLAT in perpetuity, with no growth.

Since growth is zero, free cash flow (FCF) also equals $100. If the unlevered cost of equity (k_u) is 10 percent, the unlevered value of company K (V_u) is $1,000, as follows:

$$V_u = \frac{FCF}{k_u} = \frac{100}{10\%}$$

Company K also has $400 of debt (B), which pays interest at 7 percent pre-tax (k_b), with a 40 percent tax shield (T). Using the APV model, we value the debt tax shield by discounting it at some rate. Let's assume that we can either discount the tax shield at the cost of debt (7 percent) or the unlevered cost of equity (10 percent). (We will discuss the pros and cons of the two approaches later). If we discount it at the cost of debt, the value of the tax shield (V_{tb}) is $160, as follows:

$$V_{tb} = \frac{B \times k_b \times T}{k_b} = \frac{400 \times 7\% \times 40\%}{7\%}$$
$$= 160$$

The enterprise value (V) of Company K would then be $1,160, the sum of the unlevered value ($1,000) and the present value of the tax shields ($160). The value of equity (S) would be $760, the enterprise value ($1,160) less the value of debt ($400).

To arrive at the same value using the enterprise DCF approach, the WACC would have to be 8.621 percent, derived as follows:

$$V = \frac{FCF}{WACC}$$

$$1,160 = \frac{100}{WACC}$$

$$WACC = 8.621\%$$

The relationship between the unlevered cost of equity and WACC can be derived as follows:

$$V = \frac{FCF}{WACC} = V_u + V_{tb} = \frac{FCF}{k_u} + \frac{B \times k_b \times T}{k_b}$$

$$\frac{FCF}{WACC} = \frac{FCF}{k_u} + \frac{B \times k_b \times T}{k_b}$$

$$\text{Let } B = \frac{B}{V} \times V = \frac{B}{V} \times \frac{FCF}{WACC}$$

$$\frac{FCF}{WACC} = \frac{FCF}{k_u} + \left[\frac{B}{V} \times \frac{FCF}{WACC} \times \frac{k_b \times T}{k_b} \right]$$

$$\frac{1}{WACC} = \frac{1}{k_u} + \left[\frac{B}{V} \times \frac{1}{WACC} \times T \right]$$

$$\frac{1}{k_u} = \frac{1}{WACC} \left[1 - \left(\frac{B}{V} \right) T \right]$$

$$WACC = k_u \left[1 - \left(\frac{B}{V} \right) T \right]$$

(Equation 1)

Going through the same process assuming that the tax shield from debt is discounted at the unlevered cost of equity, gives us a present value of the tax shield from debt of $112, an enterprise value of $1,112, and an equity value of $712. The WACC in this case would be 8.993 percent. The relationship between the unlevered cost of equity and WACC would be:

$$V = \frac{FCF}{WACC} = V_u + V_{tb} = \frac{FCF}{k_u} + \frac{B \times k_b \times T}{k_u}$$

$$\frac{FCF}{WACC} = \frac{FCF + \left[\frac{B}{V} \times \frac{FCF}{WACC} \times k_b \times T \right]}{k_u}$$

$$\frac{1}{WACC} = \frac{1 + \left[\frac{B}{V} \times \frac{1}{WACC} \times k_b \times T \right]}{k_u}$$

$$k_u = WACC + \left[\frac{B}{V} \times k_b \times T \right]$$

$$WACC = k_u - k_b \left(\frac{B}{V} \right) T$$

(Equation 2)

FURTHER DEVELOPMENT OF THE FORMULAS

In their original derivation of the relationship between k_u and WACC, Modigliani and Miller assume a company that does not grow and whose debt is risk free.[1] Their analysis leads to Equation 1.

Suppose we relax the assumption that growth is zero. Assuming constant growth (g) into perpetuity, the relationship between k_u and WACC becomes:

$$WACC = k_u - \left(k_b \times \frac{B}{V} \times T\right) - \frac{B}{V}\left[\frac{k_b \times T}{k_b - g}\right](k_u - k_b)$$

(Equation 3)

If you go one more step and assume discrete cash flows without constant growth, the relationship between k_u and WACC becomes:

$$WACC = k_u - \left(k_b \times \frac{B}{V} \times T\right) - \frac{PVT}{V}(k_u - k_b)$$

(Equation 4)

where,

PVT = Present value of future interest tax shields

If you accept that the tax benefit of interest expense should be discounted at the risk free rate or the cost of debt, you should use either Equation 3 or 4 to relate k_u and WACC.

Working with Equation 2, where the tax benefit of interest is discounted at k_u, and relaxing the no-growth assumption, results in the following relationship between k_u and WACC:

$$WACC = k_u - k_b\left(\frac{B}{V}\right)T$$

As you can see, this formula is the same as the original one. The same formula also holds for discrete cash flows with variable growth rates.

Exhibits A.1, A.2, and A.3 summarize the formulas for various sets of assumptions.

---

[1] F. Modigliani and M. Miller, "The Cost of Capital, Corporation Finance, and the Theory of Investment," *American Economic Review*, June 1958, pp. 261–297.

Exhibit A.1   Relationship between *WACC* and k_u

Case	Interest Tax Shield Discounted at k_u	Interest Tax Shield Discounted at k_b
Zero growth perpetuity	$WACC = k_u - k_b\left(\dfrac{B}{V}\right)T$	$WACC = k_u\left[1-\left(\dfrac{B}{V}\right)T\right]$
Growing perpetuity	$WACC = k_u - k_b\left(\dfrac{B}{V}\right)T$	$WACC = k_u - \left(k_b \times \dfrac{B}{V} \times T\right)$ $-\dfrac{B}{V}\left[\dfrac{k_b \times T}{k_b - g}\right](k_u - k_b)$
Discrete cash flows	$WACC = k_u - k_b\left(\dfrac{B}{V}\right)T$	$WACC = k_u - \left(k_b \times \dfrac{B}{V} \times T\right)$ $-\dfrac{PVT}{V}(k_u - k_b)$

where *WACC* = Weighted average cost of capital
k_u = Unlevered cost of equity
k_b = Cost of debt
B = Value of debt
V = Total enterprise value
T = Tax rate
g = Growth rate of cash flows
PVT = Present value of future tax shields

Exhibit A.2   Relationship between k_s and k_u

Case	Interest Tax Shield Discounted at k_u	Interest Tax Shield Discounted at k_b
Zero growth perpetuity	$k_s = k_u + (k_u - k_b)\dfrac{B}{S}$	$k_s = k_u + (k_u - k_b)\left(\dfrac{B}{S}\right)(1-T)$
Growing perpetuity	$k_s = k_u + (k_u - k_b)\dfrac{B}{S}$	$k_s = k_u + (k_u - k_b)\dfrac{B}{S}\left[1-\left(\dfrac{k_b}{k_b - g}\right)T\right]$

where k_s = Leveraged cost of equity
S = Value of equity

	Exhibit A.3 Relationship between $Beta_L$ and $Beta_u$	
Case	Interest Tax Shield Discounted at k_u	Interest Tax Shield Discounted at k_b
Zero growth perpetuity	$\beta_L = \beta_u + (\beta_u - \beta_b)\dfrac{B}{S}$	$\beta_L = \beta_u + (\beta_u - \beta_b)\dfrac{B}{S}(1-T)$
Zero growth perpetuity with $\beta_b = 0$ (debt is risk free)	$\beta_L = \beta_u\left(1+\dfrac{B}{S}\right)$	$\beta_L = \beta_u\left[1+\dfrac{B}{S}(1-T)\right]$
Growing perpetuity	$\beta_L = \beta_u + (\beta_u - \beta_b)\dfrac{B}{S}$	Not reducible to a formula

where β_L = Levered beta

β_u = Unlevered beta

β_b = Beta of debt

WHICH FORMULAS TO USE

The finance literature does not provide a clear answer about which discount rate for the tax benefit of interest is theoretically correct. Many point to the original work by Modigliani and Miller, which used the cost of debt (in their work they also assumed the debt was risk free). However, their purpose was to illustrate the tax impact of debt on value. They did not claim that their assumptions were realistic. When we relaxed the no-growth assumption, we saw that new formulas were needed. Similarly, Modigliani and Miller never addressed the issue of the riskiness of the tax shields from debt where a company is expected to grow and where there is uncertainty about the amount of debt that the company will have in the future.

The argument for using the cost of debt is based on the idea that uncertainty about the company's ability to realize the tax shield is best measured by the rate at which its creditors are willing to lend to the company (the cost of debt). At the extreme, consider a company with only $1 of debt. Clearly, there is low risk that the tax shield on the debt will not be realized.

The counterargument for using the unlevered cost of equity is based on the uncertainty about the size of the future tax shields. If we assume that a company sets as a target a constant debt-to-capital ratio, then the amount of debt (and the interest tax shield) will be driven by the size of the company's operating profits and cash flows. In other words, there will be a high correlation between the profits and cash flows and the interest tax shield, hence the risk will be similar. With similar risk, the interest tax shields should be discounted at the same rate as the operations, the unlevered cost of equity.

We leave it to the reader's judgment to decide which approach best fits his or her situation.[2]

---

[2] For additional reading on APV see, I. Inselbag and H. Kaufold, "Two DCF Approaches for Valuing Companies under Alternative Financing Strategies (and How to Choose Between Them)," *Journal of Applied Corporate Finance*, vol. 10, no. 1 (Spring 1997), pp. 114–122, and R. Brealey and S. Myers, *Principles of Corporate Finance*, 5th ed. (McGraw-Hill, New York, 1996), Chapter 19.

Index

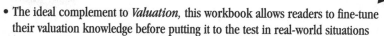